Word

If you bought the Suite version of Microsoft Works, you have the fabulous and famous Microsoft Word as your word processing program. (The regular version of Works comes with a simpler, but still very functional, word processor.) You can use Word (or the Works Word Processor) to write letters and reports, create mail merges, make fax cover sheets, and much more.

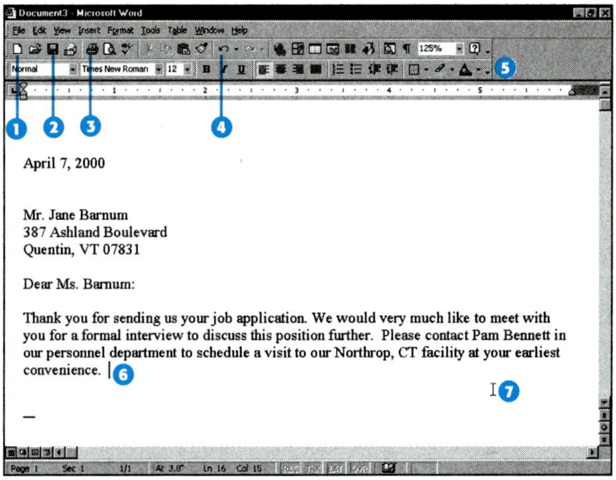

1. Start a new blank document by clicking here.
2. Save your work with the Save button.
3. The Print button prints your work.
4. Undo your last action.
5. The Formatting toolbar provides formatting shortcuts.
6. This vertical line is the insertion point.
7. Click the mouse to move the insertion point.

Word Tips

- Most common activities can be performed either with a toolbar button or by selecting a menu command. In many cases, the menu command offers more options.
- Set your page formatting first (margins, paper size) with the File, Page Setup command; then set formatting for individual paragraphs and words.
- In Word, you can have more than one document open at once. Switch between them by choosing from the Window menu or by clicking the button on the taskbar for the document you want to see.
- When you click the Print button on the toolbar, one copy of the entire document prints immediately on the default printer. To set options such as page range and number of copies, choose File, Print instead.
- A wavy red underline indicates a possible spelling error; a wavy green line represents a possible grammar error. Right-click the word and select a correction from the shortcut menu, or press F7 to run a full check.
- You can save any document in Web page format by choosing File, Save As and choosing Web Page as the file type.

The Works Spreadsheet

A spreadsheet organizes text and numbers into neat rows and columns, and enables you to perform calculations on the numbers. For example, you could set up a grade book in the Works spreadsheet or a list of employees and their sales. You can also create good-looking graphical charts representing the data.

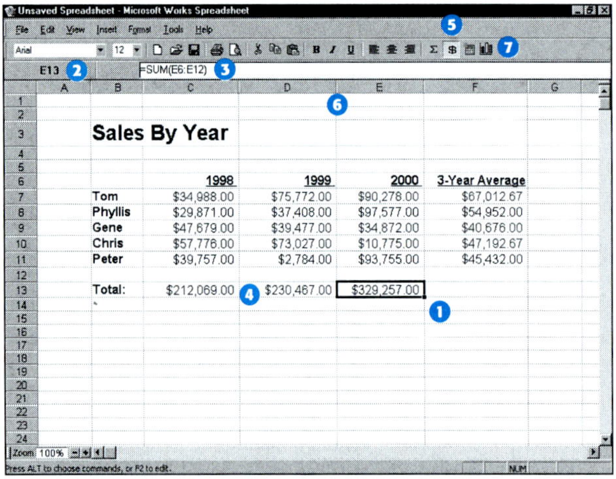

1. Selected cell (notice the dark box around it)
2. Each cell has a unique address; this box shows the address of the active cell.
3. This box shows the content of the active cell—in this case, a formula.
4. These cells contain the results of the formulas entered in them.
5. The Currency button quickly formats the content of the selected cell(s) as currency.
6. To widen a column, position the mouse pointer between column headings and drag.
7. To create a chart of the data, select it and then click the New Chart button.

Works Spreadsheet Tips

- A cell is the intersection of a row and column. Each cell has a unique name made up of the column letter and row number, such as B12 or C5.
- The formatting tools on the toolbar work the same as in a word processor. You can underline text, make it bold, change its font, and so on.
- To widen a cell, drag between the column headings. This widens the column to the left. Or, to automatically resize the column to fit its contents, double-click between the column headings.
- To insert or delete rows or columns, choose the corresponding command from the Insert menu.
- A formula begins with an equal sign (=) and uses ordinary math operators. For example, to subtract the content of B4 from B6, you would type **`=B6-B4`**.
- A function provides a shortcut for an operation. For example, to average the content of cells A1 through A6, you would type **`=AVG(A1:A6)`**. Notice that the colon (:) helps represent a range.

The Works Calendar

The Works Calendar helps you track your appointments and reminds you of special events like birthdays and anniversaries. You'll never forget an important activity again if you use the Calendar faithfully. Plus, you can combine its data with Microsoft Home Publishing to print professional-quality calendars you can take with you anywhere.

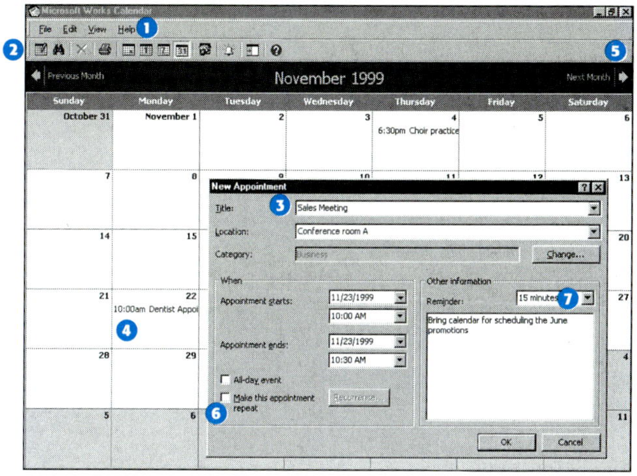

1. Click one of these buttons to switch between Day, Week, and Month views.
2. Click the New Appointment button to enter a new appointment or event.
3. Fill in the fields in the New Appointment dialog box to create a new appointment.
4. Appointments appear on the calendar; double-click one to open it.
5. Move to the next month by clicking here.
6. Click here to make the appointment recur at a regular interval.
7. Choose a reminder time, and enter the text you want to appear with the reminder alarm.

Works Calendar Tips

- To enter a new appointment, double-click any blank area of the calendar, or click the New Appointment button on the toolbar.
- In the New Appointment dialog box, enter the date, time, and other details about the appointment, and then click OK. You can reopen the appointment's details again later by double-clicking the appointment on the calendar.
- Using the controls in the New Appointment dialog box, you can categorize an appointment, set a reminder alarm for it, or set it up to recur at an interval you specify. These features are all optional.
- You can switch freely between Day, Week, and Month views by using the toolbar buttons or the View menu. Different views might be appropriate at different times.
- For a simple printout, use the Print button or the File, Print command. Or, for a fancier printout, click the Microsoft Home Publishing button on the toolbar to launch that program and create a calendar that includes special graphics, backgrounds, and so on.

Internet Explorer

Internet Explorer is a Web browser, a program that displays Web pages from the Internet. The latest version of it, version 5, comes free with Works Suite 2000 and is automatically installed when you install Works. If you have an Internet connection, you can use it and Internet Explorer to "surf the Web."

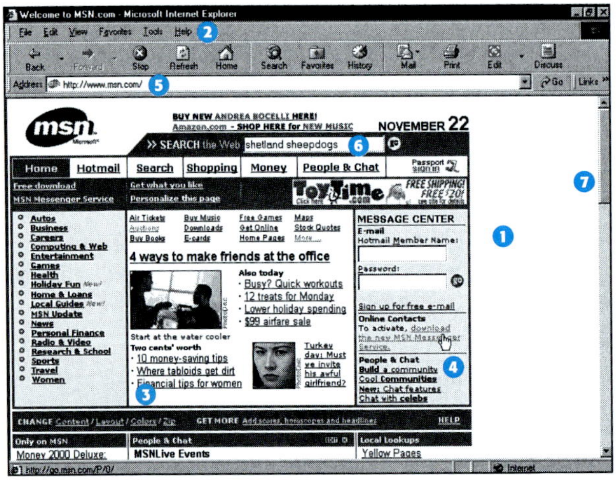

1. This is the default start page.
2. You can return to the start page any time by clicking Home.
3. Click underlined text (a hyperlink) to jump to a related page.
4. The mouse pointer becomes a hand when it is over a hyperlink.
5. To go to a specific Web address, type it here.
6. To search the Web for a specific topic, type it here.
7. Scroll down for more text to read and more hyperlinks to choose from.

Internet Explorer Tips

- There are three ways to use the Web. One is to browse by clicking hyperlinks. Another is to type a specific address in the Address bar. A third is to type a keyword to search for, and then pick from a list of pages that match your criteria.
- Your start page contains a search box at the top, but not all pages do. To search anytime, you can click the Search button on the toolbar. This opens a separate Search pane to the left of the main window, with a box into which you can type keywords to search for.
- The Back button returns to the previous page you were viewing. You can click it repeatedly to go back several pages, or open its drop-down list to select a specific page to return to.
- When you find a page you want to return to later, add it to your Favorites list. To do so, display the page and then choose Favorites, Add to Favorites.
- To change which page is used for your start page, choose Tools, Internet Options and enter a different address in the Address box.
- The Internet Options dialog box can also be used to set up tighter security than normal, to enable content filters to prevent kids from accessing adult content, and more.

Money

Microsoft Money is a financial management program. It helps you track and balance your bank accounts, but that's just the beginning. It also reminds you of bills to be paid, tracks your investments, helps you plan a budget, and directs you to Internet resources for lending services, auto and home purchasing, and more.

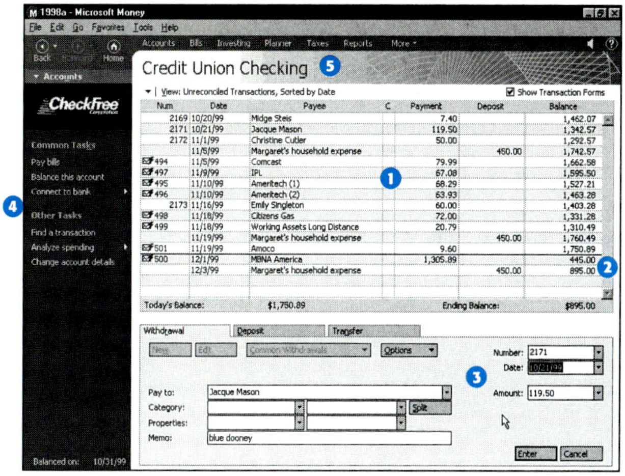

1. This checkbook register looks and functions much like a paper one.
2. Money keeps a running total of the account balance.
3. Easy-to-use forms help you enter and edit transactions.
4. Links to the most common activities appear here.
5. This Navigation bar provides quick links to other parts of the program.

Money Tips

- Each person (or each household) uses a single Money file containing multiple accounts. That way you can track your total net worth (bank accounts, investments, loans, home equity, and so on).
- Get into the habit of regularly entering all the transactions from your paper checkbook register into Money; otherwise Money won't be accurate.
- You can use Money to print checks on your printer, and even to pay bills online, so you might find yourself using your paper checkbook less and less.
- Money enables you to categorize each transaction. This takes an extra few seconds, but accurate categorization is important for setting up budgets and for printing meaningful reports.
- You can get online stock price updates through Money for free. Simply set up your stock portfolio in Money and then choose Tools, Update Internet Information.
- Money is compatible with TurboTax and other tax software, so if you have been careful to always categorize transactions, you might be able to export data directly from Money into your tax software.

Other Works Programs

There are more great programs included with the Microsoft Works Suite than can be showcased in this booklet! Here's a sampling of what else is in store for you in Special Edition Using Microsoft Works Suite 2000.

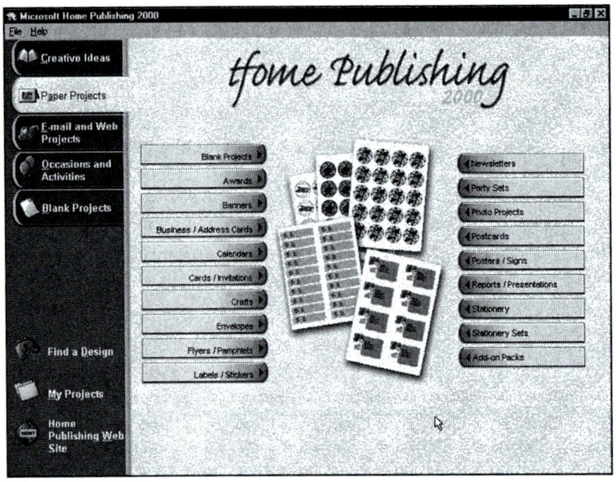

Home Publishing is a very friendly desktop publishing program that can create greeting cards, posters, calendars, Web pages, and much more.

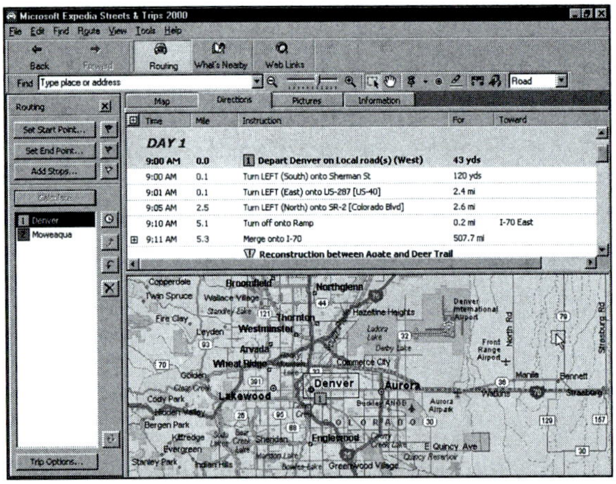

Streets & Trips is a mapping program that shows accurate maps of any region in the United States, including all roads and landmarks. It will also provide you with turn-by-turn driving directions between any two points.

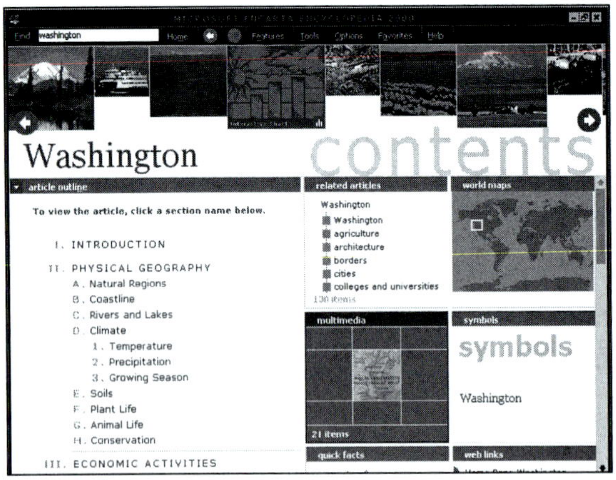

Encarta is a multimedia encyclopedia, with thousands of articles as well as pictures, video clips, sounds, narration, and other goodies. There's more than enough information here to satisfy your curiosity on almost any subject—or to write an A+ school report.

Special Edition Using Microsoft® Works Suite 2000

Faithe Wempen

QUE®
A Division of Macmillan USA
201 W. 103rd Street
Indianapolis, Indiana 46290

Special Edition Using Microsoft® Works Suite 2000

International Standard Book Number: 0-7897-2192-9

Library of Congress Catalog Card Number: 99-63883

Printed in the United States of America

First Printing: February 2000

02 01 00 4 3 2 1

Trademarks

All terms mentioned in this book that are known to be trademarks or service marks have been appropriately capitalized. Que Corporation cannot attest to the accuracy of this information. Use of a term in this book should not be regarded as affecting the validity of any trademark or service mark.

Warning and Disclaimer

Every effort has been made to make this book as complete and as accurate as possible, but no warranty or fitness is implied. The information provided is on an "as is" basis. The author and the publisher shall have neither liability nor responsibility to any person or entity with respect to any loss or damages arising from the information contained in this book.

Associate Publisher
Greg Wiegand

Acquisitions Editor
Angelina Ward

Development Editor
Gregory Harris

Managing Editor
Thomas F. Hayes

Project Editor
Lori A. Lyons

Copy Editors
Kate Talbot
Barbara Hacha

Proofreader
Jeanne Clark

Technical Editor
Mark Hall

Team Coordinator
Sharry Lee Gregory

Interior Designer
Ruth Lewis

Cover Designers
Dan Armstrong
Ruth Lewis

Copywriter
Eric Borgert

Editorial Assistant
Angela Boley

Layout Technician
Darin Crone

CONTENTS

About the Author

Faithe Wempen operates Your Computer Friend, a training and troubleshooting business that specializes in helping beginners become comfortable with their PCs. She is also an A+ Certified computer technician and the author of more than 40 computer books, including *The Microsoft Office 97 Professional 6-in-1*, *Sams Teach Yourself Access 2000 in 10 Minutes*, and *Practical Windows 98*.

Acknowledgments

Thank you to the hard-working staff at Macmillan USA, whose names appear on the Credits page of this book. You have done a great job, as usual.

Tell Us What You Think!

As the reader of this book, *you* are our most important critic and commentator. We value your opinion and want to know what we're doing right, what we could do better, what areas you'd like to see us publish in, and any other words of wisdom you're willing to pass our way.

As an Associate Publisher for Que, I welcome your comments. You can fax, email, or write me directly to let me know what you did or didn't like about this book[md]as well as what we can do to make our books stronger.

Please note that I cannot help you with technical problems related to the topic of this book, and that due to the high volume of mail I receive, I might not be able to reply to every message.

When you write, please be sure to include this book's title and author as well as your name and phone or fax number. I will carefully review your comments and share them with the author and editors who worked on the book.

Fax: 317-581-4666

Email: `consumer@mcp.com`

Mail: Greg Wiegand
Que
201 West 103rd Street
Indianapolis, IN 46290 USA

INTRODUCTION

In this chapter

Congratulations on choosing Microsoft Works Suite 2000! If you're looking for versatile software that can handle what you need to do on your home PC, you've chosen the right program. Works Suite 2000 is exactly what you need.

Although Microsoft Office is the best-selling suite of applications for business, it's not always appropriate for home use. It contains dozens of expensive features that many home users will never need and lacks such home management basics as a home finance program.

Works Suite 2000 is the right tool for the home. It contains the most-used component of Office—Word, the word processor—as well as several special programs geared specifically for the home. With Works Suite 2000, you're armed with the best available tools to tackle any computer project, from the family Christmas newsletter to your retirement planning. You will learn about Works Suite's specific tools in Chapter 1, "Introducing the Microsoft Works Suite."

About the Book

Microsoft Works Suite 2000 doesn't come with much documentation—only one slim book about Word. For the rest of the programs, you're on your own, unless you want to read the online help files (which can be somewhat awkward when you are trying to use the program at the same time). That's where this book comes in. It provides easy-to-follow, step-by-step instructions for using all the important parts of the Works Suite. Here's what you'll find in the upcoming pages.

Part I, "Using Works," covers Works, including all the main components. You'll discover how to use Works's simple but powerful word processor to create common documents, perform calculations and what-if analysis with the spreadsheet, and keep large quantities of data organized with the database. There's even a special section on using the components together—for example, to merge the addresses from the database with form letters from the word processor. If you're a beginner to computing or word processing, Works is a great warm-up program.

Part II, "Using Word," deals with Word, a powerful, yet easy-to-use, word processor. You'll learn how to create and format documents, including sophisticated ones that include columns and graphics. You'll also learn how to create your own Web page, to establish your presence on the Internet.

In Part III, "Exploring Online Offerings," you'll learn about the Internet, featuring the Internet Explorer Web browser. If you have been curious about the Internet and are ready to see what it offers, pay special attention to this section.

In Part IV, "Using Money," we'll tackle Money. You'll learn how to set up and track all your bank accounts, schedule payments, pay bills online, and plan for the future with Money's top-notch budgeting feature.

Part V, "Exploring Other Works Suite Programs," is a compilation of the best of the other Works Suite components. We'll pay visits to Home Publishing and Encarta, and learn how to plan a trip using Streets and Maps 2000.

Appendix A covers installation of the program, in case you haven't done that yet, and Appendix B is a glossary of important Works Suite terms.

Along the way, there will be many illustrations that you can use to make sure you're on the right track. You'll also find notes, tips, and cautions that spell out additional information.

The book also contains a thorough index where tasks, features, and procedures are listed in a number of ways; you should be able to find the information you seek, regardless of whether you look under the "proper" term for that item.

Conventions Used in This Book

Commands, directions, and explanations in this book are presented in the clearest format possible. The following items are some of the features that will make this book easier for you to use:

- When you should open a menu and select a command, the menu and command name are written with a comma between them, like this: Choose File, New.
- The underlined letters onscreen in command and menu names that activate commands and options are also underlined in this book.
- Text that directs you to press a key combination is written with a plus sign between them, like this: Press Ctrl+P. That means you hold down the Ctrl key and press the P key.
- Cross-references to other sections in the book help you connect similar procedures and facts conceptually to become better educated about the program.
- For all the terms that appear in the glossary, you'll find the first appearance of that term in the text in *italic* along with its definition.

Your screen might look slightly different from some of the examples in this book. This is due to various options during installation and due to varying hardware and Windows settings.

Anything Else?

That's really all you need to know to get started! Armed with this book and Works Suite 2000, you're all set with the best tools available. So get ready to tackle your home computing projects with confidence!

PART I

Using Works

CHAPTER 1

Introducing the Microsoft Works Suite

In this chapter

WHAT IS MICROSOFT WORKS SUITE?

Works Suite is a collection of programs from Microsoft designed specifically for the home user. There are more expensive packages available that offer more features, but many people have found that Works Suite contains all the software they need.

At the heart of Microsoft Works Suite is Microsoft Works itself. Works is an integrated software program (or *suite*) that combines several capabilities into one easy-to-use interface. You can purchase Microsoft Works separately, as a standalone product, or as part of the Works Suite.

Microsoft Works offers the following:

- **Works Word Processor**—Use this to write letters or create flyers, newsletters, or any other type of document that uses text.

> **Note**
>
> If you install the entire Works Suite, Microsoft Word replaces the Works Word Processor. Therefore, you might not see the Works Word Processor on the list of available programs in Works.

- **Works Spreadsheet**—Use this to create documents that work with numbers in rows and columns and to perform calculations on those numbers. You can use spreadsheets to create budgets, sales forecasts, income statements, and more.
- **Works Database**—Use this to keep track of lists of names and addresses or inventoried objects. For example, you can create an address database containing all the names, addresses, and phone numbers of people you contact the most.
- **Calendar**—Use this to keep track of your appointments and important tasks to accomplish. Each member of the family can have a separate calendar.
- **Address Book**—Use this to keep track of contact information for people you correspond with or to whom you send email.
- **Internet Explorer**—Use this to explore the World Wide Web, which is part of the Internet. You can view Web pages, shop online, research topics that interest you, and more.

> **Note**
>
> Works comes with many links to MSN (Microsoft Network) Web pages, on which you can find all sorts of useful information, from address listings to loan rates.

- **Outlook Express**—Use this to send email to and receive email from friends and business colleagues. You can send plain messages or dress them up with formatting; you can even attach Works files to a message for mailing.

In addition, when you own the Works Suite, you get the following programs:

- **Word**—Use this more powerful word processor as a replacement for the Works Word Processor.
- **Encarta Encyclopedia**—Use this just as you would use a regular encyclopedia, to look up articles and information.
- **Money**—Use this program to track your household finances, investments, loans, and other financial affairs.
- **Home Publishing**—Use this to create newsletters, flyers, greeting cards, and other projects that combine text and graphics.
- **Expedia Streets & Trips**—Use this to display and print maps and driving directions to assist you on your next trip.

STARTING THE WORKS TASK LAUNCHER

You can start Works in either of two ways:

- Double-click the Works shortcut icon on your desktop, if one is there. (When you ran the installation program, you were given the option of creating this shortcut.)
- Click the Start button, point to Programs, and click on the Microsoft Works icon.

Tip #1 from *Faithe Wempen*

If you didn't choose to create a shortcut icon on the desktop during installation, you can create one now. Right-click over the Windows desktop. Choose New from the menu that appears, and select Shortcut. This opens the Create Shortcut dialog box. In this box, type `C:\Program Files\Microsoft Works\msworks.exe`. Click Next, and the dialog box displays a default name for the shortcut. Type `Microsoft Works`. Click Finish, and the shortcut icon is placed on the desktop.

Either way, the first thing you see is the Microsoft Works Task Launcher. It is the master control for Works, and you will learn about it in the following section.

→ If you haven't installed Works yet, **see** Appendix A, "Installing Microsoft Works Suite 2000."

USING THE WORKS TASK LAUNCHER

The Microsoft Works Task Launcher is your gateway to the individual Works components, as well as to the other programs in the suite. It contains three words across the top: *Tasks*, *Programs*, and *History*. Each of these is actually a tab; click on a word to display its information.

- **Tasks**—A list of common tasks you might want to perform, without regard to which program you would use (see Figure 1.1).
- **Programs**—A list of available Works Suite tools. Click on one of them to see a list of suggested activities, like the ones on the Tasks tab, for that tool (see Figure 1.2).

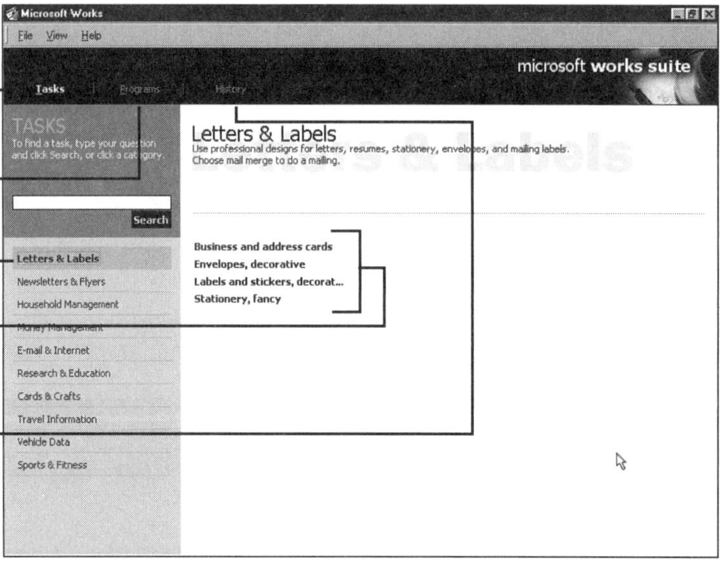

Figure 1.1
Display a list of tasks you can perform, by clicking Tasks.

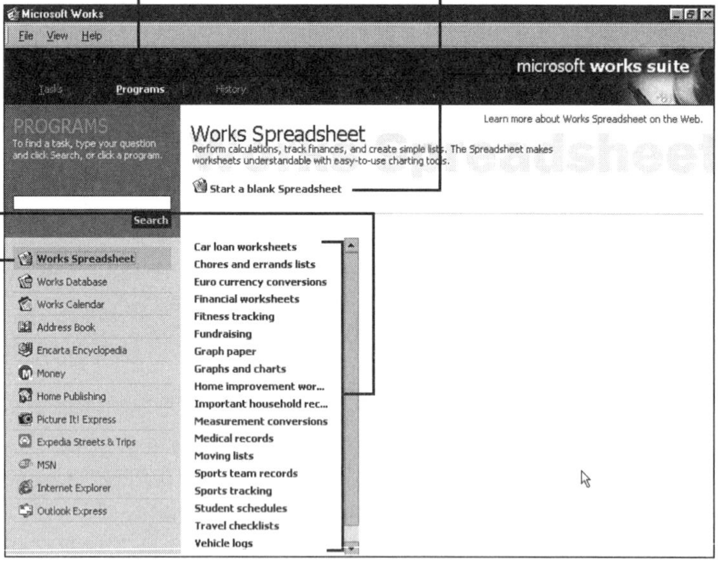

Figure 1.2
Display a list of Works Suite programs you can run, by clicking Programs.

- **History**—A list of documents you have created and saved using one of the Works Suite tools. You can reopen any of them from here. Because you haven't created any documents yet, we'll look at this tab later.

To close the Task Launcher window, click the Close (×) button in its top-right corner, or open its File menu and choose Exit.

STARTING A NEW DOCUMENT WITH A TASK

Tasks, in Microsoft Works lingo, are templates you can use to create professional-looking results, even if you have little or no experience. As you saw, the Tasks tab displays a list of tasks, organized by topic.

When you click a task, a description of it appears. An icon next to the description indicates which program will be used for the task. For example, in Figure 1.3, the selected task involves Microsoft Word. Table 1.1 shows the various icons and the programs they represent.

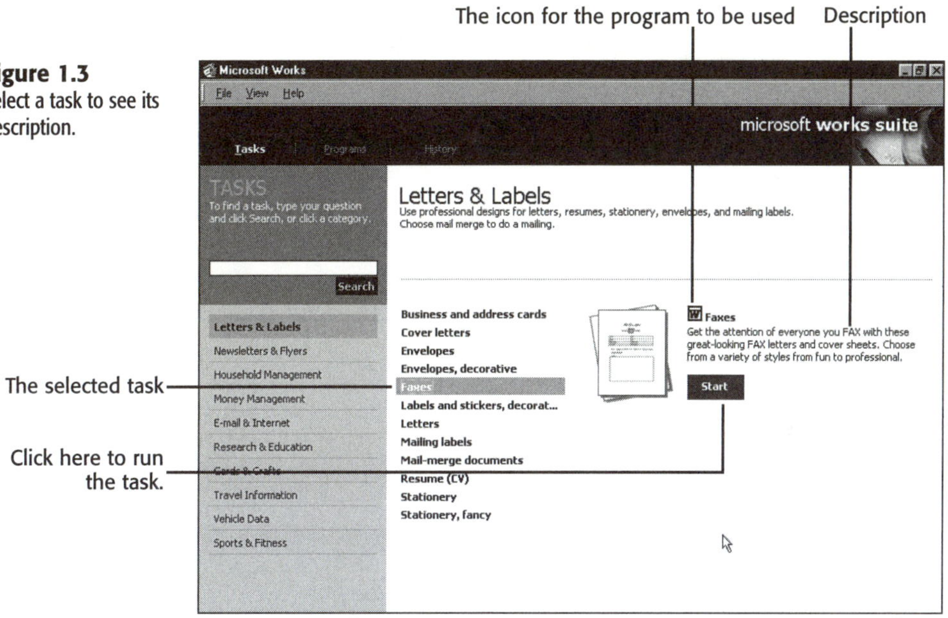

Figure 1.3
Select a task to see its description.

TABLE 1.1 ICONS REPRESENTING WORKS SUITE PROGRAMS

Icon	Program
	Word
	Works Spreadsheet
	Works Database
	Works Calendar
	Address Book

continues

TABLE 1.1 CONTINUED

Icon	Program
	Encarta Encyclopedia
	Money
	Home Publishing
	Picture It! Express
	Expedia Streets & Trips
	MSN
	Internet Explorer
	Outlook Express

In Figure 1.3, notice the Search box above the categories. You can use this to search for a task if you don't know what category it is in. Simply type a keyword in the Search box, and click the Search button. For example, in Figure 1.4, I have typed **`team`**. All the tasks from all the categories that have *team* as a keyword appear.

Figure 1.4
You can search for a task by keyword if you are not sure where to look for it.

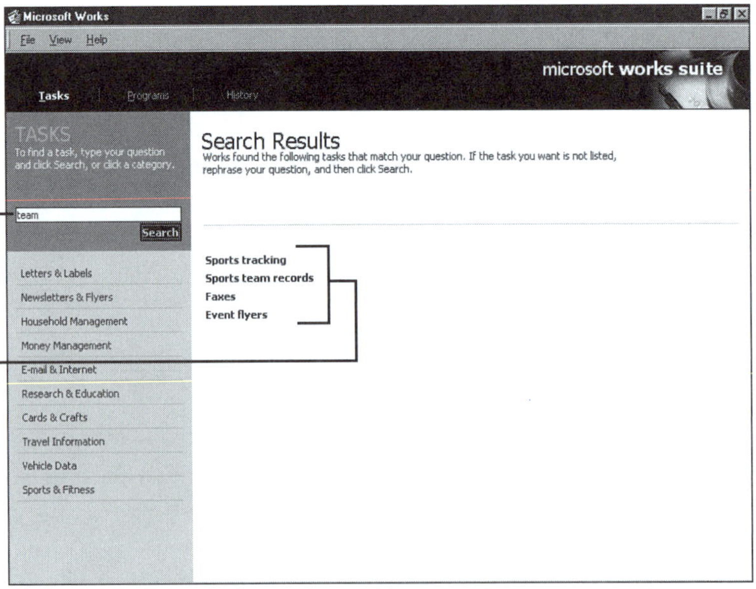

The various tasks do different things when you start them. Some tasks open *wizards*, which are dialog boxes that help you set up a particular type of document or other project. Most of the tasks associated with Word, the Works Spreadsheet, and the Works Database involve wizards. Other tasks open Web pages or start a program at a particular screen. (For example, choosing Portfolio Status under Money Management opens Microsoft Money and displays your stock portfolio.)

To start a task, follow these steps from the Works Task Launcher's Tasks tab:

1. Click the category of task you want.
2. On the list of tasks that appears, click the one you want. A description of it appears, along with a Start button.
3. Click the Start button.

If the task involves a wizard, it walks you through each step necessary to build the document. Depending on the task you choose, the options vary. For example, if you choose Faxes (refer to Figure 1.4), Word opens and the wizard shown in Figure 1.5 appears.

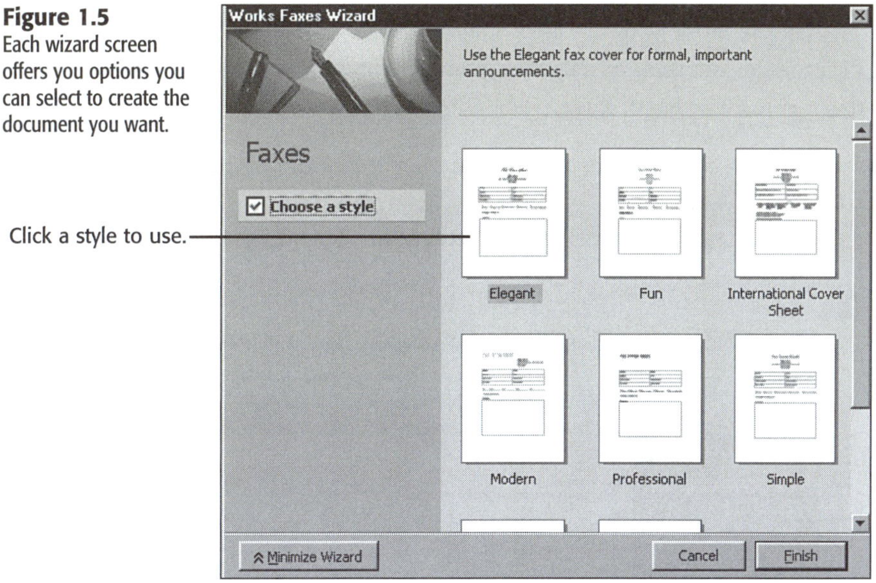

Figure 1.5
Each wizard screen offers you options you can select to create the document you want.

Make your selection in the wizard box, and click Finish.

Note

If you change your mind about completing a wizard, you can exit the process at any time by clicking the Cancel button.

When a wizard has finished, a document appears on your screen with sample text and formatting. You can customize this document and then save it for later use.

→ To save your work, **see** Chapter 2, "Performing Common Works Tasks."

STARTING A WORKS PROGRAM FROM THE TASK LAUNCHER

You don't have to start with a task; you can start one of the Works Suite programs without specifying a particular purpose. That way, you can decide what you want to do on your own.

Note

In this book, I use the term *document* to refer to any data file from any program, not just word processing files. A document can be a spreadsheet, a database, a Home Publishing project, and so on.

When you start programs such as Word, the Works Spreadsheet, and the Works Database, which are designed primarily to help you enter and edit data, a new file opens. You can use this new file or open an existing one, as you like. In other programs, such as Expedia, Encarta, and so on, there is no need to create a new file because the purpose of those programs is different.

1. Click Programs to move to the Programs tab.
2. Click the program you want to start. For example, Figure 1.6 shows Word selected.
3. Click the start line for that program. The program opens.

Note

The exact wording varies; for example, for Word, it reads `Start a Blank Word Document`. For the Works Calendar, it reads `Start the Calendar`.

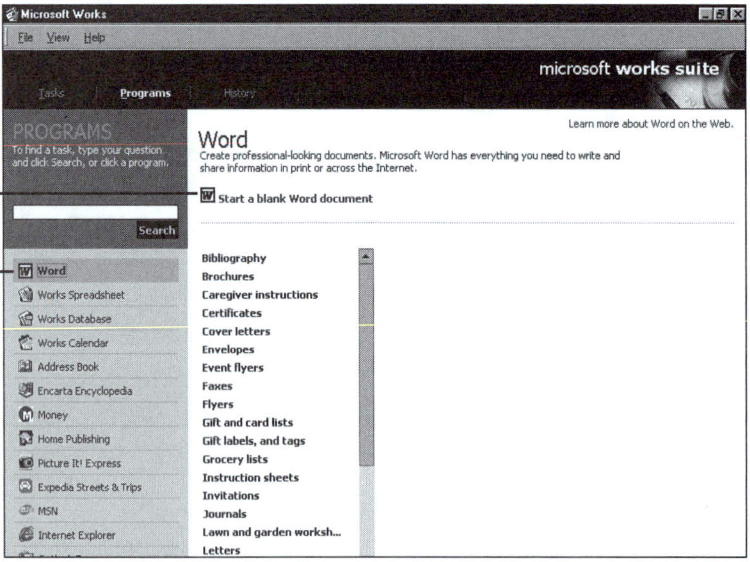

Figure 1.6
Select the program you want, and then click its Start command.

Notice in Figure 1.6 that a list of tasks appears for the program. These are the same tasks you could choose from the Tasks tab, but here they are organized according to the program used. On the Tasks tab, they are organized by task category.

OPENING AN EXISTING DOCUMENT FROM THE TASK LAUNCHER

When you create a document using a task and save your work, that document appears in the Task Launcher whenever you select that task from either the Tasks or Programs tab. For example, in Figure 1.7, you can see that I have created and saved a fax document called `fax sheet for Tony`.

To reopen a saved document from the Tasks or Programs tab, follow these steps:

1. Click Tasks or Programs, displaying the Tasks or Programs tab.
2. Click the category or program you want.
3. Click the task you want. A list of documents created from this task appears.
4. Point to the document you want to open. It becomes underlined, and the mouse pointer changes to a pointing hand.
5. Click on the underlined text. The document reopens.

The preceding steps are applicable only to documents created through the Task Launcher using a particular task. If you create a document starting with a blank or after starting a program, you will not see any record of it on the Tasks or Programs tab. However, it will appear on the History tab.

Figure 1.7
Existing documents created with a particular task appear whenever that task is selected.

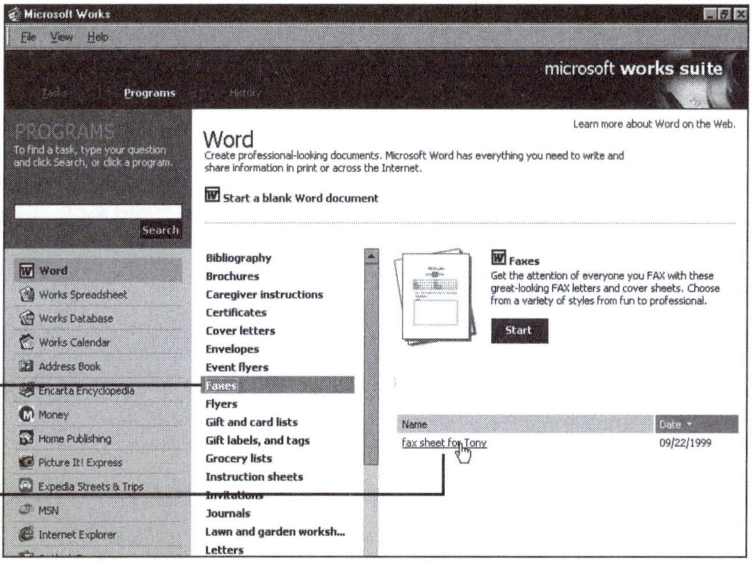

The History tab lists each document you have worked with and saved. It shows the program used to create the document, which task is associated with it (if any), and the date when it was last modified. You can reopen any document here by following these steps:

1. Click History, displaying the History tab.
2. Point to the document you want to open. It becomes underlined, and the mouse pointer changes to a pointing hand (see Figure 1.8).
3. Click the underlined text. The document opens.

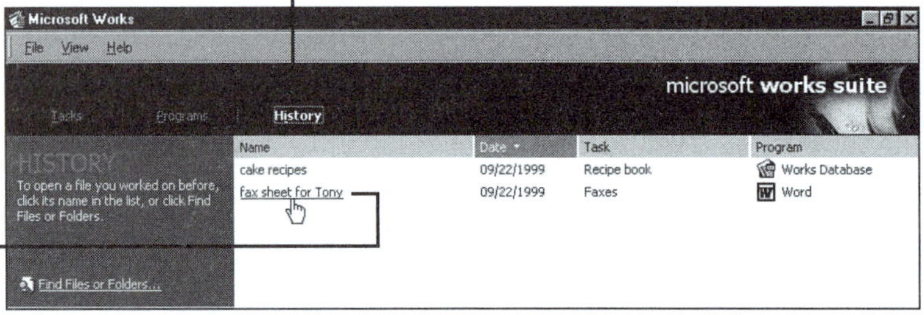

Figure 1.8
Click a document on the History tab to reopen it.

The History list in Figure 1.8 has only two documents on it, but as time goes by, your list may grow to hundreds of documents. When this happens, you might want to sort the listing in various ways to help you quickly find the document you want.

You can sort by any column on the History list by clicking that column name. An arrow appears next to the column name to let you know that it is the current sort column. For example, in Figure 1.8, the Date column is selected. Clicking on the same column again changes the sort between ascending (A–Z) and descending (Z–A) order.

Note

Want to hide your tracks? You can clear the history record by choosing View, Options and clicking the Clear History button. You can also deselect the Track History check box here to stop tracking your history from now on.

GETTING HELP

Help is on the way! If you ever get into a jam while using Works, you can find help in a variety of ways.

For starters, any time you try a Works feature for the first time, a Help box appears, offering to assist you. Figure 1.9 shows the Works Help window that opens automatically the first time you start the Works Spreadsheet, for example. Just click on underlined text for more information, or when you are finished with the Help window, click its Close (×) button.

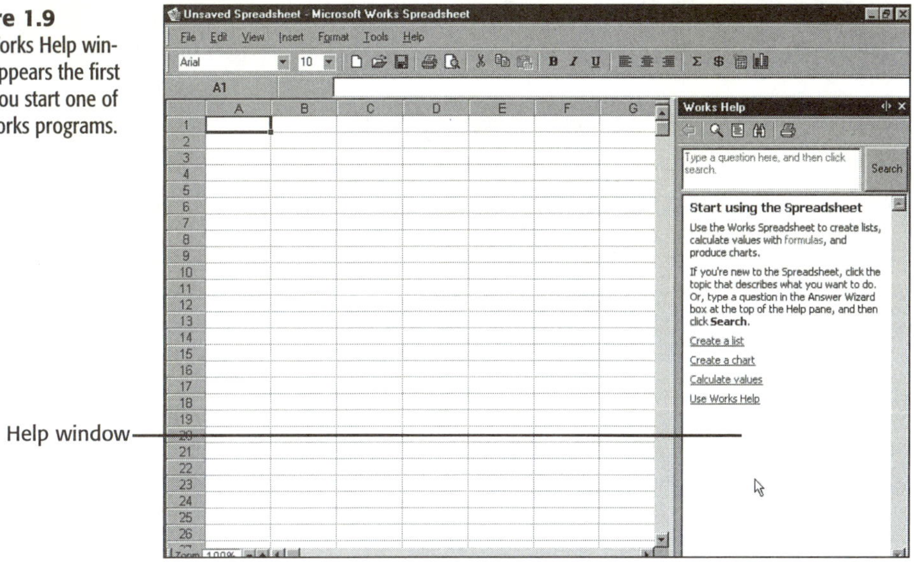

Figure 1.9
The Works Help window appears the first time you start one of the Works programs.

Note

The Help window will continue to appear each time you start that program until you close it once; then it won't appear by default anymore.

You also can use plenty of other Help features. You can access the Help system in whatever way works best for you. Take a look at the choices.

Using the What's This? Feature

The What's This? feature offers quick assistance for dialog box controls. In most dialog boxes, a question mark (**?**) button appears in the top-right corner. You can click on it and then click on any dialog box control to find out about it.

1. Start in any dialog box. (To open a dialog box just for practice, choose View, Options in the Works Suite Task Launcher window.)
2. Click the ? button. A question mark appears next to the mouse pointer (see Figure 1.10).

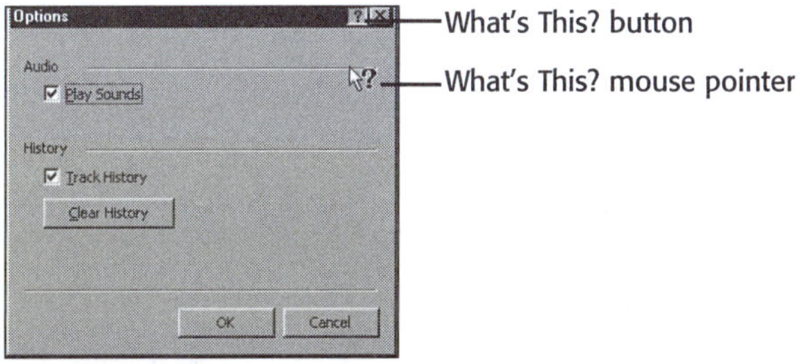

Figure 1.10
Click the question mark for What's This? Help.

3. Click any list item, button, or area of the dialog box. A short description of that option or item is displayed, as shown in Figure 1.11.

Figure 1.11
What's This? describes the Clear History button.

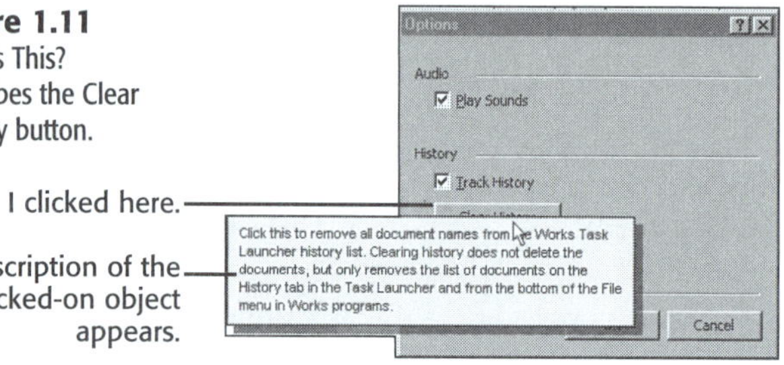

4. To clear the screen of the Help box description, click outside the Help box anywhere on the screen, or press the Esc key.

Note

In some cases, you can right-click a dialog box area, option, or list, and the Help box description activates. Another quick method is to press the F1 key. The F1 key activates a description for whatever is currently highlighted in the dialog box.

Using the Help Menu

All the programs in the Works Suite, including the Task Launcher window itself, have a Help menu, from which you can request assistance.

The programs that are part of the main Works program (the Works Task Launcher, Word Processor, Spreadsheet, Database, and Calendar) use the same Help menu. The other programs in the Works Suite have slightly different Help offerings, but all are similar enough that you should have no problem with them after learning about those for Works. Table 1.2 lists the commands on the Help menu for Works.

Table 1.2 Help Menu Commands

Menu Selection	Description
Microsoft Works Help	Opens the Answer Wizard, a pane where you can type a question and find topics that answer it. (This command is simply Works Help in some programs.)
Contents	Provides a series of Help topics organized by topics you can browse.
Index	Provides an alphabetical list of Help topics.

Menu Selection	Description
Print Help Topic	Prints whatever article is currently displayed in the Help window.
Accessibility Help	Displays information about making Works easier to use for people with disabilities.
Microsoft on the Web	Opens a submenu listing Web pages that can help with Works.
About Microsoft Works	Displays the About dialog box, which contains information about the version of Works you are using and copyright information.

Of the features listed in Table 1.2, the most important are the first three. Each of these opens the same Works Help window, but with a different "tab" on top. (They look like buttons instead of tabs, but they function as tabs.) The three tabs are Answer Wizard, Contents, and Index. Figure 1.12 shows the Help window in the Works Spreadsheet, with the Answer Wizard tab on top. You can move among the tabs by selecting the corresponding command on the Help menu or by clicking the tab's button in the Help window.

Figure 1.12
The Help window with the Answer Wizard tab displayed.

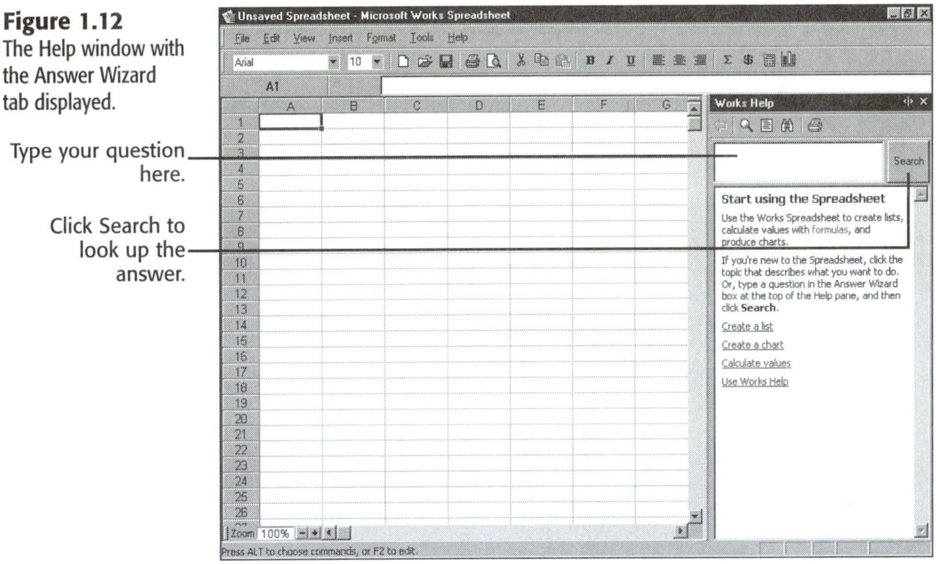

USING THE ANSWER WIZARD

When you choose Help, Microsoft Works Help (or Help, Works Help in some programs), the Works Help window opens with the Answer Wizard displayed. You can also get here by clicking the Answer Wizard button in the Help window.

To use the Answer Wizard, type your question in the text box at the top, and then click Search. A list of topics related to your question appears. Click the topic you want to read about, and it appears.

1. Choose Help, [Microsoft] Works Help, or press F1.
2. Type your question in the text box provided.
3. Click Search. A list of articles appears.
4. Click the article you want to read.

Note

Most of the Works programs have a Help toolbar button you can click to open the Help window. The Works Task Launcher is an exception in this regard; it doesn't have a toolbar at all.

USING THE CONTENTS FEATURE

The Contents feature of Works lists the available Help topics by category. It's most useful when you don't know the exact name for what you're trying to do, but you know generally what it's about. For example, suppose that you want to know how to preview the printout onscreen before you print your document, but you don't know that this feature is called *Print Preview*. You could explore the Help system by topic and find the information fairly easily.

1. Choose Help, Contents. The Help Topics: Microsoft Works dialog box appears.
2. Click a folder to expand the list of subtopics beneath it. Keep doing this until articles appear.

   You can tell the difference between a folder and article by the icon next to it, as shown in Figure 1.13.
3. Click the article you want to read. It appears.

Figure 1.13
Click a folder to expand it.

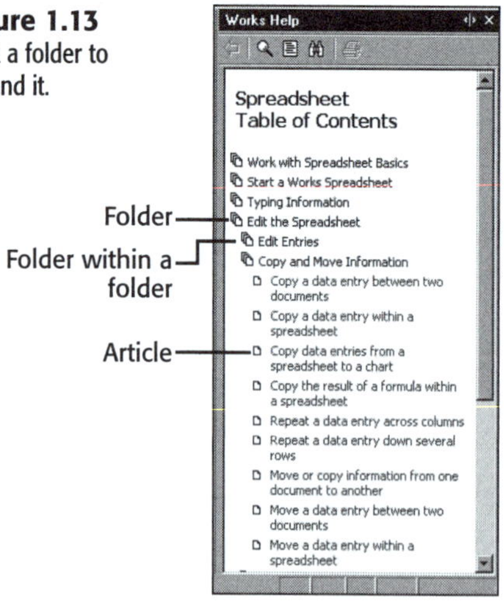

USING THE INDEX FEATURE

The Index feature of Help enables you to type a word or phrase and search the Help file for that word or phrase. As with Contents, you don't necessarily have to know the proper or technical phrase for your topic to find it. For example, if you didn't know how to change the way paragraphs align on your page, you could search for *paragraphs*, or even *changing*.

1. Choose Help, Index. The index appears.
2. Type the word you want to search for in the text box, as shown in Figure 1.14. As you type, the index entries in the bottom of the screen change, matching the word you type as closely as possible.

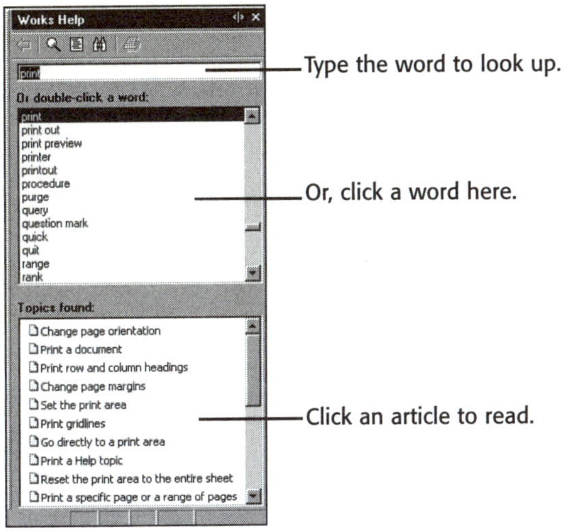

Figure 1.14
Use the Index feature of Help to search for particular topics.

3. Click the article you want to read. It appears.

RESIZING AND CLOSING THE HELP WINDOW

The Help window can appear in either of two preset sizes. You saw the larger size in Figures 1.12 through 1.14. To make it smaller, click the Resize button, which is right next to the Close (X) button on the window's title bar.

You can also manually drag the left border of the Help window to make it any size you like, even covering the entire screen. Figure 1.15 shows it enlarged to make reading an article easier.

To close the Help window, click its Close (X) button. You can reopen it at any time later.

WORKING WITH FOUND HELP ARTICLES

After finding and displaying a Help article onscreen, simply read it and follow its instructions. If you want to print it, click the Print button on the Help window's toolbar.

Notice in Figure 1.15 that the found article poses a question at the top. You can see the answer to that question by clicking the down arrow next to it, as shown in Figure 1.16.

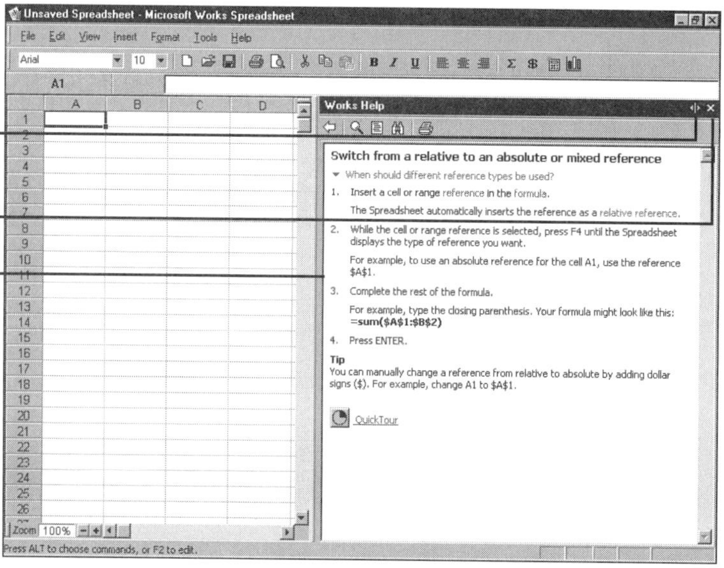

Figure 1.15
The Help window has been expanded by dragging its left border.

Resize button

Close button

Drag the border to resize.

You can also see the definitions of any words in green by clicking them; definitions expand within the text. Click on them again to collapse the definitions when you are finished reading them.

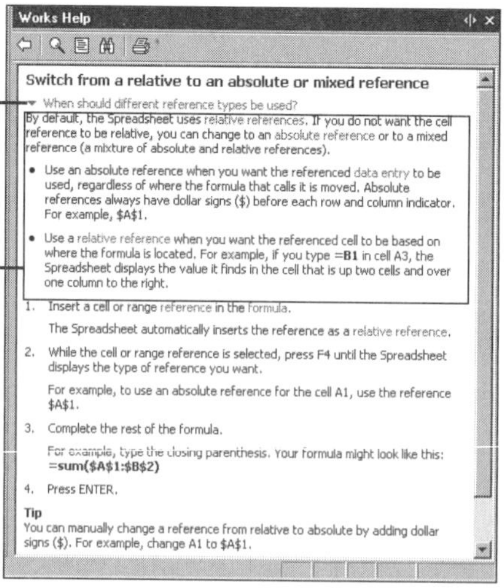

Figure 1.16
The expanded answer to the question.

Click here to collapse the answer again.

The answer to the question

NAVIGATING THE WORKS WINDOWS

It's a good idea to familiarize yourself with the onscreen elements that appear in a Works program window. Figure 1.17 points out some of these, using the Works Spreadsheet window as an example.

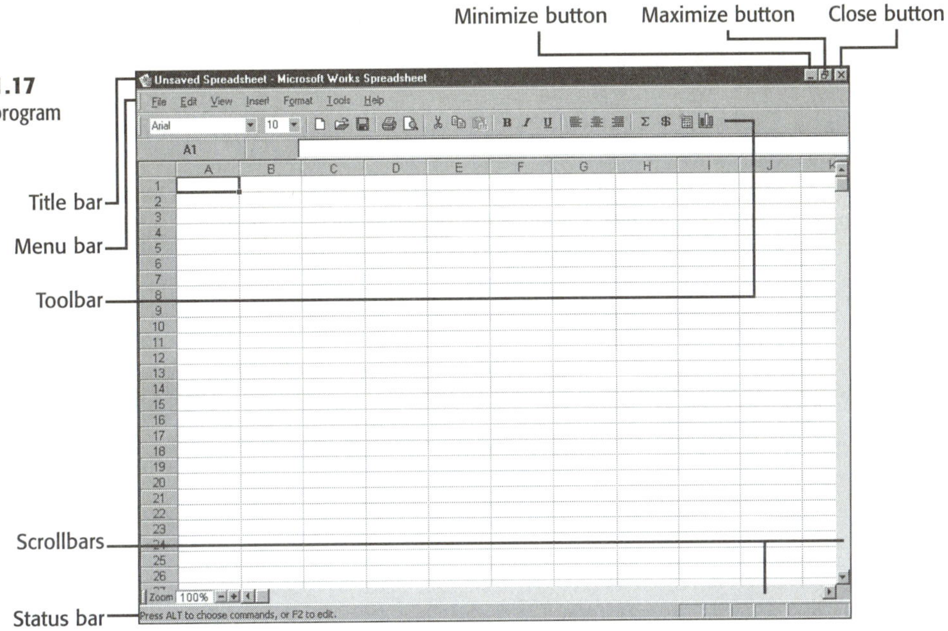

Figure 1.17
A typical program window.

Here's a brief rundown of each onscreen element in the Works window:

- **Title bar**—This bar displays the name of the program and the name of the open document. In Figure 1.17, the title bar displays the name of the program, `Microsoft Works Spreadsheet`. The document name is `Unsaved Spreadsheet` because no name has been assigned yet.
- **Menu bar**—This bar displays a collection of menus that contain commands you can select to perform different Works tasks. To display a menu, simply click on the menu name. To select a specific command from the list, click on a command.
- **Toolbar**—This bar contains shortcut buttons for common Works tasks. To select a button, click on it. Clicking toolbar buttons is much quicker than opening menus to choose commands. The Works Word Processor has two toolbars: Standard and Formatting.
- **Status bar**—This bar keeps you posted about commands you select.
- **Scrollbars**—Use the vertical and horizontal scrollbars to view different portions of your document. Click the vertical scrollbar's arrow buttons to move up or down the document. Use the horizontal scrollbar's arrow buttons to move left or right.

- **Window controls**—Use the Minimize, Maximize, and Close buttons at the far right end of the title bar to control the window. For example, if you click the Minimize button, the window is reduced to a button (click the button to restore the window to its original size). Use the Maximize button to expand the window to its maximum size. Use the Close button to close the window entirely.

Depending on which Works tool you open, the menu commands and toolbar buttons you see will vary. Each program has menus and buttons that are custom-tailored to the type of data you create and edit using it.

Which Button Is Which?

To find out about any toolbar button, hover your mouse pointer over the button; a ToolTip appears, identifying the button's name. Look on the status bar to see a brief description of the button.

USING MENUS AND TOOLBARS

The key to getting Works to create the type of documents you want is to issue commands. You can do this through menus and toolbars.

If you're an avid mouse user, selecting commands is as easy as clicking the mouse. Click on the menu name you want to view; then click on the command you want to activate.

Shortcut Menus

Mouse enthusiasts can right-click (single-click the right mouse button) on certain areas of the screen or during certain tasks to display shortcut menus listing commands applicable to the task at hand. For example, if you right-click over selected text in a document, a shortcut menu appears with commands you can apply to the text, such as formatting commands.

If you prefer to use the keyboard instead of the mouse, you can use shortcut keys to open menus and select commands. Notice the underlined letter in each menu name in Figure 1.18. Those are *selection letters*. Press the Alt key on the keyboard, and then press the menu's selection letter to display the menu. Also notice in Figure 1.18 that the commands listed on the menu have selection letters. To activate the command, press the selection letter.

As you work with the various menus in Works, you will notice key combinations listed to the right of some menu commands (refer to Figure 1.18). These are shortcut keys you also can press to activate commands with the keyboard and bypass the menu altogether. Unlike selection letters, however, you must memorize which shortcut keys to press to activate a command. For example, to quickly save a document without having to open the File menu and select the Save command, press Ctrl+S on the keyboard (press both keys simultaneously).

Sorry, Keyboard Users!

Most commands presented in this book focus on using the mouse. If you're a die-hard keyboard user, just remember to look out for selection letters and shortcut key combinations to perform the same tasks.

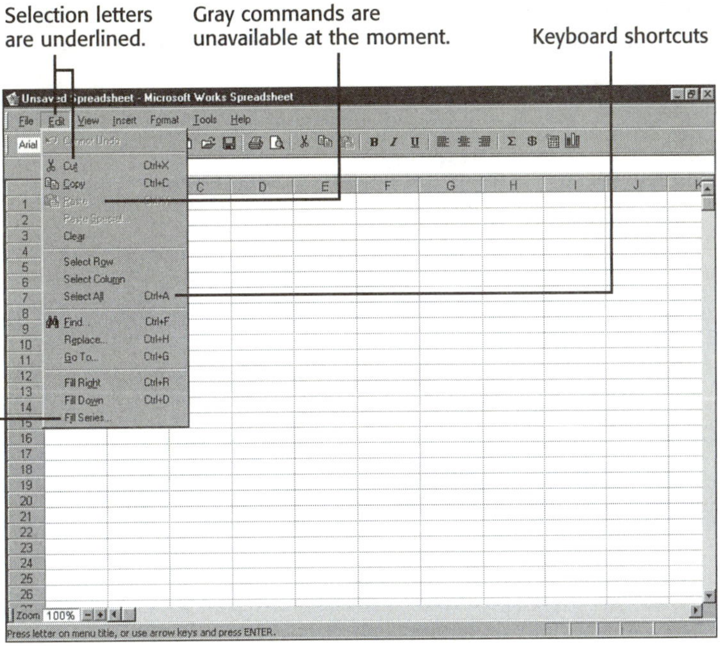

Figure 1.18
Click a menu name to display a list of commands or, if you prefer using the keyboard, press the Alt key and the menu's selection letter.

When it comes to using toolbars, keyboard users are out of luck. The only way to activate a toolbar button is to click on it with the mouse. Remember, Works toolbar buttons are simply shortcuts to common commands. Many toolbar buttons, such as Cut and Copy, have key combinations you can press to activate the commands just as quickly as clicking toolbar buttons.

USING DIALOG BOXES

Many commands you select, whether you use the mouse or the keyboard, open dialog boxes with additional options. Dialog boxes vary in complexity. Some offer only a few choices; others offer several tabs with different options on each tab. Figure 1.19 shows an example of a dialog box.

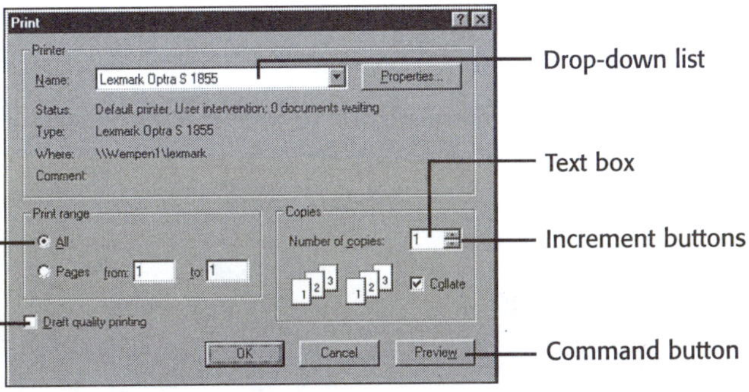

Figure 1.19
You can also issue commands in Works through dialog boxes.

You have to know how to use several common elements to make selections and issue commands using a dialog box. Table 1.3 briefly explains these common elements.

TABLE 1.3 COMMON DIALOG BOX ELEMENTS

Element	Description
List boxes	These typically list items. To choose an item from the list, click on the item name.
Drop-down boxes	You'll recognize this element by its downward-pointing arrow at the right end of the box. Click on the arrow to display a drop-down list of items. To select an item from the list, click on the item.
Text boxes	Use these boxes to enter information. Click inside the text box, and type in the required information.
Increment buttons	Text boxes that hold only numeric data have up and down arrows next to them. Click these to increment a numeric value up or down.
Check boxes	A check mark inside the check box means that the option is activated; no check mark means that the option is not activated. Click the check box to toggle the check mark on or off.
Option buttons	Either/or choices in a dialog box are represented by round option buttons. Only one button can be selected at a time.
Command buttons	Click these buttons to issue a command or open another dialog box.

Navigating with the Keyboard

You can navigate a dialog box using only the keyboard. Press the Tab key to move between options, text, and list boxes. Notice that many dialog box options have selection letters, too, just like menu commands. Use the selection letters to activate options. To exit the dialog box without applying any of the selections you made, press Esc. To apply the new selections, press Enter.

EXITING WORKS

When you exit the Works Task Launcher window, you do not close the individual programs that you have opened through it. For example, if you are working in the Works Database, and you close the Task Launcher, nothing will happen to your database window. You must close it separately.

To close the Works Task Launcher window, or any other window for that matter, click its Close (×) button (see Figure 1.20). You can also close most programs by choosing File, Exit.

Figure 1.20
To close the Works Task Launcher or any other window, choose File, Exit or click the Close button.

TROUBLESHOOTING

NO WORKS WORD PROCESSOR

The Works Word Processor doesn't appear on my list of programs.

That's normal, if you have the Suite version of Microsoft Works 2000. Word replaces it because you don't need two word processors.

The Works Word Processor is still available, even though it might not appear in the Works Task Launcher. You can run it by displaying the contents of the folder C:\Program Files\Microsoft Works in Windows Explorer and then double-clicking the WksWP icon.

NO WORD, EITHER

But what if neither Word nor the Works Word Processor appears?

If neither Word nor the Works Word Processor appears, you probably have not yet installed Word. Go ahead and do that now. See Appendix A, "Installing Microsoft Works Suite 2000," for installation help.

CHAPTER 2

Performing Common Works Tasks

In this chapter

The Works tools in the main Works program (the word processor, spreadsheet, and database) share many common procedures, such as saving your work or printing documents. The steps for performing these tasks are the same for each program. These tasks are very similar in Word, too, if you use Word instead of the Works Word Processor.

In this chapter, you will learn how to tackle common tasks such as opening new documents, saving documents, closing documents, and printing.

Although you haven't learned how to use each of the Works programs yet, this chapter can be a reference for when you're ready to perform a common task. Refer back to this chapter for quick tips and steps when needed.

RETURNING TO THE TASK LAUNCHER WINDOW

In Chapter 1, "Introducing the Microsoft Works Suite," you learned how to use the Works Task Launcher to start a Works tool and create a new document or a document based on a task. You can return to the Task Launcher to open new documents at any time, and you don't have to close the Works tool or document you're currently using. Simply click the Microsoft Works button on your taskbar, as shown in Figure 2.1, to return to the Works Task Launcher window.

Figure 2.1
Click Microsoft Works on the taskbar to return to the Works Task Launcher at any time.

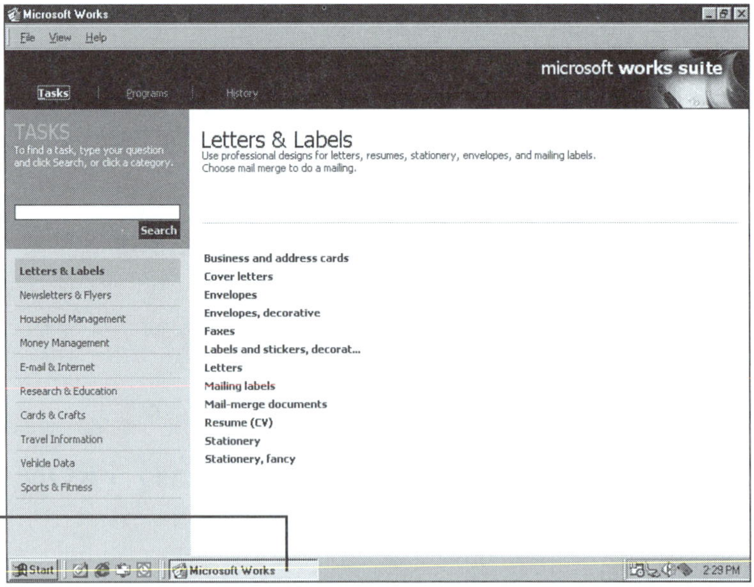

Microsoft Works on the taskbar

You can also return to the Task Launcher by choosing File, New in the Works Word Processor, Spreadsheet, Database, or Calendar program. For example, if you are using the Works Spreadsheet and you choose File, New, the Task Launcher reappears, with the Programs tab displayed and the Works Spreadsheet program selected.

If you use Microsoft Word instead of the Works Word Processor, you can still return to the Task Launcher any time. Simply choose File, New to display a submenu, as shown in Figure 2.2, and then choose Works Task Launcher from that menu.

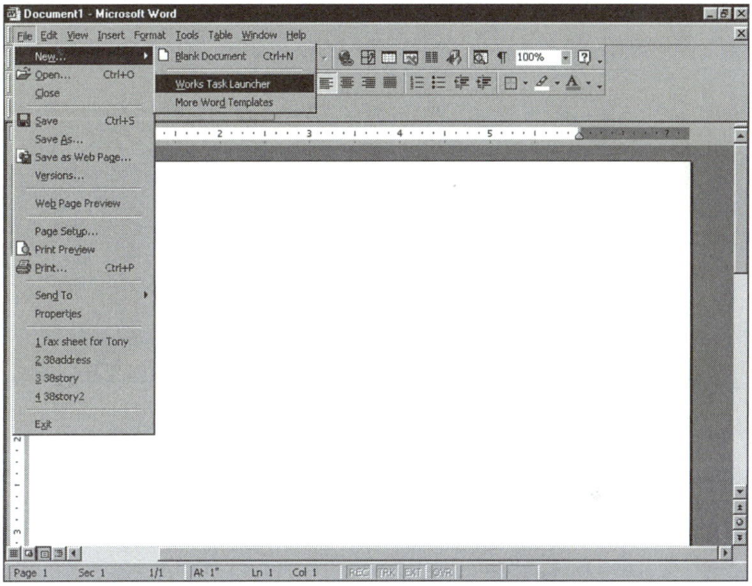

Figure 2.2
In Word, return to the Task Launcher with the File, New, Works Task Launcher command.

Note

The other Works Suite applications are not as tightly integrated with the Task Launcher; choosing File, New in one of them merely starts a new file, search, topic, or other item within that program.

STARTING A NEW, BLANK DOCUMENT FROM A WORKS PROGRAM

You don't have to return to the Task Launcher to start a new document; you can do so at any time. All Works programs (as well as Word) have a New button on the toolbar; click it to start a new, blank document with default settings (see Figure 2.3).

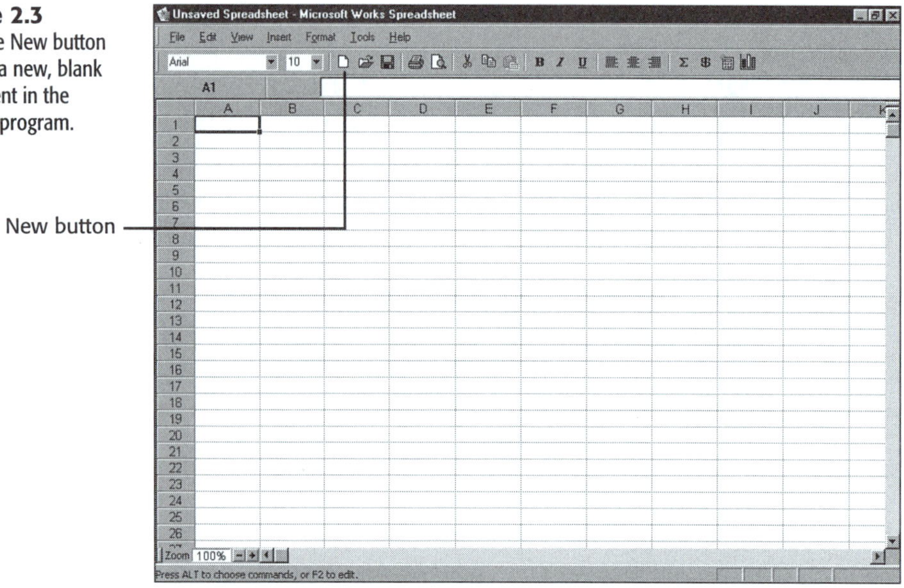

Figure 2.3
Click the New button to start a new, blank document in the current program.

OPENING EXISTING DOCUMENTS IN A WORKS PROGRAM

As you saw in Chapter 1, you can open existing documents from the Task Launcher's History tab or from the list of saved documents that appears when you select a certain task on one of the other two tabs. Here are some other ways of opening a file.

OPENING A FILE WITH THE OPEN DIALOG BOX

You can also open documents directly from within a Works program by using the File, Open command (or the Open button on the toolbar).

1. In a Works program (the word processor, spreadsheet, or database), choose File, Open. The Open dialog box appears (see Figure 2.4).
2. Click the file you want to open. (Change the location if necessary.)
3. Click Open. The file opens.

Tip #2 from *Faithe Wempen*

The last four files you have worked with appear at the bottom of the File menu. To open one of them in a hurry, simply select it from there.

If the document should not be changed (for example, a report that has already been submitted and that you are retaining for record-keeping), you can mark the Open as Read-Only check box in the Open dialog box. This prevents you from saving your changes to the document under the same name; you must use the File, Save As command to give the changed copy a new name.

Figure 2.4
Select the file to open from the Open dialog box.

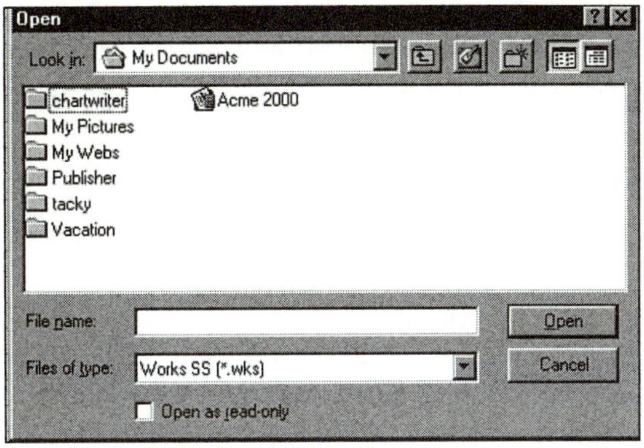

CHANGING THE FILE LOCATION

Many people store all their files in the default folder, C:\My Documents. If you do that, you will not have to change the location in step 2. However, if you use different folders to store documents, you might need to change it.

To change the location where the program should look, do the following:

1. Open the Look In drop-down list and choose the drive on which to look. A listing of all its folders appears.
2. Double-click the folder in which to look.
3. Repeat step 2, as necessary, to move through multiple levels of folders.

The Up One Level button moves you up one level in the folder structure and can be handy if you accidentally double-click the wrong folder and have to back up.

This same procedure can be used in the Save As dialog box to save a file in a location different from the default. You will learn to save files later in this chapter.

→ To create your own filing system in which to store documents, **see** "Creating a Filing System," **p. 36**.

OPENING FILES OF OTHER TYPES

You might occasionally have to open a file with a different file type, such as a plain-text file. Works can open many file types besides its own native ones, but you must tell it to display files of that type in its Open dialog box. To do so, open the Files of Type drop-down list, and select the type you want to see. If you are not sure about the type, choose All Files.

Note

Works cannot open every single file type that's out there. If it can't open the file you want, it will display an error message to let you know.

OPENING FILES IN WORD

The steps for opening a file in Word are the same as those for Works programs; the only difference is that Word's Open dialog has a few more controls (see Figure 2.5):

- The Places bar, along the left edge of the dialog box, provides shortcuts to commonly used folders when saving and opening files.
- The Tools button opens a menu of special-purpose opening and saving features, such as Find.
- The Open button has a drop-down list to let you choose whether to open the document as Read-Only.

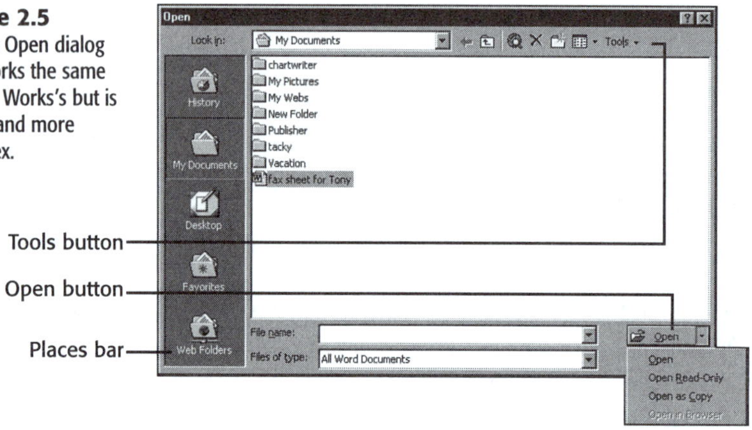

Figure 2.5
Word's Open dialog box works the same way as Works's but is larger and more complex.

SWITCHING AMONG OPEN DOCUMENTS

When you have more than one document window open at a time, you can switch between them. Each open document has its own button on the taskbar. On the taskbar, simply click on the button for the document or program you want to switch to (see Figure 2.6).

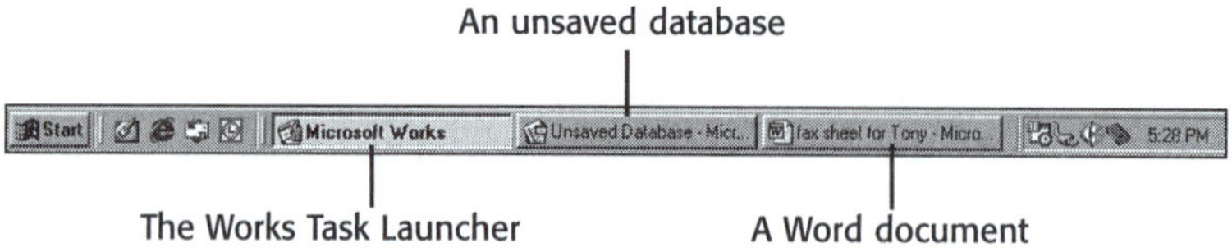

Figure 2.6
Click the document on the taskbar to bring it into view.

SAVING YOUR WORK

After you've worked on a document, you will want to save your changes so that you can open the file again. Unless you want to retype everything again, it's a good idea to save your work, even if you don't think you will ever revisit it. You can always go back and delete the file later.

When you save a document for the first time, the Save As dialog box appears, and you can assign a name to the file, as well as specify a folder in which to store it.

1. Choose File, Save, or click the Save button. The Save As dialog box opens (see Figure 2.7). (It looks slightly different in Word but works the same.)

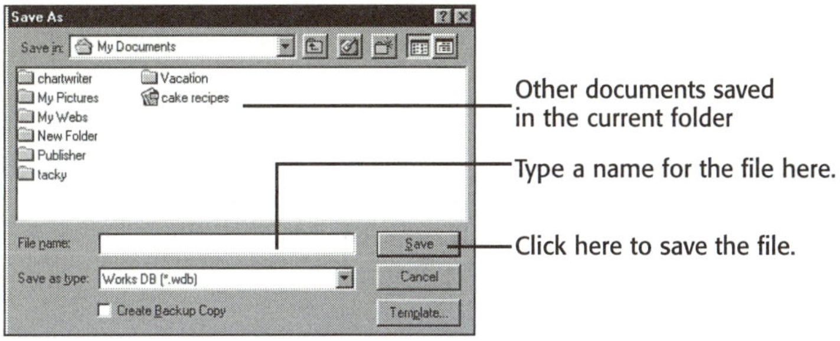

Figure 2.7
Use the Save As dialog box to assign a filename to your document and save your work.

2. Type a name in the File Name text box.
3. Click Save. The document is saved.

To save a document that's already been saved at least once, click the Save button on the toolbar, or open the File menu and select Save. Works saves your current changes without opening the dialog box.

If you want to save the document under a new filename but keep the original document intact, use the Save As dialog box again. Choose File, Save As. This reopens the Save As dialog box, and you can assign a new filename. Type a different name in the File Name text box; then click Save. Works saves the document under the new name and closes the original document.

SAVING IN A DIFFERENT LOCATION

By default, Works saves your documents in the C:\My Documents folder. You can choose to save your documents in other folders or drives as needed by changing the location from the Save In drop-down list. This works just like the Look In drop-down list you use when you open files; see "Changing the File Location" earlier in this chapter for details.

SAVING IN A DIFFERENT FILE FORMAT

You can also choose to save the file as a different file format. For example, if you've created a report in Word that you want to share with a friend who uses WordPerfect, you can save the document in a WordPerfect file format that your friend's computer can recognize. You will find numerous file format choices in the Save as Type drop-down list in the Save As dialog box.

Tip #3 from
Faithe Wempen

If the file format you want to use is not listed in the Save as Type drop-down list, try the Rich Text Format (RTF) for word processing documents or Text (TXT) for spreadsheet or database data. These are generic formats that should work in most programs.

Creating a Filing System

You might want to create your own filing system within C:\My Documents. Notice in Figure 2.7, for example, that there are several folders within C:\My Documents that I have created for storing documents for specific projects. I can switch to a folder by double-clicking it.

To create a new folder from the Save As dialog box, do the following:

1. Click the Create New Folder button in the Save As dialog box. A new folder appears in the Open dialog box in the currently displayed folder.
2. Type a name for the new folder.
3. Press Enter. The Open dialog box switches to that new folder.

Closing Documents

When you are finished with a document, close it. You can close a document in any of the following ways:

- Click the document window's Close (×) button (see Figure 2.8).
- Choose File, Close.
- Press Ctrl+W.
- Double-click the document window's Control menu icon (also shown in Figure 2.8).
- Exit the program. All open documents are closed automatically when you do so.

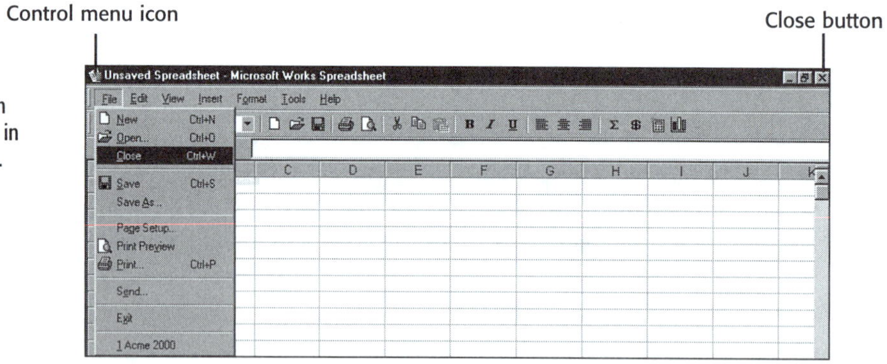

Figure 2.8
You can close an open document in numerous ways.

When you close a document after making changes to it, Works prompts you to save the file. Click Yes to save your work, No if you don't want to save your changes, or Cancel to stop the close procedure entirely.

Printing Your Work

One of the main reasons people create documents in Works is to share information with other people. Creating a printout of your work is one of the best ways to share it.

To print a single copy of the entire document using the default print settings, click the Print button on the toolbar. The document prints immediately. This is the fastest, easiest way to print! However, there might be times when you want to check your work or specify print options. The following sections explain what to do.

Using Print Preview

The Works programs (and Word, too) have a Print Preview feature that enables you to see how your pages will look when printed before you actually print them. This can save you paper because you do not have to print a draft to check layout.

> **Note**
>
> Another way to proofread your work onscreen is to adjust the zoom. Zoom controls how large or small the document looks on your monitor; it has no effect on the printout. You might want to zoom in for an up-close look or zoom out for an overall view.
>
> To zoom, click the - or + button next to the Zoom box in the bottom-left corner of the spreadsheet or database screen, or enter a specific zoom percentage. (The default is 100%.) In Word and the Works Word Processor, you can select from the Zoom drop-down list on the toolbar.

To use Print Preview, choose File, Print Preview, or click the Print Preview button on the toolbar. This opens the document in Print Preview mode, as shown in Figure 2.9.

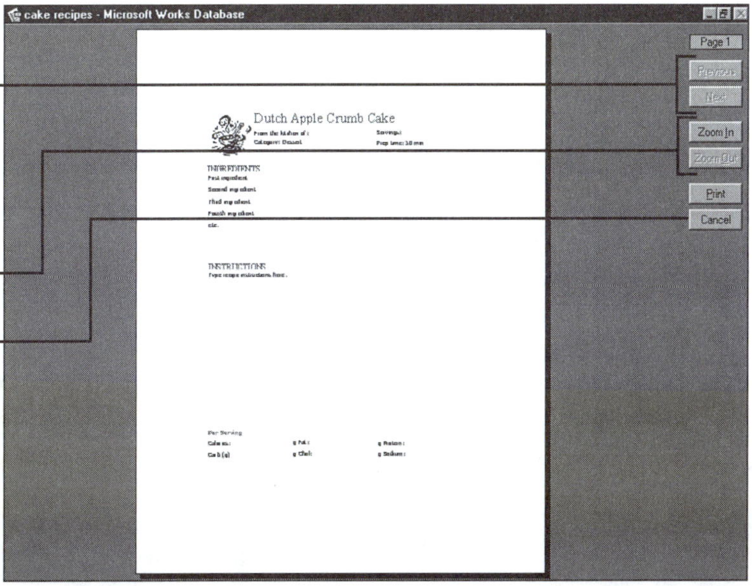

Figure 2.9
The Works Print Preview feature lets you check your document's appearance before printing.

View the preceding or next page.

Zoom in or out.

Close Print Preview.

Print Preview looks a bit different in Word but functions basically the same way.

By default the document appears in full-page view in Print Preview. To zoom in for a closer look, click the mouse pointer over the area of the document you want to see, or click the Zoom In button. To zoom out again, click the Zoom Out button.

If your document has more than one page, use the Next button to display another page. To return to a previous page, click the Previous button. These buttons will be unavailable if your document has only one page, like the one shown in Figure 2.9.

To exit the Print Preview window, click Cancel.

If everything appears as you want it in Print Preview mode, you can choose to print the file. Click the Print button. Works sends the file to your default printer and closes the Print Preview window.

SETTING PRINT OPTIONS

As mentioned earlier, you can print immediately by clicking the Print button on the toolbar. If you want to set print options, however, you must choose File, Print to display the Print dialog box (shown in Figure 2.10) and make any adjustments to the printing options. For example, you can specify how many copies to print and exactly which pages to print, and you can change which printer to print to.

Note

Each program's Print dialog box is a bit different. The one shown in Figure 2.10 is for the Works Database. They all work the same way, however.

1. Choose File, Print. This opens the Print dialog box shown in Figure 2.9.
2. Do any of the following:
   - To change the printer to use, click the Name drop-down list box and choose another printer.
   - To specify a page range, such as pages 2–4, or the entire document, select an option under Print Range. By default, the All option is selected. To print certain pages, click the Pages option. In the From and To text boxes, enter the page numbers you want to print.
   - Some programs (such as the Works Database) have a control that lets you specify certain data to print; make a selection in the What to Print section.
   - To print more than one copy of the document, set a new number in the Number of Copies text box. Use the increment buttons to set a number, or click inside the text box and type a number.
3. When finished selecting print options, click OK to print the document.

Figure 2.10
Use the Print dialog box to specify printer options.

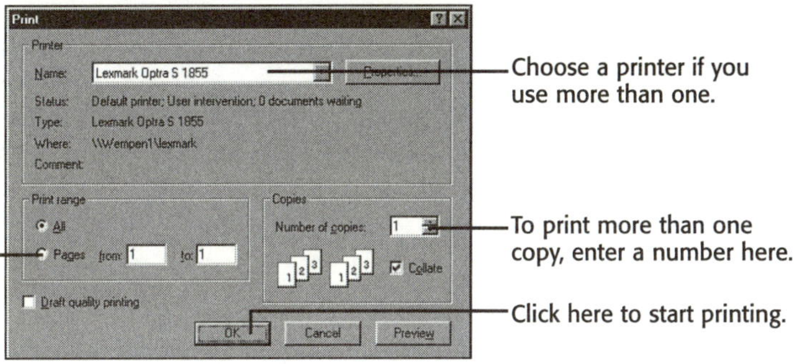

Note

You can also click the Properties button next to your printer name for printer-specific settings you can control. These are different for each printer and may include settings such as draft mode, graphics resolution, color/black-and-white mode, page orientation, and so on.

TROUBLESHOOTING

FILE NOT FOUND

I'm trying to open an existing document, but I get a message that the file is not found.

Perhaps it has been moved. You might want to use the Find command in Windows (Start, Find, Files or Folders) to look for it.

FILE OPENS UNREADABLE

I opened a file of a type that is not native to the program, and gibberish appears in the document.

This *usually* means that the file type is not supported by the program in which you are trying to use it. Try reopening that file in the original program that created it and then using that program's Save As command to save it in a different file format.

CAN'T OPEN A FILE FROM A FLOPPY

I saved my data files on a floppy, but now when I try to open one of them, I see a message about a "data error."

Many people think that they are being "safe" by saving their work to floppy disks rather than on the computer's hard drive, but they are mistaken. Floppy disks fail much more often than hard disks do.

Try running ScanDisk on the floppy (Start, Programs, Accessories, System Tools, ScanDisk) to identify and seal off the bad areas, and then try opening the data file again. It might not open perfectly; some data might be lost. Resolve in the future never to save your only copy of an important file to a floppy disk.

DOCUMENT WON'T PRINT

My document won't print!

Use some deductive reasoning. Try printing a different document in the same program. Try printing from a different program. In this way, you can narrow down what might be the problem.

CHAPTER 3

Introducing the Works Word Processor

In this chapter

WHO USES THE WORKS WORD PROCESSOR?

Both the Works Word Processor and Word do the same thing, but Word does it better. If you have a choice, I suggest that you use Word and skip this chapter and the next.

However, if you don't own the Suite version of Works 2000, you might not have access to Word, so you don't have a choice. Don't feel bad about being stuck with the Works Word Processor! It's a fine little program, and it has more word processing features than the average person will ever use, anyway.

When you install Word as part of the Works Suite, it replaces the Works Word Processor in the Works Task Launcher. Your Works Word Processor is still there, still installed on your PC, but through the Works Task Manager, it has been disabled.

Tip #4 from *Faithe Wempen*

Should you ever want to run the Works Word Processor instead of Word (if you want to play around with this chapter, for example), you can start it by double-clicking the file WksWP.exe in the C:\Program Files\Microsoft Works folder.

STARTING THE WORKS WORD PROCESSOR

With the Works Word Processor, you can create all kinds of interesting documents, including reports, letters, résumés, envelopes, and so on. The method you use for starting the Word Processor depends largely on what you want to do with it after it's started. Starting from the Task Launcher in Works, your choices include the following:

- To start a new, blank document, click the Programs tab and then click the Start a Blank Document button. A blank page appears in the Word Processor, as shown in Figure 3.1.
- To open an existing word processing document, click the History tab and then click the document you want to open.
- To start a new document based on a task, click the Tasks tab and then click the category and task you want to use. Or, to choose a task specifically for the Word Processor, click the Programs tab, click Works Word Processor, and then choose a task.

To follow along with the lessons in this chapter, you should do the first one: Create a new document. Your new document should look like Figure 3.1.

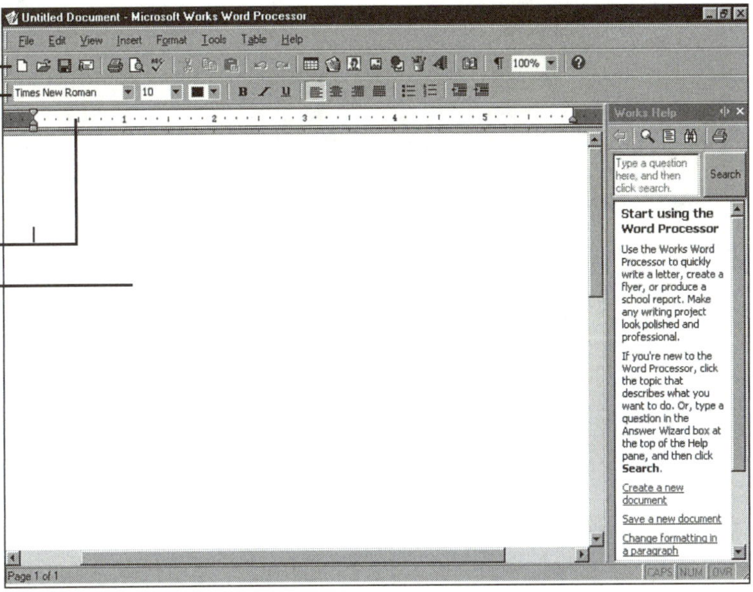

Figure 3.1
When you start the Word Processor tool, a blank document appears, ready for you to start typing.

Note

If the Works Help window appears at the right, you can click its Close (×) button to close it.

→ To learn more about the parts of the screen in a Works program, **see** Chapter 1, "Introducing the Microsoft Works Suite."

THE WORD PROCESSOR TOOLBAR

The Word Processor has two toolbars: Standard (on top) and Formatting (below the Standard). They contain buttons that represent the most commonly used menu commands. (Many of the same buttons are found on all Works program toolbars.)

Some of the buttons, such as bold, italic, and underline, work like toggle switches—one click turns on a feature, and a second click turns it off. (When a toggle button is switched on, it looks as though it's pressed on the toolbar.) Other toolbar buttons, such as Save and Spell Check, open a dialog box. Still others, such as the ones that control paragraph alignment, all work as a group; one of them is always on, and if you select another, the first one turns off.

The first three tools on the toolbar are *drop-down lists*. To see the list of alternatives, click the drop-down arrow. When you select an item from the list, it becomes the current setting, and it appears in the box to the left of the drop-down arrow. Figure 3.2 shows the Works Word Processor toolbar with one of these drop-down lists open.

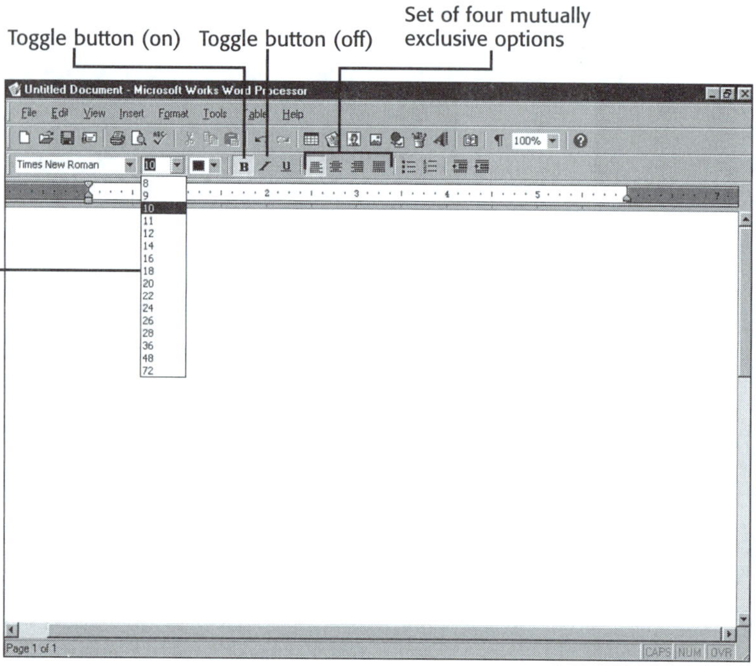

Figure 3.2
The Word Processor toolbar lets you issue commands and change settings with a click of the mouse.

TYPING TEXT

Typing appears at the cursor, a.k.a. the *insertion point* (see Figure 3.3). It's the short vertical line you see blinking on your blank page.

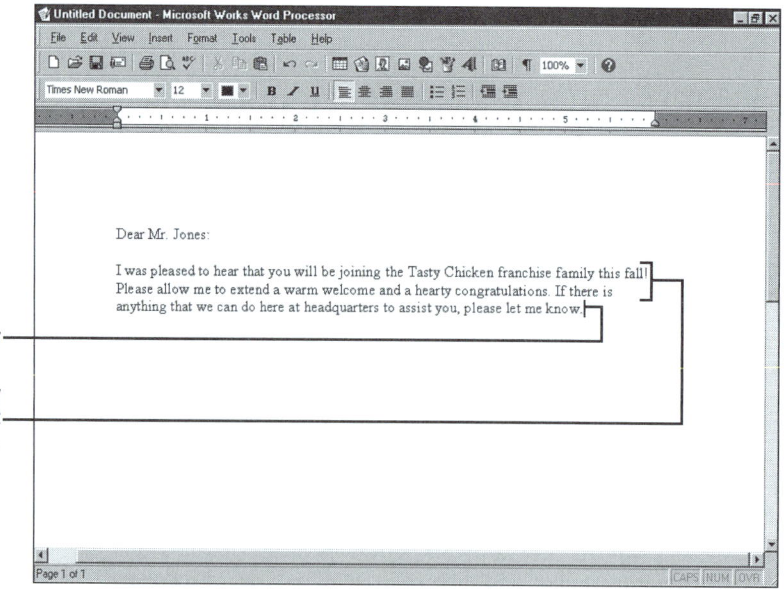

Figure 3.3
Don't worry about pressing Enter when your text nears the right margin. Works automatically wraps the text to the next line for you.

Here are some typing basics:

- Don't press Enter when your text is approaching the right margin. A feature called *Word Wrap* automatically moves your text to the next line when you reach the margin (refer to Figure 3.3). Press Enter to start a new paragraph or to separate items in a vertical list.
- Use the arrow keys or the scrollbars (not Enter, Backspace, or the spacebar) to move around your page. The Enter key inserts a blank line every time you press it, Backspace deletes a space or character, and the spacebar inserts a blank space.
- The Delete key erases the text to the right of the cursor.
- The Backspace key erases the text to the left of the cursor.
- Don't use letters (lowercase *l* and uppercase *O*) in place of numbers. Works can't figure out that you intend for the letters *lO* to represent the number 10, which is common practice with many typewriters.

Moving Around in a Document

As you type your document, you might want to move quickly to the beginning of a previous paragraph, go to the next page, or move to the end of a line. To navigate and reposition the cursor (the insertion point) within your document, you can use the scrollbars and then click your mouse on the document. You can also use these shortcuts:

- Ctrl+Home takes you to the top of the document.
- Ctrl+End takes you to the end of the document.
- The arrow keys on your keyboard move you up or down one line and left or right one character. You can press and hold down the arrow key to scroll.
- Press the Ctrl key while pressing the arrows, and you move up or down one full paragraph and left or right one full word.
- The Home key takes you to the beginning of the line you're on.
- The End key takes you to the end of the line you're on.
- Press Page Up or Page Down to move up or down one full screen (a full screen doesn't always correspond to one printed page).
- Press Ctrl+G to open the Go To dialog box, and enter the page number where you want to go. This feature works only on documents of more than one page.

Positioning Your Cursor

Your cursor marks the place in the document where your keyboard actions—typing text, pressing Delete, pressing Enter, and so on—take effect. Using the scrollbars to view another section of your document does not move your cursor to a new insertion point. If you scroll to another section of the document, you must click your mouse in the new location to place your cursor there. Make sure that you can see your cursor before you begin typing; otherwise, you might be adding or deleting text in the wrong place in your document.

At the end of the document is an invisible end-of-file marker. Many beginners become frustrated because they can't move their cursor below the end-of-file marker. To position the insertion point further down on the page, move the insertion point to the end of the last line of text and press the Enter key to move the end-of-file marker down.

DISPLAYING HIDDEN MARKERS

There are many nonprinting characters in a typical document. The end-of-paragraph markers, the spaces between words, and the end-of-file marker are all important parts of the document, but you won't see them on your screen by default.

¶ Sometimes, however, it's useful to know where these lie, to check spacing or help in positioning the insertion point. To toggle between displaying and hiding these nonprinting characters, click the Show All button, or choose View, All Characters. Figure 3.4 shows the same text as in Figure 3.3, but with Show All turned on.

Figure 3.4
Nonprinting characters.

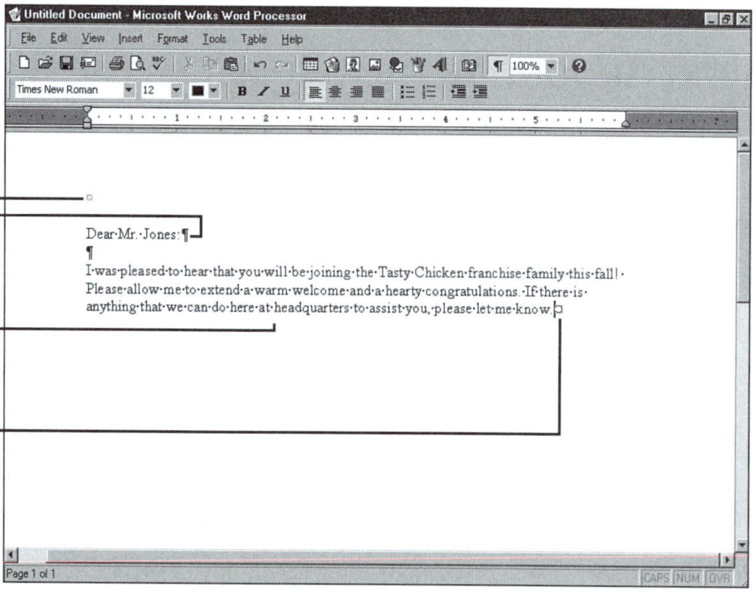

EDITING TEXT

Typing text is only half the battle—you then have to read what you've written, realize that it isn't quite right, and change your mind. At that point, you're ready to edit your document. To change a word or short phrase, you can just reposition the cursor, use the Backspace or Delete keys to remove the words you don't want, and then type your changes. To change more than a few words, however, take advantage of the Works Word Processor's more powerful editing features.

Insert and Overtype Modes

By default, the Word Processor operates in *insert mode*, which means that characters to the right of the cursor scoot over to make room for new text. If you prefer to type over existing text, switch to *overtype mode*. To turn insert and overtype modes on or off, press the Insert key on your keyboard. (The status bar displays OVR in the far-right side to indicate that overtype mode is on.)

Selecting Text

Before you can act on blocks of typed text—whether that action is formatting, deleting, moving, or whatever—you must select it. A big mistake beginners often make is to forget to select the text they want to act on. The Word Processor's editing features require the same structure as a common sentence: To structure an edit, you must define both a subject (what you're acting on) and a verb (which action you want). Figure 3.5 shows an example of selected text.

Figure 3.5
Selected text appears surrounded by a black box, or highlighted.

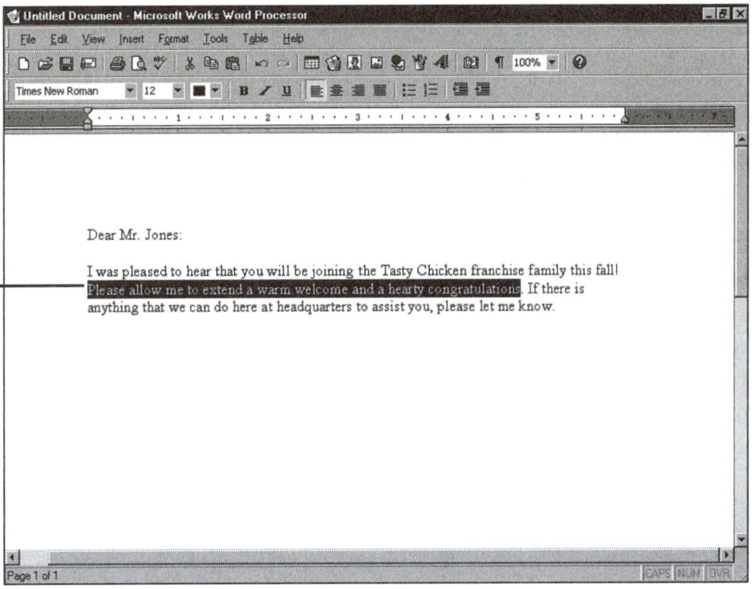

You can select text with your mouse, the keyboard, or a combination of the two. When selecting text with the mouse, your mouse pointer changes, depending on its location in the Word Processor window:

- When your mouse is within your existing text, the mouse pointer looks like a capital *I* and is called an *I-beam*. You can use this pointer for selecting smaller portions of text, such as a word within a sentence or a sentence within a paragraph.
- The mouse pointer turns to a right-pointing arrow when it's in the left margin of your document window. Use this mouse pointer for selecting large areas of text, such as entire lines or paragraphs.

- Your mouse returns to a standard left-pointing arrow when it's on the menus, toolbar, scrollbars, or page/view controls.

Whether your mouse is an I-beam or a right-pointing arrow, clicking your mouse can select text:

- To select a single word, double-click it.
- To select a line of text, place your mouse pointer in the left margin next to the line, and click once.
- To select an entire paragraph, place your mouse pointer in the left margin next to the paragraph, and double-click.

To select text with the keyboard, use the Shift key and the arrow keys together:

- Press the Shift key with the left or right arrow to select text one character at a time.
- Press Ctrl+Shift with the left or right arrow to select entire words.
- Press Shift with the up or down arrow to select text one line at a time.
- Press Ctrl+Shift with the up or down arrow to select entire paragraphs.

If you want to add more text to a selection with either the mouse or the keyboard, press the Shift key and click the mouse at the end of the additional text you want to select.

INTRODUCING THE CLIPBOARD

We're going to talk about moving and copying text momentarily, but to understand those processes, you must understand the Windows Clipboard. The *Clipboard* is a temporary holding area in your computer's memory. The Clipboard enables you to move or copy text, graphics, or data from one document to another, from one file to another, and from one application to another.

It works like this: When you select some text and then issue either the Cut or Copy command, the material is placed on the Clipboard. Then you reposition your cursor and issue the Paste command, and whatever is on the Clipboard appears at the cursor.

Some ground rules for the Clipboard include the following:

- You can place only one selection on the Clipboard at a time. When you place a new selection on the Clipboard, the preceding selection disappears from memory.
- Material stays on the Clipboard until it is replaced by something else being cut or copied.
- You can use the Clipboard to move or copy between different Windows-based programs. You aren't restricted to using it just in Works. For example, you could copy text from Works and paste it into Microsoft Word or into an email program.
- Exiting Windows empties the Clipboard. If you accidentally exit Windows or shut down your computer, you lose whatever is stored in the Clipboard. However, exiting an individual Windows program like Works does not disturb the Clipboard contents.

Moving and Copying Text

Moving and copying are closely related. The only difference is that with moving, the original is deleted, whereas with copying, the original stays put. You can move or copy selected text to another location in your current document, to another document, or to a completely different application.

No "Move" command exists per se; moving is a combination of two commands: Cut and Paste. You cut the selection from its original location and paste it into its new home, effectively moving it. When you copy, you issue the Copy command to copy the selection to the Clipboard and then the Paste command to put the copy where you want it. Here's how:

1. Select the text you want to move or copy.

2. Open the Edit menu and then choose Cut to move or Copy to copy, or click the Cut button or the Copy button on the toolbar.
3. Position your cursor where you want to insert the selection (the target location). If your target location is in another document, open the document and place your cursor where you want to insert the Clipboard's contents.

4. Choose Edit, Paste, or click the Paste button on the toolbar.

Tip #5 from
Faithe Wempen

You can also right-click on the selected text to display a shortcut menu from which you can choose Copy, Cut, and Paste.

Another way to move or copy selected text is by dragging and dropping it. To move the text, select it and drag it to a new location. (Press and hold down the left mouse button on the text, and then move the mouse.) A box appears next to the mouse pointer as you drag. To copy, press the Ctrl key while performing the drag and drop.

Using Undo

You can reverse your last action with the Works Undo command. Choose Edit, Undo Editing; press Ctrl+Z; or click the Undo button on the toolbar. If you've just made a mistake, *you must use Undo immediately*. The Undo command applies only to the last action performed.

As soon as you've undone an action, that action appears on the Edit menu as an action you can Redo. Shortcuts for Redo include Ctrl+Y and the Redo button on the toolbar.

Finding and Replacing Text

Whether it's your car keys or a bit of text you've lost, it can be frustrating not to find what you're looking for. Fortunately, you can search for a particular word or phrase in your Works document to assist you with proofreading, and you can replace the text you find with another word or phrase.

To find text, do the following:

1. Choose Edit, Find or press Ctrl+F. The Find tab of the Find and Replace dialog box appears (see Figure 3.6).
2. In the Find What text box, enter the text you're looking for.
3. Click Find Next.
4. If the text you're looking for appears more than once in the document, click Find Next again to go to the next incidence.
5. When you've come to the last occurrence of the text, you are prompted with `Works did not find a match`. Click OK and then click Cancel in the Find dialog box.

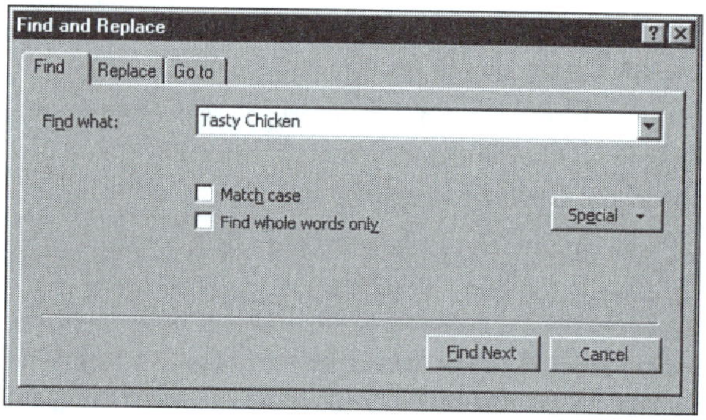

Figure 3.6
Use the Find tab to search for particular words and phrases.

Tip #6 from
Faithe Wempen

If you start the Find feature in the middle of your document, Works stops at the end and asks whether you want to start looking again at the beginning of the document. To avoid this extra step, make sure that your cursor is at the top of the document before you begin the Find process. You can get to the top of the document quickly by pressing Crtl+Home.

Sometimes you just want to find things, but more often you want to find them for a purpose—so that you can replace them with something else. For example, suppose that your company changed its name from *Acme Corporation* to *Friendly Foods Corporation*. You could use the Replace feature in Works to change all instances of the old name to the new name.

To replace text, do the following:

1. Choose Edit, Replace or press Ctrl+H; the Replace tab of the Find and Replace dialog box appears (see Figure 3.7).
2. In the Find What box, enter the text you want to find.
3. Enter the replacement text in the Replace With box exactly as you want it to appear in the document.
4. If you want to replace every occurrence of the text without seeing each one, click Replace All. Clicking Replace instead enables you to skip some of the found items if you don't want to replace all of them. To skip an item, click Find Next.
5. When you're finished, click the Cancel button to close the dialog box.

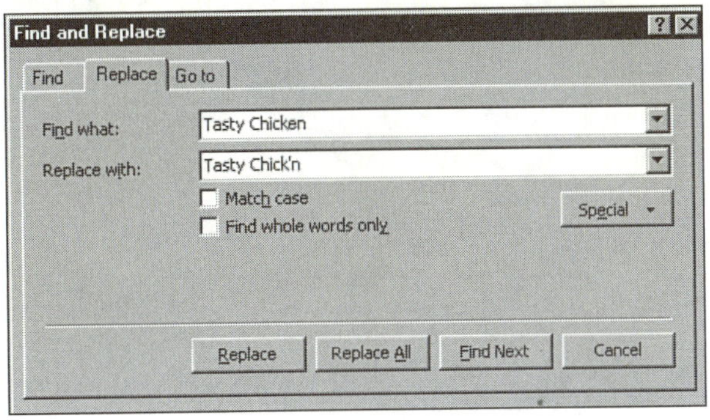

Figure 3.7
Use the Replace tab to replace one text string with another.

Tip #7 from *Faithe Wempen*

If you leave the Replace With text box empty, you can delete every occurrence of the word without replacing it with anything else.

As you might have already noticed, I haven't talked about all the controls in the Find and Replace dialog box yet. You can use the Match Case check box to specify that your search match the case of the text that you enter in the Find What box, and you can check Find Whole Words Only. For example, a search that uses both these options would keep you from finding *candy* when you're looking for *Andy*.

You can also enter a variety of special search characters into the Find What text box. Each of these begins with a caret character (^). For example, `^p` stands for *paragraph mark*, and `^t` stands for *tab stop*. You don't have to memorize these, however; you can choose them from the Special drop-down list.

CHECKING SPELLING AND GRAMMAR

You can check your document for misspelled words and grammar errors by using the Works Spelling and Grammar checker. You can do so at any point in your editing process and as many times as you like. You can add your own words, such as people's names, peculiar terminology, and abbreviations to the Works dictionary. This is the same spelling checker used in Word.

Caution

Spell checking programs work on the basis of a spelling dictionary. If a word doesn't appear in that dictionary, Works flags it as a spelling error. It might not be—it could be a proper name or jargon peculiar to your industry. In addition, the grammar checker isn't perfect and may suggest some changes that turn a perfectly okay sentence into a mess. You still have to use common sense!

As you type, a red underline appears under words that are not in the dictionary. You can right-click a red-underlined word to see and then select from the alternatives (see Figure 3.8).

You can also check the spelling and grammar for the entire document. With your document

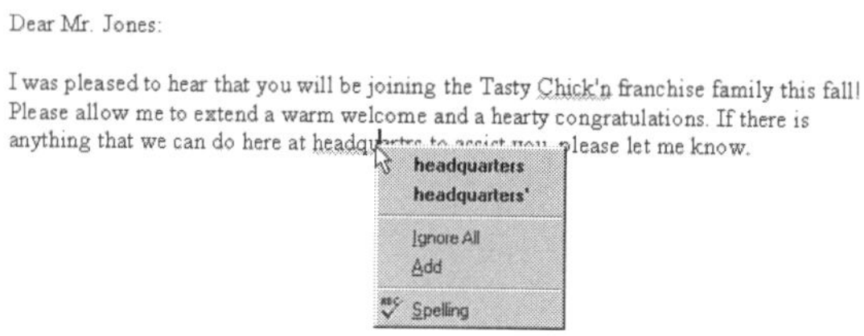

Figure 3.8
Right-click a red-underlined word to check or correct its spelling.

open onscreen, choose Tools, Spelling and Grammar; press F7; or click the Spelling and Grammar button on the Standard toolbar.

The Spelling and Grammar dialog box opens and displays the first problem it finds. This could be either a spelling error or a grammar error. Figure 3.9 shows a grammar error, and Figure 3.10 shows a spelling error so that you can see the difference.

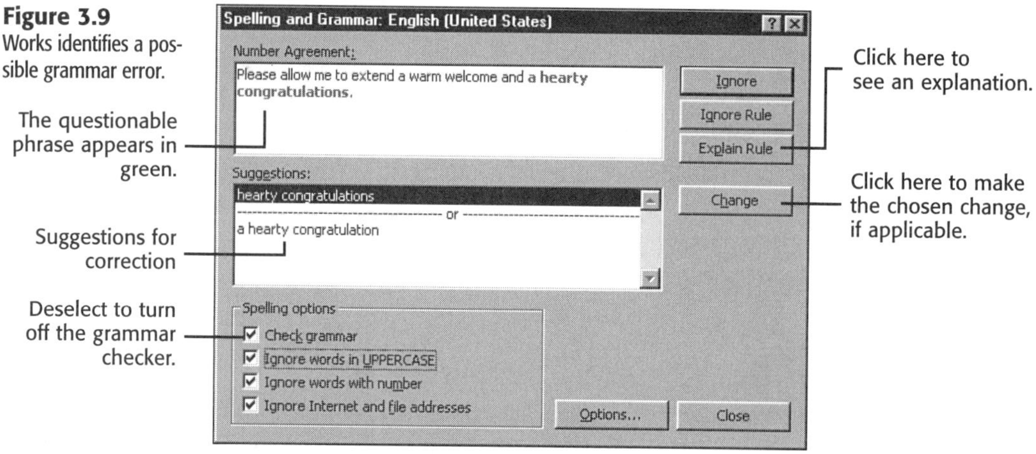

Figure 3.9
Works identifies a possible grammar error.

For a grammar error, choose one of these options:

- If you believe the sentence to be correct as is, click Ignore.
- To prevent the grammar checker from checking for that same grammar rule again in this document, click Ignore Rule.
- If you are not sure why the grammar checker has flagged a problem, click Explain Rule.
- To change to one of the suggestions, click it and then click Change.

For a spelling error, choose from any of the following options:

- If one of the suggestions is appropriate, select it from the list and click Change. Click Change All if you've used the word more than once.

- If none of the suggestions are appropriate or no suggestions are offered, click in the document (behind the dialog box), and type your own correction.
- If the word is spelled correctly, click Ignore or Ignore All. Choose Ignore All if all instances of the word should be ignored.
- If the word is spelled correctly and you know you will be using it in future documents, click Add. This adds the word to the dictionary, preventing it from appearing as misspelled the next time you use it.

When you are finished with the check, a message appears to that effect; click OK. To end the check early, click Close.

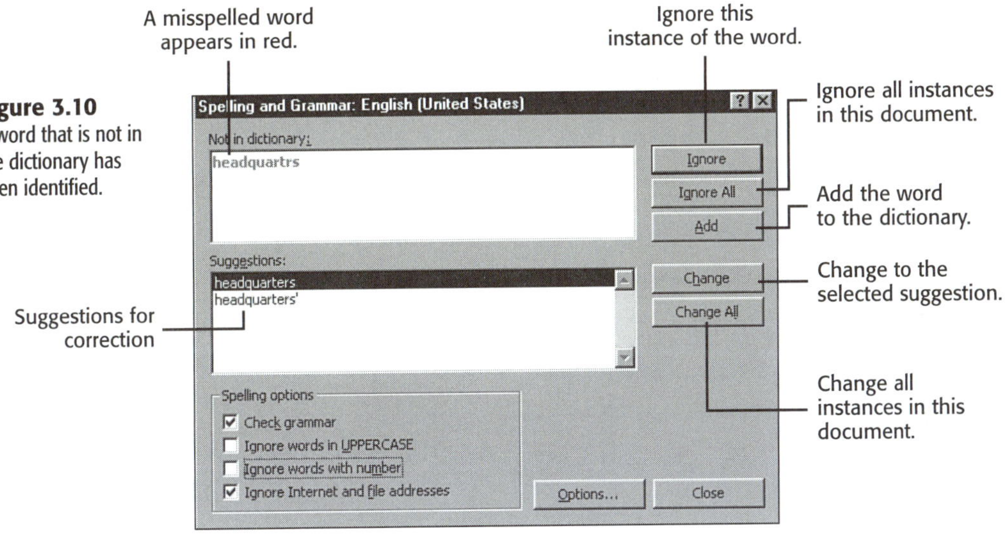

Figure 3.10
A word that is not in the dictionary has been identified.

Tip #8 from *Faithe Wempen*

To set up how the spelling and grammar check works, you can click the Options button to open a configuration box. You can define grammar levels, edit the dictionary, and more.

Caution

The spelling check can't catch improperly used words. For example, if you meant to type `here` but instead typed `hear`, the spelling check will note nothing wrong because both are legitimate words.

Using the Thesaurus

You can use the Thesaurus to look up alternative words (synonyms) or words you feel you're using too often and to get a word's definition by looking at other words that mean the same thing:

1. Select the word you want to look up.
2. Choose Tools, Thesaurus, or press Shift+F7. The Thesaurus dialog box displays your word and two lists:
    - A list of potential meanings for your word appears on the left. In Figure 3.11, you see the meanings for the word *congratulations*.
    - A list of synonyms (alternative words) appears on the right in the Replace with Synonym box. Depending on which meaning you choose, the list of synonyms changes.
3. If multiple meanings exist for the word, choose the one that's appropriate for your context from the Meanings list.
4. Click the word you want to use from the Replace with Synonym box.
5. Click Replace.

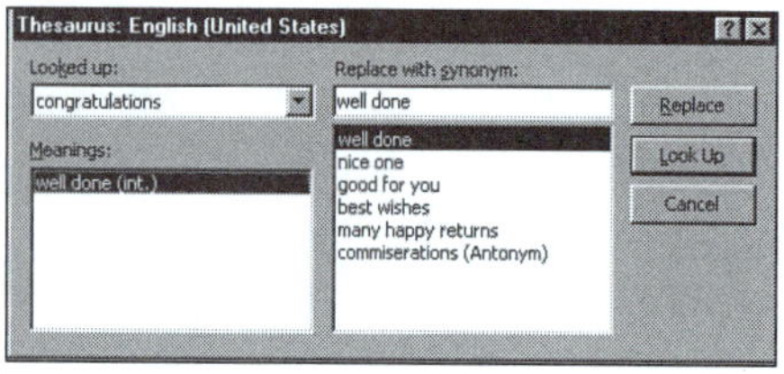

Figure 3.11
Choose the synonym you want to use.

Tip #9 from
Faithe Wempen

You can use the Thesaurus to look up the meaning of a word. Just type the word, select it, and then open the Thesaurus. Note the meanings that appear, and click Cancel to close the Thesaurus without making a change.

You can also use the Thesaurus to look up words that aren't in a document. In an open document with no text selected, choose Tools, Thesaurus. In the dialog box, type the word you want to look up in the Replace with Synonym box, and click Look Up. The word you inserted moves to the Looked Up box. A list of meanings appears on the left, accompanied by synonyms on the right.

→ When you're ready to save your document or print it out, **see** Chapter 2, "Performing Common Works Tasks," for all the details on performing these common Works tasks.

TROUBLESHOOTING

ICONS TOO SMALL

I have trouble seeing those icons on the toolbar.

Choose View, Toolbars, Large Icons to make them bigger. (They take up more space onscreen this way, of course, so there's a tradeoff.)

NON-KEYBOARD CHARACTERS

I sometimes type words or phrases in other languages, such as Spanish, and I need to type characters with accent marks over them. How can I do that?

Try the Insert, Special Character command. This lets you insert any character from the full set, not just the characters that appear on a keyboard.

PASTING FROM OFFICE 2000

Sometimes I copy and paste between the Works Word Processor and a Microsoft Office 2000 program, such as Excel. Those programs have a better Clipboard. Can I use that Clipboard in the Works Word Processor?

Unfortunately, no. Office 2000 has an enhanced Clipboard that can hold more than one clip at a time. That Clipboard is available only in Office 2000 programs. Although you can copy multiple selections onto this enhanced Clipboard from an Office program, you can paste only the last selection into Works programs.

SETTING SPELLING AND GRAMMAR OPTIONS

How do I change my spelling or grammar options?

To set spelling and grammar options, the Spelling and Grammar dialog box must be open, and it opens only when it finds an error. If you have to make changes to those options in a document that does not contain any errors, you might have to create an error, such as a misspelling, so that the Spelling and Grammar dialog box will open. Some of the spelling options, however, can be set from the Options dialog box (Tools, Options) without running the Spelling and Grammar checker.

CHAPTER 4

Formatting with the Works Word Processor

In this chapter

Formatting Text

In this chapter, you learn about formatting in the Works Word Processor. *Formatting* is what makes word processing programs fun. Formatting commands let you change the look of text in your document. For example, you can make a word bold to stand out on the page, or you can increase its point size. Use formatting commands to make your documents easier to read, more interesting to look at, and more professional in presentation.

The most basic, fundamental level of formatting involves the actual characters themselves. You can change the typeface (font) and size of the lettering; apply bold, italic, and underline attributes; and more. Changes like these can be used strategically to make headings more noticeable, emphasize important words and phrases, and make the document more readable overall.

Selecting a Font

The choice of font is probably the most important decision you make with each document. If the lettering is difficult to read, your reader might stop reading and not receive your whole message. Choose a font that attracts readers and makes people care about your message.

Tip #10 from *Faithe Wempen*

For the main body of a document, stay away from novelty fonts (unless that's the look you're going for). Stick with plain, easy-to-read fonts such as Arial and Times New Roman. These fonts look great both in printouts and on the screen. Don't use a broad mix of fonts in any single document; one or two fonts in a single document usually are enough. Choose a font that promotes readability and reflects the spirit of your document. You can vary the size of the font and apply bold, italic, or underline formatting to emphasize individual words or phrases.

You can format your text by changing its typeface, commonly known as *font*. You can also change the *font size* (that is, the size of each letter) and *font style* (in other words, the attributes applied to the text, such as bold or underline). These changes can be made from the toolbar or the Format menu.

To change the font from the toolbar, do the following:

1. Select the text you want to change, or if you're starting a new document, make the change before you start typing.
2. Open the Font drop-down list. A list of available fonts appears, as in Figure 4.1.
3. Click the font you want. Your selected text changes to that font.

The fonts on the list with TT next to them are *TrueType* fonts. These fonts are *scalable*, which means that they can be used at any size. Any fonts that are missing the TT label are not TrueType; perhaps they are fonts built in to your printer, or some other kind of font. Try to choose TrueType fonts whenever possible because they look good both on the screen and in print.

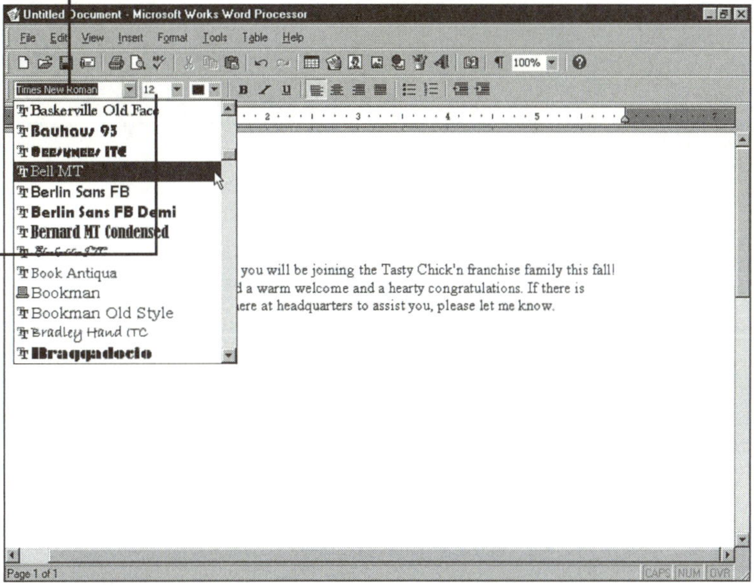

Figure 4.1
The Font drop-down list shows the available fonts installed on your computer.

Note

Depending on the other types of programs you've installed on your computer, the fonts in your Font list box might differ from the ones in Figure 4.1.

Even though the font has changed, the text is still the same size. To increase or decrease the font size (measured in *points*), open the Font Size drop-down list. A list of point sizes drops down. The higher the number, the bigger your text. Select a point size by clicking the number in the list.

If you make your text bold, italic, or underlined, you're changing the *font style*. The Bold, Italic, and Underline buttons on the toolbar work like toggle switches—one click and they're on, a second click and they're off. Figure 4.2 shows the toolbar with the Bold button turned on. To apply these styles to your text, select the text and then click the appropriate button. You can apply one, two, or all three styles to any text. To remove the attribute, select the text again and click the attribute button.

You can also change the text's font, size, and style by using the Format menu to open the Font dialog box, shown in Figure 4.3. This dialog box lets you set all the font formatting in one place, and it offers formatting effects not available on the toolbar. You can also see a sample preview of the settings you change, before applying them to your own text.

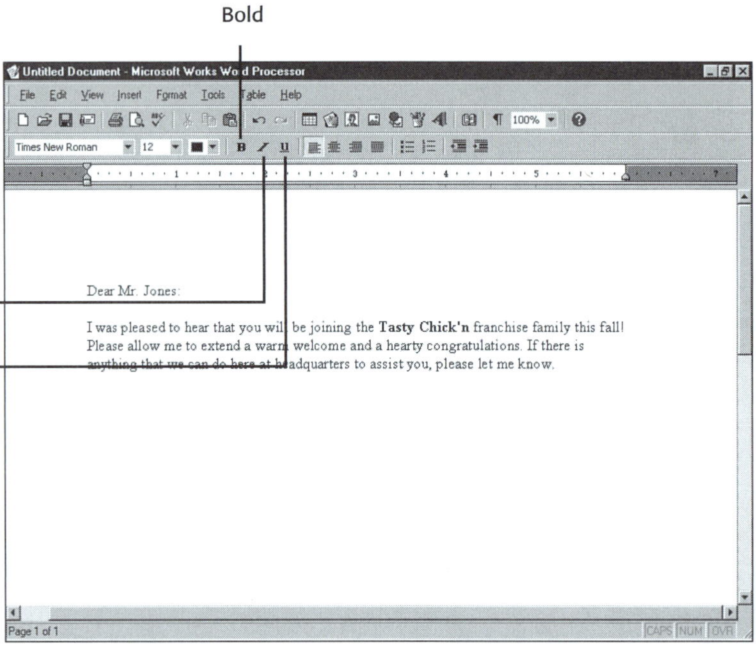

Figure 4.2
Use the Bold, Italic, and/or Underline buttons to change the selected text's style.

To change the font, size, and effects from the Font dialog box, do the following:

1. Choose Format, Font. The Font dialog box appears (see Figure 4.3).
2. On the Font list, click the font you want.
3. On the Font Style list, choose Bold, Italic, both, or neither.
4. In the Size list, click the size you want.
5. If you want underlining, open the Underline drop-down list, and choose a line style.
6. If you want the text to be a certain color, open the Color drop-down list, and select it.
7. In the Effects area, select check boxes for any special effects you want.
8. Look in the Sample area to see a preview of what your selections will look like.
9. Click OK to exit the dialog box and apply the new settings.

Note

If you leave the color set to Automatic, Works will choose a font color for you (either black or white) to contrast with the background color chosen. To choose a background color to appear behind the text, use Format, Borders and Shading, and choose a fill color in the Shading area.

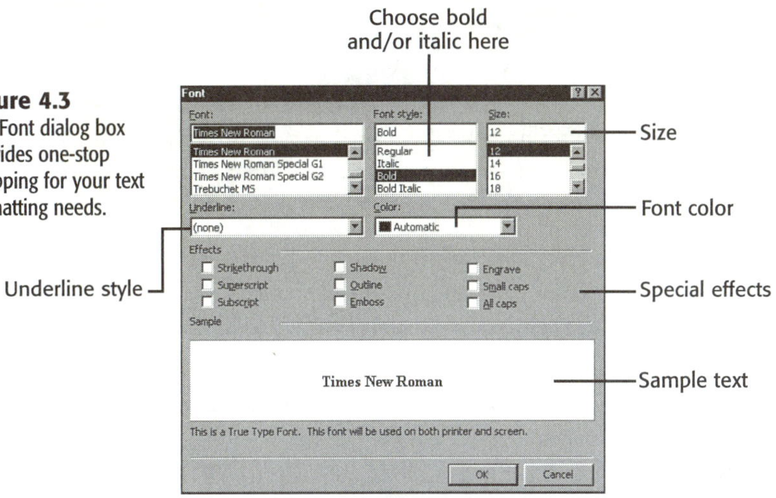

Figure 4.3
The Font dialog box provides one-stop shopping for your text formatting needs.

Figure 4.4 shows a sample document with some character formatting applied, so you can see the dramatic effects you can create with simple text formatting.

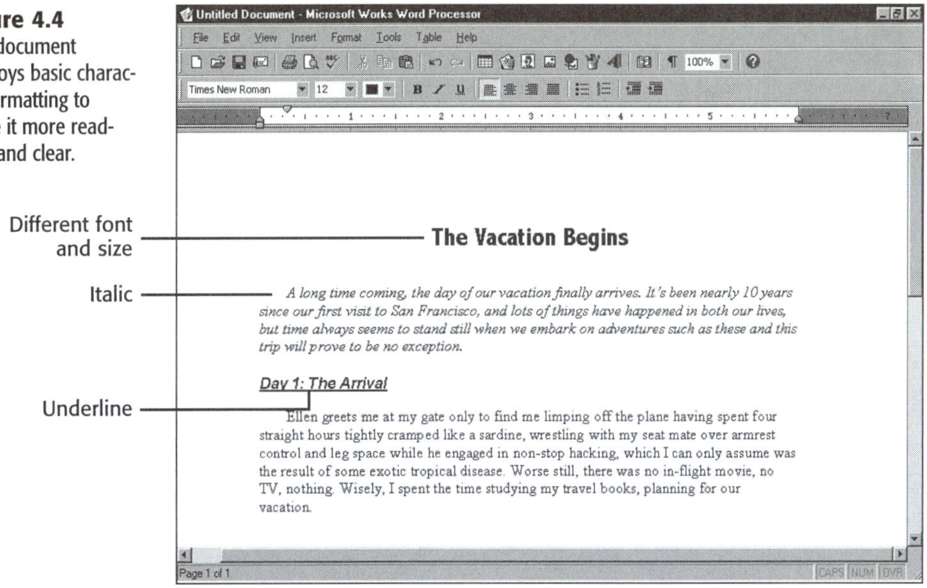

Figure 4.4
This document employs basic character formatting to make it more readable and clear.

→ To select text, **see** Chapter 3, "Introducing the Works Word Processor."

PART I
CH 4

USING WORDART

WordArt is an accessory program that runs within Works (and Microsoft Word, too). It helps you dress up plain text to be really special, for headings, posters, and other special uses. You can add *textures* to the lettering, give them shadows, twist them into different shapes, and so on. Spend some time experimenting with these effects—they can make all the difference in attracting readers.

To add WordArt to a document, follow these steps:

1. Place your cursor where you want to place your WordArt text.

2. Choose Insert, Picture, WordArt or click the Insert WordArt button on the toolbar.
3. When WordArt is activated, its toolbar replaces the Works toolbar. Figure 4.5 shows the WordArt window and toolbar. A box appears in your document, with sample text that reads `Enter Your Text Here`.
4. Type your text in the box, and click the Update Display button. The WordArt text appears in your document, and the WordArt tools and text box remain onscreen.
5. Apply any special effects by clicking the toolbar buttons.
6. When you're finished, close the Enter Your Text Here window by clicking its Close (×) button.

Note

If you click the Font Size drop-down list on the WordArt toolbar, you will see that the default is Best Fit. Using Best Fit means that if your text box is enlarged or reduced, the text size is automatically adjusted to fit the box.

When you're finished formatting your WordArt text, click anywhere outside the WordArt text box to deactivate WordArt and return to Works.

After you've created WordArt, you can

- Move the WordArt object by dragging it with your mouse.
- Resize your WordArt object by clicking once on the text. Then, grab one of the *handles* and drag it outward to increase the item's size or inward to make it smaller (see Figure 4.6).
- Return to WordArt to reformat your text. Just double-click the WordArt object. The WordArt program is activated, and the WordArt tools return to the screen.
- Delete a WordArt object by clicking it once to select it (the handles appear) and then pressing the Delete key.

Tip #11 from
Faithe Wempen

It takes a bit of experimenting to get a WordArt object to look just the way you want it, so don't be afraid to try out different effects to see what they look like. You can always go back and edit the object later.

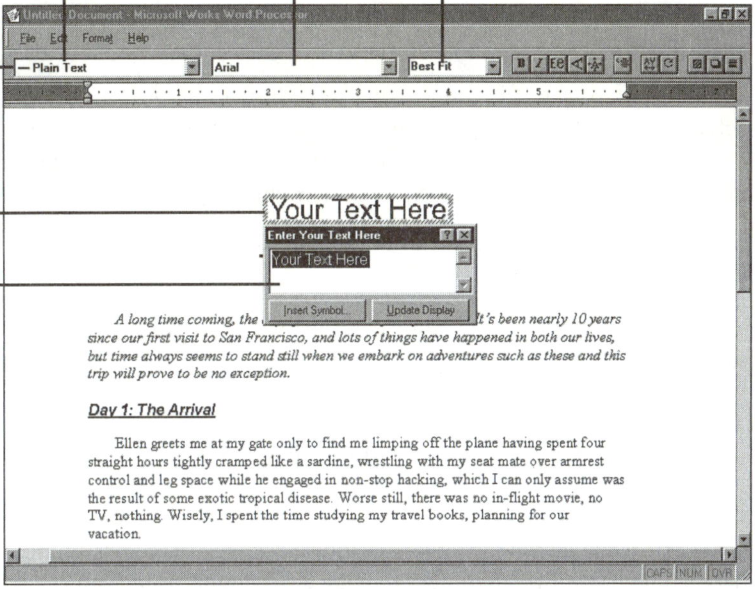

Figure 4.5
The WordArt window and toolbar invite you to customize the text and effects.

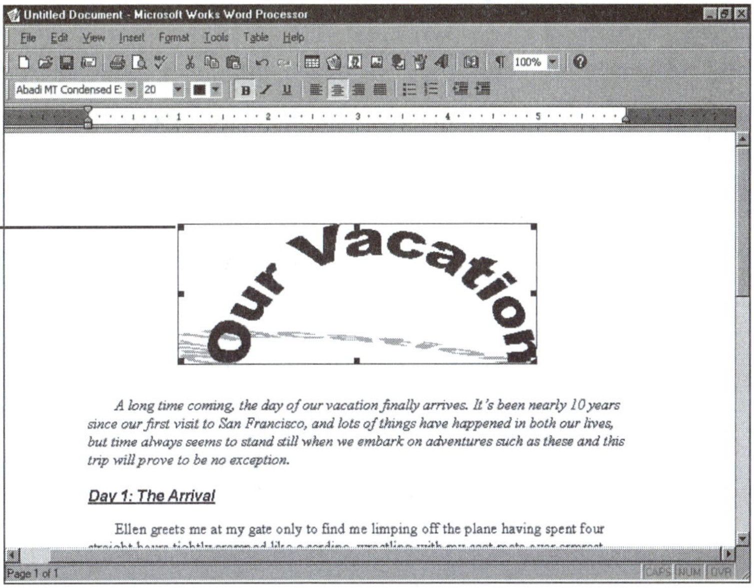

Figure 4.6
Resizing a WordArt object is as simple as dragging a corner of its box.

Formatting Paragraphs

So far in this chapter, I've concentrated on the text itself. Now it's time to think about the paragraphs in which the text lies. Every time you press Enter, you create a new paragraph.

Each of these paragraphs is a discrete unit that can be formatted separately from the others; each can have its own alignment, tabs, and indents.

ALIGNING TEXT

You can *align* your text by the left and/or right margin, or from the center of the page. By default, your text is left aligned, meaning that when you type, your text starts on the left side of the page, and the left side of your text stays even with the left margin. The right edge of the text doesn't have to stay even with the right margin (it's *ragged right*).

Alignments can be applied to existing text or set before you start typing. If you want to align existing text, select it first.

The easiest way to set alignment is with the toolbar buttons. In addition to the default left alignment, you can choose

- **Center**—Text centered between margins, often used for titles and headings

- **Right**—Text aligned to the right margin, often used for the date at the top of a page

You can also set alignment with the Format Paragraph dialog box, shown in Figure 4.7. The Format Paragraph dialog box has the advantage of having a fourth alignment method: Justified. Use Justified alignment to align a paragraph from both the left and the right, eliminating the ragged right edge. Justified alignment is often used to create smooth text columns in newsletters.

To set alignment with the Format Paragraph dialog box, do the following:

1. Choose Format, Paragraph to display the Format Paragraph dialog box (see Figure 4.7).
2. Click on the text alignment you want to use.
3. Click OK to exit the dialog box and apply the new setting.

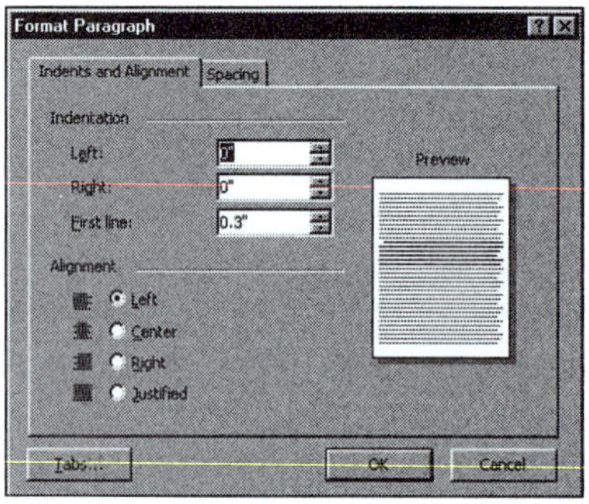

Figure 4.7
The Format Paragraph dialog box contains four alignment types; the toolbar has only three.

SETTING AND USING TABS

Tabs are places on your document ruler where you place a mark (called a *tab stop*) that controls the movement of the Tab key. In a new, blank document, tabs are set by default to every half inch, starting at the left margin. You can set custom tabs at any place on the ruler and use them to indent the first line of a paragraph or for typing multicolumn lists.

Note

If the ruler does not appear, open the View menu and choose Ruler.

The "normal" kind of tab stop is left-aligned with no *leader* (just blank space). Most of the time, you want this kind of tab stop. However, other types can be useful in certain circumstances. Figure 4.8 shows some tab stop variations with text. *Decimal tabs*, for example, are particularly helpful for typing numbers with an irregular number of characters to the right of the decimal point but can also be used for currency when dollars and cents are involved. Right alignment works well for aligning whole numbers or for positioning text in a column so that it evenly lines up on its right edge.

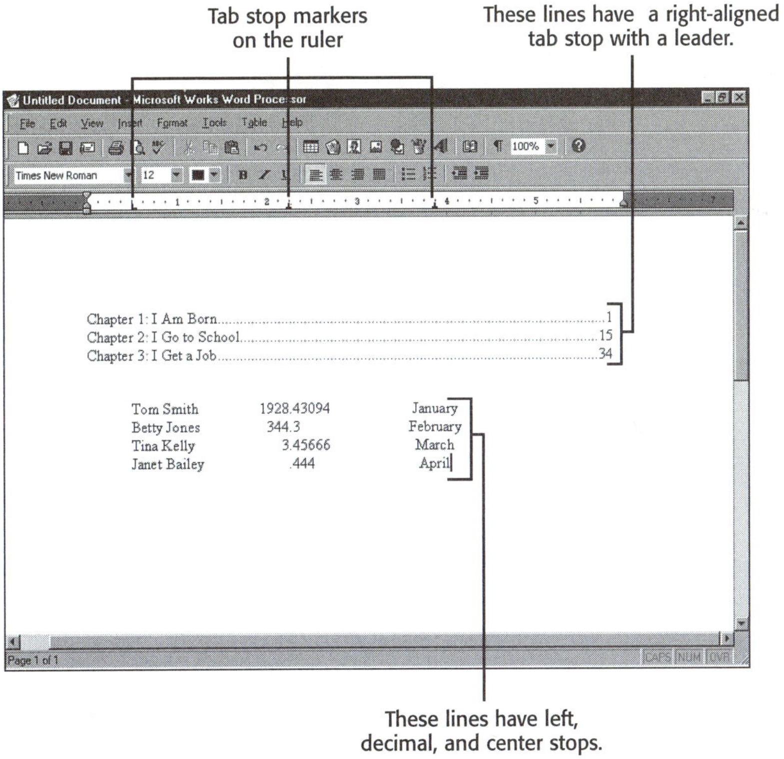

Figure 4.8
Notice the different kinds of tab stops at work.

Note

A *leader* is a repeated character, usually a dot, that fills the blank space between text and a tab.

One way to set tabs is to click the ruler where you want a tab stop to appear. This is easy but is lacking somewhat in flexibility. Left-clicking on the ruler places a left tab stop, and right-clicking on it places a right stop. There's no way to place the other types of tabs with this method. A more precise way is described in the following steps.

Tip #12 from *Faithe Wempen*

To set tab stops for multiple paragraphs at once, select those paragraphs before setting the stops.

1. Double-click the ruler, or choose Format, Tabs, to open the Tabs dialog box.

   Any tabs you have already set up by clicking the ruler will appear on the Tab Stops list. Figure 4.9 shows three tab stops already set up.
2. To create a new tab stop, type a number in the Tab Stop Position text box to indicate where on the ruler you want to place a tab stop.

   To format an existing tab stop, select it from the Tab Stops list.
3. Click a button in the Alignment area to choose how text aligns with the tab stop.
4. Choose a leader from the Leader area. The default is None, which works with most tabbed text.
5. Click Set.
6. If you have to set more tabs, repeat steps 3–5.
7. Click OK to accept your settings and close the dialog box.

Note

Default tab stops appear every 0.5 inches on the ruler. Each time you press Tab, if no custom tab stops are set for the paragraph, those defaults are used. You can change the default interval in the Default Tab Stops text box.

When tabs are set, they appear as small symbols on the ruler. Refer to Figure 4.8 to see a ruler with a series of tab stops. The stops on the ruler are for whatever paragraph the cursor is in at the moment. If you move the cursor to another paragraph, that paragraph's tab stops appear on the ruler instead.

You can change tab settings that you've made in your document by dragging the tab stops on the ruler with your mouse or by making changes to your tab settings in the Tabs dialog box. If you want the change to apply to more than the current paragraph, you must select all the paragraphs to be involved *before* you make the change.

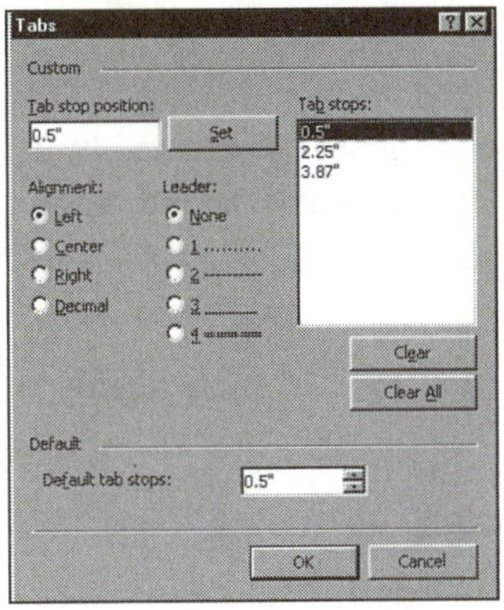

Figure 4.9
You can set tab stops with great accuracy and control from the Tabs dialog box.

Note

As you are initially typing your text, you can set tab stops for your first paragraph, and then each time you press Enter to start a new paragraph, those same tab stops will be used.

To remove a tab stop, drag it down and off the ruler. When you release your mouse, the tab stop is gone. To remove a tab when you're in the Tabs dialog box, select the tab from the Tab Stop Position list box and click Clear. Click Clear All to remove all the tab stops and return to the default tab stops.

INDENTING PARAGRAPHS

Indenting a paragraph increases the distance between the text and the margin. You can set a variety of indent types, indenting the text from the left or right margin or from both margins. For example, you might indent a quotation from the rest of a report to make it stand out, or you might indent a list of items from the regular paragraphs.

Paragraphs have two parts—a first line and a body (the rest of the lines). You can indent one or both of these parts. For example, some people like to have the first line of every paragraph indented five spaces. You can also indent the body and leave the first line flush with the left margin; this is called a *hanging indent*, and it's used to create bulleted lists. (To do that, you set the Left indent to a positive number, for example, 1.0, and the First Line indent to a negative one, for example, 0.5.) When you set an indent to a negative number, it's called an *outdent*.

Here's how to set paragraph indents:

1. Place your cursor in the paragraph you want to indent. You don't have to select any text unless you want to apply the indents to more than one existing paragraph.
2. Choose Format, Paragraph. The Format Paragraph dialog box opens.
3. On the Indents and Alignment tab (see Figure 4.10), type a value in the text box for the indentation you want, or click the increment buttons to increment the number up or down:
   - **Left**—The left edge of all the lines in the paragraph move to the left by an amount you specify.

- **Right**—The right edge of all the lines in the paragraph move in a specified distance from the right margin.
- **First Line**—The first line of the paragraph is indented by a distance you specify. The body of the paragraph remains at the left margin.

The Preview area of the dialog box shows how your indent settings look in your document.

4. Click the OK button to accept your settings and close the dialog box. Figure 4.11 shows some sample indents.

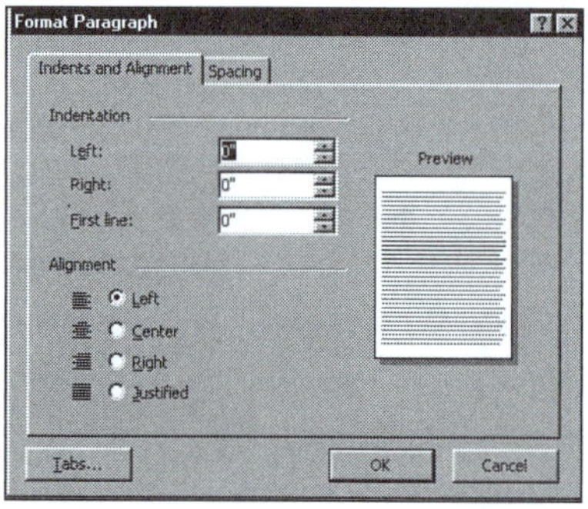

Figure 4.10
Use the Format Paragraph dialog box to change the indents.

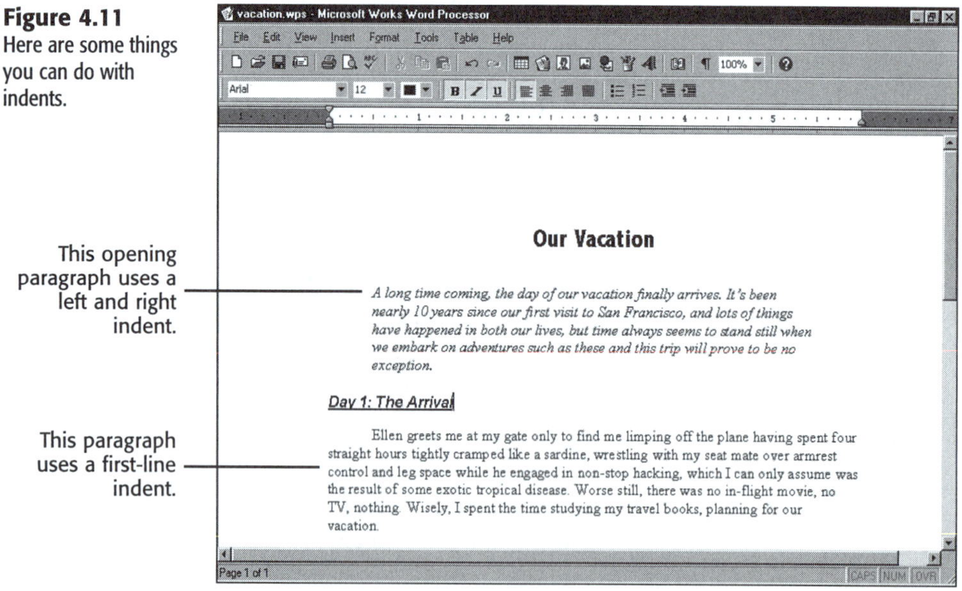

Figure 4.11
Here are some things you can do with indents.

CREATING BULLETED LISTS

Bullets are small symbols used to mark the beginning of all paragraphs within a list, or to add emphasis to a single, inset paragraph. Notice that this book contains many bulleted lists.

The Bullets feature in Works makes creating a bulleted list easy. This feature adds a bullet character in front of the selected paragraphs *and* sets the indents appropriately, all in one step. You can place bullets in existing paragraphs, or you can add them as you type. The choice is yours.

To type bulleted paragraphs, do the following:

1. Position the cursor where you want to begin the first bulleted paragraph.

2. Click the Bullets button on the toolbar. A bullet appears before the current line.
3. Type the paragraph and press Enter. A bullet automatically appears in front of the following paragraph, too.
4. Keep repeating step 3 until you are finished with the bulleted list. Then click the Bullets button again to turn off the Bullet feature. Figure 4.12 shows an example of bulleted text.

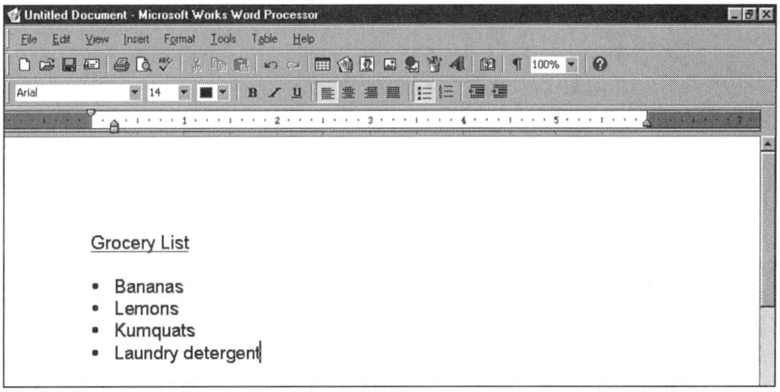

Figure 4.12
Use bullets to make a list of items stand out.

You can also make existing paragraphs into bullets by following these steps:

1. Select the paragraphs to which you want to add bullets.

2. Click the Bullets button on the toolbar. A bullet appears before each selected line.
3. Click anywhere away from the paragraphs to deselect them.

If there were blank lines between your lines or paragraphs that are now bulleted, click each line individually and click the Bullet button on the toolbar. This turns off the bullet for that line.

The default bullet is a generic dot. To choose from a group of other symbols for your bullets or to set custom positioning for the bullet character, do the following:

1. Select the paragraphs to receive the different bullet. They need not already have bullets.

2. Choose Format, Bullets and Numbering. The Bullets and Numbering dialog box appears, with the Bulleted tab on top (see Figure 4.13).
3. Click the bullet symbol you want to use.
4. In the Bullet Indent At box, enter the position (on the ruler) at which you want the bullet character to appear.
5. In the Text Indent At box, enter the position at which you want the paragraph next to the bullet to appear.
6. Click OK to accept your selection and close the dialog box.

Figure 4.13
The Bulleted tab enables you to choose the bullet character you prefer.

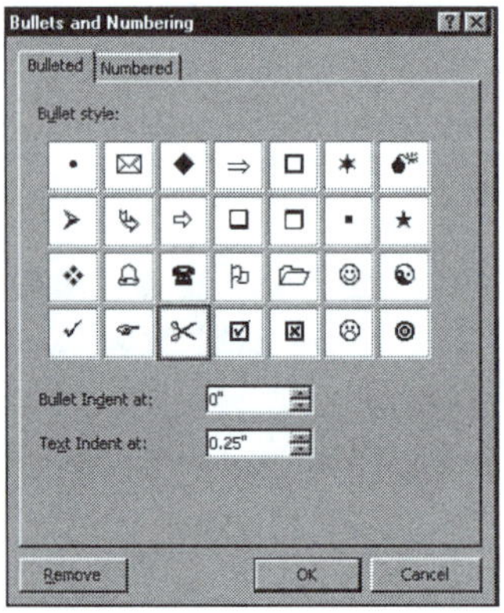

Your selection now becomes the default bullet that appears when you click the Bullets button on the toolbar. To return to the generic dot, you must go back and choose it from the Bullets and Numbering dialog box.

→ In Word, you can use any character in any font, not just the 28 characters that Works provides. **See** Chapter 10, "Formatting Documents in Word."

FORMATTING PAGES

So far in this chapter, you have learned about formatting individual characters and individual paragraphs. Now, let's move one step further and talk about formatting that applies to entire pages or documents. You can use such formatting to affect the overall presentation of your document.

INSERTING PAGE BREAKS

Page breaks occur naturally every time your text exceeds the length of a page. As you're entering text and you reach the bottom margin of the page, Works creates a new page, and the rest of the text flows onto it. This is known as a *soft page break*. However, you might have to force a page break where one would not occur naturally, to keep text on a particular page or move the text to the next page. This is a *hard* or *manual page break*.

To create a hard page break, position your cursor where you want the page break to occur, and press Ctrl+Enter.

A hard page break is a hidden character that Works places in your document. To delete your hard page break, simply delete that symbol. Position the insertion point at the top of the next page, and press the Backspace key.

Changing Margins

Your document margins are the areas around the edge of the page—top, bottom, and both sides—where there is no text. Works's default margins are 1 inch from the top and bottom and 1 1/4 inches from the left and right sides of the page.

To change the page margins, follow these steps:

1. Choose File, Page Setup. Click the Margins tab (see Figure 4.14).
2. You will see a series of four boxes for the Top, Bottom, Left, and Right sides of your page. Use the up and down increment buttons next to each field to increase or decrease the defaults, or select the contents of the boxes and type the new measurement. You don't have to type the inch marks.
3. Click OK to accept your changes and close the dialog box.

Note

In the Page Setup dialog box, you can also set how far from the edge of the paper you want to put the header or footer. In the From Edge section, specify an amount in the Header or Footer text box.

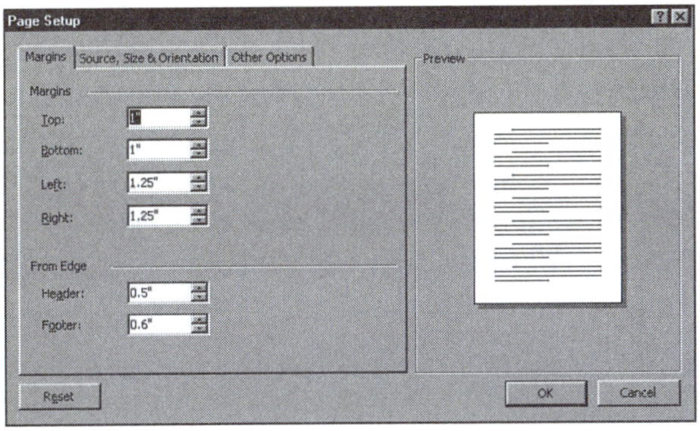

Figure 4.14
Change the document margins here.

Setting the Paper Size and Orientation

Most business and personal documents are letter size, or 8 1/2 by 11 inches, and this is the default paper size for a Works word processing document. Also, by default, Works prints documents in *portrait orientation*, in which the long edge of the paper is vertical. If you want to print on another size paper or in *landscape* orientation (with the long edge of the paper horizontal), you can do so through the Page Setup dialog box, shown in Figure 4.15. For example, you might want to print on special stationery for party invitations or formal announcements (such as enclosures for a wedding invitation). You can also use the Page Setup dialog box to choose a different paper source if your printer has more than one paper tray.

Tip #13 from
Faithe Wempen

You don't have to change the paper size to print on an envelope. Instead, choose Tools, Envelopes, and follow the prompts there to set up to print on an envelope.

1. Choose File, Page Setup. This opens the Page Setup dialog box.
2. Click the Source, Size & Orientation tab (see Figure 4.15).
3. Choose the appropriate paper size, orientation, and paper tray. Click OK to accept your settings and close the dialog box.

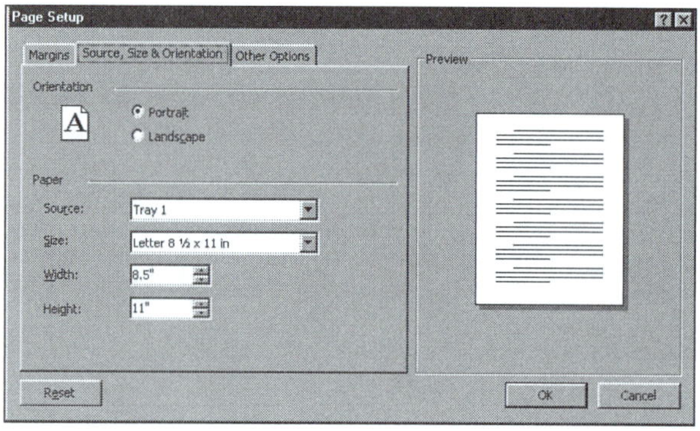

Figure 4.15
With these controls, you can change information about the paper you are using.

Adding Page Numbers

It's a good idea to add page numbers to any documents longer than one page. Page numbers can make your collating job easier if you're producing multiple copies of the document, and they make it easier for your readers to keep the document pages in order. Page numbers are also a lifesaver for reassembling your work after you have accidentally dropped all the printed pages on the floor and they have scattered every which way! (I speak from sad personal experience here.)

Page numbering codes should be placed in the document header or footer. These are special areas at the top and bottom of the page in which you place information that should be repeated on every page. (You will learn more about them in the next section.)

To place page numbers on your pages, follow these steps.

1. Choose View, Header and Footer. The Header box for the page becomes active, and the Header and Footer toolbar appears (see Figure 4.16).

2. (Optional) If you want to place the page number in the footer, click the Switch Between Header and Footer button.

3. Choose Insert, Page Numbers, or click the Insert Page Number button on the Header and Footer toolbar.

   This places a page number code, also known as a *placeholder*. It might look like a regular number onscreen, but when the document is printed, the actual page number replaces the code on each page.

4. To center or right-align your page number, highlight the code, and click the appropriate alignment button on your toolbar.

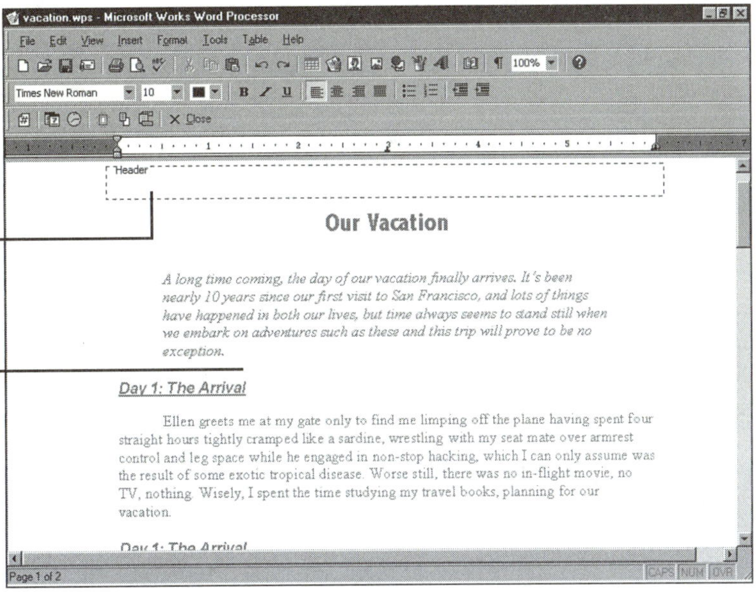

Figure 4.16
Activate the header and footer so that you can place a page number code in one of them.

You can set a few extra options for page numbering. To remove your page number from the first page of your document, choose File, Page Setup. Click the Other Options tab, and select the No Header on First Page and No Footer on First Page check boxes. Then click OK. Figure 4.17 shows the Page Setup dialog box.

To start your page numbering with a number other than 1, use that same dialog box. Choose File, Page Setup. Click the Other Options tab, and enter a number in the Starting Page Number box (or use the up or down arrow to change the number). Click OK.

Tip #14 from *Faithe Wempen*

> If your page 1 is a cover page, you can make page 2 into page 1 by setting the starting page number to 0. The starting page number can also be set to negative numbers, so you can count the number of unnumbered pages that precede the page you want to be page 1 and set the starting page number to that negative number. This can be useful if your document has several introductory pages or a table of contents. For example, if you have a cover and a three-page table of contents, set the starting page number to –3 (counting backward, that's 0, –1, –2, –3).

Part I
Ch 4

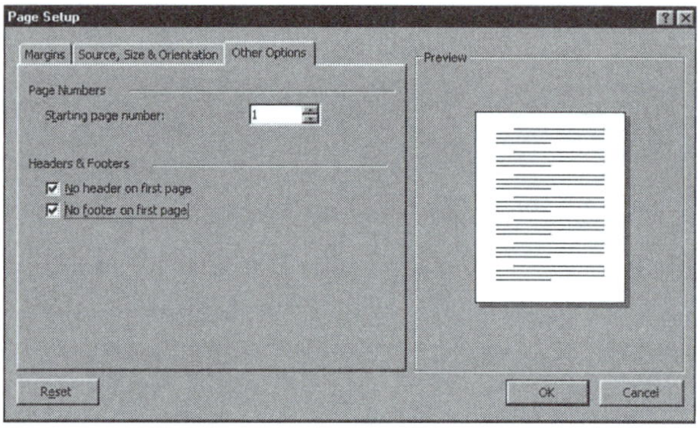

Figure 4.17
You can use the Page Setup dialog box to suppress the header and footer on the first page.

USING HEADERS AND FOOTERS

Just as page numbers help readers see which page they're on, headers and footers provide information to assist the reader in following long documents. A *header* is text that appears at the top of every page in your document, and a *footer* is text that appears at the bottom of every page in your document. You can place the title, date, copyright, and other information in your header and footer. Figure 4.18 shows a sample header. (This page has a footer, too, but you can't see it onscreen right now. You can scroll down in your own document to see the footer area.)

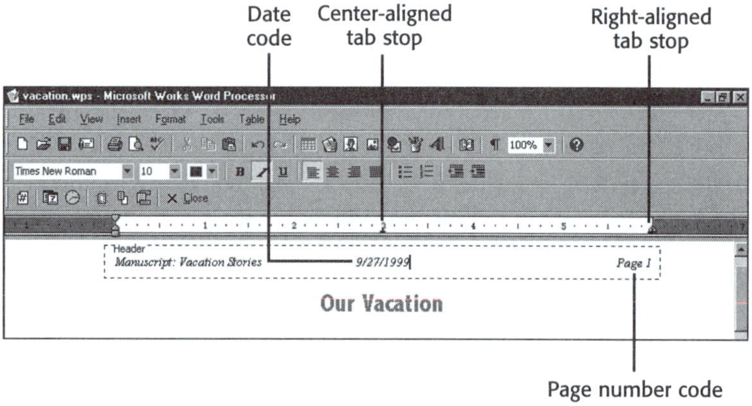

Figure 4.18
This document header prints the same useful information on every page.

By default, each header and footer has two tab stops: a center-aligned one in the middle of the line and a right-aligned one at the right edge. This makes it easy to enter text at any or all of the three positions in the header: left, center, and right. For example, in Figure 4.18, I typed the first bit of text, pressed Tab, and then clicked the Insert Date button to insert the date code. I pressed Tab again and typed Page. Then I clicked the Insert Page Number button to insert the page number code.

Here's how to create your own header and/or footer:

1. Choose View, Header and Footer. The Header box becomes active, and the Header and Footer toolbar appears.

2. Type your header text. You can format this text as you would any other text in the body of the document.

   To switch between the header area and the footer area, click the Switch Between Header and Footer button.

3. (Optional) To insert codes in the header or footer, such as a page number code or a code that produces the current date, click one of the buttons on the Header and Footer toolbar (see Table 4.1).

4. When you are finished working with the header and footer, choose View, Header and Footer, or click the Close button to return to the main document.

TABLE 4.1 TOOLBAR BUTTONS FOR INSERTING CODES

Button	Name
	Insert Page Number
	Insert Date
	Insert Time
	Insert Document Name

Note

The Insert Document Name button places the filename in the header or footer. It's not covered in this chapter because most people don't use it very often.

Just as page numbers shouldn't be placed on the first page of a business or personal letter, headers and footers shouldn't appear on the first page, either.

To suppress the header and footer on the first page, do the following:

1. Choose File, Page Setup.
2. Click the Other Options tab (refer to Figure 4.17).
3. Check No Header on First Page to remove the header from the first page. Check No Footer on First Page to remove the footer.
4. Click OK to accept your settings and close the dialog box.

CREATING COLUMNS

When you create a newsletter or similar document, you can divide your page into columns like a newspaper. Although you can set up many columns per page, two or three columns are the easiest for you to use and for your audience to read.

Column settings apply to your entire document. You can format existing text in columns or set up columns in a blank document before you begin typing.

Tip #15 from
Faithe Wempen

When creating something complicated like a newsletter that involves multiple columns, it's much easier to start with a task from the Works Task Launcher than try to build from scratch. The Newsletter task is highly worth your while to check out. Also, if you have the whole Works Suite (not just Works), you might try creating a newsletter using Word or Home Publisher instead. Both these programs contain more sophisticated layout features than the Works Word Processor.

To divide your document into multiple columns, follow these steps:

1. Choose Format, Columns. This opens the Format Columns dialog box, shown in Figure 4.19. In this dialog box, you can change any or all of these three settings:
    - **Number of Columns**—You can enter up to seven columns for portrait, letter-size paper. If you choose a higher number, Works advises you that your number of columns and the paper size don't match.
    - **Space Between**—This setting controls the space between columns. The default is 0.5 inches. You might have to print your document before you can judge whether this distance is too small or too large. Then adjust the gap between the columns by changing this measurement.
    - **Line Between Columns**—Vertical lines serve two purposes: They can add a polished look to a newsletter, and they can help the reader follow the text.
2. After entering your selections, click OK to close the dialog box.

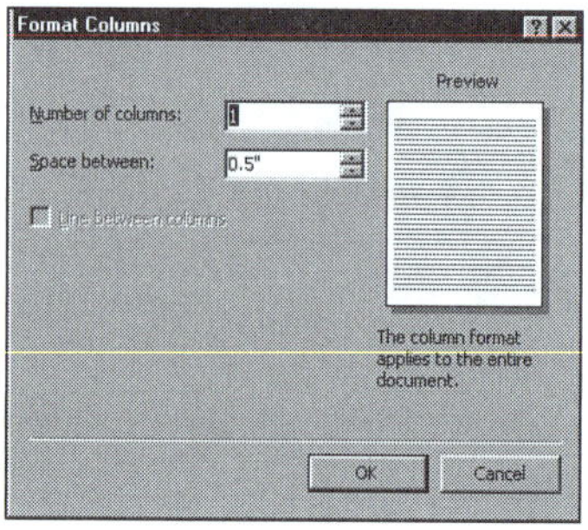

Figure 4.19
Specify the number of columns and the space between them, and choose whether to have a vertical line between columns.

WORKING WITH TABLES

A *table* is a group of rows and columns added to a document for storing and organizing text. The intersections of the columns and rows in a table are called *cells*. Tables can be used to create multicolumn lists, parallel paragraphs, and fill-in forms.

Tip #16 from
Faithe Wempen

If your table is going to contain many calculations and be filled with numbers instead of text, you're better off creating a spreadsheet in Works's Spreadsheet program. If you have to include the spreadsheet in your word processing document, you can always copy the spreadsheet to the Clipboard and then paste it into the document.

➔ For more information about spreadsheets, **see** Chapter 5, "Using the Works Spreadsheet."

To create a table in an open document, do the following:

1. Place your cursor at the point in your document where you want to place the table.
2. Choose Insert, Table, or click the Table button on the toolbar. The Insert Table dialog box appears (see Figure 4.20).
3. Enter the number of rows and columns you want in the Number of Rows and the Number of Columns text boxes.
4. (Optional) Choose one of the predesigned formats, if desired, from the Select a Format list. The Example area shows what the format looks like.
5. Click OK to accept your settings and close the dialog box.

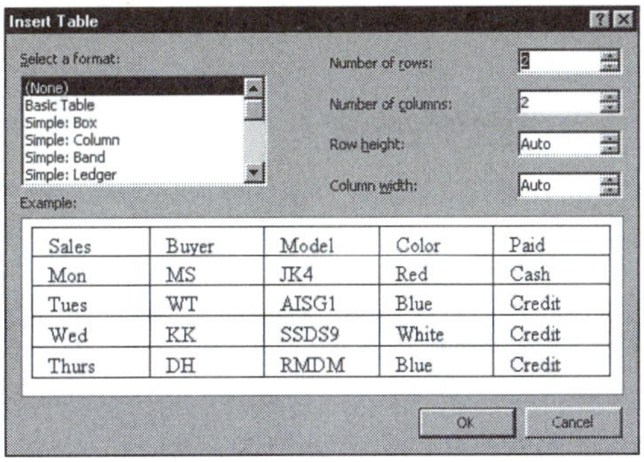

Figure 4.20
Choose your table settings from the Insert Table dialog box.

After you've inserted your table, you will see a large rectangle appear on your screen. To enter text into a cell, click in it to move the insertion point there; then type. Press the Tab key to move to the next cell (or press Shift+Tab to move to the preceding cell). You can also use the arrow keys to move from cell to cell or click in a cell to place the cursor there. *Do not* press Enter to move from cell to cell. Pressing Enter begins a new paragraph within the cell. Figure 4.21 shows a table with information entered into some cells.

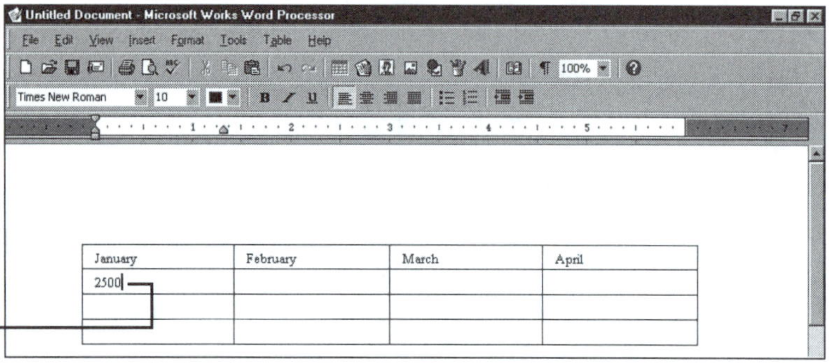

Figure 4.21
Type text in a cell as you would in a regular paragraph.

Insertion point

SELECTING TABLE CELLS

To format your table cells or the text in your table, you have to select the cells first. To select a cell in your table, point at the left edge of the cell so that the mouse pointer turns into a right-pointer. (This is like your normal mouse arrow except that it points to the upper right instead of the upper left.) Then click to select that cell (see Figure 4.22). To select more than one cell, drag across multiple cells.

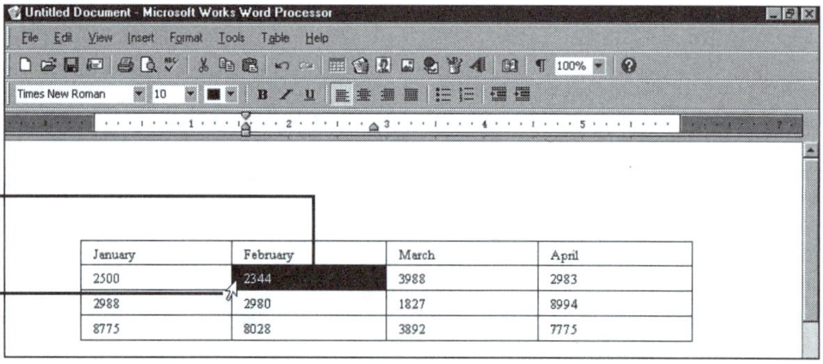

Figure 4.22
To select a cell, point to its left edge and click.

Selected cell

Right-pointing mouse pointer

To select the entire row, click to the left of that row *outside the table*. To select an entire column, click above that column *outside the table*. The mouse pointer becomes a small black down-pointing arrow when it is positioned appropriately for selecting a column (see Figure 4.23). To select multiple rows or columns, drag after selecting a single one.

FORMATTING TEXT IN A TABLE

You can format text in table cells as you would any other text—you can change the text's alignment, font, style, and size. You can type paragraph text into a cell (the text wraps within the horizontal dimensions of the cell) and set indents for the text. The only thing you can't do in a table cell is use the Tab key to indent text, because the Tab key moves you to the next cell.

Figure 4.23
To select a column, point above it and click.

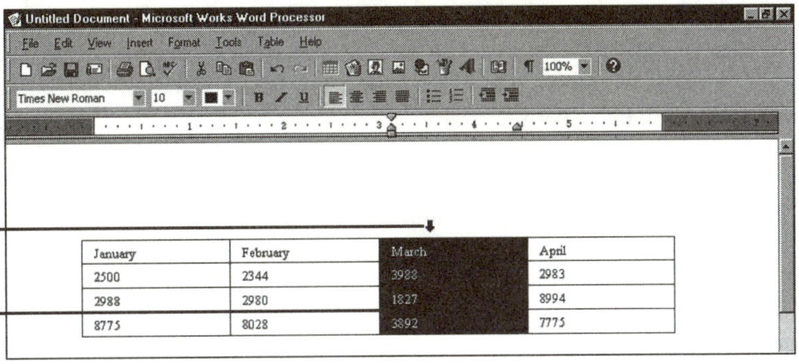

➔ For more information about formatting text in or out of a table, **see** "Formatting Text," **p. 58**.
➔ For more information about the Spreadsheet tool, **see** Chapter 5, "Using the Works Spreadsheet."

Changing Table Dimensions

Before you create your table, think about what will go into it. For example, if the table will contain a list of employees and the hours they worked on a given day, think about how many columns that will require—one column each for the employee name, date, and hours worked. That's three columns. The number of employees plus the number of column headings will tell you how many rows you need.

Even if you plan ahead, you might have to make changes. After you've created the table and entered the text, you might decide that you want to add a column for Social Security numbers. If you forget to put in an employee and his or her hours, you will have to add a row.

To add a column, place your cursor in any cell in the column to the right of where you want to add your new column. Choose Insert, Column (or right-click the cell and choose Insert Column from the pop-up menu). A new column appears, sized to fit within your current table dimensions.

To add a row, click to place your cursor in any cell in the row below where you want to add your new row. Choose Insert, Row (or right-click the cell and choose Insert Row from the pop-up menu).

Changing Column Width

Does the text you type into a cell not fit into a single row? If you're not happy with the appearance of your table because of weird widths, you can change the width of your columns to accommodate the width of the text in your cells.

1. Position the mouse pointer on the line between two columns, to the left of the column you want to adjust. The mouse pointer becomes a vertical line with a double-headed arrow.
2. Drag the line to change the column width.

You can also change column width from the Column Width dialog box. This method has the advantage of giving you more precise control, but it's a bit more trouble. Use it when the exact width (and not just an eyeball "guesstimate") is important to you. To use the dialog box method, follow these steps:

1. Place your cursor in any cell in the column to be adjusted.
2. Choose Table, Cell Height and Width. The Cell Height and Width dialog box opens.
3. Enter the width you want, in inches, in the Column Width box.
4. Click OK to accept your setting and close the dialog box.

Note

Although the row height adjusts automatically depending on the size of type in the row, you can adjust the row height manually by dragging between a row, the same as you do for a column. You can also use the Row Height setting in the Cell Height and Width dialog box to adjust row height.

Adding Table Borders and Shading

Adding borders and shading to your table clarifies its information and helps to draw your readers' attention to specific columns, rows, or cells. Works supplies a series of preformatted table shading and border designs, which can make the process of enhancing a table much easier.

To AutoFormat a table, do the following:

1. Place your cursor anywhere in the table.
2. Choose Table, Table Format. This opens the Table Format dialog box (see Figure 4.24).
3. Scroll through the list of formats and preview them by clicking them. The Example area shows you a preview of the selected format.
4. When you find one you like, click OK to accept your selection and close the dialog box.

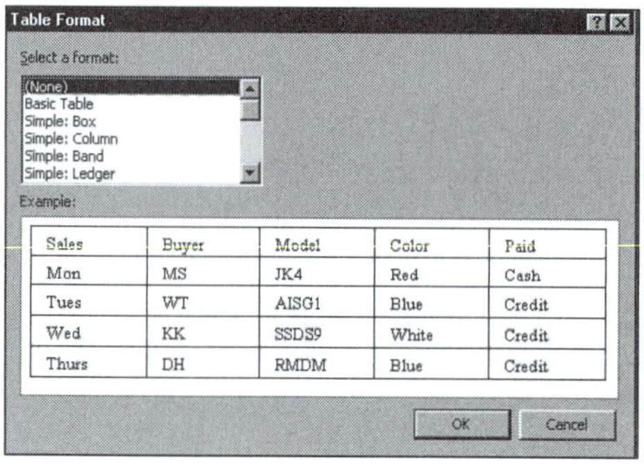

Figure 4.24
AutoFormat makes it easy to create professional-looking tables.

If you'd prefer to apply your own borders and shading on a cell-by-cell basis, you can use the Format, Borders and Shading command, as described in the following steps. (You might want to start with an AutoFormat and then use the controls to fine-tune.)

1. Select the cell or cells you want to shade and/or border.
2. Choose Format, Borders and Shading. The Borders and Shading dialog box opens (see Figure 4.25).
3. Do any of the following:
   - Choose a line style from the Line Style drop-down list.
   - Choose a line color from the Line Color drop-down list
   - Choose a fill style from the Fill Style drop-down list.
   - Choose colors for the fill from the Color 1 and Color 2 lists. (Color 2 is applicable only if a pattern is chosen for the Fill Style.)
   - Choose a button to indicate which part of the selection the settings should apply to: Outline, Top, Bottom, Left, and/or Right.
4. Click OK to accept your settings and close the dialog box.

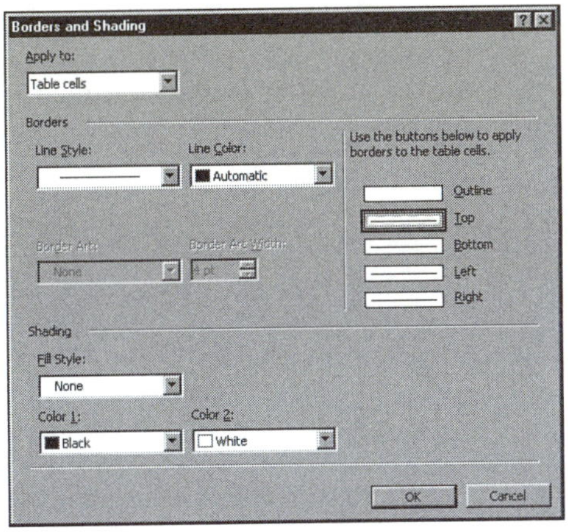

Figure 4.25
Apply your own border and shading settings to the table here.

DELETING THE TABLE

If you decide you don't need the table in your document, select the table by clicking it once. The table displays gray handles (if a solid border shows, click outside the table, and the gray handles will appear). Press the Delete key.

This concludes the coverage of the Works Word Processor tool. In the next chapter, you will learn to use the Spreadsheet tool to work with numbers and calculate data.

TROUBLESHOOTING

TOO MANY FONTS

I have so many fonts that it's hard to find the ones I actually use on the list.

You might want to remove some of the fonts from your system. Do so in the Windows Control Panel. Choose Start, Settings, Control Panel, and double-click the Fonts icon. Then click a font you want to delete, and press the Delete key. Be careful not to delete a font that you think you will want in the future, however.

BLACK BLOBS INSTEAD OF SYMBOLS

Certain typographical characters such as ellipses (…) and curly quotes ("") appear as black blobs rather than in their normal form in some cases.

Perhaps the font you are using does not support those characters. Select the text, change it to a different font, and see whether those characters reappear.

PRINTING CUTS OFF LAST LINE OF TEXT

On certain documents, the printer always cuts off the last line or two. This doesn't happen on all documents, though.

Perhaps your bottom margin is set too low for your printer's capability. Increase the bottom margin slightly until the problem is resolved.

CHAPTER 5

Using the Works Spreadsheet

In this chapter

Starting a Spreadsheet

A *spreadsheet program* is a software application that organizes data into *rows* and *columns*. In a spreadsheet program, numeric values can be calculated and text can be sorted. The pages or documents these programs create are called *spreadsheets* or *worksheets*. They work great for organizing material into rows and columns, much like tables in the Works Word Processor but with more precision and features.

The tasks included with Works offer dozens of great spreadsheet ideas, from price lists to business forms such as invoices.

You can start a spreadsheet in much the same way you start a word processing document:

- From the Tasks tab in the Task Launcher, double-click one of the tasks with a spreadsheet icon next to its description.
- From the Task Launcher's Programs tab, start a new spreadsheet document by clicking Works Spreadsheet and then Start a Blank Spreadsheet.

If you want to follow along with this chapter's activities, do the latter—start a blank spreadsheet.

→ For information about tasks, **see** Chapter 1, "Introducing the Microsoft Works Suite."

Understanding the Spreadsheet Window

The Spreadsheet window has a lot in common with the Word Processor window you saw in Chapter 3, "Introducing the Works Word Processor," and Chapter 4, "Formatting with the Works Word Processor." The main difference is the area where you enter your work. Unlike the large blank document where you enter text in the Word Processor tool, you have a series of rows and columns in the Spreadsheet tool's document that intersect to form *cells*. Figure 5.1 points out the important features of the spreadsheet, and the following list describes them:

- **Formula bar**—Displays any formula that is in the active cell. The cell itself displays the results of the formula.
- **Row header**—Lists the numbers that label each row.
- **Column header**—Lists the letters that label each column.
- **Active cell**—This cell is marked by a black border (called a *cell cursor*). Any characters or commands you type act on the active cell.
- **Cell address area**—This area shows the address of the active cell. The cell address identifies the cell's location, the intersecting column and row of the cell. The address A1, for example, identifies the cell in the first column and first row of the spreadsheet.

A *cell* occurs at the intersection of a column and a row. Columns are identified by letters of the alphabet (A through IV). Rows are identified by numbers (1 through 16384). Those rows and columns make up more than 3.3 million total cells.

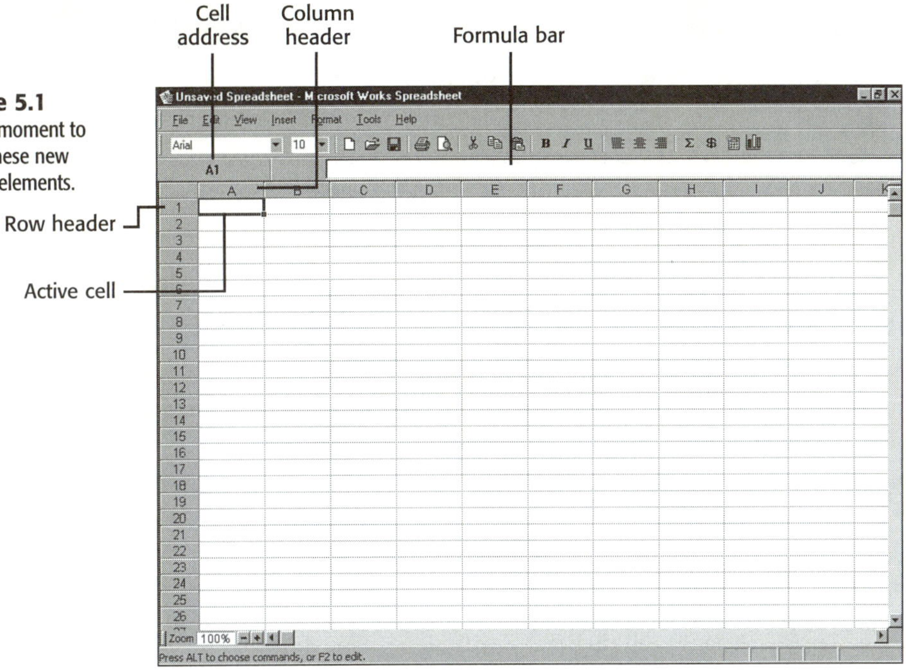

Figure 5.1
Take a moment to learn these new screen elements.

Because each cell address consists of the column name and the row name, the cell address of the top cell in the first column is `A1`; the cell address of the last cell on the spreadsheet is `IV16384`.

➔ For more information about some of the common features in Works tools, such as the toolbar, menu bar, and scrollbars, **see** Chapter 1, "Introducing the Microsoft Works Suite."

WORKING WITH THE SPREADSHEET TOOLBAR

Although you might be familiar with some of the tools on the Spreadsheet toolbar, it also includes tools not found elsewhere in Microsoft Works Suite 2000. You can see a name and description of any tool on the toolbar by resting your mouse pointer on it; the tool's name (a *ScreenTip*) appears below the tool, and a brief explanation of the tool's function appears in the status bar. Table 5.1 describes some of the Spreadsheet tools.

TABLE 5.1 TOOLBAR BUTTONS UNIQUE TO THE SPREADSHEET

Tool	Name	Description
Σ	AutoSum	Inserts the `SUM` function in the current cell and proposes a range of cells to total
$	Currency	Applies the currency format to numbers in the selected cell(s)

continues

TABLE 5.1 CONTINUED

Tool	Name	Description
	Easy Calc	Starts Easy Calc, which helps you create formulas
	New Chart	Creates a new chart

WORKING WITH SPREADSHEET FILES

You probably already know how to handle files in Works because I covered it in some detail in Chapter 2, "Performing Common Works Tasks." In case you need a refresher, turn back to that chapter now.

→ To learn how to open, save, close, and print spreadsheets, **see** Chapter 2, "Performing Common Works Tasks."

MOVING AROUND THE SPREADSHEET

To designate the active cell (in other words, to position your cursor in a specific cell), click it with the mouse. The cell cursor appears as a black border around the active cell. If you can't see the cell you want to work with, scroll the display to bring the necessary cell into view.

As you place information into the cells, you might work with so many cells that you won't be able to see them all onscreen at once. You can use the scrollbars to move around the spreadsheet, just as you would with a document. Notice that the spreadsheet has both a vertical (on the right) and horizontal (on the bottom) scrollbar, so you can move in two dimensions. You can also move around using keyboard shortcuts, as shown in Table 5.2.

TABLE 5.2 KEYBOARD SHORTCUTS FOR MOVING AROUND THE SPREADSHEET

Press...	To...
←	Move to the left one cell.
→	Move to the right one cell.
↑	Move up one row.
↓	Move down one row.
Tab	Move to the right one cell.
Shift+Tab	Move to the left one cell.
Home	Move to beginning of the row.
End	Move to the end of the row (the last cell containing data).
Page Down	Move one screen down the spreadsheet.
Page Up	Move one screen up the spreadsheet.
Ctrl+Home	Go to A1 (the first cell on the spreadsheet).
Ctrl+End	Go to the last cell in the spreadsheet that contains data.

Tip #17 from
Faithe Wempen

A quick way to move to a cell in a large spreadsheet without scrolling is to use the Go To command. Choose Edit, Go To, or press F5 on your keyboard. This opens the Go To dialog box, where you can enter the cell address to which you want to move.

ENTERING YOUR DATA

Building a spreadsheet has a natural flow to it. First, enter the text labels for the rows and columns. Then, enter the data (the text or numbers you're tracking). Finally, enter any formulas or functions that you will use to calculate the results.

ENTERING TEXT

The first thing you will probably want to do is enter text into some of the cells. This might seem like an odd thing to do in a program designed to calculate numbers, but you will understand the numbers better if they're clearly labeled. For example, if you are setting up a spreadsheet that keeps track of your diet plan for the day, you must enter a title for the list and then some column labels, as shown in Figure 5.2.

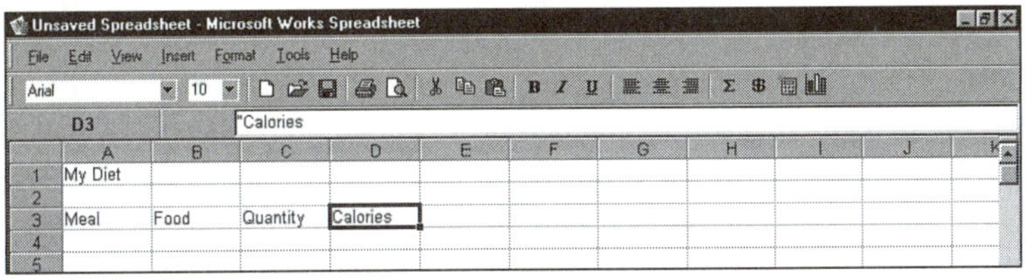

Figure 5.2
Most spreadsheets start out with some text.

To enter text in a cell, do the following:

1. Click the cell in which you want the text to appear (or use the keyboard shortcuts to go to the cell). That cell then becomes the active cell.
2. Type the text. As you type, the text appears both in the cell and in the formula bar at the top of the spreadsheet.
3. Press Enter or click the check mark next to the formula bar to accept your text entry.

Tip #18 from
Faithe Wempen

If you're entering information in a series of cells, you don't have to press Enter after each entry. Instead, press the arrow key pointing in the direction of the next cell. Works accepts the entry and moves to the next cell, all in one motion. If you're entering data into adjacent cells in a row, you can press Tab after each entry to accept the data and then move one cell to the right.

ENTERING NUMBERS

Entering numbers works the same as entering text; just position the cell cursor in the cell in which you want to enter the numbers, and then type them. If the numbers you are entering require special symbols, such as currency ($) or percent (%), you can enter them now if you want, or you can format the cells with a special formatting that applies those symbols automatically. (You will learn about that later in this chapter.)

Note

If you're typing figures with decimal points, your trailing zeros disappear. For instance, the number 55.10 appears as `55.1`. This is normal. It happens because the spreadsheet is automatically set in the General format. Later in this chapter, you will learn how to apply various number formats. Meanwhile, don't worry—the calculations are still correct even without the zero.

ENTERING DATES AND TIMES

Dates and times are considered "numbers" by the Spreadsheet, and it can perform calculations on them. For example, if you have `7/7/98` in one cell and `7/1/98` in another, and you ask the Spreadsheet (through a formula) to subtract the second from the first, the result is `6` (for 6 days).

A date's number is the number of days between it and January 1, 1900. For example, January 1, 1900, would be `1`, and December 31, 1999, would be `36,525`. Times are measured in decimal points after the whole number. For example, if `1` is midnight on January 1, 1900, then `1.5` would be noon on that day, and `1.75` would be 6:00 p.m.

However, you don't see these raw numbers on your spreadsheet because Works formats dates in a more readable date format, such as `1/1/00` or `6:00 p.m.`

To enter a date or time, do the following:

1. Click the cell where you want the date or time to appear (or use the keyboard shortcuts to go to the cell). That cell then becomes the active cell.
2. Type the date or time in your preferred format (for example, *`xx/xx/xx`* or *`xx:xx`*). As you type, the date or time appears in both the cell and in the formula bar at the top of the spreadsheet.
3. Press Enter or click the check mark next to the formula bar to accept your date or time entry.

The best way to enter dates is with slashes (1/12/97), especially if you want to use them for calculations such as figuring ages or length of employment. You can always format these later to appear in some other format (such as January 12, 1997). Avoid entering the date with dashes (such as 1-12-97) because Works treats that as text and won't recognize it as a date for calculations.

When entering times, add AM or PM for morning or afternoon (for example, `10:00 PM`) or use the 24-hour or military clock (for example, `22:00`). You can specify time to the second (as in `10:00:03 PM`).

➔ To choose different date and time formats, **see** "Changing Date and Time Formats," **p. 107**.

USING UNDO

If you make a mistake in an entry as you are typing it, just backspace and enter the correct text. Don't use the arrow keys to move back and forth, because you will end up in one of the cells next to the one in which you wanted to enter the data.

After you accept the entry (by pressing Enter), the fastest way to fix it is to undo the mistake. Choose Edit, Undo Entry, or press Ctrl+Z. You must use Undo immediately after making the error, because you can undo only the last thing you did.

SELECTING CELLS AND RANGES

Before you can delete, move, copy, or format data, you must select the cells to be involved in the operation. The active cell is automatically selected, but you also can select a range of cells. A *range* is a rectangular group of cells connected either horizontally or vertically. It can be as small as one or two cells or as large as the entire spreadsheet.

The range is referenced by the first cell in the upper-left corner of the range and the last cell in the lower-right corner of the range. When written, a range reference always has a colon (`:`) between the cell addresses that define it, such as `A1:C9`.

The selected cells in a range are surrounded by a thick border, and all but the first cell in the selection appear in reverse highlighting (see Figure 5.3). The range reference appears in the Cell Address area.

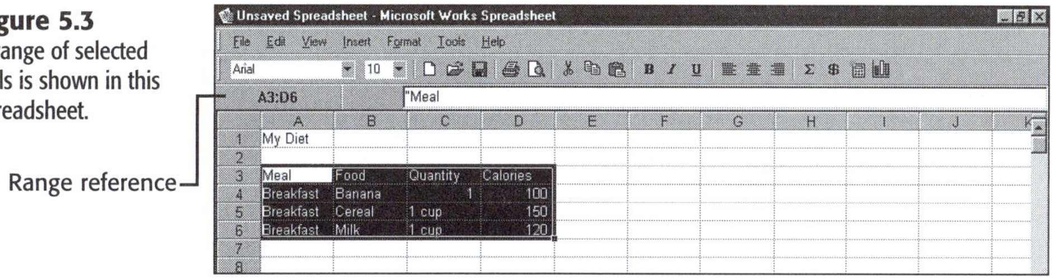

Figure 5.3
A range of selected cells is shown in this spreadsheet.

Table 5.3 lists the methods (both keyboard and mouse) for highlighting cells in your spreadsheet.

Table 5.3 How to Highlight (Select) Cells

To Highlight...	Mouse Method	Keyboard Method
A cell	Click the cell.	Press an arrow key.
A group of cells	Click the first cell, hold down the mouse button, and drag to the last cell in the group.	Position the cursor in the first cell in the upper-left corner of the group, press F8, and then use the arrow keys to highlight the rest of the cells.
A row	Click the row header.	Highlight one cell in the row, and then press Ctrl+F8.
A column	Click the column header.	Highlight one cell in the column, and press Shift+F8.
The entire spreadsheet	Click the corner header cell in which the column headers and row headers meet (the upper-left corner of the spreadsheet).	Press Ctrl+Shift+F8.

Tip #19 from *Faithe Wempen*

When you have to enter data in a large block of cells, highlight the cells first. Then, starting in the first cell in the upper-left corner of the block, enter the data and press Enter. Works automatically moves you to the next cell, first going down one column, then moving to the top of the next column to the right, down that column, then to the next column on the right, and so on.

Modifying Cell Contents

These next few sections deal with ways to make changes to what you've entered in your cells, short of wiping it all out and starting over. Changes are inevitable, even if you carefully plan ahead of time. You might have to change the data in a cell, move or copy it, clear it out completely, or perform any of several other operations.

Editing Data

If you've entered data incorrectly and it's too late to undo the entry with the Edit, Undo command, you can correct the data by replacing the entry or by editing the entry. To replace information in a cell, click the cell containing the information you want to replace, type the new information, and press Enter. The new entry wipes out the old one.

To edit a cell, click it and then press F2, or click in the formula bar to move the insertion point into that cell for changes. Use the Backspace or Delete key to remove what's there, as needed, and type your changes. Press Enter when you're done.

DELETING CELL CONTENT

To delete data from a cell or group of cells, highlight the cell or cells that contain the data, and then press the Delete key on the keyboard or choose Edit, Clear.

If you accidentally delete data in the wrong cell, choose Edit, Undo Clear before taking any other action.

MOVING OR COPYING CELL CONTENT

You can move or copy data from one part of a spreadsheet to another or from one spreadsheet to another spreadsheet. For example, perhaps you have decided that the column on the left side would look better on the right. Or the rows are in the wrong order. Or maybe you want a copy of a particular row to appear on a different spreadsheet.

Caution

When you move cells, the destination cells must be blank. If you move cells onto cells with existing content, the existing content goes away. Therefore, before you move cells, you might have to insert some blank ones. See "Inserting and Deleting Rows and Columns" later in this chapter to learn how to do that.

To move or copy cells, you can either cut and paste them, as you learned how to do with text in Chapter 2, or you can use a different technique, called *drag and drop*.

To move or copy with drag and drop, follow these steps:

1. Select the cell(s) you want to move or copy.
2. Point to the edge of the highlighted cell or group of cells so that the word DRAG appears on the mouse pointer (see Figure 5.4).
3. Hold down the left mouse button, and drag the highlighted cell(s) to a new location.

   If you want to copy (as opposed to move), hold down the Ctrl key, too.

   An outline of the cells appears as you drag, and the word MOVE or COPY replaces DRAG under the mouse pointer. Release the mouse button, and the data is relocated.

Caution

As you drag, make sure that the mouse pointer says the right thing. If you are trying to copy, but the mouse pointer says MOVE, you didn't press and hold down the Ctrl key before pressing and holding down the mouse button. Release both buttons and try again.

→ For a reminder of how to use the cut-and-paste method, **see** Chapter 2, "Performing Common Works Tasks."

FINDING AND REPLACING DATA

The Spreadsheet tool uses the same Find and Replace procedures as the Word Processor, which you learned about in Chapter 3. Turn back to "Finding and Replacing Text" in that chapter and try out the same steps on your spreadsheet, just to reinforce the skills.

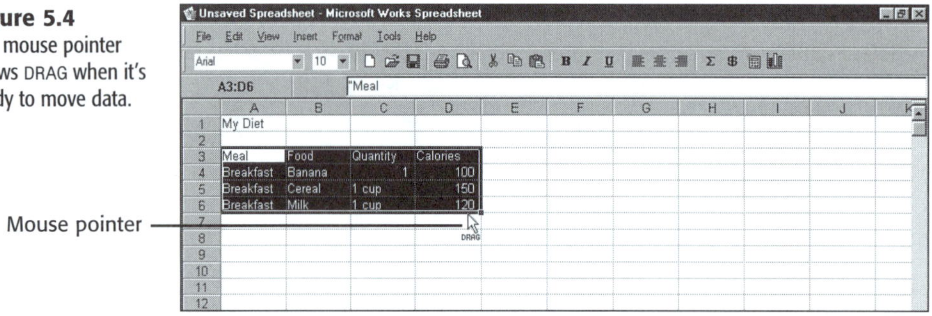

Figure 5.4
The mouse pointer shows DRAG when it's ready to move data.

Working with Formulas

A *formula* is an algebraic expression using numbers, functions, and cell addresses that tells a spreadsheet program what operations to perform on those numbers or the contents of the designated cells. A formula can be as simple as `1+1`. The result of that formula, of course, is `2`.

In a spreadsheet, formulas are often written using cell references instead of actual numbers. For example, a formula in cell `C1` might be `=A1+B1`. (The equals sign preceding the formula tells Works that it is a formula and not regular text.) Such a formula would add up whatever numbers happened to be in cells `A1` and `B1` at the moment and place the answer in cell `C1`. For example, in Figure 5.5, cell `A1` contains `10`, and cell `B1` contains `12`. The formula in cell `C1` (`=A1+B1`) results in an answer of `22`.

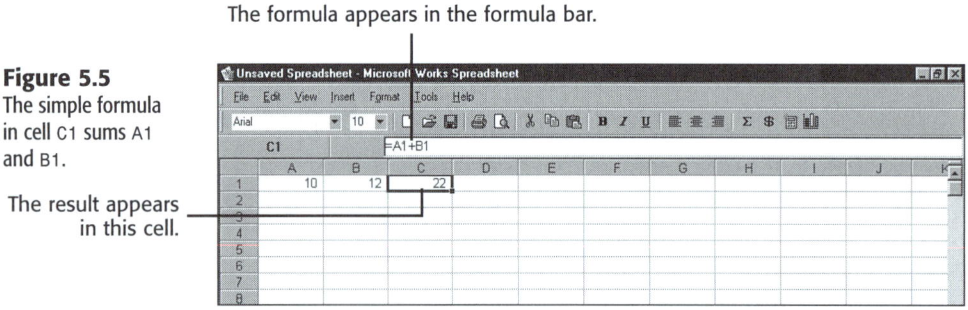

Figure 5.5
The simple formula in cell C1 sums A1 and B1.

Formulas are always written with no spaces and starting with an equals sign. To indicate the type of operation you want the spreadsheet to perform, you must use *operators* in a formula. You assign, modify, or combine values into new values by using operators. The most common operators are *arithmetic operators*, as listed in Table 5.4.

Table 5.4 Arithmetic Operators

Operator	Use to...	Example
+	Add two numbers or cell addresses.	=C5+C9
-	Subtract two numbers or cell addresses.	=C5-C9

Operator	Use to...	Example
*	Multiply two numbers or cell addresses.	=C5*C9
/	Divide two numbers or cell addresses.	=C5/C9

A formula is calculated from left to right. For example, if the formula is =C6+C9-C10, the contents of cell C6 are added to the contents of cell C9, and the contents of cell C10 are then subtracted from that result.

Arithmetic operators evaluate in the following order: exponents, multiplication and division, and then addition and subtraction. Therefore, the result of the formula =6+4/2 is 8 because the division (4/2) is evaluated first and then added to the 6.

If the formula contains an *exponent*, it's calculated first, so the result of the formula $=6+4^2/2$ is 14. The exponent (4^2) is calculated first, the result of 16 is then divided by 2 for an answer of 8, and that answer is added to 6.

If your formula is more complicated, you might want to group expressions by using parentheses. For example, in algebra, a formula might be (x*y)/(z-y). When parentheses are used in a formula, the calculation within the parentheses is performed first. In this formula, you would calculate the answer to x*y first and then divide it by the answer to z-y. So in a spreadsheet formula such as =(C5*C9)-(D11/D12), the answer to C5*C9 is calculated first, then the answer to D11/D12 is calculated, and finally the two answers are subtracted.

For example, the formula =6+4/2 results in 8, but the formula (6+4)/2 results in 5 because the addition in the parentheses is calculated first and then the division occurs.

To enter a formula, follow these steps:

1. Click in the cell in which you want the result of the formula to appear.
2. Type an equal sign (=) to indicate that you're entering a formula.
3. Type the values, cell addresses, range references, and operators necessary to create your formula.

Tip #20 from *Faithe Wempen*

When you want to use a range reference in a formula, enter the formula up to the point where you need the range reference, and then highlight the range of cells you want to reference. Works automatically displays the cell reference on the formula bar. Type the next character of the formula or press Enter, and the range reference becomes part of the formula. If you've assigned a name to that range of cells, the range name automatically appears in place of the cells' addresses.

4. Press Enter, or click the check mark next to the formula bar. The formula results appear in the cell, and the formula itself appears in the formula bar.

USING AUTOSUM

One of the most common formulas involves adding a column or row of numbers. Works provides a special function called *AutoSum* that efficiently handles such activities.

For example, suppose that you want to add the numbers for each quarter in Figure 5.6. You should place formulas that sum each column in row 11. For example, in cell `B11` you could enter `=B7+B8+B9+B10`. That's a bit tedious, however, because you have to type all those cell references. There is a better way.

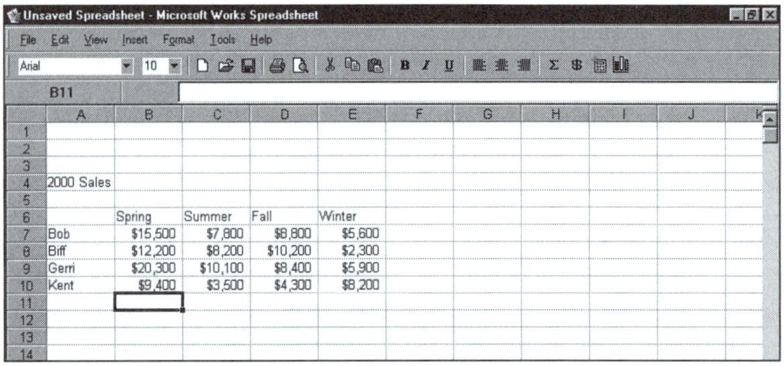

Figure 5.6
Columns and rows of numbers like these can be easily summed with AutoSum.

To sum a column of numbers with AutoSum, perform these steps:

1. Enter the numbers in your spreadsheet that you want to sum. For example, from Figure 5.6 you will sum the values in `B7` through `B10`.
2. Click in the cell in which you want the result to appear (for example, `B11` in Figure 5.6).
3.  Click the AutoSum button on the toolbar.
4. Works makes a guess at what you want to sum (see Figure 5.7). If the range outlined is correct, press Enter. If not, drag across the cells that you actually want to sum, and then press Enter.

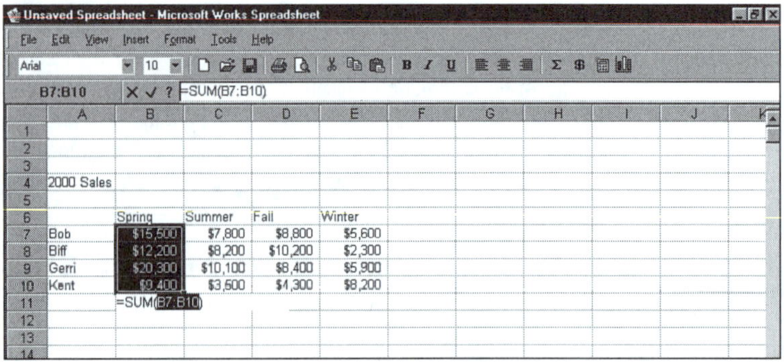

Figure 5.7
AutoSum makes its best guess about what you want to sum, based on the position of the cell.

After you press Enter, you will see a formula in the formula bar, like this: `=SUM(B7:B10)`. You have just created your first formula that uses a function! A *function*, as you will learn later in this chapter, is a special keyword that applies a certain bit of math to the selected cells. In this case, the function is `SUM`, and the math it applies is addition. Don't worry too much about this now; just keep it in mind for later use.

Note

If you see the error message `Missing Operand` when you use AutoSum, this means that your formula ends in an operator instead of a cell reference. This can happen if you enter the cell addresses manually rather than select the cells or stick with the cells that AutoSum chose. Double-check your formula and make sure that it ends in a cell reference.

➔ To learn more about functions, **see** "Working with Functions," **p. 97**.

MODIFYING FORMULAS

You can edit formulas in basically the same way you edit text and numbers in cells. Just click in the cell, and then do your editing on the formula bar. Use the arrow keys to position the cursor within the formula bar, and use Backspace or Delete to remove unwanted characters.

MOVING AND COPYING FORMULAS

You can move and copy formulas the same way you move and copy regular text: with either the drag-and-drop or cut-and-paste techniques described earlier. (The result is slightly different when you move formulas than when you move regular text, but I'll go into that momentarily.)

➔ To recall how to move cell contents with drag and drop, **see** "Moving or Copying Cell Content," **p. 91**.
➔ For more information about cut and paste and the Clipboard, **see** "Moving and Copying Text," **p. 49**.

COPYING WITH FILL

You can copy a formula cell as you would any data cell. Point at the cell's handle (small black box) in the lower-right corner of the cell border. The word `FILL` appears beneath the mouse pointer. Drag to the right to fill a row or down to fill a column, highlighting the number of cells to which you want to copy the formula, and then release the mouse button.

You can also copy with the Fill command on the menu. Highlight the formula cell, and then drag across the cells you want to fill to highlight them. Choose Edit, Fill Right (Ctrl+R) for a row or Edit, Fill Down (Ctrl+D) for a column.

UNDERSTANDING RELATIVE AND ABSOLUTE REFERENCES

Your formula may contain cell addresses. When you move or copy a formula, you probably don't want those addresses to stay the same. For example, in Figure 5.8, cell `B11` has an AutoSum formula that totals the values in that column. I want to copy that formula to cell

C11, but I want the formula to refer to column C, instead of B, so the result in C11 is =SUM(C7:C10) instead of =SUM(B7:B10). Works handles this change automatically. When you move or copy a formula, the new version refers to the cells in similar positions relative to its new home rather than to the original positions. This is called *relative addressing*.

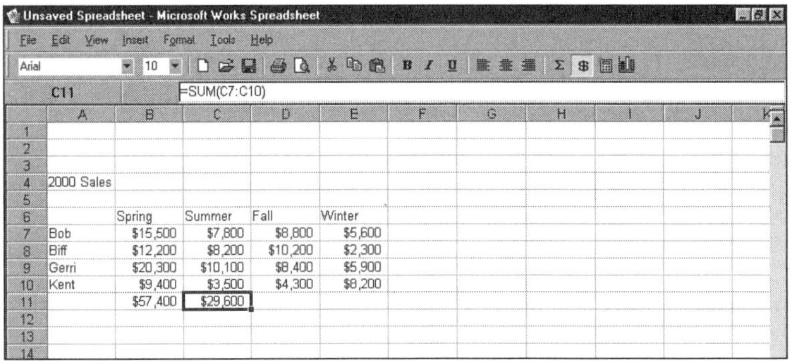

Figure 5.8
The formula in B11 was copied to C11, where it changed its references automatically to refer to column C.

Relative addressing changes the cell addresses relative to the position of the formula. This is true if you copy the formula from one row or column to the next or from one side of your worksheet to the other.

All this works beautifully until you want every copied formula to refer to the same exact cell. For example, take a look at Figure 5.9. You have the current sales commission rate in cell F3. In rows F7 through F10, you have values for the total sales for each salesperson. To calculate the amount of commission due each salesperson, you want to multiply the total sales amount by the rate of commission, so you enter the formula =F7*F3 in cell G7. However, if you copy that formula down the column, the commission due amounts will be obviously incorrect for the remaining salespeople.

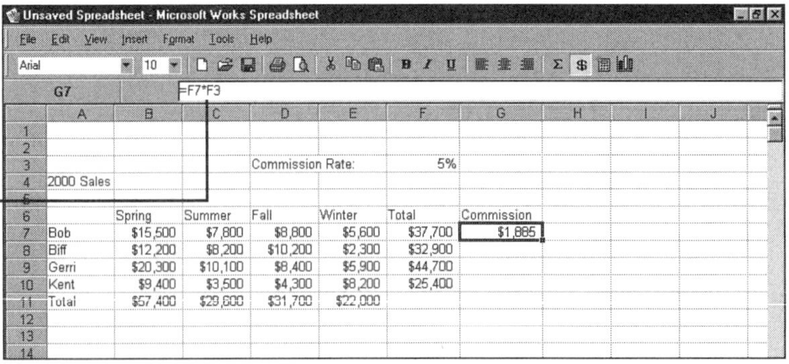

Figure 5.9
In this case, copying the formula would not give the desired result.

F3 must remain static in all copies.

The solution to this problem is to use *absolute addressing*. Absolute addressing marks the exact, original location of a cell in a spreadsheet. To reference such a location in a formula, use dollar signs ($) before the column letter and row number (F3).

For example, in Figure 5.9, the formula entered in cell G7 should have been =F7*F3. The F7 cell address could change as the formula was copied to another cell (it's relative), but the F3 cell address, which is absolute, should remain the same in every copied formula.

See Table 5.5 to learn where to put the dollar signs in your cell address and how it affects the copied formula.

Tip #21 from *Faithe Wempen*

You can type the dollar signs manually, but there's an easier way. Highlight the cell reference in the worksheet to place the cell address in your formula in the formula bar. Then press F4, which cycles you through absolute, relative, and mixed reference types each time you press it. Mixed references keep row references absolute while the column references are relative, or row references relative while column references are absolute (dollar signs mark which references are absolute).

Table 5.5 Where Does the Dollar Sign Go?

Type of Reference	Example	How It Acts in a Copied Formula
Absolute column, absolute row	F3	Refers to an exact cell. The cell address doesn't change in the copied formula.
Absolute column, relative row	$F3	The column of the address always remains the same, but the row can change.
Relative column, absolute row	F$3	The row of the address always remains the same, but the column can change.
Relative column, relative row	F3	The row and the column can change.

Working with Functions

Functions are built-in formulas that can save you time when you have to do complicated calculations. The amount of time they save you is proportional to the complexity of the math that the function performs. You have already seen one function at work: SUM. Recall that entering =SUM(B7:B10) is the same as entering =B7+B8+B9+B10. Here is another example that saves even more time.

Suppose that you need to find the average of five cells of values. To do it with a formula, you would add all the values and divide by the number of cells. This could result in a formula like this: =(C1+C2+C3+C4+C5)/5. Works has a function (AVG) that averages for you and writes the formula using a function name (=AVG(C1:C5)). Much simpler, isn't it?

Types of Functions

Functions fall into eight categories:

- **Financial**—These functions deal with monetary matters, such as calculating interest on a loan or the term of a loan.

- **Date and Time**—These functions perform operations to put the current date and time on your spreadsheet or pull out the serial number for the date or time for calculation purposes.
- **Math and Trig**—These functions help you calculate logarithms, absolute numbers, rounded numbers, integers, exponents, and trigonometric functions (cosine, sine, tangent, cotangent, and so forth).
- **Statistical**—These functions do many of the everyday calculations such as sums, averages, and counting.
- **Lookup and Ref**—These functions work with lookup tables that you create within your spreadsheet. They also pull information from those tables into your formulas.
- **Text**—These functions help you manipulate text strings by pulling out portions or by converting some portions of text for other use.
- **Logical**—These functions enable you to work with conditional statements (*if this, then that*).
- **Informational**—These functions are used to notify you of errors in formulas and values.

FUNCTION SYNTAX

Several rules apply when you are writing formulas, and these rules are referred to as the *syntax rules*. You must follow syntax rules, or your formulas will not work. Those rules that apply specifically to functions are

- Precede the function formula with an equals sign (=).
- Function names must be capitalized (such as `SUM`).
- If functions use arguments, the argument must follow the function (see the following section, "Using Arguments"). These arguments must be enclosed in parentheses.
- Arguments must be separated by commas.
- If you use a text string as an argument, the text must be in quotes (`"  "`).

Note

If text in a formula consists of single characters that aren't part of a cell address or of one or more words, it is considered a text string. For example, in an inventory spreadsheet you might want the words `out of stock` to appear if the inventory of an item is 0. Such a formula might be written `=IF(C7=0,"out of stock",C7)`. The phrase `out of stock` is a text string.

USING ARGUMENTS

An *argument* in a function is the information you provide for the function to perform properly. An argument can be a number, formula, cell address, range reference, text string, or another function.

For example, in the function `=IF(condition,action,else-action)`, `condition`, `action`, and `else-action` are the arguments.

Arguments are always enclosed in parentheses and separated by commas.

ENTERING FUNCTIONS IN CELLS

You can insert a function into a cell in several ways, ranging from quickest to most foolproof:

- You can enter the function manually by typing it directly into the cell. This is fast, but it requires that you know exactly what the function name is and what arguments to enter.
- You can insert the function by choosing Insert, Function and then replacing the placeholders with real arguments, as explained in the steps that follow this list.
- You can use Easy Calc to choose and insert a formula, which takes the most time but requires the least knowledge of functions.

To insert a function in a cell with the Insert Function dialog box, do the following:

1. Click in the cell where you want to use the function.
2. Choose Insert, Function. The Insert Function dialog box appears (see Figure 5.10).
3. Under Category, choose the type of function you want. If you aren't sure, leave it set to All.
4. Click the function you want to use from the Choose a Function list box.
5. Click Insert. The function appears in the cell, with the first argument highlighted.
6. Click the cells or type in the argument information required by the function. For example, if you want to average some cells, this is the time to drag across those cells to select them.
7. Delete any extraneous argument placeholders in the function. For example, if there were multiple placeholders for arguments but you entered only one argument, remove the rest with the Backspace or Delete key.
8. Press Enter to complete the function.

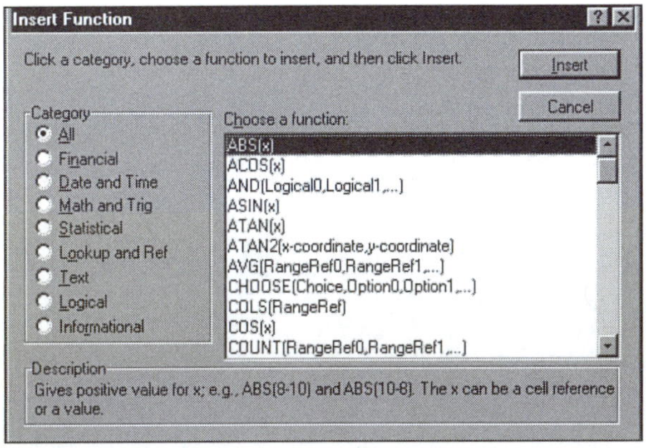

Figure 5.10
The Insert Function dialog box helps you choose a function to use.

As you just learned, entering a function with the Insert Function dialog box is fairly easy—if you know what you are doing, that is. What if you aren't sure about which function to use or what arguments you need? In that case, Easy Calc is a better bet.

To insert a function with Easy Calc, do the following:

1. Click in the cell where you want the results of the formula to appear.

2. Choose Tools, Easy Calc, or click the Easy Calc button on the toolbar. The Easy Calc dialog box appears (see Figure 5.11).

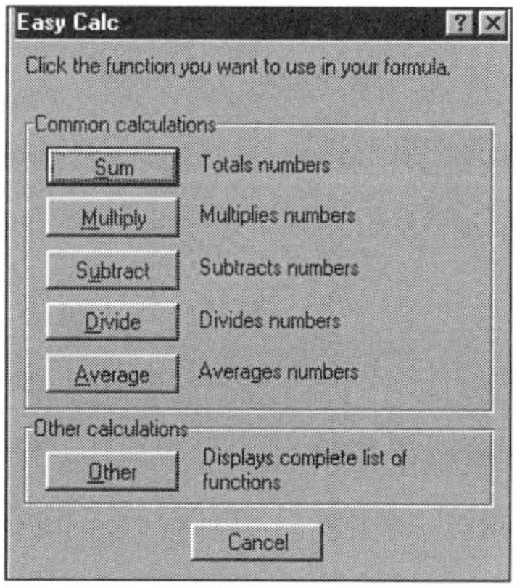

Figure 5.11
Use Easy Calc to choose a function and enter its arguments.

3. Click the button for the function you want and skip to step 7, or click Other to see a full list of functions and continue on to step 4.
4. The Insert Function dialog box appears (refer to Figure 5.10). Under Category, choose the type of function you want.
5. Click the function you want to use, in the Choose a Function list box.
6. Click Insert. A dialog box specific to the selected function appears (see Figure 5.12).

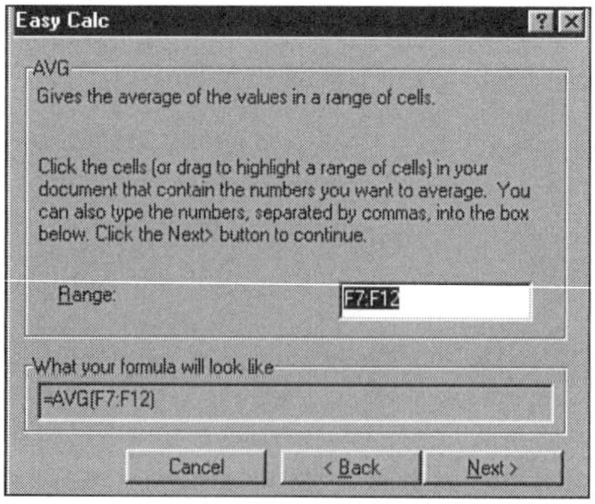

Figure 5.12
Easy Calc shows controls specific to the function you chose.

7. Enter whatever values or cell addresses you need in order to complete your formula (or click the appropriate cells to enter the addresses).
8. Click Next.
9. Easy Calc asks you to confirm the cell address where the formula goes. Enter the correct cell address if it isn't already showing in the Result At box.
10. Click Finish. The result of the function appears in the cell (you can see the function in the formula bar).

Tip #22 from *Faithe Wempen*

If the Easy Calc dialog box is blocking your view of the spreadsheet, you can move it out of the way. Just click and drag the dialog box title bar to another location on your screen.

Moving Data Around in a Spreadsheet

Even after you enter all your data and set all your formulas and functions, you still might not be satisfied with your work. Sometimes rows and columns have to be moved around or sorted in a different order. The following sections offer some advice aimed toward organizing your spreadsheet in the most pleasing way.

Sorting Data

Another use for a spreadsheet, besides raw calculations, is keeping track of lists of things. The Database tool also does this, but if the list contains one or more columns of numbers that have to be totaled, it is sometimes easier to use the Spreadsheet. Figure 5.13 shows how I have entered my tax-deductible medical expenses on a spreadsheet and entered a `=SUM` function to give me a total.

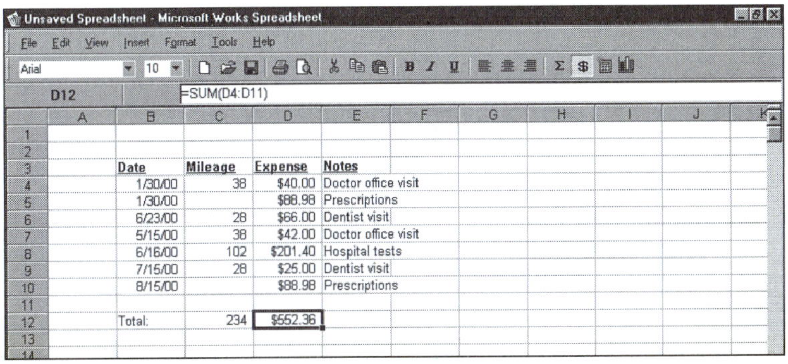

Figure 5.13
Keeping a list on a spreadsheet can sometimes make sense.

When you keep such records on a spreadsheet, you might find that you must sort the rows differently than you had originally entered them. You can sort rows of data by any column, and all the items in that row stay together. For example, you could re-sort the lines in

Figure 5.13 by the Expense column, from either least to most or most to least, and the appropriate dates, descriptions, and notes would stay with each expense.

To sort data, follow these steps:

1. Select the data you want to sort. Make sure that you select the entire range, including all the columns that you want to stay together. For example, in Figure 5.13 you would select `B4:E10`. Do not select column or row labels or lines containing totals.
2. Choose Tools, Sort. (The first time you do this, an extra dialog box appears; click OK to clear it.) The Sort dialog box appears (see Figure 5.14).

Figure 5.14
Specify what kind of sorting you want.

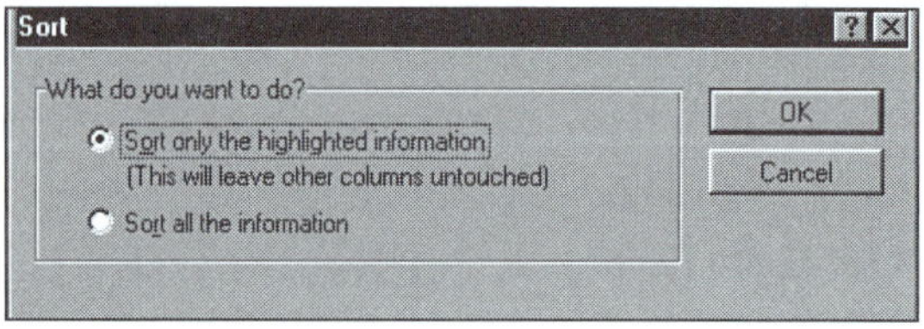

3. Leave the Sort Only the Highlighted Information marked, and click OK.
4. When the dialog box changes (see Figure 5.15), choose the column you want to use for sorting from the Sort By drop-down list.

Figure 5.15
Select the column you want to sort by and the sort order.

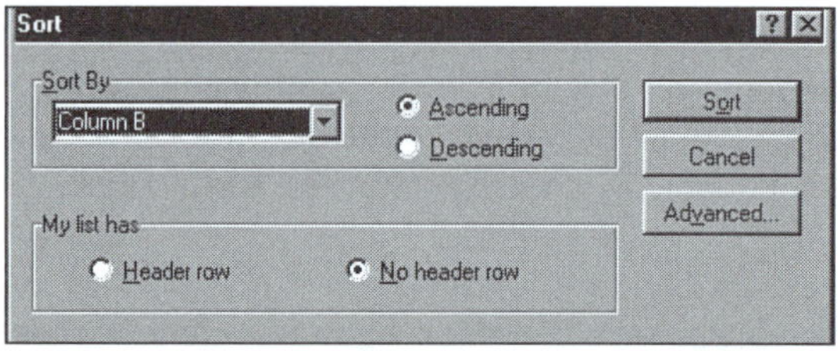

5. Choose your sort order: Select Ascending to sort the column A–Z, 1–100 or Descending to sort Z–A, 100–1.
6. If the first row of your highlighted sort range has column headings, select Header Row under My List Has so that Works ignores that row when it sorts. Otherwise, select No Header Row.

Note

If you followed my advice in step 1 when selecting, you will choose No Header Row in step 6 because the column labels are not included in your selected range. After you become familiar with this process, you might sometimes want to include the column labels in your selected range and then choose Header Row in step 6; this has the advantage of putting the labels from that row in the Sort By drop-down list, instead of generic names like *Column B*.

7. Click Sort. The dialog box goes away, and your data is sorted.

If you want to sort by more than one column, click the Advanced button in the Sort dialog box. As you can see in Figure 5.16, you can then specify a second and a third column to sort by. (This is useful if the first column contains last names, and the second column holds first names. You might want to sort first by last names and then by first names in case you have more than one person with the same last name.) To start the sort from the Advanced Options box, click Sort.

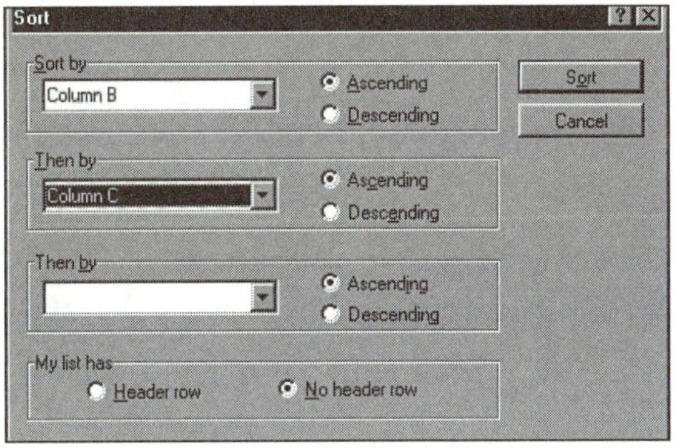

Figure 5.16
Click Advanced to display the controls shown here, which let you sort by more than one column.

Inserting and Deleting Rows and Columns

As you build your spreadsheet, you might find that you need to make some changes. Perhaps you have to add a column to accommodate another type of data, remove an extraneous row, or widen a column. Let's take a look at the changes you can make.

To insert columns, do the following:

1. Click the column header to the right of where you want to add the column. This action highlights that column.
2. Choose Insert, Insert Column. The columns move over to make room for the new column.

To insert rows, perform the following:

1. Click the row heading *below* where you want to add the row. That row is highlighted.
2. Choose Insert, Insert Row. The rows move down to make room for the new row.

To delete a column or row, just click its row or column header to highlight it, and then choose Insert, Delete Column or Insert, Delete Row.

Moving Columns and Rows

Moving columns and rows is actually more common than deleting them. You might have to move a column or row to reorganize your spreadsheet. (Your idea of the perfect layout might change as you enter your data. Mine often does.)

As I mentioned earlier in the chapter, when moving or copying cell data, you have to be careful about pasting data over the top of—and thereby overwriting—existing data. If you select a range of cells and drag them onto the top of another range that already contains data, the old data is replaced.

When moving and copying entire rows and columns in Works, you don't have this problem. That's because the existing rows and columns automatically move over to make room for the incoming stuff. That's good because you don't have to create new rows and columns to hold the moved or copied material, so it saves you a step.

You can use the cut-and-paste method to move or copy rows and columns, as you learned earlier in this chapter. However, the easiest way to move or copy rows and columns is with drag and drop.

To move or copy rows or columns, do the following:

1. Click the gray column header to highlight the column you want to move, or click the gray row header to highlight the row you want to move.
2. Position the mouse pointer on the edge of the row or column, so that the mouse pointer reads DRAG.
3. If you are copying (rather than moving), press and hold down the Ctrl key.
4. Hold down the mouse button and move the mouse until a dark line appears where you want the row or column to go. The mouse pointer reads MOVE, as shown in Figure 5.17.
5. Release the mouse button (and the Ctrl key, if necessary).

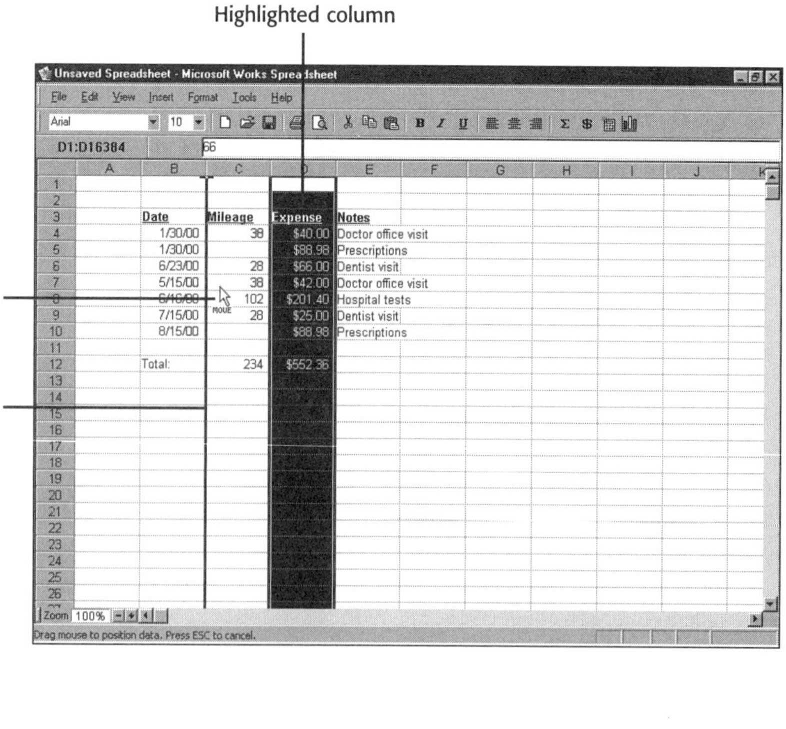

Figure 5.17
The dark line shows where the new row or column will be placed.

→ To learn how to rearrange rows through sorting, **see** "Sorting Data," **p. 101**.
→ To move or copy data in cells, **see** "Moving or Copying Cell Content," **p. 91**.

FORMATTING YOUR SPREADSHEET

In some ways, formatting a spreadsheet is the same as formatting a word processing document. You have text to which you can apply different fonts and sizes, margins to set, and a paper size and orientation to specify. I won't bore you by repeating the steps for the procedures that are the same, but I do want to introduce you to some new formatting procedures unique to spreadsheets.

→ To format text in cells, **see** "Formatting Text," **p. 58** .
→ To set page margins, **see** "Changing Margins," **p. 71**.
→ To set the paper size and orientation, **see** "Setting the Paper Size and Orientation," **p. 71**.

CHANGING NUMBER FORMATS

Number "helpers," such as dollar signs and percentages, are not considered real characters in a number within a cell. Instead, they are *formats*, somewhat like bold and italic. When you apply the Currency format to a cell, a dollar sign is placed in front of whatever number it contains. When you change the number in the cell, the dollar sign remains associated with the cell, as long as the cell is formatted as Currency.

If you type a dollar sign (or some other sign) as you are entering a number, Works interprets it as a message to format that cell with the specified number format. That's one way to apply a number format, but there's an easier way. You can enter the numbers "plain" and then apply the number formatting to an entire range of cells at once. For example, you could enter an entire column of sales figures, then highlight the column, and apply the Currency format to the entire column at once.

The number formats you can choose from are

- **General format**—Displays numbers as precisely as possible. The number of decimal places appears as it is typed. Trailing zeros, however, disappear (if you type **12.30**, it appears as 12.3). Larger numbers are shown in exponential format (1.23E+03).
- **Fixed format**—Displays the numbers with the specified number of decimal places (if you specify 3 decimal places and you enter **12.3**, it appears as 12.300).
- **Currency format**—Automatically adds a dollar sign ($) to the beginning of the number and includes a comma separator if the number is 1,000 or more. You may specify the number of decimal places you want to see, but 2 is the default setting.

Note

You can quickly apply the Currency number format by clicking the Currency button on the toolbar.

- **Comma format**—Automatically includes a comma separator if the number is 1,000 or more.

- **Percent format**—Automatically shows the number as if it had been multiplied by 100 and adds the percent sign (`%`) at the end of the number.

Caution

If you're entering numbers that you intend to later format as percentages, make sure that you write them in the correct decimal format (`0.15` becomes `15%`).

- **Exponential format**—Shows larger numbers as a base number with an exponent. For example, the number 1,000,000 shows as `1.00E+06`.
- **Leading Zeros format**—Adds zeros to show the specified number of places (if you enter `1`, it appears as `00001` if you specify five places).
- **Fraction format**—Changes a fraction entered in decimals to a standard fraction preceded by a zero (`0.03125` becomes `0 1/32`). If you enter a number in fraction format, this format is automatically applied to that cell. However, the decimal equivalent of the number appears on the formula bar.
- **True/False format**—Displays all zeros as `FALSE` and all nonzero values as `TRUE`.
- **Date/Time format**—Displays the number as a date or time.
- **Text format**—Enables you to specify a numerical entry as text. For example, if you enter a phone number, you want to format it as text.

Formatting affects only the appearance of the number. Works still uses the unformatted number when calculating. Therefore, if you have formatted a cell to display the number 0.751 with one decimal place, it appears as `.7`, but when you refer to that cell in a formula, it uses the actual value of `0.751`.

Follow these steps to change a cell's number format:

1. Select the cell or cells you want to format. You can format entire rows and columns at a time, or even the entire worksheet.
2. Choose Format, Number. The Format Cells dialog box appears with the Number tab in front (see Figure 5.18).

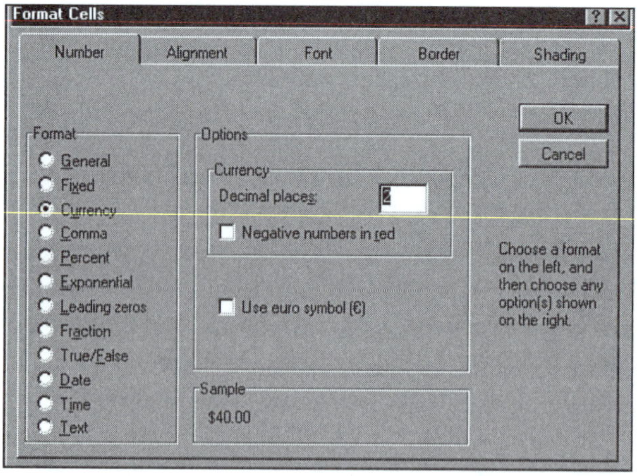

Figure 5.18
The Format Cells dialog box with Currency selected.

3. Under Format, select the type of format you want to use.
4. Under Options, specify any options you want for that format, such as the number of decimal places. Check the Sample area to see how your choice affects the number.
5. Click OK. Any formatting you chose is applied to the cell(s).

CHANGING DATE AND TIME FORMATS

Dates and times are considered numbers in Works, so you can perform calculations on them. For a cell to properly display a date or time, it must be formatted with the Date or Time format. Otherwise, the cell's contents appear as a meaningless string of numbers or characters.

Times are actually decimals of whole numbers. For example, 3:00 a.m. is 0.125 because that's the percentage of 24 hours that 3 hours represents. (24 hours represents a whole day, or 1.)

You can choose from many date and time formats. To look at the formats, enter a date or time into a cell, and then follow these steps:

1. Select the cell or cells you want to format with a date or time format (or a different one).
2. Choose Format, Number. The Format Cells dialog box appears with the Number tab in front.
3. Under Format, select Time or Date.
4. Under Options, choose the format you want from the list (see Figure 5.19). You will find many ways to express the date or time here, from simple ones such as 2/99 to fancy ones such as February 23, 1999.
5. Click OK. The formatting you selected is applied to the cell(s).

Figure 5.19
Choose from a variety of date formats.

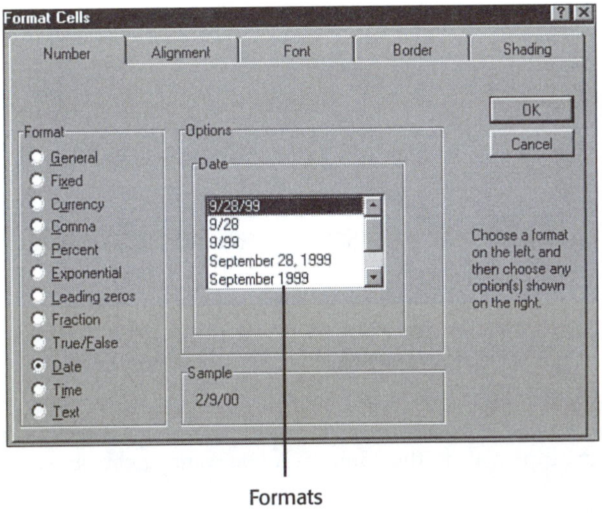

→ To learn more about entering dates and times, **see** "Entering Dates and Times," **p. 88**.

CHANGING COLUMN WIDTH AND ROW HEIGHT

By default, the columns in your spreadsheet are set to a width of 10 characters. If you type more into a cell than it can hold, the extra spills over into the next cell to the right. If that cell isn't empty, the content is truncated, so you see only a portion of it. (Even though you might not be able to see a cell's full content, the content is still there and is still applicable to any calculations you perform on that cell.)

Row heights are somewhat different; they adjust automatically to accommodate whatever is in the cell. For example, if you have 26-point type in a cell, the cell's height increases so that you can see the text. If you then reformat that text to 12-point, the cell's height decreases.

The easiest way to change the column width or row height is to drag it with the mouse. Point to the line to the right of the column or below the row you want to adjust. The mouse pointer reads ADJUST. Then drag in the appropriate direction to increase or decrease the width or height (see Figure 5.20).

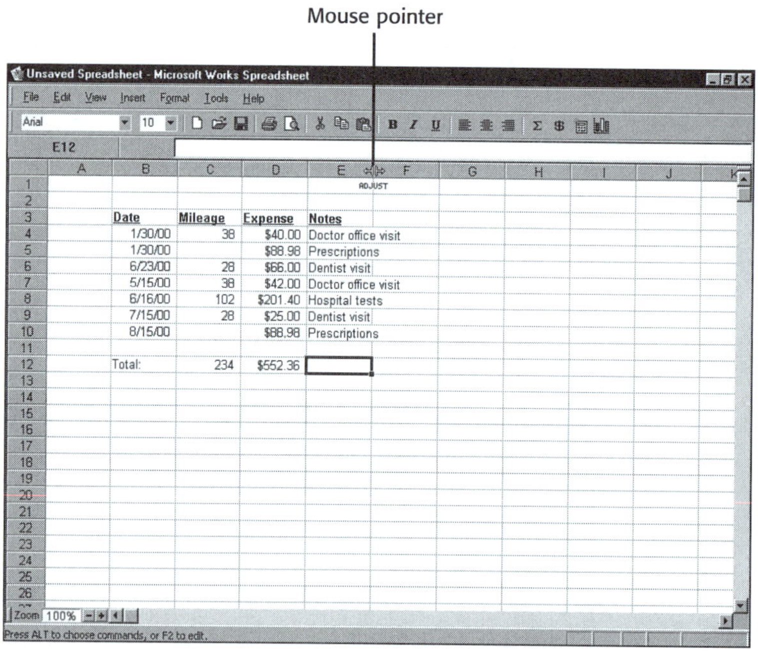

Figure 5.20
Position the mouse pointer between columns, and drag to change the width.

If you need more precise changes (for example, if all the columns must be exactly the same width), you must open a dialog box and make your changes there.

To change a column using the Column Width dialog box, perform the following steps:

1. Click in one of the cells in the column. If you want to change several columns at once, select them.

2. Choose Format, Column Width. The Column Width dialog box appears (see Figure 5.21).

Figure 5.21
Use the Column Width dialog box to set the precise column width.

3. To specify the exact column width in number of characters, enter a figure in the Column Width text box. Then click OK. You can also do one of the following:
   - Click Standard to immediately return the column width to 10 characters wide and close the dialog box.
   - Click Best Fit to have Works automatically select a column width that best fits the text in the column and immediately resize the column. This also closes the dialog box.

The row height works the same way, except that you use the Row Height command on the Format menu instead of the Column Width command.

→ Cell height can also be affected by *wrapping*, which lets the text in a cell wrap to multiple lines. To learn more about wrapping, **see** "Using Word Wrap," **p. 110**.

ALIGNING TEXT

You already know something about aligning text from reading the word processing chapters in this book: Text can align to the left, center, or right. In the case of a spreadsheet, text aligns within its cell rather than within the entire printed page.

When you enter text in a spreadsheet, Works automatically aligns that text to the left within each cell and numbers to the right. This might not be the most attractive placement for your spreadsheet; you can decide this for yourself and make a change to one or more cells as needed. For example, you might want to center labels you enter at the head of columns, or you can make the word `Total` appear on the right side of a cell.

The quickest way to change the text alignment is to use the buttons on the toolbar. They work the same as in the Word Processor.

Other special alignment options are available that pertain only to spreadsheets, but you can't access them from the toolbar; you must open the Format Cells dialog box.

To set cell alignment with the Format Cells dialog box, here are the steps:

1. Select the cell or cells whose alignment you want to change.
2. Choose Format, Alignment. The Format Cells dialog box appears with the Alignment tab selected (see Figure 5.22).

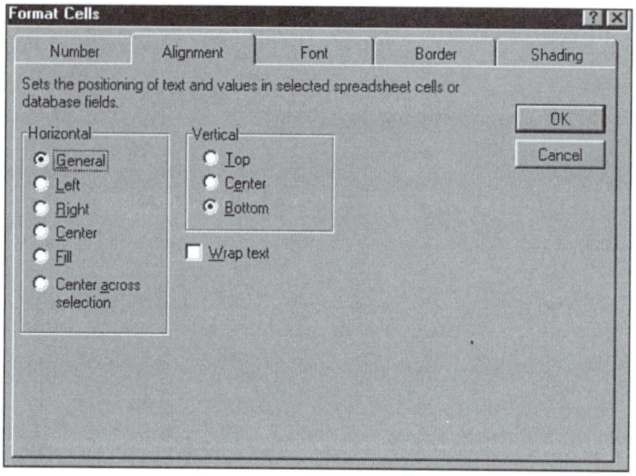

Figure 5.22
Set cell alignment on the Alignment tab.

3. Under Horizontal, choose one of the following:
   - **General**—Aligns text to the left, numbers to the right, and errors and logical values in the center
   - **Left**—Aligns the text on the left side of the cell
   - **Right**—Aligns the text on the right side of the cell
   - **Center**—Centers the text between the left and right sides of the cell
   - **Fill**—Repeats the characters until they fill the cell from left to right (such as putting asterisks across the cell)
   - **Center Across Selection**—Centers the text across the cells you've selected
4. If your row is taller than the normal height of your text, select an option under Vertical to align your text with the Top of the cell, the Center of the cell from top to bottom, or the Bottom of the cell.
5. Click OK.

→ To learn more about text alignment options, **see** "Aligning Text," **p. 64**.

Using Word Wrap

As you've already learned, when your text overflows the size of a cell, it flows into the cell to the right only if that next cell is blank. If the cell to the right isn't empty, Works displays only the portion of the text that fits inside the left and right borders of your current cell.

However, the Word Wrap option in Works allows the text to wrap within the cell, making multiple lines of text within one cell. When you choose this option, be aware that the height of the cell increases, affecting the height of the entire row. This works especially well for cells that contain a lot of data, such as whole sentences. You won't want to widen such columns enough to accommodate the entire sentence, but you also won't want the sentence to be unreadable (see Figure 5.23).

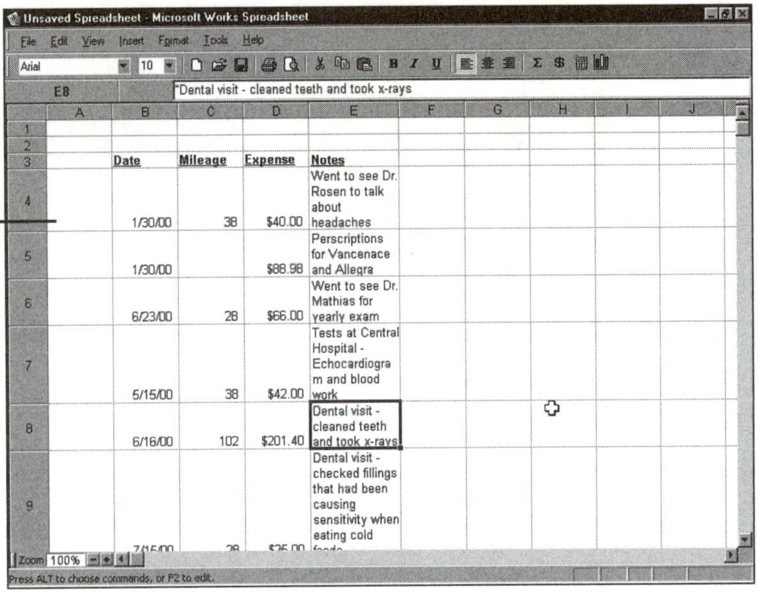

Figure 5.23
Word Wrap can be the answer to a tough formatting problem like this.

Row heights increase to accommodate extra lines.

To set up word wrap for one or more cells, do the following:

1. Highlight the cell (or cells).
2. Choose Format, Alignment. The Format Cells dialog box appears with the Alignment tab selected (refer to Figure 5.22).
3. Click the Wrap Text check box.
4. Click OK.

APPLYING BORDERS AND SHADING

Using borders and shading organizes your spreadsheet into definite areas and produces a professional-looking printout. For example, you might want to shade the column headings to distinguish them from the data underneath, or apply a bottom border to "draw a line" between heading and data.

A border can be applied to any or all sides of a cell individually. By applying a four-sided border around a group of cells, you "box them in." By applying a bottom border to a row, you draw a horizontal line under that row. Figure 5.24 shows some examples of what borders can do.

Note

Don't confuse *borders* with *gridlines*. Those fine gray lines you see on the screen that separate each row and column are gridlines. They do not print unless you specifically set them to do so (by choosing File, Page Setup). Borders are lines around cells that you manually apply yourself. They always print.

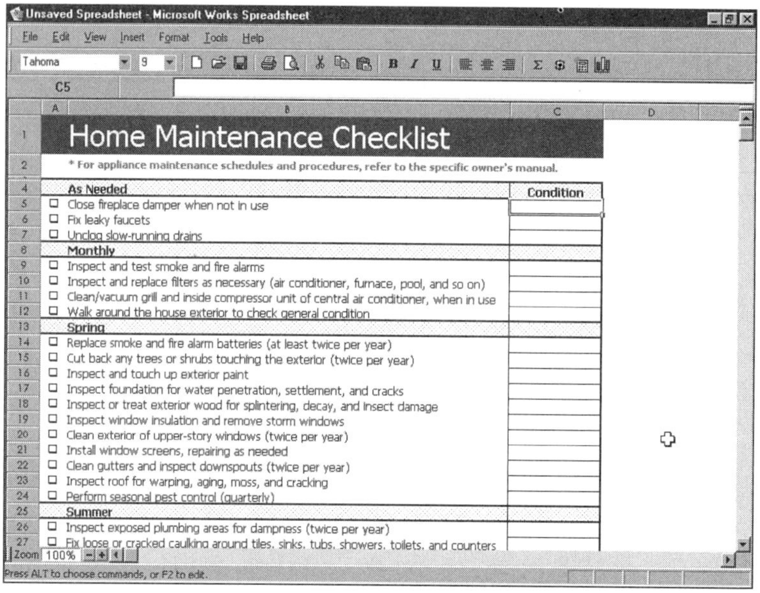

Figure 5.24
Borders can separate your work into meaningful groupings or create divisions.

To add cell borders, do the following:

1. Highlight the cells to which you want to apply a border.
2. Choose Format, Border. The Format Cells dialog box appears with the Border tab selected (see Figure 5.25).

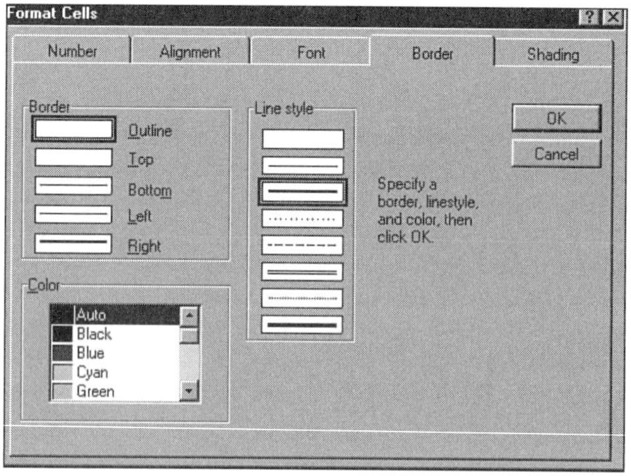

Figure 5.25
The Format Cells dialog box appears with the Border tab selected.

3. Under Border, select whether you want to apply the border to the Outline of the selection or to just the Top, Bottom, Left, or Right side. The Outline choice puts an outside border around the group of selected cells; the other choices refer to each of the individual cells in the selected range.

4. Under Line Style, select the style of line you want to use.
5. From the Color list box, select a color to apply to the line.
6. If you want other kinds of borders around other sides of the selected range, go back to step 3 and choose another area; then work through steps 4 and 5 again to set a different style and color for it.
7. Click OK.

Shading works much the same way in a spreadsheet, calling attention to certain areas that you want the user to pay attention to. You can shade a cell that contains a total, for example, to draw the reader's eye there.

To apply cell shading, follow these steps:

1. Highlight the cells to which you want to apply shading.
2. Choose Format, Shading. The Format Cells dialog box opens with the Shading tab selected (see Figure 5.26).

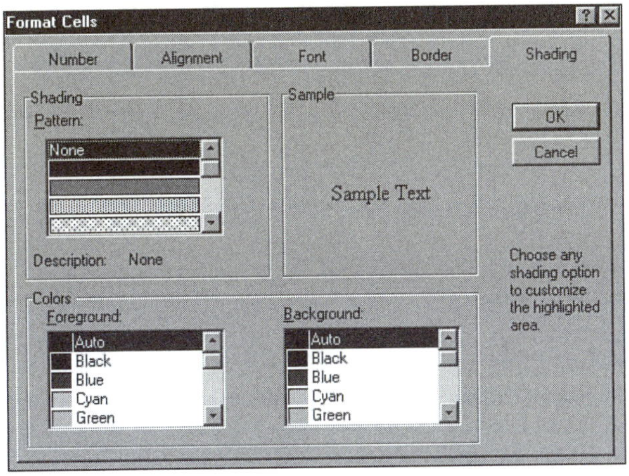

Figure 5.26
The Format Cells dialog box appears with the Shading tab selected.

3. Under Colors, select a Foreground color and a Background color (for example, you could have blue checks on a yellow background). To use only one color, set the background color to white.
4. Under Shading, make a selection from the Pattern list box.
5. Preview your selections in the Sample area. Click OK to accept your choices, and close the dialog box.

WORKING WITH CHARTS

Works uses the words *chart* and *graph* interchangeably, and for the most part, you can, too. A chart is a pictorial representation of the numerical information on the spreadsheet. A chart makes it easier to understand a series of numbers, interpret numbers as trends, or compare groups of numbers.

One of the most basic kinds of charts is a pie chart. A *pie chart* is a circle divided into sections that represent percentages of a whole (see Figure 5.27). It's a good way to illustrate how one segment fits into the whole picture or how a whole is being divided (such as how your tax dollar is being used).

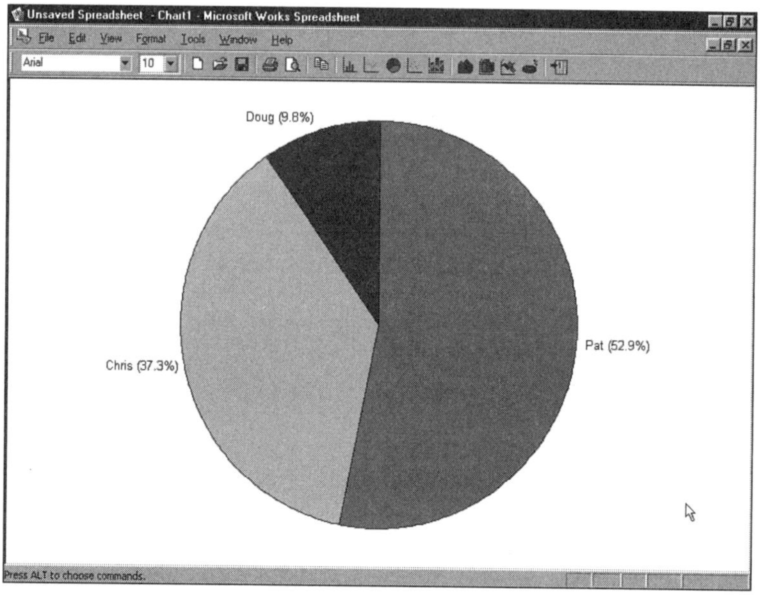

Figure 5.27
A pie chart shows how parts compose the whole.

Another kind of chart plots numbers on an X and Y axis. (Professionals call this kind of chart a *graph*, but Works doesn't make the distinction.) The *X axis* is the horizontal line at the bottom of the chart, and the labels are *categories*. The *Y axis* is the vertical line at the left of the chart and displays the *values* (see Figure 5.28).

Works has several types of charts available:

- The *bar* chart is useful for comparing information.
- The *line* chart is useful for showing trends.
- Use the *area* chart to show trends versus a quota amount (as in actual sales versus planned sales) over a time period.
- *Scatter* charts are a favorite tool of statisticians who are plotting populations versus figures by showing just the data points.
- *Radar* charts are plotted around a center point and are used more by mathematicians.
- Works also has a *combined bar-line* chart.

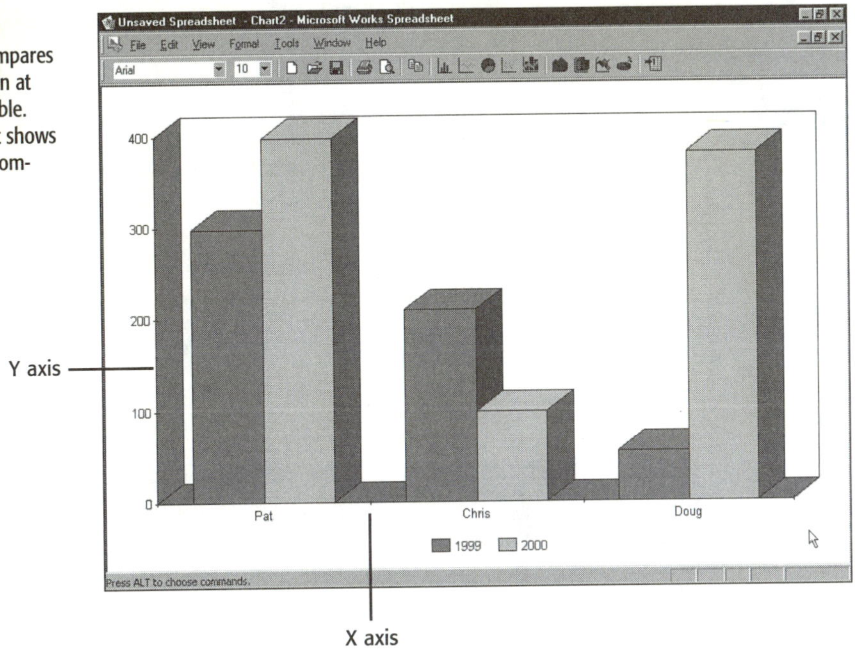

Figure 5.28
A bar chart compares values based on at least one variable. Here, the chart shows sales in 1999 compared to 2000.

Caution

Don't use a chart just because it's pretty. If it doesn't have a point, don't bother with it. Don't spend much time picking colors and line styles, either. Customizing a chart takes time, and a blue bar next to a red bar is just as readable as a blue bar next to a green bar. If the chart gets the point across, changing the appearance isn't really necessary. Play with the colors only if you have a lot of time.

After you've opened a spreadsheet and entered the data, the first step in creating a chart is to select the data to chart. If the chart is a pie chart, this involves only two sets of data: the slice labels and the values each slice represents. If the chart is some other kind, the data can involve several columns and rows.

To select the data, highlight the range. If you have rows that end in totals or columns that end in totals, don't include the totals in the chart range (unless you just want to chart the totals). If you have rows or columns that contain labels, however, you should include them because they become labels on the chart.

Note

A chart requires *contiguous* data (all in one place on the spreadsheet). If yours isn't that way, use a nonprinting area of the spreadsheet, and copy the data to that area. For example, to create a pie chart of the total sales for the year by salesperson, you need only the names of the salespeople and their totals. Copy just the names of the salespeople and their totals to another area of the spreadsheet, and highlight that range to create the chart.

Using the general information provided in the preceding section, you should know what type of chart you want to make.

Note

Like many other Works features, the first time you create a chart, the First-Time Help dialog box appears and offers to assist you. Click OK to continue.

To create a chart, follow these steps:

1. Select the data range you want to chart. Include any text labels that should be in the chart.

2. Choose Tools, Create New Chart, or click the New Chart button on the toolbar. The New Chart dialog box opens (see Figure 5.29).

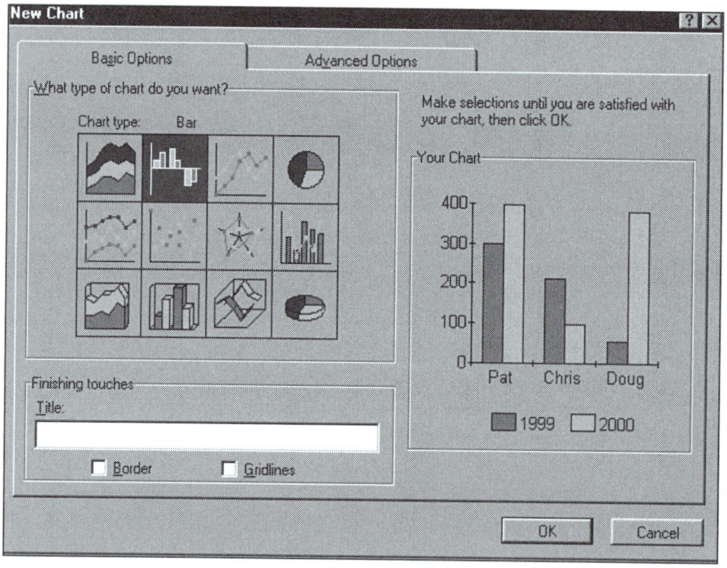

Figure 5.29
Select the chart type from the New Chart dialog box.

3. Under What Type of Chart Do You Want?, Works displays 12 chart types. Click one of the pictures to select that chart type. The Your Chart area displays the name of the chart and a sample of how your data looks using this chart type.
4. (Optional) Type a chart title in the Title text box, and mark the Gridlines and Border check boxes if you want either of those items.

Note

Gridlines are lines that run behind a chart (such as a bar or line chart) and help your eye follow the Y-axis measurement across the screen. A *border* is a box around the entire chart.

5. Click OK to create the chart. The chart appears on your screen, and a Chart toolbar is now available to use in modifying your chart.

The chart you create appears in a separate window, but it's still considered part of the current spreadsheet you are working with. You can have up to eight charts for your spreadsheet, and each can have a different name.

From here, you can dress up and customize your chart with the tools on the toolbar and with the commands on the Format menu. (All the menus have special commands for modifying a chart whenever a chart is displayed.) Here's a sampling of what you can do:

- You can change the chart type or subtype by choosing Format, Chart Type. Click a different chart type to change it. You can also click the Variations tab in the dialog box that appears and choose a different subtype. For example, with a pie chart, you can choose a subtype that displays the percentages next to each slice.
- On the Edit menu, you will find commands that let you modify the data series, title, and other text and data on the chart. For example, choose Edit, Titles to add a title to your chart.
- The Format menu contains many commands that fine-tune the chart appearance. For example, choosing Format, Horizontal Axis lets you specify at what number that axis begins. Choosing the Font and Style command lets you choose the fonts in use on the chart.
- You can use the Tools menu commands to duplicate the chart, delete the chart, or start a new one.

Tip #23 from *Faithe Wempen*

You can delete the chart. From the chart window, choose Tools, Delete Chart. Choose the chart you want to remove; then click the Delete button. Click OK to exit the dialog box.

After you've created a chart, give it a unique name and save it as part of the spreadsheet file. From the chart window, choose Tools, Rename Chart. This opens the Rename Chart dialog box. Select the chart to name; then click inside the Type a Name Below text box, and enter a new name for the chart. Click Rename, and the name is added. Click OK to exit the dialog box.

You can switch back and forth between the chart window and the spreadsheet window as needed, using the same skills you learned in Chapter 2 for working with multiple windows.

TROUBLESHOOTING

FORMULA CREATION

Is there any online help available for formulas and functions?

Yes, indeed. If you aren't sure which variables to use for a particular formula, press F1 while you are creating the formula. The Help system opens to the appropriate topic.

FORMULA COPYING

I copied a formula, but the result wasn't what I expected. I think I need some of the references to stay static.

Set an absolute reference for one or more of the addresses. Remember, to make an address absolute, precede the part that should stay fixed with a dollar sign, like this: `$B$5`.

GRIDLINE PRINTING

Why don't the gridlines print?

Gridlines do not print by default. If you want them to, choose File, Page Setup, and on the Other Options tab, select Print Gridlines.

CHAPTER 6

USING THE WORKS DATABASE

In this chapter

What Is a Database?

A *database program* automates the process of creating, collecting, sharing, and managing almost any kind of information. That information might be a list of names and addresses used for club membership or a record of your videotape purchases.

Like a spreadsheet, a database program keeps track of little bits of information in a well-organized format, but a database is designed specifically for organizing data rather than making calculations. As such, a database can organize and present information even more efficiently than a spreadsheet.

Typical database applications include these:

- **An address book**—This is a list of names and addresses that can be sorted by name, address, zip code, or phone number. You can also extract a list of people in a particular area code or zip code. Because Works already comes with an Address Book application, however, you might want to use it instead of the Works Database for storing addresses.
- **An inventory**—This is a list of personal or business items that can be sorted by status (on hand, on order), location (dining room, warehouse), ordering information, vendor, value, or price of an item.
- **A customer list**—This is a list of customers that can be sorted by location, salesperson, status (active or inactive), or contact name.

A database is a table of information. As with a spreadsheet, a table has rows and columns. The primary components of any database are *fields* and *records*. Fields are the smallest pieces of data in the database. Fields represent information such as first name, last name, address, city, and so forth. A record is a set of fields. In a customer database, for example, each customer is a record.

Fields are displayed in columns in the database table, with the field name at the top of the column. Records are displayed in rows in the database table. For example, in a dog kennel database, each dog's data would be a record in its own row, and fields such as Name and Birthdate would be the columns. Figure 6.1 shows a database table with records and fields.

You can add information to the database by typing directly into the table, or you can create forms for entering data. *Input forms* are easier to read than tables. Figure 6.2 represents an input form for an address database.

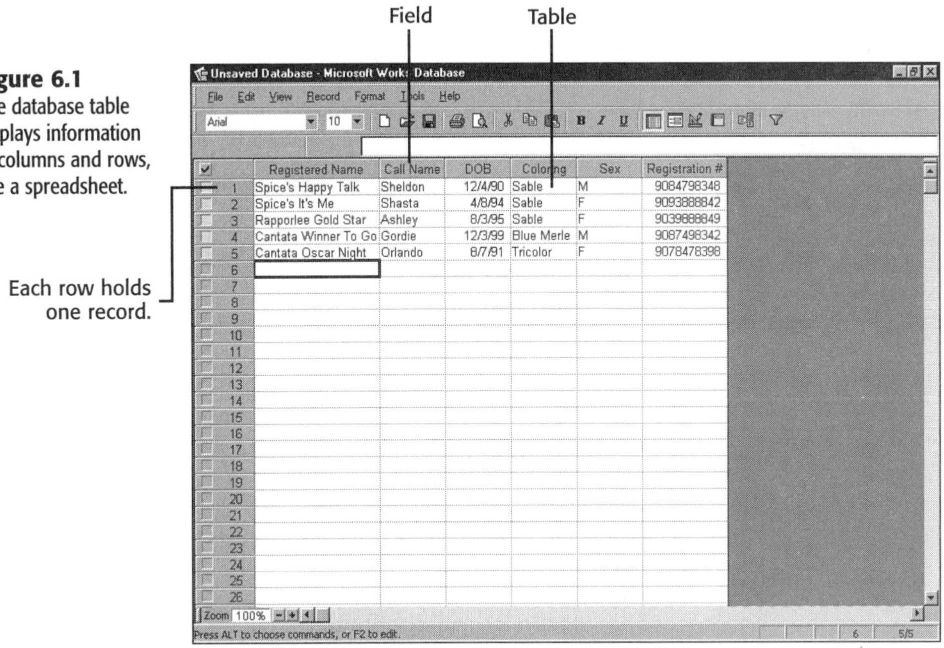

Figure 6.1
The database table displays information in columns and rows, like a spreadsheet.

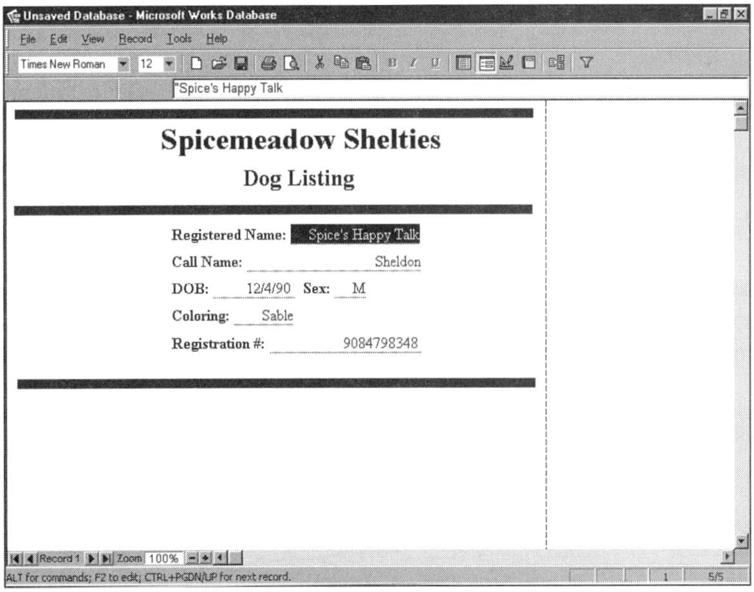

Figure 6.2
You can use forms for inputting data.

You create reports when you want to print information from your database. With a report, you can print all or some of your data, and you can sort, extract, and format the appearance of that data. Figure 6.3 is a report from a dog kennel register; the data is sorted according to date of birth (DOB).

Figure 6.3
Create reports and print your data. Data can be sorted, manipulated, or extracted using reports.

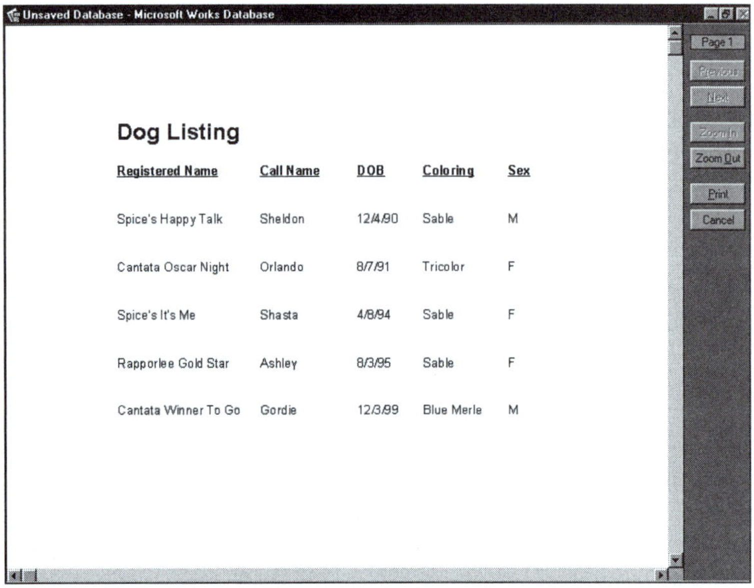

Creating a Database File

You can create the database file using a task from the Task Launcher, or you can create it from scratch. A task defines the fields for you and creates an attractive form—and perhaps a report, too. This is a fast and easy way to get a professional-looking database. However, Works does not come with very many database tasks, so you might not be able to locate one that fits your needs. In that case, you would create one from scratch.

Tip #24 from *Faithe Wempen*

In the Task Launcher, use the Works Web Site link on the Programs tab to go to Microsoft on the Internet and possibly download additional tasks.

Note

Don't use Works to create an address book; use the Address Book utility built in to Works instead. See Chapter 7, "Using the Address Book," for details about it.

When you create a database from scratch, you must define each field you are going to use. You must tell Works the name of the field, its size, its data type, and so on. This can be time-consuming, but it results in a database that's tailor-made for you. For example, suppose that you want to create a database that keeps track of the purebred dogs in a kennel. You will need fields such as AKC Registration Number, Call Name, Registered Name, Coat Color, and so on.

To create a new database, do the following:

1. From the Works Task Launcher, click the Programs tab, and then click the Works Database button. Then click Start a Blank Database.
2. If the First-Time Help box appears, click OK to move past it.

   A Create Database dialog box appears, prompting you for your first field name, as shown in Figure 6.4.

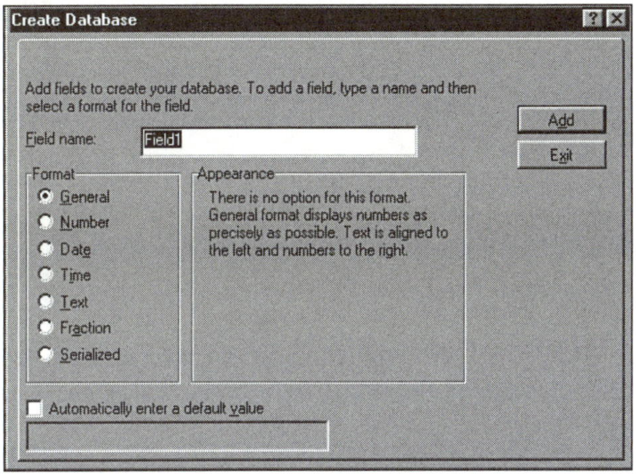

Figure 6.4
Works prompts you to describe the fields you will need.

3. Enter the first field name in the Field Name text box. Each field name must be unique.
4. Choose a data type from the Format list (they're explained in Table 6.1).
5. If applicable, choose an appearance from the Appearance area. Not all data types have appearance options.
6. (Optional) If you want the field to have a *default value* (a value that appears unless you change it), click the Automatically Enter a Default Value check box, and enter the default value in the text box below it. This is not an option for some data types.

Tip #25 from *Faithe Wempen*

Default values can save you some data-entry time if you have certain fields that are almost always the same. For example, if almost everyone in your database lives in the United States, you could create a Country field and set its default value to USA. Then when entering new records, you could skip that field unless it needed a non-USA value.

7. Click Add to add the field. The settings clear, so you can enter another field.
8. Continue entering fields until you are finished, and then click Exit to close the dialog box.

TABLE 6.1 FIELD FORMATTING OPTIONS

Type of Field	Used For
General	No formatting at all, and no restrictions on entry.
Number	Numbers that have numeric value and on which you might want to perform calculations. You cannot enter any text in these fields.
Date	For dates only. You cannot enter anything except valid dates.
Time	For time only. You cannot enter anything except valid times.
Text	For text and numbers that have no value (such as zip codes and phone numbers). No restrictions on entry.
Fraction	For numbers that have to be expressed as fractions instead of decimals (such as stock prices).
Serialized	For record numbers or fields in which you want to increment the value every time you add a record.

Tip #26 from
Faithe Wempen

The Serialized data type can be useful. Suppose, for example, that you must assign an account number to each new record. You can set up the Account Number field to automatically increment to the next available account number each time you enter a new record.

As with the other Works tools, it's a good idea to save your database early and often. To save your database, choose File, Save, or press Ctrl+S. You can also save by clicking the Save icon on the toolbar.

UNDERSTANDING THE DATABASE VIEWS

The Database window (refer to Figure 6.1) opens when you finish creating and entering new fields into a new database or when you finish creating a database with a task template. This window has a menu bar and toolbar just like the other Works tools, so things should look familiar.

The main thing to know about the Database window is that your database is always displayed in one of four *views*. To switch views, you can open the View menu and choose the view you want, or you can click the appropriate button on the toolbar:

- **List view**—This view looks like a spreadsheet, with field names as columns and records as rows. You saw this view in Figure 6.1.
- **Form view**—A list of your fields appears with a blank next to each one; you can enter data by filling in the blanks. This view appeared in Figure 6.2.
- **Form Design view**—Here's where you can customize your form.

- **Report view**—You can change the layout of an existing report here or create new reports. When you get the report the way you want it, you can preview it in Print Preview (refer to Figure 6.3) and/or print it.

If you use a task template to create your database, it puts you in Form view so that you can do your data entry. If you create the database from scratch, you're left in List view when it's all finished. Whatever view you're starting in, go ahead and try some of the other views right now. If you use the template you will have fully designed reports and forms at your disposal in those views; if not, you will have a plain list of fields in Form view, and you will be prompted to create a report when you enter Report view. (Click Cancel to avoid that for now.)

Tip #27 from *Faithe Wempen*

To quickly switch views, press F9 for Form view or Shift+F9 for List view.

Editing Your Database Structure

The best time to modify a database's structure (that is, change its fields) is before you start entering data into it. If you add fields after you have some records in your database, you will have to go back through all your data and "clean up" by making entries in the new fields. If you delete fields after entering data, you will have wasted the time it took you to populate that field originally. What a pain! Think about your database now, and try to make the changes upfront.

Adding and Deleting Fields

After you have created your initial database fields (either manually or with the task template), you might want to make some changes. Perhaps you forgot about a field or have decided that one of the fields is unnecessary.

To add a field, perform these steps:

1. Choose View, List.
2. Click on a field name that is adjacent to the spot where the new field should go.
3. Choose Record, Insert Field. A submenu appears with Before and After on it. Click 1 Before if you want the new field to be placed to the left of the selected one, or click 2 After if you want it placed to the right.
4. The Insert Field dialog box appears. It is almost identical to the Create Field dialog box in Figure 6.4.
5. Follow the steps in the earlier section "Creating a Database File" to fill in the necessary information for the new field.

To delete a field, select the field in List view. Then choose Record, Delete Field. A dialog box appears, asking you whether you are sure; click OK.

Tip #28 from
Faithe Wempen

When filling out the database form, you use the Tab key to move from field to field (left to right and then down to the next field). If you add a field, you change the tab order. To use a different order, perhaps to fill out all the fields on the left side of the form first, choose Format, Tab Order. From the Format Tab Order dialog box, change the tab order by moving the field names up or down in the list, and click OK.

➔ To rearrange fields in the database, which works just like moving columns in a spreadsheet, **see** Chapter 5, "Using the Works Spreadsheet."

EDITING THE FIELD NAME OR TYPE

It's not unusual to want to change a field name after you have completed the initial design of your database. For example, you might find that you want to shorten the Registration # field name to Reg#. You might also want to change the field's type. For example, perhaps you formatted the Registration # field as Number, but you realize now that some registration numbers also have letters in them. You think that you might want to set the field type to Text, instead.

To change a field's properties, follow these steps:

1. Switch to List view, if you're not there already.
2. Select the field you want to edit by clicking on its name.
3. Choose Format, Field. The Format dialog box appears with the Field tab in front, as shown in Figure 6.5.

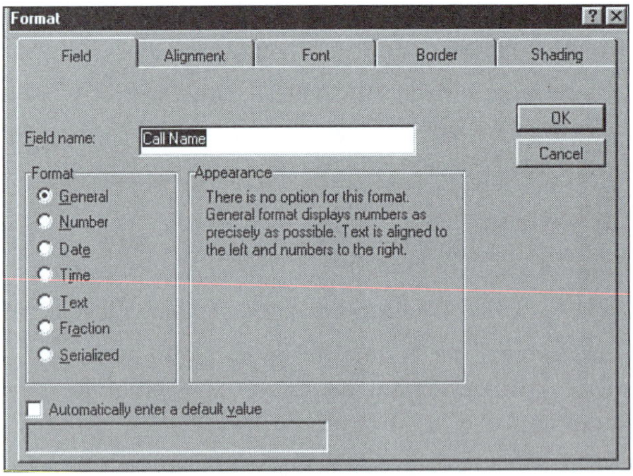

Figure 6.5
Change the field's properties from the Format menu.

4. In the Field Name text box, change your field name by typing your new field name. The new text replaces the old field name.
5. If you have to change the field type, choose a different one from the Format area.
6. Click OK to save your changes, and close the dialog box.

Moving Fields

Fields appear in your database in List view in the order in which you entered them when you first created the database. You can change these at any time.

To rearrange the fields in List view, do the following:

1. Click on the field name to select that column.
2. Position the mouse pointer at the edge of the field. The pointer reads DRAG.
3. Hold down the mouse button, and drag the field to the position you want. Then release the mouse button.

If you make a mistake while rearranging fields, use the Undo command immediately. Choose Edit, Undo.

Deleting Fields

You can delete a field in one of several ways. Remember that when you delete a field, you delete all the data contained in that field for every record. When you cut or delete a field, Works displays a dialog box asking whether you want to permanently delete this information. This is a safety measure designed to make you pause and think before you delete. When you see the dialog box and are sure you want to delete the field, click OK to close the box and delete the field.

To delete a field, do one of the following:

- Select the field and choose Edit, Cut.
- Select the field and press Ctrl+X.
- Right-click the field and choose Delete Field from the shortcut menu.

Tip #29 from *Faithe Wempen*

If you accidentally delete a field, or if you delete the wrong field, you can undo the delete if it is the very next step you take. To undelete, press Ctrl+Z, or choose Edit, Undo Delete Field.

Tip #30 from *Faithe Wempen*

If you can't seem to delete a field, it's probably protected. Choose Format, Protection, and deselect the Protect Form check box. Click OK.

Changing the Way a Field Appears Onscreen

In a database, the appearance of the fields in List view is not your primary concern. You should be more interested in how the data will look when printed in reports, which are designed especially for printing. The List view is designed to be rough and unformatted.

Note

When you change the width of a field in List view, it does not change in Form view. Any changes to the field width in either view are independent of each other.

However, if this roughness bothers you, you can easily make some small changes that will enhance the database's readability onscreen. These changes are the same as the changes you learned to make to spreadsheets and word processing documents. Refer back to these sections.

Tip #31 from *Faithe Wempen*

If a column in List view displays #### marks, it means that the column is too narrow to display the data. To quickly widen a column just enough so that it can display the data in it, double-click on the divider between that column and the one to the right, next to the field name.

→ To format text in fields, **see** "Formatting Text," **p. 58**.
→ To widen the columns, **see** "Changing Column Width and Row Height," **p. 108**.
→ To align text differently in the field, **see** "Aligning Text," **p. 109**.

ENTERING AND EDITING DATA

The most cumbersome part of creating a database is *populating*, or adding records to, the database. When you do your initial data entry, the upkeep of your database will seem like a piece of cake because all you will have to do is make a few additions and deletions occasionally to keep everything updated.

ADDING RECORDS

When you add records, you don't have to be concerned about the order in which you add them. The purpose of a database program is that it enables you to sort, filter, and manipulate data when you want to rearrange or find information. The only exception to this is when you are using a Serialized field and need the serial numbers to be in a particular order.

Most people find it easier to enter records in Form view, so you will want to switch to that view before you begin. To add records, simply position your cursor in the field of the database in which you want to add information. Click in the field where you want to start, enter the information for that field, and then press Tab to move to the next field (press Shift+Tab to move back to the preceding field).

When you press Tab at the last field, Works starts a new record, and your cursor moves to the first field of a new record. If you make a mistake and must return to a previous record, you can do so by clicking the left-pointing arrow button at the bottom of the screen (you learn more about moving between records in the next section of this chapter).

In List view, the database is displayed as a table. You can enter records by filling out each field in the database and then moving down the table to the next record. Use the Tab key to move from field to field and from record to record if you have reached the last field in a record. Experienced spreadsheet users might prefer List view for data entry because it is familiar, but most people prefer Form view for data entry.

Note

If you are entering data in List view, the columns might be too narrow for you to see your entire entry in some fields.

You can widen the column to bring the data fully into view. Just position the cursor field column header on the separator line between columns. The cursor changes, displaying two arrows and the word ADJUST. Holding down the mouse button, click and drag the column header to expand or shorten the column width. You can also double-click between the field names (column headings) to automatically widen the column.

Tip #32 from
Faithe Wempen

To prevent others (or yourself) from deleting or accidentally changing data in your database, protect your fields with the Protection options. In either List view or Form Design view, select the field (or fields) you want to protect and choose Format, Protection. This opens the Format Protection dialog box. Select the Protect Field check box, and click OK. (You can use these same steps to unprotect the fields again and make changes to them.)

Moving Among Records

In List view, you can move among records exactly as you would in the Spreadsheet tool. Just click the cells you want, and type into them, using the scrollbars, as necessary, to move around.

→ For more detailed instructions on how to navigate within a spreadsheet, **see** "Moving Around the Spreadsheet," **p. 86**.

In Form view, you can click in the field in which you want to type and use the scrollbars to see any fields that might not fit on the screen. (Some data-entry forms are larger than a single screen.) To move from record to record, use the navigation buttons in the bottom-left corner of the screen.

- Go to first record.

- Go to preceding record.

- Go to next record.

- Go to the last record.

If you click the Go to Next Record button when you are already on the last record in the database, Works displays a blank data entry screen in which you can enter another record.

Caution

Don't forget to save your new database often as you enter new records. Choose File, Save, or click the Save button on the toolbar.

EDITING DATA

You can edit data just as you entered it: Simply move the cursor to the field, and type your changes. It's just like making edits in a spreadsheet.

When you move the cursor into a field that contains data, you can edit it using two methods: by deleting the characters you don't want and typing new ones or by clearing out the whole field and starting afresh. To clear a field, press the Delete key on the keyboard.

To delete an entire record, you must select it. In List view, select its row by clicking the row number, and then press Delete. In Form view, choose Edit, Cut Record, or press Ctrl+Shift+X.

ADDING MORE RECORDS

When inserting a new record, you don't have to pay too much attention to its position in the database. If you are trying to enter your records alphabetically, for example, and you later find that you missed one in the *A*s, you don't have to insert the new entry in any particular spot. Just add it to the end of the database, and then sort the records alphabetically.

In List view, click on the first empty row in the table, and type the new entry there. In Form view, click the Go to Next Record button, and then click the Go to Last Record button to display a blank form.

However, if it is important to you to place a new record in a certain position in the database, you can do so from List view, as described in the following steps:

1. Switch to List view, if it is not already displayed.
2. Place your pointer on the record below where you want to insert the new record (row).
3. Right-click with your mouse and select Insert Record from the shortcut menu (see Figure 6.6), or click the Insert Record button—or you can choose Record, Insert Record. The new, blank record appears above your current cursor position.
4. Using the Tab key to move between fields, enter the field information in the new record.

Tip #33 from
Faithe Wempen

If you need to insert several records in the same spot, select a number of rows in step 2 equal to the number of rows you want to insert. For example, to insert three records, select three rows. Then continue with the steps.

Figure 6.6
Right-click on the record below which the new one should go.

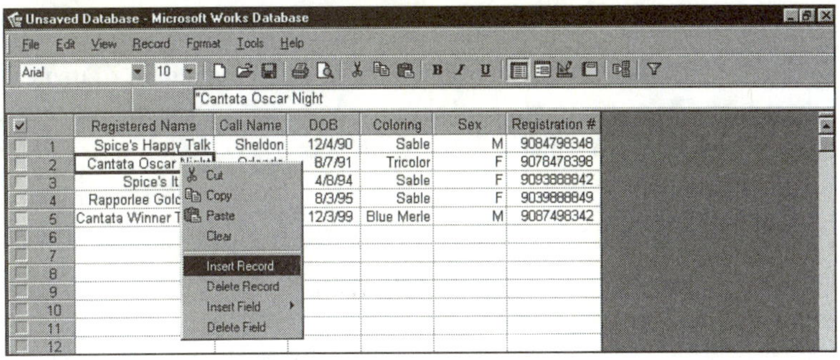

MODIFYING THE FORM

When you create a database, Works automatically creates a form from your database fields. If you use a task template, the form might be more attractive and graphical than that of a database you create from scratch.

You can modify the form by switching to Form Design view. Choose View, Form Design or click the Form Design button on the toolbar. In Form Design view, your form appears, but each part of it is movable, so you can rearrange, reposition, and add fields and descriptive text.

Figure 6.7 shows some modifications you can make to a form to make it more interesting and easy to read.

These lines are actually thin rectangles.

Figure 6.7
This form has been improved with formatting.

Labels added and text formatting applied

Field names made bold

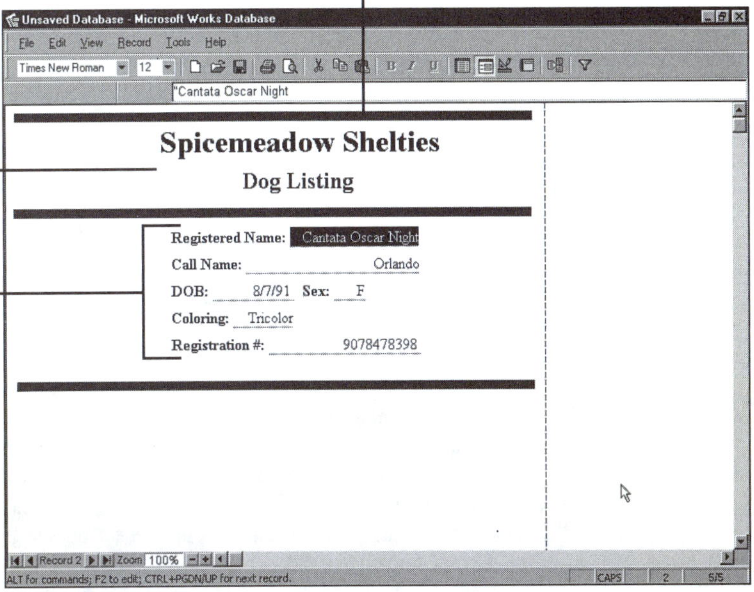

PART I
CH 6

REPOSITIONING FIELDS

You can move fields in Form Design view by dragging a field to its new location. As you design your form, you might find that you want to change the order of fields, perhaps to list first all the fields into which you generally input data, followed by all the default and calculated fields.

You can also move fields around the screen for aesthetic purposes. Perhaps you want to move the fields higher on the screen so that they are clustered more tightly together and you don't have to scroll down to see them all. Perhaps you want to create space between certain fields to group the fields into logical units. Moving fields is a simple drag-and-drop operation in Form Design view.

To move a field on a form, perform these steps:

1. Click the field to select it.
2. Holding down the mouse button, drag the field to its new position. An outline shows where the field is going, as shown in Figure 6.8.
3. When you have positioned the field where you want it, release the mouse button.

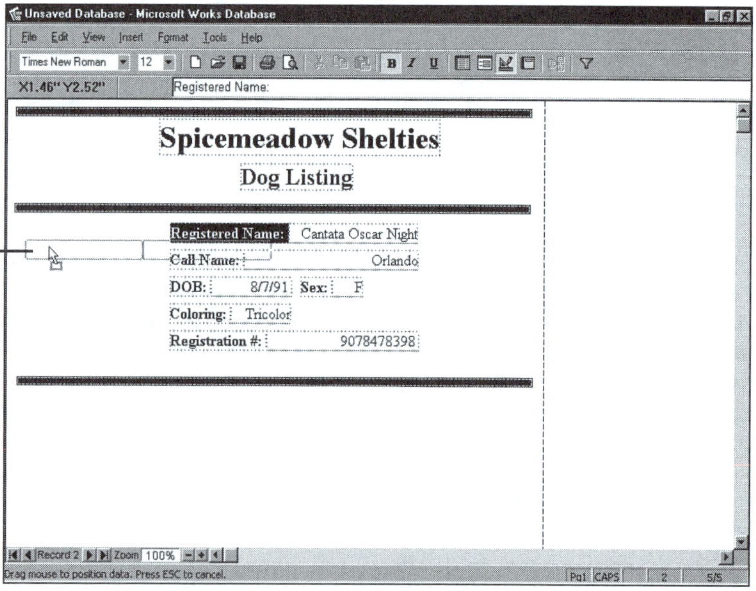

Figure 6.8
Drag fields around on the form to reposition them.

Tip #34 from *Faithe Wempen*

To move several fields at a time, select them by holding down the Ctrl key as you click on each field; then drag them as a group. You can also select a group of fields by drawing a selection box around them. To draw a selection box, press and hold down the mouse button, and drag over the group of fields. You can see a selection box surround the fields. Release the mouse button. The selection box disappears, but the group of items remains highlighted, ready for you to move.

Changing the Tab Order of Fields

The tab order is the path that the cursor takes when you press Tab to move from field to field as you enter records. In Works, the default order of the tab is left to right, top to bottom on your form. If you move a field, the tab order changes.

You can override the default tab order. You might want to do this, for example, if your database has a field that is rarely populated and often skipped over. You can make that field last in the tab order but keep it in its original location on the form.

To set a different tab order, follow these steps:

1. From Form Design view, choose Format, Tab Order. The Format Tab Order dialog box appears, as shown in Figure 6.9.
2. Select the field you want to move in the tab order. Use the Up or Down buttons to reorder the field. To return to the default order, click the Reset button.
3. When you have the order you want, click OK to save your changes and close the dialog box.
4. To test the new tab order, press the Tab key to move through your fields in Form view or Form Design view.

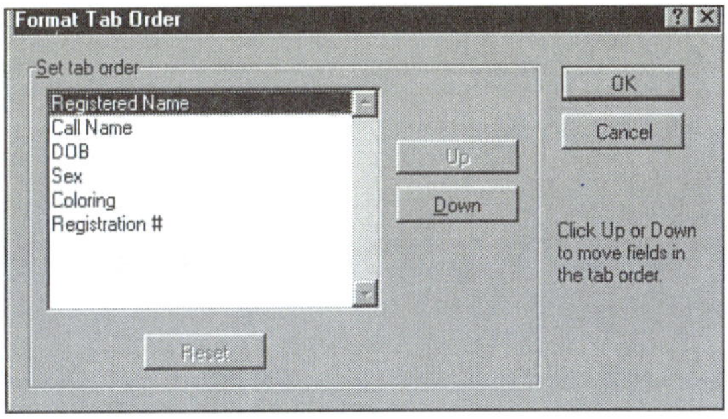

Figure 6.9
You can modify the default tab order from this dialog box.

Adding Labels to the Form

You might want to add labels to your database to assist others when they are working in it. For example, descriptive text such as "Enter Mr. or Mrs. or Miss" next to a field called Title helps others to understand that the field is for common prefixes rather than for royalty. You can also use labels to divide one section of the form from another. Labels are just like any other text on the form, and they print normally when you print the Form view. (Labels don't appear on reports, though, and they don't show up in List view.)

To add a text label to a form, do the following:

1. In Form Design view, position the cursor where you want to place the label. Be sure that your cursor is not on an existing field but in a blank area of the form. If there is no room where you want to place the label, move the fields.
2. Type the text and press Enter.

Edit labels as you would edit any text; click on one to select the label, and then type. Delete by selecting the label and pressing the Delete key.

ADDING RECTANGLES

Rectangles can help separate one section of a form from another. You can place rectangles around groups of fields or make extremely thin rectangles and fill them with color to create colored vertical or horizontal lines (refer to Figure 6.7).

To place a rectangle on the form, perform these steps:

1. In Form Design view, choose Insert, Rectangle. A rectangle appears on the form.
2. Drag the rectangle (by its center) to the desired position.
3. Drag a selection handle around the outside of the rectangle to change its shape as desired.

The rectangles that form the dividers in Figure 6.7 have been filled with a solid blue. If you want to fill a rectangle, do the following:

1. Select the rectangle.
2. Choose Format, Shading. The Format dialog box opens with the Shading tab displayed (see Figure 6.10).
3. Select a Pattern (choose the solid block at the top of the list for solid fill).
4. Choose a Foreground and Background color.
5. Click OK to finish.

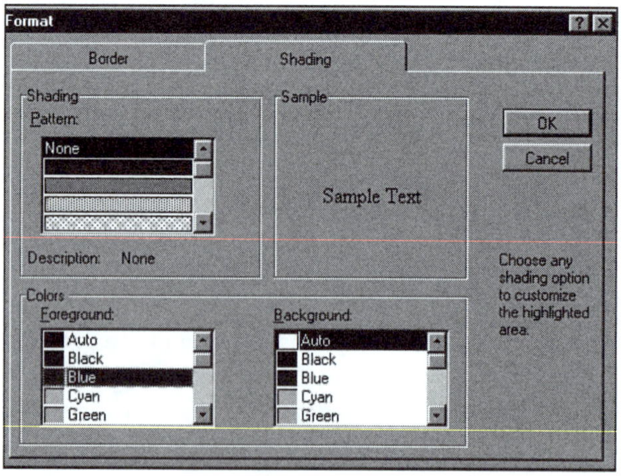

Figure 6.10
Format your rectangle here to fill it with shading.

FINDING RECORDS

If you don't have many records, you might find it easy to browse through each of them. In List view, it is easy to skim the page and locate a record you want if the list is not too long. You can use the arrow keys on the status bar to move from record to record in Form view.

Works provides another tool that you can use if the list is long enough to be unwieldy: the Find command. This command works much like the Find command in other applications; in the database, Find looks for data in any field.

To find a record containing specific data, do the following:

1. Choose Edit, Find or press Ctrl+F. The Find dialog box appears, as shown in Figure 6.11.
2. Fill in the information you want to find in the Find What box.
3. Click OK.

Figure 6.11
Use the Find dialog box to locate a record.

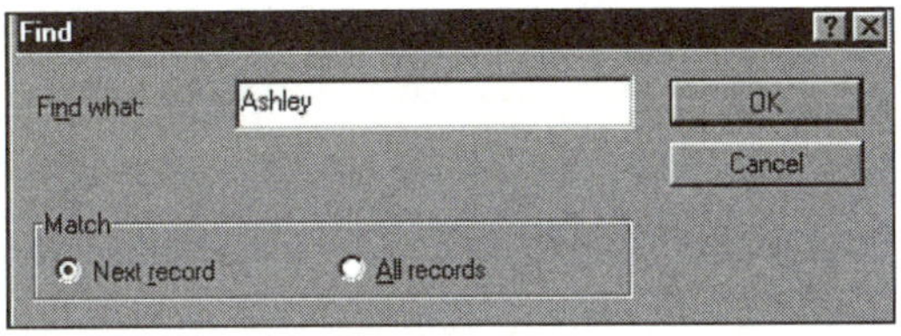

Works displays the next instance of the word that it finds in the database. If you want to see *all* such entries in the database, click the All Records option in the Find dialog box (refer to Figure 6.11). When you select this option, Works displays all occurrences of the search word, one record (form) at a time. Click the next record indicator to move through the records.

SORTING RECORDS

A key feature of any database program is the capability of sorting records. Sorting records enables you to populate the database without concern for alphabetical or numerical order. When you have populated the database, you can sort any of your fields. To refine your sort order, you can sort up to three fields, giving you the ability to sort a database by committee, last name, and first name, for example.

Although you can sort while in either Form Design or List view, it is easier to see the effects of sorting if you work in List view, which shows multiple records. Form Design view displays only one record at a time.

To sort your database, do the following:

1. In List view, choose Record, Sort Records. (If you see an extra dialog box asking whether you want a quick tour, click OK to bypass it.) The Sort Records dialog box appears (see Figure 6.12).
2. Using the drop-down lists, select the fields you want to sort in the order you want them sorted.
3. Choose Ascending or Descending for each field as the order to sort.

4. Click OK to save your sort preferences, and close the dialog box. Your database now appears in the order you indicated in the Sort Records dialog box.

Figure 6.12
Sort up to three fields using the Sort Records dialog box.

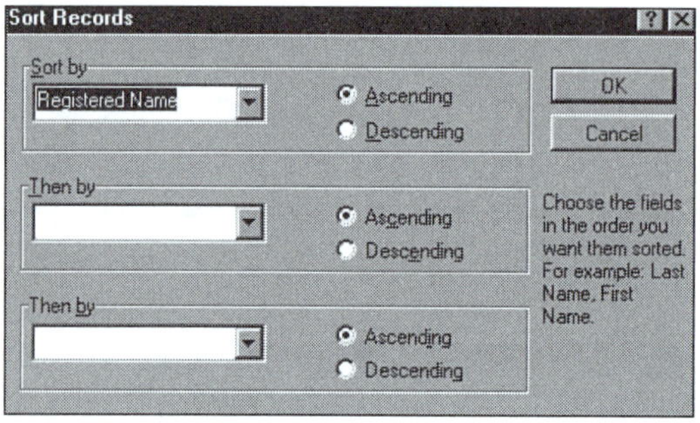

Note

Use the Undo command to undo a sort; choose Edit, Undo Sort or press Ctrl+Z.

WORKING WITH FILTERS

A *filter* is a search that gives you greater abilities to locate information than a simple search performed with the Find command. You use the Find command when you want to search for John Jones, but you use a filter when you want to search for members in your database who have joined your organization after December 31, 1998, and before December 31, 2000, for example.

Works has two kinds of filters, the *easy filter* and the *filter using formula*. This book focuses on the easy filter. An easy filter uses a comparison when searching for records.

Note

In Access and some other more powerful database programs, you can create powerful filters called *queries*. Filters are Works's version of queries.

At a minimum, you must supply three pieces of information for the easy filter:

- **Field Name**—The name of the field whose contents you are searching.
- **Comparison**—Comparison phrases are selected from a drop-down list. They contain phrases representing *operators*, such as *is less than*, *is equal to*, and *does not contain*.
- **Compare To**—The search criteria.

For example, you could find everyone with Indianapolis as their city by entering **`City`** for the Field Name, **`Equals`** as the Comparison, and **`Indianapolis`** as the Compare To.

When you apply the filter, you see only those records that match the filter criteria. The other records in your database are not deleted; they are simply filtered from the view.

Here's how to create a filter with the easy filter:

1. From List view, choose Tools, Filters, or click the Filters button on the toolbar. The Filter Name dialog box appears, as shown in Figure 6.13.

   If this is the first time you have created a filter in Works, the First-Time Help dialog box appears. Click OK to move past it.

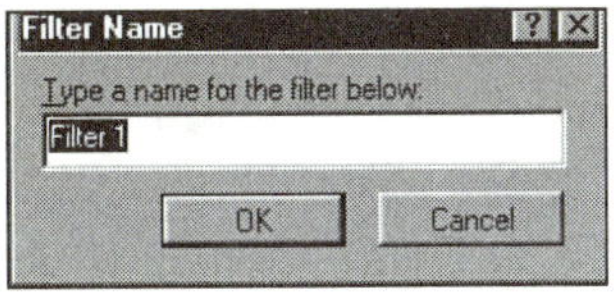

Figure 6.13
Name your filter in the Filter Name dialog box.

2. A default name of Filter 1 is supplied. If you do not want this name, type a descriptive name for your filter.
3. Click OK to save your filter name, and close that dialog box.
4. Use the drop-down menus to select a Field Name and Comparison.
5. In the Compare To text box, type the value for your filter criteria. Figure 6.14 shows a completed filter comparison that finds all records where the DOB field has a date later than 9/28/96.

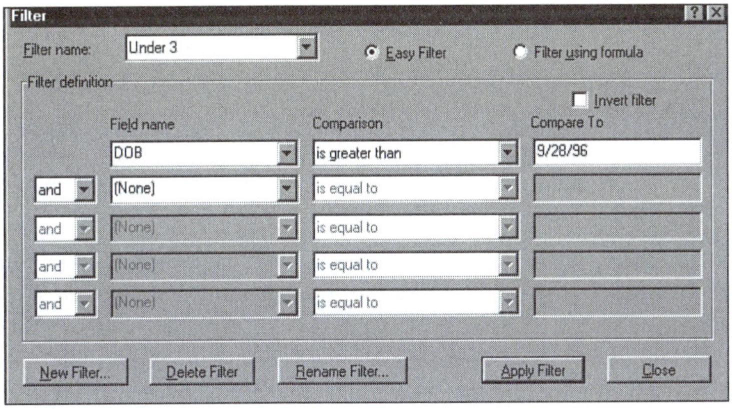

Figure 6.14
This filter finds all records where the DOB field is a date that comes after 9/28/96.

Note

If you need to add a second filter, you must choose And or Or from the drop-down list to the left of the second line. Use the Or to search for records that match any of your comparisons; use And for records that match all your comparison criteria.

6. Click the Apply Filter button to close the dialog box and finish your filter. Works displays the search results. If no match is found for your filter, you see a message to that effect, and the Filter dialog box remains open.

To redisplay all records in the database, effectively removing the filter, choose Record, Show, 1 All Records.

To reapply the filter, choose Record, Apply Filter, and choose a filter from the list.

CREATING ADDITIONAL FILTERS

You can create multiple filters in a database, and each is saved. (In other words, when you create a second filter, the first one doesn't go away; it's still accessible.) To create additional filters, you must click the New Filter button in the Filters dialog box (refer to Figure 6.14). The New Filter dialog box reappears, and you can type a new name.

DELETING FILTERS

You might find yourself with filters that you don't want or need. It's good to clear them out so that they don't unnecessarily muck up your list of filters (which you see when you choose Record, Apply Filter).

To delete a filter, do the following:

1. Choose Tools, Filters. The Filter dialog box appears.
2. In the Filter Name drop-down box, select the filter you want to delete.
3. Click the Delete Filter button.
4. A message appears, confirming that you want to delete the filter and display the filter name. Click Yes.

CREATING REPORTS

Reports are designed to be printed. You can create a report using any or all fields in your database, and you can arrange and format them on the report in whatever way you want.

For example, suppose that Barbara is your club member responsible for recruiting other club members into committees, such as the Spring Dance committee or the Fund-Raising committee. Supplying Barbara with a list of club members who are not active committee members and their phone numbers would help Barbara recruit new committee members. Other member information contained in your database, such as dues and addresses, would not be contained in your report to Barbara because she doesn't need that information.

When you create a report, you can apply filters or create new filters during the report creation process. After the report is created, you can edit or fine-tune it in the Report view.

Note

Because of space limitations, this book does not cover changing a report in Report view, but you can easily figure it out. Just use the same controls that you have already learned to use in Works to change fonts, font sizes, alignments, and so on. Move items around by dragging them, just as you do when you edit forms.

You can create up to eight reports per database. To create a report, you use a wizard called *ReportCreator*:

1. Choose Tools, ReportCreator. The Report Name dialog box appears. (If the First Time Help box appears, click OK.)
2. Type a descriptive name in the Report Name text box. For example, if you are creating a report that lists the dog names in the kennel, you might call it **`Dog Names`**.
3. Click OK. The ReportCreator dialog box appears, as shown in Figure 6.15. Your report name appears in the title bar of the dialog box, and the Title tab is displayed.
4. Change the name in the Report Title box, if desired.

Tip #35 from *Faithe Wempen*

You can shorten the name of the report by deleting the database name. (By default, the title is the name of the database plus the title you typed in step 2.)

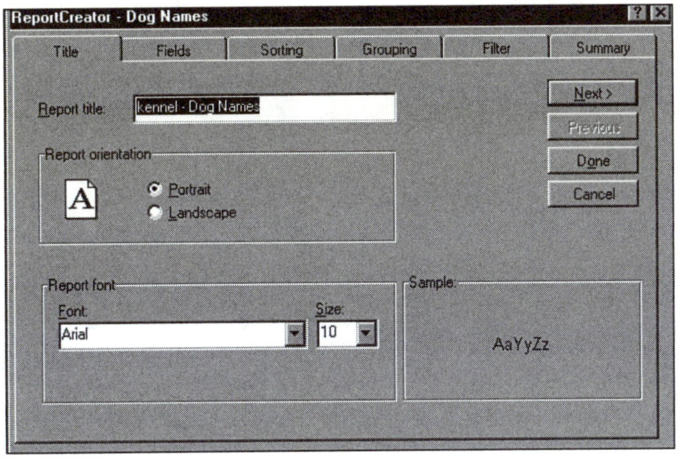

Figure 6.15
On the starting page of ReportCreator, you specify a title, font, and orientation.

5. Select an orientation for your report (Portrait or Landscape) and a Font. Then click Next.

➔ For information about font controls, **see** "Selecting a Font," **p. 58**.

6. Works displays the Fields tab. Here, you indicate which fields appear on your report and specify the order in which they appear. Highlight the field in the Fields Available list, and click the Add button. Repeat for each field you want to use. Figure 6.16 shows a report with two fields added.

Tip #36 from *Faithe Wempen*

To add all the fields in the database at one time, click the Add All button. You can also double-click a field to quickly add it to the Field Order list box.

Part I
Ch 6

Note

If you change your mind about using a field in the report, you can select the field in the Field Order list box and click the Remove button. If you need to start all over again, click the Remove All button.

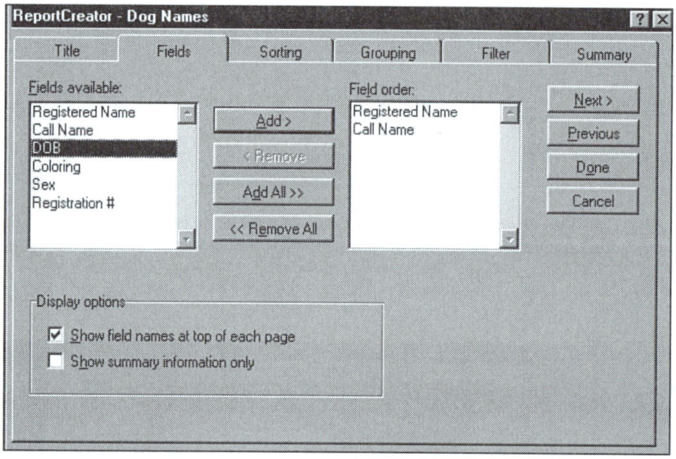

Figure 6.16 Add fields to the report by selecting them and clicking Add.

Caution

Do not add a field to the report if you intend to group by that field. For example, if you are grouping by the Committee field, you don't have to see the Committee field in each record.

7. Select or deselect either of the two Display Options check boxes as appropriate:
    - **Show Field Names at Top of Each Page**—Mark this if you want the field names to print. For example, next to each first name, you might want to say `First Name`.
    - **Show Summary Information Only**—Mark this if the individual records are not important, but the summary of them is. For example, if it is not important who is on the list but only that there are eight people on it, use this.

    When you have finished, click the Next button to continue.
8. The Sorting tab appears next. Select the order in which you want your records to appear in the report. This works just like the sorting you did earlier in this chapter. Click Next when finished.

Tip #37 from *Faithe Wempen*

If you intend to group your report, choose the field you are grouping by in the Sort By box on the Sorting tab. This places your groups in order. For example, if you are going to group by committee, choose Committee as the first Sort By field, and choose Ascending as the order. This will result in a report grouped by committee, and the committees will be in alphabetical order.

9. Next, the Grouping tab appears. Any fields that you selected in the Sorting tab appear here (for example, Committee), but in a turned-off state. Click the When Contents Change check box to enable a grouping (see Figure 6.17). This inserts a blank line in the report whenever a group of records that have a different value for the chosen field appear.
10. After you enable a grouping, choose from the following options for each field:
    - **Use First Letter Only**—Inserts a blank line in the report whenever the first letter of the field changes. This is appropriate when you are grouping by a field for which there are few or no duplicates, such as Last Name. This option groups by the first letter of the chosen field rather than by the entire content of it.
    - **Show Group Heading**—Prints the group header on the report. When sorting by committee, for example, each committee type (such as Public Relations) appears as a group heading.
    - **Start Each Group on a New Page**—Forces a page break each time this group changes, resulting in one group type per page. This is handy if you need to give the different lists to different people.

    When you have finished, click the Next button to continue.

Figure 6.17
Select the grouping options for sorted records.

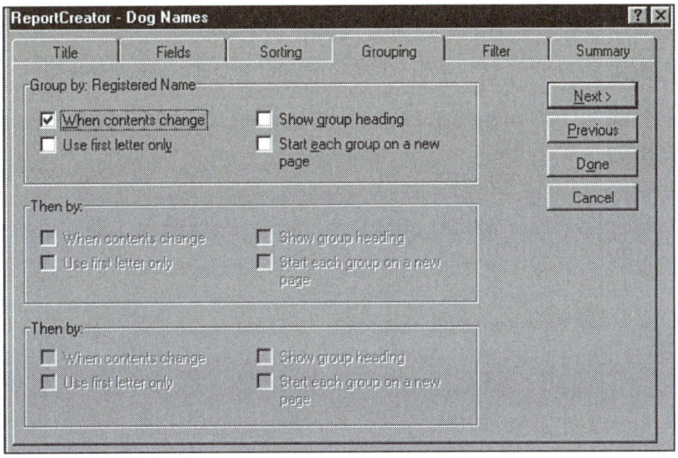

Note

The Grouping tab is grayed out if you have not selected any fields on the Sorting tab. If you want to change or add the sorting information, click the Sorting tab, make your changes, and click on the Grouping tab to return to step 10.

11. The Filter tab appears. Choose any existing filter, or click Create New Filter to create a new one, as you learned to do earlier in this chapter. Then click Next to continue.

→ To learn more about filters, **see** "Working with Filters," **p. 136**.

12. The Summary tab appears next, as shown in Figure 6.18. Summaries generally apply to number fields, not text fields. For example, you would *not* elect to sum the contents of a field called Registered Name, because there would be no numbers to sum in that field. You can, however, elect to count the number of items in a field. Choose the field you want to calculate (or count) in the Select a Field box, and check off your options in the Summaries box.

Figure 6.18
Use the Summary options to perform calculations on your report, if appropriate.

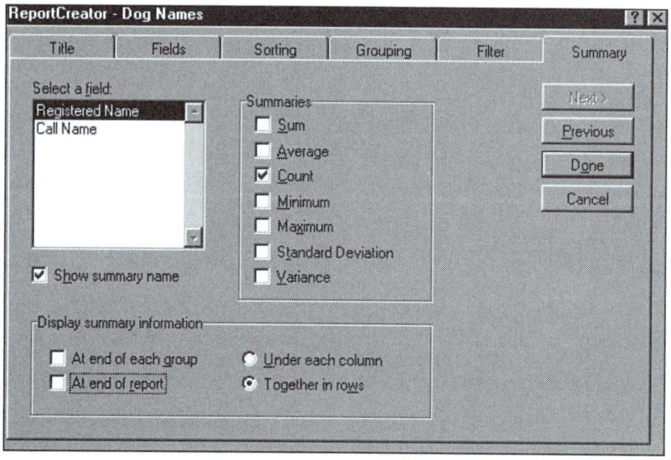

13. Select any of the summary options from the Display Summary Information section, as appropriate. (These are all fairly self-explanatory.) When you have completed your summary options, click Done.

14. A message indicates that the ReportCreator is finished. Click Preview to see your report in Print Preview.

Note

You can select Modify in step 14 to modify the report, but you see the report without data. It is much more useful to see the report with data in Print Preview mode.

When you have finished previewing your report in Print Preview mode, click Print to print it or Cancel to return to your database.

Tip #38 from *Faithe Wempen*

To print a single record in your database, display the record in Form view; then open the File menu and select Print. From the Print dialog box, select Current Record Only; then click OK.

TROUBLESHOOTING

IMPORTING RECORDS FROM OTHER DATABASES

I have an existing database created in another program, and I would like to use it in the Works Suite 2000 database.

If your data is in some other format, you might be able to import it into the Works Database. Use the File, Open command, but choose the appropriate file type from the Files of Type box. Works supports either Text or dBASE format, and most other database programs will save in one of these formats.

REMOVING FIELD PROTECTION

I want to delete some data, but the database prevents me from doing so.

Perhaps you have turned on protection for that field. Choose Format, Protection, and make sure that the Protect Field check box is not selected.

VIEWING SUPPRESSED DATA

I can't see some records that I know are in my database. Is there something wrong with my database file?

If some of your data appears to be missing, make sure that no filter is applied. Choose Record, Show, 1 All Records.

CHAPTER 7

USING THE ADDRESS BOOK

In this chapter

WHAT IS THE ADDRESS BOOK?

The Address Book has been around in Windows and in many Windows applications for a long time; Works Suite 2000 features it more prominently than ever before. It is a minidatabase set up specifically to track your contact information (names, addresses, email addresses, and so on). You can use it to store information about people that you need to contact, and pull that information into any other Works Suite application as needed. For example, you could do a mail merge with the Works Word Processor or with Word, or you could pull addresses from it to address email messages in Outlook Express.

→ To perform a mail merge, **see** Chapter 16, "Mail Merging and Data Sharing."

→ To send email, **see** Chapter 20, "Working with Email and Newsgroups."

OPENING THE ADDRESS BOOK

You can open the Address Book from the Works Task Launcher by selecting it from the Programs tab, just like any other Works program (see Figure 7.1).

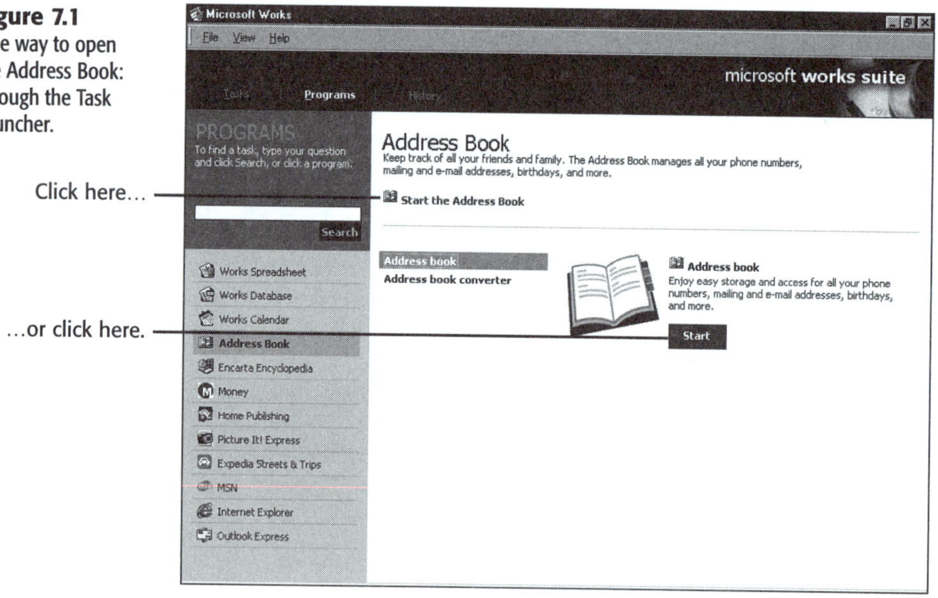

Figure 7.1
One way to open the Address Book: through the Task Launcher.

Many Works programs also have an Address Book button on their toolbar, so you can access it that way, too.

When you open the Address Book, a list of your current contacts appears. (If this is the first time you are using the Address Book, your list might be blank.) Figure 7.2 shows the Address Book window with several addresses already in it.

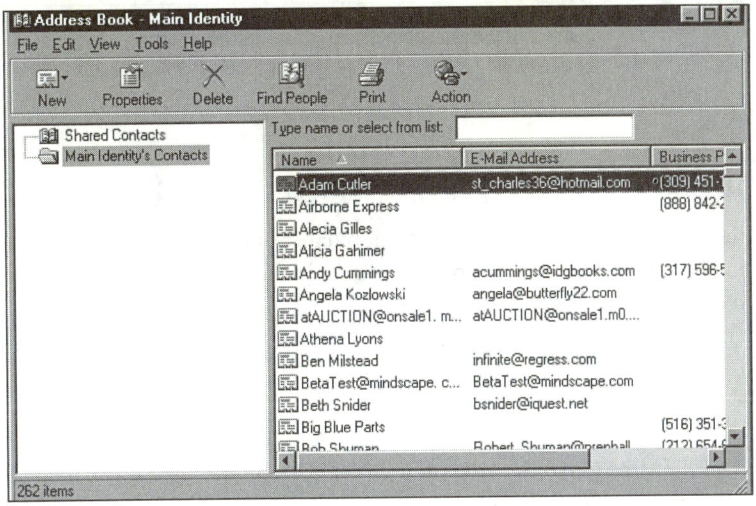

Figure 7.2
The Address Book's main screen shows a contact listing.

Note

When you send email in Outlook Express or reply to email you received, that person's email address is automatically entered in your Address Book. If you see some names on your Address Book listing that you did not put there, Outlook Express might have entered them.

If you have Outlook installed on your PC when you install Works, the Address Book is installed in Outlook Compatibility mode. This limits its capabilities but ensures that you will be able to select addresses from the Address Book while using Outlook. If your Address Book looks more like Figure 7.3, you are in Outlook Compatibility mode. To switch, choose Tools, Options, and choose whether to share contact information with Outlook.

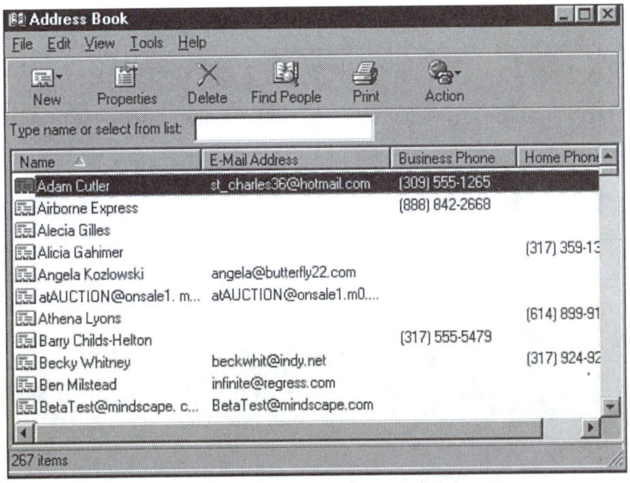

Figure 7.3
The Address Book when in Outlook Compatibility mode.

Part I
Ch 7

Caution

Unless you need compatibility with Outlook or some other external program, you should not run the Address Book in Outlook Compatibility mode because it reduces its capabilities.

ADDING A NAME TO THE ADDRESS BOOK

First things first—you will want to populate your Address Book with the contact information for the people and businesses you deal with regularly. The following steps explain how to create a new Address Book entry:

1. Open the Address Book, if it is not already open.

2. Click the New button to open a menu, and then click New Contact. A Properties box for the new contact appears.
3. Fill in the person's name on the Name tab in the boxes provided (First, Middle, Last, and so on)—see Figure 7.4.
4. Type the person's email address (if you know it) in the E-Mail Addresses box.
5. If the person has more than one email address, click the Add button, and then repeat step 4 to add another.

Note

If there is more than one email address for a person, choose which should be the default. Click it on the list, and then click the Set as Default button.

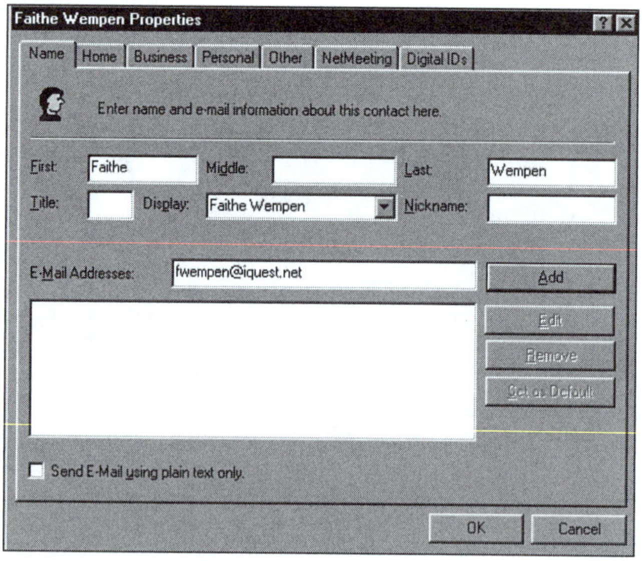

Figure 7.4
Enter the name and email address for the person.

6. (Optional) To record any extra information about the person, click one of the other tabs in the dialog box, and fill in the other fields.
7. Click OK. The name is added to your Address Book.

Note

Whenever you receive a message from someone in Outlook Express, you can add that person's email address to your Address Book by selecting the message in the Inbox listing and then choosing Tools, Add Sender to Address Book. You will learn more about Outlook Express in Chapter 20, "Working with Email and Newsgroups."

EDITING CONTACT INFORMATION

To make changes to a person's information, simply double-click on the name in the Address Book list. The Properties dialog box for that person reopens, and you can make changes there.

The Properties dialog box for an existing contact has an extra tab, Summary, that appears at the front of the stack. It's a read-only tab; you can't make changes there (see Figure 7.5). Click one of the other tabs (which are the same as the ones you used to enter the contact initially) to make your changes.

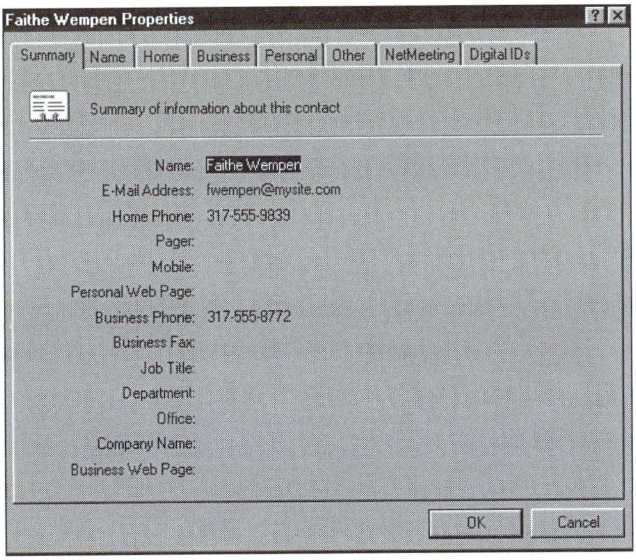

Figure 7.5
The Summary tab is read-only; click one of the other tabs to change the information on it.

FINDING A PERSON

The Find People feature is useful when you need to filter the address list by a certain criterion or when you want to find someone whose name you have forgotten. It lets you specify criteria in any or all of these fields: Name, E-mail, Address, Phone, and Other.

As with many other searches, you can use *wildcard characters* when entering criteria. The `?` stands for a single character, and the `*` stands for multiple characters. For example, to find everyone whose name begins with *S*, enter **`S*`**. To find a person named either *Smith* or *Smyth*, enter **`Sm?th`**.

To find a person in your Address Book, do the following:

1. Choose Edit, Find People, or click the Find People button on the toolbar, or press Ctrl+F. The Find People window opens.
2. Enter the criteria for your search in one or more of the boxes provided. For example, Figure 7.6 shows a search that will locate everyone with 317 in their phone number.

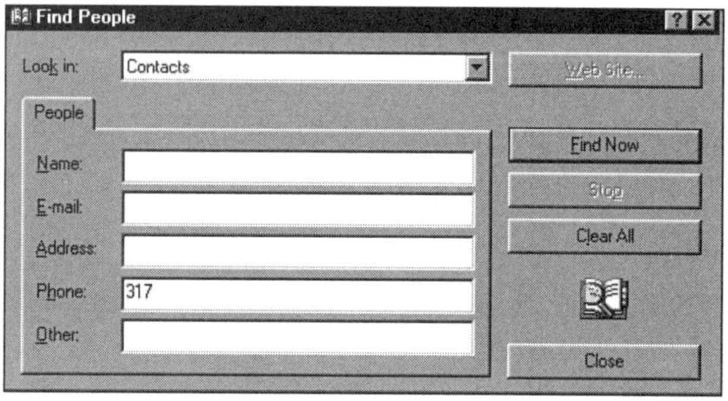

Figure 7.6
Enter criteria for narrowing down the list.

3. Click Find Now. The window expands to show a list of found contacts at the bottom, as in Figure 7.7.

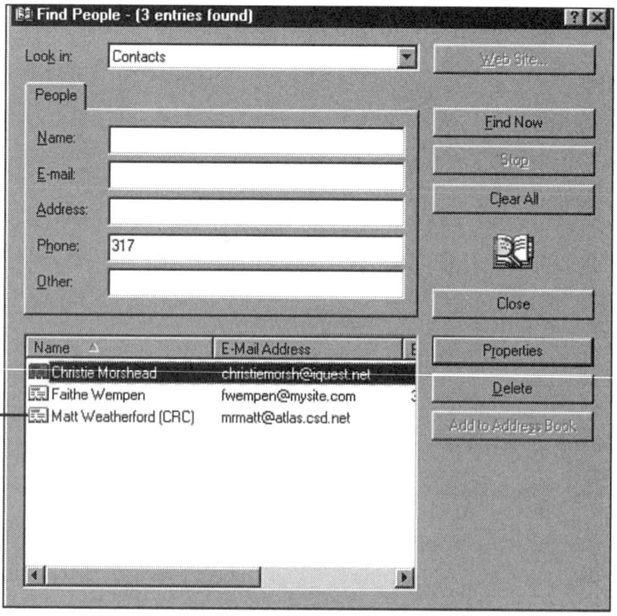

Figure 7.7
Contacts matching the criteria appear on the list.

Contacts that match the criteria entered

4. Do any of the following with the found contacts:
   - Display one's information by double-clicking the name or clicking it once and then clicking Properties.
   - Delete a contact by clicking it and then clicking Delete or pressing the Delete key on the keyboard.

Tip #39 from *Faithe Wempen*

You are not limited to searching your own Address Book! Open the Look In drop-down list in the Find People dialog box, and you will see a list of Internet directories. If your computer is connected to the Internet, you can use any of these directories to search for a person. Then, after locating the person's contact information, click the name and click the Add to Address Book button at the bottom of the dialog box.

Sorting the Address List

By default the address list is sorted by name, but you can sort by any other field by clicking the field name. Clicking once on it sorts it in descending order (A–Z); clicking again on the same field sorts it in ascending order (Z–A).

You can tell which field is currently used for the sorting because a little arrow appears next to its name. A down-pointing arrow indicates a descending sort; an up-pointing one appears for ascending sort.

The Name field has an extra sorting feature: You can sort by either first name or last name. By default, the names appear in this format: *First Last*. Click the Name field once, and that's how it's sorted: ascending, by first name. Click again on it, and it's sorted descending by first name. However, if you click on it a third time, the names switch to this: *Last*, *First*, and the sort becomes ascending by last name. A fourth click changes to descending by last name. (A fifth click takes you back to the beginning of the cycle again.)

Removing a Person from the Address Book

There are lots of ways to delete a person from your Address Book. One way, as you saw earlier in this chapter, is to use the Find feature to locate a contact and then delete it from there. Here are some other ways.

Locate and select the contact to delete, and then do any of the following:

- Click the Delete button on the toolbar.
- Press the Delete key on the keyboard.
- Choose File, Delete.
- Right-click the contact, and choose Delete from the shortcut menu.

When you choose to delete a contact, a confirmation box appears, asking whether you want to permanently delete it. Click Yes to confirm.

PRINTING AN ADDRESS LIST

You can print your address list in any of several formats. For example, you might want to print a phone listing to stick inside your daily planner or print a business card for a single contact.

To print, follow these steps:

1. If you want to print only a single contact, or only certain contacts, select the one(s) you want. To select more than one, hold down the Ctrl key as you click on the ones you want.
2. Choose File, Print, or click the Print button on the toolbar, or press Ctrl+P. The Print dialog box opens (see Figure 7.8).

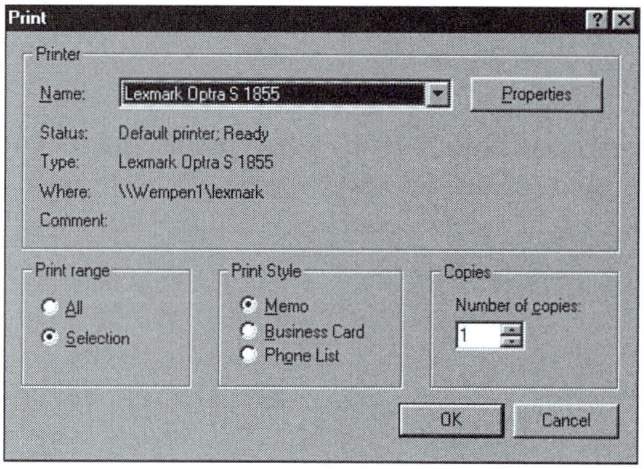

Figure 7.8
Choose what you want to print and how many copies.

3. In the Print Range area, choose what you want to print: All (for all contacts) or Selection (for just the ones you chose in step 1).
4. In the Print Style area, choose how you want them to print: Memo, Business Card, or Phone List.

Note

You might want to print a sample of each format so that you can see how they compare. The Memo and Business Card formats are very similar, except the Business Card format uses smaller print.

5. If you want more than one copy, enter the number in the Number of Copies box.
6. Click OK.

Using the Address Book to Dial Your Telephone

One of the advantages of using the Address Book is that, if you have a modem, it will dial your telephone for you when you want to call a person on your list. Here's how to do it:

1. Select the person you want to call.
2. Choose Tools, Action, Dial, or click the Action button and then choose Dial from its menu. The New Call dialog box opens (see Figure 7.9).

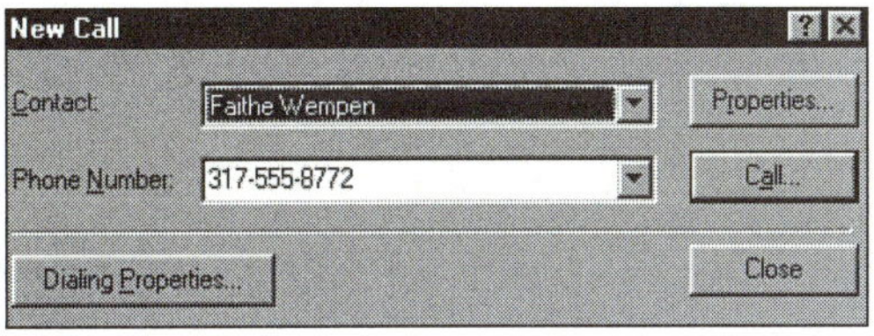

Figure 7.9
Place a call to a person in your Address Book.

3. If the person has more than one phone number in your Address Book (for example, Home and Business), select the one you want from the Phone Number drop-down list.

> **Note**
>
> You can adjust the dialing properties, such as whether to dial a 9 to get an outside line, by clicking the Dialing Properties button.

4. Click Call.
5. If the Phone Dialer dialog box appears, click the Dial button.
6. Pick up the phone and talk!

You can also place Internet calls from the Address Book. Just choose Internet Call instead of Dial from the Action menu, and follow the prompts. To do this, however, you must have set up conferencing information for the person. Do so on the NetMeeting tab of the person's Properties dialog box.

Creating New Address Folders

You can create additional folders in which to store addresses in the Address Book. That way, you can organize addresses according to any category you like, such as separating business contacts from friends or family.

To create a new address folder, perform the following steps:

1. Choose File, New, New Folder, or click the New button and then choose New Folder. A Properties dialog box appears with a single text box in it.
2. Type the new folder name, and then click OK. A new folder appears on the folder tree.

3. Click the Main Identity's Contacts folder on the tree to see your original list of contacts again.
4. Select and drag any contacts you like from the contact list onto the new folder on the folder tree, moving them there.

CREATING CONTACT GROUPS

Contact groups are useful for mass mailings. If you have to send the same email address to multiple people, for example, you can create a group containing all their email addresses and then send a message with the group as the sole recipient. Each person will receive a copy.

To create a group, do the following:

1. Choose File, New, New Group, or click the New button and then choose New Group. A Properties dialog box appears for the group.
2. Enter a group name in the Group Name box.
3. Click the Select Members button. The Select Group Members dialog box opens.
4. Click the first person you want to place in the group, and then click Select. (Or, to select more than one person at once, hold down the Ctrl key as you click on each one.)
5. Repeat step 4 for each person to add to the group (see Figure 7.10).

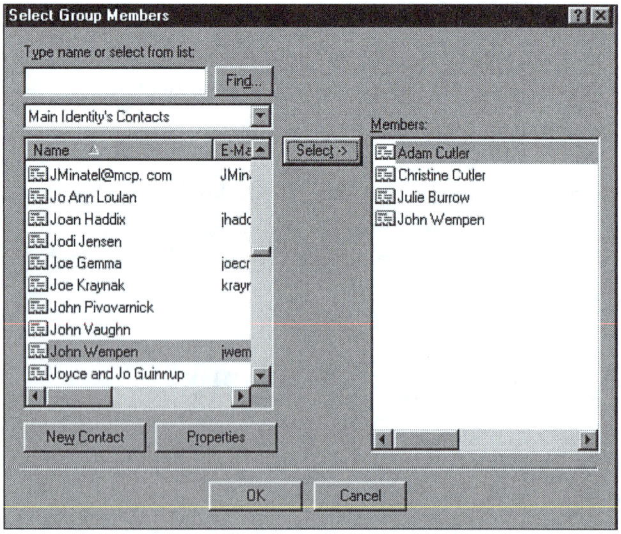

Figure 7.10
Add contacts to the new group.

6. Click OK. The names appear in the Properties dialog box under Group Members.
7. Click OK to create the group.

Tip #40 from *Faithe Wempen*

You can also add names to the list that are not already in your Address Book. Type the name in the Name box and the email address in the E-Mail box, and click Add (see Figure 7.11).

Figure 7.11
The group with contacts added.

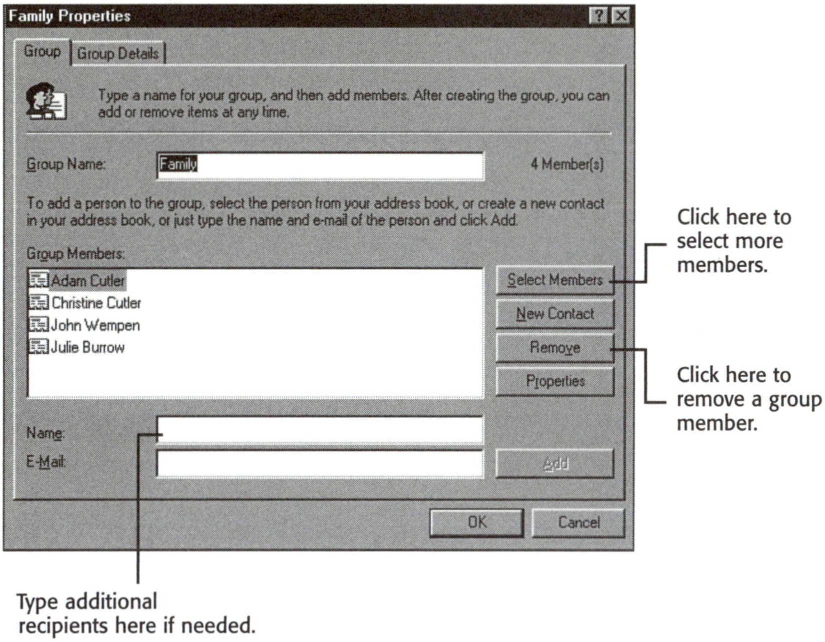

TROUBLESHOOTING

THE LINE IS BUSY

I'm trying to place a call from the Address Book, but Windows reports that another program is using the phone line.

When you are using the Address Book to dial your phone, if you see a message that an other program is using the selected Telephony device, click OK and then use the Taskbar to switch to the Phone Dialer window, which opens in the background. From there, click the Dial button.

CAN'T IMPORT IN OUTLOOK MODE

The Address Book won't let me import records. What's wrong?

If you are running the Address Book in Outlook Compatibility mode, the Import command is not available, so you can't directly import contacts into the Address Book. However, you can import them into Outlook, and they will automatically spill over into the Address Book. Use the File, Import and Export command in Outlook.

CHAPTER 8

Using the Works Calendar

In this chapter

WHAT IS THE WORKS CALENDAR?

Microsoft's Works Calendar is a handy organizational tool you can use to help you track your appointments and daily tasks. If you're like most busy people, you rely on paper notes and paper calendars to keep track of things you need to do, places you need to go, or things you need to see. But, as we all know from firsthand experience, paper notes can be lost easily, and paper calendars can quickly become a mess of jumbled markings as you enter new appointments and cross off canceled ones.

With Works Calendar, you won't have to worry about losing your notes about upcoming appointments or tasks you have to accomplish for the day. You can keep track of such things electronically in one central place—Works Calendar. Use Works Calendar to schedule appointments, make note of events (such as birthdays, anniversaries, trips, or conventions), and even remind yourself of important meetings.

Works Calendar looks much like an ordinary day planner—the notebook and paper kind that you can carry along with you—and lets you view your schedule in daily, weekly, and monthly views. Rather than drag the Works Calendar around with you, however, you will find it handy on your computer, and you can easily print out appointments or tasks as needed. Works Calendar is the perfect tool for tracking your daily comings and goings.

To start Works Calendar, you can choose it from the Task Launcher, or you can choose Start, Programs, Microsoft Works, Microsoft Works Calendar. A blank calendar opens onscreen, as shown in Figure 8.1.

Note

When you start Works Calendar for the first time, you might see a prompt box that asks whether you want Microsoft Works Calendar to be your default calendar. Click Yes if you do, or No if you use another calendar program. Deselect the Always Perform This Check When Starting Works Calendar check box, and you won't be bothered by this prompt again.

The Help pane opens the first time you use the Calendar. You can use the Help system in the Calendar the same way you do in other Works applications.

→ For help with the Works Help system, **see** "Getting Help," **p. 16**.

→ To recall how to use the Task Launcher, **see** "Using the Works Task Launcher," **p. 9**.

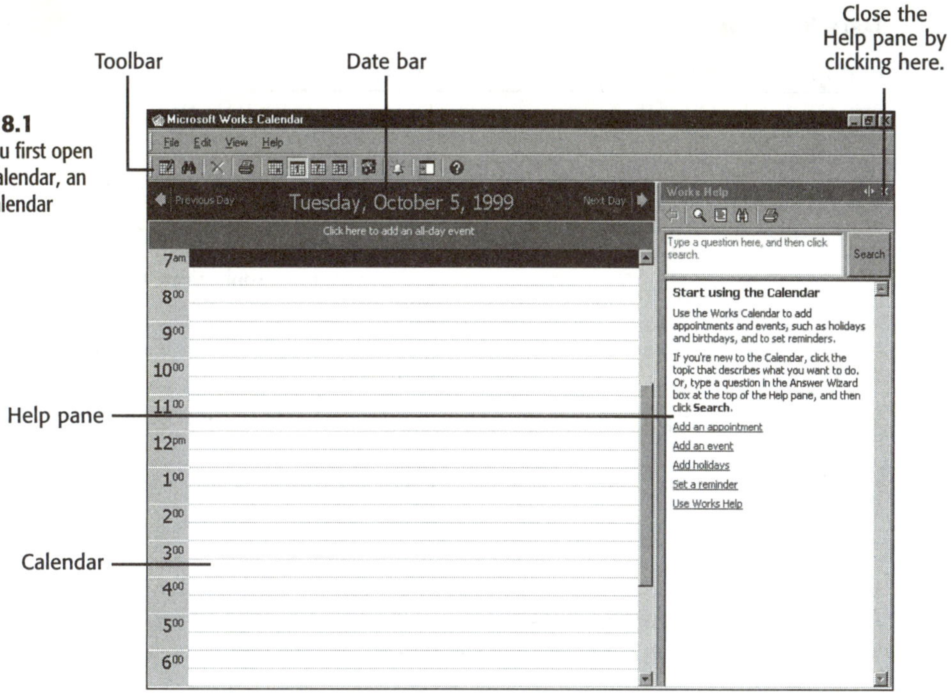

Figure 8.1
When you first open Works Calendar, an empty calendar appears.

USING THE WORKS CALENDAR TOOLBAR

Use the Works Calendar toolbar to quickly activate commands and features with a click of a button. Table 8.1 describes the buttons on the toolbar.

TABLE 8.1 TOOLBAR BUTTONS

Button	Name	Function
	New Appointment	Opens the New Appointment dialog box for recording new appointments in the Calendar
	Find	Opens the Find dialog box for searching the Calendar
	Delete	Deletes the selected appointment
	Print	Opens the Print dialog box
	Go to Today	Displays the current date
	View Day	Displays the Calendar in Day view

continues

Table 8.1 Continued

Button	Name	Function
	View Week	Displays the Calendar in Week view
	View Month	Displays the Calendar in Month view
	Launch Home Publishing	Starts the Home Publishing program so that you can create a more sophisticated printout of your calendar
	Reminders	Opens the View Reminders dialog box for viewing set reminders
	Category Filter	Toggles the Category Filter pane on and off
	Help	Opens the Help pane

Tip #41 from *Faithe Wempen*

The Works Calendar toolbar icons are a bit small. If you prefer larger toolbar buttons, choose View, Toolbar, Use Large Icons. Do the same again to toggle the size back to small.

Changing Views

There are several ways to look at the Works Calendar. You can choose to look at your calendar in Day, Week, or Month view. Each view gives you a different perspective of your scheduled appointments and tasks. You can quickly switch between views as needed, which is explained in this section.

Tip #42 from *Faithe Wempen*

Regardless of which calendar view you're using, a click on the Go to Today button always takes you to the current date.

Using Day View

Day view lets you see what appointments or tasks you have scheduled for a particular day. By default, the first time you open Works Calendar, Day view, shown in Figure 8.2, displays the current day with time slots for each hour, broken into half-hour increments. If Day view isn't displayed, click the View Day button on the toolbar, or press Alt+1. You can also choose View, Day.

With Day view, you have the option of viewing the daily schedule by hour (refer to Figure 8.2) or by sections (see Figure 8.3). To switch between them, choose View, Show Day in Hours to toggle the hours on and off.

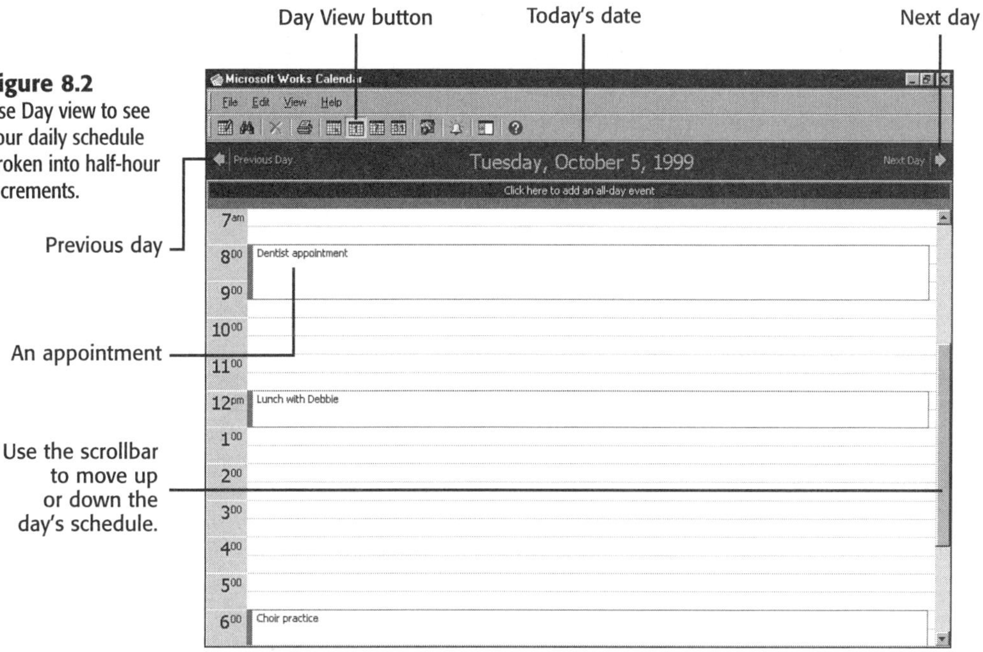

Figure 8.2
Use Day view to see your daily schedule broken into half-hour increments.

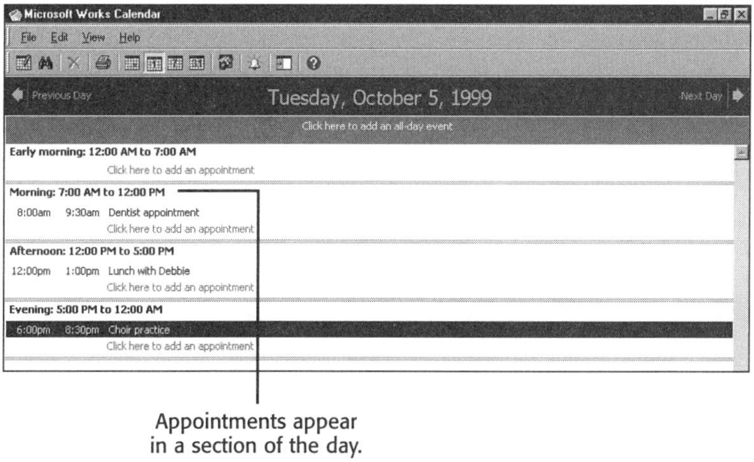

Figure 8.3
Here's a view of the schedule without hourly increments displayed.

As you can see in Figure 8.3, turning off the hour slots lets you view your daily schedule in four sections: Early Morning, Morning, Afternoon, and Evening. This view lets you target the appointments you currently have scheduled.

Regardless of which view option you're using to see your daily schedule, you can navigate the schedule in the same way:

- To view the preceding day's schedule, click the Previous Day button at the top of the Day view area.

- To view the next day's schedule, click the Next Day button.
- To move your view of the hours up or down, drag the scrollbar.
- To select another date to view, click on the banner date to display a pop-up month calendar, as shown in Figure 8.4; then, click on the date to view or use the arrows at the top of the pop-up calendar to select another month.

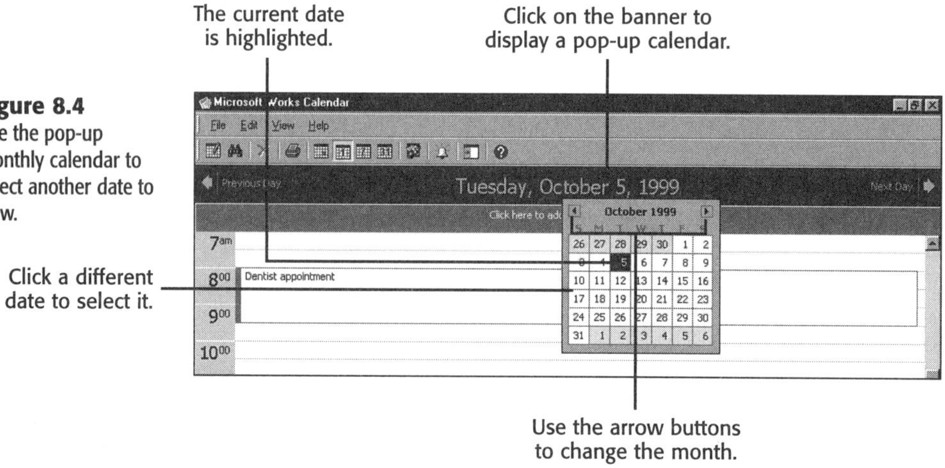

Figure 8.4
Use the pop-up monthly calendar to select another date to view.

Works Calendar, by default, starts a week on Sunday and displays the hours in Day view starting with 7:00 a.m. You can change which day the week starts with and which hour begins the day in Day view.

To change the start date and time, do the following:

1. Choose View, Options. This opens the Calendar Options dialog box, as shown in Figure 8.5.

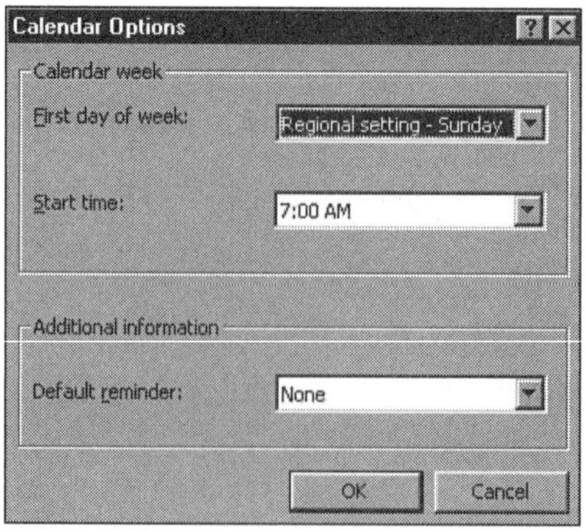

Figure 8.5
Use the Calendar Options dialog box to change the day your week starts with and the start time.

2. To change the day your week begins on, click the First Day of Week drop-down arrow, and choose another day.
3. To change the start time you view in the daily schedule, click the Start Time drop-down arrow, and select another time from the list (refer to Figure 8.5).
4. Click OK to exit the dialog box and apply the new settings.

USING WEEK VIEW

Week view lets you see your entire week's schedule at a glance, as shown in Figure 8.6. This view shows all seven days and any appointments scheduled. As you add appointments to the schedule, your weekly schedule might become too full to view onscreen. In which case, you use the scrollbars to see portions of the weekly schedule.

To switch to Week view, click the View Week button on the toolbar, or choose View, Week.

Tip #43 from *Faithe Wempen*

You can also press Alt+- to switch to Week view.

Figure 8.6
Here's an example of Week view, which shows a week's worth of dates.

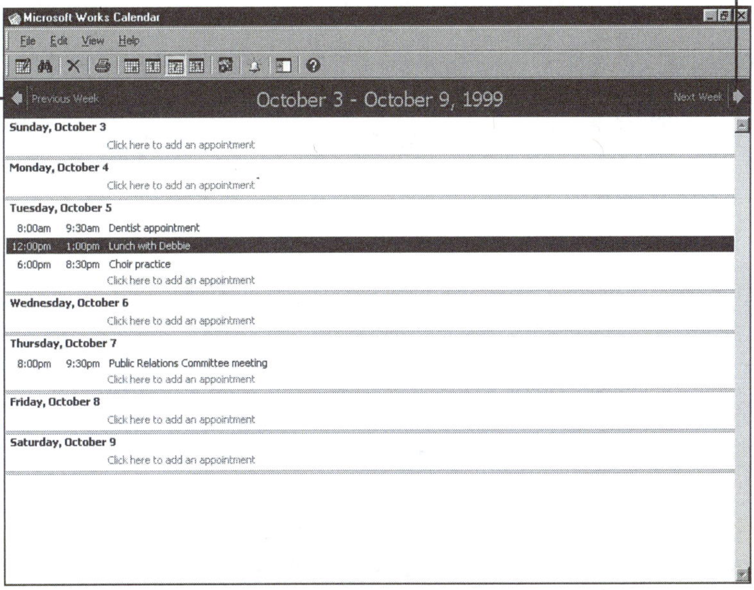

To navigate the Week view of your schedule, use the same methods that you used in Day view.

- To view the preceding week's schedule, click the Previous Week button at the top of the Week view area.
- To view the next week's schedule, click the Next Week button.
- To move your view of the weekly schedule up or down, click the appropriate scrollbar arrow.
- To select another date to view, click on the banner date to display a pop-up month calendar (refer to Figure 8.4); then click on the date to view, or use the arrows at the top of the pop-up calendar to select another month.

USING MONTH VIEW

Last, but not least, you can view your calendar by month using Month view, shown in Figure 8.7. To switch to Month view, click the View Month button on the toolbar, or choose View, Month (or press Alt+= on the keyboard).

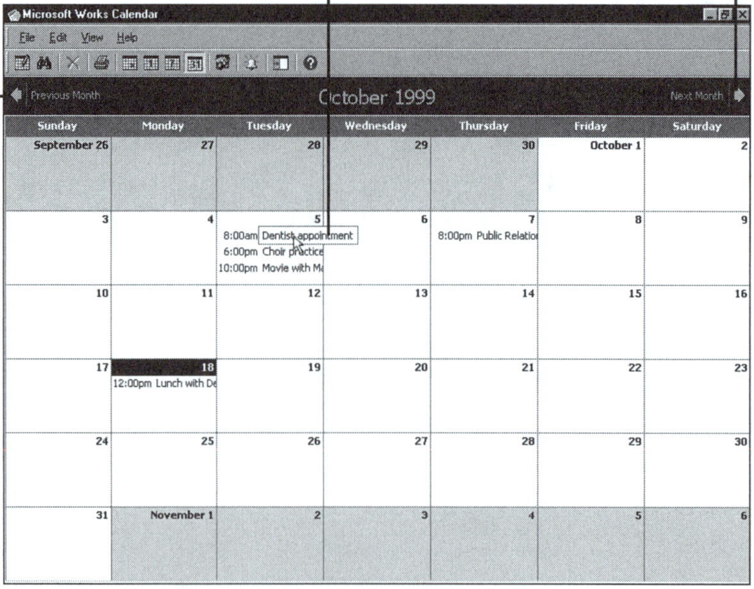

Figure 8.7
Month view lets you see an entire month's worth of dates.

As you can see in Figure 8.7, the text describing each appointment is cut off because of the monthly calendar's size. To quickly see the appointment text, hover your mouse pointer over the appointment. If a day has more appointments than can be listed in a Month view date, click the button at the bottom of the date square to switch back to Day view and see the entire list. For example, in Figure 8.7, October 5 has more appointments than can possibly appear in the date's square. If I click the button in the bottom-right corner of the date's square, I switch the view to Day view and can then see each appointment I have scheduled.

Use these methods to navigate the Month view of your schedule:

- To view the preceding month's schedule, click the Previous Month button at the top of the Week view area.
- To view the next month's schedule, click the Next Month button.
- To select another month to view, click on the banner month to display a pop-up list of months, as shown in Figure 8.8; then click on the month to view.

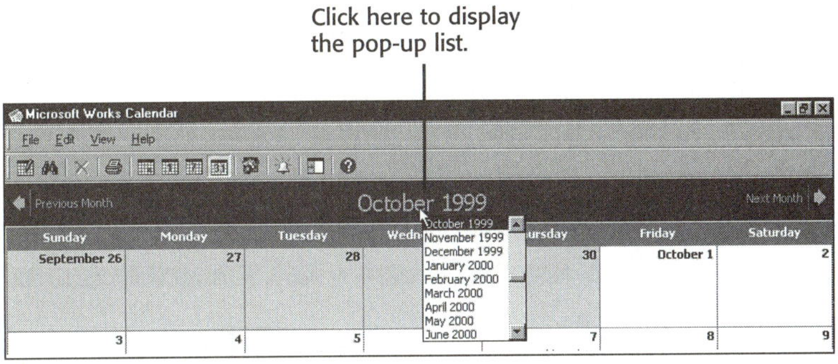

Figure 8.8
When you click on the banner month in Month view, a list of months appears.

Setting an Appointment

To start using Works Calendar, just begin entering appointments and scheduling tasks. When you open Works Calendar, the current date is displayed, and you can immediately start adding appointments to your schedule for that day.

In Works Calendar, the information you enter as an appointment can be just about anything—a note, a description of a meeting, a list of things you have to do, whatever suits your needs for organizing and detailing your schedule. Anything that fits on a single line of text can be used as an appointment description. Figure 8.9 shows some examples of appointments listed in Day view. As you can see, the descriptions vary in how the appointed time is to be used.

➔ To learn more about the Calendar's views, **see** "Changing Views," **p. 160**.

Entering Appointments with the New Appointment Dialog Box

One way to enter an appointment is through the New Appointment dialog box. Open it in any of these ways:

- Click the New Appointment button on the toolbar.
- Double-click an empty spot on the calendar.
- Open the File menu and select New Appointment.
- Press Ctrl+N.
- Right-click over an empty area of the calendar, and choose New Appointment from the pop-up menu.

Figure 8.9
Here's an example of appointments listed in Day view.

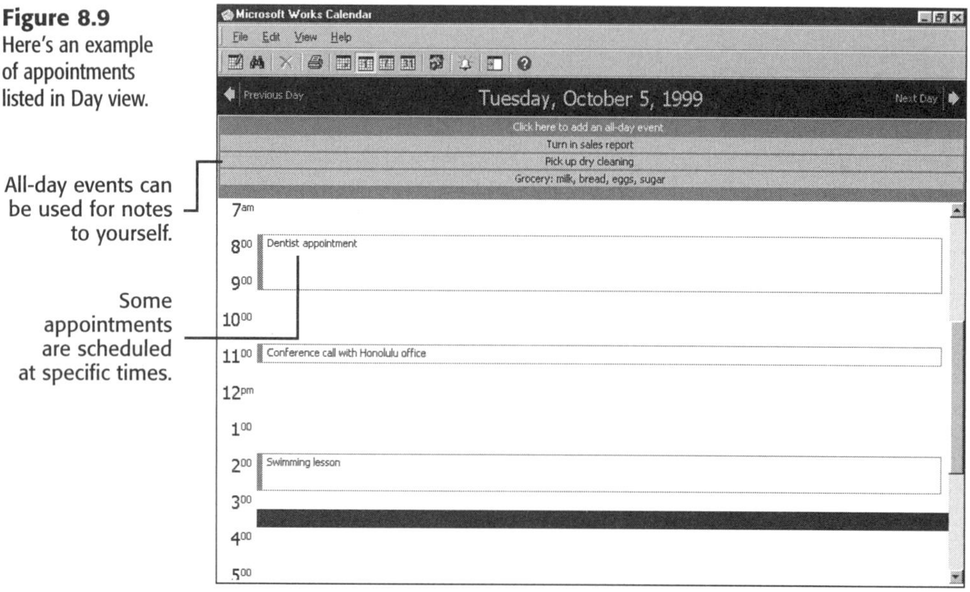

Any of these methods displays the New Appointment dialog box, as shown in Figure 8.10. From this dialog box, you can give the appointment or task a title, assign a location or category, specify a starting date (and time, if appropriate) and ending date/time, and even assign a reminder with a note about the item. (Use only the fields that are applicable; none of them are specifically required.)

Figure 8.10
Use the New Appointment dialog box to enter information about the appointment.

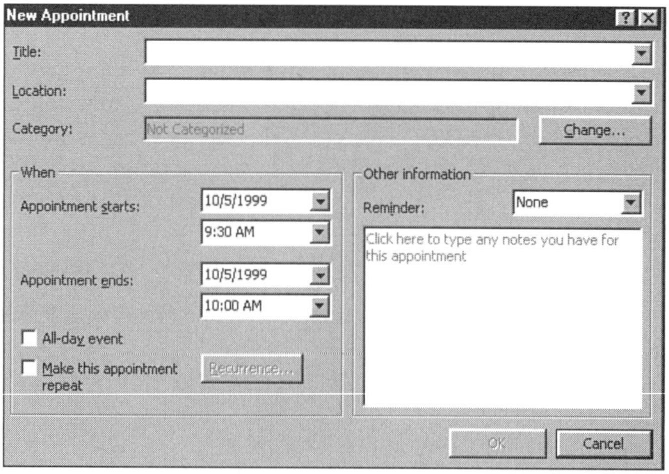

1. Click inside the Title text box, and enter a description for the appointment or task. If the appointment is a duplicate of a previous appointment, use the drop-down list for that box to assign the same title.

2. [Optional] Click inside the Location field, and enter a location where the appointment takes place (or choose a previously used location from the drop-down list).

Note

If you double-clicked over a specific date or time to open the dialog box, that date and time will be entered as the Appointment Starts selection in the When section. You can change them as needed.

3. To set a start date, click the Appointment Starts date drop-down arrow, and choose a date from the pop-up calendar, as shown in Figure 8.11.

Note

You can also type a date or time directly into the appropriate text boxes in the New Appointment dialog box, if you prefer not to use the pop-up calendar or the list box.

Figure 8.11
Use the pop-up calendar to set a specific date.

Click here to display the pop-up calendar.

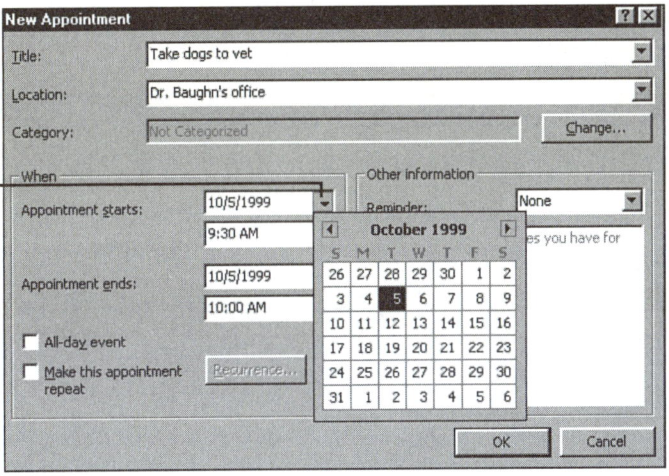

4. [Optional] If this is an all-day event (that is, if you don't want to assign a specific time to it), select the All-Day Event check box, and skip to step 6.

Tip #44 from *Faithe Wempen*

Use the All-Day Event option to enter to-do items and other reminders to yourself that are not real appointments occurring at a specific time.

5. To set a start time, click the Appointment Starts time drop-down arrow, as shown in Figure 8.12, and select a time.
6. Set the Appointment Ends date and time fields to the ending date and time, just as you did with the starting date and time.

Figure 8.12
Use the list of times to choose a start time for the appointment.

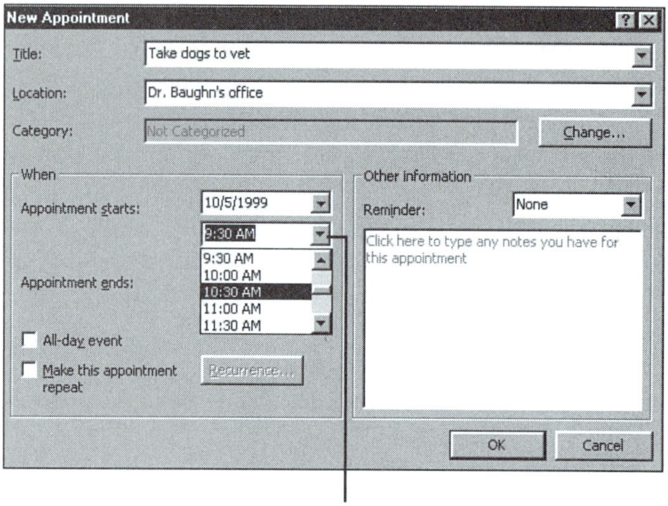

Click here to open the list of times.

Note

By default, Works Calendar attempts to set every appointment for 30 minutes. If your appointment requires more time, set the end time for a longer length of time.

7. Click OK. The new appointment is added to your schedule.

Don't worry about the other options you see in the New Appointment dialog box. I cover those in the next few sections of this chapter.

CREATING RECURRING APPOINTMENTS

If your schedule includes appointments that repeat, don't retype the appointment each time; create a repeating appointment instead. For example, you might have a meeting that you attend at the same time each week, or perhaps you have a long-standing series of appointments with your doctor. You can enter the details about the appointment once and set the appointment as a recurring appointment in Works Calendar.

1. Start creating the appointment normally, as described in the preceding section. Make sure that you have entered the correct starting and ending dates and times.
2. Select the Make This Appointment Repeat check box. The Recurrence button becomes available.
3. Click the Recurrence button. The Recurrence Options dialog box opens (see Figure 8.13).
4. Select from a variety of recurrence options, as explained here:
   - From the Recurring options at the top of the dialog box, specify how often the appointment repeats. For example, if the appointment occurs each week on a Wednesday, select Weekly and Wednesday.

- Use the Range of Recurrence options to specify when the recurring appointments start and end. This creates a time frame for the appointments so that they don't go on indefinitely (unless you want them to). To create a start date, click the Start drop-down arrow, and choose a new date from the pop-up calendar.
- To select a particular date to end the recurrence, click the End By option, and use the pop-up calendar to set an end date.
- To end a recurring appointment after a certain number of appointments has passed, click the End After option, and choose the number of occurrences.
- Use the Appointment Time area of the dialog box to set an appointment start and end time.

5. Click OK to exit; then click OK again to exit the New Appointment dialog box.

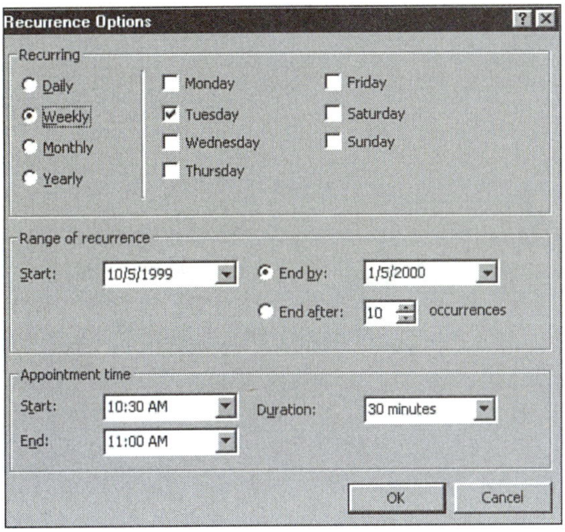

Figure 8.13
Use the Recurrence Options dialog box to specify the frequency of the repeating appointment.

Entering Appointments Directly into the Calendar

Another way to enter appointments is to do so directly into the Calendar. Unlike the New Appointment dialog box, you won't be able to add appointment details, such as location or recurring dates, but you can type in an appointment title or other text that describes the appointment.

If you're using Day view with the hour slots displayed, you can click inside any time slot and start entering an appointment's description (see Figure 8.14).

If you're using Week view or Day view without the hour slots displayed, you might notice some grayed-out text reading `Click here to add an appointment`. You can click on this text and start typing to enter an appointment.

Figure 8.14
You can enter an appointment directly into the Calendar in Day view.

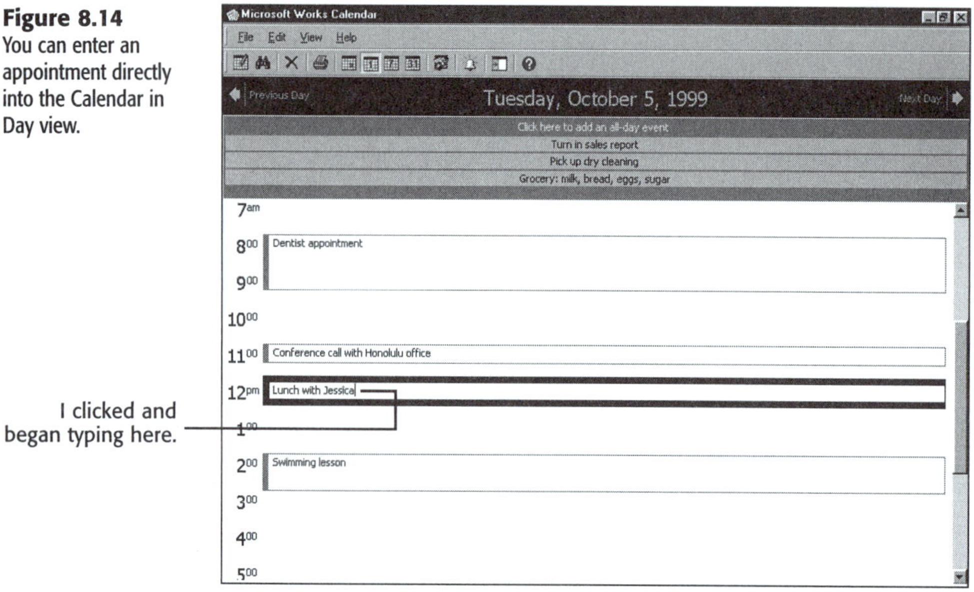

Caution

When you add an appointment by typing in a view without hour slots, the appointment time defaults to 7:00 a.m. If that's not the time you want to use, double-click the entry to open the Edit Appointment dialog box, and change the time as described in the next section.

EDITING APPOINTMENTS

After committing an appointment to the Works Calendar, you can easily go back and edit it at any time. For example, you might have to change the time or date.

Open the Edit Appointment dialog box using any of these methods:

- Double-click on the appointment in any Calendar view.
- Open the File menu and select Open Appointment.
- Right-click over the appointment in the calendar, and choose Open from the pop-up menu.

The Edit Appointment dialog box appears, as shown in Figure 8.15. This dialog box is exactly the same as the New Appointment dialog box you used to create the appointment. Make changes to the various fields just as you did when you created the appointment, and then click OK.

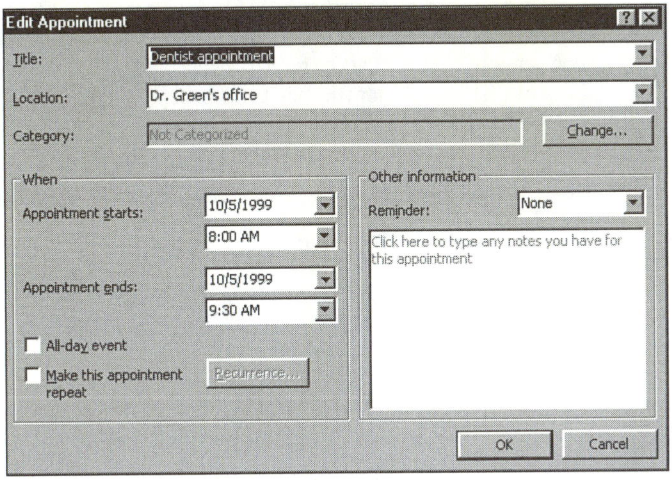

Figure 8.15
The dialog box for editing appointments is similar to the dialog box for creating appointments.

Dragging and Dropping Appointments

If you have to move an appointment to a new date or time, you can click and drag the appointment on the calendar.

1. Switch to Day view with the Show Day in Hours option selected (you can see exactly which time slot you're moving the appointment to in this view mode).
2. Locate and select the appointment you want to move. A selected appointment is surrounded by a highlighted border.
3. Move your mouse pointer to the far left side of the selected appointment until the pointer takes the shape of a four-sided arrow pointer. Click on the appointment, hold down the mouse button, and then drag the appointment to a new time slot.
4. Release the mouse button, and the appointment is moved.

When moving appointments from one day to another but keeping the same time, use Month view. Use the preceding steps, but drag the appointment from one date to another date.

Editing Recurring Appointments

When editing recurring appointments, you can choose to edit one appointment or the entire series. For example, if you have a recurring appointment with your chiropractor for three months but need to change the time for one appointment only, you can edit the one occurrence. If you need to change any details for every appointment, you can edit the entire series.

1. From any Calendar view, double-click on the recurring appointment you want to edit. This opens the Open Recurring Item dialog box, shown in Figure 8.16.

Tip #45 from
Faithe Wempen

You can also select a recurring appointment in the Calendar and choose File, Open Appointment to display the Open Recurring Item dialog box, or right-click on the appointment and select Open from the pop-up menu.

Figure 8.16
Works Calendar warns you about the recurring appointment and offers two options for editing.

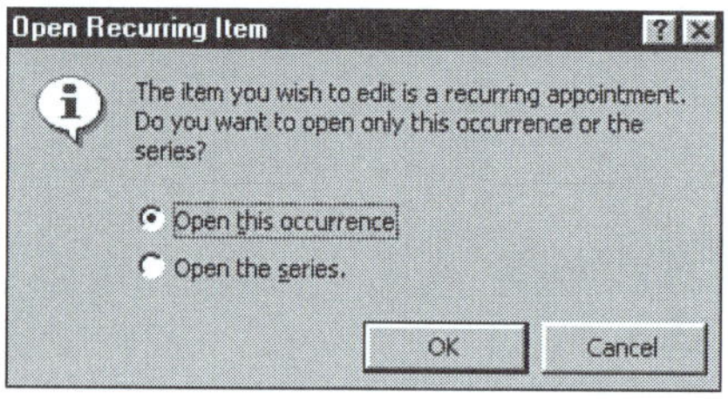

2a. To edit only the one occurrence, select the Open This Occurrence option, and click OK. This opens the Edit Appointment dialog box, and you can make changes to the appointment's date or time as needed. Skip to step 4.

Or

2b. To edit all the recurring appointments in the series, select the Open the Series option, and click OK. This opens the Edit Appointment dialog box.

3. Click the Recurrence button to open the Recurrence Options dialog box.
4. Make your changes to the series details; then click OK to return to the Edit Appointment dialog box.
5. Click OK to exit the Edit Appointment dialog box.

DELETING APPOINTMENTS

If you find that you no longer need an item scheduled on the calendar, you can delete it.

Select the appointment from any Calendar view; then use any of these methods to delete the appointment:

- Click the Delete button on the toolbar.
- Open the Edit menu and select Delete Appointment.
- Press Ctrl+D on the keyboard.
- Right-click over the appointment in the Calendar, and choose Delete Item from the pop-up menu.
- Press the Delete key on the keyboard.

When you attempt to delete an item, Works Calendar displays a prompt box asking you to confirm the deletion. Choose Yes to finish deleting the item or No if you change your mind about deleting.

After you delete an item, you can't get it back. That's why Works Calendar wants to make sure that you're sure.

Tip #46 from *Faithe Wempen*

By default, Works Calendar always prompts you about the deletion before actually deleting the item. However, if you're relatively sure of all your deletions, deselect the Always Confirm Before Deleting check box. Works Calendar won't prompt you anymore about future deletions.

WORKING WITH REMINDERS

You can assign a reminder to any appointment, and Works Calendar prompts you as the appointment time approaches. Best of all, you don't have to have Works Calendar up and running for the reminder to work.

Caution

For Works Calendar's reminder feature to work accurately, make sure that your computer's clock is accurate. If it's not, you can reset it, provided that you have the correct time. Return to the Windows desktop; then double-click on the time display in the lower-right corner of the screen (located at the far right end of the taskbar). This opens the Date/Time Properties dialog box. Click the Date & Time tab, and set the correct time. Click OK to exit.

SETTING REMINDERS

You can assign a reminder to your appointment as you enter details about the appointment in the New Appointment (or Edit Appointment) dialog box. When you assign a reminder, you have a choice of times you can assign. The time you select specifies exactly when the remind prompt appears. For example, if you schedule a meeting in the office and assign a reminder time of 15 minutes, the prompt appears on your screen 15 minutes before the meeting.

1. Begin creating or editing the appointment normally.
2. Open the Reminder drop-down list, and choose when you want to be reminded, in relation to the appointment time (see Figure 8.17).

Note

To set a time other than one on the list in Figure 8.17, type a time directly into the Reminder text box (in minutes).

3. Click in the text box beneath the Reminder box, and type the reminder text there. In Figure 8.18, for example, I'm reminding myself to bring my insurance card to my dentist appointment.

Select or type a reminder time.

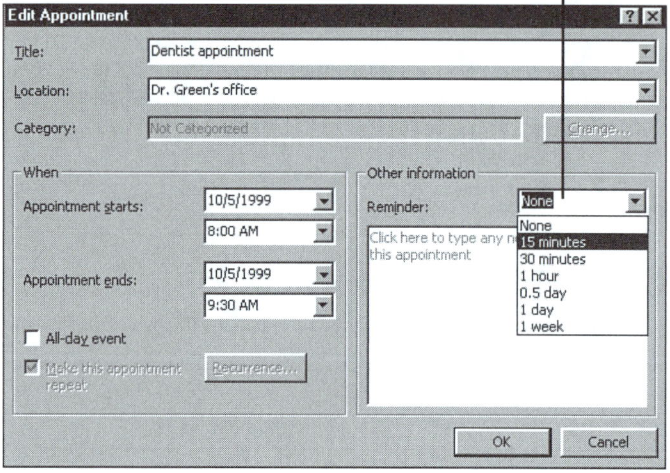

Figure 8.17
You can assign reminders to any appointment you create in the New Appointment dialog box.

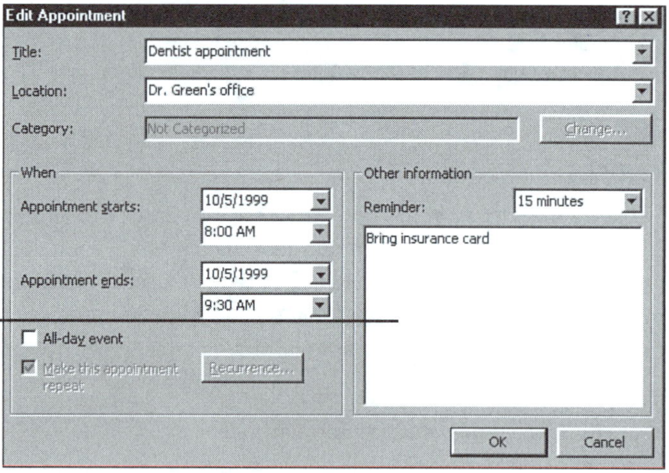

Figure 8.18
You can add notes to yourself in the Reminder text box.

Type your reminder text here.

Tip #47 from
Faithe Wempen

The notes text box is a good place to jot down phone numbers, lists, or any other data you want to remember about the appointment. You don't have to use the notes box just for reminders; you can use it when setting appointments without reminders, too.

4. Click OK to close the New Appointment dialog box.

WORKING WITH REMINDER PROMPTS

When the set reminder time occurs, a View Reminders prompt box appears, as shown in Figure 8.19. Regardless of what program you are working in, the prompt box opens on your screen.

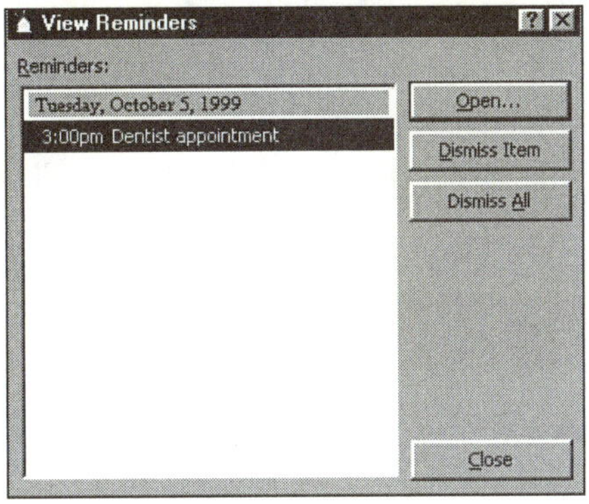

Figure 8.19
The View Reminders prompt box tells you about your appointment.

The View Reminders prompt box has four options you can choose. Select the appointment from the list box, and then do one of the following:

- Click the Open button to view details about the appointment. This opens the Edit Appointment dialog box. (Click OK to exit the dialog box.)
- Click the Dismiss Item button to delete the reminder.
- Click the Dismiss All button to delete all the reminders currently set.
- Click the Close button to close the prompt box.

To view your active reminders, click the Reminders button on the toolbar, or open the View menu and select Reminders.

USING CATEGORIES

Works Calendar lets you assign categories to your appointments to help you keep them organized. For example, you can assign the Business category to all business-related appointments. You can assign the Personal category to all nonbusiness appointments. Then, using Works Calendar Category Filter feature, you can choose to display only the business-related appointments in your calendar or only the nonbusiness appointments. You can even print out appointments assigned to a specific category. You can use Works Calendar's categories or create your own.

Tip #48 from *Faithe Wempen*

To fully utilize this feature, you must consistently assign categories to all your appointments. You might find that you need to use only two categories, Business and Personal. This way, you can choose to view all your business-related appointments at once and then view all your personal appointments.

ASSIGNING CATEGORIES

You can assign categories while creating a new appointment or when editing existing appointments. Remember, the New Appointment and Edit Appointment dialog boxes are the same, so the steps for assigning categories apply to new appointments, as well as existing appointments.

1. Start creating or editing the appointment normally.
2. To assign a category, click the Change button. This opens the Choose Categories dialog box, as shown in Figure 8.20.

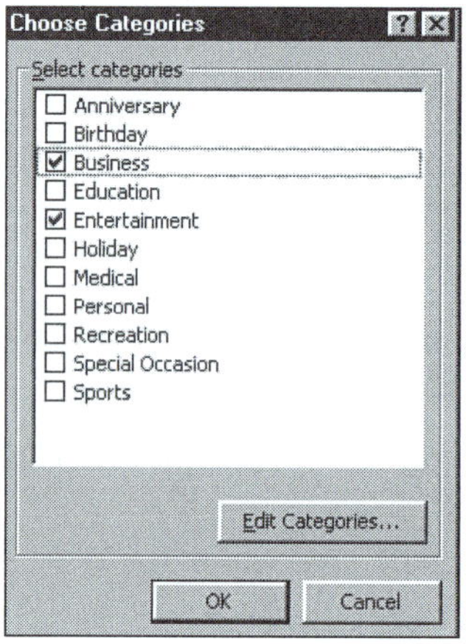

Figure 8.20
You can assign categories to any appointment you create.

3. Select the category you want to assign to the appointment (you can check as many as apply).
4. Click OK to exit the Choose Categories dialog box; then continue creating or editing the appointment as desired.

CUSTOMIZING CATEGORIES

Works Calendar offers nine categories you can choose from, but if nine isn't enough, or if some of the categories don't fit your situation, you can add or edit categories.

1. From the Works Calendar's main screen, choose Edit, Categories. This opens the Edit Categories dialog box, as shown in Figure 8.21.

Tip #49 from *Faithe Wempen*

To edit categories while creating a new appointment or editing an existing appointment, click the Change button, and then click the Edit Categories button in the Choose Categories dialog box.

2. Do any of the following:
   - To add a category to the list box, click inside the text box, and type in a category name. Then click the Add button. The category is added to the list box.
   - To rename a category, select it in the list box, type a new category name, and click Rename.
   - To delete a category, select it from the list box, and then click the Delete button.

Figure 8.21
You can add new categories, delete categories, or rename categories in the Edit Categories dialog box.

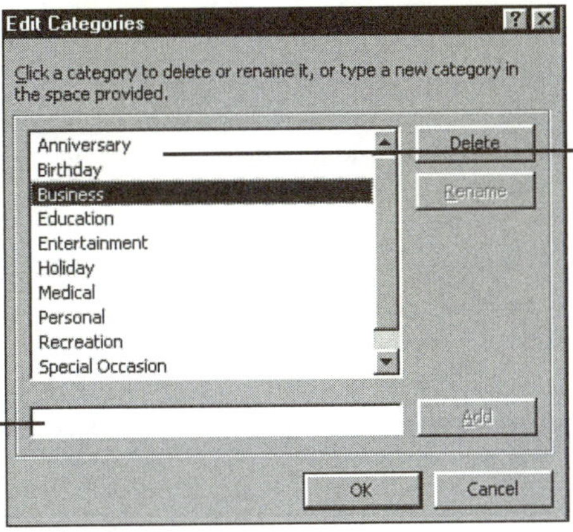

Existing categories

Type a new category name here.

3. Click OK to exit the Edit Categories dialog box.

Using the Category Filter

The best part of using categories is that you can filter how they are viewed in your calendar. To open the category filter, click the Show Category Filter button on the toolbar, or choose View, Show Category Filter. This opens the Category Filter pane on the left side of the program window, as shown in Figure 8.22. You can use the Category Filter pane in any Calendar view.

Click here to open the Category Filter.

Figure 8.22
Use the Category Filter pane to control which categories appear on the calendar.

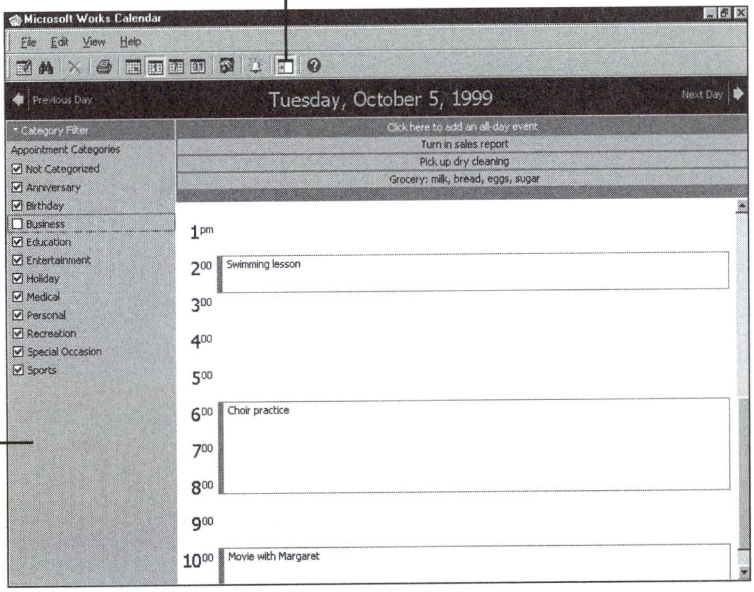

The Category Filter pane

Each category is represented by a check box. A check mark in the check box indicates that the category is selected. For example, in Figure 8.22, the Business category is unselected. This means that none of the appointments with the assigned category of Business is displayed on the calendar (unless those appointments also have another category assigned whose check box *is* selected).

To show every category in the calendar, click the Category Filter drop-down arrow, as shown in Figure 8.23, and choose Show Appointments in All Categories. You can also choose View, Category Filter, Show Appointments in All Categories.

Figure 8.23
You can use the drop-down list to view every categorized appointment or every uncategorized appointment.

Click here to display the list.

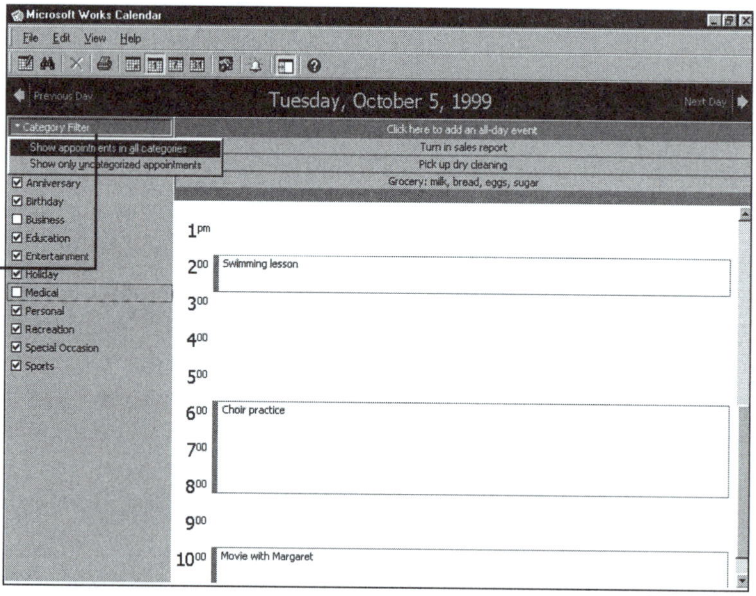

To see all the uncategorized appointments on your calendar, select Show Only Uncategorized Appointments.

To turn off the category filter, click the Show Category Filter button. This button toggles the feature on and off.

SEARCHING YOUR CALENDAR

The more appointments and tasks you enter into the Calendar, the harder it becomes to keep everything organized. When you want to look up a specific appointment, you could spend time looking through each day, week, or month until you find it. To make things easier, however, Works Calendar has some search tools you can use to look up items you've entered into the Calendar.

Use the Find dialog box, shown in Figure 8.24, to search for keywords (specific text entries), times, or categories.

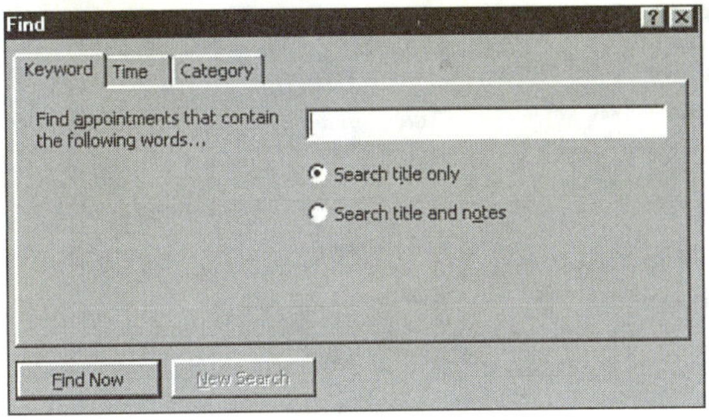

Figure 8.24
Use the Find dialog box to conduct several kinds of searches.

1. Click the Find button or choose Edit, Find. The Find dialog box (refer to Figure 8.24) opens onscreen.
2. With the Keyword tab displayed, click inside the text box and enter the text for which you're searching.
3. To search only the appointment title text, select the Search Title Only option, or to search title text and note text, select the Search Title and Notes option.
4. If you want to narrow your search to a specific time frame, click the Time tab (see Figure 8.25), and use the drop-down lists to specify a time period.

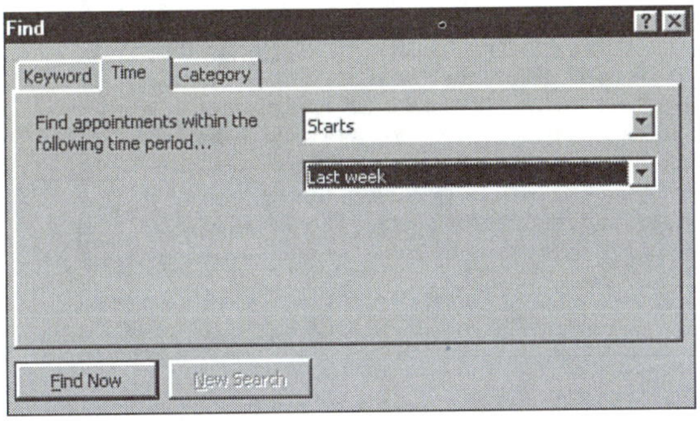

Figure 8.25
Use the Time tab to specify a time period to search.

5. To search only certain categories, click the Category tab (see Figure 8.26), and select or deselect the categories to include in the search.
6. When you're ready to start the search, click the Find Now button.
7. Works Calendar presents any matches in an extended portion of the Find dialog box, as shown in Figure 8.27. To investigate any item, select it from the list box and click the Open Item button, or just double-click on the item.
8. If the search didn't reveal the results you were looking for, try again. Click the New Search button. This clears the preceding search criteria, and you can start a new search.
9. To close the Find dialog box at any time, click the Close (×) button located in the upper-right corner of the dialog box.

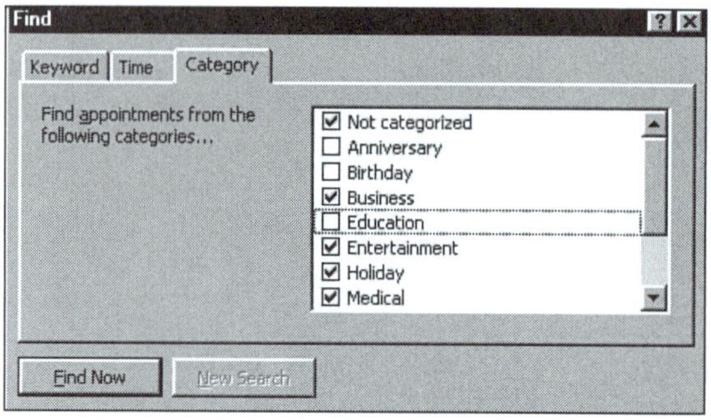

Figure 8.26
Use the Category tab to designate which categories to search.

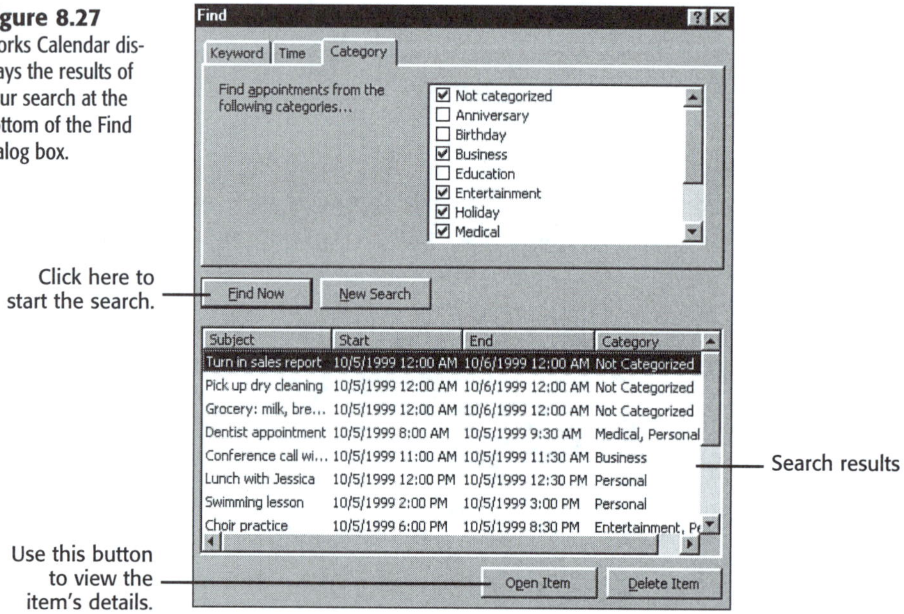

Figure 8.27
Works Calendar displays the results of your search at the bottom of the Find dialog box.

Tip #50 from
Faithe Wempen

Use the Delete Item button in the Find dialog box (refer to Figure 8.27) to remove the found item from your calendar.

SHARING CALENDAR INFORMATION

What if you're going on a sales trip and want to let your secretary know where you will be throughout the day? You can give him or her a copy of your detailed daily business-related schedule. Are you going on vacation and need to leave Grandma a schedule of which child is at which lesson during the week? Print her a copy of your personal schedule. There are numerous ways to share the information you enter into your calendar:

- Print out your calendar to give to others or take with you as you travel.
- Turn an appointment into an email message.
- Export your calendar into another calendar program.
- Import information from someone else's calendar program into yours.
- Save the Calendar data as an HTML document to post on a Web site.

Printing Your Calendar

Works Calendar offers a variety of ways to print your Calendar data. You can choose to print a single day's schedule or a week's or month's worth of appointments. You can also print different styles; for example, print your daily schedule without the times, or print only certain categories.

Works Calendar's printing features are found in the Print dialog box, as shown in Figure 8.28. You can choose from seven print styles:

- **Day by Appointments**—Prints the Day view of your schedule, including every hour time slot and appointment
- **Day by Hours**—Also prints the Day view of your schedule, with hour time slots and appointments
- **Day List**—Prints your daily schedule of appointments as a list
- **Day List by Sections**—Prints your daily schedule listed in sections (early morning, morning, afternoon, and evening)
- **Week**—Prints a weekly view of your schedule
- **Month – Portrait**—Prints the Month view of your calendar with the top of the page starting at the short end of the paper (vertical orientation)
- **Month – Landscape**—Prints the Month view of your calendar with the top of the page starting at the long edge of the paper (horizontal orientation)

To print your calendar, follow these steps:

1. Click the Print button on the toolbar, or choose File, Print. This opens the Print dialog box shown in Figure 8.28.

Tip #51 from *Faithe Wempen*

You can also right-click over the appointment you want to print and then choose Print from the pop-up menu, or press Ctrl+P on your keyboard.

2. From the Style list box, select the icon representing the print style you want to use.

Note

If you choose the Day List or Day List by Sections styles, the Appointment Details option is enabled in the Print dialog box. Select this option to print appointment details along with the appointments.

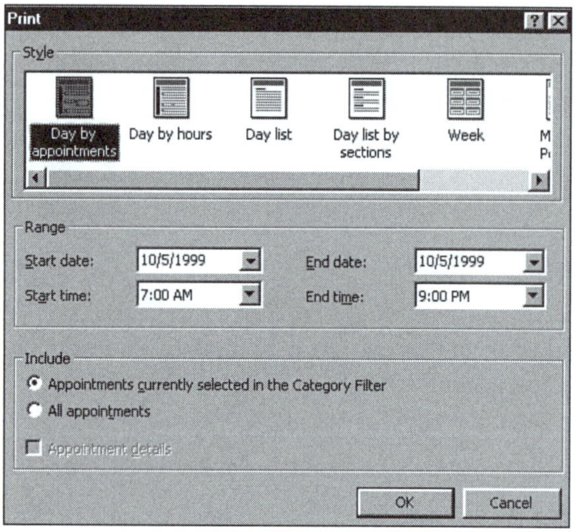

Figure 8.28
Use the Print dialog box to specify which part of the schedule to print and a print style to use.

3. From the Range options, select the date or date range to print and, if applicable, the hours.

   Depending on which style you selected in step 2, the range options can vary. For example, if you select the Day List style, you can choose a Start Date and End Date. If you select the Day by Hours style, you can choose both starting and ending dates and times.
4. To print all the appointments, leave All Appointments selected. To print only the categorized appointments shown in the Category Filter, choose the Appointments Currently Selected in the Category Filter option.
5. Click OK. A second Print dialog box appears, as shown in Figure 8.29.

Tip #52 from
Faithe Wempen

If you chose to print Month - Landscape in step 2, click the Properties button in the second Print dialog box (see Figure 8.29), and change the page orientation to Landscape.

6. If necessary, select the printer to use from the Name drop-down list.
7. Enter the number of copies you want in the Number of Copies box.
8. Click OK to start printing.

Emailing Your Appointments

Here's a convenient idea—if you do a lot of emailing, you can email your schedule to someone else. If you've installed Internet Explorer and have a modem and an Internet account, you're ready to go. (Learn all about using Outlook Express to send email in Chapter 20, "Working with Email and Newsgroups.") You must log on to your Internet connection to send the schedule.

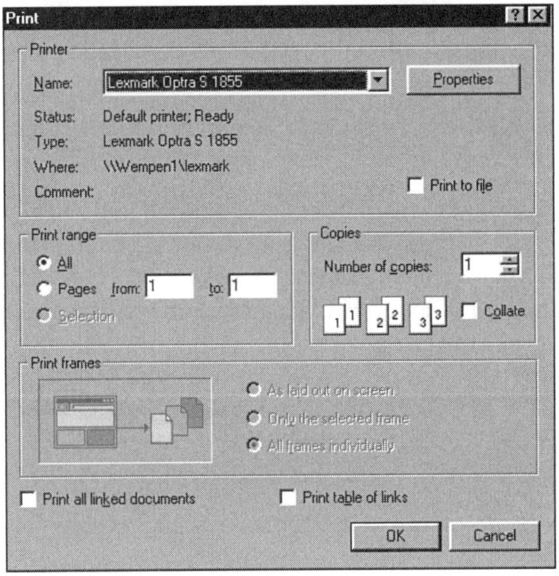

Figure 8.29
Choose a printer and the number of copies.

To send your schedule as an email message, choose File, Send. The Send to E-Mail dialog box opens (see Figure 8.30). It's very similar to the Print dialog box, in Figure 8.28. Like the Print dialog box, you can choose from several styles. Instead of seven, you're limited to three styles, all of which are based on Works Calendar's views:

- **Day List**—Presents your daily schedule of appointments as a list
- **Week List**—A weekly view of your schedule
- **Month List**—The Month view of your calendar

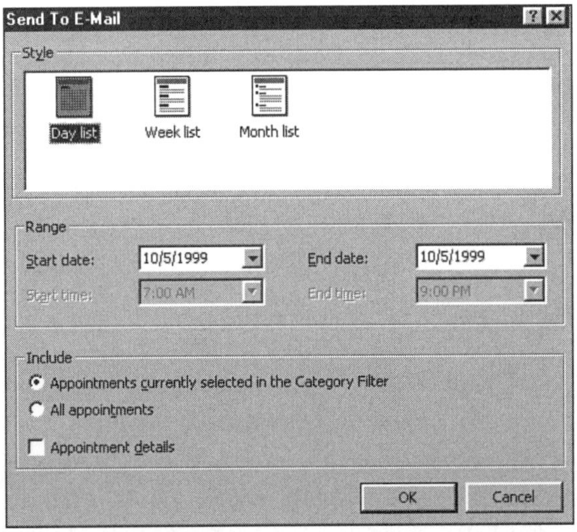

Figure 8.30
The Send to E-Mail dialog box looks familiar—it's a slightly altered version of the Print dialog box.

Depending on the style you select, the options in the Range area of the dialog box can differ. Use the range options to specify a date and time range for the schedule, just as you did in the Print dialog box.

Choose a range and a page style, just as you did in the preceding section when printing. Then click OK. This opens Outlook Express and the New Message window.

In the Outlook Express window (see Figure 8.31), you will notice that there are two attachments: Calendar.htm and Calendar.vcs. The .vcs version is in a format specific to the Works Calendar program. If your intended recipient uses the Works Calendar, he will be able to open this file. The .htm version is an HTML document, which the recipient can use if he does not have the Works Calendar program.

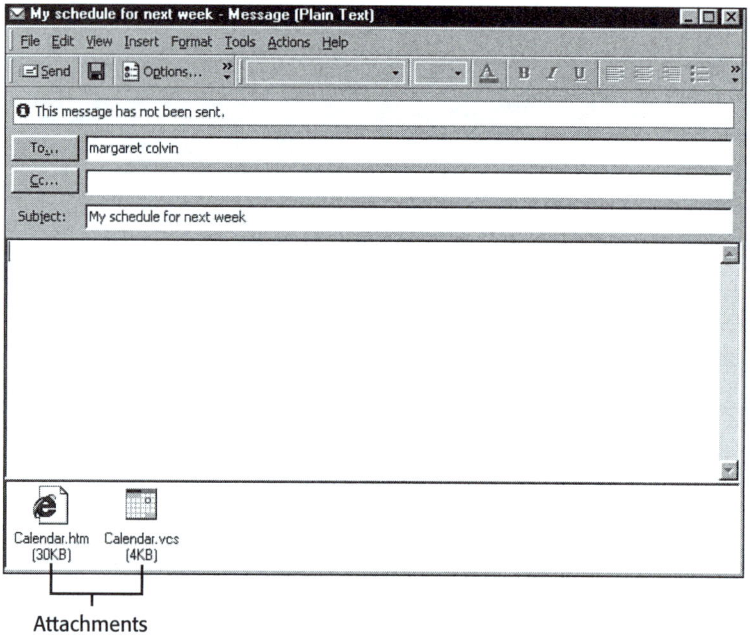

Figure 8.31
This message in Outlook Express contains two attachments.

Compose the email message normally (refer to Chapter 20 for help, if necessary), and then click Send to send it.

TROUBLESHOOTING

SUPPRESSING THE HELP PANE

The Help pane appears every time I start, and I'd like to get rid of it.

If you don't want the Works Help pane to appear each time you start the program, make sure the Help pane is closed when you exit the program. When you start the program, the Help window will be in whatever state you left it when you exited (displayed or hidden).

MORE CALENDAR HELP

I'm looking for help with the Calendar program, but I can't find much in Works Suite Help.

If you need more help with the Calendar than the Help system can provide, try browsing the Works online help on the Internet. To do so, choose Help, Microsoft on the Web, Microsoft Works Home Page.

SUPPRESSING REMINDERS

I scheduled a reminder for an appointment, but now I've decided that I don't want to be reminded after all. Is there an easy way to turn it off?

If you have set a reminder for an appointment, but you have changed your mind about it and want to turn it off, you don't necessarily have to locate the appointment on the calendar. Just click the Reminders button on the toolbar to open the list of active reminders, and use Dismiss Item on it.

IMPROVING CALENDAR PRINTOUTS

I've printed my calendar, but the printout could stand some improvement.

If you are not happy with the printout of your calendar, try importing it into Home Publishing. To do so, display the calendar, and then click the Launch Microsoft Home Publishing button on the toolbar. Home Publishing opens and begins creating a graphical calendar based on the data from your Works calendar. Chapter 26, "Using Microsoft Home Publishing," deals with Microsoft Home Publishing; turn there if you need more information.

PART II

USING WORD

CHAPTER 9

Getting Started with Word

In this chapter

How Word Fits into the Works Suite

Microsoft Word is the most popular and most powerful word processor program around today. Use it to create all kinds of text-based documents, including memos, newsletters, reports, Web pages, and more. In addition to text, you can add graphics and special effects, create columns and tables, and swap data with other programs. There's no end to the type of documents you can create in Word; whether you're using the program at work or at home, you can quickly put its numerous features to work for you.

Word does everything that the Works Word Processor does, and much more. That's why if you bought the Works Suite 2000 package, rather than the standalone Works program, Word replaced the Works Word Processor in the Task Launcher. This book spends several chapters on Word because it is the most popular component in Works Suite, and the one that you will likely spend the most time using.

Starting a Word Document

To start Word 2000, choose Start, Programs, Microsoft Word. Word opens and automatically creates a new, blank document with the generic name Document1 (see Figure 9.1). At this point, you can simply start typing to begin creating a document. You can also begin any of a variety of special projects through the tasks in the Task Launcher, as you learned in Chapter 1, "Introducing the Microsoft Works Suite."

Note

The first time you start Word, the Office Assistant (a paperclip, by default) appears, asking if you need any help. Click the Start Using Microsoft Word option to go on.

Familiarize yourself with these screen elements:

- **Insertion point**—The flashing vertical line shows where text you type will go.
- **Mouse pointer**—When in the document window, the mouse pointer is an I-beam with a representation of the current alignment (Left, in Figure 9.1).
- **Standard toolbar**—These buttons offer quick shortcuts to some of Word's most commonly used commands. To activate a command, click on the appropriate button.
- **Formatting toolbar**—Word's most popular formatting commands are available as shortcuts on this toolbar.
- **Ruler**—Use this element to set margins and tabs and to see how your text lines up in the document.
- **Document window**—The document window holds the text you type.

Note

To quickly find out the name of any toolbar button, hover your mouse pointer over the button, and a ScreenTip appears with the button's name.

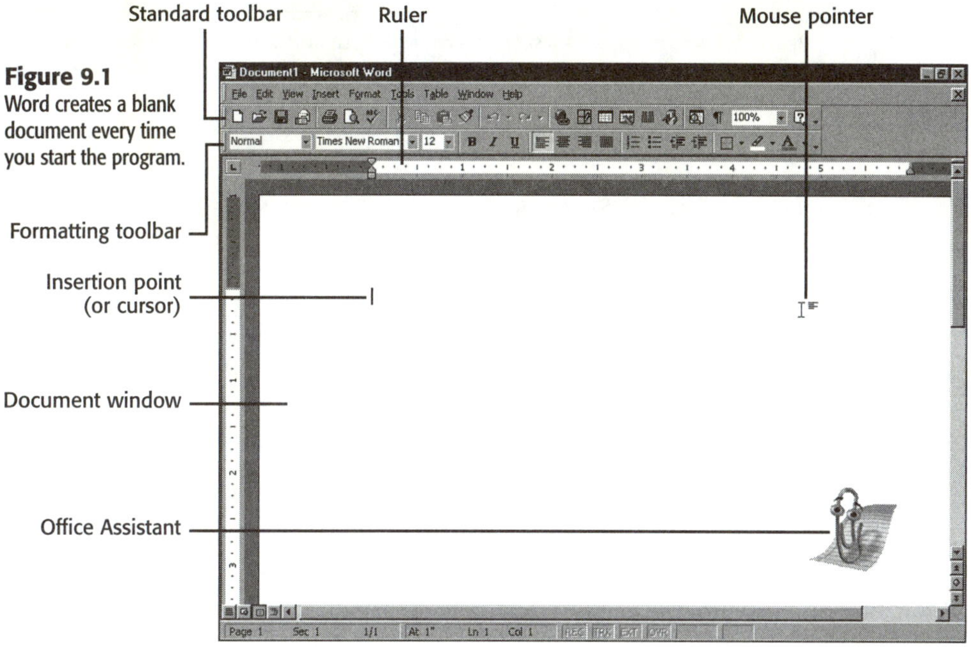

Figure 9.1
Word creates a blank document every time you start the program.

To turn off the Office Assistant, right-click it and choose Hide. To display it again, click the Help button on the Standard toolbar.

CREATING A NEW DOCUMENT

When you start Word, it automatically starts a blank document for you. Go ahead and use it.

If you later want another blank page, use one of the following techniques:

- Click the New button.
- Press Ctrl+N.
- Choose File, New, Blank Document.

When you use any of these techniques, the new document you create looks like a blank sheet of paper. Although no text appears on the page, your new document is actually based on the Normal document template, which is contained in a file called Normal.dot.

The Normal document template is a tremendously important part of Word. Settings stored here define the basic look of every new document you create. Table 9.1 lists the basic settings for Normal.dot.

Tip #53 from *Faithe Wempen*

Remember, you can use the Tasks in the Works Task Launcher to create a variety of documents using Word. You can also choose File, New, More Word Templates to see additional templates that come with Word.

Table 9.1 Document Options Saved in the Normal Document Template

Document Option	Default Setting
Default margins	1 inch at top and bottom of page, 1.25 inches on each side
Default paper size and orientation	In the United States, Word uses 8.5×11-inch (Letter) paper in portrait orientation
Default font and font size	10-point Times New Roman
Default paragraph spacing	Single-spaced
Styles	More than 90 built-in paragraph and character styles for specifying the look of text, lists, headings, and so on

Using Ready-Made Templates

Word's templates offer great head starts for creating common document types such as reports, letters, faxes, résumés, and much more. If a template exists for the kind of document you want, you can really save some time by using it. (The downside is that the template has many of the decisions made already, such as font and spacing, so you have less creative freedom.)

There are two ways to start a template. One is to use one of the Tasks in the Task Launcher, as you learned in Chapter 1. The other is to use a template directly from Word, as in the following steps:

1. Choose File, New, More Word Templates. The New dialog box appears with tabs for the various kinds of templates available.
2. Click a tab to look at the templates available in each category. Then click a template icon to see a preview in the Preview box (see Figure 9.2).
3. When you find the one you want, click OK to open it.

Note

The New dialog box has two different types of icons. The wizards have magic wands on their icons; the templates don't. You learn about wizards in the following section.

In some templates, generic text is formatted using Word fields, which enables you to click to select the entire block of text and then type to replace it. In other cases, such as the company name at the top of the Contemporary Letter template (see Figure 9.3), you have to use the mouse to select the sample text and then replace it before you can use the document.

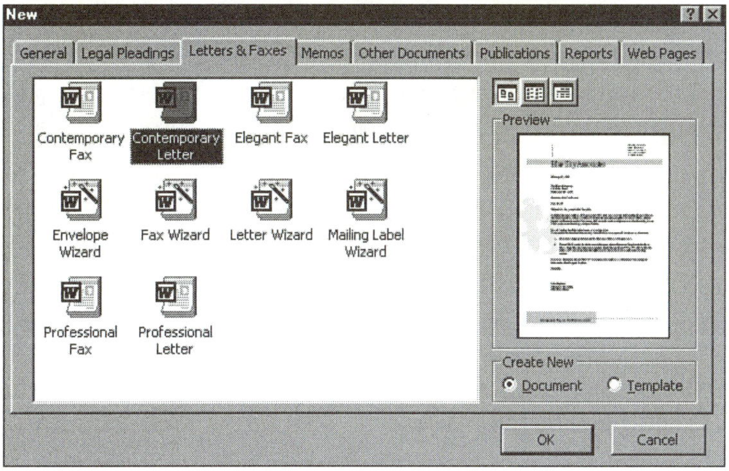

Figure 9.2
Pick a template from this dialog box.

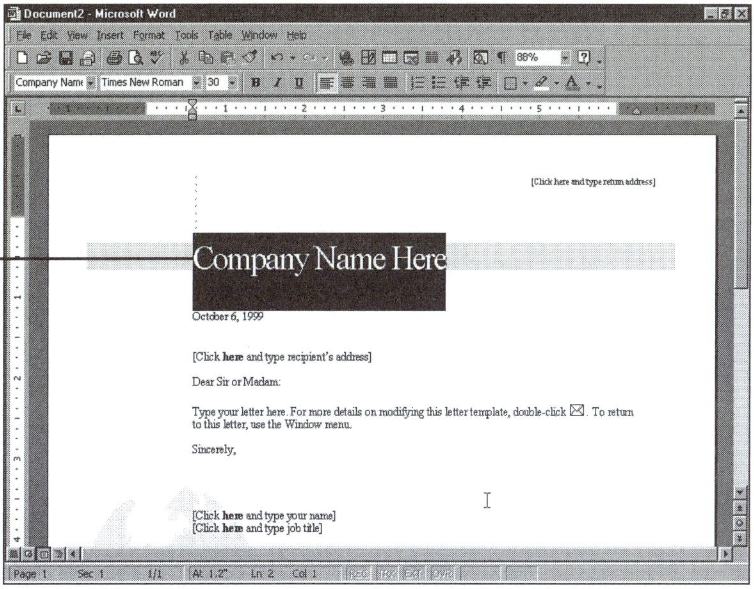

Figure 9.3
Select the "generic" text in a document template; it disappears as soon as you start typing.

Caution

Whenever you use a document template for the first time, check the results carefully. Nothing is more embarrassing than sending a fax cover sheet that identifies you as an employee of *Company Name Here*.

➔ If you use a particular template regularly and you want instructions on customizing it for your own use, **see** "Customizing Word Templates," **p. 250**.

USING A WIZARD TO CREATE A NEW DOCUMENT

Word 2000 offers a total of ten wizards. These choices appear in the New dialog box mixed in with the regular document templates; you can tell a wizard at a glance by its name (which invariably includes the word *Wizard*) and its distinctive icon (which includes a magic wand).

The wizards can be a great help, especially if you are unfamiliar with the type of conventions for the document that you need to create. For example, the Letter Wizard produces and formats a letter in your choice of three styles. The Fax Wizard creates a cover sheet that you can fax through a fax-modem or print out to use with a regular fax machine.

To use a wizard, double-click it in the New dialog box and then follow the prompts. Most Word wizards include easy-to-follow help. Choose options or fill in information on each of the wizard's dialog boxes, as in the Fax Wizard shown in Figure 9.4. Use the Next button as you complete each step and click Finish when you're done.

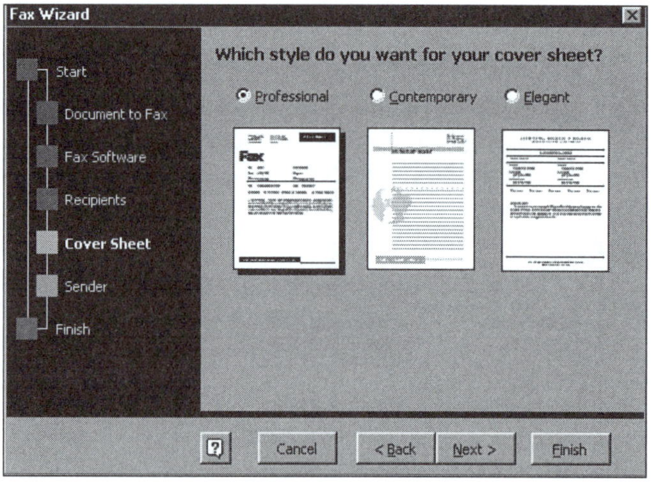

Figure 9.4
Wizards let you build a document by entering your own data or selecting from a number of customizing options.

→ You will want to save your work in Word; **see** "Saving Your Work," **p. 34**.

→ To open a saved document, **see** "Opening Files in Word," **p. 34**.

MOVING THE INSERTION POINT

When you open a new document based on the Normal document template, just start typing. The insertion point marks the spot where your characters appear when you start typing. It moves as you type.

To move the insertion point into existing text, so you can make a correction or an addition, click there. Clicking the mouse pointer moves the insertion point.

If there is no existing text where you clicked (for example, it is below the end of the document), the insertion point won't move there. However, you can *double-click* to place the insertion point *anywhere*, even outside the existing document area.

➔ To find out how to modify the settings listed in Table 9.1, **see** "Customizing Word Templates," **p. 250**.

CHOOSING THE RIGHT DOCUMENT VIEW

Word lets you choose one of four distinct views when you're creating or editing a document. Which view should you choose? The answer depends on what you're trying to do. Are you concentrating on writing? Trying to make your document look great? Organizing your thoughts? Word has a special view for each step in the writing process, as described in the following sections.

Word's viewing options are all available on the View menu. You can also switch between Normal, Web Layout, Print Layout, and Outline views using the four buttons in the lower-left corner of the document window (see Figure 9.5). Hover the mouse pointer over each button to identify it.

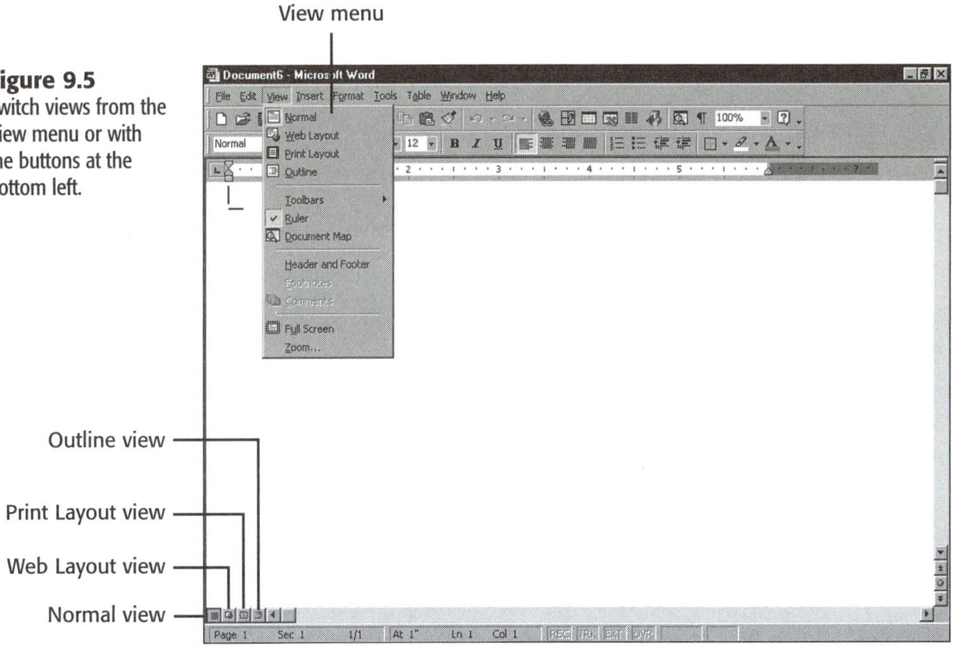

Figure 9.5
Switch views from the View menu or with the buttons at the bottom left.

Three of these views (Normal, Page Layout, and Outline) are suitable for working with a variety of documents. I'll explain them in the following sections. The fourth view, Web Layout, is a specialized view for working with Web content; you'll use it in Chapter 15, "Creating Web Pages with Word."

USING NORMAL VIEW

Normal view is perfect for when you just want to get the words out of your head, and you aren't concerned about exactly how they'll look when printed. Normal view shows you all text formatting, graphics, and other objects on the page; you see placeholders where page breaks, margins, columns, and other page layout options should appear. Figure 9.6 shows this simplified view of a document.

Figure 9.6
Normal view uses the entire window to display your document. It's perfect for quickly typing a first draft.

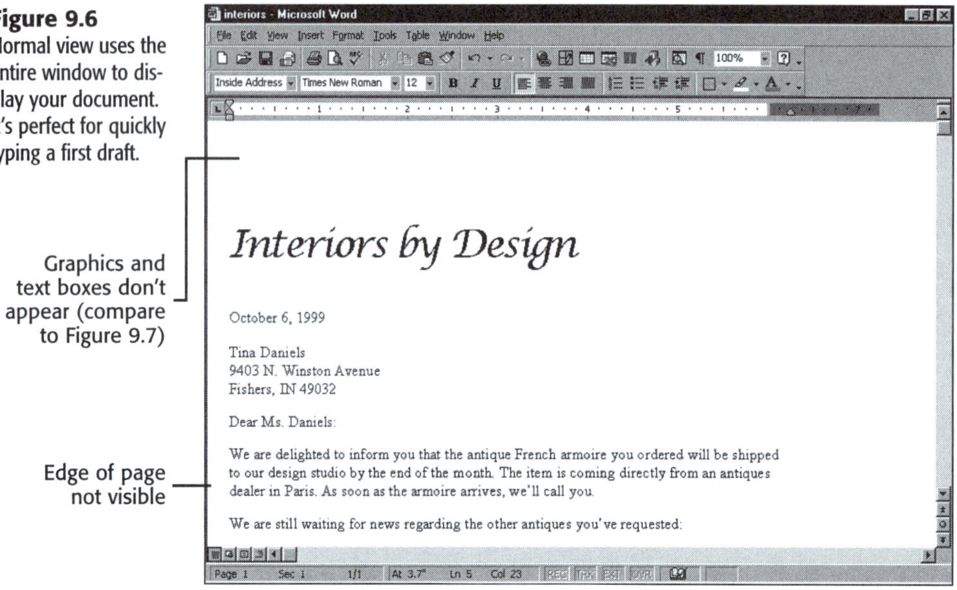

Using Page Layout View

When you select Page Layout view, you can see how much space is available in the margins on each side of the page. As you scroll through your document, you can see the bottom and top margins of each page as well. If you've put page numbers or a title on the page, they are visible too. Page Layout view is particularly appropriate for tasks that involve fine formatting and precise placement of headers, footers, graphics, text boxes, and other screen elements. Figure 9.7 shows what you see when you choose this view.

Tip #54 from *Faithe Wempen*

If toolbars, rulers, and other screen elements are too distracting, choose View, Full Screen. In this view, all you typically see is the document itself and a simple toolbar with one button; all other toolbars, menus, and screen elements, including the Windows taskbar, disappear. Click the Close Full Screen button to switch back to the regular program window.

Using Outline View

Outline view is ideal for making sure that your thoughts are well organized. When you use Word's built-in heading styles, you can switch to Outline view and collapse your document to see just its main points. The Outlining toolbar helps you collapse and expand each section (see Figure 9.8).

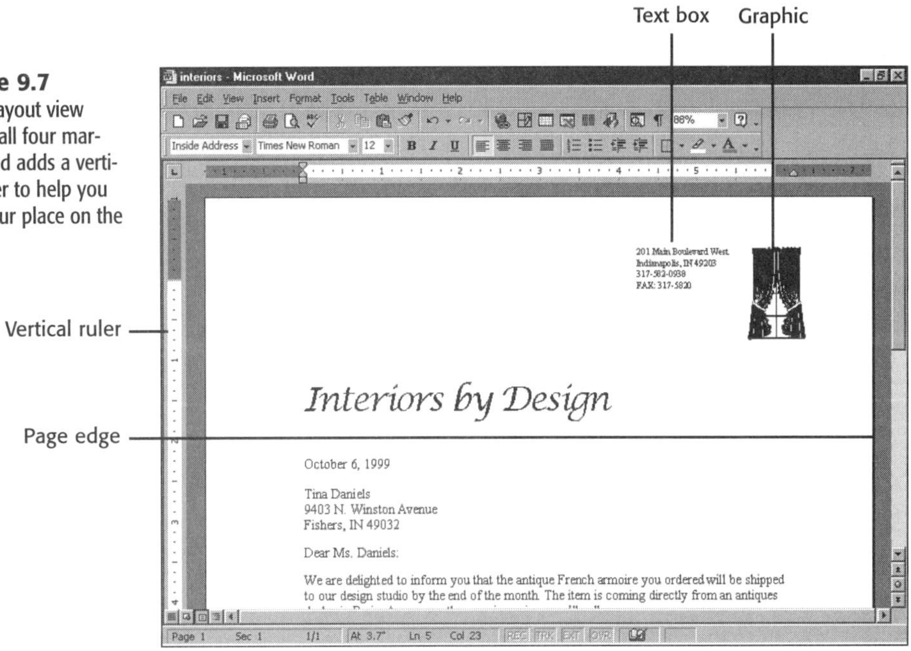

Figure 9.7
Page Layout view shows all four margins and adds a vertical ruler to help you find your place on the page.

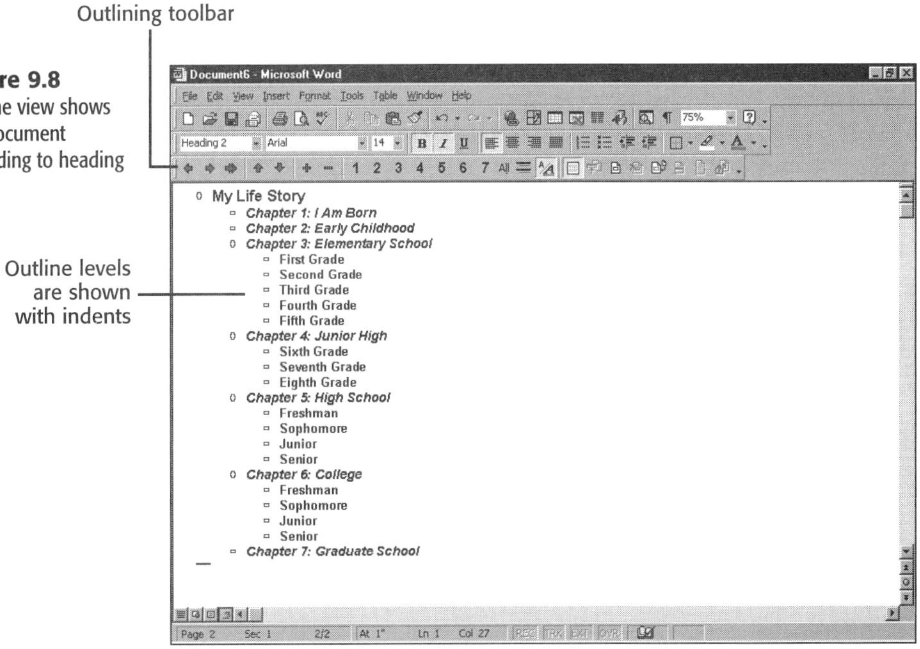

Figure 9.8
Outline view shows the document according to heading level.

ZOOMING THE DISPLAY

Regardless of which view you've selected, you can increase or decrease the size of the document displayed on the screen. Zooming in makes it easier to read or edit text when the words on the screen are too small to read easily. Zooming out lets you see the overall design of the page. Zoom does *not* affect the size at which the document will print.

Use the Zoom drop-down list on the Standard toolbar, shown in Figure 9.9, to choose a predefined magnification from 10 to 500 percent of normal size. Choose Page Width to expand the text so that it's as large as possible without running off the edge of the screen. Try Whole Page to fit the entire page on the screen, or Two Pages for a side-by-side view. (Those two options are available only from Print Layout view.) To see more Zoom options, choose View, Zoom.

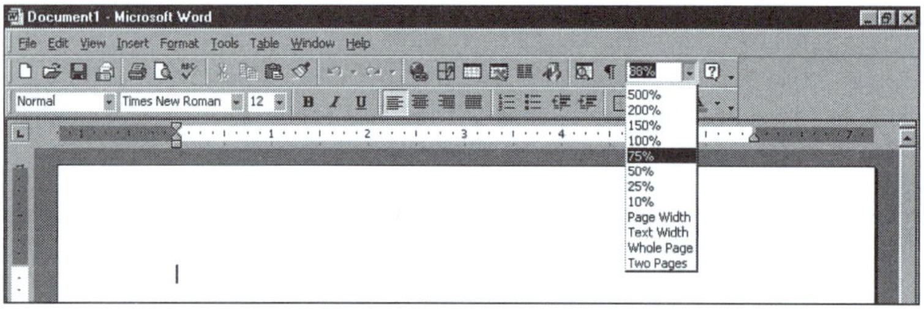

Figure 9.9
Select a Zoom percentage to zoom in or out on your document.

MOVING AROUND IN A WORD DOCUMENT

Knowing the right navigation shortcuts can dramatically increase your productivity as you edit in Word. Instead of using arrow keys to move at a snail's pace through your document, mouse and keyboard shortcuts can help you move to the precise point where you want to be.

When you're editing text, the fastest way to move through the document is with the help of the keyboard shortcuts shown in Table 9.2.

TABLE 9.2 MOVING THROUGH A DOCUMENT USING THE KEYBOARD

To Do This	Press This Key Combination
Move to the beginning or end of the current line	Home or End
Move one word to the right or left, respectively	Ctrl+Right arrow or Ctrl+Left arrow
Move to the previous or next paragraph, respectively	Ctrl+Up arrow or Ctrl+Down arrow
Move up or down one window	PgUp or PgDn
Jump to the top or bottom of the documentd	Ctrl+Home or Ctrl+End

An additional keyboard shortcut is worth noting. Shift+F5 is one of my all-time favorites. When you press this key combination, Word cycles the insertion point through the last three places where you entered or edited text. Use this cool shortcut if you've scrolled through a long document, and you want to jump back quickly to the place where you started.

You can also move with the mouse using the scrollbars, of course, just like in any other Windows program. You can click above or below the scroll box to move one screen in that direction. Click the arrows at the ends of the scroll bar to move slightly in one direction or the other, or drag the scroll box to move quickly. As you drag the scroll box, a note appears telling you what page you're on, and in some views even what heading you'll find there (see Figure 9.10).

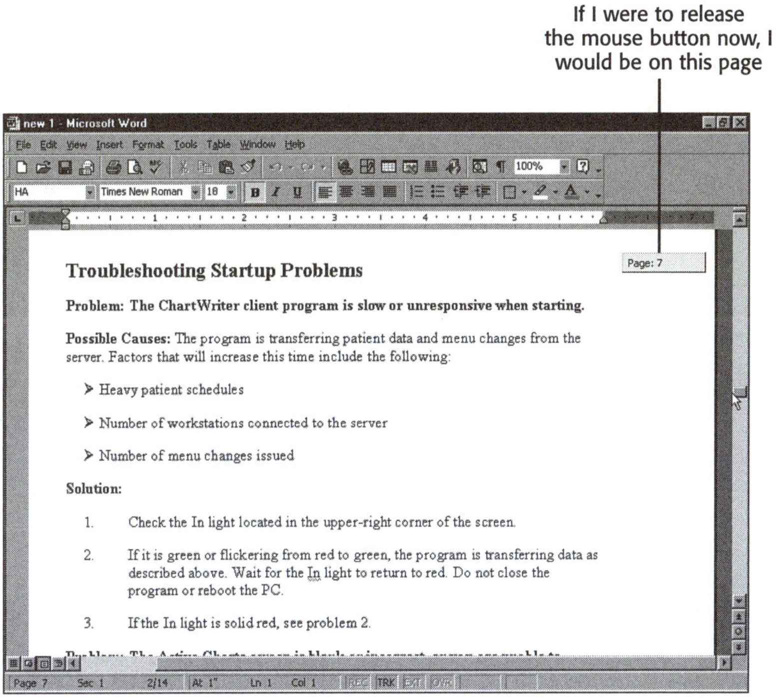

Figure 9.10
As you drag the scroll box, Word tells you what page you're on.

SELECTING TEXT IN WORD

Before you can move, copy, delete, or reformat text, you first have to select it. (You can tell when text has been selected because it appears in a dark bar, with white letters on a black background.) Selecting text using the mouse is easiest, but if you prefer to keep your hands on the keyboard, you can find plenty of shortcuts.

SELECTING TEXT USING THE MOUSE

Word enables you to use an assortment of mouse techniques to select chunks of text, as shown in Table 9.3.

TABLE 9.3 MOUSE TECHNIQUES FOR SELECTING TEXT

To Select	Do This
A word	Point to the word and double-click.
A sentence	Point to the sentence and triple-click, or hold down the Ctrl key, point to the sentence, and click.
A paragraph	Point in the margin to the left of the paragraph; when the mouse pointer turns into an arrow, double-click.
A whole document	Move the mouse pointer to the left margin until it turns into an arrow and then triple-click.

You don't have to be precise to select an entire word using the mouse. Aim the mouse pointer anywhere within a word; as you drag the pointer left or right, the selection changes to include each new word. Most of the time, that's the correct action because you typically want to move, copy, or format an entire word rather than a few characters within a word.

What if you really want to select the end of one word and the beginning of another? To override automatic word selection temporarily, hold down the Ctrl and Shift keys as you drag the selection.

Tip #55 from *Faithe Wempen*

If automatic word selection bugs you, you can easily disable this feature. Choose Tools, Options, click the Edit tab, and remove the check mark next to the box labeled When Selecting, Automatically Select Entire Word. Click OK to exit the dialog box.

SELECTING TEXT USING THE KEYBOARD

If you're a speedy typist, nothing slows down your productivity more than having to take your fingers off the keyboard, find the mouse, click to select a block, and then move back to the keys. Every touch typist should learn to select text using the keyboard shortcuts; in most cases, you can hold down the Shift key while you use the same shortcuts that you use to move through a document. Table 9.4 lists these techniques.

TABLE 9.4 KEYBOARD SELECTION TECHNIQUES

To Select	Do This
One or more characters	Hold down the Shift key as you press the left- or right-arrow keys one or more times.
A word	Move the insertion point to the beginning of the word; then press Ctrl+Shift+Right arrow.

To Select	Do This
To the beginning or end of the line	Press Shift+Home or Shift+End.
To the beginning or end of the paragraph	Press Ctrl+Shift+Up arrow or Ctrl+Shift+Down arrow.
To the beginning or end of the document	Press Ctrl+Shift+Home or Ctrl+Shift+End.
The whole document	Press Ctrl+A.

My favorite keyboard shortcut lets you quickly select a word, a sentence, a paragraph, or the whole document. Just move the insertion point where you want to begin selecting and then press the F8 key to turn on Extend Selection mode. (To see an onscreen reminder that you've turned on this feature, look in the center of the status bar at the bottom of the document window. If you see the letters EXT, Extend Selection mode is on.)

After you've pressed F8, you can press any key to extend the selection. If you press the period key, for example, Word extends the selection to the next period, which is usually the end of the sentence. Press the period key again to select to the end of the next sentence.

After pressing F8 the first time, you can extend the selection farther. Press F8 a second time to select a whole word, a third time to select the entire sentence, a fourth time for the current paragraph, and a fifth time to select your entire document. To exit Extend Selection mode, press the Esc key. To deselect your selection, move any arrow key.

Tip #56 from *Faithe Wempen*

If you inadvertently press any character on the keyboard, including the Spacebar, whatever you type replaces whatever is currently selected. To bring back the original selection, click the Undo button or press Ctrl+Z.

Entering and Deleting Text

When you start a new document, all you have to do is type. Don't press Enter to start a new line; Word does that for you automatically. Press Enter only when you are ready to start a new paragraph. If you make a mistake, back up using the Backspace key. (If you make a big mistake, or need to back up a long way, see the editing suggestions later in this section.)

Note

How many times has your finger slipped as you struck the Shift or Tab key, accidentally pressing the Caps Lock key and producing text like the preceding headline? Touch typists can go for a paragraph or even a full page before they notice that all the text has been entered incorrectly. Word 2000 is smart enough to detect when Caps Lock comes on inappropriately, automatically undoing the scrambled text and restoring Caps Lock to its correct setting.

Replacing Text as You Type

Normally, Word lets you enter text in *Insert mode*—whatever you enter pushes any existing text out of the way to make room. Pressing the Insert key, deliberately or inadvertently, toggles into *Overtype* mode, in which each new character you type replaces the character immediately to its right. Be careful! When you press the Insert key by accident, you can wipe out massive amounts of work before you even realize anything is wrong.

Word offers a subtle clue that tells you when you've shifted from Insert to Overtype mode. In the center of the status bar at the bottom of the document window are five small indicator boxes. If the letters OVR are visible, you've switched into Overtype mode. Press the Insert key to switch back to Insert mode.

Tip #57 from *Faithe Wempen*

If you regularly find yourself accidentally shifting into Overtype mode, you can disable the Insert key's capability to switch into it by choosing Tools, Options, and then clicking the Edit tab. Click the Use the INS Key for Paste check box; then click OK to exit. This reassigns the mission of the Insert key, so that it no longer toggles between Overtype and Insert mode.

Deleting Text

Keyboard shortcuts offer the fastest way to get rid of text. Touch typists should memorize the key combinations shown in Table 9.5.

Table 9.5 Keyboard Shortcuts

To Perform This Action	Use This Key or Combination
Delete the current selection; if no text is selected, delete the character to the left of the insertion point	Backspace
Delete the current selection; if no text is selected, delete the character to the right of the insertion point	Del
Delete the word to the left of the insertion point or selection	Ctrl+Backspace
Delete the word to the right of the insertion point or selection	Ctrl+Del
Cut the currently selected text and put it on the Clipboard	Ctrl+X

Adding Symbols and Special Characters

If you use the standard U.S. keyboard layout, you can find all the letters of the alphabet, the numbers 0 through 9, and most punctuation marks on the keyboard. Often, however, you may want to enter characters that aren't available on the keyboard: accented characters from foreign alphabets, currency symbols other than the dollar sign, or copyright and trademark indicators.

If a character is not on the standard keyboard, Word considers it a symbol or a special character. To insert one, follow these steps:

1. Position the insertion point where you want the symbol or special character to appear.
2. Choose Insert, Symbol to open the Symbol dialog box.
3. Click the Special Characters tab in the dialog box and choose from some commonly used special characters (such as copyright symbols and foreign currency symbols) as shown in Figure 9.11. If you see the symbol you want to insert there, double-click it, and you're finished. If not, go on to the next step.

Figure 9.11
The Special Characters tab contains many of the most popular symbols that users need to insert.

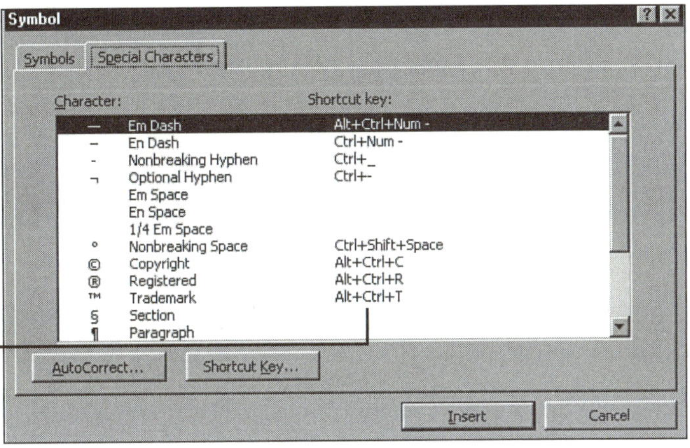

Some characters have shortcut keys.

Tip #58 from *Faithe Wempen*

If you regularly use any of these special characters, memorize the keyboard shortcut listed to its right on the Special Characters tab.

4. Click the Symbols tab to display the full list of characters in the currently displayed font. These include not only the characters available from the keyboard but also some special ones, such as vowels with accent marks over them for foreign spellings (see Figure 9.12).
5. If needed, click a character to enlarge it so that you can see it better. If you do not see the character you want, try choosing a different font from the Font drop-down list.
6. When you find the character you want to insert, double-click it to place it in your document, or click once on it and then click Insert.
7. Click the Close button to close the dialog box.

Tip #59 from *Faithe Wempen*

Word's AutoCorrect feature lets you enter some special symbols directly from the keyboard. If you type `(tm)` or `(r)`, for example, Word automatically changes the entry to the trademark (™) or registered trademark (®) symbols. To see other such AutoText characters, choose Tools, AutoCorrect, and click the AutoCorrect tab. There, you can find smileys, "frownies," and "who cares" faces, as well as some lines and arrows. You learn more about this feature in Chapter 12, "Correcting and Polishing Your Document."

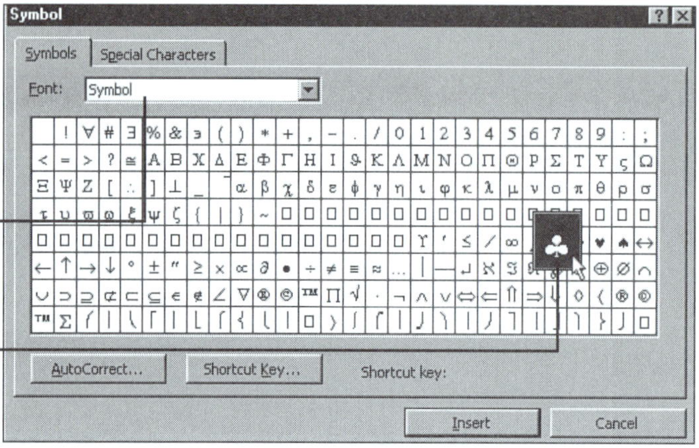

Figure 9.12
The Symbols tab lets you select any character from any font installed on your system.

Select a different font if desired.

Click on a symbol to view it enlarged.

Undoing (and Redoing) What You've Done

What happens when you inadvertently delete an important part of your document? Relax. You can put everything back the way it was by using Word's Undo button on the Standard toolbar. Click once to undo your last action. Keep clicking, and the Undo button rolls back as many as your last 100 actions.

If you know you want to undo a lengthy sequence of actions, click the arrow at the right of the Undo button and then scroll through the drop-down list of steps Word can undo for you (see Figure 9.13). If you click the fourth step in the list, for example, Word automatically undoes the last four actions in a single motion.

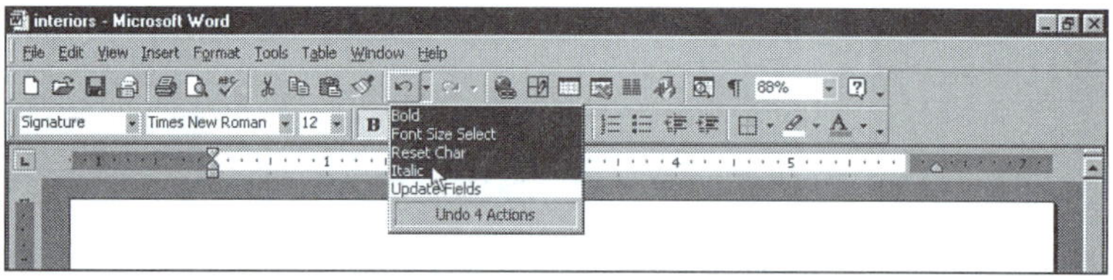

Figure 9.13
Word's Undo key can reverse the effects of 1, 50, or even 100 recent keystrokes and mouse clicks.

Use the matching Redo button or its keyboard shortcut Ctrl+Y when you change your mind after using the Undo button. In combination, the two buttons can let you restore a chunk of text you deleted earlier in the current session, without losing other changes you've made since then. Use the Undo button to roll back your changes until the deleted text is visible again. Select the text, copy it to the Clipboard, and then use the Redo button to return to the most recent version of the document.

Finding and Replacing

The longer and more complex a document is, the more likely you'll need Word's help to find a specific section of the document. Have you used the same phrase too many times in the current document? Have you misspelled the name of a person or company? Where is the section that talks about second-quarter budget results?

To answer any of these questions, use Word's Find and Replace feature. Day in and day out, it is probably the most valuable Word editing tool you can master.

FINDING TEXT

You can easily find a word or phrase anywhere in your document by using Word's Find feature. Here's how it works:

1. Choose Edit, Find or press Ctrl+F. The Find and Replace dialog box appears, shown in Figure 9.14.

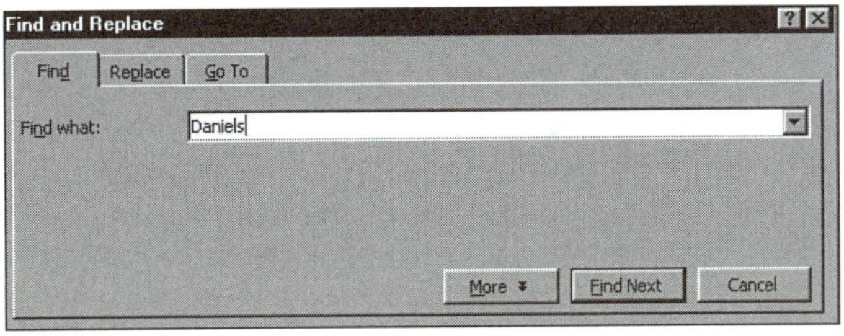

Figure 9.14
The Find and Replace dialog box lets you search for a word or phrase anywhere in your document.

2. Click in the Find What box and type the text for which you want to search—a word, name, phrase, or complete sentence.
3. Click the Find Next button to jump to the first occurrence of the text you entered.
4. Keep clicking the Find Next button to jump to each successive location in the document where the selected text appears.
5. Press Esc or click the Cancel button to close the Find and Replace dialog box.

Normally, Word ignores the case of the text you enter in the Find What box. If you want to restrict the search further, click the More button and select one or more of the check boxes in the bottom of the dialog box. Turning on the Match Case option, for example, forces Word to distinguish between upper- and lowercase letters. Right-click and choose What's This? for a brief description of how you can use these options.

REPLACING TEXT

If you can find a piece of text, you can change it. That capability comes in handy if you've written a lengthy pitch for Acme Corporation and then discover the company's legal name is actually Acme Industries, Inc. Instead of searching through your document and painstakingly retyping the name each time it appears, let Word replace the existing text with the new text you specify.

Replacing takes place from the Replace tab of the Find and Replace dialog box, so if that dialog box is already open, you can click that tab to switch to those controls.

1. If the Find and Replace dialog box is visible, click the Replace tab. If this dialog box is not visible, choose Edit, Replace or press Ctrl+H.
2. Type the text you want to search for in the Find What box; type the replacement text in the box labeled Replace With. The dialog box should look like the one in Figure 9.15.
3. Click the Find Next button to jump to the first occurrence of the text you specified.
4. To replace the text in that location, click the Replace button. Word makes the substitution and moves on to the next spot where the search text appears.
5. To find the next occurrence of the search text without changing the current selection, click the Find Next button.
6. To change every occurrence of the selected text automatically, click Replace All.
7. Press Esc or click Cancel to close the Find and Replace dialog box.

Figure 9.15
Use the Find and Replace dialog box to substitute one word or phrase for another automatically.

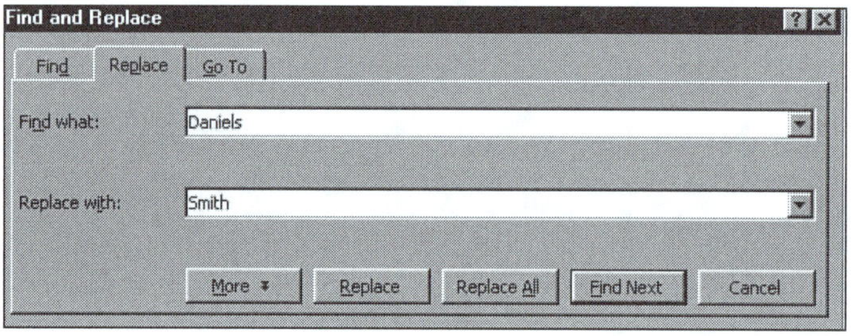

Tip #60 from
Faithe Wempen

With the Find and Replace dialog box, you don't need to close it to resume editing your document. Leave the dialog box open if you want, and click in the document editing window to add a new sentence or make another change. Click in the dialog box to resume working with it.

Finding and Replacing Formatting and Special Characters

Sometimes you might want to search for (and replace) more than just text. For example, I might want to open a document, find every place where I've used Bold Italic, and change that formatting to Bold Underline. Or, if I've received a document that someone else formatted, I might want to remove all manual page breaks that were inserted.

Two buttons at the bottom of the Find and Replace dialog box (the Format and Special buttons) let you expand the scope of a Word search. (If you don't see these buttons, click the More button to display the additional dialog box controls.) Use these buttons to search for formatting (including fonts and styles) or special characters (such as tabs and paragraph marks). You can combine these attributes, searching for a specific word or phrase that matches the formatting you specify.

After assigning any formatting or special characters as part of the search, look just underneath the Find What and Replace With text boxes to see the selected formatting. To remove formatting, click the No Formatting button.

ADDING HEADERS, FOOTERS, AND PAGE NUMBERS

Page numbers, chapter titles, and section names help readers understand how a document is organized. You can add these and other milestones to long Word documents, enabling readers to find their way more easily around the printed page.

When this sort of information is at the top of the page, it's called a *header*; at the bottom of the page, it's a *footer*. You can put just about anything in a header or footer, but most often you use these spaces for information such as titles, page numbers, dates, and labels (such as "Confidential" or "Draft"). Usually, you don't need to add these details to short documents such as letters and memos or to documents that you expect will be read online.

WORKING WITH HEADERS AND FOOTERS

Word's default document includes space for a header and footer 1/2 inch from the top and bottom of each page. Before you can add text or graphics to a header or footer, you first have to make these editing boxes visible. Choose View, Header and Footer (see Figure 9.16). Word switches to Page Layout view, if necessary.

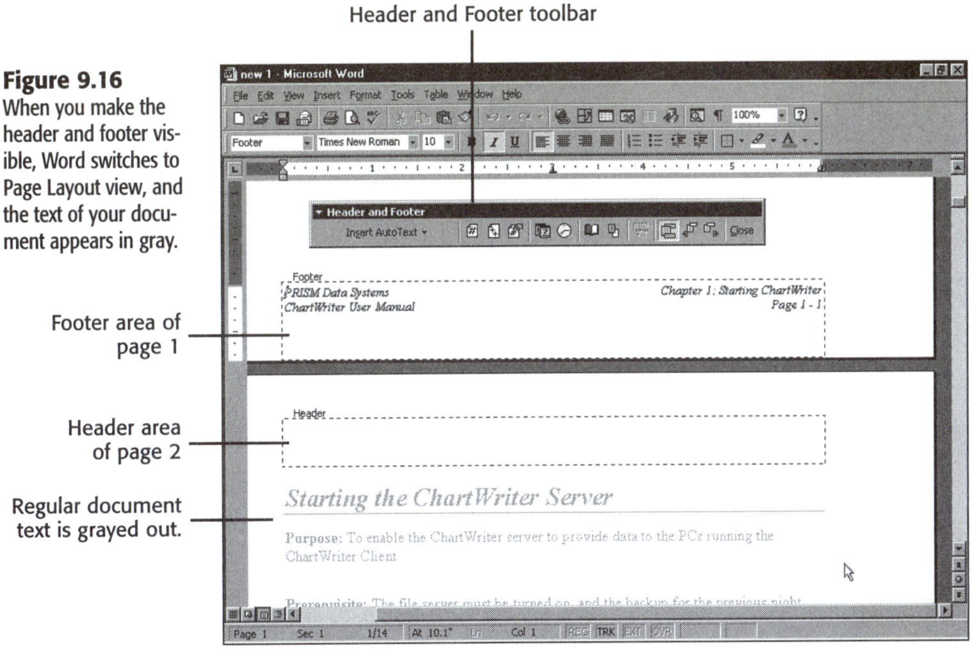

Figure 9.16
When you make the header and footer visible, Word switches to Page Layout view, and the text of your document appears in gray.

You can enter any type of data in a header or footer box, including text, text boxes, drawings, pictures, tables, and hyperlinks. You can also change typefaces and sizes, realign text, and adjust the space between the header or footer and the body of your document.

While you work, the Header and Footer toolbar floats nearby with buttons you can use to navigate through your document or to insert page numbers, dates, and other information. Table 9.6 shows the buttons that are useful for working with headers and footers.

TABLE 9.6 BUTTONS ON THE HEADER AND FOOTER TOOLBAR

Button	What It Does
Insert AutoText ▾	Adds an AutoText entry, such as your name or company name, at the insertion point
	Inserts the page number
	Inserts the number of pages
	Formats the page number
	Inserts the date
	Inserts the time
	Opens the Layout tab of the Page Setup dialog box
	Shows or hides document text
	Uses the header/footer from a previous section in the document, if you have used multiple sections
	Jumps from header to footer and vice versa
	Jumps to the header or footer in the previous section of the document, if applicable
	Jumps to the header or footer in the next section
Close	Hides the Header and Footer boxes and toolbar; returns to the previously selected view

Note

You can create section breaks in a document and have different headers, footers, margins, and so on for each section. To create a section break, choose Insert, Break. Choose one of the section breaks from the dialog box and click OK.

One of the most popular uses for a document footer is to keep a running total of pages in the current document, automatically updating this information as you make a document longer or shorter.

Here's an example of placing page numbering in a footer:

1. Choose View, Header and Footer if the header and footer are not already displayed.
2. Click in the Footer box. Click the Switch Between Header and Footer button if needed to display it.
3. Type **`Page`** and press the Spacebar.
4. Click the Insert Page Number button.
5. Press the Spacebar, type **`of`**, and press the Spacebar again.
6. Click the Insert Number of Pages button.

Note

When you click the Insert Page Number or Insert Number of Pages button, Word actually inserts a field code in the header or footer. As you edit a document and it gets longer or shorter, Word keeps track of the total page count. When you view or print a document, Word updates the numbers on each page as needed. Date and time fields work the same way.

7. Select and format the text you entered, if you want. Click the Close button to return to the main body of the document.

CUSTOMIZING HEADERS AND FOOTERS

Do you want the exact same header and footer on every page? Maybe not. If you've created a custom title page, the header and footer would mess up its careful design. Likewise, if you're planning to print on both sides of the paper and bind your work in book format, you might want to set up different headers and footers on left and right pages, with the title of your report on the right page header only, for example. (Look at this book to see an example of different headers for left and right pages.)

Word lets you handle both instances with ease. To open the Page Setup dialog box (shown in Figure 9.17), just click the Page Setup button on the Header and Footer toolbar.

Figure 9.17
The Page Setup dialog box lets you tell Word where you want your headers and footers to appear.

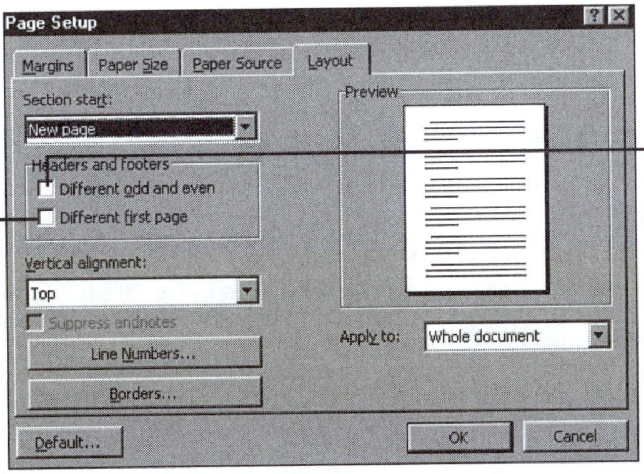

Click here to set up separate headers and footers for left and right pages.

Click here to set up a separate header or footer for the first page of a document or section.

If you've created separate sections in a long document, you can use different headers for each section. By default, each section uses the same header information as the previous section. Click the Same as Previous button to toggle this setting on and off.

Tip #61 from
Faithe Wempen

Look at the top of the header or footer box to see at a glance which header you're currently working with. A simple Header or Footer label means that you have only one of each. If you've set up additional headers or footers, you see different labels for each one—First Page Header or Even Page Footer, for example.

Use the navigation buttons on the Header and Footer toolbar to jump back and forth between different headers and footers, like the ones you've created for left and right pages. In Page Layout view, double-click the header or footer area to activate it at any time and double-click anywhere on the page (outside the header or footer area) to return to the text of your document.

ADDING PAGE NUMBERS ONLY

If all you want to do is number the pages in your document, you don't have to hassle with headers or footers. When you choose Insert, Page Numbers, the Page Numbers dialog box opens (see Figure 9.18). Use it to specify how you want the pages numbered. Word then creates a footer (or a header, if you prefer) in your document and adds a page number code to it.

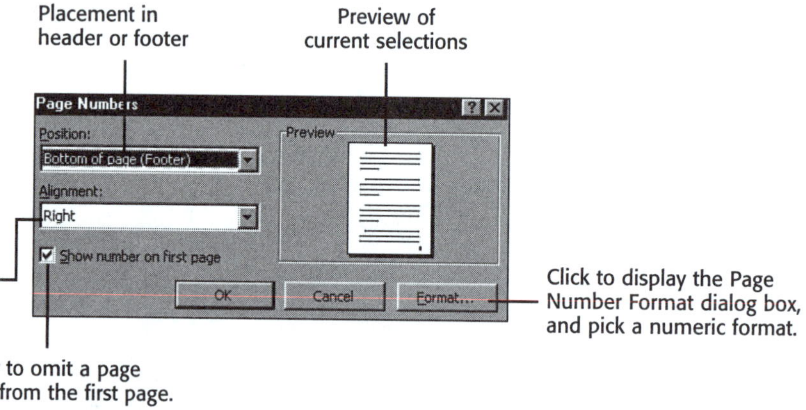

Figure 9.18
Choose Insert, Page Numbers to add page numbers quickly to any document.

Note

The Page Numbers command is grayed out and unavailable when you're working in Outline or Online Layout view. Switch to Normal or Page Layout view and try again.

→ After setting up your header and footer, you might be ready to print the document; **see** "Printing Your Work," **p. 37**.

TROUBLESHOOTING

RECOVERING AFTER A POWER OUTAGE OR LOCKUP

I was working in Word when a power outage occurred. Is there any chance of recovering my work?

If you lose a document you were working on due to a computer lockup or power outage, the next time you start Word the document might appear automatically, recovered with Word's AutoSave feature. Save it right away under a new name if this happens.

I restarted Word after the power outage, but there's no recovered document. Is all lost?

If you lost a document that does not automatically open when you restart Word, look for a file with a .tmp extension in your default document folder (probably C:\My Documents). Open the file in Word; it may be a more recent AutoSave copy of your document than the last one saved on your hard disk.

TURNING OFF CERTAIN EDITING FEATURES

Word won't let me drag across a part of a word to select it; the whole word becomes selected the moment I start to drag across it.

When you drag across text to select it, Word automatically extends the selection to entire words. If you don't like this, choose Tools, Options and, on the Edit tab, deselect the When Selecting, Automatically Select Entire Word check box.

I find myself frequently dragging and dropping text unintentionally.

If you find yourself accidentally moving text with drag-and-drop that you did not intend to, you might want to turn Drag-and-Drop editing off. To do so, choose Tools, Options and, on the Edit tab, deselect the Drag-and-Drop Text editing check box.

AutoCorrect keeps "helping" me by correcting mistakes, but I don't agree with some of the changes it makes.

If Word uses its AutoCorrect to replace text in a way that you don't want (for example, if you don't want it to replace (c) with the © symbol), choose Tools, AutoCorrect. Find the correction to remove on the list of existing corrections, and then click Delete to remove it.

CHAPTER 10

Formatting Documents in Word

In this chapter

UNDERSTANDING YOUR FORMATTING OPTIONS

Formatting is all about making your documents easier to read, helping them convey your message, and giving them polish and pizzazz to impress the reader. Formatting can be as simple as a change in font or as complex as a set of styles assigned to various headings and body text in a document. With Word, formatting options are nearly limitless.

You can exercise pinpoint control over every part of a document's design, from the white space around pages, to the placement of objects on the page, to the size and shape of text. In general, you can use three formatting options to turn plain text into well-designed documents: page setup options, character formatting, and paragraph formatting.

- **Page Setup options**—Control margins, paper size, header and footer placement, the printer's paper tray, and so on.
- **Character formatting**—Affects the appearance of individual characters. It includes font changes, size changes, character attributes (bold, italic), and text color.
- **Paragraph formatting**—Controls the alignment, spacing, and arrangement of entire paragraphs. You can use indents, tab stops, line spacing, and other methods to control a paragraph.

In this chapter, you will learn how to apply all three kinds of formatting in a document.

Note

This chapter teaches you about *direct formatting*, in which you select some text and then apply formatting to it. You can also apply formatting indirectly, by defining a style and then applying that style to some text. You will learn about that in Chapter 11, "Using Templates and Styles in Word."

CHANGING THE LOOK OF A PAGE

If you use the default settings in the Normal document template, Word assumes that you want all your documents on 8.5-by-11-inch letter paper, with roughly an inch of white space on all four sides. You can adjust any of these settings, however, and your changes can apply to the entire document or to individual sections of it.

➔ To learn more about sections, **see** "Working with Sections," **p. 217**.

STARTING A NEW PAGE

Word inserts page breaks automatically when you reach the bottom of a page. These breaks are called *soft page breaks* because they float as needed. For example, if you added two paragraphs to page 1, the break between pages 1 and 2 would float to accommodate the new text.

Sometimes, however, you might want to end the current page early and force Word to start a new one—for example, to put a table on its own page. This is called a *hard page break*.

Press Ctrl+Enter to add a hard page break, or choose Insert, Break and then select Page Break from the Break dialog box and click OK. In Normal and Outline views, you see a dotted line with the words `Page Break` where you added the break (see Figure 10.1).

Figure 10.1
Page break lines appear in Normal and Outline views.

Soft page break

Hard page break

You can delete a page break the same as you delete any single character in your document. Select the page break in Normal view and press Delete, or position the insertion point directly below it and press Backspace.

ADJUSTING THE MARGINS

You can leave extra room on either side, both sides, on the top, or on the bottom of your page. For example, when distributing a report to reviewers, you might leave room for comments in the right or left margin. You can also trim the margins to pack more words on the page, although that might make the document more difficult to read.

Caution

With most printers, you cannot set the margins to zero because standard laser and inkjet printers have an unprintable area that Windows doesn't let you use. If you try to set a margin to a value that is within the *unprintable area,* Word offers to change it to the minimum setting.

Follow these steps to adjust the margins in a document:

1. Choose File, Page Setup. This opens the Page Setup dialog box.
2. Click the Margins tab (see Figure 10.2) to view the available margin settings. You can set margins for all four edges, as well as the gutter, which is the inside of each page (on the right side of the left page and the left side of the right page) when you're printing a book or other bound document.
3. To change a margin setting, click inside the appropriate box (Top, Bottom, Left, or Right) and enter a new margin.

Tip #62 from *Faithe Wempen*

(Optional) Click the box labeled Mirror Margins to change the Left and Right boxes to Inside and Outside when printing documents you plan to bind book-style.

4. Click OK to exit the dialog box and apply the new margins.

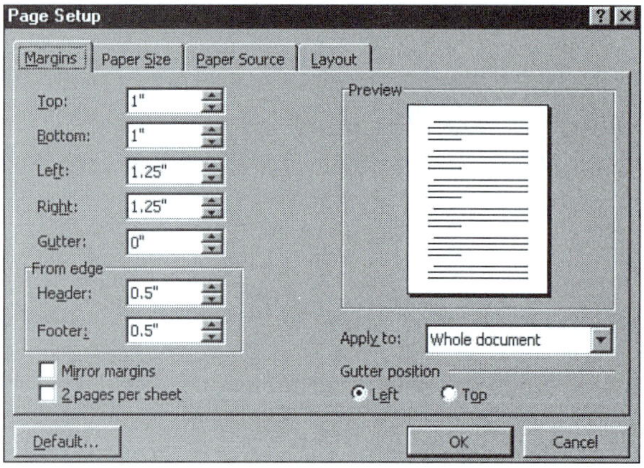

Figure 10.2
Click the Margins tab in the Page Setup dialog box to adjust the amount of white space around your pages.

Tip #63 from *Faithe Wempen*

You can easily change margins and even paper size in the middle of a document. To do so, position your cursor where you want the new settings to begin. Then just choose This Point Forward from the Apply To drop-down list. This creates a section break in the spot where your cursor lies and applies the changes to the new section.

In addition to setting margins with the Page Setup dialog box, you can change the margins using the ruler. You can drag the margin markers in Page Layout view or Print Preview to adjust the page margins for your document.

→ To learn more about using the ruler, **see** "Positioning Text with Tabs," **p. 227**.

→ To find out more about section breaks, **see** "Working with Sections," **p. 217**.

CHANGING PAPER SIZE AND ORIENTATION

You will print most business documents on plain letter paper. But what do you do when you want to use legal-size paper or odd-size stationery? Or when you want to print a table in landscape mode, with the wide edge of the paper at the top and bottom of the page? In those cases, you must change the paper size and/or orientation.

Orientation refers to the direction the text runs on the page. The default is *Portrait*, in which the text is parallel to the narrow edge. The alternative is *Landscape*, in which the text runs along the wide edge.

1. Choose File, Page Setup to open Word's Page Setup dialog box.
2. Click the Paper Size tab to display the dialog box shown in Figure 10.3.
3. Open the Paper Size drop-down list, and choose a predefined size (if the size you want is listed).

   If the paper size you want is not listed, choose Custom Size from the bottom of the list, and enter the dimensions of the paper in the Width and Height boxes.

Caution

Before you specify a custom paper size, make sure that your printer can handle it. Some printers require that you use a manual feed for nonstandard sizes, and thick papers (such as the stock used for postcards or placards) can jam your printer. Read the printer's documentation if you're not sure.

4. To use the selected paper size for all documents, click the Default button.
5. Click OK to close the dialog box.

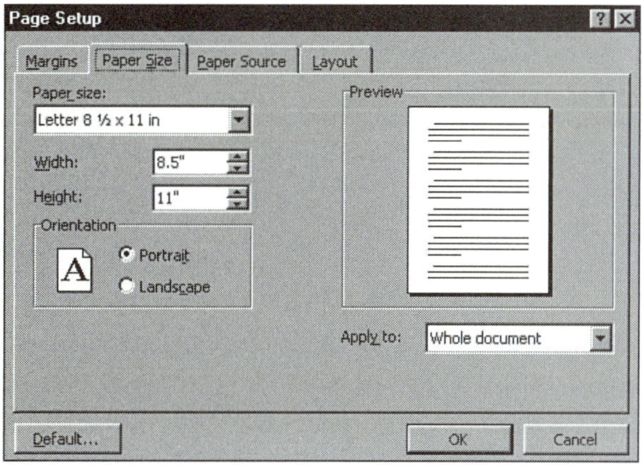

Figure 10.3
Use these options to change paper sizes and switch from Portrait (tall) to Landscape (wide) orientation.

Tip #64 from *Faithe Wempen*

Does your laser printer use letterhead in one tray and plain paper in another? Use the Page Setup dialog box to tell Word which tray to use. You can find the specific options for your printer under the Paper Source tab. The exact choices vary by printer; on some printers, you can specify an upper or lower tray, a manual tray, or an envelope feeder. Alternatively, you can let the printer automatically select the correct paper source.

Working with Sections

You can divide your document into sections by inserting *section breaks*. Each section can then have its own margins, columns, headers, and footers. For example, you might format the first page of a letter for printing on your company's letterhead, with remaining pages on ordinary letter stock. In this example, each section has its own page setup settings.

Another example would be a newsletter with a masthead across the top that runs the entire width of the page. Beneath it is an article in three columns. Because each section can have only one number-of-columns setting, a section break separates the one-column text from the three-column text.

→ To learn how to create multiple columns, **see** "Working with Multiple Columns," **p.280**.

To insert a section break:

1. Choose Insert, Break. This opens the Break dialog box, as shown in Figure 10.4.

Figure 10.4
Set section breaks using the Break dialog box.

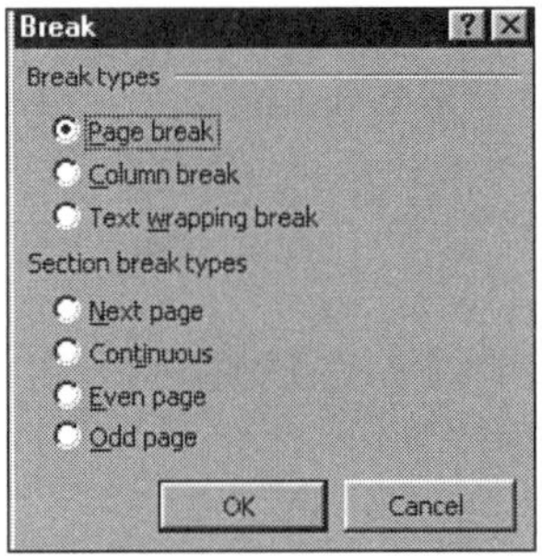

2. Under the Section Break Types area, choose from one of the following options:
   - Choose the Next Page option when you want to insert a section break and start a new page, as you would when changing paper types.
   - Select Continuous if you want text to continue on the same page, with different margins and other page settings, as with the newsletter example.
   - The Even Page and Odd Page options are most useful if you're creating a bound booklet.
3. Click OK to exit the dialog box and apply the section break.

After you insert a section break, it is invisible in Page Layout view, but you can see it just like a page break in Normal view, as shown in Figure 10.5. To delete it, just select the break in Normal view, and press the Delete key.

Figure 10.5
Section breaks appear as dotted lines in Normal view.

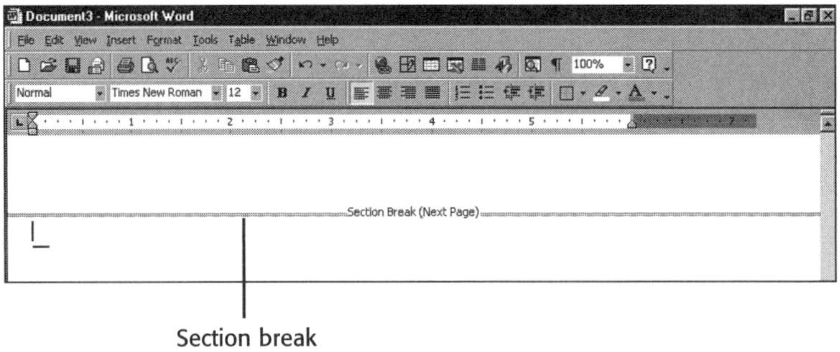

To apply a page layout change to a section, position the insertion point anywhere in that section and then make the change, as described in the following sections.

FORMATTING TEXT

By changing the appearance of words, numbers, symbols, and other text, you can dramatically enhance the readability of a document. (Of course, if you make lousy design decisions, you will only make things more difficult for your readers.) Fonts and font effects, such as underlining, can help the reader distinguish between headings and body text or help draw the reader's eye to individual words or phrases within a paragraph.

Tip #65 from *Faithe Wempen*

Any character formatting you apply to text can be instantly removed by selecting the text and pressing Ctrl+spacebar.

UNDERSTANDING FONTS

Fonts, or *typefaces*, are sets of distinguishing characteristics applied to an entire set of characters, including numbers, letters, and even punctuation. For example, Arial and Times New Roman are both popular fonts used in Word documents.

By default, Word assigns Times New Roman every time you start a new document using the Normal template. Plenty of other fonts are available to use, and your list will vary based on which ones are installed on your computer.

Windows uses several kinds of fonts, but the most popular variety is called *TrueType*. TrueType fonts are scalable, which means that Windows can stretch (scale) them into the exact size you specify, in virtually any size. They also look identical on the printer and onscreen. Printer fonts and screen fonts, on the other hand, usually come in a limited number of sizes and can cause problems when displaying or printing documents. If you choose a printer font that doesn't have a matching screen font, for example, Windows has to substitute an installed screen font when displaying the document. This means that what you see onscreen will not look the same as what you get from the printer.

Note

Typefaces come in all levels of complexity, but they can generally be divided into two broad categories: serif and sans serif. Serifs are the small decorative flourishes at the ends of some characters in some typefaces. *Sans* means "without," so a sans serif face has none of these decorations. Look at the tips of the capital *T* in the following type samples to see the difference clearly:

- This is a SERIF typeface.
- This is a SANS SERIF typeface.

Most designers agree that serif typefaces are best for big blocks of text because they're easier to read, whereas sans serif typefaces are better for headlines and short paragraphs.

CHANGING THE FONT AND SIZE OF TEXT

The easiest way to change a font is to select the text and then choose a different font from the Font drop-down list on the Formatting toolbar, as shown in Figure 10.6. The fonts you've used most recently appear at the top of the list, so they're easy to find; the rest of the fonts appear in alphabetical order. You can choose a font size from the Font Size drop-down list, right next door to it.

Click here to display the list.

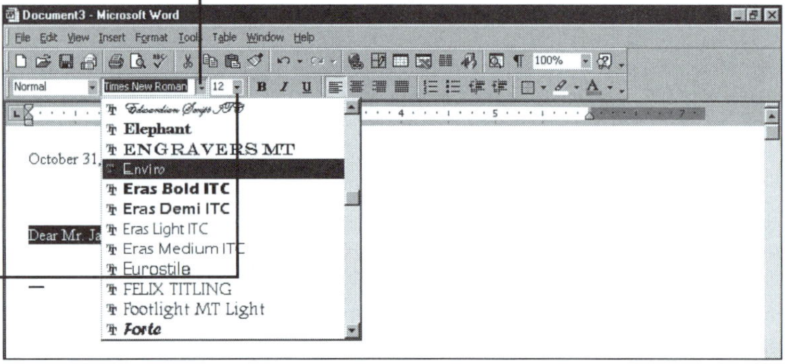

Use the Font Size drop-down list to change the size of text.

Figure 10.6
Use the Font drop-down list on the Formatting toolbar to quickly assign a new font.

Note

If you select no text at all and select a new font, the font selection applies to anything you type at the insertion point. When you create a new document and immediately change fonts, for example, the change applies to all text until you change it again.

An alternative method of changing the font involves the Font dialog box. With this method, you can see a preview of the font before you apply it. The Font dialog box is rather like one-stop shopping for setting character formatting controls, because you can also choose a font size, font color, font style, and other attributes from this same dialog box.

To change text with the Font dialog box, do the following:

1. Select the text you want to change.
2. Choose Format, Font, or right-click on the selection and choose Font from the shortcut menu. You then see the Font dialog box, shown in Figure 10.7.
3. Choose a typeface from the Font list. For a preview of what your text will look like, see the panel at the bottom of the dialog box.
4. Pick a font style: Regular, Bold, Italic, or Bold and Italic.
5. Specify the font size (in points). You must enter a number between 1 and 1,638 here. For most business documents, use 10 or 12 points for text.

Note

For more than 500 years, printers have used the point as a standard unit to measure the size of letters on a typeset page. There are approximately 72 points to an inch, so a six-line paragraph set in 12-point type fills an inch, and a 72-point character is one inch tall.

6. Choose a text color from the drop-down palette of available colors.

7. Select the check boxes for any additional font effects, if desired.

   The Preview area shows you an example of how the settings you selected will appear in the document.

8. Click OK to exit the dialog box and apply the new settings.

Figure 10.7
Use a full range of text-formatting settings in the Font dialog box.

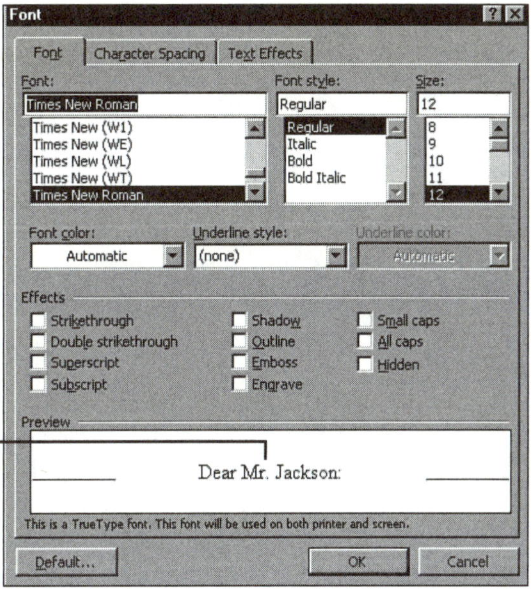

Preview your selections here.

APPLYING TEXT ATTRIBUTES

Besides choosing the font, which dictates the shape and general appearance of characters, you can specify effects to be applied to that font. These options are independent of font selections; when you choose to underline the selected text, for example, underlining remains even if you change fonts.

The Formatting toolbar contains buttons for the three most common text effects:

B Bold

I Italic

U Underline

You will find additional effects, such as Strikethrough or Shadow available in the Font dialog box, as you saw in the preceding steps. Figure 10.8 illustrates the effects you can apply with these and additional font effects in the Font dialog box. Hidden text, another available option, is discussed in the following section.

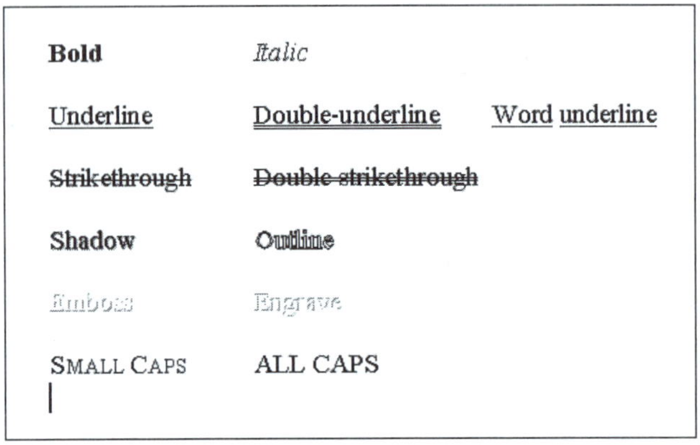

Figure 10.8
Word can apply these character effects.

→ To learn which of these character effects will work with Web pages, **see** "Changing the Appearance of Text," **p. 317**.

HIDING TEXT

One effect available in the Font dialog box is Hidden. Select this font effect when you want the option to see text on the screen without seeing it on the printed page. Text formatted as hidden never prints out, and under most circumstances, it's not visible on the screen, either. To reveal hidden text, choose Tools, Options, click the View tab, and check the Hidden Text box.

Hidden text can be used for comments or notes to yourself as you work or for directives to a layout person or proofreader. However, Word also provides another feature (not covered in this book) that you can use to add nonprinting notes: comments. Look up "Tracking Changes" in Word's Help system index for more information.

CHANGING TEXT CASE

There are a number of ways you can change the case of certain text (that is, change from uppercase to lowercase or vice-versa).

If you simply want to make the text all uppercase, two options in the Font dialog box can help: Small Caps and All Caps. Small Caps makes all the letters capital in shape, but the uppercase letters appear taller. All Caps makes all letters true capitals. These do not actually change the case of the text you typed; they merely apply a formatting attribute that makes the letters appear uppercase. When you remove that attribute, the text goes back to its normal case.

Note

Certain fonts include only capital letters in their character set. If you format text using the Algerian font, for example, the lowercase and uppercase letters are identical. Whatever you type appears in caps, regardless of other formatting options.

You can also change the case of the actual letters. Select the text, and then press Shift+F3 to toggle from lowercase, to *mixed* case (initial caps only), to all caps. Each time you press the key combination, it cycles one step through the formats.

You can also use the Change Case dialog box to specify a case for selected text. Select the text and then choose Format, Change Case. Choose which case option to use, and click OK.

Using a Drop Cap

Professional designers often enlarge the first letter of a paragraph to make it easier for readers to find the beginning of a section. Because the larger initial letter drops below the base of the first line, designers call this feature a *drop cap*. Word enables you to create drop caps easily in documents you create. Click in the paragraph where you want to add a larger first letter, and choose Format, Drop Cap. You then see a dialog box like the one in Figure 10.9.

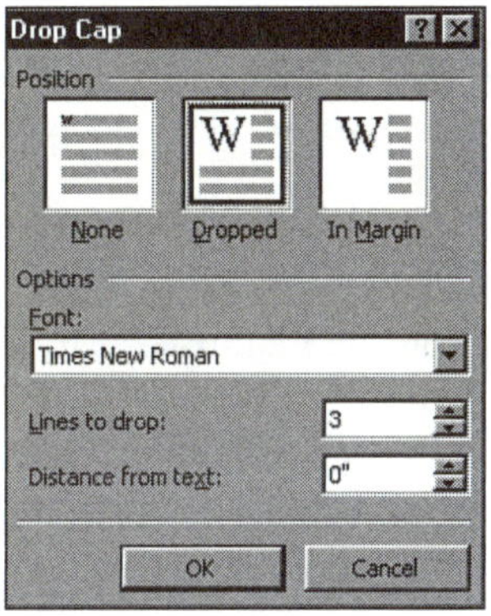

Figure 10.9
Set up a drop cap here.

Tip #66 from *Faithe Wempen*

A drop cap should never be larger than the headline above it. In 12-point body text, a three-line drop cap goes with a 36-point headline.

Choose a font (which need not be the same as the font in the rest of the paragraph), pick the number of lines you want the first letter to extend downward, and specify how much of a gap you want between the drop cap and the text. Click OK to add the drop cap.

Formatting Paragraphs

By choosing the right fonts and applying other text formatting options, you can make words and sentences stand out on the page. When you design a document, arranging the words so that they fall in the right place on the page is equally important. Large headlines, for example, look better when centered between the left and right sides of the page, with ample white space above and below. Summary information stands out on the page when it's indented slightly. If you want to leave room for changes in a draft of a document, you can add extra space between lines.

With Word's paragraph formatting options, you can set off text with extra spacing, stack your words neatly on top of one another, center words on the page, and control precisely when Word ends one page and begins a new one.

ADJUSTING SPACE BETWEEN LINES

For most documents, most of the time, you will use the default single spacing. Some kinds of documents, though, are more readable when extra space appears between each line. (Double-spacing is especially useful if you expect someone to add comments and corrections to your work. Sometimes school papers must be double-spaced, too, as part of the assignment.) You can allow Word to adjust the spacing automatically, based on each line's font size and any graphics or other embedded objects. Or, to maintain precise control over the look of a page, you can specify an exact amount of space between lines.

Tip #67 from *Faithe Wempen*

Line spacing is most important in running text, when you have paragraphs that wrap around to multiple lines. To control space above and below headings, captions, and other one-liners, use paragraph spacing options instead.

To change line spacing, follow these steps:

1. Position the insertion point in the paragraph you want to format, or select multiple paragraphs to format.
2. Choose Format, Paragraph, or right-click anywhere within the selection and choose Paragraph from the shortcut menu.

Note

Paragraph formatting options are not available in Outline view. To adjust these options, switch to another view.

3. Click the Indents and Spacing tab if it is not already on top (see Figure 10.10).
4. To adjust line spacing, choose one of the following options:
   - Select Single, 1.5 Lines, or Double from the Line Spacing drop-down list.
   - Select Multiple from the Line Spacing drop-down list; then choose the number of lines in the At box. You can enter a decimal, such as **1.25**; to use triple spacing, enter **3** here.
   - Choose Exactly from the Line Spacing list, and enter the spacing you want (in points) in the At box. When you choose this option, Word maintains the precise line spacing you selected, even if you increase or decrease the font size or insert graphics.
   - If you have large type or graphics mixed with small type, select At Least from the Line Spacing list. Enter the minimum spacing in the At box; make sure that this number is at least as big as the biggest type size you're using.
5. Click OK to close the dialog box.

Figure 10.10
Change the vertical spacing for a paragraph from here.

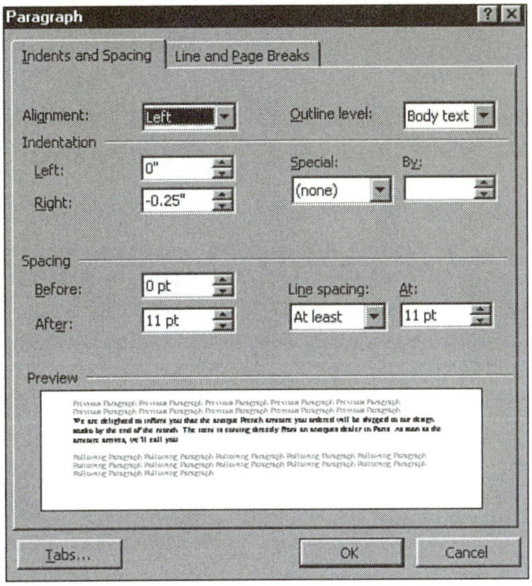

ADJUSTING SPACE BEFORE AND AFTER PARAGRAPHS

Some people prefer to add space after each paragraph by pressing the Enter key twice. Don't! There's a better way to separate one paragraph from the next. To add space before or after a paragraph, select it and choose Format, Paragraph, or right-click and choose Paragraph from the shortcut menu. Then click the Indents and Spacing tab (refer to Figure 10.10). The default setting in the Before and After boxes is 0 points; add space here to provide extra separation between paragraphs. For example, if you're using a 12-point font and you want to add half a line at the end of each paragraph, enter **6** points in the box labeled After.

Note that this setting is separate from the line spacing settings described in the preceding section. Line spacing affects the lines *within* a paragraph; Before and After set the spacing *outside* the paragraph.

All these settings build on one another, so if you've selected double spacing with 12-point text, and you add 6 points after each paragraph, the effect is to add 2.5 lines between paragraphs. The 2 comes from the double-spacing chosen from the Line Spacing list, and the .5 comes from the half line (6 is half of 12) specified in the After field.

INDENTING PARAGRAPHS

The final controls to talk about in the Paragraph dialog box (refer to Figure 10.10) are the Indentation settings. When you set the margins for a document, they apply to every paragraph in that document (or in a section, if you've created multiple sections). Sometimes, though, you want to vary the relation between the text in one or more paragraphs and the white space in the document margins.

You might *indent* the first line to help make the beginning of a paragraph more noticeable. Indenting an important paragraph on both sides adds white space on the left and right so that it stands out from the rest of the page. Adding negative indents, which extend into the left margin, is a useful way to set off headings and lists. Finally, you might use a hanging indent to set off paragraphs in a list. Figure 10.11 shows examples of these three indent styles.

Figure 10.11
You can use paragraph indents in a variety of ways to help set blocks of text apart from the rest of your document.

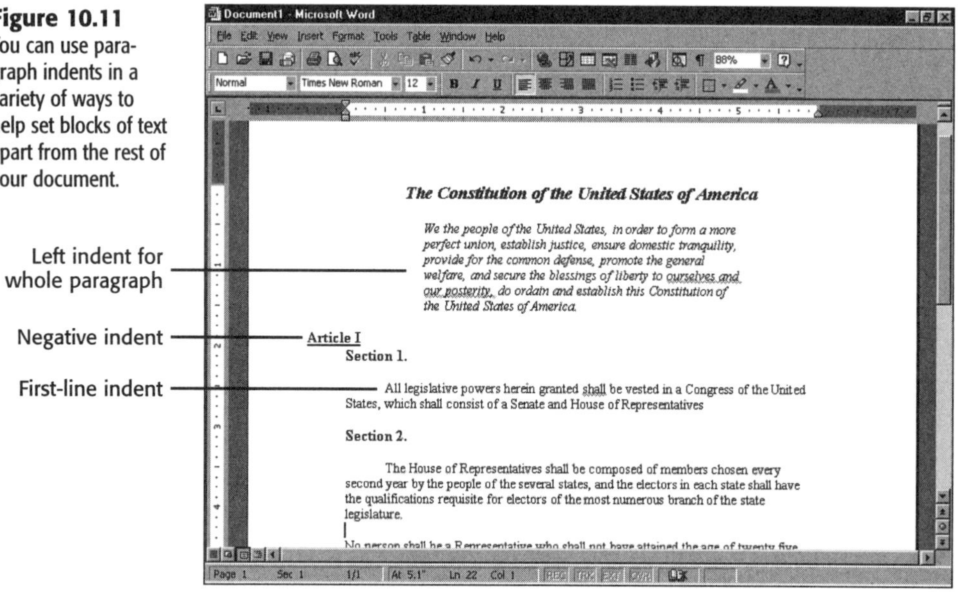

To set paragraph indents using the Paragraph dialog box, follow these steps:

1. Select the paragraph(s) to affect.
2. Choose Format, Paragraph to display the Paragraph dialog box.
3. Enter a positive or negative number in the Left or Right text box in the Indentation section.
4. For a hanging or first-line indent, open the Special drop-down list, choose either of those, and then enter the amount in the By text box next to it.
5. The Preview area shows an example of the new settings. Click OK to apply them to the paragraph.

You can also set indents with the indent markers on the ruler. Notice, at the right end of the ruler, an up-pointing triangle; this controls the right indent for the current paragraph. At the left end are two triangles and a rectangle; the triangles control the first and subsequent line indents separately; the rectangle moves them both at once (see Figure 10.12). Drag these markers along the ruler to change the indents for a selected paragraph.

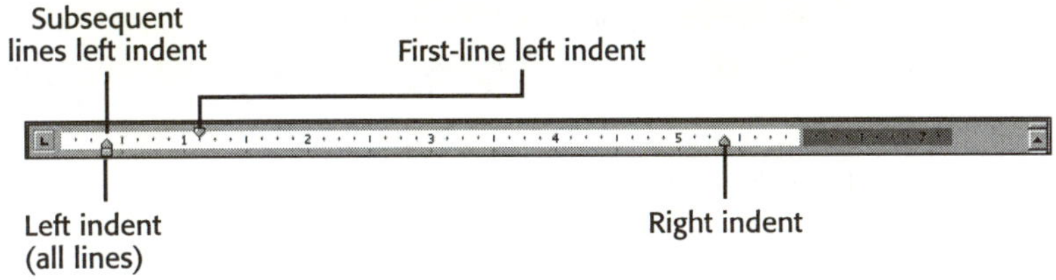

Figure 10.12 Drag the indent markers on the ruler to quickly change a paragraph's indents.

Aligning Text

For every paragraph, you can also choose how it lines up on the page. You have four distinct alignment choices, and you can quickly assign one with a click of a button. All four are available as buttons on the Formatting toolbar.

- **Left**—Because most Western languages read from left to right, this alignment is the most popular choice for text. Every line starts at the same place on the left edge and ends at a different place on the right, depending on how many characters are in each line.

- **Centered**—Use centered text for headlines and short blocks of text. Do not center lengthy passages.

- **Right**—As you type, the text begins at the right edge, and each new letter pushes its neighbors to the left so that everything lines up perfectly on the right edge. Use this choice only for short captions alongside pictures or boxes or when you want a distinctive look for a headline on a flyer or newsletter. Right alignment is also appropriate when numbering pages.

- **Justified**—When you choose this option, Word distributes extra space between words so that lines of text align at both the left and right margins. Justified text works best with formatted columns, as in a newsletter. Don't use it in memos because it makes them difficult to read.

Because this setting applies to the entire paragraph, all you have to do is click anywhere in the paragraph and then click whichever button you prefer.

Tip #68 from *Faithe Wempen*

You can also assign the alignment commands using the Paragraph dialog box (Format, Paragraph). Click the Indents and Spacing tab; then open the Alignment drop-down list, and select an alignment command.

Positioning Text with Tabs

Tabs are one of the most common ways to position text in a document. When you create a new tab stop, you define a point on the horizontal ruler. Each time you press the Tab key, the insertion point moves to the next tab stop. Each of the five types of tab stops is defined by the text alignment at that location. The most common use for tab stops is to mix and match different text alignments on the same line. For example, in a document footer you might set a center tab in the middle of the page and a right tab at the right margin; then you could enter a chapter number, press Tab to enter the chapter name and center it on the page, and then press Tab again to add a page number at the right margin.

Table 10.1 describes how each type of tab stop works and shows what each one looks like when placed on the ruler in Word.

TABLE 10.1 TAB STOP TYPES

Symbol	Tab Alignment	How It Works
	Left	Moves the insertion point to the tab stop; when you enter text, it extends to the right.
	Center	Moves the insertion point and centers text you enter at the tab stop.
	Right	Moves the insertion point to the tab stop; when you enter text, it extends to the left.
	Decimal	Text or numbers align at the decimal point, with all other text extending to the left; this type is used most often to align columns of numbers in currency format.
	Bar	Draws a vertical rule at the tab stop; pressing the Tab key does not move the insertion point.

Tip #69 from
Faithe Wempen

You might be tempted just to press the Tab key and keep pressing, but for most documents, you should consider two alternative formatting options. For lining up columns of text and numbers, tables (with hidden borders) are easier to work with than tabs. Constructing a block-style résumé, for example, is a nightmare using tabs, but it's simple with tables. Likewise, simple paragraph alignment is easier, and the results are more predictable when you use indents (described later in this chapter) instead of tabs.

→ To learn more about using Word tables, **see** Chapter 13, "Working with Tables and Columns."

SETTING TABS WITH THE RULER

The quickest way to set a tab is with the help of Word's ruler, which sits just above the document editing window. To set a tab, click the Tab Type button (at the far left end of the ruler) until the symbol for the tab type you want appears (refer to Table 10.1). Then, on the ruler, click where you want the tab stop to appear. Figure 10.13 shows some tab stops placed on the ruler.

To remove a tab stop from the ruler, drag it down (off the ruler) and drop it. It disappears. To reposition a tab stop, drag it to the right or left.

WORKING WITH THE TABS DIALOG BOX

The Tabs dialog box is not as quick and convenient as the ruler method, but it offers some additional capabilities that you can't have by simply clicking on the ruler.

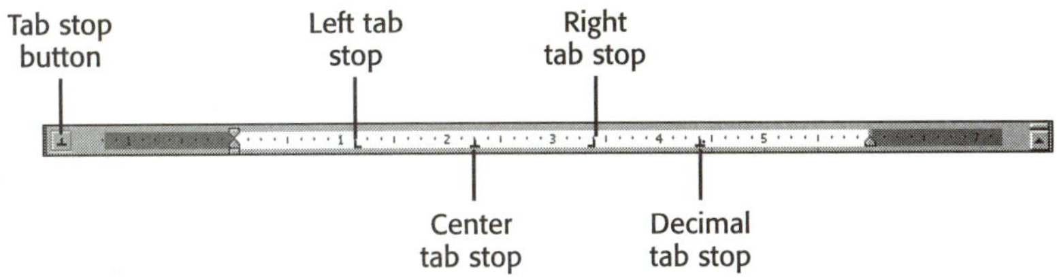

Figure 10.13
To place a tab stop on the ruler, click where you want one.

When you press a Tab key, the insertion point usually moves to the next tab stop. However, you can also tell Word to add a *leader character*, such as a row of periods, between the text and the tab stop. These characters are commonly used with tables of contents and invoices, where you want the reader's eye to clearly see the relationship between the entry at the left and the matching entry to its right.

To set tabs with leaders, you must use the Tabs dialog box, shown in Figure 10.14. Choose Format, Tabs. Set the tabs as you want; then click OK to exit the dialog box.

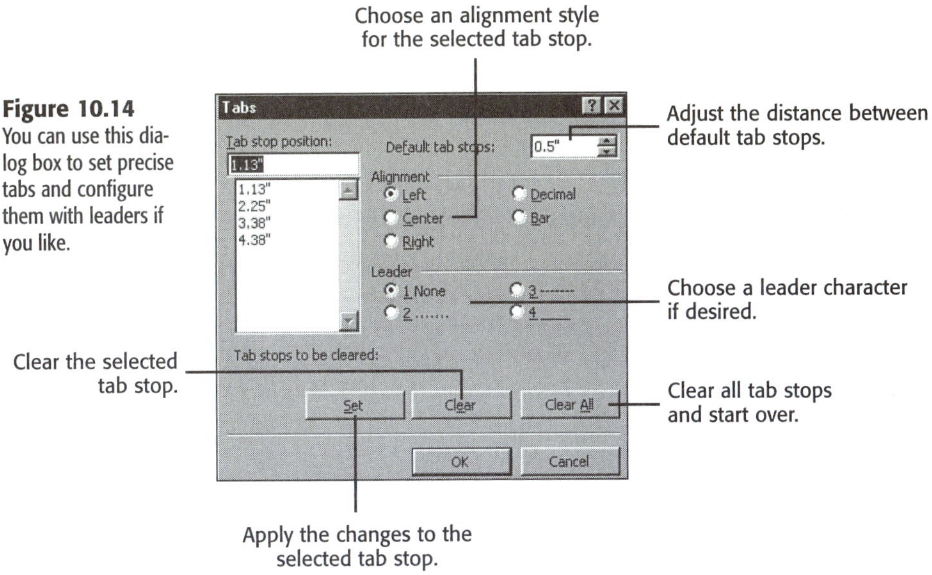

Figure 10.14
You can use this dialog box to set precise tabs and configure them with leaders if you like.

Creating Bulleted and Numbered Lists

When you want to communicate with other people, lists are among your most powerful tools. Whether the list items are single words or full paragraphs, bullet characters and numbers help set them apart from normal body text.

Creating a Bulleted List

To create a bulleted list on-the-fly as you type, just click the Bullets button. Type the first item in your list, and then press Enter to add another bulleted item. The items in a list can be anything—numbers, words, phrases, whole paragraphs, even graphics. To stop adding bullets and return to normal paragraph style, click the Bullets button again.

To add bullets to a list you've already typed, first select the items in the list; then click the Bullets button. The default bullet is a simple black dot in front of each item, as shown in Figure 10.15. See the next section to learn how to use a different character.

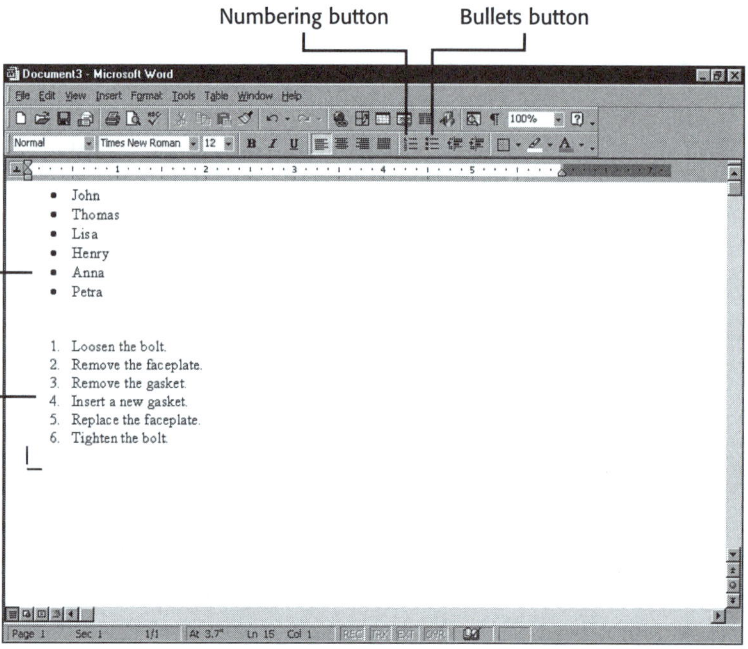

Figure 10.15
Bulleted and numbered lists help the reader focus on important information.

CHANGING THE BULLET CHARACTER

When you first create a bulleted list, Word sets off each item with a big, bold, boring dot. If you would prefer a more visually interesting bullet, you're in luck. With Word, you can choose from seven predefined bullet types, or you can replace the bullet character with practically any symbol.

To change the bullet character, select the entire list and then choose Format, Bullets and Numbering. The Bullets and Numbering dialog box appears, with the Bulleted tab on top. To use one of the seven predefined bullet characters, click the bullet style you want from the list shown in Figure 10.16. Then click OK.

If you don't like any of those seven choices, you can select your own bullet character by doing the following:

1. From the Bullets and Numbering dialog box, click the Customize button on the Bulleted tab. The Customize Bulleted List dialog box appears (see Figure 10.17).
2. Choose the bullet type you want to replace.
3. Click the Bullet button. The Symbol dialog box appears.

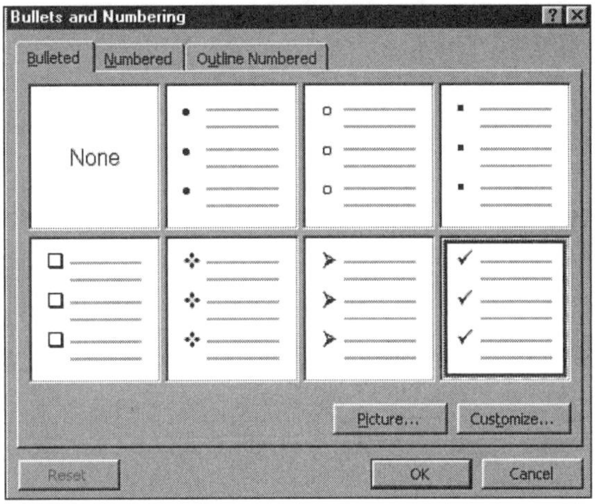

Figure 10.16
When you choose Bullets and Numbering from the shortcut menu, Word offers you these seven choices.

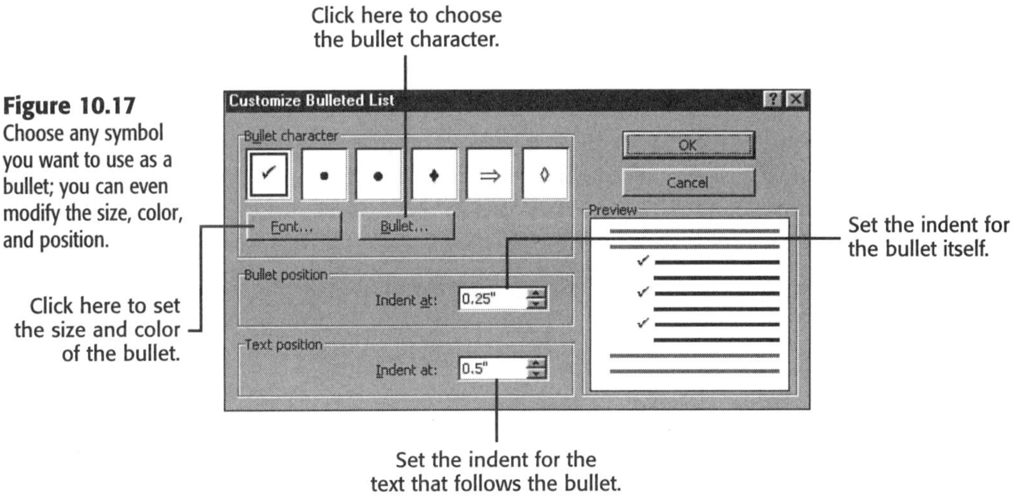

Figure 10.17
Choose any symbol you want to use as a bullet; you can even modify the size, color, and position.

4. Choose the symbol you want for the bullets. (Select a different font from the Font list if desired.)
5. Click OK to return to the Customize Bulleted List dialog box.
6. To change the size or color of the bullet, click the Font button. The Font dialog box appears.
7. Select a different size from the Size list if desired.
8. Open the Font Color drop-down list, and choose a different color for the bullet if desired.
9. Click OK to return to the Customize Bulleted List dialog box.
10. If desired, enter a different bullet position in the Indent At box under Bullet Position.

11. If desired, enter a different text position (for the text that follows the bullet) in the Indent At box under Text Position.
12. Click OK to apply the new bullet. This becomes the default bullet for the document until you change it to something else.

CREATING NUMBERED LISTS

Bullets signify that the items on the list are of equal importance. If the order of items in a list is important, as when you're writing step-by-step instructions, use a numbered list instead (refer to Figure 10.15).

When you choose to number the items in your list, Word doesn't simply plop a number in front of each paragraph; instead, it adds a hidden numbering code. If you add a new item or move items around, Word automatically renumbers the list to keep each item in the proper order.

To start a numbered list, click the Numbering button and then begin typing. Word adds the numeral 1, followed by a period and an indent. Type whatever you want—a word, sentence, or whole paragraph. When you press Enter, Word begins the next paragraph with the next number in the sequence.

Note

Although they're called numbered lists, Word also recognizes Roman numerals and letters as appropriate ways to order a list. You can begin a numbered list by typing `1,` `I),` `a.` or whatever style you want to use. Press the spacebar or the Tab key; then enter the text you want for that item. When you press Enter, Word automatically converts the paragraph you just typed into numbered format and continues the list in the paragraph you're about to type.

CHANGING NUMBERING OPTIONS

The basic format of a numbered list is a simple 1, 2, 3, but Word enables you to choose another format if you want. You can switch to Roman numerals or capital letters, or you can add descriptive text to the bare numbers. If you're writing a list of instructions, for example, you might add the word **`Step`** before each number and a colon afterward, so your readers see `Step 1:`, `Step 2:`, and so on, in front of each item.

To change to a different numbering style, select the existing numbered list, and choose Format, Bullets and Numbering. The Bullets and Numbering dialog box appears, with the Numbered tab on top. Seven numbering styles appear (see Figure 10.18); click the one you want and then click OK.

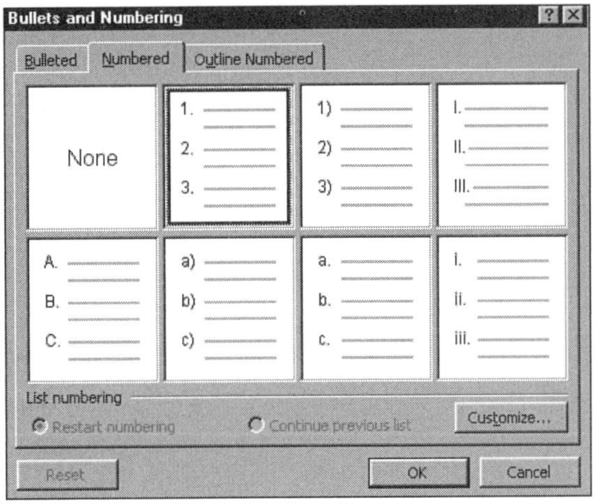

Figure 10.18
Select one of the seven numbering styles.

If you want more flexibility, you can define a custom numbering style, as explained in the following steps:

1. Click the Customize button on the Numbered tab. The Customize Numbered List dialog box appears (see Figure 10.19).

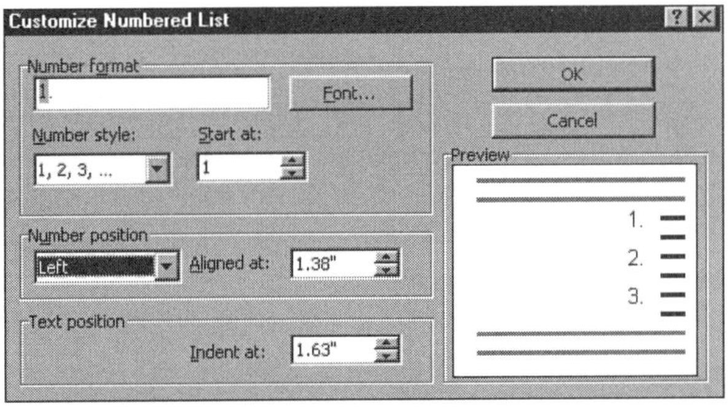

Figure 10.19
Replace Word's default numbering scheme with your own format.

2. Open the Number Style drop-down list, and choose a numbering style.
3. Set the Start At number to start at some other number than 1, if desired.
4. To create a custom format that includes text, click in the box labeled Number Format, and add the text before the number field. Be sure to add a space after the text.

   For example, if you wanted each step to read *Step #1*, *Step #2*, and so on, you would type **`Step #`** in front of the number code.
5. If desired, change the number position from the Number Position drop-down list.

   Number position affects the alignment of numbers with one another. For example, in a list with 10 steps, with Left number position, the 1 in "10" will align vertically with the single-digit step numbers. With Right number position, the 0 in "10" will align.

6. If desired, change the number position in the Aligned At box. This affects how the number will be indented.
7. If desired, change the indent for the text to follow the numbers in the Indent At box.
8. Click OK to apply the new numbering format.

REARRANGING AND EDITING LISTS

Because bullet and number codes are contained in Word fields, you can easily rearrange, reorder, or expand items in a list. Here's how:

- To move a list item to a new position, first select the entire item, including the paragraph mark (¶). Then use the Cut and Paste shortcut menus, or simply drag the item to its new spot.

Tip #70 from
Faithe Wempen

> To move a bulleted or numbered item properly, make sure that you've selected the paragraph mark (¶) at the end of the item. (Click the Show/Hide ¶ button to make it easier to see paragraph marks.) If you don't select the entire paragraph, the bullet or numbering formatting stays where it is, and only the text moves.

- To add a new item to the end of the list, move the insertion point to the end of the last paragraph in the list, and press Enter. Pressing Enter twice in a row turns off numbering or bullets.
- To insert a new item, click to position the insertion point at the beginning of the paragraph where you want to add the new item, and then press Enter.
- To skip or stop numbering, right-click on the paragraph where you want to skip an entry, and choose Paragraph. Click the Line and Page Breaks tab; then check the box labeled Suppress Line Numbers. This technique is especially useful when you want to add a comment in the middle of a long list.
- To restart or continue a list when Word doesn't do it correctly, right-click the numbered paragraph, and choose Bullets and Numbering. Then click either Restart Numbering (to set the selected item to 1) or Continue Previous List (to pick up where the last numbered paragraph left off).
- To restore a list to plain text format, select the entire list, and click the Numbering button or the Bullets button.

USING FORMAT PAINTER

A quick way to copy formatting from one block of text to another (either an entire paragraph or individual characters) is with the Format Painter tool. Select the paragraph containing the formatting you want to copy; then click the Format Painter button on the Standard toolbar. Drag across the text you want to copy the formatting to, and the formatting is immediately applied.

USING AUTOFORMAT

Word's AutoFormat feature is a great idea that doesn't always work as promised. It's supposed to make your documents look great, effortlessly and automatically. The bigger the document, however, the more likely that AutoFormat will make some mistakes. The most common one is to apply the wrong style tag, turning body text into lists, for example. AutoFormat works best on short documents. It also works well on blocks of text, such as numbered lists and addresses.

Note

Don't confuse AutoFormat with the AutoFormat as You Type feature. Although the two features share some of the same settings, they're completely independent of each other.

When you use AutoFormat, Word works its way through your document from top to bottom, replacing standard quotes with *smart quotes*, taking out extra spaces and unnecessary paragraph marks, and so on. AutoFormat also tries to guess which style is best for each block of text. You can tell Word to skip one or more of these steps: Choose Tools, AutoCorrect, click the AutoFormat tab, and add or remove check marks as necessary.

To format the current document automatically, choose Format, AutoFormat. You then see a dialog box like the one in Figure 10.20, where you can choose whether to review the changes made. To decline a review of the changes, choose the AutoFormat Now option. Then click OK. Word whizzes through your document, makes all its changes, and displays the newly formatted document in the editing window.

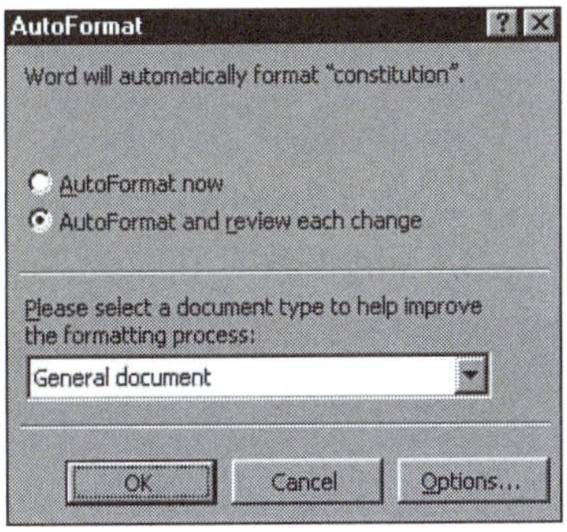

Figure 10.20
Choose whether to review changes.

If you choose the second option, AutoFormat and Review Each Change, Word formats the document and then asks whether you want to Accept All, Reject All, or Review Changes. Click Review Changes, and then click Find to find the first change, as in Figure 10.21. To accept a change, simply skip over it by clicking Find again to find the next change. To reject it, click the Reject button. When you are finished, click Cancel to return to the AutoFormat dialog box, and then click Accept All to accept all the changes (minus those that you rejected individually).

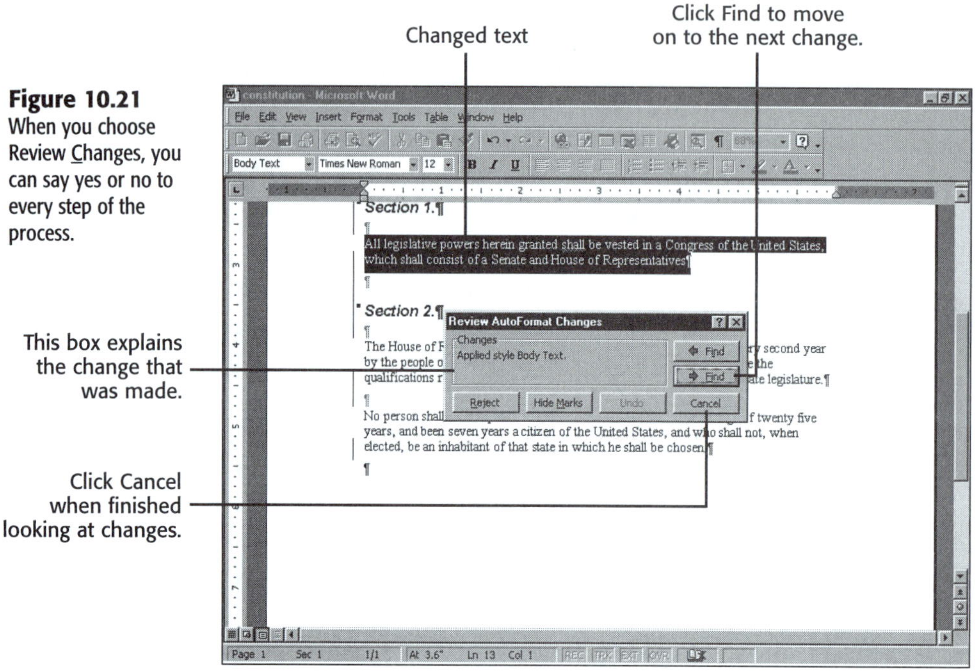

Figure 10.21
When you choose Review Changes, you can say yes or no to every step of the process.

Troubleshooting

Printer Cuts Off Documents

I printed a document and discovered that the last few lines at the bottom of the page are missing, yet they appear in the Print Preview.

If part of your document is cut off at the bottom of the page when you print it, but looks okay onscreen, perhaps your printer cannot print as low on the page as the Word document requires. Increase the bottom margin setting and try again.

Courier Font Limitations

I'm typing a document in Courier, but some of the characters don't look right onscreen.

If you are using Courier font and the text appears broken up onscreen, or quotation marks or other symbols appear as black bars, try switching to Courier New font. This is the same font, but with additional character capabilities.

Hidden Text Causes Printout Discrepancies

I printed a document, but the printed copy is a different length than the onscreen version.

If you have hidden text in your document, the document might not look the same onscreen as it does when you print it. Use Print Preview to check how the document will actually look.

Paragraphs Spaced Too Far Apart

My paragraphs print with too much space between them.

If you have set extra space before and after some paragraphs, but you are getting twice the desired space between paragraphs, remove either the Before or After entry, leaving only one of the two set. These settings build on each other; 12 points after paragraph 1 and 12 points before paragraph 2 equals 24 points.

More Bullet Choices

I'd like to customize my bulleted list, but I don't see a bullet option that I like.

If you don't like any of the bullet characters available from any of the fonts, try clicking the Picture button on the Bulleted tab of the Bullets and Numbering dialog box. A Picture Bullet dialog box opens, through which you can select a graphical bullet from the Clip Gallery.

Automatic Changes Not Desired

Word automatically makes formatting changes as I type, but I don't want that.

If Word insists on automatically making corrections you don't want as you type, such as automatic bulleted or numbered lists, choose Tools, AutoCorrect, and deselect check boxes for certain corrections on the AutoFormat As You Type tab.

CHAPTER 11

Using Templates and Styles in Word

In this chapter

HOW STYLES WORK

The letters, memos, reports, and faxes you create every day use many of the same elments—body text, headings, signatures, address blocks, and so on. Rather than format each of these elements from scratch when you start a new document, you can save format specifications, called *styles*, and reuse them any time. When you attach a saved style to a word or paragraph, the effect is the same as if you had applied formatting directly—fonts, colors, line spacing, tab stops—you name it.

Using styles offers two significant advantages over direct formatting. First, it makes even complex formatting tasks easy, bypassing all the check boxes, lists, and dialog boxes that you would otherwise have to use. Second, it lets you create and share consistent formatting for all documents you create; that's especially important if you're using Word for a small business, where typefaces and other design elements can be as important as a company's logo in creating a visual identity.

Note

Early versions of Word, as well as some other word processing programs you might have used, employ *style sheets* to keep track of groups of styles. Word 2000 doesn't use style sheets; instead, it organizes the styles in template files, which you learn about later in this chapter.

PARAGRAPH STYLES VERSUS CHARACTER STYLES

Word enables you to create and use two types of named styles: *paragraph styles* and *character styles*.

As the name implies, a paragraph style applies to an entire paragraph. A named paragraph style can include alignments, line spacing, tab settings, and other paragraph formatting options. It also contains character formatting, such as a default font and font size. When you create a document using the Normal document template, the default paragraph style is also called *Normal*. It uses 10-point Times New Roman, with single spacing and left alignment. When you apply the built-in Heading 1 style, the selected paragraph changes to 14-point Arial Bold, with 12 points of extra spacing before the heading and 3 points of extra spacing after, in addition to the single line spacing.

Character styles, on the other hand, apply font, border, and language information to selected text or characters. When you use a character style, it overrides the font information contained in the paragraph style. When you enter a Web address in a Word document, for example, Word's AutoFormat as You Type feature applies the Hyperlink character style, which uses the Default Paragraph font but displays the selection in blue, with a single underline.

You might want to create and use a custom character style for your company's name so that it always appears in the proper typeface and size. When writing this book, I used a custom character style to define words and terms that I planned to add to the glossary. By redefining the glossary style (a 60-second job), I was able to change the appearance of every glossary entry when the book designer decided to use a different format.

→ To find detailed explanations of all your paragraph formatting options, **see** "Formatting Paragraphs," **p. 223**.

→ To learn how to add emphasis to text, **see** "Formatting Text," **p. 219**.

Understanding Paragraph Marks

Before you get started working with styles, stop a moment for a quick lesson on end-of-paragraph markers and their significance.

Many characters in your Word document don't print and don't display onscreen by default. To view them onscreen, click the Show/Hide ¶ button. The hidden characters that appear include spaces (represented by dots), end-of-paragraph markers (¶), and tabs (represented by arrows). Figure 11.1 shows a document with these hidden characters displayed.

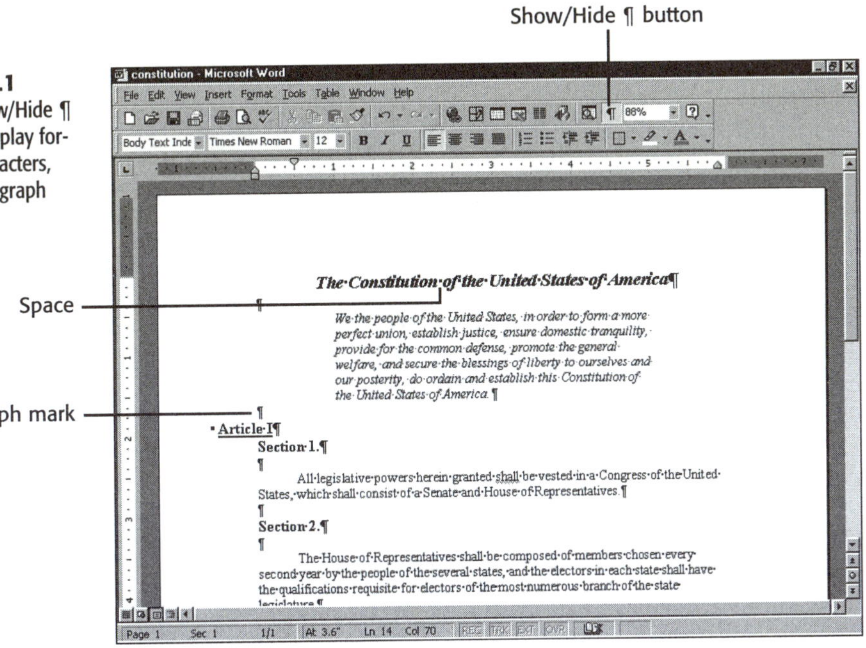

Figure 11.1
Use the Show/Hide ¶ button to display formatting characters, such as paragraph marks.

Turning on these hidden characters is useful because you can see where the end-of-paragraph markers lie. Word stores all the paragraph formatting and style data for the paragraph in those paragraph marks. If you choose a paragraph style that instructs Word to display text in the Arial font with triple-line spacing, for example, Word dutifully saves your instructions (along with any direct formatting) inside that paragraph mark.

Why does this information matter? Because if you copy or move that paragraph mark, you also move the styles that go with it. On the other hand, if you don't include the paragraph mark in your selection, the text you paste changes to the style of the paragraph into which you paste the text.

Tip #71 from *Faithe Wempen*

Some Word experts recommend that you leave paragraph marks visible all the time when working with Word. I consider that advice extreme, but I do recommend that you click the Show/Hide ¶ button to see all your paragraph marks whenever you plan to move one or more paragraphs. Make sure that you move a paragraph mark only if you also want to move the formatting that goes with it.

VIEWING AVAILABLE STYLES

Every document contains the styles stored in the template on which the document is based. When you create a new style or edit an existing one, you can choose to save the style only in the current document, or you can revise the template's style collection. To see which style is applied to the paragraph in which the insertion point currently lies, look in the Style box at the left of the Formatting toolbar.

Note

If you position the insertion point within a word that is formatted with a character style, the Style box displays that style's name. If no character style appears at the insertion point, or if you select two or more words formatted with different character styles, the Style box displays the name of the current paragraph style. When you select text from two or more paragraphs formatted with different paragraph styles, the Style box is empty.

To see a list of available styles, open the Style drop-down list on the Formatting toolbar. The default list shows only the styles in use for the current document, as well as a few standard styles. To see every style choice available in the current document template, including those not currently in use, hold down the Shift key when you click the drop-down arrow. The full list for a document based on the Normal template resembles the one shown in Figure 11.2.

For complete details about each style, choose Format, Style. By default, you see only the styles currently in use in the document; open the List drop-down list, and choose All Styles to see them all. Figure 11.3 shows how to decipher the entries in this dialog box.

Tip #72 from *Faithe Wempen*

If you'd rather see exactly which style is applied to which paragraph, you can choose to see the style name in the left margin. Choose Tools, Options. Click the View tab, and change the Style Area Width setting to .5. Click OK to exit; then switch to Normal view to see the style area in the margin.

Notice that the Delete button is unavailable in Figure 11.3. That's because you can delete only styles you yourself have created; you cannot delete styles that come with the template.

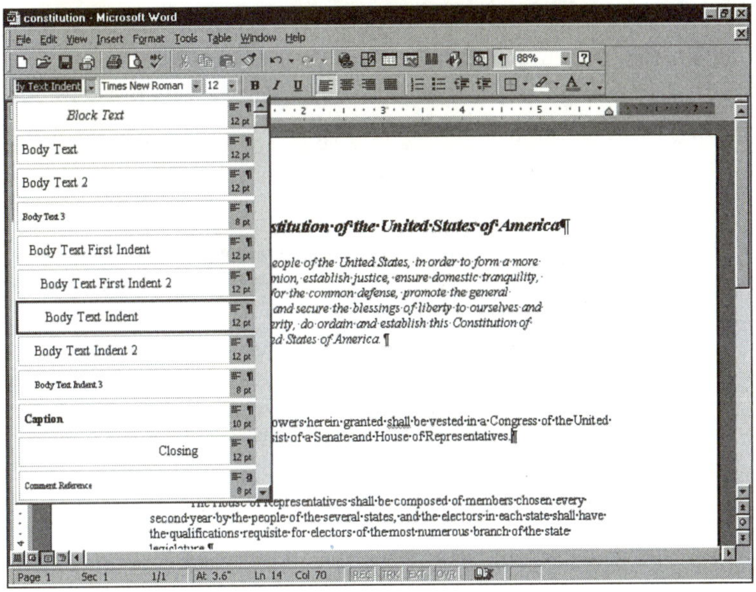

Figure 11.2
Hold down the Shift key to see a list of every available style; the icon at the right of each entry identifies the type of style.

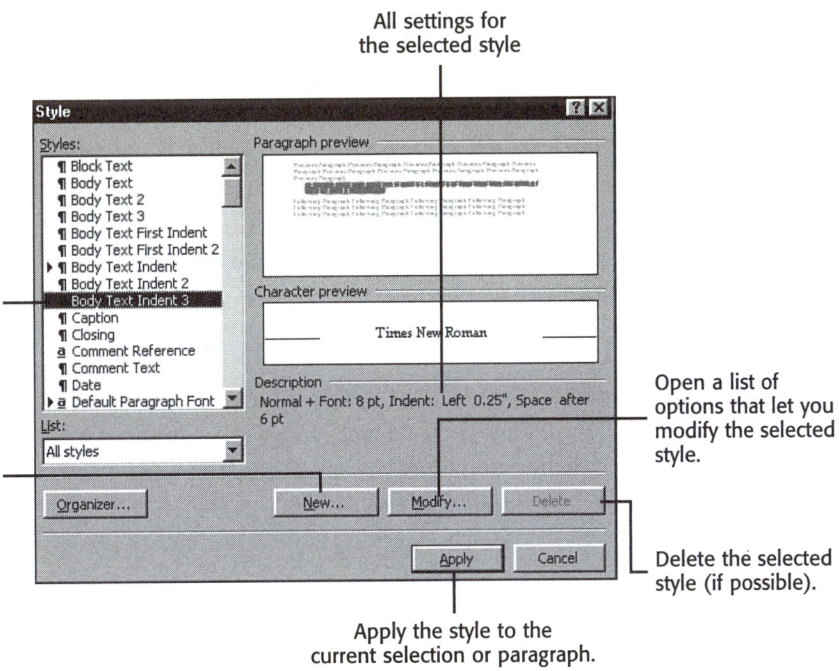

Figure 11.3
Use the Style dialog box to see and edit details about styles in the current document and template.

→ For details on how styles and templates work together, **see** "Collecting Styles (and More) in Document Templates," **p. 248**.

→ For details on how to use the templates included with Word, see "Using Ready-Made Templates," **p. 192**.

APPLYING STYLES TO WORD DOCUMENTS

The simplest way to apply a style to a document is with the help of the drop-down Style list on the Formatting toolbar. You can change the style for a text selection or a paragraph.

1. Position the insertion point where you want to change the style, or select the text that you want it to affect.

Note

If you position the insertion point in a word without making a selection and then choose a character style, Word applies that style to the entire word. If you apply a paragraph style without selecting, the style applies to the entire paragraph.

If you select text before applying a style, Word applies the style only to the selected words or characters. Paragraph styles always apply to the entire paragraph, regardless of whether you make a selection, except if they contain character formatting, too. If they do, the character aspects of the style apply to only the selected text.

2. Open the Style drop-down list, and click the style you want.

   To choose a new style that is available in the current document template but not yet in use, hold down the Shift key as you open the drop-down Style list.

Tip #73 from *Faithe Wempen*

After you choose any Word command, you can repeat the command by pressing the F4 key. This shortcut is especially useful when you want to format a few widely separated paragraphs using the same style. Apply the style to a selection; then position the insertion point in the next paragraph you want to reformat, and press F4.

You can also apply a style from the Style dialog box (refer to Figure 11.3). Just open that dialog box (choose Format, Style), click the style you want, and then click Apply to apply it.

SAVING YOUR FAVORITE FORMATS AS NAMED STYLES

Although the predefined styles in standard Word templates are a useful starting point, sooner or later you will want to create and edit styles for documents you've designed. Word lets you define a style by example, or you can modify the styles included with Word templates, including the Normal document template.

DEFINING A STYLE BY EXAMPLE

If you've formatted an existing document, you can easily save some or all of your settings as named paragraph styles so that you can reuse them later.

You cannot use these steps to create a character style; for that task, you have to open the Style dialog box, as explained in the next section.

To create a new paragraph style by example, follow these steps:

1. Position the insertion point in the paragraph that contains the formatting you want to save as a style.
2. Click in the Style box on the toolbar, and type a name for the new style.
3. Press Enter. If the name you typed is not already in use, Word creates a new style with that name.

   If the name you type is already the name of a style in the current template, one of two things happens. Either the paragraph changes immediately to the existing formatting of that style, or a dialog box appears, asking what to do (see Figure 11.4). Choose Update the Style to Reflect Recent Changes, and click OK.

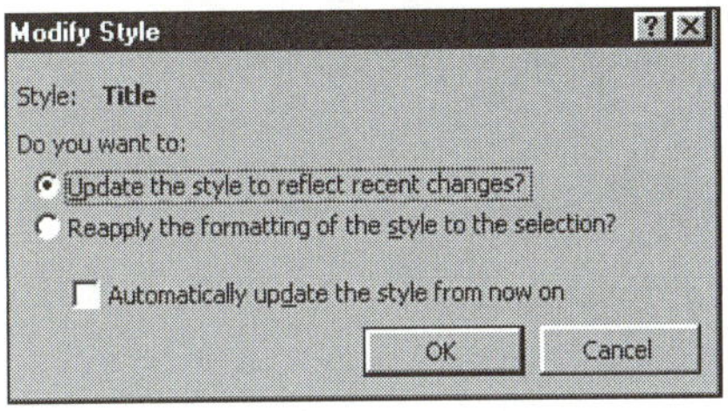

Figure 11.4
When you apply manual formatting and then enter the name of an existing style in the Style box, Word offers you these choices.

Caution

When you update an existing style, Word offers to apply further format changes automatically. (Notice the check box in Figure 11.4.) Think carefully before you decide to allow automatic style updates. When you enable this feature, every manual formatting change you make applies instantly to other paragraphs formatted using that style. The results can be unwelcome.

Creating a New Style Based on Another Style

If you want to create a character style, or create a style that is not based on some text you have already formatted, you must use the Style dialog box. The general procedure is this: Define a new style by naming it, and specify which existing style it is based on. Then, enter formatting specifications that differentiate it from the original. For example, you might create a style named `Normal Indented` that is just like the Normal style (based on it) except that each paragraph is indented one-half an inch on the first line. If you later change the Normal style to use a different font, for example, Normal Indent's font also changes because it is based on Normal and follows its lead.

To create a new style based on another style, do the following:

1. Choose Format, Style. The Style dialog box opens (refer to Figure 11.3).
2. Click the New button. A New Style dialog box opens, as shown in Figure 11.5.

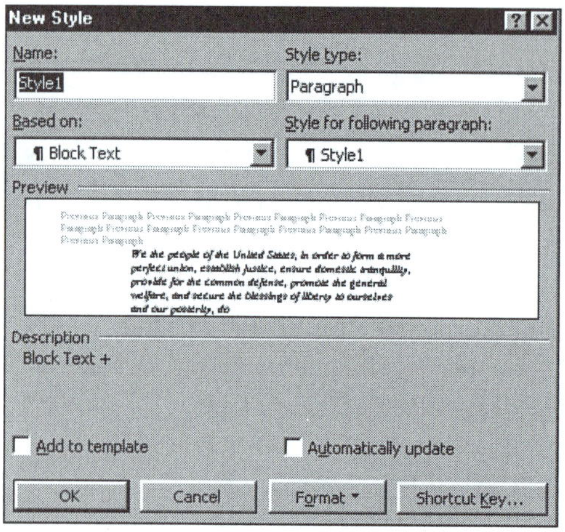

Figure 11.5
Define the new style, and choose which existing style it is based on.

3. Type a name for the new style in the Name box.
4. Open the Style Type drop-down list, and choose Character or Paragraph, as appropriate.
5. Open the Based On drop-down list, and choose the style on which the new style should be based. (If in doubt, choose Normal.)
6. Open the Style for Following Paragraph drop-down list, and choose the style for paragraphs that follow this one. This specifies what the default style of the next paragraph should be following a paragraph formatted with this one.

> **Note**
>
> The Style for Following Paragraph setting can be useful if you use it correctly. If you are creating a new style that will primarily be used for single, sporadic lines in the document (such as a heading, for example), set the Style for Following Paragraph to the style that you use for normal text. That way, when you press Enter at the end of a paragraph formatted with this style, the style resets itself back to your normal paragraph style.

7. Click the Add to Template check box to make sure that the style is added to the template, if you want that. If this style is for use only in the current document, you can skip that step.
8. Skip to step 4 in the following section to modify the style's definition.

MODIFYING A NAMED STYLE

You can modify any character or paragraph style, including the Normal paragraph style. You can then choose precise formatting options for a style after you've created it.

Follow these steps to change an existing style with the Style dialog box:

1. Choose Format, Style. The Style dialog box opens.

2. Select an entry from the Styles list. Check the Preview and Description boxes at the right to confirm that you've selected the correct style.
3. Click the Modify button. The Modify Style dialog box appears. (It looks virtually identical to the New Style dialog box shown previously in Figure 11.5.)
4. Click the Format button, and choose one of the following entries from the drop-down menu (see Figure 11.6). For paragraph styles, all choices are available; for character styles, some of the seven choices are grayed out.
   - **Font**—Adjust the current font, font size, color, effects, and other options for character and paragraph styles.
   - **Paragraph**—Set line spacing, paragraph spacing, indents, and other paragraph options (not available for character styles).
   - **Tabs**—Set and edit tab stops (not available for character styles).
   - **Border**—Use rules and shading around the selected text or paragraph.
   - **Language**—Select a language for the selected text or paragraph; this setting tells Word which dictionary to use when spell-checking documents.
   - **Frame**—Choose size, text wrapping, and position options for text that appears in a frame (not available for character styles).
   - **Numbering**—Define bullet and numbering options (not available for character styles).

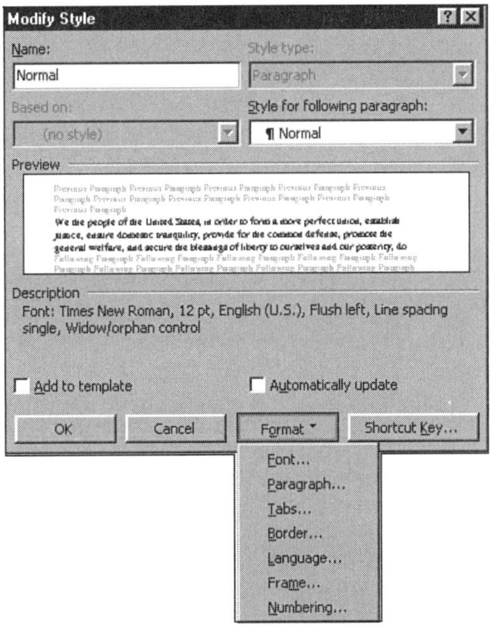

Figure 11.6
Choose the type of modification you want to make to the style.

5. Each choice leads to a different dialog box. Adjust formatting options as you want, and click OK. Repeat step 4 to set other formatting options, as needed.

6. Check the Add to Template box if you want to save your changes in the current template and have them automatically applied to other documents based on that template. Leave this box blank if you want the style changes to apply only to text in the current document.
7. Click OK to save your changes, and return to the Style dialog box. Click Apply to return to the editing window.

COLLECTING STYLES (AND MORE) IN DOCUMENT TEMPLATES

Templates provide a handy way to start new documents, but they also play an important role as a storage place for styles, macros, AutoText entries, and custom Word commands and toolbar settings. When you attach a template to a document originally created using a different template, Word can automatically update document styles whose names match those in the new template.

Note

Document templates can contain boilerplate text that automatically becomes part of any new document you create using that template. You can open a new file by choosing the File, New, More Word Templates command.

When you attach a template to an existing document, however, Word ignores boilerplate text in the document and gives you access to styles and other document elements stored in the template.

➔ To start a new document based on a template, **see** "Using Ready-Made Templates," **p. 192**.

CHANGING THE TEMPLATE FOR THE CURRENT DOCUMENT

Document templates are powerful tools for maintaining a set of standards. For example, if you create a template that contains many of the styles you use frequently, you can attach that template to other documents and thereby gain access to those styles in the other documents. This is done a lot in publishing, for example—a publisher provides a template to an author, and the author attaches that template to each chapter file he or she creates. You will find many home uses for it, too.

To change the template for the current document, follow these steps:

1. Choose Tools, Templates and Add-Ins. The Templates and Add-ins dialog box shows which template is currently associated with the document (see Figure 11.7).
2. Click the Attach button to browse through a list of all available templates.
3. Select the template you want to use with the document, and click the Open button.
4. If you want to open the attached template and update formatting every time you open the current document, check the box labeled Automatically Update Document Styles. Leave this box blank if you want to base the document on the current version of the template only.

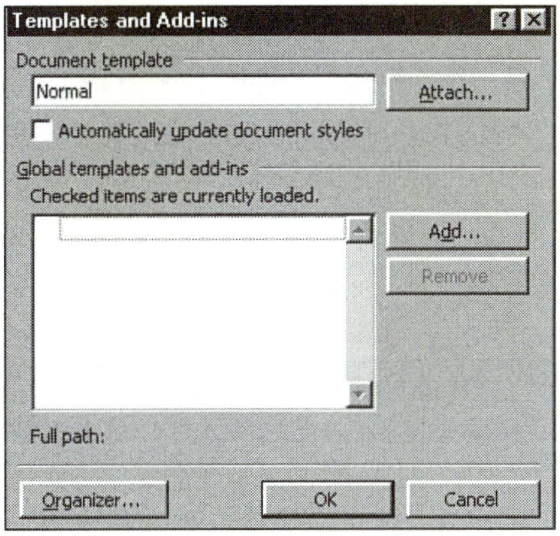

Figure 11.7
Use the Templates and Add-ins dialog box to change the look of a document by using styles stored in another template.

Tip #74 from *Faithe Wempen*

If you have some text in the document that is already formatted with a style that has the same name as a style in the incoming template, you must make sure that the Automatically Update Document Styles check box is marked if you want the text to be reformatted with the new version of the style being attached. Otherwise, you will have to reselect the text and reapply the style manually after attaching the new template.

5. Click OK to save your changes. The formatting of your document changes immediately.

What happens when you open a document created by someone else using a template you don't have? Word stores all the formatting information for the styles used in that document within the document itself, which means that you see the formatting as the author intended it. If the author updates the template, however, your copy won't reflect those updates.

MANAGING STYLES AND TEMPLATES

Although you can save a template in any folder, you should make it a habit to store document templates in one of two locations. For personal templates, use the C:\Program Files\Microsoft Office\Templates folder. Word also lets you specify a secondary location where you store templates that you share with other members of your workgroup. (You can find this setting on the File Locations tab when you choose Tools, Options.

CREATING A NEW TEMPLATE

To create a new document template, start with a document. Although you can edit the template file later, most people find it easier to create styles, AutoText entries, and other document elements first and then save the file as a document template.

To create a new template from a document, do the following:

1. Create the Word document you want to use as a template. Do not include any text, unless you want text to appear when you create a new document based on the template.
2. Choose File, Save As.
3. Choose Document Template (*.dot) from the Save as Type list. Word switches to the Templates folder (see Figure 11.8).

Figure 11.8
Make sure that you set the document type to Document Template.

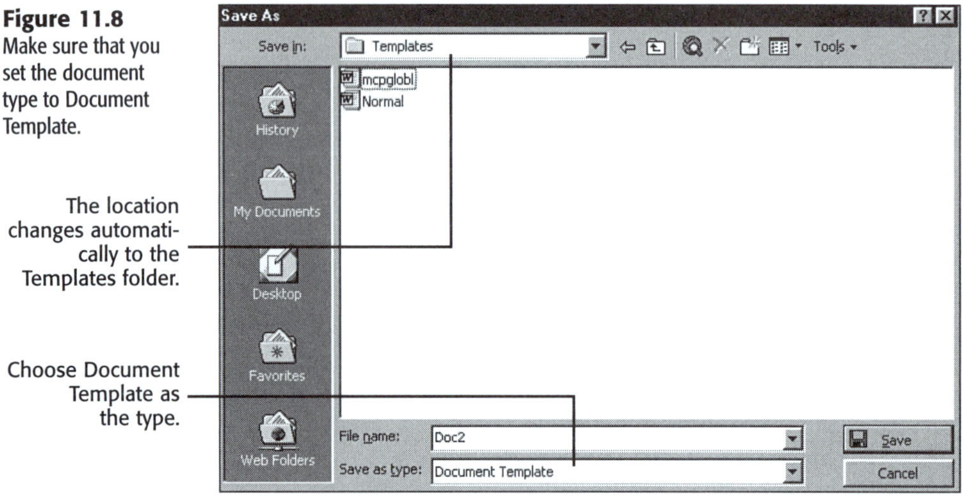

4. Give the template a descriptive name in the File Name text box.
5. Click Save to save the template.

Caution

After you save a file in Document Template format, you cannot save it in any other format. When you open the template file for editing and make changes, Word grays out the Save as Type list to prevent you from inadvertently damaging a template. To save the document using another format, first create a new document based on the template, and then save that document.

Customizing Word Templates

Most built-in Word templates are made to be customized. You can remove sample text and graphics, replacing them with names, logos, and other details appropriate for you or your company and adding text and graphics of your own. You can also adjust styles, change or delete AutoText entries, edit macros, and rearrange toolbars and menus for use with documents you create using the template.

The most straightforward way to customize a document template is to choose File, Open, and then select Document Templates from the Files of Type list. Select one of the templates to customize, and then click Open.

Tip #75 from
Faithe Wempen

To make a copy of a template rather than overwrite the original, choose File, New, More Word Templates. In the New dialog box, click the Template button, and select the template you want to copy. Then click OK, and a copy of that template opens for editing. Save the template under a new name when you are finished editing it.

After you open the document template, make any changes that you want to have on every document that you create with the template. For example, if you want documents based on the Elegant Letter template to use 12-point type instead of 10, select all the text areas (drag across them), and then change the font size to 12.

You might also want to type some *boilerplate* text (text that you will use every time you use the template) so that you don't have to type it each time. For example, for a letter, you might pre-enter your return address and your signature block.

After making your changes, don't forget to save your work.

Note

If you want to use a template to start new documents, you must save it in the designated Templates folder. (By default, it's C:\Program Files\Microsoft Office\Templates, but you can change this location on the File Locations tab of the Options dialog box.) If you save a template anywhere else, the template won't appear in the New dialog box so that you can choose it.

COPYING STYLES AND SETTINGS BETWEEN TEMPLATES

If you design many documents, eventually you will wind up with a large collection of templates. If you've saved a style in a special-purpose template, you might want to make it available to all your documents. Alternatively, you might want to consolidate styles, AutoText entries, macros, and other document elements from several templates. To manage styles and templates, Word includes an all-purpose tool called the *Organizer*.

Although you can open the Organizer in several ways, the easiest way is through the Style dialog box.

To copy a style from one template to another, perform these steps:

1. Open a document that contains the style you want to copy to another document or template.
2. Choose Format, Style. The Style dialog box opens.
3. Click the Organizer button. The Organizer dialog box appears, as shown in Figure 11.9. Click the Styles tab, if it's not currently visible.
4. The left pane displays styles from the current document. If you prefer to see styles in the current template, select the template from the Styles Available In drop-down list. (Be sure to use the left pane.)

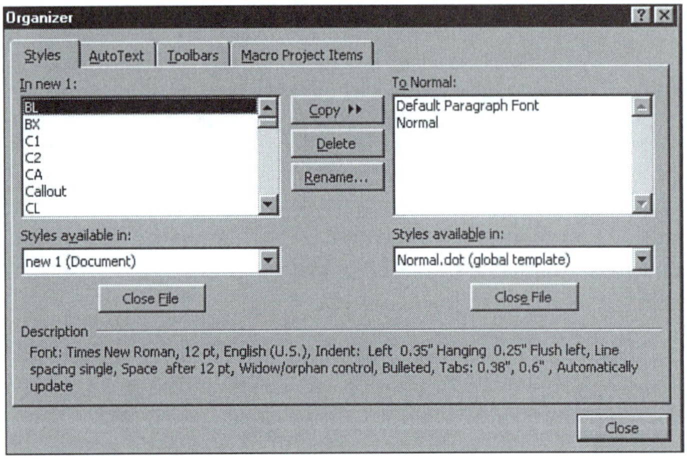

Figure 11.9
Use Word's Organizer to copy styles between documents and templates.

5. By default, the right pane displays styles in the Normal document template. If you want to copy files to another template, click the Close File button beneath the right pane; when that button changes to Open File, click and open the template or document you want to use instead.

Tip #76 from *Faithe Wempen*

Remember, you can store styles in documents or in templates. If you want to reuse a style from a document, and you don't expect to reuse the style in other documents, just copy it to the document rather than store it in a template.

6. To copy a style, select its entry in the left pane, and click the Copy button.
7. To manage styles in either pane, select the style, and click the Delete or Rename button.
8. Use the other tabs to manage other document and template items. Click the Close button to save your changes.

TROUBLESHOOTING

DISPLAYING ALL STYLES

I can't find a particular style in the style list.

If you don't see the style you want on the Style list (from the Formatting toolbar), hold down the Shift key as you open the drop-down list; this action displays every available style, not just the ones currently in use.

APPLYING STYLES TO ENTIRE PARAGRAPHS

I applied a style to a paragraph, but the style affected only a character.

If you click in a paragraph before applying a style to it, make sure that you have not inadvertently selected a character or a space. If you apply a style with text selected (even a single character or a single space), the character features of the style will apply only to the selection. Either position the insertion point in the paragraph without selecting, or select the entire paragraph.

SUPPRESSING AUTOMATIC UPDATES

I formatted a section of text, and those changes were automatically applied to some other paragraphs too, without my permission.

If a certain style changes itself every time you change some text formatted with it, perhaps the Automatically Update feature has been turned on for that style. To turn it off, choose Format, Style. Select the style from the list, and click Modify. Deselect the Automatically Update check box from the dialog box that appears.

REPEATING STYLES

I need to apply the same style to a number of noncontiguous paragraphs, but it's really tedious.

If you become tired of applying the same styles over and over, try assigning a shortcut key to a style. Choose Format, Style, and select the style; click Modify. Then, click the Shortcut Key button. Type the shortcut key combination you want to assign, and then click the Assign button.

REVERTING TO STYLE

I want to remove manual formatting from some text but retain the properties of the original style.

To strip off all manual formatting, leaving some text formatted according to the paragraph style applied to it, select the text and press Ctrl+spacebar.

CHAPTER 12

Correcting and Polishing Your Document

In this chapter

USING WORD TO CHECK YOUR SPELLING

If you studied the spelling and grammar checker in the Works Word Processor in Chapter 3, "Introducing the Works Word Processor," this section will seem like a review. That's because both Word and Works share the same spelling and grammar checker controls.

As you create or edit a document, Word automatically flags, with a wavy red underline, words it can't find in its built-in dictionary. With a green wavy underline, it flags grammar constructions it doesn't recognize. When you click the Spelling and Grammar button on the Standard toolbar, Word zips through the current selection or your entire document, stopping at each possible misspelling and grammatical error. You can accept its suggestions, make your own corrections, or ignore the advice.

WHAT THE SPELLING CHECKER CAN AND CAN'T DO

Word comes with its own dictionary of words, as well as a custom dictionary, in which you can add your own terms (such as proper names and technical jargon). When Word checks the spelling of words in your document, it compares them with the contents of its built-in dictionary and your custom dictionary and reports any words that do not appear in either place.

The spelling checker also flags consecutively repeated words, which is good news if you sometimes type **`the the end`**.

Note

When you first run Word, it adds your last name and your company's name to the custom dictionary file.

Word's spelling checker alerts you only when you use a word that isn't in its dictionary. If you've chosen the wrong word—typing **`profit and less`** instead of **`profit and loss`**, for example—Word does not flag the error. The moral? Spelling checkers are useful for catching obvious typos, but you should still proofread important documents carefully.

HOW TO CHECK YOUR SPELLING

Word gives you two options for correcting spelling and typing mistakes. You can fix typos as you work, or you can type the words on the screen as fast as you can and clean up the misspellings later. Either way, as you go, Word marks words that it cannot identify with a wavy red underline.

Note

The red marks that flag possible misspelled words are visible only on the screen. They don't show when you print.

To correct a typo right away, right-click the marked word, and then make a selection from the pop-up menu you see in Figure 12.1.

Figure 12.1
Choose the correct spelling from the list of suggestions, or select one of the other commands.

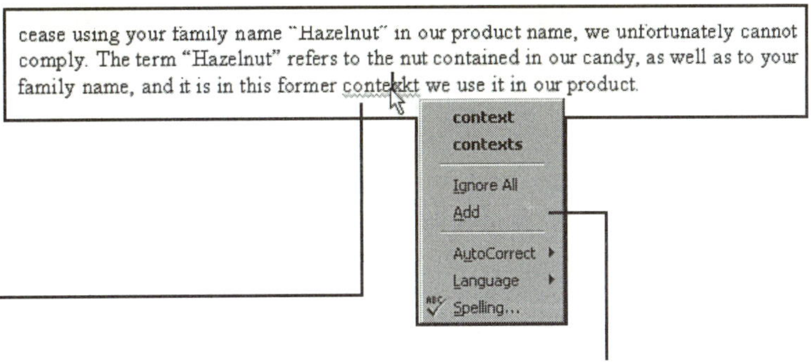

Your choices are as follow:

- **Use one of the suggestions**—Word usually takes its best shot at guessing what you tried to type, offering one or more options. If the correct spelling is in this boldface list, select it.
- **Tell Word that the spelling is correct**—The word in question might be a foreign word or a proper name, or it just might not be in Word's dictionary. In either case, click Ignore All, and Word stops flagging all future occurrences of that word in the current document.
- **Add the word to your custom dictionary**—Select Add, and Word will never again mark the selected word as misspelled.
- **Add the word to your AutoCorrect list**—If you regularly misspell the word in question, and the correct spelling is listed as a boldface entry at the top of the shortcut menu, add the word to your AutoCorrect list. Click AutoCorrect, and choose the proper spelling from the cascading menu that appears at the right. From now on, Word will automatically substitute the word you chose for the one you mistyped.

Caution

AutoCorrect can get you into trouble if you're indiscriminate in its use. For example, suppose that you sometimes misspell *pain* as *pian*, but you also sometimes misspell *piano* as *pian*. If you set AutoCorrect to change all instances of pian to pain, it may correct some instances you did not intend, and no wavy red underline will help you notice. To learn more about AutoCorrect, see "AutoCorrect: Fixing Typos On-the-Fly," later in this chapter.

If the wavy red and green underlines bother you onscreen, you can turn off their display. See "Changing Your Spelling and Grammar Options," later in this chapter.

Checking the Spelling and Grammar in the Entire Document

Even when automatic spell-checking is turned off, you can still use the spelling checker to look up a word, check a paragraph, or go through your entire document.

1. Select the text to check. If you don't make a selection, Word checks the entire document.

2. Choose Tools, Spelling and Grammar, or click the Spelling and Grammar button, or press F7.
3. If any misspellings or grammatical mistakes appear in the selection, Word highlights the possible error and pops up a list of suggested alternatives, as shown in Figure 12.2. (Figure 12.2 shows a spelling mistake; the controls might be slightly different for a grammar mistake.) Do whatever is appropriate to resolve the problem:
   - Click the AutoCorrect button to add this typo and its correction to the AutoCorrect list.
   - Select the correct spelling, and then click Change to fix the typo instantly.
   - Click Change All to fix every instance of this misspelling in the current document.
   - Click Add to add the word to your custom dictionary so that Word stops flagging it as misspelled.
   - Click Ignore to tell Word to ignore this instance of this word.
   - Click Ignore All to tell Word to ignore all instances of this word in the current document.
   - Click in the Not in Dictionary box, and type the correction yourself if Word's suggestions aren't correct.

Tip #77 from *Faithe Wempen*

If you decide not to accept that last change you made in the Spelling and Grammar dialog box, you can undo it with a click of the Undo button.

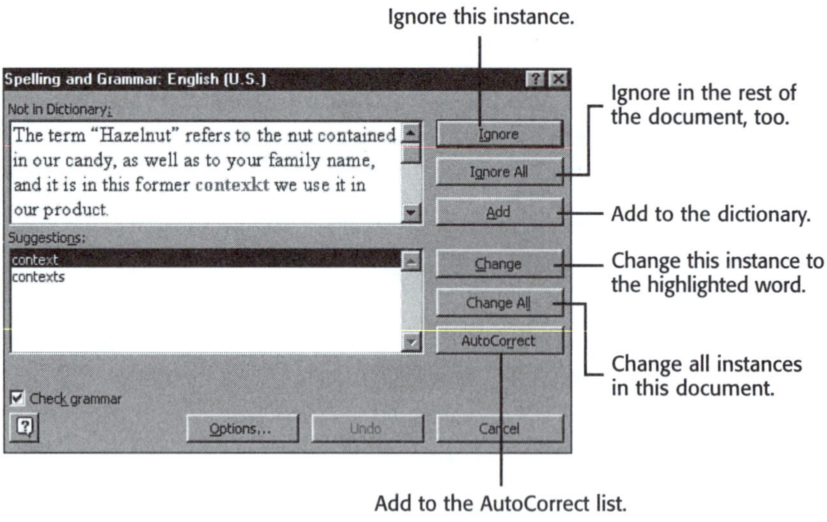

Figure 12.2
When Word identifies a word it doesn't recognize, you can ignore it, change it, or mark it as okay.

4. After Word has finished checking the entire document, it pops up a dialog box telling you that the spell check is complete. Click OK to return to the editing window.

Note

If you are checking a selected block of text, and no errors appear in the selected text, Word offers to check the rest of your document. Click Cancel to return to the document.

MORE ABOUT THE GRAMMAR CHECK

Grammar-checking works basically the same as spell-checking. Possible mistakes have a wavy underline, but in green instead of red. You can right-click a green-underlined word or phrase to see what Word thinks is the appropriate correction. If you agree, accept the correction by clicking it on that menu. You can also check all the grammar at the same time that you check the spelling.

The main difference between the spelling check and the grammar check is that the Spelling and Grammar dialog box has fewer options when it finds a grammar error. You can either Ignore, Ignore All, Change, or go to the Next Sentence. You can't change all at once because every instance is unique. A sample grammar error appears in Figure 12.3.

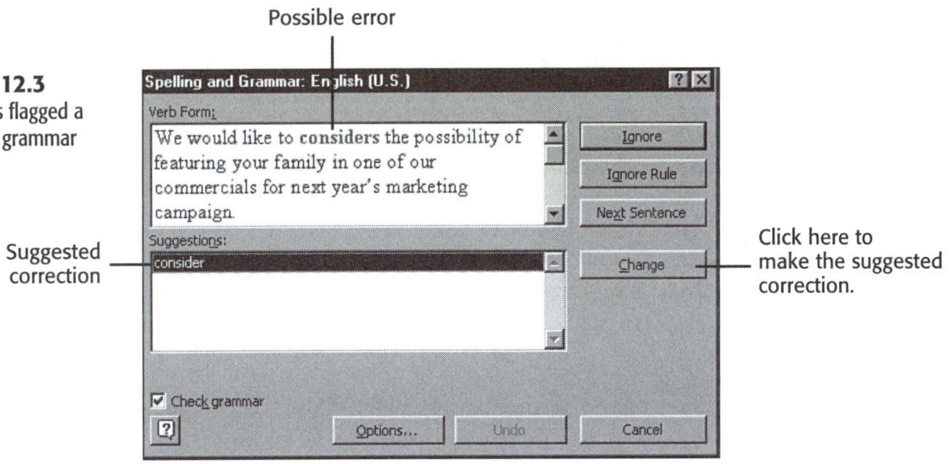

Figure 12.3
Word has flagged a potential grammar error.

Caution

Word's grammar checker can sometimes steer you wrong. It can suggest a correction for a perfectly good sentence, and the correction, if made, causes the sentence to lose its meaning or become incorrect. For example, it might incorrectly suggest *whom* when *who* is appropriate, or it might recommend that you lowercase the words in a heading that should be all uppercase. Take its advice with a grain of salt.

CHANGING YOUR SPELLING AND GRAMMAR OPTIONS

You can set a number of options to make the spelling and grammar checks go more according to your plans. You can set up special dictionaries, for example, and ignore certain types of false alarms.

From the Spelling and Grammar dialog box (refer to Figure 12.3), click the Options button to see your spelling and grammar choices (see Figure 12.4).

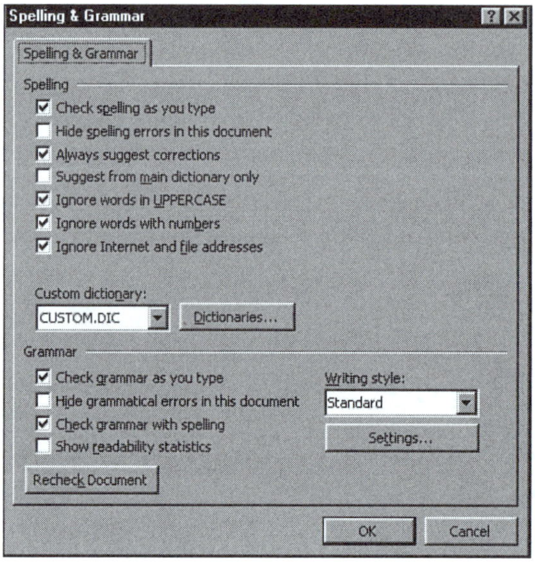

Figure 12.4
Customize how the spelling and grammar checks work.

For example, you can turn off the red and green wavy lines on the onscreen display. To some people, those wavy lines are a distraction. You can still run the regular spelling and grammar checks with the Spelling and Grammar button, even with the word-by-word check off.

To turn off Word's on-the-fly spell-checking, deselect the Check Spelling as You Type check box at the top of the list. To hide the green marks (grammar errors), deselect the Check Grammar as You Type check box. These changes affect not only the current document but all future documents you work on.

You can also hide the red and green marks only in the current document. To hide the marks only in the current document, select the Hide Spelling Errors in This Document and/or Hide Grammatical Errors in This Document check boxes.

The grammar checker offers a choice of several writing styles. Formal is the pickiest and identifies the most problems. Casual is the least picky and allows the most leeway. The default is Standard. You can change the writing style by choosing a new one in the Writing Style drop-down list.

If you are knowledgeable about grammar, you might have your own opinions about some of these rules. To set the grammar-checking rules, follow these steps:

1. From the Spelling and Grammar dialog box, click Options, or from the main Word screen choose Tools, Options and click the Spelling & Grammar tab.
2. Click the Settings button under Writing Style. The Grammar Settings dialog box opens (see Figure 12.5).

Figure 12.5
You can make your own decisions about various grammar rules from here.

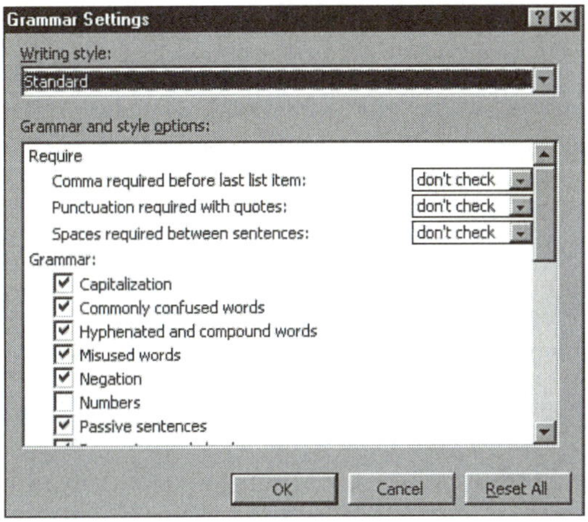

3. Choose the writing style you want to modify from the Writing Style drop-down list. Choose Custom if you want to leave the existing styles undisturbed.
4. Scroll through the Grammar and Style Options list, and select or deselect check boxes for each rule.
5. In the Require section, open any of the drop-down lists, and make your selection for these special grammar and punctuation rules.
6. Click OK to return to the Spelling and Grammar Options dialog box.
7. Click OK again to return to the spelling and grammar check.

SAVING TIME WITH AUTOMATIC CHANGES

Does Word 2000 have more *Autos* than a Ford factory, or what? That's the way it seems sometimes. Word alone has *AutoText*, *AutoComplete*, and *AutoFormat as You Type*, which all fall under the general heading of *AutoCorrect*. The names can be confusingly similar, but each one of these "AutoSomethings" has a specific purpose: to fix obvious mistakes automatically and eliminate unnecessary keystrokes as you work.

To see and adjust all the Auto- options available, choose Tools, AutoCorrect. Each tab in this dialog box serves a slightly different purpose.

AUTOCORRECT: FIXING TYPOS ON-THE-FLY

AutoCorrect helps you with your spelling. Word watches as you type, waiting for combinations of keys that it finds on the AutoCorrect list. In some cases, Word automatically replaces what you typed, usually so quickly that you don't even notice (if you type **`teh`**, for example, AutoCorrect changes it to `the` immediately).

Word's AutoCorrect feature is turned on by default. To check it yourself, try misspelling the word *the* (type **`teh`**). When you add an entry to the AutoCorrect list, Word makes the substitution without asking for your permission. For this reason, AutoCorrect entries are generally limited to replacements for words that you know are incorrectly spelled.

However, you can also add entries for long words or phrases you use often. For example, if your company's name is *Willard & Sechrest Distributors Unlimited*, that's a lot to type in each time. You can add the company name as an AutoCorrect entry and type in an abbreviation instead. Every time you enter the abbreviation, AutoCorrect replaces it with the full name.

Tip #78 from *Faithe Wempen*

Any time Word makes an AutoCorrect change, you can cancel the change by clicking the Undo button. When Word turns your `(c)` into a copyright symbol, for example, press Ctrl+Z or click the Undo button to change it right back, and then continue typing.

You can add AutoCorrect entries through the Spelling and Grammar dialog box; that's the easiest way. You can also add them through the AutoCorrect dialog box (see Figure 12.6). Open it by choosing Tools, AutoCorrect.

Make sure that the Replace Text as You Type check box is selected. Then enter a new error-and-correction pair in the Replace Text as You Type list, and click Add. For example, if you want an abbreviation for a long company name, enter the abbreviation in the Replace text box; then, enter the actual company name in the With text box. Click Add to add the entry to the list. Click OK to exit the dialog box. The next time you type the abbreviation, AutoCorrect enters the full company name.

If you find yourself becoming annoyed with certain AutoCorrect corrections that you don't want, you can remove them from the list. Simply select the AutoCorrect entry from the list in the AutoCorrect dialog box, and click the Delete button.

AUTOTEXT: INSERTING BOILERPLATE TEXT

If you create business documents, you probably find yourself using the same sentences and paragraphs over and over again. Word lets you automatically insert this kind of boilerplate text by defining a shorthand name for it and then using pull-down menus or a shortcut key to expand the shorthand name into the full text.

In a press release, for example, the last paragraph is usually a standard description of the company issuing the release. You could define an AutoText entry for that paragraph and assign the shorthand name *pr-close* to it. Now all you have to do is type that shorthand name and press Enter or F3 to stuff the entire paragraph into your document at the insertion point.

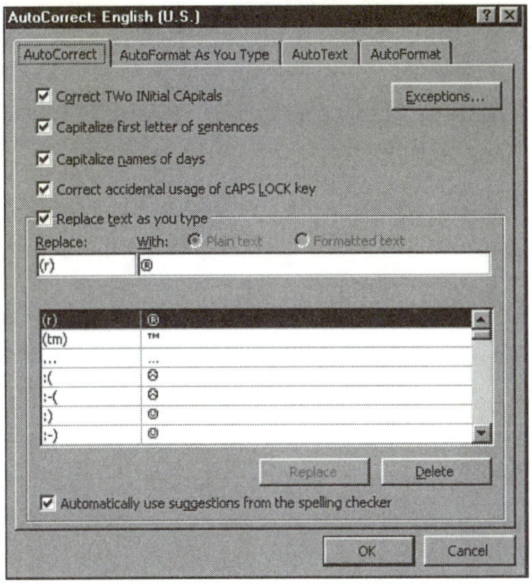

Figure 12.6
AutoCorrect lists all the "errors" and replacements it currently has on file.

Note

When you first install Word, the AutoText list includes more than 40 entries, most of them elements in common business letters. It also recognizes the days of the week and the months of the year, so if you type `febr` and press F3, `February` appears in your document.

To create a new AutoText entry, follow these steps:

1. In the current document, select the text and/or graphics you want to insert into future documents. (If your entry is a paragraph, make sure that you include the entire paragraph in the selection.)
2. Choose Tools, AutoCorrect; then click the AutoText tab.
3. Check the Preview window at the bottom of the dialog box shown in Figure 12.7. If that entry is correct, type the shorthand name for your boilerplate text (in this case, **`pr-close`**) in the box labeled Enter AutoText Entries Here.
4. If you want the AutoText entry to be available to all documents, choose Normal (Global Template) from the list labeled Look In. To assign the entry to another template, choose its name from the same list.
5. Click Add to save the new AutoText entry.

Tip #79 from *Faithe Wempen*

When you type the first four letters of some (but not all) AutoText items, such as months, Word displays a pop-up tip that suggests the complete word or phrase. When you see this ScreenTip, you can press Enter or F3 to accept the suggestion and insert the AutoText entry. Just continue typing if you want to ignore the AutoText suggestion.

To prevent these AutoComplete tips from popping up at all, clear the check box labeled Show AutoComplete Tip for AutoText and Dates at the top of the AutoCorrect dialog box.

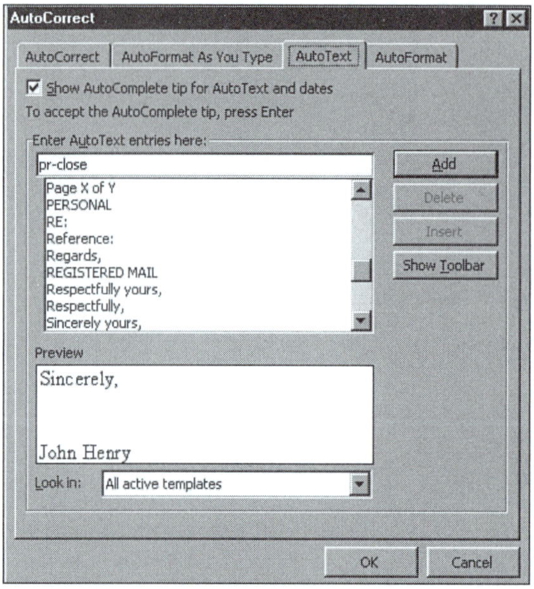

Figure 12.7 AutoText entries can be entire documents or simple words and phrases. Word includes a list of predefined AutoText entries that include dates and common business phrases.

After you've added an AutoText entry, you can use it in any document based on that template. When you store the AutoText entry in the Normal document template, it's available to all documents.

To use AutoText in a document, perform these steps:

1. Position the insertion point in the document where you want to add the AutoText entry.
2. Type the name of the AutoText entry (you don't have to follow the name with a space).
3. If you've turned on the AutoComplete option, Word pops up a ScreenTip as soon as it recognizes what you've typed. Press Enter to insert the AutoText item.

   Alternatively, if AutoComplete is turned off, enter the shorthand name for your boilerplate text, and press the F3 key.

Word inserts the boilerplate text at the insertion point.

To change an AutoText entry, follow the preceding steps to create a new AutoText entry with the same name as the old one. Answer Yes when Word asks whether you want to redefine the entry.

To delete an AutoText entry, just highlight its name and click the Delete button.

AutoFormat as You Type

By default, Word changes some characters you type into a different format. For example, when you enter a fraction such as 1/2, Word replaces those three characters with a single, neat publishing character— ½. Any time you find Word changing what you've typed for no apparent reason, this feature is probably the reason.

To see all the formatting changes that Word can make automatically, choose Tools, AutoCorrect. Click the tab labeled AutoFormat As You Type, and you see the dialog box shown in Figure 12.8.

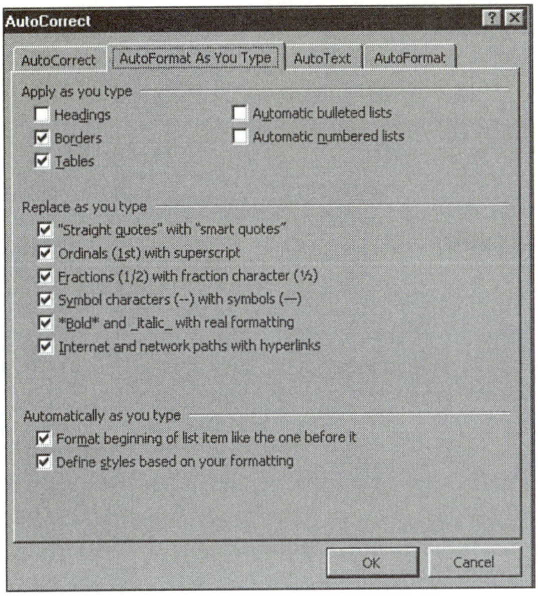

Figure 12.8
Adjust the AutoFormat options in this dialog box to match your preferences.

I like the way Word changes my straight quotes to the curly variety and changes a pair of hyphens to a dash, so I routinely leave these items turned on. I prefer seeing fractions as I type them, however, so I clear that check box. Also, because I usually create documents destined for paper instead of the Web, I turn off Word's option to convert Internet paths to clickable hyperlinks.

Tip #80 from *Faithe Wempen*

If formatting documents isn't your cup of tea, try out Word's AutoFormat feature. AutoFormat looks over your document and automatically suggests formatting changes. To use this feature, choose Format, AutoFormat.

→ To learn how to format text, **see** "Formatting Text," **p. 219**.
→ To learn how to format entire documents, **see** "Changing the Look of a Page," **p. 214**.

FINDING THE RIGHT WORD

Sooner or later, every writer needs help finding exactly the right word. When you're stuck, use Word's built-in thesaurus to look up other words that might work in your current document.

To look up synonyms in the Word Thesaurus, do the following:

1. Click to move the insertion point into the word you want to replace (you don't have to select the entire word).
2. Choose Tools, Language, Thesaurus, or press Shift+F7. The Thesaurus box appears, as in Figure 12.9, with the word you chose in the Looked Up drop-down list box.

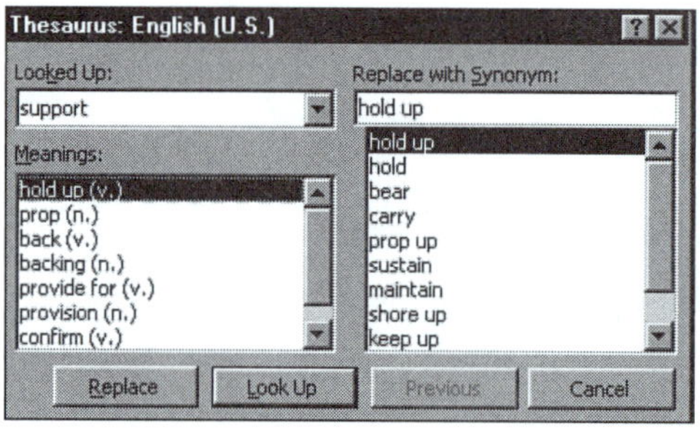

Figure 12.9
Use Word's Thesaurus to search for a more appropriate word.

3. Select the appropriate meaning for the context in which you are using the word from the Meanings list. This list can also allow you to select related words or antonyms—words that are opposite in meaning to the one you selected.
4. If you find a suitable word in the Replace with Synonym list, select it and click the Replace button.
5. If one of the suggested synonyms is close but not quite right, select that word and click the Look Up button.
6. To exit without making a change, just click the Cancel button or press Esc.

TROUBLESHOOTING

SETTING SPELLING OPTIONS IN A CLEAN DOCUMENT

I'd like to set spelling options, but I don't have any misspelled words to use to get into the spelling checker.

If you want to set spelling options, but there are no misspelled words in the document (so the Spelling and Grammar dialog box won't open), you can access the same controls by choosing Tools, Options and clicking the Spelling & Grammar tab. Alternatively, you can deliberately type a misspelled word and then delete it after making changes in the Spelling and Grammar dialog box.

REMOVING ERRONEOUS WORDS FROM THE DICTIONARY

Oops! I just added a misspelled word to the dictionary! Now Word won't mark it as mispelled anymore.

If you accidentally add a word to the dictionary, you can remove it. From the Spelling & Grammar options, click the Dictionaries button. Then click Edit and then OK to open the dictionary list as a Word file. Delete any words you don't want (and/or add any additional words, pressing Enter after each one), and close the file, saving your changes to it.

CHAPTER 13

Working with Tables and Columns

In this chapter

USING TABLES TO ORGANIZE INFORMATION

How do you handle complex lists in which each item consists of two or more details? Word tables are the perfect tool to organize this kind of information into neat rows and columns. When you give each item its own row and break the details into separate columns, you wind up with an easy-to-read, information-packed table. With the help of tables, you can perform the following tasks:

- Align words and numbers into precise columns (with or without borders).
- Put text and graphics together with a minimum of fuss.
- Arrange paragraphs of text side by side, as in a résumé.
- Create professional-looking forms.

Word tables include faint gridlines that help you see the outlines of the rows and columns when you're entering text. If you want, you can add borders, shading, and custom cell formats to give your tables a professional look. Also, if you've ever tried to line up columns using tabs, you will appreciate how much more easily you can work with tables.

HOW WORD TABLES WORK

As with spreadsheets, Word tables organize information into rows and columns. You add text (or numbers or graphics) inside cells; if you enter text that's wider than the cell, it wraps to a new line, increasing the height of the cell automatically. You can insert and delete rows and columns or move entire columns by dragging from one location to another. You can also change column width and row height, or you can merge cells to form headings and labels. The parts of a typical Word table, shown in Figure 13.1, are as follows:

- **Border**—Unlike the nonprinting gridlines, these lines show up when you print. You can adjust their thickness and location.
- **Cell**—The basic unit of a table. Each cell is formed by the intersection of a row and a column.
- **Column**—Each table can have up to 63 columns.
- **Heading**—Designate one or more rows to serve as labels for the columns below them.
- **Row**—A table can have up to 32,767 rows.

→ To learn more about merged cells, **see** "Merging and Splitting Cells," **p. 277**.

Caution

Word tables enable you to perform basic mathematical calculations, including totals, averages, and counts. The procedures for adding formulas are daunting, however, and you have to update the results manually if you change the numbers that go into a formula. If you have to perform calculations on data in a table, use an embedded Works spreadsheet instead (see Chapter 5, "Using the Works Spreadsheet").

Figure 13.1
Use Word tables to organize detailed information in easy-to-follow rows and columns.

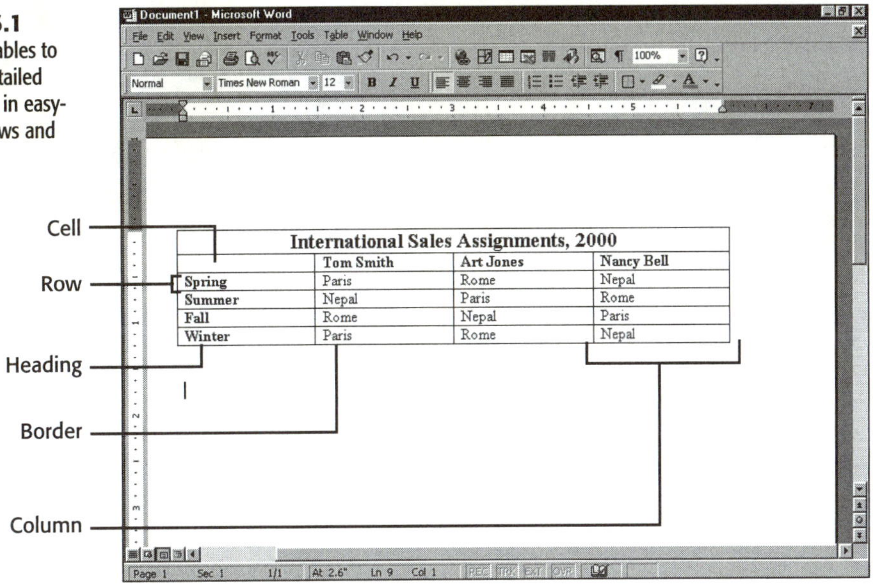

By default, Word tables include *borders*—lines that separate cells and define the boundaries of the table itself on the printed page. Using tables with borders is a good way to insert feature comparisons, price lists, and other tabular material in documents. Remove the borders to use tables as a way to arrange blocks of text and other objects on the page without having to fuss with columns and tabs stops.

Tip #81 from *Faithe Wempen*

If you want to hide all traces of a table, turn off gridlines after you've entered data. Choose Table, Hide Gridlines. If gridlines are hidden, choose Show Gridlines to reveal them again. This command affects all tables in the current document.

➔ To find details on how to set tab stops, **see** "Positioning Text with Tabs," **p. 227**.

ADDING A TABLE TO A DOCUMENT

There are several ways to create a table; the following sections give you the rundown on each method.

CREATING TABLES QUICKLY WITH A FEW CLICKS

Click the Insert Table button to add an unformatted table to your document quickly. When you click the button, a table grid (like the one in Figure 13.2) drops down from the toolbar. Drag the pointer down and to the right to select the number of rows and columns for your table.

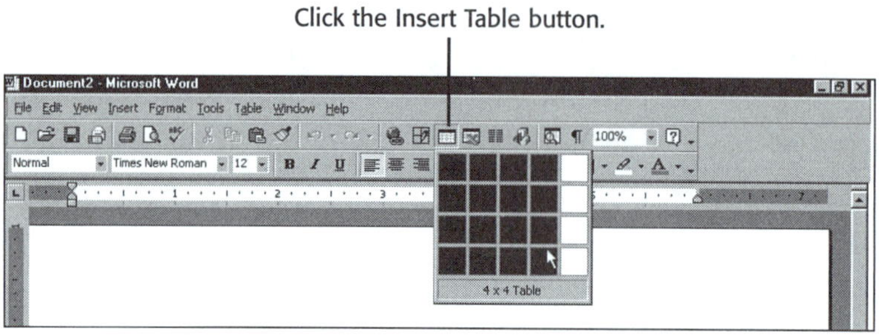

Figure 13.2
Click and drag to insert an unformatted table. The caption tells you that this table will include four rows of four columns each.

When you use the Insert Table button, the resulting table is completely unformatted. It fills the entire width of the current page, with columns of equal size and rows that match the height of the font defined in the Normal paragraph style. If you're willing to go through the extra formatting steps, using this button is an acceptable way to add a few rows and columns to a document. However, there's a much faster and easier way to create the exact table you want, as explained in the next section.

Drawing a Complex Table

For anything more complex than a few simple rows and columns, you can use Word's extremely effective Table Drawing tool. Rather than drop a simple rectangle in your document, forcing you to rearrange the cells to fit your data, use this feature to turn the mouse pointer into a "pen." You can use this pen to draw the table exactly as you want it to appear on the page.

To draw a table within a Word document, follow these steps:

1. Click the Tables and Borders button. Word switches into Page Layout view if necessary, displays the floating Tables and Borders toolbar, and changes the shape of the pointer to a pen.
2. Point to the place in your document where you want the upper-left corner of the table to appear.
3. Click and drag down and to the right until you've drawn a rectangle that's roughly the size you want your final table to be.
4. Use the pen to draw lines for the rows and columns inside the table. You don't have to draw full lines; as you draw, you will see the lines "snap" to connect with those you've already drawn, as in Figure 13.3.

Tip #82 from *Faithe Wempen*

As you draw, rows and columns can appear in varying sizes, with uneven spacing between them. Don't worry. Just draw the proper number of rows and columns; then, select some or all of them, and click the Distribute Rows Evenly and/or Distribute Columns Evenly buttons to resize them all in one smooth motion.

5. If you make a mistake, click the Eraser button. Then, click the line to erase; it disappears. Click the Eraser button again to turn it off when finished.

6. If the mouse pointer is still a pen, click the Draw Table button to turn it off.

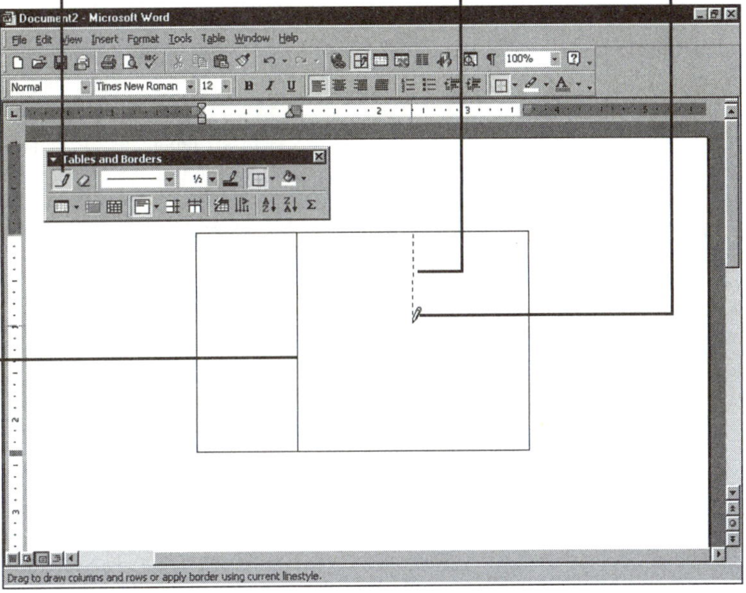

Figure 13.3
Use this pen-shaped pointer to draw the table you want. Use lines of varying lengths to create merged cells for titles and group headings.

Don't worry about neatness when you're using the Table Drawing tool. After you have the basic outline of your table in place, you can use the Tables and Borders toolbar to give it a slick, professional appearance.

Tip #83 from *Faithe Wempen*

If you regularly use the same type of table in documents, create a blank table and save it as an AutoText entry, complete with formatting and headings. To reuse the table, insert that AutoText entry into your documents whenever you need it.

→ To save a table with AutoText, **see** "AutoText: Inserting Boilerplate Text," **p. 262**.

Converting Text to a Table

What do you do when you've already entered text in a document and you know it would work better in a table? You don't have to cut and paste. Instead, you can convert the block of text to a table.

To convert text to a Word table, follow these steps:

1. Select the entire block of text you want to convert. Be sure to include the paragraph mark for each row you plan to convert (see Figure 13.4).

Tip #84 from *Faithe Wempen*

Click the Show/Hide ¶ button on the Standard toolbar to see tabs and paragraph marks when you're getting ready to convert text to a table. This step enables you to see easily whether you need to add another tab character to a row.

2. Click the Insert Table button to surround the selected text with a table instantly.

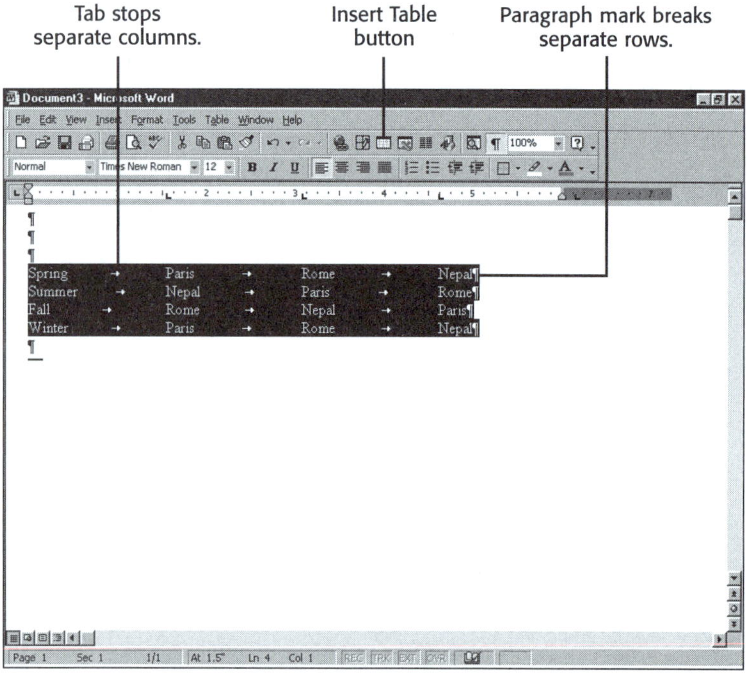

Figure 13.4
Highlight the text with separators in place, and then click the Insert Table button.

Note

If you want to split data into two or more columns per row, the data must include separator characters that define the end of each row and each item within the row. Word can use tabs, commas, or other characters as separators. If the text-to-table conversion doesn't give the expected results, you might have to edit your raw data to add separator characters in one or more places.

3. If the one-button approach doesn't work (if it comes out with the gridlines in the wrong places, for example), click the Undo button on the Standard toolbar, and try again. This time, choose Table, Convert Text to Table.

4. In the Convert Text to Table dialog box (see Figure 13.5), choose the separator character your text uses. Look in the Number of Columns box. If the number displayed here doesn't match the number of columns you expect to see in the new table, click Cancel and make sure that the selected text contains no stray paragraph marks.
5. If you want to apply automatic formatting options during the conversion process, click the AutoFormat button and adjust options as needed.
6. Click OK to complete the conversion.

To convert the contents of a table to text, reverse the process: Select the entire table, and then choose Table, Convert Table to Text. Word enables you to choose tab characters or paragraph marks to separate items in each row.

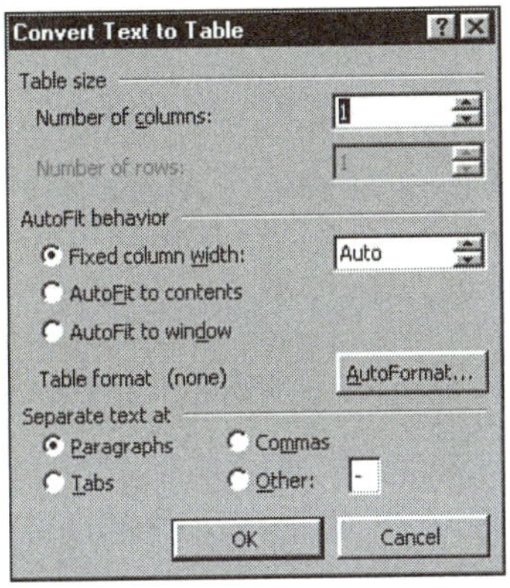

Figure 13.5
Before you convert text to a table, specify which character separates items in each row.

WORKING WITH TABLES

Anything you can put in a Word document can also go into a table: text, numbers, symbols, or graphics, for example. You can even add automatic numbering to the items in a row or column of a table; as you move items around, they stay in the right sequence.

After you have stashed your information neatly in a table, you can rearrange it to your heart's content. You can move cells, rows, or columns; change the height of a row or the width of a column; and even instruct Word to reformat your entire table automatically—all with a few mouse clicks.

➔ To learn how to format simple lists with bullets and numbers, **see** "Creating Bulleted and Numbered Lists," **p. 229**.

SELECTING CELLS, ROWS, AND COLUMNS

Before you can rearrange, resize, or reformat a part of a table, you must select it. Table 13.1 lists the specific techniques required to select parts of a table.

Table 13.1 Selecting Parts of a Table

To Select This Part of a Table	Do This
Cell contents	Drag the mouse pointer over the text you want to select.
Cell	Point to the inside left edge of the cell and click.
Entire row	Point and click just outside the left edge of the first cell in the row.
Entire column	Point to the gridline or border at the top of the column; click when you see a small arrow pointing downward.
Multiple cells, rows, or columns	Select a cell, row, or column; then, click and drag to select additional cells, rows, or columns.
Whole table	Choose Table, Select Table.

Entering and Editing Table Data

To begin entering data into a table, click to position the insertion point anywhere in the cell, and then start typing. Don't press Enter unless you want to start a new paragraph within the cell; if Word runs out of room, it wraps the text within the cell. To move to the next cell, press Tab. (If you're already at the end of a row, this action moves the selection to the first cell in the next row.) To move to the preceding cell, press Shift+Tab. Use the arrow keys to move up or down, one row at a time.

Tip #85 from *Faithe Wempen*

Pressing the Tab key moves the cursor from cell to cell within a table. If you want to insert a tab character, hold down the Ctrl key and then press Tab.

Moving and Copying Parts of a Table

If you know how to move and copy text and objects in a Word document, you will have no problem moving and copying parts of a table. You can use the Windows Clipboard or drag cells, rows, and columns from one place to another.

Similar to the Cut or Copy menu commands (or their keyboard shortcuts) used to place one or more cells, rows, or columns on the Clipboard, Windows adds a Paste Cells, Paste Rows, or Paste Columns command on the Edit menu. You can also find the command on right-click shortcut menus. To use drag-and-drop techniques, select the object you want to copy or move first, and then drag it to its new location.

When you move or copy cells, the contents of the Clipboard replace the cells in the new location. When you move or copy rows or columns, existing rows and columns slide out of the way to make room.

→ To learn more details about cutting and pasting in a Windows program, **see** "Moving and Copying Text," **p. 49**.

Tip #86 from *Faithe Wempen*

The commands on Word's Table menu vary depending on what is selected. Before you can use the menus to delete a row or a column, for example, you must select a row or column; otherwise, you will never see the menu choices you're seeking.

CHANGING COLUMN WIDTHS AND ROW HEIGHTS

One way to make a table more readable is to adjust its column widths so that each column takes up just enough room to accommodate the information in it.

Tip #87 from *Faithe Wempen*

When the insertion point is within a table, markers on the horizontal ruler define the margins and tab settings for each cell. Although you can adjust column and table widths using the rectangles, triangles, and other symbols, manipulating the table directly is far easier.

To adjust the width of a column, point to the right border of the column; when the mouse pointer changes to a two-headed arrow, click and drag to the left or right. Hold down the Alt key while dragging to see column and table measurements in the ruler, as in Figure 13.6.

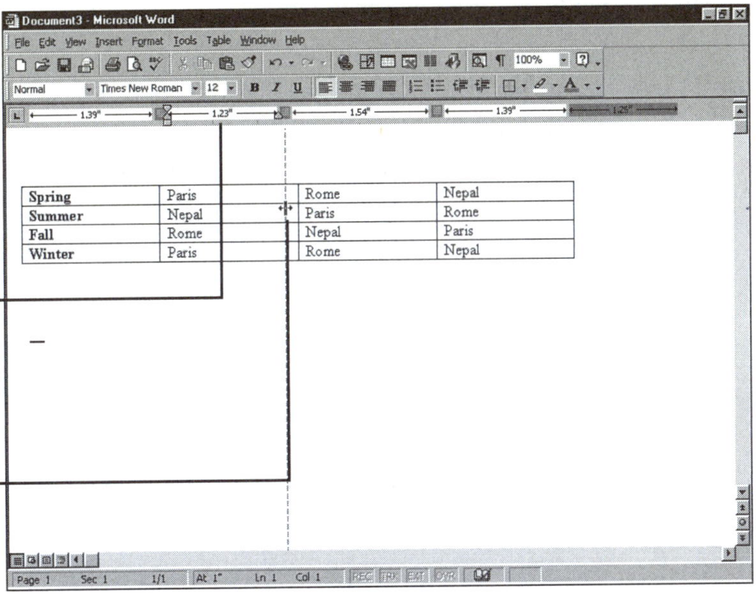

Figure 13.6
To change a column's width, point to the right border until the pointer changes to this shape, and then drag.

Column measurements in the ruler

Mouse pointer

When you use the mouse pointer to reduce the width of a column, Word automatically increases the width of the adjacent column, and vice versa. To maintain all other column widths, hold down the Shift key while you drag the ruler markers or the column boundaries; when you do so, the width of your table increases or decreases the same amount as the change you make in the selected column.

Tip #88 from *Faithe Wempen*

Want to adjust the width of your columns automatically according to what you've already typed in them? If you want to use AutoFit for the entire table, be sure to select the entire table. Then, choose Table, Cell Height and Width, and click the AutoFit button on the Column tab. Note that this choice might not work properly if your table contains any merged cells.

Adding and Deleting Rows and Columns

You can easily add or remove rows and columns in your table. If you're comfortable with Word's Table and Borders toolbar, use the Draw Table and Eraser tools to add and delete new rows within an existing table. You can also follow the mouse-based and menu-based procedures listed in Table 13.2.

Tip #89 from *Faithe Wempen*

After you insert a row or column, you can easily add another in the same location. Just press F4 (the keyboard shortcut for Repeat Last Action).

If you get to the last row in a table and see that you have to add another row, press Tab. Word automatically creates a new row in the table.

Table 13.2 Table-Editing Techniques

To Perform This Action	Do This
Add a new row at the bottom of the table.	Click in the last cell of the last row; then press Tab.
Insert a row within the table.	Click in the row just below the place where you want to insert a new row; then click the Insert Rows button, or right-click and choose Insert Rows from the shortcut menu.
Insert a column within the table.	First, select the column to the right of the place where you want to add the new column; then click the Insert Columns button, or right-click and choose Insert Columns from the shortcut menu.
Add a new column to the right of the last column.	Aim the mouse pointer just to the right of the top-right edge of the table until it changes to a down-pointing arrow. Click to select the column; then click the Insert Columns button, or right-click and choose Insert Columns from the shortcut menu.
Delete one or more rows or columns.	Select the row(s) or column(s), right-click, and choose Delete Rows or Delete Columns from the shortcut menu.

Tip #90 from *Faithe Wempen*

When you add a new column, it might extend well beyond the right margin. In Page Layout view, you cannot see the right edge of the table to resize the column and bring the table back within the page margins. Switch to Normal view, and then use the horizontal scrollbar to see and modify the entire table.

If you want to remove rows or columns, don't use the Delete key. Pressing this key simply clears the contents of the selected cells, leaving the basic structure of the table intact. To remove rows or columns, you have to choose the appropriate command from the pull-down or shortcut menus.

Merging and Splitting Cells

For part of an effective table design, you might want to use a single large cell that spans several rows or columns. This technique is a great way to add a title to the first row of a table, as shown in Figure 13.1 at the beginning of this chapter. It's also the best way to label subgroupings within a table.

If you know that your table has to include this design element, you can add it when you create the table. Use the pen-shaped Draw Table tool to create rows or columns of the appropriate size and shape. On the other hand, if you've already created a table, you can merge two or more cells into a single larger cell.

Select the cells you want to merge; choose Table, Merge Cells. Note that this action preserves the contents of the first cell in the selection but erases the contents of everything else. To reverse the process and split a merged cell back into the original cells, choose Table, Split Cells.

Making Great-Looking Tables

Every table starts out as a collection of cells, rows, and columns, with identical character formatting in each cell. To make a table easier to read, you must resize rows and columns, reformat headings, add decorative borders, and use background colors and shading to set off individual sections. You can tackle each of these tasks individually, or you can use Word's Table AutoFormat feature to jump-start the process.

Letting Word Do the Work with AutoFormat

Any time the insertion point is within a table, you can choose Table, Table AutoFormat. Although I don't recommend that you use Word's AutoFormat feature for general documents, the Table AutoFormat feature usually works well. Because information is contained in neat rows and columns, Word can more easily analyze and format rows, columns, and headings automatically—and you can control each part of the process.

Caution

Before you start using Table AutoFormat, save your work (choose File, Save). That way, you can revert to the original if you are unhappy with the changes that Table AutoFormat makes.

To apply an AutoFormat to a table, do the following:

1. Position the insertion point anywhere in the table.
2. Choose Table, Table AutoFormat.
3. Choose one of the prebuilt designs (see Figure 13.7).

Tip #91 from
Faithe Wempen

Different formats are appropriate for different types of data; for example, some AutoFormats work perfectly with lists, and others give you your choice of grids. The Preview area in the Table AutoFormat dialog box shows you how each element of the table will look with the selected format. As you add and remove formatting options, the Preview display changes.

4. Adjust other format options in this dialog box:
   - AutoFormat can add borders, adjust colors and shading, and resize columns. To skip any of these steps, clear the associated check mark in the section labeled Formats to Apply.
   - To preserve the fonts you've already defined for the table, deselect the Font box.
   - AutoFormat assumes that your table has labels in the first column and headings in the first row. If your table doesn't include these elements, remove one or both check marks in the section labeled Apply Special Formats To.
   - In tables that contain numbers, AutoFormat assumes that the last row or last column contains totals. If this is not the case in the current table, deselect these check boxes in the section labeled Apply Special Formats To.
   - The AutoFit feature doesn't work properly if you've merged cells to form a single cell in one row. Deselect this option if you have trouble.
5. Click OK to apply the selected formats to the entire table.

Tip #92 from
Faithe Wempen

If the Table AutoFormat feature doesn't work when you try it, choose Edit, Undo AutoFormat (or press Ctrl+Z), and start again, choosing different options this time.

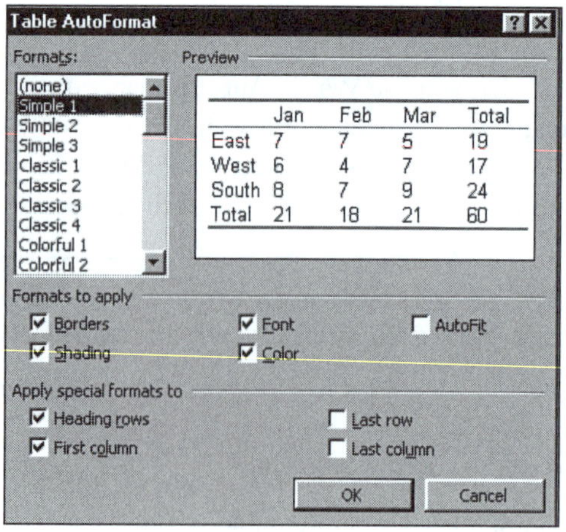

Figure 13.7
The Table AutoFormat feature gives your table more than 30 different formats.

Adding Emphasis to Rows and Columns

Use lines and shading to help your readers follow along as they read items in the same row or column. This formatting step is especially important when you have wide rows and long columns filled with details. Format column headings in bold, easy-to-read fonts so that they stand out clearly from the details in each row.

Adding borders to a table is simple. Use the Tables and Borders toolbar to specify thick or decorative lines around the outside of the table, thin lines between rows and columns, custom borders to separate headings and totals, or colored borders anywhere.

To add custom borders to a Word table, follow these steps:

1. Select the cells, rows, or columns where you want to add borders. If you click in the table without making a selection, Word assumes that you want to add borders to the current cell only.

2. Click the Tables and Borders button to display the Tables and Borders toolbar.

Note

All the choices on the Tables and Borders toolbar are also available in a three-tabbed dialog box. If you prefer dialog boxes to toolbars, choose Format, Borders and Shading.

3. Open the Line Style drop-down list, and choose the look you want for your borders.
4. Open the Line Weight drop-down list, and choose a border thickness. The default setting is a relatively thin .5-point line.

5. Click the Border Color button. Choose the default setting (Automatic) for printed documents; select one of 13 available colors if you plan to use your table in a Web page or send it to a color printer.

6. Click the drop-down arrow to the right of the Borders button to display all 10 available combinations of borders. If you plan to set multiple borders, click the horizontal bar just above the two rows of buttons, and drag the Borders menu off the toolbar so that it floats.
7. Click the button that corresponds to the border you want to adjust. The All Borders button adds a line to all sides of all cells in the current selection, and the Bottom Border button is useful for putting a thin double line under headings or under the last row before totals.

Tip #93 from *Faithe Wempen*

To remove an individual border, choose No Border from the list of Line Style options; then click the Borders button that corresponds to the border you want to change. To remove all lines around and within the selected cell or cells, click the Borders button; then click the No Border option at the far right of the second row.

8. If necessary, select another cell or cells, and repeat steps 3 through 7.

To add a gray or colored background within one or more cells, first select the cells, rows, or columns; then, click the arrow to the right of the Shading Color button on the Tables and Borders toolbar. The palette includes 40 choices, most of them representing various shades of gray.

Tip #94 from *Faithe Wempen*

Let the mouse pointer hover over the squares in the color palette to display the name of each one in a ScreenTip. For the sake of readability, avoid using more than a 20% gray background behind ordinary text.

Working with Long Tables

Two special format settings can help make reading and following long tables easier. First, if your table includes column headings and you expect it to print on two or more pages, tell Word that you want to repeat the headings on subsequent pages. Select the row or rows you want to repeat; then choose Table, Headings.

Note

Word assumes that the first row of your table includes headings. If this assumption is correct, click anywhere in that row before you define headings to repeat on subsequent pages. If you want to use multiple rows, select them before choosing the Headings command. You must include the first row in your selection; otherwise, the command is grayed out and unavailable.

Second, if your table includes some cells whose contents wrap to two or more lines, you can prevent those rows from splitting across page breaks. Select the cell or cells (or the entire table) and choose Table, Cell Height and Width. Click the Row tab, and clear the check mark next to the box labeled Allow Row to Break Across Pages.

Working with Multiple Columns

You can insert multiple columns of text in Word in several ways. One, as you have already seen, is to create a table and put text in each cell. This method is called *parallel columns* because you can make information of varying lengths align perfectly in parallel lines. Figure 13.8 shows an example. You can also create the same effect with tabs, but it is much more difficult to keep everything aligned if you edit the text later.

Tip #95 from *Faithe Wempen*

You might want to selectively apply borders to certain sides of certain cells to create divider lines. For example, you might add borders to the bottom of the cells in a header row, or you might create vertical lines between parallel columns by applying borders to the sides of the cells. In Figure 13.8, all borders have been removed except the one under the first row.

The other kind of columns you can create are the snaking kind, like those in a newspaper, where an article runs down one column and then the next. You set up this kind of column with Word's Columns feature.

Figure 13.8
Placing text in a table is one of the easiest ways to make parallel columns.

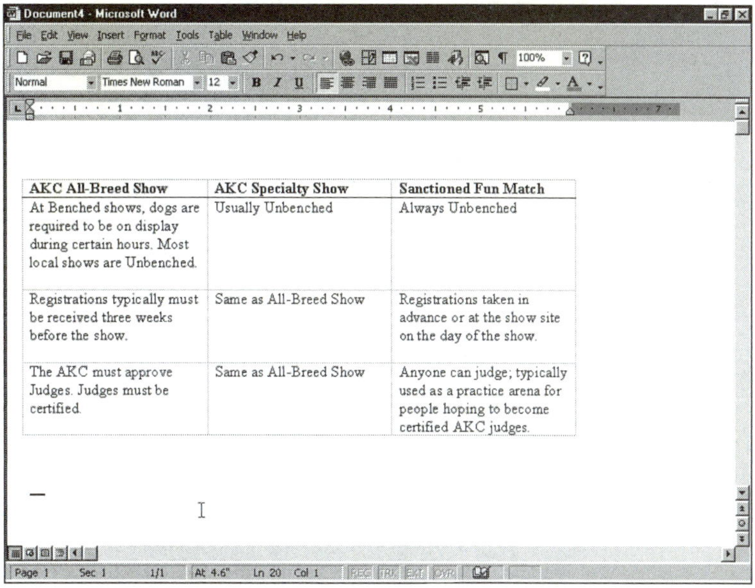

To format an article in multiple newspaper-style columns, perform these steps:

1. If only a portion of your document should be formatted in multiple columns, select all the text that should be included. If you don't, the change applies to the entire section (or the entire document, if you have not created any section breaks).

Note

When you select some text before changing the Columns setting, Word inserts section breaks before and after the text so that the formatting change is in its own section. You can create your own section breaks in documents, too, by choosing Insert, Break.

2. Click the Columns button on the Standard toolbar.
3. Drag across the number of columns you want, much as you did with tables (see Figure 13.9).
4. To change the number of columns at any time (for example, to go back to a single-column layout), just repeat the steps.
5. To fine-tune your columns (for example, to change the spacing between them or to change the width of one or more), use the Columns dialog box (choose Format, Columns). In this dialog box, you will find controls to set specific column widths, change the number of columns used, and add vertical gridlines between columns (see Figure 13.10).

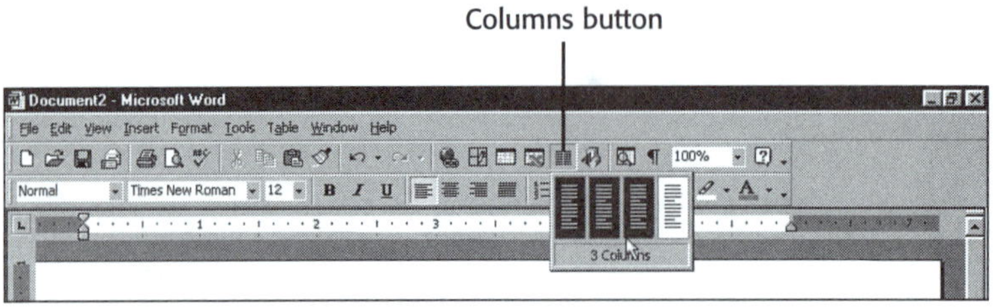

Figure 13.9
You can quickly format text in multiple columns using this button.

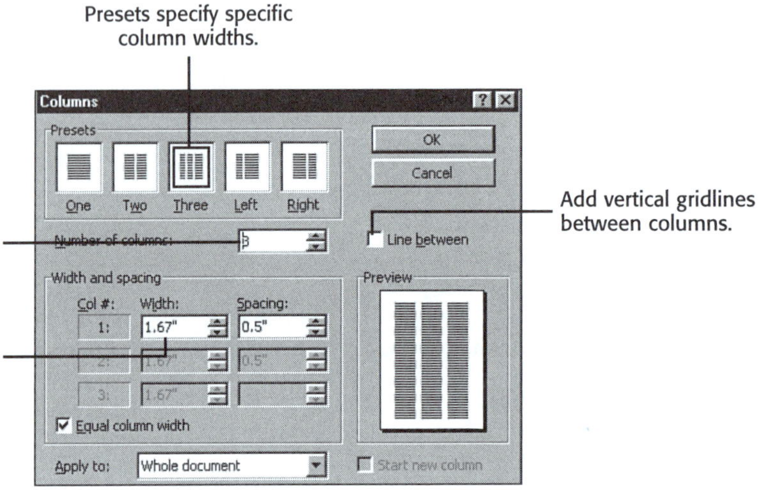

Figure 13.10
Adjust your columns with the Columns dialog box.

As you are typing and editing text in multiple columns, you might want to end a column early—for example, to force a heading to be at the top of the next column. To do so, insert a column break by pressing Ctrl+Shift+Enter. A column break is like a page break, except that it moves the text to the next column rather than to the next page. If you have only one column on the page, a column break and a page break have the same effect.

TROUBLESHOOTING

ADDING LINES TO THE BEGINNING OF A TABLE

I started my document with a table at the top. How do I go back and add non-table lines before it? Word won't let me place the insertion point above the table.

If you place a table at the beginning of the document and later realize you have to add some lines above it, position the insertion point in the beginning of the first cell, and press Enter. This creates a new paragraph above the table.

CONVERTING TABLES TO TEXT

I converted a table to text, but Word didn't correctly identify the column breaks.

If you are converting text to a table, but the number of columns doesn't come out right, check to make sure that you do not have any missing separator characters (such as tab stops) or any extra ones. Sometimes, when people are aligning text with tabs, they add an extra tab to move some text over, for example, and this can cause misalignment when converting the text to a table.

RESIZING TABLE COLUMNS

Resizing one column changes the width of surrounding columns too, so that I end up having to resize the other columns to put them back the way they were.

When resizing table columns, start with the leftmost column, and work your way toward the right. That way, if columns to the right change as a result of the change you make, you will not have to repeat your efforts.

TABLE RESIZING OPTIONS

Resizing table columns can be pretty tedious. Are there any special shortcuts?

Yes, there are. When resizing table columns, be aware of the overall effect you want, and hold down the appropriate key as you drag. Drag "plain," without any key press, to adjust the bar between cells without changing the overall table width. Hold down the Shift key to resize the entire table along with it, changing only the cell to the left. Hold down the Ctrl key to adjust the widths of all the other columns in the table proportionally, along with the one you are resizing.

MULTIPLE COLUMN DOCUMENTS

I want a certain section of the document to appear in a different number of columns than the rest. What's the easiest way to make this happen?

When setting a document for multiple columns, you might have some text in the document that you want to be a different number of columns. If so, select that text, and then apply a special number-of-columns setting for just that text. Word creates section breaks around the text to accommodate your wishes.

CHAPTER 14

INCORPORATING GRAPHICS

In this chapter

ADDING PICTURES TO YOUR DOCUMENTS

Word's desktop-publishing capabilities could easily fill a book. With the creative use of imported graphics, columns, sections, and text boxes, you can create sophisticated newsletters, brochures, flyers, and other complex documents. To make these types of publications more professional-looking, and more appealing to your audience, add illustrations. The term *illustration* includes pictures, graphics, or any kind of image created in a drawing program. An illustration can go a long way toward explaining your text or getting a point across. Illustrations you can add in Word include clip art (predrawn collections of pictures and graphics), photos, shapes, and text effects.

To add a picture or a graphics image to any Word document, position the insertion point at the spot where you want the picture to appear, and choose Insert, Picture. A submenu appears:

- **Clip Art**—This selection opens the Microsoft Clip Gallery application. Your options include hundreds of drawings and a smaller number of high-quality scanned photos.
- **From File**—Import a file saved in any of several graphics formats.
- **From Scanner**—If you've installed a scanner, you can convert photographs, documents, magazine pages, and other hard copy to editable images. Choose this menu option to launch the scanner's software.
- **AutoShapes**—Word includes drawing tools that enable you to create and edit basic shapes, such as squares, stars, and arrows. Use these building blocks to create logos, flowcharts, or simple illustrations.
- **WordArt**—Start with a word or two; then stretch the text and add background colors, shadows, and other effects. This tool is useful for creating logos and headlines.
- **Chart**—This menu option inserts a Microsoft Chart object into the current document. Use the spreadsheet-style data entry window to add numbers and quickly convert them to a chart.

The following sections take you through some of the most popular kinds of graphics that beginning and intermediate users need for their documents: clip art, WordArt, Word drawings, and AutoShapes.

USING A GRAPHIC FROM A FILE

When you choose Insert, Picture, From File, an Insert Picture dialog box opens. From it, you can navigate to the folder containing the picture you want, select it, and click Insert.

Word recognizes and imports many common graphics file formats, such as Windows Metafile (WMF) and Enhanced Metafile (EMF), JPEG File Interchange Format (JPG and JPEG), Windows Bitmap (BMP), and PC Paintbrush (PCX). For a detailed list of compatible file formats, search for the Help topic "Graphics file types Word can use."

Caution

"Borrowing" an image from any Web page is easy. When you see a graphics image you want to save and reuse, right-click and choose Save Picture As from Internet Explorer's shortcut menu. Be aware, though, that many images are copyrighted material and you legally cannot reuse them without the permission of the copyright owner. Pay particular attention to copyrights when your document is intended for the Web or for distribution to a wide audience. A major advantage of most clip art collections (including the images in the Microsoft Clip Gallery) is that you're free to reuse them without additional payments or permissions.

USING CLIP ART

Clip art is predrawn artwork that comes with Word. You access it from the Clip Gallery, a picture-organizing program built in to Word.

To open the Clip Gallery, choose Insert, Picture, Clip Art. The Clip Gallery appears, as shown in Figure 14.1. (Its title bar reads *Insert ClipArt*, but don't let this fool you.)

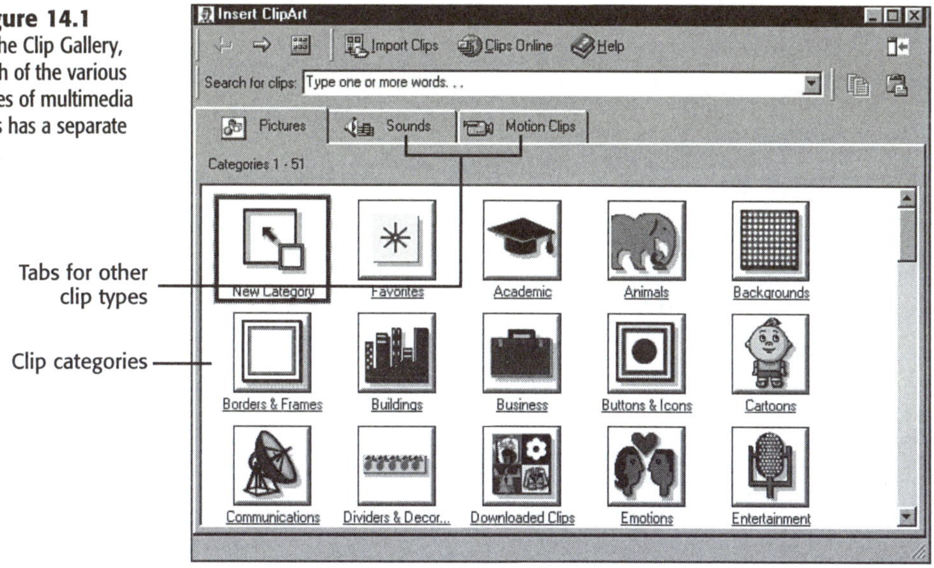

Figure 14.1 In the Clip Gallery, each of the various types of multimedia files has a separate tab.

The Clip Gallery does more than just display clip art; in Figure 14.1, notice the three tabs, one for each type of clip that Word helps you organize. This chapter focuses mainly on the clip art, but keep in mind that you can use the Clip Gallery for sounds and motion clips (videos), too.

Note

If a dialog box appears, telling you that additional clip art is on the CD, and if your CD is handy, go ahead and put it in your CD-ROM drive. (If it's not handy, don't worry about it.)

The Clip Gallery begins by showing you various categories. If you have a specific topic in mind, click on a clip category to see the clips in it. Or, to search for a clip by keyword, type a word in the Search for Clips box, and press Enter; this displays only the clips that match your criterion. Figure 14.2 shows the result of searching for all the clips with the word `child` as a keyword.

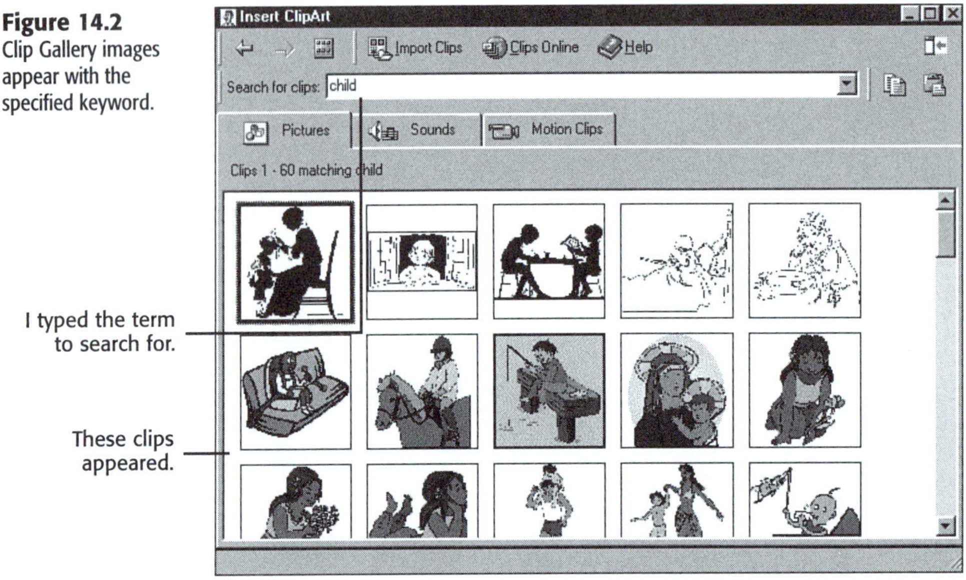

Figure 14.2
Clip Gallery images appear with the specified keyword.

When you see the clip you want, click on it. This displays a palette with four buttons on it. Click the top button, Insert Clip, shown in Figure 14.3. This inserts the clip into your document. Then, close the Clip Gallery window.

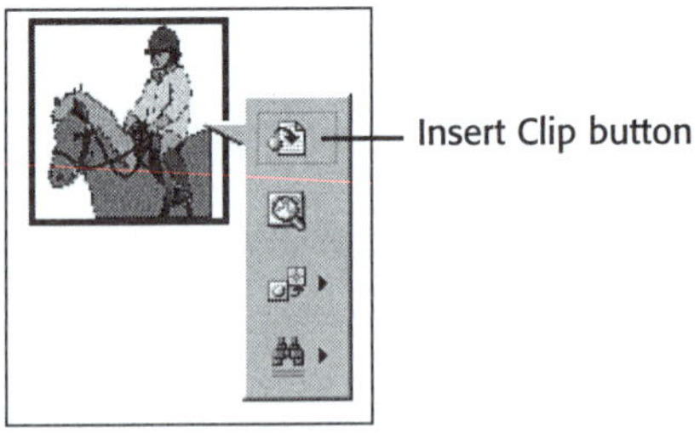

Figure 14.3
Click the clip, and then click the Insert Clip button.

Note

Depending on what programs you have installed, all the clip art available may not be stored on your hard disk. If you see a message to insert a certain CD in your drive when you click the Insert Clip button, insert the CD and click Retry.

→ To resize and format a clip, **see** "Working with Graphic Images," **p. 293**.

Importing Clips to the Clip Gallery

If you use your own pictures frequently in Word, you might want to import them into the Clip Gallery so that they'll be available for browsing there. (This is entirely optional; you can continue to insert them with the Insert, Picture, From File command if you prefer.)

To import a picture to the Clip Gallery, perform these steps:

1. If the Clip Gallery isn't open, choose Insert, Picture, Clip Art.
2. Click the Import Clips button. The Add Clip to Clip Gallery dialog box appears (see Figure 14.4).
3. Change the drive and folder to display the contents of the folder where the art is located.

Figure 14.4
Choose the graphics file to place in the Clip Gallery.

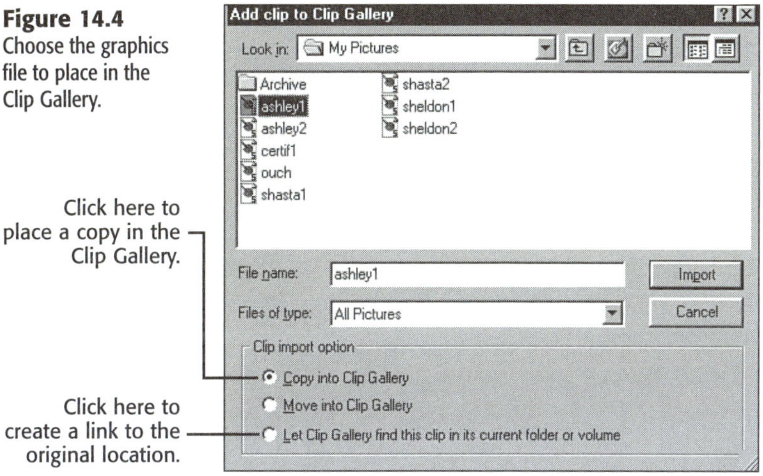

4. Click the file that you want.

Tip #96 from *Faithe Wempen*

To import more than one file, click on the first file, and then hold down the Shift key while you click on the last one. This selects all the files between those two.

5. Click the Import button. A Clip Properties dialog box appears for the first clip, as shown in Figure 14.5.
6. Do any of the following as desired. (The more of these you do, the more ways you will be able to find the clip later.)
   - Type a description in the Description of This Clip box on the Description tab.
   - Choose the categories into which to put the clip on the Categories tab. (You can create a new category by clicking New Category.)
   - Add keywords on the Keywords tab to identify the clip. To add a keyword, click the New Keyword button, type a keyword, and click OK.

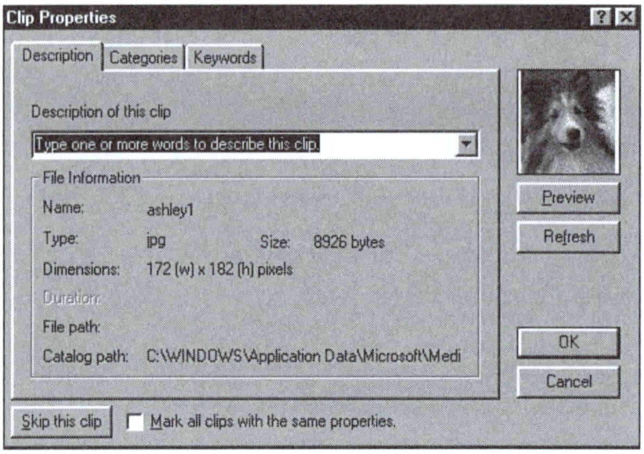

Figure 14.5
For each imported clip, you must give Clip Gallery some information.

7. Click OK.

   If you are importing multiple clips, the Properties box for the next clip appears; return to step 6.

   When you have finished with the properties for all clips, the image(s) appear in the Clip Gallery, as shown in Figure 14.6.

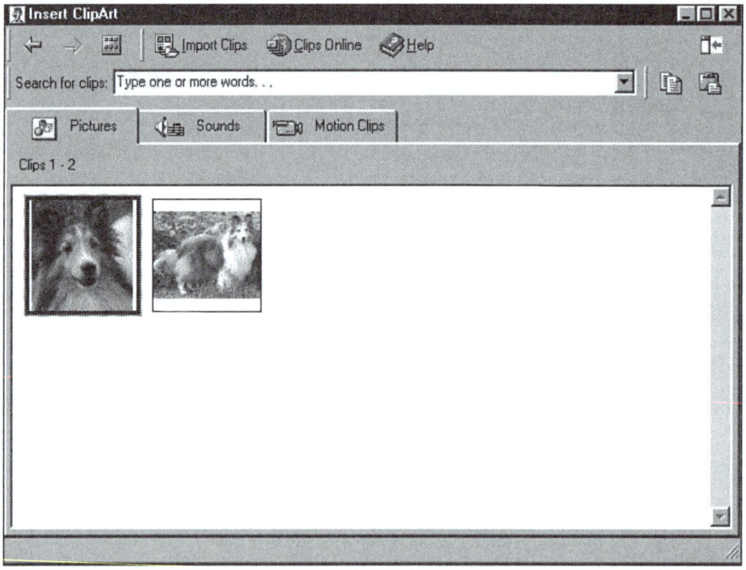

Figure 14.6
Two imported photographs now appear in the Clip Gallery.

GETTING MORE CLIPS FROM THE INTERNET

Microsoft has a Web site on the Internet that offers a number of clips you can download. These include sounds, videos, pictures, and clip art. To get them, you must have a way to connect to the Internet (an online service or a dial-up or network Internet connection).

Follow these steps to download clips from the Microsoft Clip Gallery Live online:

1. Establish your Internet connection. This might involve starting your online service software and connecting, or using Windows Dial-Up Networking to connect to your Internet service provider.
2. Start Word, or switch back to Word if it is already open.
3. Open the Clip Gallery (Insert, Picture, Clip Art).
4. Click the Clips Online button.
5. If you see a dialog box telling you that you should click OK to browse the Web, do so. (You might not see this dialog box at all, depending on your setup.) Internet Explorer opens, and the Clip Gallery Live page loads.
6. If a licensing agreement appears, read it and then click the Accept button to move on. The Clip Gallery Live loads, as shown in Figure 14.7.

Note

Microsoft periodically changes its online offerings, so the page you see might not look exactly like Figure 14.7.

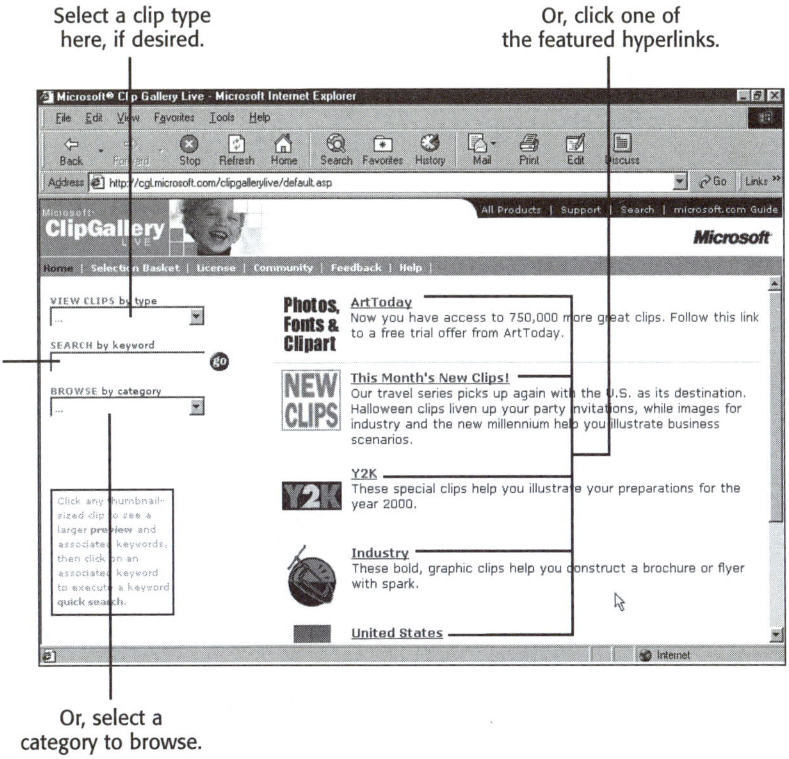

Figure 14.7 Microsoft's Clip Gallery Live page enables you to browse the available clips or search by keyword.

7. Do any of the following to display some clips:
    - Open the VIEW CLIPS by Type drop-down list, and choose a clip type, such as Clip Art.
    - Type one or more keywords in the SEARCH by Keyword box, and then click Go.
    - Open the BROWSE by Category drop-down list, and select a category.
8. Click to place a check mark next to each clip that you want, as shown in Figure 14.8. If more clips are available, click the >> hyperlink to display the next screenful.

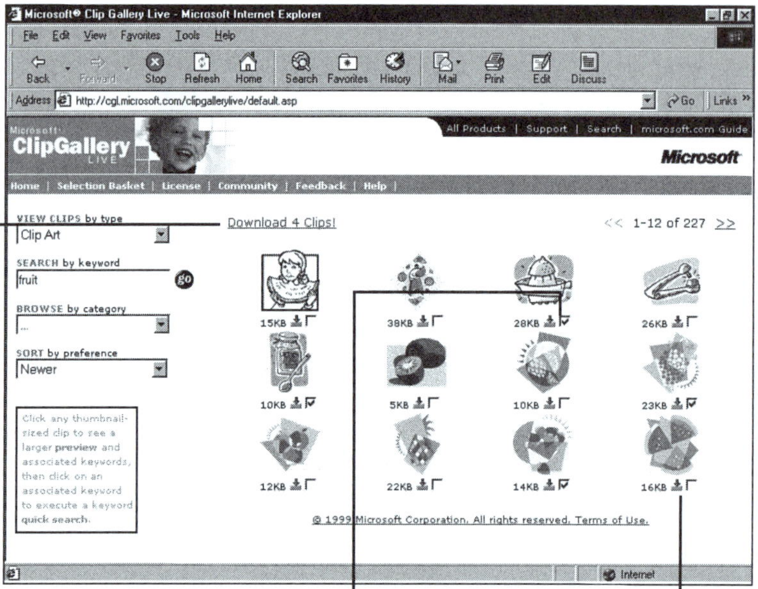

Figure 14.8
Select the clips you want, and then click the Download hyperlink.

Tip #97 from *Faithe Wempen*

To quickly download a single clip, click the button to the left of its check box, as pointed out in Figure 14.8.

9. Click the Download *x* Clips! hyperlink. A number appears in place of *x*, depending on how many clips you have selected.
10. Click the Download Now! hyperlink. The clips are transferred to your PC, and the Clip Gallery opens to display them.

Note

Downloaded clips are placed in the Downloaded Clips category and come with their own keywords. To add a downloaded clip to additional categories, right-click on it and choose Clip Properties.

11. Jump back to your browser and get more clips, if you want. When you are finished, terminate your Internet connection, and jump back to the Clip Gallery to use your new clips.

➔ For information about connecting to the Internet and using Internet Explorer, **see** Chapter 17, "Internet Basics."

WORKING WITH GRAPHIC IMAGES

After placing a graphic image (either from a file or from the Clip Gallery), you will likely want to format it, move it, resize it, or alter it in some other way.

To select a graphic, click on it. Selection handles (black squares) appear around it, and the Picture toolbar appears. You can use the tools on the Picture toolbar to modify the graphic, as you will learn in the following sections.

MOVING A GRAPHIC

To move a graphic, select it and then drag it where you want it, or use cut-and-paste as you do with text.

If you try to drag a graphic to a new spot but it won't "stick" there, perhaps the text wrapping settings for it need to be adjusted (see "Positioning Graphics with Text" later in this chapter).

RESIZING A GRAPHIC

Drag a selection handle on the graphic to resize it. A dotted line shows the space the graphic will occupy (see Figure 14.9). By default, graphics maintain their aspect ratio (their ratio of height to width) when you drag a corner selection handle; drag a side selection handle if you want to resize in only one dimension (and distort the image).

CHANGING THE GRAPHIC IMAGE

In addition to changing the size and position of the graphic, you can also change the image itself. The Picture toolbar provides several buttons that let you adjust the graphic's appearance. Table 14.1 summarizes them.

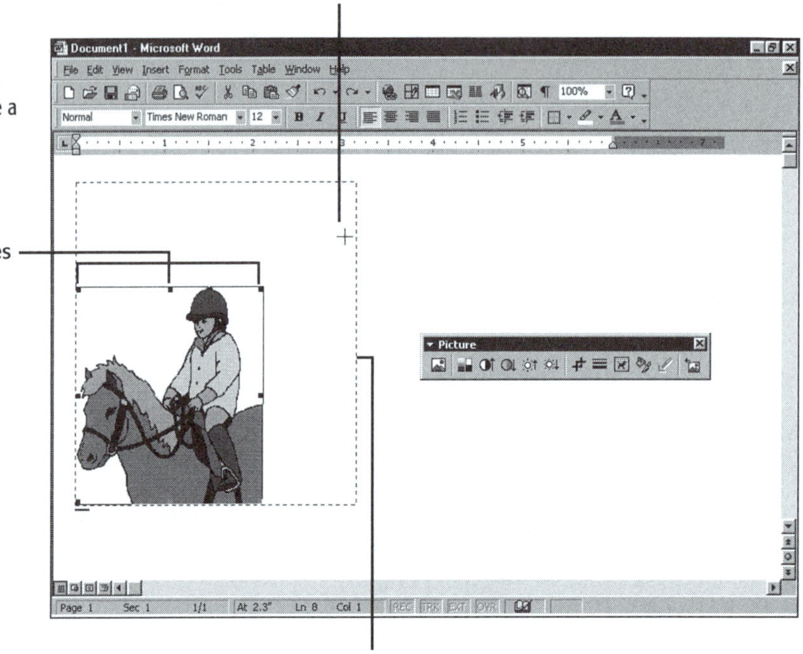

Figure 14.9
Drag a corner selection handle to resize a graphic without distorting it.

TABLE 14.1 IMAGE ADJUSTMENTS ON THE PICTURE TOOLBAR

Button	Name	Purpose
	Image Control	Opens a menu of four image choices: Automatic, Grayscale, Black & White, and Watermark
	More Contrast	Increases the contrast in the image
	Less Contrast	Decreases the contrast in the image
	More Brightness	Increases the brightness in the image
	Less Brightness	Decreases the brightness in the image

CROPPING A GRAPHIC

Especially when working with photographs, you might want to crop an image to remove extraneous parts from one or more sides. The Picture toolbar contains a Crop tool that does exactly that.

To crop a picture, follow these steps:

1. Select the picture so that selection handles appear around it.

2. Click the Crop tool on the Picture toolbar. The mouse pointer changes to an arrow with a Crop symbol.
3. Drag a selection handle toward the center of the image until the undesired part of the image is cropped out. You can drag either a corner or a side handle.
4. Repeat step 3 to crop other sides of the image as needed.
5. Click the Crop tool again, turning off the feature.

POSITIONING GRAPHICS WITH TEXT

When a page contains both text and graphics, you will want to specify how the graphic will interact with the text. Here are your choices:

- **In line with text**—The graphic is treated as a single character of text would be; it floats along with the surrounding text. This might be useful, for example, when placing a very small graphic within a paragraph.
- **Square**—The text wraps around the rectangular frame of the graphic (outside the selection handles).
- **Tight**—The text wraps around the image itself, ignoring any white space around the image but inside the frame. This is useful for wrapping text tightly around an irregular-shape clip art image.
- **Behind text**—The text runs right over the top of the image, as if it were not even there. This is useful for placing a faint watermark image behind text.
- **In front of text**—The text runs behind the image, with the image obscuring part of the text.

To set wrapping from the toolbar, select the image, and then click the Text Wrapping button. A menu appears, as shown in Figure 14.10. Click the text wrapping option you want for the graphic. Note that text wrapping is controlled by the graphic itself, not by the text that interacts with it.

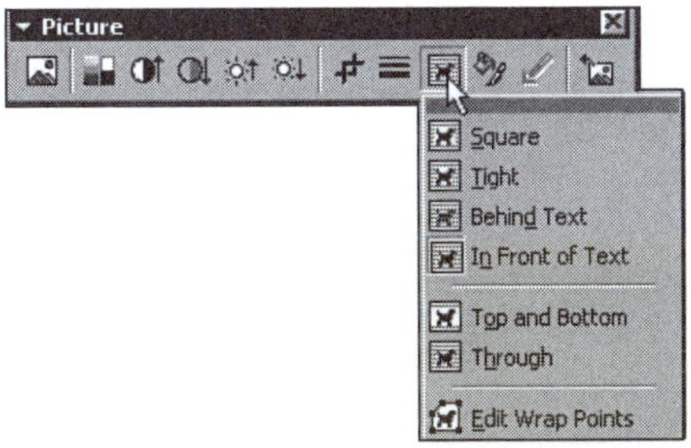

Figure 14.10
Set text wrapping for a graphic the fast and easy way: from the Picture toolbar.

Notice in Figure 14.10 that you can choose Edit Wrap Points. This displays an outline around the image, as shown in Figure 14.11; text will wrap outside this outline. Drag a square around the outline border to change the wrapping for that spot. When finished, click away from the image to deselect it.

Figure 14.11
You can adjust the wrapping points for an image.

The other way to change an image's wrapping setting is through its Format dialog box. This method, while not as convenient, offers some additional options. Follow these steps:

1. Select the image.

2. Choose Format, Picture, or click the Format Picture button on the Picture toolbar. The Format Picture dialog box appears.
3. Click the Layout tab. Buttons for each wrapping style appear, as shown in Figure 14.12.

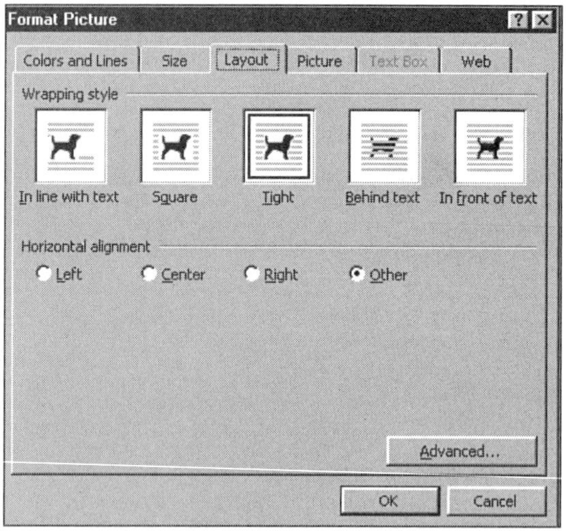

Figure 14.12
Additional wrapping options are available from the Format Picture dialog box.

4. Click the wrapping style you want.
5. Click a button in the Horizontal Alignment section to describe how you want the image to align on the page. These buttons are not available for the In Line with Text wrapping style.

6. (Optional) If desired, click the Advanced button. Additional controls appear for wrapping, such as boxes in which you can specify precise measurements for the distance of the text from the graphic. Click OK when finished with the Advanced controls.
7. Click OK to accept the changes and close the dialog box.

Creating WordArt

Microsoft WordArt is a text manipulation program within Word. This program enables you to type short bits of text and then mold, twist, and otherwise reshape the text to make it look more interesting. Figure 14.13 shows some examples of WordArt.

Figure 14.13 Here are some examples of the hundreds of effects you can create with WordArt.

To create a new piece of WordArt, follow these steps:

1. If it is not already displayed, display the Drawing toolbar at the bottom of the Word screen by clicking the Drawing button.

2. On the Drawing toolbar, click the WordArt button. The WordArt Gallery dialog box appears (see Figure 14.14).
3. Click on one of the samples that's similar to what you want. (You can change later, so don't agonize over it.)
4. Click OK. The Edit WordArt Text dialog box appears.
5. Type the text you want in the title, replacing the "Your Text Here" text (see Figure 14.15).

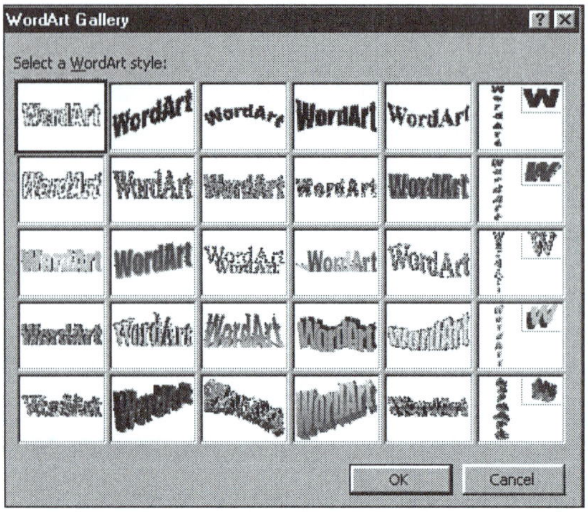

Figure 14.14
Choose a basic WordArt design.

Figure 14.15
Type your own text here.

Caution

Try to keep it short; WordArt looks best when the text is not cluttered. If you use more than two or three words, it often ruins the effect.

6. (Optional) If you want a different font or font size, or different attributes, change them using the controls at the top of the Edit WordArt Text dialog box.
7. Click OK. Your text appears as WordArt in the document, and the WordArt toolbar appears, as shown in Figure 14.16.

Now that you have some WordArt in a document, you can do any of the following:

- Drag the WordArt to a new position by dragging it from its center (when the mouse pointer is a four-headed arrow).
- Resize the WordArt by dragging one of the selection handles.

Figure 14.16 The WordArt now appears in the document.

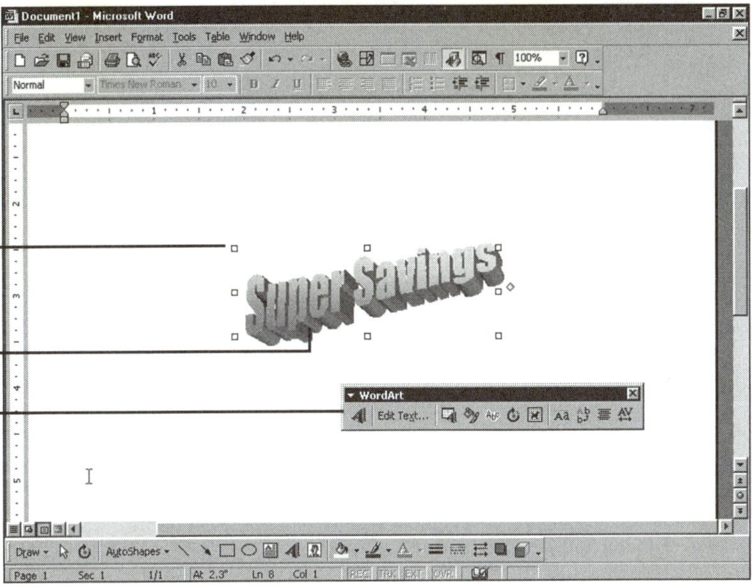

Notice that WordArt has its own toolbar, made especially to help you make changes to your WordArt objects. This toolbar appears automatically when you create a piece of WordArt. Table 14.2 explains the functions of these buttons.

TABLE 14.2 WORDART TOOLBAR BUTTONS

Button	Purpose
	Opens the WordArt Gallery dialog box for a new WordArt object
Edit Text...	Reopens the Edit WordArt Text dialog box
	Reopens the WordArt Gallery dialog box for the existing WordArt object
	Opens the Format WordArt dialog box, where you can change the lines and colors used
	Opens a pop-up array of shapes to which you can conform your WordArt
	Enables you to rotate the WordArt (works the same way as the Free Rotate tool on the Drawing toolbar)
	Opens a list of text wrapping options from which to choose
	Makes all the letters the same height

continues

PART II CH 14

Table 14.2 Continued

Button	Purpose
	Toggles between vertical and horizontal text orientation
	Opens a pop-up menu of text alignments (centered, left aligned, and so on)
	Changes the spacing between letters

To edit a piece of WordArt, click it. This displays the WordArt toolbar (if it isn't visible already). To edit the text, click the Edit Text button, or double-click the WordArt.

When you are finished making changes to the WordArt, click outside it to deselect it. As with any other drawn object, you can drag the WordArt around the worksheet to reposition it, or you can resize it using the selection handles in the corners.

Drawing Your Own Shapes and Lines

You saw the Drawing toolbar in the preceding section; to display it, click the Drawing button on the Standard toolbar. You can use this Drawing toolbar to place lines and shapes in your document.

Drawing Lines and Shapes

The Drawing toolbar contains two types of tools: tools that draw shapes and tools that manipulate shapes. Because you can't manipulate a shape before you've drawn it, let's look at the drawing tools first:

 Line

 Line with arrow

 Rectangle

 Ellipse

The procedure is basically the same for all these tools, although it might take you a bit of practice to master them. To draw with one of the tools, do the following:

1. Click the drawing tool you want.
2. Point the mouse pointer where you want the line or shape to begin.
3. Hold down the mouse button, and drag to where you want the line or shape to end.
4. Release the mouse button to view the finished line or shape.

Tip #98 from *Faithe Wempen*

If you double-click rather than click in step 2, you can repeat the procedure from step 3 to draw more of the same shape. Otherwise, you must go back to step 2 each time.

Practice with the lines and shapes for a while until you get comfortable.

DRAWING AUTOSHAPES

AutoShapes are predrawn shapes that function just like the lines and boxes you draw. They're great for people who want shapes such as arrows and starbursts but aren't coordinated enough to draw them (or simply don't have the time to do so). To use an AutoShape, follow these steps:

1. Click the AutoShapes button on the Drawing toolbar. A menu pops up listing categories of shapes.
2. Point your mouse at the category you want (for example, Block Arrows). A menu of the available shapes in that category appears (see Figure 14.17).
3. Click on the shape you want. Your mouse pointer turns into a crosshair.
4. Drag on the document to draw a box where you want the shape to appear. When you release the mouse button, the shape appears on your document.

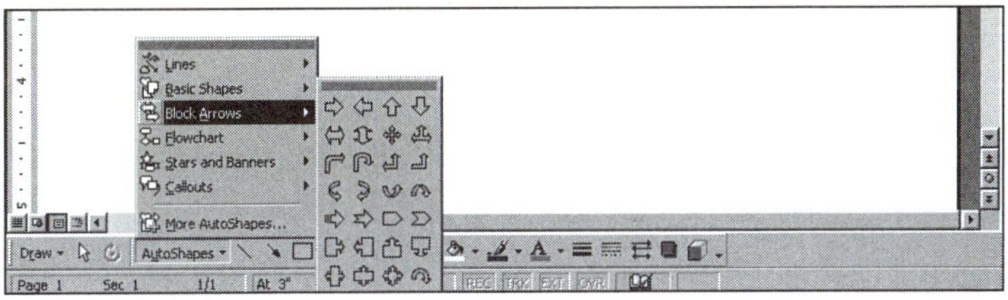

Figure 14.17
Choose the category of AutoShape you want, and then choose the shape itself.

MANIPULATING LINES AND SHAPES

Moving lines and shapes is the same as moving WordArt, which you learned earlier in this chapter. To move a line or shape, simply click on it to select it, and then position the mouse pointer over it so that your pointer becomes a four-headed arrow. Then drag the line or shape to its new position.

Resizing a line or shape is the same as resizing WordArt, too: Just point to one of the line's or shape's selection handles, and drag it to change the line or shape.

COPYING AND DELETING LINES AND SHAPES

You can copy lines and shapes the same way you copy anything else in Word. Here's one easy way:

1. Select the line or shape.
2. Choose Edit, Copy, click the Copy button on the toolbar, or press Ctrl+C.

3. Click in your document to indicate where you want the copy of the line or shape to go.
4. Choose Edit, Paste, click the Paste button, or press Ctrl+V.
5. If necessary, reposition the copy in the exact location where you want it.

You can also copy a line or shape by selecting it and then holding down the Ctrl key as you drag it somewhere else. The original will stay in place, and a copy will be moved.

Deleting is just what you'd expect: Select the object, and then press the Delete key on the keyboard.

ROTATING AND FLIPPING LINES AND SHAPES

Suppose that you've drawn an arrow that points up with the AutoShape feature, but you want it to point down. No problem—just flip it.

To flip a drawn object, perform these steps:

1. Select the object.
2. Click the Draw button on the Drawing toolbar. A menu appears.
3. Choose Rotate or Flip on that menu. Another submenu appears.
4. Choose Flip Vertical or Flip Horizontal, depending on what you're after.

As you saw while you had the menu open, the Rotate or Flip submenu also has commands for Rotate Right and Rotate Left. You can use these to rotate your shape 90 degrees in either the left or right direction.

If you want to control the precise amount of rotation, use the Free Rotate feature. Here's how that feature works:

1. Click the Free Rotate button on the Drawing toolbar. The selection handles around the shape turn into green circles.
2. Position the mouse pointer over one of those circles so that the mouse pointer turns into a circular arrow. Then, drag that selection handle to rotate the shape to the exact position you want (see Figure 14.18).
3. Click anywhere away from the shape to finish.

CHANGING THE APPEARANCE OF A LINE OR SHAPE

The Drawing toolbar contains several tools that control how a drawing appears:

- **Fill Color**—Open the drop-down list to choose a fill color, and then click the button to apply the color to the selected shape. (This does not work with lines.)

- **Line Color**—Open the drop-down list to choose a line color, and then click the button to apply the color to the line or shape. (If you're working with a shape, this changes the outline color around the shape.)

Note

The Line Color, Fill Color, Shadow, and 3D buttons also work with WordArt.

- **Line Thickness**—Select the line or shape; then open this drop-down list, and select the line thickness to use. If applied to a shape, this changes the border around the shape.
- **Line Style**—Select the line or shape; then open this drop-down list, and select the line style (dotted, dashed, and so on). If applied to a shape, this changes the border.
- **Arrow Style**—Select the line; then open this drop-down list, and select the type of arrow to use (including None to remove an arrow). This doesn't work with shapes.
- **Shadow**—Select the shape and then click this button to open a list of shadow types. Click on the one you want to apply. This doesn't work with lines.
- **3D**—Select the shape, and then click this button to open a list of 3D types. Click on the one you want to apply. This doesn't work with lines.

Note

You can access all the controls from the Drawing toolbar in a more formal form, with more precise controls, by right-clicking on the shape or line and then choosing Format AutoShape from the shortcut menu. (It doesn't matter whether you actually created the shape or line with the AutoShape button; Word considers all shapes and lines AutoShapes after they're drawn.)

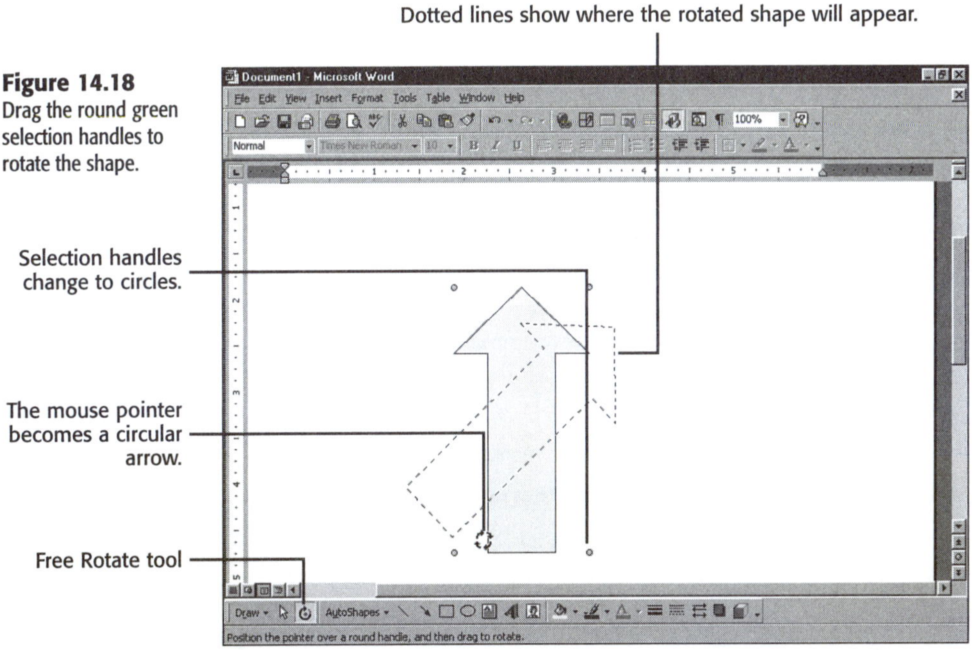

Figure 14.18
Drag the round green selection handles to rotate the shape.

Troubleshooting

Invoking the Insert Picture Preview

I don't see any previews in the Insert Picture dialog box.

Click the Views button until the Preview pane appears, or open the Views button's drop-down list and choose Preview from it.

Filtering Graphic File Types

I'm searching for a particular image in the Insert Picture dialog, but the folder is so crowded that I'm having trouble locating it.

If too many pictures are listed in the Insert Picture dialog box and you want to narrow down the listing to a particular image type, open the Files of Type drop-down list, and choose a format (for example, JPEG File Interchange Format).

Using Object Linking and Embedding (OLE) with Images

I want to insert an image into a document. However, I expect to edit the image later, and I want to ensure that the document's copy reflects these changes.

If you have to create a link between the original picture and the copy you are placing in your document, open the Insert button's drop-down list from the Insert Picture dialog box, and choose Insert and Link. You will learn more about creating links in Chapter 16, "Mail Merging and Data Sharing."

Locating Sounds

I can't find a particular sound in the Clip Gallery.

If you are trying to place sounds from the Clip Gallery into a document, but are having trouble locating any clips of that type, try using the keyword `sound` from the Sounds tab.

Rotating Graphics

I've placed a graphic in a document, but I can't rotate it.

Not all graphics can be free-rotated. If the Free Rotate button is not available when a certain graphic is selected, you cannot free-rotate it. However, you may be able to rotate or flip it using the Draw, Rotate, or Flip menu commands.

Setting AutoShape Defaults

I find myself frequently having to change the border or fill color in AutoShapes I draw.

If the AutoShapes you create are a different color or have a different outline than you would prefer, format an AutoShape the way you want them all to be, and then choose Draw, Set AutoShape Defaults.

CHAPTER 15

Creating Web Pages with Word

In this chapter

IS WORD THE RIGHT WEB TOOL FOR YOU?

A *Web page* is a document designed to be published on the Internet. Each Web page has a unique name and address (that is, *uniform resource locator*, or *URL*) that people who want to read it can use to bring it up on their screens, using a special program called a *Web browser*. (You will learn about Internet Explorer, the Microsoft-provided Web browser, in Chapter 17, "Internet Basics.")

Word 2000 has a very easy-to-use Web page–creation utility built in. It's head and shoulders above other word processing programs in this area and far ahead of the preceding version, Word 97.

With Word 2000, you can create either single Web pages or entire Web sites. If you opt for an entire site, the pages you create will all be linked together via a navigation bar that your visitors can click to jump from page to page. It's very handy, for both you and your Web audience. You can also base a Web page on any of several templates.

Word 2000 is not the perfect Web creation tool for everyone, however. If you have to create a sophisticated Web site for commercial use, you will want to look elsewhere. Likewise, if you have to incorporate special features—such as an online ordering system, a search utility, or special programming such as Java or CGI—Word 2000 might not serve your needs. In such cases, try Microsoft FrontPage instead.

For home users wanting to create simple Web sites for hobbies, organizations, and even some small businesses, however, Word 2000 is an excellent choice.

➔ If you are new to the Internet, **see** the first part of Chapter 17, "Internet Basics," for an introduction. This explains terms such as *Web*, *hyperlink*, and so on.

CREATING WEB PAGES IN WORD

You can use Word to create Web pages in any of several ways. You can use the Web Page Wizard, you can start with a Web template, or you can convert content you've already created in other documents into Web pages.

If you want to create a multipage Web site, the best way is to use the wizard. That way, the hyperlinks between pages are inserted automatically, and you don't have to worry about them.

The Web Page Wizard assumes that you want to create a multipage Web site. If you are creating a single page only, you can either use the Web Page Wizard (and delete all but one of the pages) or start with one of the Web templates. The wizard employs these same templates when it creates a multipage site, so you aren't getting a lesser layout by using a template. However, the wizard does enable you to choose a visual theme (a color and design scheme), which you will have to do manually later if you use a template (more on that later in this chapter).

If you have existing text that you want converted to Web format, and you just want that single page saved, use File, Save As, and choose Web Page from the Save as Type drop-down list.

To add an existing document to a new, multipage Web site you are creating, include it during the wizard process. (I'll show you how in the next section.) Or, you can use the wizard to create a new Web site and then use Copy and Paste to insert text from an existing document on one of the new Web pages.

→ To recall how to use Save As, **see** "Saving Your Work," **p. 34**.

→ For more information on Copy and Paste, **see** "Moving and Copying Text," **p.49**.

Creating a Web Site with the Web Page Wizard

The Web Page Wizard makes it easy to create a Web site with multiple pages. If you have tried to do so in other programs, including Word 97, you will be amazed at how easy it is in Word 2000 to create a good-looking set of pages that are seamlessly linked together.

To start a new Web site, follow these steps:

1. Choose File, New, More Word Templates. The New dialog box opens.

Note

If you are using a standalone version of Word, rather than integrated with Works Suite, the command in step 1 is File, New.

2. Click the Web Pages tab, and then double-click Web Page Wizard. The Web Page Wizard opens.
3. Click Next to begin.
4. Type a title for the Web site in the Web Site Title box. This title will appear in the title bar in your visitors' Web browsers (see Figure 15.1).

Figure 15.1
Choose the Web site title and its storage location.

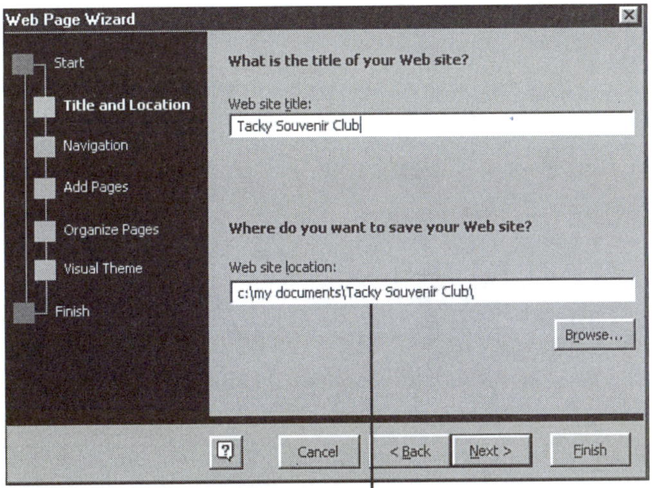

This folder name changes when you change the Web site title entry above.

5. If you want to save the files in a different location than the default, enter that location in the Web Site Location box. Then click Next.

Note

The default location is a new folder in your C:\My Documents folder, with the same name you entered for the Web site title. If you want to save files directly to a corporate Web server, see your system administrator for the path to use. However, for home use, you will want to create and perfect the pages *locally* (that is, on your own hard disk) before you transfer them to your Internet service provider's server.

6. Select a navigation style for your Web site. For a multipage site, choose Vertical Frame or Horizontal Frame. (I myself prefer Vertical.) For a single-page site, choose Separate Page. Then click Next.
7. The next screen lists the current pages to be included (see Figure 15.2). Do any of the following to customize this list:
   - To remove a page from the list, click it and then click Remove Page.
   - To add another blank page, click the Add New Blank Page button.
   - To add a template page, click the Add Template Page button. The Web Page Templates dialog box opens. Select the template you want (a sample of the selected one appears behind the dialog box, as in Figure 15.3), and click OK.
   - To add an existing document as a Web page, click the Add Existing File button. The Open dialog box appears. Select the file to add (it can be any document that Word can open), and click Open.

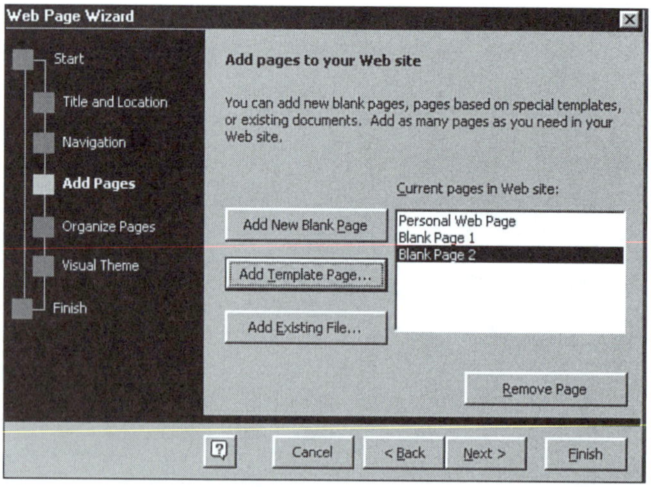

Figure 15.2
Add or remove pages to the list as desired.

8. Click Next to move on. The next screen (see Figure 15.4) prompts you to specify the order for the pages in the navigation bar.
9. To move a page in the presentation order, click it and then click the Move Up or Move Down button. When you are finished moving pages, click Next to continue.

Figure 15.3
Select a template to use for an added page.

Sample of selected page

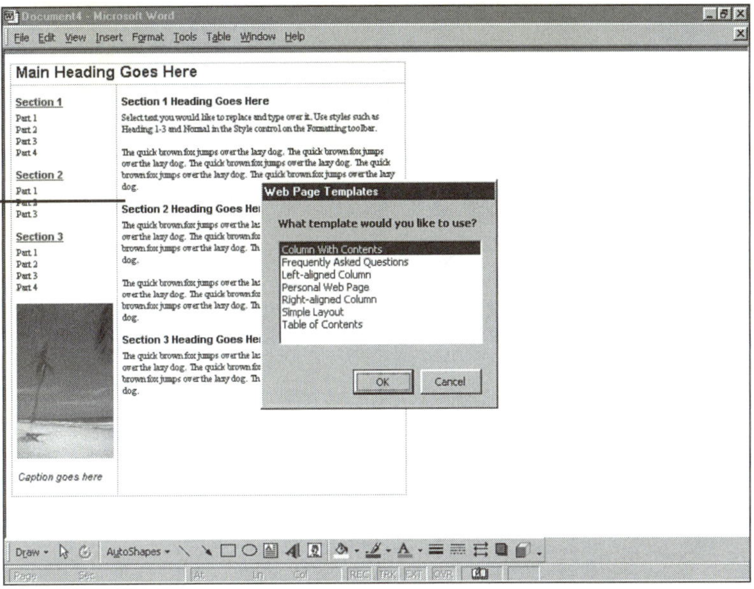

Figure 15.4
Select a page, and then click Move Up or Move Down.

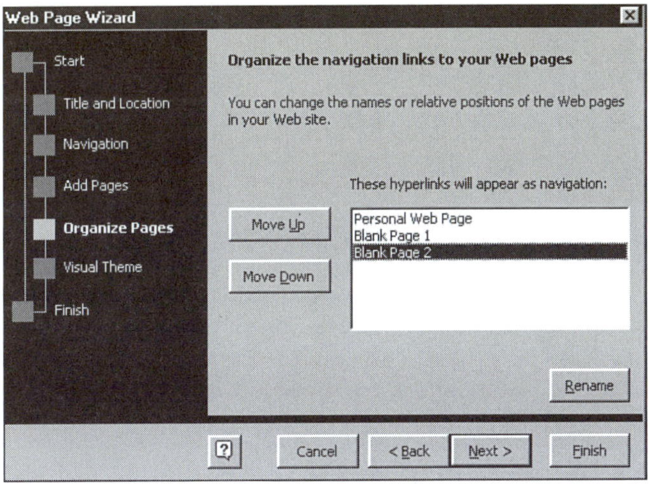

10. If you *don't* want a theme (that is, if you want a plain white page with no special formatting), click No Visual theme, and skip to step 12.

    If you *want* to use a theme, click the Browse Themes button. The Theme dialog box appears.

11. Select a theme from the Choose a Theme list. A sample of it appears in the sample pane, as shown in Figure 15.5. Click OK when finished.

Note

The default installation of Word does not install all the themes. If you choose a theme and an Install button appears instead of a sample of it, click the Install button, and follow the prompts onscreen to install it.

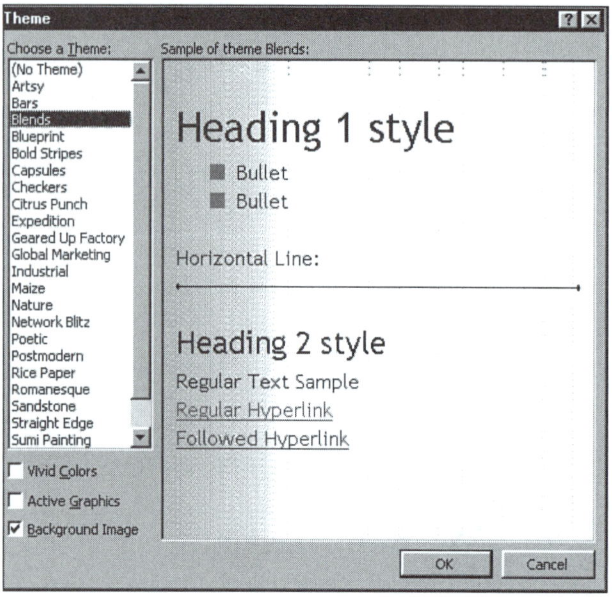

Figure 15.5
Select a theme to control the colors and fonts on your pages.

Note

There are three check boxes at the bottom of the Theme dialog box. Vivid Colors uses colors brighter than normal in the theme. Active Graphics employs animated graphics where possible. (This effect might not show up on all visitors' Web browsers.) Background Image displays a background graphic behind the text. Background graphics look great, but loading a graphic through a slow Internet connection can be time-consuming; your visitors might resent this. Select or deselect any of these check boxes as appropriate for your situation.

12. Click Next.
13. Click Finish. Word creates the new Web site, using your specified settings. Figure 15.6 shows an example.

What next? Start replacing the sample text with your own content. Edit and format the pages normally, as you would any document. I'll cover some special features, such as inserting hyperlinks, later in this chapter.

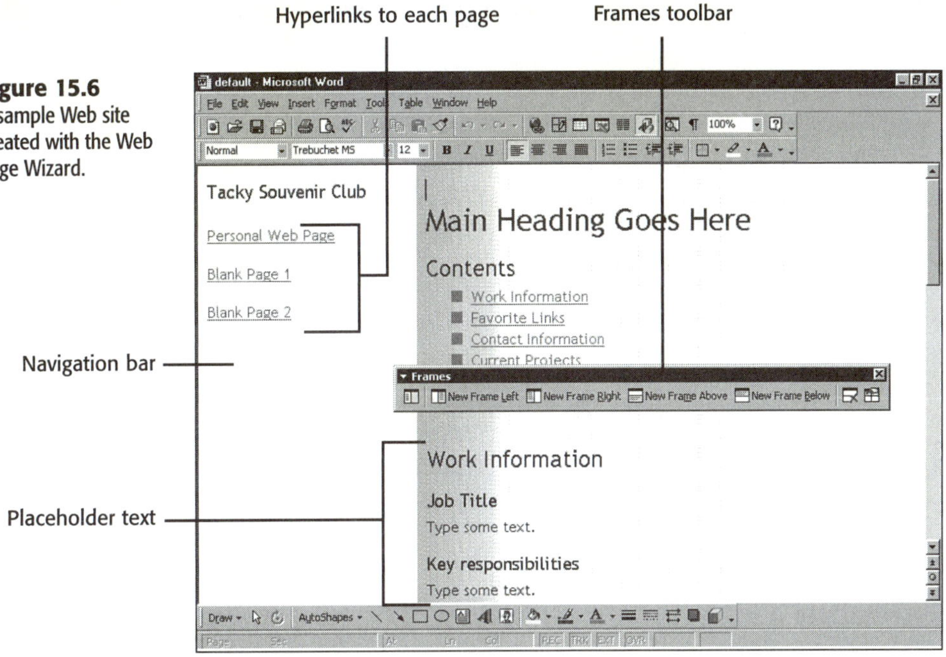

Figure 15.6
A sample Web site created with the Web Page Wizard.

CREATING A WEB PAGE FROM A TEMPLATE

If you are creating a single Web page, you might prefer to use one of Word's templates instead of the full-blown wizard. The templates provide placeholders for text and graphics; you can replace these with your own material.

To create a Web page from a template, do the following:

1. Choose File, New, More Word Templates. The New dialog box opens.
2. Click the Web Pages tab.
3. Click one of the templates listed there. (Choose any of them except the Web Page Wizard.)
4. Click OK.

After creating and customizing a single Web page, you will want to save it. See the next section for details.

SAVING WEB PAGES

If you were saving an ordinary document as a Web page, you would use the command File, Save as Web Page to open a special version of the Save As dialog box. However, when you start a Web page based on a Web template or the Web Page Wizard, the correct Save As dialog box appears no matter how you save. Therefore, you can use either Save As or Save as Web Page. Either will open the correct dialog box.

The special Save As dialog box, shown in Figure 15.7, is typical in most ways. Its special features are

- You can set a page title separately from the document title. The page title will appear in the browser window's title bar when the page is displayed on the Web. To change the page title, click the Change Title button.

Tip #99 from *Faithe Wempen*

You can also assign (or change) the page title at any time by choosing File, Properties and changing the title in the Title box.

- The Save as Type setting is automatically set to Web Page.

Figure 15.7
When saving a Web page, the Save As dialog box is slightly different.

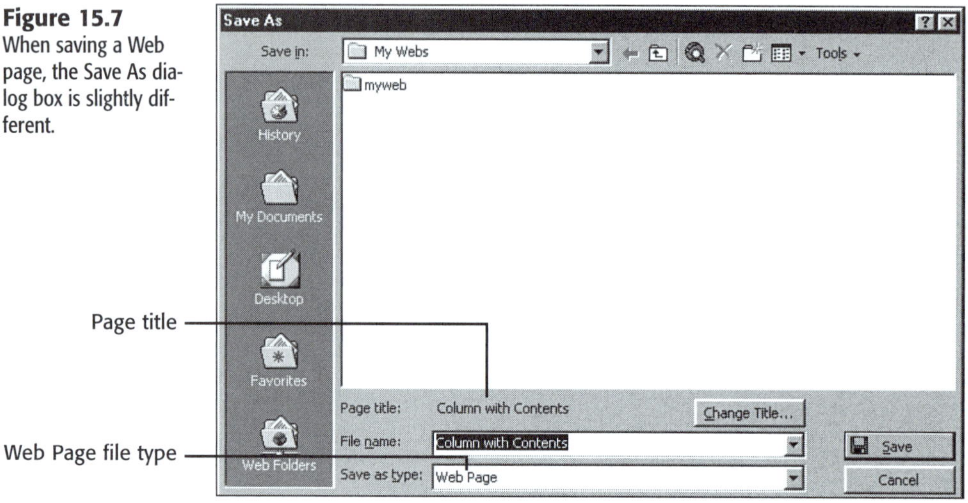

In addition, you can set a few options for Web page saving. These allow you to customize the save format for special situations.

To access the Web save options, click the Tools button in the Save As dialog box. This opens a menu; choose Web Options to open the Web Options dialog box, shown in Figure 15.8.

I won't go through all the options here because many of them are obscure and you won't want to change them. However, here are a couple of options to pay attention to.

On the General tab, there is a Browser drop-down list. By default, Word saves pages optimized for Microsoft Internet Explorer 5.0 (the Browser box's current setting). However, if most of your visitors will be using Netscape (assuming that you could possibly know this), you might want to open the Browser drop-down list and choose Internet Explorer 4.0 and Netscape Navigator 4.0 instead.

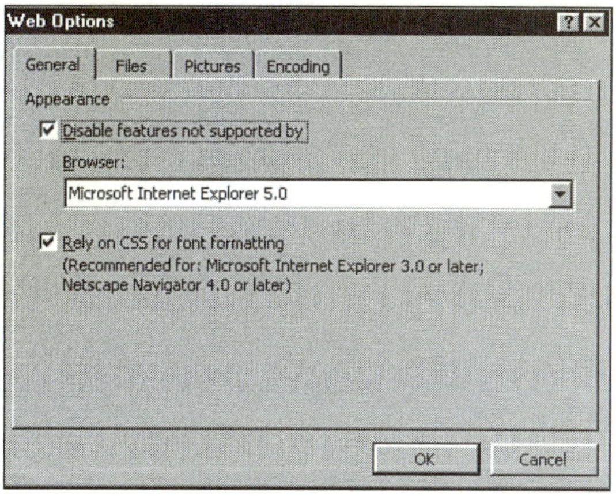

Figure 15.8
Set Web options here to control how Word saves Web pages.

On the Files tab, there is an Organize Supporting Files in a Folder check box. You might recall from the Web Page Wizard that it saves your Web site in its own folder within the C:\My Documents folder. To place all the needed files directly in My Documents rather than in a newly created subfolder, deselect this check box. (Warning, though—this can make your My Documents folder very cluttered, and it will be difficult later to discern which files have to be included when you transfer the Web site to a server.)

On the Pictures tab, you can set a screen size. This optimizes the display for a particular screen resolution. If you know that most of your visitors use 640×480 screen resolution, you might set Screen Size to that setting.

FORMATTING A WEB PAGE

Now that you have a Web page in front of you (by one method or another) in Word, what can you do to change it? Generally, you edit the page the same way as you edit any other document. The differences are explained in the following sections.

ADDING BACKGROUNDS AND TEXTURES

The Web Page Wizard creates a default background matching the theme for the page you've created. You can customize the background or add one (if one isn't chosen already) through the Format menu.

To change the page background, choose Format, Background. A palette of colors appears. Then, do any of the following:

- Click the color you want on the pop-up palette.
- Click More Colors if you want additional choices.
- Click Fill Effects to select from a palette of woven, marble, and other background textures.

Of these, the first two are self-explanatory, but the Fill Effects could use some clarification. Choosing this command opens a Fill Effects dialog box (see Figure 15.9) containing four tabs:

- **Gradient**—Enables you to select two-color blends (or one color plus black or white).
- **Texture**—Lets you choose from among many tiled graphics that look like various materials, such as cloth or marble.
- **Pattern**—Lets you choose any of dozens of patterns, created with two colors of your choosing.
- **Picture**—Helps you select a graphic to use for the background. (Most of the Themes employ a graphic as a background.)

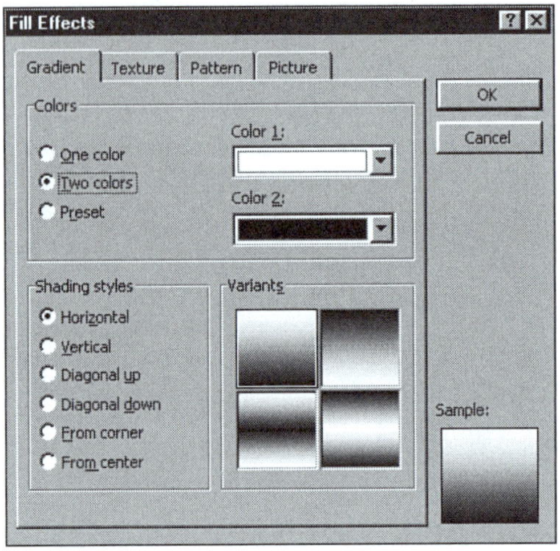

Figure 15.9
Here's the Gradient tab; click one of the other tabs to use a different fill effect.

Caution

Be careful not to pick a background color or pattern that obscures your text. For example, if your text is black, make sure that the background is a light, contrasting color. If you choose a pattern, make sure that it is not a busy, high-contrast pattern, or the text in front of it will be unreadable.

Word saves your background as a separate graphics file, such as Image.gif, in the folder in which your Web page was created. If you move your page to a different folder or another location (such as a Web server), be sure to move the image file, too.

Note

Word saves your background texture as a Graphics Interchange Format (GIF) file because it is a format compatible with the Web environment and because it displays in most browsers. Another type of image file you're likely to see on the Web is Joint Photographic Experts Group (JPEG), a popular format for photographs.

INSERTING FRAMES

Frames are an advanced feature that many Web browsers today support. They divide the screen into separate areas, each of which can display a different page. Frames are ideal for inserting material such as hyperlinks, logos, advertisements, or other items that you want to remain on the screen at all times, regardless of which page of your site the visitor is viewing.

Caution

> The drawback to using frames—not all browsers support them. If a visitor views your site in a browser that does not support frames, the site will not look as you intended. The visitor will be able to see only the main frame.
>
> Some people get around this by creating two versions of their Web site: frames and non-frames. Then, on their opening page, they supply links to both versions, allowing the visitor to choose. This is probably overkill for a noncommercial Web site, however.

When you create a Web site using the Web Page Wizard, it places the navigation bar in a separate frame. You can create additional frames in the document by clicking the button on the Frames toolbar that corresponds to the frame you want (for example, New Frame Right or New Frame Left). You can also access all the same commands that are on the toolbar, with the Format, Frames menu command. Figure 15.10 shows the Frames toolbar.

Figure 15.10
Create, format, and delete frames with the Frames toolbar.

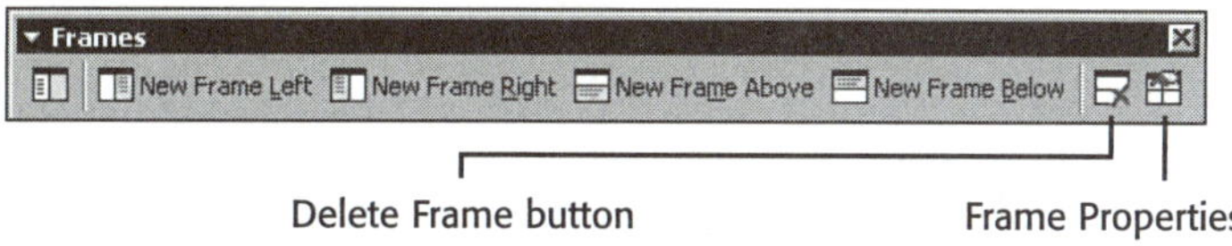

To delete a frame, click inside that frame and then click the Delete Frame button on the Frames toolbar, or choose Format, Frames, Delete Frame.

To format a frame, click inside that frame and then click the Frame Properties button, or choose Format, Frames, Frame Properties. A Frame Properties dialog box appears, in which you can set the options for the chosen frame.

INSERTING GRAPHIC LINES AND DIVIDERS

Adding lines to your Web page can help you organize your information and make it more visually appealing.

You can use the line-drawing tools on the Drawing toolbar in a Web page, as you learned in Chapter 14, "Incorporating Graphics," but these don't give the polished look that you might want. Instead, I recommend using graphic line images that come with Word's Clip Gallery.

While you are in the Clip Gallery, you might also want to check out the other Web categories: Web Bullets & Buttons, Web Backgrounds, and Web Banners. Any of these can be a source of nice-looking artwork for a Web page. You are free to use any clip art from the Clip Gallery on your Web page, of course, but the ones in the Web categories are especially appropriate.

➔ To add a graphic line to your Web page, insert one from the Web Dividers category in the Clip Gallery. **See** "Using Clip Art," **p. 287**.

Adding Bullets

Adding bullets to your Web page is similar to adding bullets to any other type of document in Word. However, you can also use graphics images, as well as standard bullet symbols. As I mentioned in the preceding section, the Clip Gallery has some special categories for Web use, and the Web Bullets & Buttons category offers many good-looking graphics that are ideal for bulleted lists.

1. Highlight the text in front of where you want the bullet to appear.
2. Choose Format, Bullets and Numbering. The Bullets and Numbering dialog box opens.
3. Click the Bulleted tab if it is not already on top.
4. Click the Picture button. The Picture Bullet dialog box appears (a version of the Clip Gallery), listing all the bullets from the Web Bullets & Buttons category (see Figure 15.11).

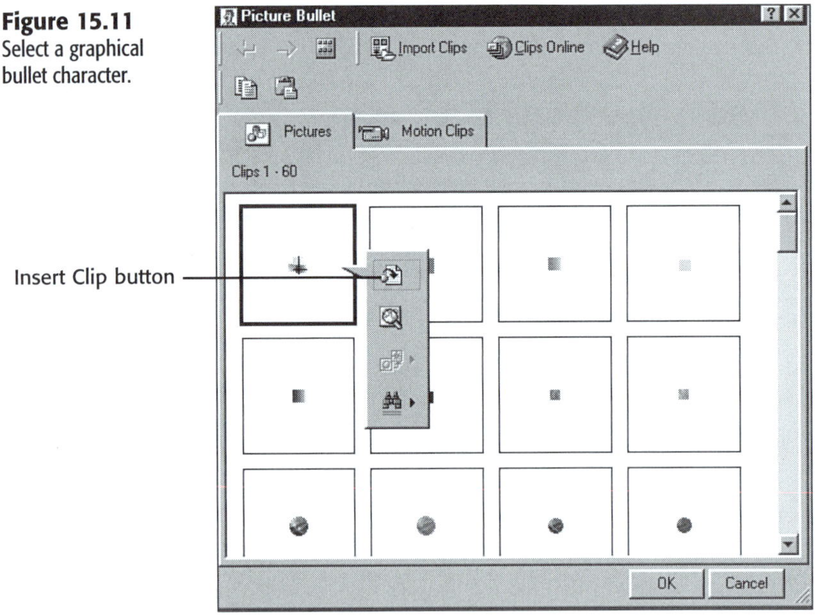

Figure 15.11
Select a graphical bullet character.

5. Click the graphic you want to use for a bullet character. A palette of four icons appears (refer to Figure 15.11).
6. Click the Insert Clip button (the top icon). The selected text becomes a bulleted list using that graphic as a bullet.

Changing the Appearance of Text

You can customize the text on your Web page much as you do any other text in a document. Change the fonts, the font sizes, the font colors, and so on.

One of the best ways to format text on a Web page is with Styles. When you are editing a Web page, your Styles list contains standardized, widely recognized styles for Web pages. Applying these styles inserts codes in your document that help Web browsers know how to format your text. Use styles whenever you can on Web pages. (Refer to Chapter 11, "Using Templates and Styles in Word," for help as needed.)

Note

Not all formatting is supported in Web format. You can't use these attributes, for example: Double Strikethrough, Shadow, Outline, Emboss, or Engrave.

Adding Hyperlinks

Hyperlinks are the primary navigation tools on the Web. You can use them to enable your readers to jump from one of your pages to another, from one section to another on the same page, or from one of your pages to a completely different Web site. You also can turn your email address into a hyperlink so that people can contact you easily.

When you create a Web site using the Web Page Wizard, hyperlinks for jumping among the pages are included automatically in the navigation pane. You can also add your own hyperlinks. The following sections explain how to do so.

Note

Hyperlinks are embedded in an element (usually a word, phrase, or image) of an electronic document. When you click a hyperlink on a Web page, it instructs your browser to retrieve and display a different document or a different section of the same document. You can tell when an object on a Web page is a hyperlink: If you pass your mouse pointer over it, the pointer changes from an arrow to a pointing finger.

Inserting a Hyperlink

With Word, you can use both text and images as hyperlinks. You can link from a word, phrase, or image to another page in your Web site. This is especially helpful if you elected not to use the navigation bar or if you created a single Web page with a template rather than use the wizard.

1. Select the text or image you want to turn into a hyperlink. (If using text, modify its wording first so that it accurately reflects your link.)

2. Choose Insert, Hyperlink, or click the Insert Hyperlink button on the toolbar.

   If you haven't already done so, Word prompts you to save your file. After you do, the Insert Hyperlink dialog box appears (see Figure 15.12).

3. Click the existing file or the Web Page button.
4. Do one of the following:
   - Type the Web page address in the Type the File or Web Page Name box.
   - Click the Web Page button. Your Web browser window opens. Navigate to the page to which you want to link, and then use the taskbar to return to Word. The page's address appears in the Type the File or Web Page Name box.

Tip #100 from *Faithe Wempen*

Another way to place an address in the box–click one of the Recent Files, Browsed Pages, or Inserted Links buttons, and choose a page from one of those lists.

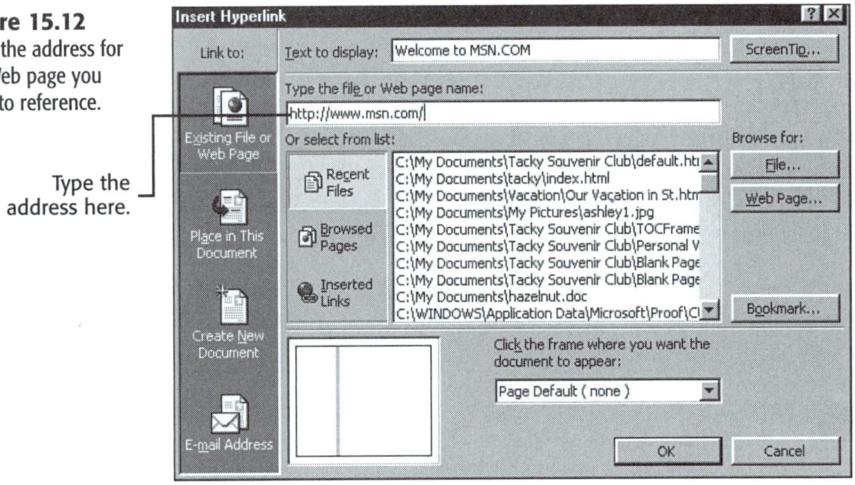

Figure 15.12
Enter the address for the Web page you want to reference.

5. Type the text that should appear on your page in the Text to Display box. (If you are creating a graphical hyperlink, this text will appear only if the graphic is unable to load in a person's Web browser.)
6. Click OK. The hyperlink is created.

To display the destination of a hyperlink you've inserted, rest your mouse pointer over it. To test it, click on the hyperlink; the referenced page should open.

TYPING A HYPERLINK

Besides using the Insert Hyperlink dialog box, you can use Word's automatic formatting feature to create links to other Web sites just by typing URLs on your page.

First, however, you must make sure that this feature is enabled, by doing the following:

1. Choose Tools, AutoCorrect.
2. Choose the AutoFormat as You Type tab.

3. Under Replace as You Type, make sure that the Internet and Network Paths with Hyperlinks check box is selected.
4. Click OK.

Now, when you type an URL and a space after it on your Web page, the URL automatically becomes a hyperlink.

Tip #101 from *Faithe Wempen*

You can highlight the address of a Web page in Internet Explorer (Edit, Copy) and then switch to Word and choose Edit, Paste to paste its address directly into your Web page.

TURNING AN EMAIL ADDRESS INTO A HYPERLINK

When someone visiting your Web page clicks a hyperlinked email address, a message composition screen with the address already inserted in the To: line is created—if the visitor has an email program (also known as an *email client*) installed on his or her system.

You can turn email addresses into hyperlinks just by typing them on your page, if Word's automatic formatting feature is active. (See the preceding section to turn it on.)

You can also create an email hyperlink using the Insert Hyperlink dialog box you saw earlier in this chapter. Click the E-mail Address button in it, and then type the email address you want to use.

PREVIEWING A WEB PAGE AS YOU WORK

If you have a Web browser installed on your system, you can choose File, Web Page Preview to see how the page you're working on will look in a Web browser. After you've viewed the page, you can go back to Word by closing the browser or by switching back to Word using the taskbar.

USING GRAPHICS IN WEB PAGES

Tip #102 from *Faithe Wempen*

You can download free images for your Web page from a Microsoft site on the Web. Refer to "Getting More Clips from the Internet" in Chapter 14, "Incorporating Graphics."

On your Web page, Word enables you to add images in many file formats (TIF, for example), but they are converted to the GIF format when you save the page. The only type of image that isn't converted is a JPEG file, which remains in that format. (JPEG and GIF are the two image types supported on the Web.)

To insert an image in a Web page, follow these steps:

1. Place the insertion point where you want the picture to appear.

2. Choose Insert, Picture, and select the appropriate image source, as you learned in Chapter 14. You can choose Clip Art, From File, WordArt, and so on.

   The associated dialog box opens for the image source you selected. If you chose Clip Art, for example, the Clip Gallery opens.

3. Choose and insert the image you want in the dialog box as you normally would in a document.

Tip #103 from
Faithe Wempen

When you save your Web page, Word automatically copies the image into the same folder as the page. If you insert a graphic from a file (instead of clip art) and you want to link to an image at a fixed location, such as another Web server, click Link to File in the Insert Picture dialog box.

When you insert a graphic on a Web page, it is aligned by default with the left margin. To resize or reposition the image, select it and drag it, or drag the resize handles.

As you drag, the surrounding text and objects move to accommodate the image, but by default, text doesn't flow around it. You can control how the picture interacts with text by clicking the Text Wrap button on the Picture toolbar and selecting an alignment, just as you did in Chapter 14.

Tip #104 from
Faithe Wempen

To turn an image into a hyperlink, select the image; choose Insert, Hyperlink, or click the Hyperlink button. Then, enter the appropriate information in the Insert Hyperlink dialog box (see the section "Inserting a Hyperlink," earlier in this chapter). On your Web page, you might want to add some explanatory text (`click here`, for example) in front of the image so that your readers know that it is a hyperlink.

➔ To insert various types of graphics, **see** Chapter 14, "Incorporating Graphics."

➔ To set text wrapping around a graphic, **see** "Positioning Graphics with Text," **p. 295**.

Publishing to a Web Server

To publish your pages to the Internet, you copy them to a server. The *server* is a computer connected to the Internet full-time. It's usually owned by the company where you get your Internet service (your ISP or an online service such as America Online). The monthly fee you pay for your Internet connection (in most cases) also entitles you to a small amount of space on its server to publish your own Web pages. All you have to know is the address of the server and the directory on it where you should copy your files.

Determining Your Save Location

Before you can publish your pages to the Internet, you must contact your service provider and find out where on its server you should put your pages. (If you are using an online service such as America Online, information is available in the online Help.) For example, your service provider might give you a path like this one:

`ftp.servername.com/pub/web/homepage/members/`*`yourname`*

This is the physical location on the server where you will send your files via File Transfer Protocol (FTP). FTP is an alternative way of transmitting information on the Internet and is used for file transfers from computer to computer. This is *not* the address you will give to other people who want to access your page, however. The Web address to your page will likely be much simpler, like this one:

`http://www.servername.com/~`*`yourname`*

These addresses are just made-up examples; your service provider must tell you which addresses to use.

Choosing a Transfer Method

There are two ways to save Web pages directly to a Web server from within Word. One uses the FTP address, and the other uses a new feature in Word 2000 called *Web Folders*. The Web Folders method is easier, but not all servers support it.

I suggest that you try the Web Folders method, and if that doesn't work, you can fall back on the FTP method.

> **Note**
>
> You can also use a utility called the *Web Publishing Wizard*, which comes with Works Suite (and also with Windows 98, if you have that), to transfer a file or folder from outside Word.

Saving to the Server with Web Folders

Web Folders are shortcuts to folders on the Web server to which you are saving your work. You create the shortcut, and then you can use it from the Web Folders folder in the future.

1. Choose File, Save as Web Page.
2. Click the Web Folders button.
3. If you are saving to an *existing* Web folder, double-click the folder to open it.

   If you have to create a *new* Web folder to save in, do the following:

   - Click the Create New Folder button. The Add Web Folder Wizard runs.
   - Type the Web address of the location to add (for example, **`http://www.something.com/foldername`**), as shown in Figure 15.13. Then click Next.

> **Note**
>
> If you see a message that the server cannot connect to the location, even though you know the address is correct, try one of the other methods. Your server might not support Web-based uploading, or there may be some other problem. Try the FTP method or the Web Publishing Wizard.

   - If prompted, enter a username and password for the site. Then choose Next.

- If you wish to change the name of the Web folder, type the new name in the box.
- Choose Finish.

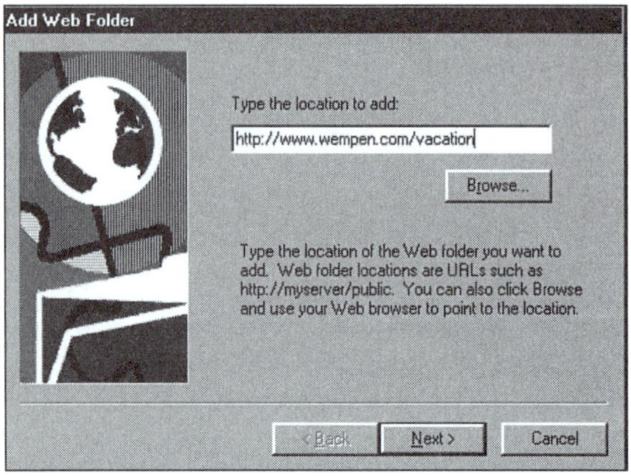

Figure 15.13
Enter the address for the Web page you want to reference.

4. Choose Save.

TRANSFERRING FILES WITH FTP LOCATIONS

In most Microsoft applications (including Word 2000), you can save a file to an FTP location directly from the Save As dialog box. This method is not quite as easy as the Web Folders method you learned about earlier, but it makes a good fall-back if you can't make the Web Folders method work for some reason. (Another good fall-back is the Web Publishing Wizard, covered in the next section.)

1. Choose File, Save as Web Page.
2. To work with an *existing* FTP location, skip to step 7.

   To add a *new* FTP location, open the Save In drop-down list, and choose Add/Modify FTP Locations.
3. Type the FTP site's address in the Name of FTP Site box.

   Do *not* include anything after the first slash (/). (If you do, you will receive an error message, and it won't work.) For example, if the address you were given was `ftp.iquest.net/fw/fwempen`, you would type **`ftp.iquest.net`** here.
4. If you must log in (which is very likely), click the User button and type your username. Then type your password in the Password box (see Figure 15.14).
5. Click the Add button.
6. Click OK. The new FTP location appears on the list.
7. Double-click the FTP location to connect to it.
8. Using the path you were given, navigate to the folder in which you are supposed to save your files.

9. Make sure that the filename in the File Name box is what you want it to be.
10. Click Save.

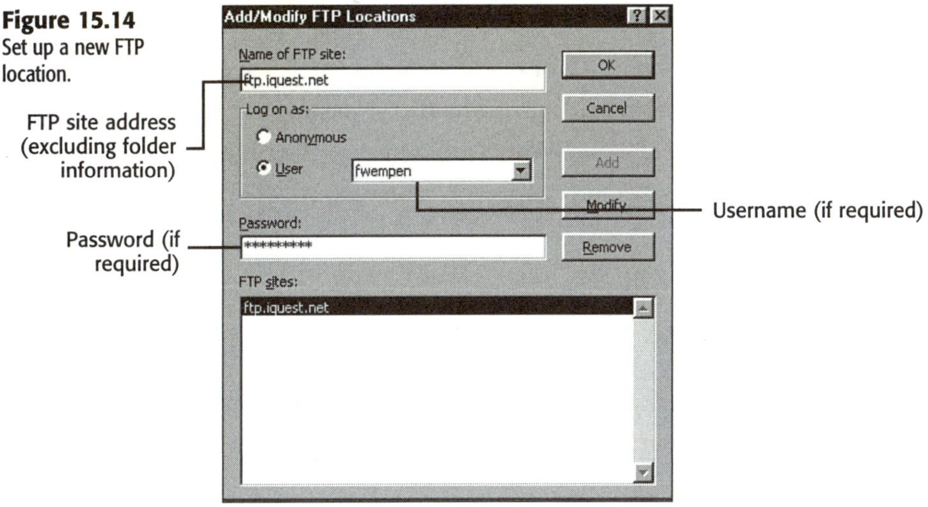

Figure 15.14
Set up a new FTP location.

Transferring Files with the Web Publishing Wizard

The Web Publishing Wizard is more out of the way than the other methods, but it is also foolproof and thorough. It walks you through the transfer, step by step, allowing for any quirks or peculiarities of your server.

> **Note**
>
> The Web Publishing Wizard transfers a single file or a single folder each time you use it, so you might want to put all the files to be transferred into a folder before you transfer them; that way, you can do them all at once.

1. From Windows, choose Start, Programs, Accessories, Internet Tools, Web Publishing Wizard.

   If the Web Publishing Wizard is not there, install it in Windows 98 using Add/Remove Programs in the Windows Control Panel. If you do not have Windows 98, you can download it from Microsoft's Web site (`http://www.microsoft.com`).
2. Click Next to begin.
3. Click the Browse Folders or Browse Files button, and locate the file or folder you want to transfer. Click Open to accept it and then Next.
4. Type a descriptive name for the Web server that you will recognize later. Then click Next.

Tip #105 from
Faithe Wempen

If the Web Publishing Wizard has not worked for you in the past, you might want to click the Advanced button instead of Next in step 4. This brings up a drop-down list of connection methods; ask your ISP which one you should use.

5. Type the Web address in the URL or Internet address box. Then click Next.
6. If prompted, enter your username and password, and click OK.
7. Click Finish. The Web Publishing Wizard transfers the file or folder to the server.
8. When a message appears that the transfer was successful, click OK.

TROUBLESHOOTING

DIFFERING MENU COMMANDS

This chapter directed me to choose File, New, More Word Templates to open the New dialog box, but that doesn't match what I see onscreen. I do have a New command on the File menu, but there's no submenu.

If you are using a standalone version of Word, rather than Word integrated with Works, you should substitute File, New instead to open the New dialog box.

WEB STYLES NOT AVAILABLE

I don't have any of the Web styles available on my Style drop-down list.

If you start with a regular Word document and use File, Save as Web Page, it does not change the template attached to the document. Therefore, you might not have the Web styles that you want available. To fix this, you can create a new, blank Web document (File, New, More Word Templates) and then cut and paste all the text from the existing document into it. Then, format that text using the styles available in the Web document.

ADDITIONAL PAGES NOT LISTED ON NAVIGATION BAR

I have added more pages to my Web site after creating it initially with the Web Page Wizard. How do I get the new pages to appear on the navigation bar?

If you have to add more pages to a multipage Web site after creating it, add hyperlinks to the additional pages to the navigation bar, using the Insert, Hyperlink command.

If you add a lot of new pages, you might find it easier to re-create the Web site using the Web Page Wizard and add any of the pages you want to keep, when given the opportunity in the wizard to add pages. That way you do not have to manually insert the extra hyperlinks in the navigation bar.

BACKGROUNDS IN MULTIFRAME PAGES

Does the navigation bar have to be the same color as the rest of the page?

Not at all. You can apply different backgrounds to each frame in a multiframe layout. For example, if you have a navigation bar, click in it, and then change the background to set it to contrast with the main pane. This can look very sharp.

TURNING OFF AUTOMATIC HYPERLINK CREATION

Every time I type a Web address or email address in a document, Word turns it into a hyperlink. How do I prevent this from happening?

If you type a Web address and Word makes it into a hyperlink automatically, but that's not what you want, press Ctrl+Z or choose Edit, Undo immediately. This undoes Word's automatic change, leaving you with plain text.

If you have to un-make a hyperlink, right-click on it and choose Hyperlink, Remove Hyperlink. This leaves the regular text but removes its link-ability.

To prevent Word from making the automatic change in the future, choose Tools, AutoCorrect, and on the AutoFormat As You Type tab, deselect the Internet and Network Paths with Hyperlinks check box.

CHAPTER 16

Mail Merging and Data Sharing

In this chapter

Moving and Copying Between Documents

The simplest way of sharing data between two Windows-based programs is to use the Clipboard, as you learned in Chapter 3, "Introducing the Works Word Processor." You cut or copy to the Clipboard and then switch to the program into which you want to paste. Then, you issue the Paste command from that program. This works with almost all Windows programs, not just Word and Works.

For example, suppose that you want to include a few cells from a Works spreadsheet in a report you are creating in Word. Here's how you would do it:

1. In the spreadsheet (or the other program of your choice), select what you want to copy. To select, simply drag the mouse across your selection, with the left button held down.
2. To *copy*, choose Edit, Copy, or click the Copy button. To *move*, choose Edit, Cut, or click the Cut button.
3. Switch to the program into which you want to paste, and position the insertion point where you want the data to go.
4. Choose Edit, Paste, or click the Paste button. The data appears in the open document.

Tip #106 from *Faithe Wempen*

You can also use Ctrl+C to copy, Ctrl+X to cut, and Ctrl+V to paste.

Figure 16.1 shows an example of a Works spreadsheet pasted into a Word document.

If you paste data into a tool that is not its native format (for example, spreadsheet data in a word processor document), you will not be able to edit the data directly. The table in Figure 16.1, for example, might look like a regular table created in Word, but you cannot click inside it to make changes.

To change a pasted object, double-click on it. This opens the pasted data's native controls, as shown in Figure 16.2. From there, you can do your editing. When you are finished, click anywhere away from the object to return to your normal controls.

→ For more information about the Clipboard, **see** "Editing Text," **p. 46**.

Figure 16.1
Pasted spreadsheet cells in a Word document.

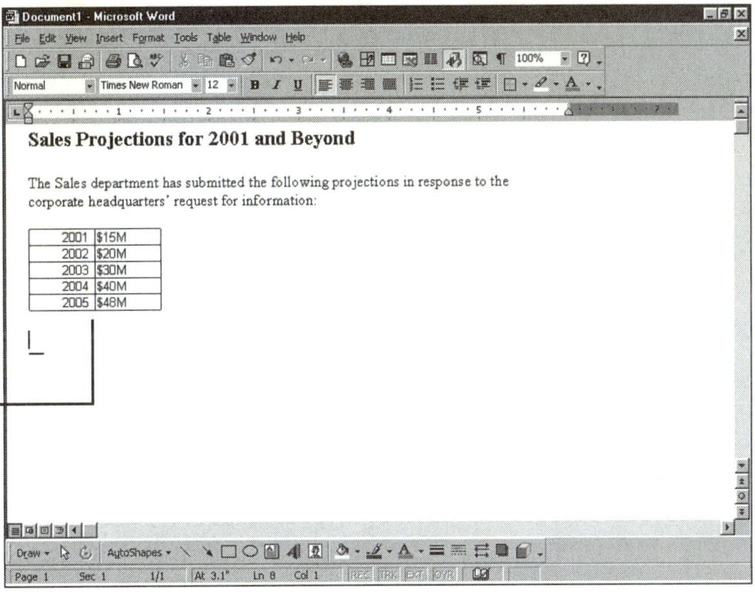

Spreadsheet Cells

Notice that the toolbar buttons are those of the Spreadsheet tool.

Figure 16.2
Double-click a pasted object to open its native tool's controls.

To guide you, row and column headers appear.

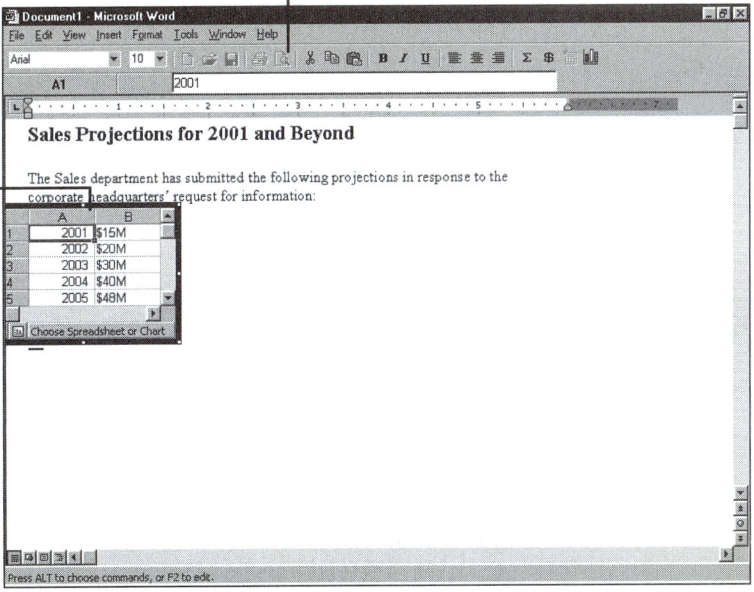

CREATING DYNAMIC LINKS BETWEEN DOCUMENTS

When you copy or paste something, as in the preceding section, it is a *static* copy, which means that no tie exists to the original. If you change the original, the copy does not change. You can also paste *dynamic* copies from one tool to another. With a dynamic copy, if the original changes, the copy also changes.

Note

The process of pasting dynamic copies is sometimes referred to as *object linking and embedding* (OLE).

Suppose that you have a chart in the Spreadsheet tool that changes every month when you input the latest financial data into the spreadsheet on which it is based. You want that chart to appear each month in a word processor report that is always up-to-date. To do this, you insert an object. *Object* is a generic term that means any bit of data (usually in a format other than the native one to the program in which you're working). When you dynamically link an object to a spot in another program, you do not actually paste a copy of the object. Instead, you paste a *link* to the original. Every time the document containing the link is opened, the link is updated with a copy of the latest version.

To create a dynamic link between data in one program and a reference to it in another program, perform the following steps:

1. Make sure that you have saved your work in the program that contains the object you are copying.
2. Select the object (or range, text, whatever), and then copy it to the Clipboard. If you are pasting a chart from the Spreadsheet tool, you don't select it; you merely display it and issue the Copy command.
3. Switch to the document where you want to paste the dynamic link.
4. Choose Edit, Paste Special. The Paste Special dialog box appears (see Figure 16.3).

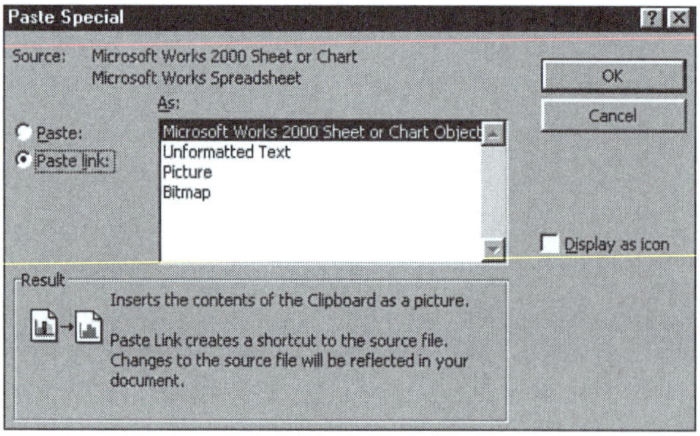

Figure 16.3
Use the Paste Special dialog box to paste a dynamic link.

5. Click the Paste Link option button. The As list changes to show only the valid formats for a pasted link. (There will probably be only one item on the list.)
6. If there is more than one item on the As list, make sure that the one that ends in the word *object* is selected—for example, Microsoft Works 2000 Sheet or Chart Object.
7. Click OK. The object is pasted into the document with a dynamic link.

To test this link, close both documents. Then, open the one containing the original of the object, and make a change to it. Save your work, and then open the document containing the link. The document should display the updated version of the object.

INTRODUCING MAIL MERGE

Many people shudder when they hear the words *mail merge* because mass mailings have traditionally been difficult to set up in word processing programs. With Word, however, it's easy to create a mass mailing.

A *mass mailing* can be any form letter in which you want a personalized copy of the same text to go to multiple recipients. You probably get sweepstakes entries in the mail all the time with your name on them; these are mass mailings, just like the ones you can create in Works.

Mail merge refers to the process of creating a generic letter in a word processor and then "merging" it with a list of addresses. These addresses can be taken directly from a Works database, from your Address Book, from a table in Word, from the Works word processor or spreadsheet, from Microsoft Excel, or from virtually any other program that organizes data in columnar format.

UNDERSTANDING DATA SOURCES

Normally, for a mail merge, your data source will include names and addresses of people. However, it doesn't have to, if you are merging to create some other kind of document (such as merging product names and prices into a catalog, for example).

The data source should have well-defined *fields*, with each field holding unique information. For example, in your Address Book (see Chapter 7, "Using the Address Book"), there is a First Name field, a Last Name field, and so on. The Works database also organizes data neatly into fields like that. Each person's collection of information is a *record*.

If your data source is some sort of table, such as a spreadsheet or a table in a word processing program, each column serves as a field, and each row as a record. To help Word recognize the data for your merge, you should have field names in the first row. If your data source is not currently set up like that, edit it in its native program before you begin the mail merge process.

Understanding Field Codes

The mail merge works by placing field codes into an otherwise ordinary document. Each code stands for a field. When you perform the merge, it generates a separate copy of the document for each record in the data source, with the fields filled in for that record. For example, you might have a letter with a `<<FIRST>>` field code in it like this:

```
Dear <<FIRST>>:
```

The mail merge would create a copy of the letter for each record in the data source, each one with the correct name filled in, like this:

```
Dear Dennis:
```

As you can imagine, it's critical to use the correct field names and place them in the right spots. You'll choose the fields names from a drop-down list, so you don't have to type them (and risk typos), but the field code placement is up to you. Make sure that you remember the little things, like leaving a space between the `<<FIRST>>` and `<<LAST>>` fields so that a space will appear in the letter between those inserted words.

Understanding Merge Output

The most common kind of merge output is a form letter, but you can create several other kinds of output. Word specifically supports form letters, labels, envelopes, and catalogs, and you can use one of these output types to fudge almost any other merge project.

In this chapter I'll show you how to do a form letter, but you can try the other output types on your own whenever you like.

Performing a Mail Merge

After you have chosen and prepared your data source and decided on your output type, you're ready to roll! The following steps walk you through the process of creating a mail-merged form letter, using the names and addresses from your Address Book. I'll explain how to handle other output types and other data sources later in the chapter.

Note

The steps for mail merging with the version of Word that comes with Works Suite 2000 are a bit different from those for the standalone version of Word. This chapter covers the Works Suite version.

1. Start in a new, blank document.
2. Choose Tools, Mail Merge, Document Type. The Document Type dialog box appears.
3. Select the output type you want. (For this example, choose Form Letter.) Then click OK. The Open Data Source dialog box appears.
4. Click Merge from the Address Book. You will return to your document, with the Mail Merge toolbar displayed.

5. Begin typing your letter normally, until you get to the first spot where you want to insert a field.
6. Click the Insert Merge Field button on the Mail Merge toolbar. A list of available fields will appear.
7. Click the field you want to insert. A code for it will appear in the document.
8. Repeat steps 5–7 to compose the rest of the letter and insert the other field codes. Figure 16.4 shows a completed letter.

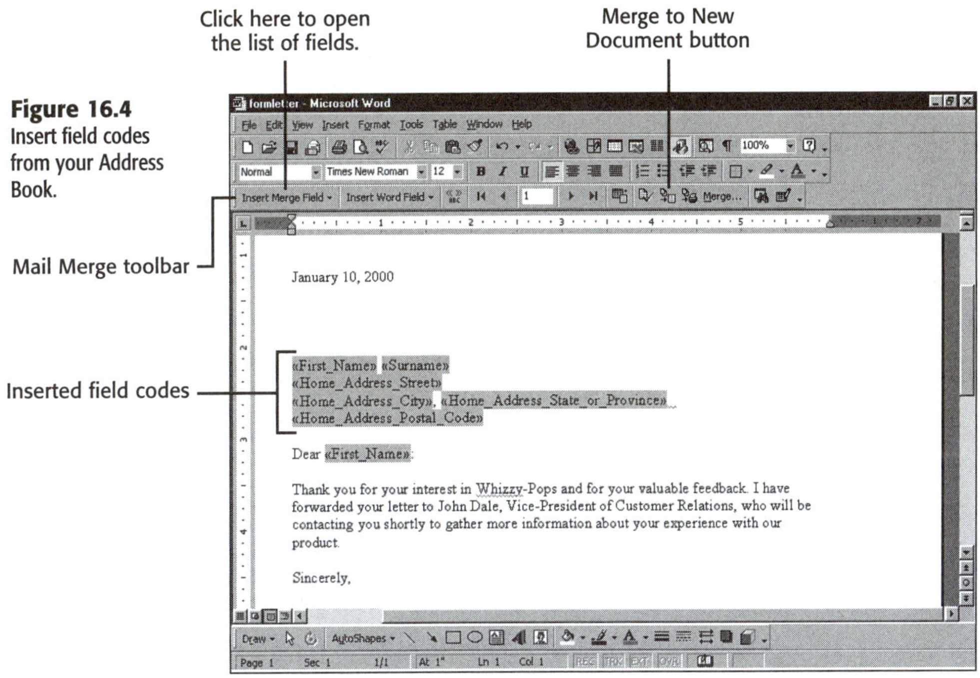

Figure 16.4
Insert field codes from your Address Book.

9. Click the Merge to New Document button on the Mail Merge toolbar. A new document appears, with a page for each of the customized letters.
10. Examine the merge results. If you are happy with them, print them (File, Print). If not, close the merge results document window without saving its changes, and then make adjustments to the merge, as explained next.

FILTERING THE DATA SOURCE

If you are merging from your Address Book, you might not want to include every single person from it in the merge. One way to eliminate some people is to delete their copies of the letter from the merge document before you print it. However, you might prefer to exclude them *before* you merge to the new document.

After step 8 in the preceding procedure, do the following to filter the data:

1. Click the Mail Merge Helper button on the Mail Merge toolbar. The Mail Merge Helper dialog box opens.
2. Click the Query Options button. The Query Options dialog box appears.
3. On the Filter Records tab, create a criterion for filtering by doing the following:
   - Open the Field drop-down list, and choose the field to apply the criterion to.
   - Open the Comparison drop-down list, and choose the comparison you want.
   - Type the value to use for the comparison in the Compare To box.

   For example, you might want records in which the Home Address, Street field is not empty. This would eliminate records for people for whom you don't have a mailing address. Or, you might want to limit the merge to only certain zip codes by setting the Home Address, Postal Code field to be within a certain range of values. Both these criteria are shown in Figure 16.5.

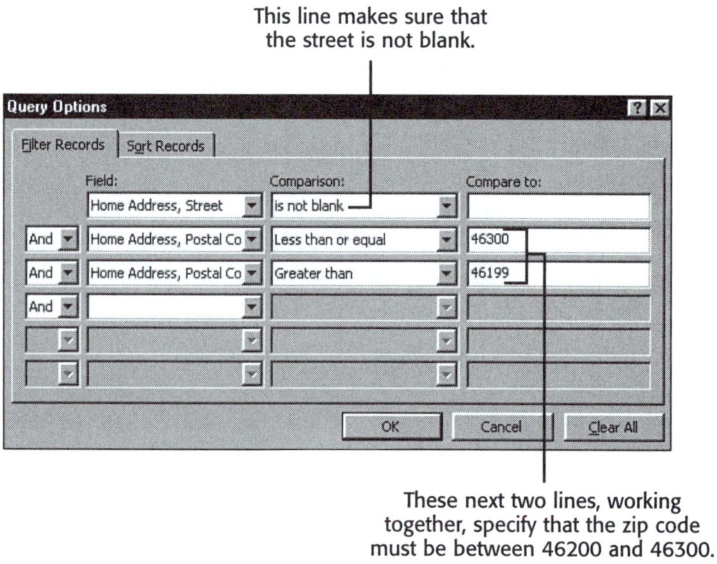

Figure 16.5
Filter the data to exclude records you don't want in the merge.

4. Repeat step 3 to set up additional criteria as desired.
5. Click OK.
6. Return to step 9 in the preceding procedure.

USING OTHER DATA SOURCES

So far, you have used your Address Book for the mail merge, which is easy because you don't have to worry about the fields being set up correctly. However, you can also use other data sources in various formats.

To perform a merge using an alternative data source, follow these steps:

1. Start in a new, blank document.
2. Choose Tools, Mail Merge, Document Type. The Document Type dialog box appears.
3. Select the output type you want. (For this example, choose Form Letter.) Then click OK. The Open Data Source dialog box appears.
4. Click Merge Information from Another Type of File. The Open Data Source dialog box appears.
5. Select the file you want to use as the data source.

   The default file type is Microsoft Works Database, so if you want to use some other data type, choose it from the Files of Type drop-down list.
6. Click Open.

Note

For certain data types, you will see extra prompts or dialog boxes. Work through them. For example, when using a table or spreadsheet, you are asked whether you want to use the entries in the first row as your field names.

Another example–if you are working with a delimited text file (where fields are separated by tabs or commas instead of actual column breaks), you will be prompted to specify the separator character that is in use.

7. Complete the mail merge normally. (Pick up at step 5 of the procedure "Performing a Mail Merge," earlier in this chapter.)

WORKING WITH OTHER OUTPUT TYPES

When you create types of output other than letters, you see some extra prompts during the mail merge setup. For example, when creating labels, you see a message that Word has to set up your mail merge document. Click OK to bypass this, and the Mail Merge Helper dialog box appears. From there, click the Setup button to choose your label size, and insert fields in a Create Labels dialog box (see Figure 16.6).

Note

The Address Book's field names are very long, so the last three fields wrapped to their own lines in Figure 16.6. I did not press Enter after them, however, so they will all appear on the same line when the label prints.

You will run into similar extra dialog boxes and settings with each of the other output types. Just follow the prompts and roll with the punches; none of it is difficult.

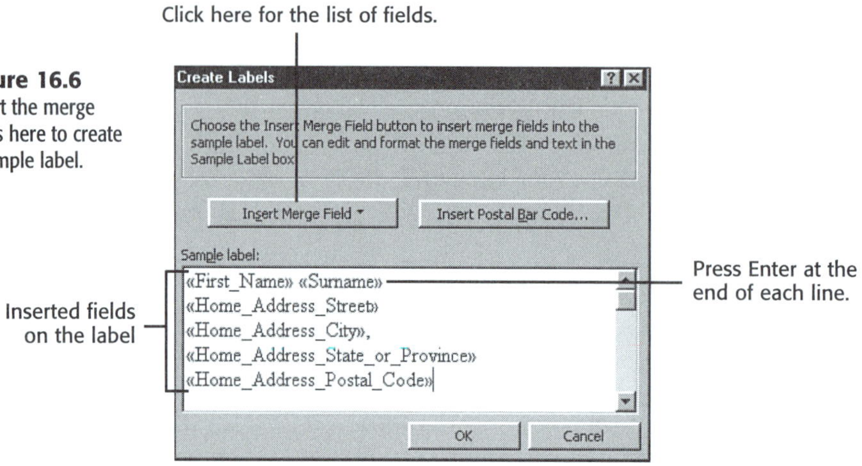

Figure 16.6
Insert the merge fields here to create a sample label.

TROUBLESHOOTING

MAIL MERGE CONTROLS ARE DIFFERENT THAN EXPECTED

I've used Word before, and mail merge didn't work the same way it's described here.

The version of Word that comes with Works Suite is slightly different than the standalone version you may be familiar with. If you are accustomed to Word 2000's "regular" mail merge features, instead of the specialized ones for Works Suite, click the Mail Merge Helper button on the Mail Merge toolbar to open the old familiar Mail Merge Helper window. This is the same as in the regular version of Word, and you can access all of Word's mail merge features from it.

USING DIFFERENT ADDRESS BOOKS

I already have an address book in another program that I would like to use for the mail merge.

If you want to use a different address book than the one that comes with Works (for example, the Outlook Address Book if you use Outlook), start with your regular Works Address Book. Then click the Mail Merge Helper button, and then click the Get Data button to open a menu of data sources. Choose Use Address Book, and a dialog box will appear, from which you can select any address book on your system.

EMPTY LINES NOT PRINTED

Word seems to automatically close up the space whenever there is an empty field in the merge, but I want it to retain the blank space. How can I set it up to do that?

By default, Word doesn't print blank lines when a particular data field is empty. (For example, if there is no address in the Address field for a particular person, it closes up the space reserved for that field on that copy of the letter.) If that's not what you want, click the Merge button on the Mail Merge toolbar, and then choose Print Blank Lines When Data Fields Are Empty.

PART III

Exploring Online Offerings

CHAPTER 17

Internet Basics

In this chapter

WHAT IS THE INTERNET?

The *Internet* is a vast, interconnected network of computers all over the world. They hook together to share data. It started out as a hard-to-use system for computer geeks and scientists, but advances in software and in computing power have made it easy and cost-effective for the average person to explore the Internet, too.

When someone mentions the Internet, the first thing most people think of is the World Wide Web (or *Web*, for short). The Web is a network of Web pages containing text and graphics. If you know the address of a Web page and it's available to the public, you can view it in your Web browser. (Internet Explorer is the default Web browser in the Works suite—more on it later in this chapter).

But there are other parts of the Internet, too. Email is a very popular one, for example. You can exchange email messages with individuals all over the world, as you will learn in Chapter 20, "Working with Email and Newsgroups." Sending and receiving email requires a special program, such as Outlook Express.

Newsgroups are yet another popular Internet feature. Newsgroups are like public bulletin boards on which you can post public messages available to anyone who wants to read them. You must use a newsreader program to read newsgroups; Outlook Express provides this capability, as you will see in Chapter 20.

Note

Because the Web is by far the most popular Internet tool, clever programmers have come up with ways to use some of the other tools through the Web. You can send and receive email using a special Web-based account at some Web sites, for example, and other Web sites enable you to search for and read newsgroup messages. You can also download some files directly from Web pages, using FTP.

Another Internet tool is File Transfer Protocol (FTP). It's a method of transferring files from one computer to another. (You saw it at work at the end of Chapter 15, "Creating Web Pages with Word," for example.) You can use a separate FTP program, or you can access FTP from within programs like Word.

In this chapter, you will learn how to use Internet Explorer (IE) to check out the Web. You will continue learning about IE in Chapter 18, "Looking Up Information Online," and Chapter 19, "Customizing Internet Explorer," and about email and newsgroups in Chapter 20, "Working with Email and Newsgroups."

INTRODUCING INTERNET EXPLORER

Internet Explorer is a *Web browser*, a program designed specifically for viewing pages found on the Web. The Web is a collection of documents, called *pages*, scattered all over the Internet. Each page is linked to others, so you can move from page to page. One minute you might be reading about financial news found on a *server* (a computer that stores large quantities of data) in Los Angeles—the next minute you can view the latest local news from a server in Hong Kong. Figure 17.1 shows a sample Web page in Internet Explorer.

Note

Do not confuse Internet Explorer (which is the Web browser) with Windows Explorer (which is a file management tool for your PC).

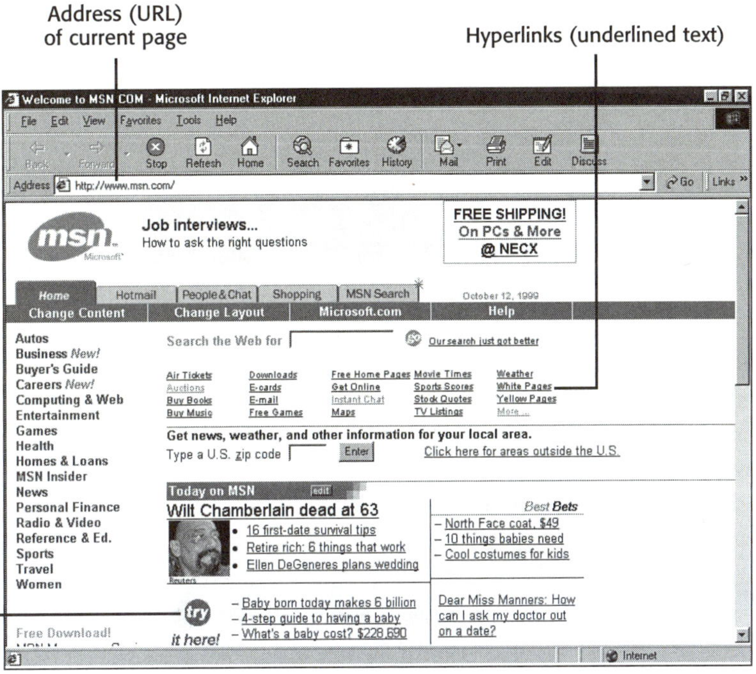

Figure 17.1
Internet Explorer in action, displaying a page from Microsoft.

Web pages use *Hypertext Transfer Protocol* (HTTP) technology, which means that an underlined link on a page can be clicked and another page appears on your screen for viewing. Links make Web pages so easy to use. By moving from link to link, you can view all kinds of information on the Web.

Each Web document can be identified by its URL (pronounced "earl"), which stands for *uniform resource locator*—its address on the Internet. Besides jumping from link to link on a page, you can type in an URL to go directly to that page. (You can find URLs all over the place, in advertising, computer magazines, and so on. Even your friends might give you some URLs to check out.)

Microsoft Internet Explorer 5.0 comes bundled with Microsoft Works Suite 2000. When you install Works Suite 2000 (see Appendix A, "Installing Microsoft Works Suite 2000"), you automatically install Internet Explorer 5.0, too. This also includes Outlook Express, a complete email program that lets you send and receive email and access *newsgroups* (public discussion groups) on the Internet.

SETTING UP AN INTERNET CONNECTION

You need a couple of things before you can begin using Internet Explorer or Outlook Express. For starters, you need a modem (that is, assuming you do not have a network connection through your company's LAN). Most computers come with modems these days, so you're probably covered on that issue. Second, you must have an Internet connection. Windows makes it easy for you to configure your Internet connection. However, it's up to you to set up an account with an *Internet service provider (ISP)*. An ISP provides you with all the information you need—IP address, DNS address, host name, phone number to dial, and so on—to configure Windows for the Internet.

Note

Whenever you set up an Internet connection, you must deal with a certain amount of technical mumbo-jumbo. Terms such as *IP address, DNS address, mail server*, and so on, probably don't mean a lot to you–and they don't have to, either. Just copy the information given to you by your ISP into the appropriate blanks to perform the setup once, and then you never have to worry about those things again.

It's easy to find an Internet service provider these days; you can start by looking in your local Yellow Pages directory. You can check computer magazines, newspapers, and computer stores or ask your friends or colleagues what service they use. You can even let Microsoft's Internet Connection Wizard suggest a list of service providers and provide information on how to contact them to establish an account. When you sign up for an account with an Internet service provider, you can log on to the Internet via the service provider's computer, for a small fee (of course).

Caution

When signing up with an Internet service provider, make sure that you write down the correct names of the mail server and news server used to send and receive email and subscribe to newsgroups. The server names are important for setting up Outlook Express to work with the Internet service provider's computers.

Windows makes it easy to set up and use the Internet by providing a wizard that guides you through the steps. The following steps assume that you already have an Internet account set up with your local ISP and are ready to configure it on your PC. If that's not the case, your procedure might be slightly different, but just follow the prompts and you will be fine.

1. Choose Start, Programs, Accessories, Internet Tools, Internet Connection Wizard. This opens the Internet Connection Wizard dialog box, shown in Figure 17.2.

Note

Step 1 shows the path to the file in Windows 98 Second Edition; if you have an earlier version of Windows, it could be in a different place on the Start menu system. Look for Start, Programs, Internet Explorer, Internet Connection Wizard on a Windows 95 system, for example.

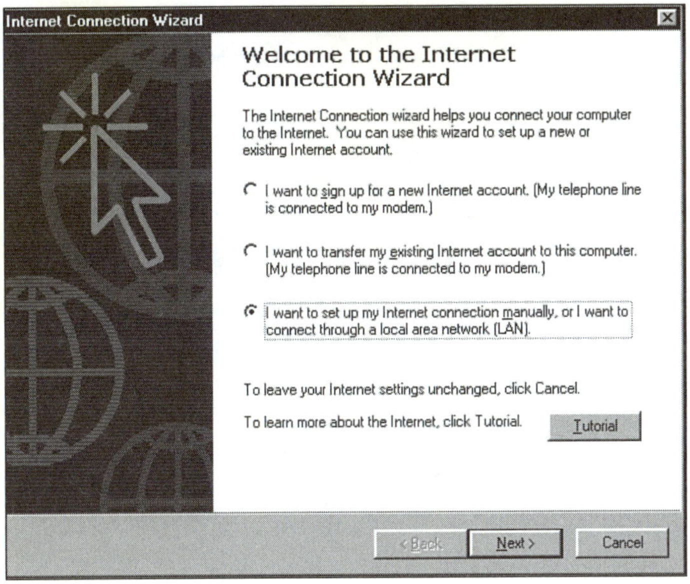

Figure 17.2 The Internet Connection Wizard walks you through the steps necessary for setting up Internet Explorer to work with your Internet account.

2. Choose the last option (I Want to Set Up My Internet Connection Manually), and then click Next.

Note

In step 2, you choose to set up the connection manually because you already have an account with an ISP and you just need to configure Windows to recognize it. If that's not the case and you would like Microsoft's recommendation of a provider, choose the first option. (You will probably be able to find a better provider locally on your own, though.)

The second option, to transfer an existing account to this computer, is misleading. Its name makes it sound as though it works for all ISPs, but it actually works with only a select few service providers.

3. Leave the I Connect Through a Phone Line and a Modem selected, and click Next to continue.

Note

If you connect through a LAN, choose that instead in step 3, but the rest of these steps will not be applicable; you will have to complete the process on your own.

4. The next dialog box, shown in Figure 17.3, asks you to enter your ISP's phone number. Do so.
5. If you have to dial the area code along with it, leave the Dial Using the Area Code and Country Code box marked; otherwise, deselect it. Then click Next.

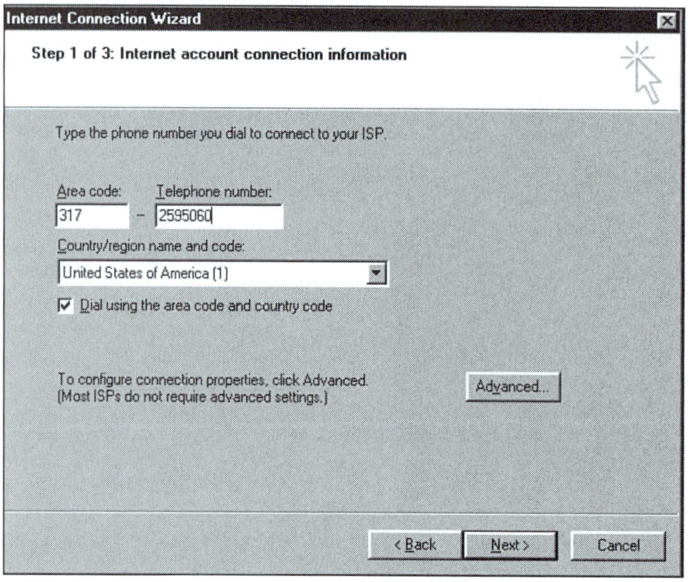

Figure 17.3
Enter your ISP's phone number (the number the modem should dial).

Note

If your ISP requires special settings, such as entering a specific IP address or DNS address, click the Advanced button for extra dialog boxes in which to enter that information. Most providers these days do not require this, however—check with yours to make sure.

6. Next, enter your username and password. These were given to you by your ISP when you signed up for an account. Then click Next.
7. Enter a "friendly" name for the connection in the Connection Name box. This text will appear under the connection icon. For example, you might call it `Connect to Internet`. Then click Next.
8. The wizard then asks whether you want to set up an Internet mail account. Click Yes, and click Next to continue.
9. Click Create a New Internet Mail Account, and then click Next.

Note

To use the existing Internet mail account, select Use an Existing Internet Mail Account in step 8, and choose the account; then click Next to continue, and skip to step 15.

10. Type the name that you want to appear on the mail messages you send. This could be your full name, your first initial and last name, or whatever you like. Then click Next.
11. Enter your email address. Then click Next.
12. Enter your incoming mail server name in the Incoming Mail (POP3, IMAP or HTTP) Server box. Normally, this is `pop.xxxxx.xxx`, where the `xxxxx.xxx` is whatever comes after the `@` sign in your email address.

13. Enter your outgoing mail server name in the Outgoing Mail (SMTP) Server box. Normally, this is `smtp.xxxxx.xxx`, again, where *`xxxxx.xxx`* is whatever comes after the `@` in your email address.
14. In the Account Name box, type the account name your ISP has given to you. This is probably the text that comes *before* the `@` sign in your email address.
15. Type your password in the Password box. Then click Next.

Tip #107 from *Faithe Wempen*

If you are the only person who uses your computer, you might want Windows to remember your password and enter it automatically each time. Mark the Remember Password check box if so. If not, you will be prompted for it each time you connect.

16. Click Finish. Your connection is set up.

At this point, your new connection is established, and Internet Explorer loads.

Accessing the Internet

After you have set up your Internet connection (in the preceding steps), that connection starts whenever you start Internet Explorer.

To start Internet Explorer, do any of the following:

- Double-click the Internet Explorer icon on your desktop.
- Click the Internet Explorer icon on the Quick Launch toolbar (next to the Start button), if you have Windows 98 (or Windows 95 with Internet Explorer 4.0).
- Choose Start, Programs, Internet Explorer.

If you are not already connected to the Internet, the Dial-up Connection dialog box appears (see Figure 17.4) with your connection information pre-entered.

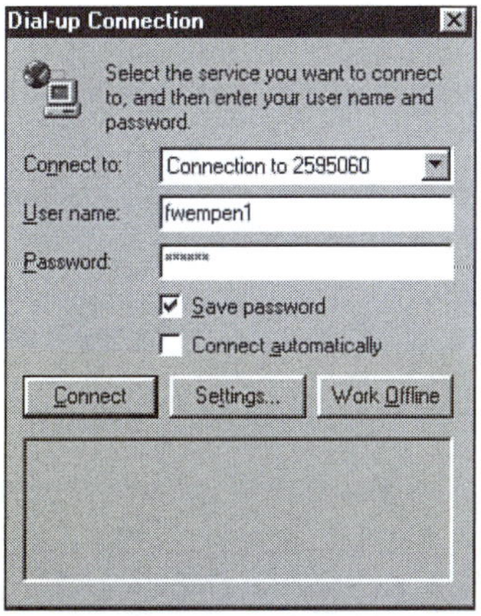

Figure 17.4 Windows prompts you to establish your Internet connection.

If your password is not in the Password text box, enter it. Then click Connect to dial and connect to the Internet. The Explorer dials your ISP and then displays the Internet Explorer window and the Microsoft home page.

The Welcome to MSN.COM page is the first Web page you see after connecting to the Internet with Internet Explorer. (You see it in Figure 17.1.) This page tells you about Microsoft, as well as other services you can access over the Internet. The start page changes frequently, so the page shown in Figure 17.1 might differ from the page you see when you log on to Microsoft's Web site.

USING INTERNET EXPLORER

The Internet Explorer window, shown in Figure 17.5, looks similar to other program windows used in Windows. The familiar title bar, menu bar, and toolbar appear, and the Web page itself is displayed in the middle of the window.

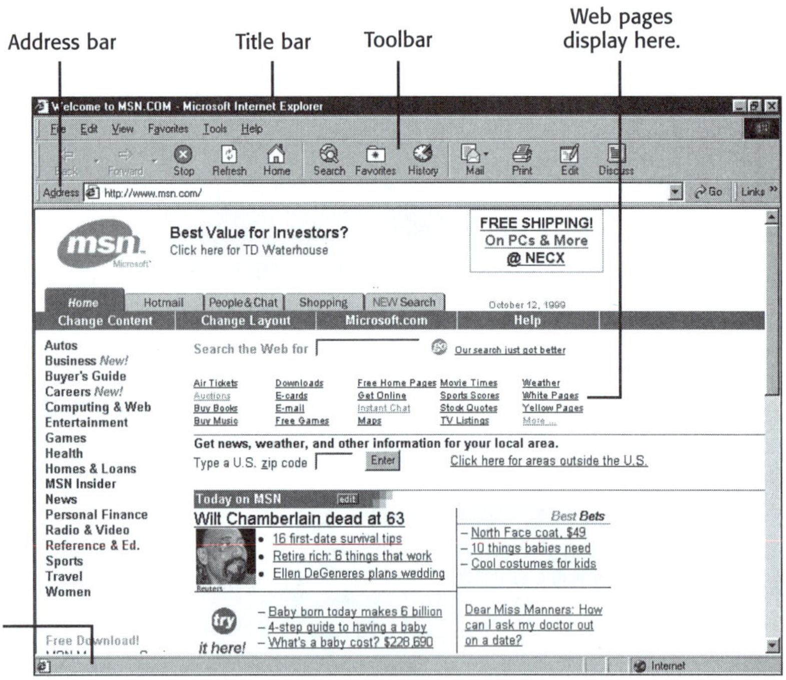

Figure 17.5
The Welcome to MSN.COM page appears by default each time you start Internet Explorer.

Take a few moments and acclimate yourself to the Internet Explorer window and its onscreen elements:

- **Title bar**—Displays the name of the program and the title of the current Web page.
- **Toolbar**—As in Word and Works, IE employs a toolbar to provide shortcuts for the most common menu commands.

- **Address bar**—The address bar shows the address of the current page you're viewing. You can visit other pages by typing their addresses here and pressing Enter.
- **Status bar**—This bar shows the status of the current page. As a page is loading, it tells you what percentage of the loading process is done.

Tip #108 from *Faithe Wempen*

By default, Internet Explorer automatically starts your Internet session with the page shown in Figure 17.5. You don't have to stick to the Microsoft Web site that appears by default; you can make any Web page your home page. To do so, choose Tools, Internet Options. On the General tab, type a different URL in the Address text box. Click OK. The next time you start Internet Explorer, the new start page will appear.

VIEWING PAGES

The easiest way to begin viewing Web pages is to click on links. As I explained at the beginning of the chapter, links connect Web pages from computers all over the world. When you click on a link, another Web page appears. On most Web pages, links appear as underlined text. Graphics objects also can be links. One way to find out whether Web page text and graphics are links is to hover your mouse pointer over the object. If the pointer takes the shape of a pointing hand, it's a link. Both kinds of hyperlinks appear in Figure 17.5, although there are more text hyperlinks than graphic ones.

Some Web documents are longer, and even wider, than others. Use the scrollbars to view various parts of the page. You will probably encounter pages that even have links to other areas of the page. For example, you might click a link at the top of the page and end up viewing a section near the bottom of the page.

Links are definitely the way to explore the Web, but after viewing several pages, you might want to return to a page. Internet Explorer has two important toolbar buttons for moving among pages:

- **Back**—Each time you click Back, you return to the preceding page. You can click it as many times as you want, until you are finally back at your original default starting page. You can also open the button's drop-down list and go back several steps at once.

- **Forward**—If you have clicked Back, you can go forward again by clicking this button. (Note that you can't go forward unless you have gone back.) This button also has a drop-down list to move ahead multiple steps at once.

GETTING OUT OF TROUBLE

Occasionally, you might become "lost," or a page might not load correctly. Here are a few ways to get out of one of these messes:

- **Stop**—This button stops the loading of a page. You might use it, for example, to stop either a page that you didn't intend to load or a page that is taking too long to load.

- **Refresh**—Sometimes there is a snafu in sending the data from the Internet to your browser, and a page might not look right. Maybe some pictures are missing, or the text is out of whack. You can sometimes correct this by refreshing the page. Refreshing also updates the page information from the server, so if you are looking at a page that updates frequently (for example, to show the current stock prices), the figures will be updated each time you click Refresh.

- **Home**—If you ever get lost and you aren't sure where to go, why not go home? Click the Home button to return to your default Internet start page.

Going to a Specific Address

These days, it seems as though everybody and his corporate sponsor have a *Web site* (a collection of pages), and they all want you to visit. Even TV commercials show Web site addresses. Chances are good that, if you haven't already, you will soon find an address you want to visit.

> **Note**
>
> Another term for a Web address is *uniform resource locator* (URL). The terms *address* and *URL* are used interchangeably when referring to the Internet.

To go to a specific page, do the following:

1. Click in the address bar. The address that's currently there becomes highlighted.
2. Type the new address. The old one disappears immediately when you start typing.
3. Press Enter. Internet Explorer takes you to that page.

If an error message appears, perhaps you typed something wrong. Check the address in the address bar. If you see an error, correct it. To correct an error, click once on the address to highlight it, and then click on it a second time to move a cursor into it. Use the arrow keys to move the cursor and the Backspace key to delete, just as in a word processor.

> **Tip #109 from** *Faithe Wempen*
>
> Many of the Web addresses you come across resemble this one: `http://www.mcp.com`. You don't have to type in the entire address when entering an URL in Internet Explorer 4; you can drop the `http://` prefix and start with the www part.

Internet Explorer keeps track of all the Web sites you visit during an online session. To quickly revisit a site, click the drop-down arrow at the right end of the address bar to display a history list. To select a site from the list, click the descriptive name (see Figure 17.6).

You can also click the History button on the toolbar to open the History pane. Use this feature to revisit pages you viewed in previous sessions. To clear your History list and start fresh, choose Tools, Internet Options. Click the Clear History button on the General tab, and click OK.

→ To search for Web pages for which you don't know the exact address, **see** Chapter 18, "Looking Up Information Online."

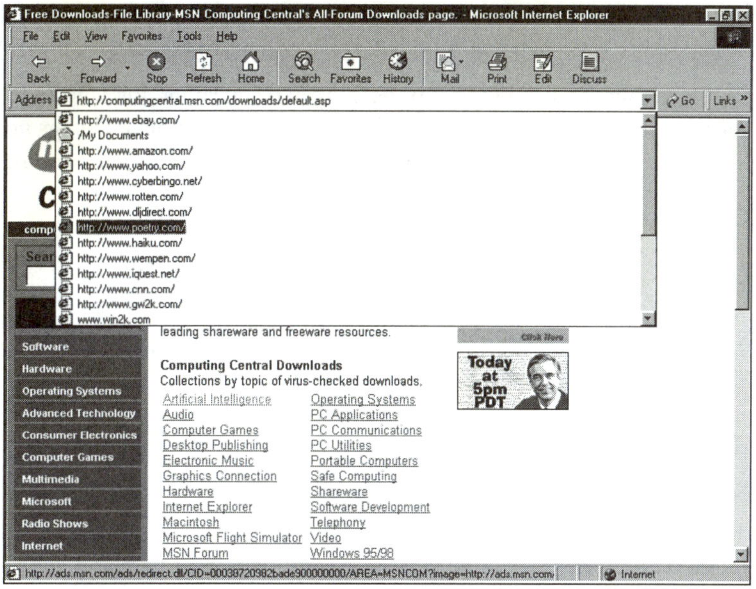

Figure 17.6
By opening the Address box's drop-down list, you can see a list of sites you have visited and can select from the list.

SHUTTING DOWN YOUR INTERNET CONNECTION

When you're finished surfing the Web and you're ready to close Internet Explorer, you can either remain connected or disconnect from the Internet. If you remain connected, you can access the Outlook Express email features, as explained in Chapter 20.

To exit Internet Explorer, close the Internet Explorer window. You can do so by choosing File, Close or by clicking the window's Close (×) button.

To disconnect from the Internet, double-click the connection icon on the taskbar (down by the clock) to open the Connected To dialog box. Depending on your setup, the icon might look like two computers hooked together with a cable or like a modem with two flashing red and green lights. Click the Disconnect button to disconnect from the Internet. If you connect through a LAN, you don't have to disconnect from the Internet when you are finished; your connection is "up" at all times.

TROUBLESHOOTING

CAN'T KEEP CONNECTED

Almost every time I try to connect to my ISP, it hangs up on me after about 30 seconds to a minute.

Your dial-up connection is probably not configured right for your ISP. Open the My Computer window, and double-click Dial-Up Networking. Find the icon for the connection, and right-click on it; then choose Properties. Use this dialog box to change the settings for your connection. (Call your ISP's technical support department to find out what changes to make.)

If you only occasionally lose your Internet connection after about 30 seconds of being connected, there is probably no problem with your settings. Most likely, your ISP is just busy.

If your modem makes all kinds of beeping and squealing noises for a few seconds as you connect, that's normal. However, if it continues until it finally hangs up on itself, there's likely a problem with your telephone line quality. Static on the line can cause this problem.

CAN'T GO ANYWHERE

I can connect to my ISP, but it won't let me do anything after I'm connected. Everything seems to be moving as slow as mud.

Try hanging up and dialing again. Sometimes I have to dial my ISP four or five times to get a good, fast connection.

THIS PAGE TAKES FOREVER TO LOAD

Sometimes I wait and wait for a Web page to load.

The overall speed at which pages load depends partially on the amount of traffic on the Internet at the moment. Sometimes you can get caught behind a "slow driver" in making a certain request. To try again loading a certain page, click Stop and then Refresh. Sometimes this shakes things up to load faster.

CHAPTER 18

Looking Up Information Online

In this chapter

Visiting a Web Site Through the Task Launcher

Looking for some common information, such as the zip code for Cleveland or the postage rates to send a letter to France? Before you start digging around on the Internet, check the Works Task Launcher first. There could be a link for the site you want, and you can save yourself the search.

The Works Task Launcher provides links to many of the most popular and useful reference sites on the Internet through the MSN (Microsoft Network) server. To visit one, do the following:

1. Start the Works Task Launcher.
2. Click Programs.
3. Click MSN. A list of sites appears.
4. Click the site you want to go to (see Figure 18.1).
5. Click the Start button for that site. Internet Explorer opens and displays information about that site.

Figure 18.1
Select one of these useful sites to visit.

Choose the site to visit.

Click Start to open Internet Explorer.

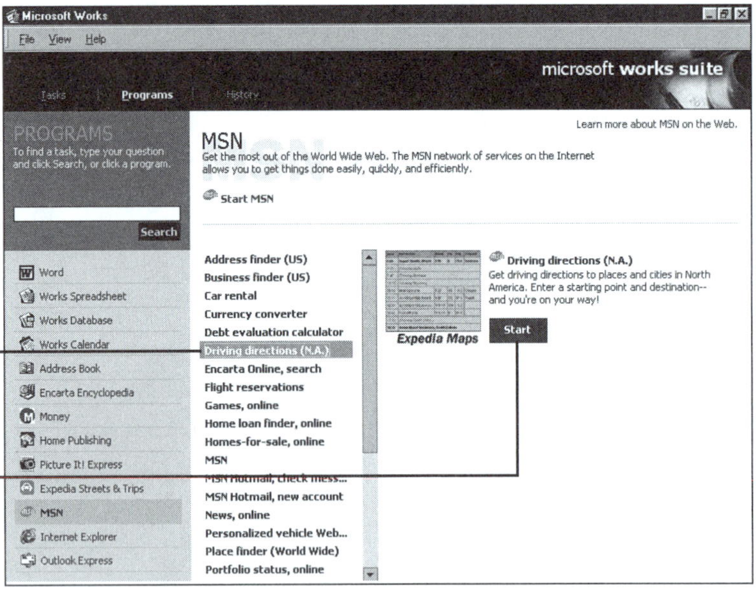

Searching the Internet

When you're trying to locate information on the Web, jumping from link to link is like looking for a needle in a haystack. To find information in a more organized way, try an *Internet search engine*, a program designed specifically for looking up data on the Web. By typing in a keyword, the search engine looks through its most recent database of Web page sites for a match. When it finds a match, it displays it as a link you can click to check out the information.

Numerous search engines are available that you can use. Unfortunately, there is no complete "yellow pages" of the Internet. Many so-called directories or indexes exist, but none list every single Web page. That's the "cup is half empty" approach; the optimistic thought is that millions of interesting sites are readily available through hundreds of online search engines.

Note

A *search engine* is a program that looks up keywords or other criteria you specify in a huge database collection of information about Web pages. To use a search engine, you first go to the page where it is located.

Each of the hundreds of search engines available on the Internet maintains its own database, and each produces different results. If you're doing serious research, you should work with several search engines. If you're just using the Internet for fun, you can get by with one or two.

PERFORMING A QUICK SEARCH FROM THE START PAGE

The Welcome to MSN page (the page that first appears when you start Internet Explorer) offers a shortcut to the MSN search engine right there, so you don't even have to visit any other sites. Just type a subject of interest into the Search the Web For text box, and click the Go button (see Figure 18.2). A list of sites about that subject appears, as in Figure 18.3. Click on the hyperlink for any site you want to visit.

Figure 18.2
Search from your starting page by typing a subject and clicking Go.

Type the search term here.

Press Enter or click Go.

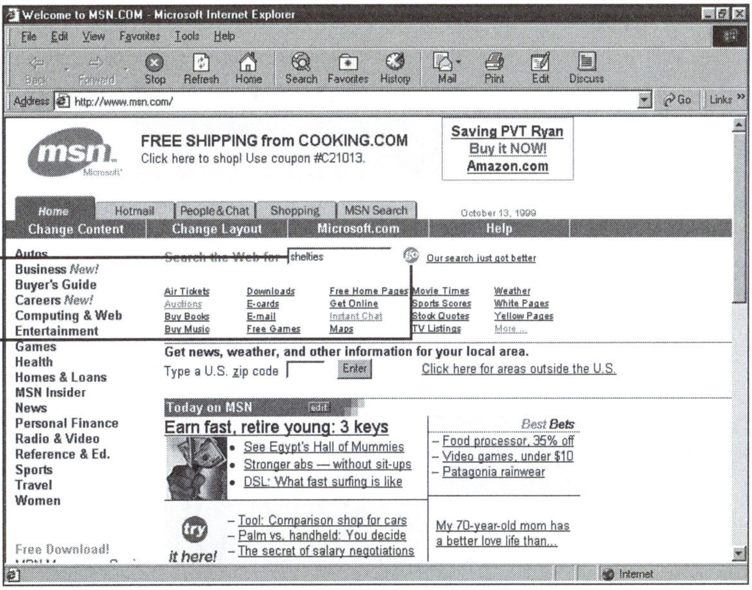

Figure 18.3
Search results for the word *Sheltie*.

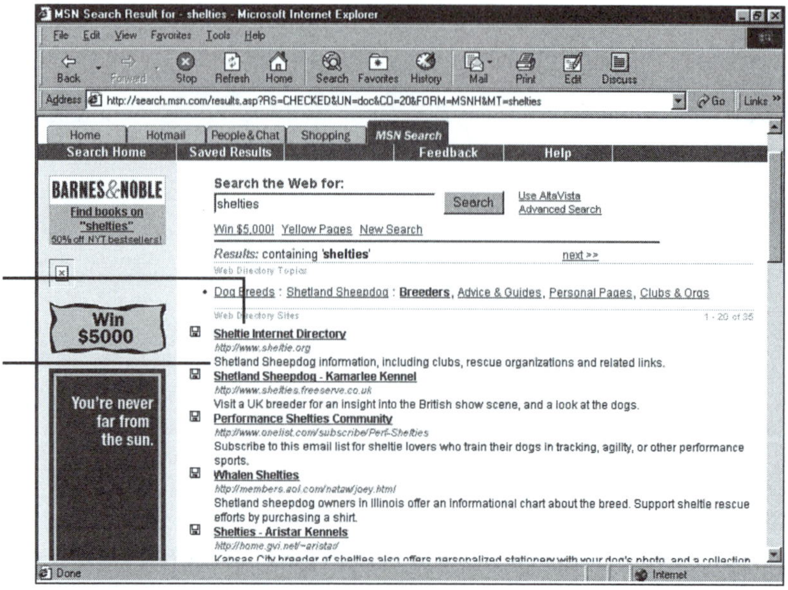

USING THE SEARCH PANE IN INTERNET EXPLORER

For quick access to a search engine, click the Search button on the Internet Explorer toolbar. This opens the Search pane, as shown in Figure 18.4.

Figure 18.4
The Search pane displays a default search engine, but the search engine you see can change from time to time.

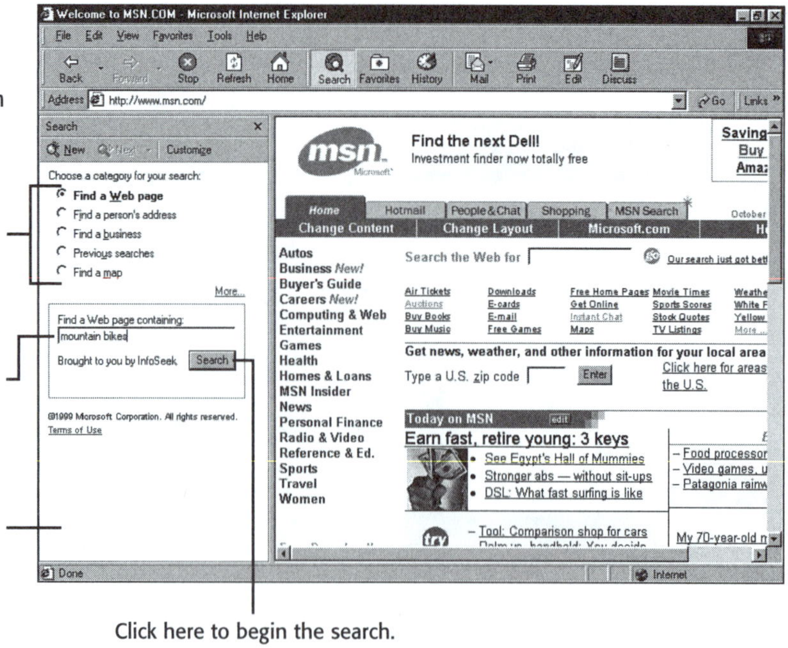

For example, suppose that you are searching for Web pages related to mountain bikes. You would type the words `mountain bikes` into the search text box shown in Figure 18.4 and then press Enter or click Search. A list of topics appears in the Search pane. Click on the one that most closely matches your interest, and its results appear in the main pane, as shown in Figure 18.5. From there, you could click on any of the found sites to visit it.

Figure 18.5
Here are the results of searching for *mountain bikes* and then choosing the Mountain Bicycles topic.

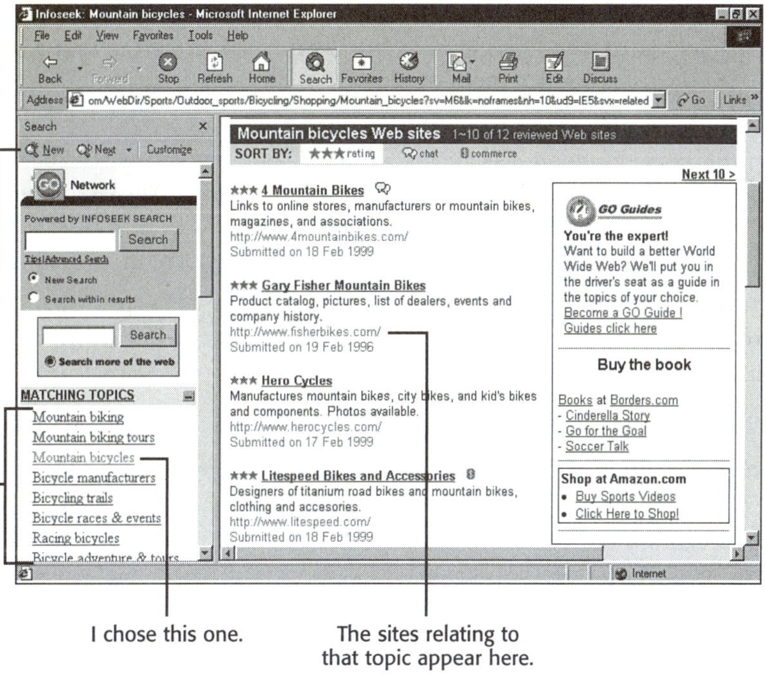

To start a new search, returning to the text shown in that pane in Figure 18.4, click the New button at the top of the Search pane.

You just saw how to search for Web pages, but you can also search for people, businesses, or maps by choosing one of the other option buttons in Figure 18.4. Then, just fill in the fields provided. For example, when searching for a person, you are prompted for the person's name.

When you are finished with the Search pane, close it by clicking its Close (×) button or clicking the Search button again on the toolbar.

SEARCHING WITH OTHER SEARCH ENGINES

The Search pane in Internet Explorer employs a variety of search engines on a rotating basis. If you want to use other search engines instead, you can visit their Web sites directly and work in a single-pane view. Here are some of the more popular ones:

```
http://www.infoseek.com
http://www.altavista.com
```

```
http://www.lycos.com
http://www.goto.com
http://www.yahoo.com
http://www.webcrawler.com
```

Tip #110 from
Faithe Wempen

Of all the major search engines, only Yahoo! limits its sites to those that the Yahoo! staff has checked and approved. Use Yahoo! if you want to see fewer–but better–sites. If you're looking for quantity, use one of the other search engines.

If you would like more specific information about a certain search engine, check out Que's book *The Complete Idiot's Guide to Online Search Secrets* by Michael Miller.

Customizing the Search Pane in Internet Explorer

You don't have to give up the handy Search pane to use one particular search engine that you like. Simply do the following to choose which search engine the Search pane should use:

1. Display the Search pane.
2. Click the Customize button. The Customize Search Settings dialog box opens.
3. Click Use One Search Service for All Searches. A list of search services appears (see Figure 18.6).
4. Click the search service you want to use.
5. Click OK.

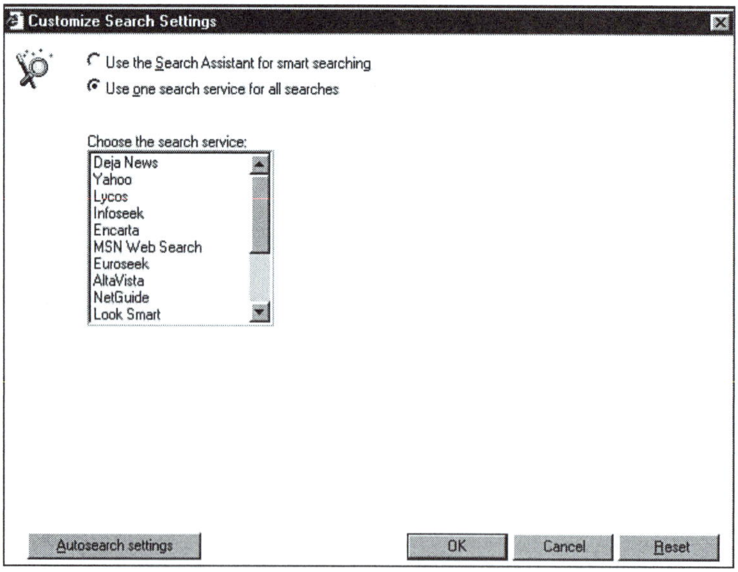

Figure 18.6
Select the search engine to use.

WORDING SEARCH QUERIES

So far, you have searched by entering a single keyword, but much more sophisticated search methods are available. Unfortunately, each search engine has its own search syntax, so they're all slightly different. On some of them, for example, when you enter more than one word, they display only pages that contain both words. Other sites display pages that contain *either* word unless you enter some special code to indicate that a word is required (such as a plus sign before or after it). It's impossible to generalize; each one works differently.

At each search site you visit, however, there should be some explanation. Look for a Search Options, Advanced Search, or some such button or hyperlink, and click it. Directions should appear to help you with the necessary syntax, or a more complex search form. For example, when I click Search Options at `http://www.infoseek.com`, I see the powerful search form shown in Figure 18.7.

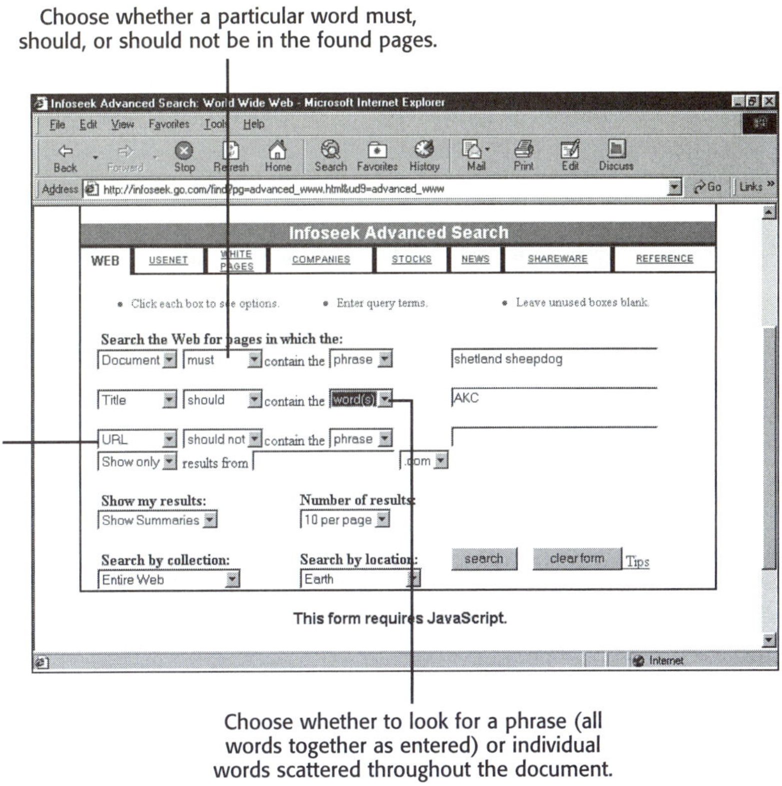

Figure 18.7
The advanced version of the search form at Infoseek.

WORKING WITH SEARCH RESULTS

In general, when you get a list of results, you simply click the hyperlink for a page to visit it. That's common for all search engines.

However, some search engines offer special features to help you refine your search. For example, search results from Infoseek include a hyperlink under each found site, named Find Similar Pages. This re-does the search using the selected page as a model of what you are looking for. Because each site is different, you will want to play around with the options offered, to see what each search engine provides.

WORKING WITH FAVORITE PLACES

Sometimes you will stumble by accident on a site that is really cool, and you will want to remember to come back to it later. That's where the Favorites list comes in.

Note

If you have worked with other Web browsers (such as Netscape) before, you might be more familiar with the term *bookmarks* than with *favorites*. They both mean the same thing: saved Web page addresses.

You can use Internet Explorer's Favorites feature to mark and record sites in a convenient listing; to revisit the site, you need only click its name in the list. You also can sort and edit the list to manage this time-saving feature.

ADDING A FAVORITE WEB PAGE

Adding a Web site to your Favorites list takes only a moment—and can save you lots of time later.

1. Display the Web page you want to save in your Favorites list.
2. Choose Favorites, Add to Favorites. (Use the Favorites menu, not the Favorites toolbar button.) This opens the Add Favorite dialog box, shown in Figure 18.8.
3. (Optional) To save the favorite in a subfolder of the Favorites menu, click the Create In button. The dialog box expands, as in Figure 18.9.

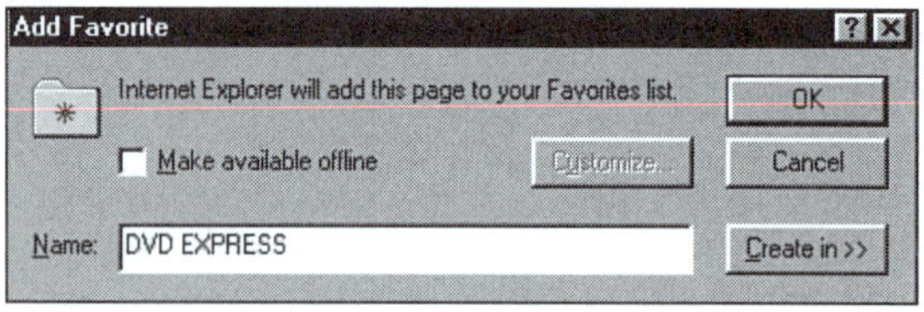

Figure 18.8
Save your favorite Web pages using the Add Favorite dialog box.

4. If desired, change the descriptive name in the Name text box. This text will appear on your Favorite menu.

Tip #111 from *Faithe Wempen*

Your Favorites list can become crowded over time. One way to organize lots of favorites is to place them into separate folders that you create. Each folder becomes a submenu of the Favorites list.

Figure 18.9
You can save a favorite in a different folder if desired.

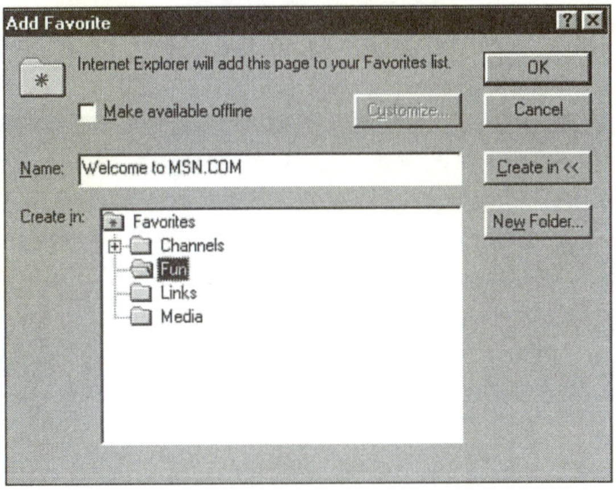

5. Do one of the following:
   - Click an existing folder in which you want to save it.
   - To create a new folder, click the New Folder button. Type the name for a new folder, and then click OK.
6. Click OK. The favorite is created.

USING THE FAVORITES LIST

To view your Favorites list, open the Favorites menu. Then, select a favorite from the menu.

You can also open the Favorites list in a separate pane, like the Search pane. To do so, click the Favorites button on the toolbar. This opens the Favorites pane, as shown in Figure 18.10. To open a folder, click the folder name. To go to a page, click on its name.

MANAGING THE FAVORITES LIST

In the preceding sections, you saw how you can create new favorites either directly on the Favorites menu or within a subfolder. You can also move favorites among subfolders after they have been created, as well as create new folders and delete favorites that no longer interest you.

1. Choose Favorites, Organize Favorites. (Use the Favorites menu, not the Favorites button.) This opens the Organize Favorites dialog box, as shown in Figure 18.11.

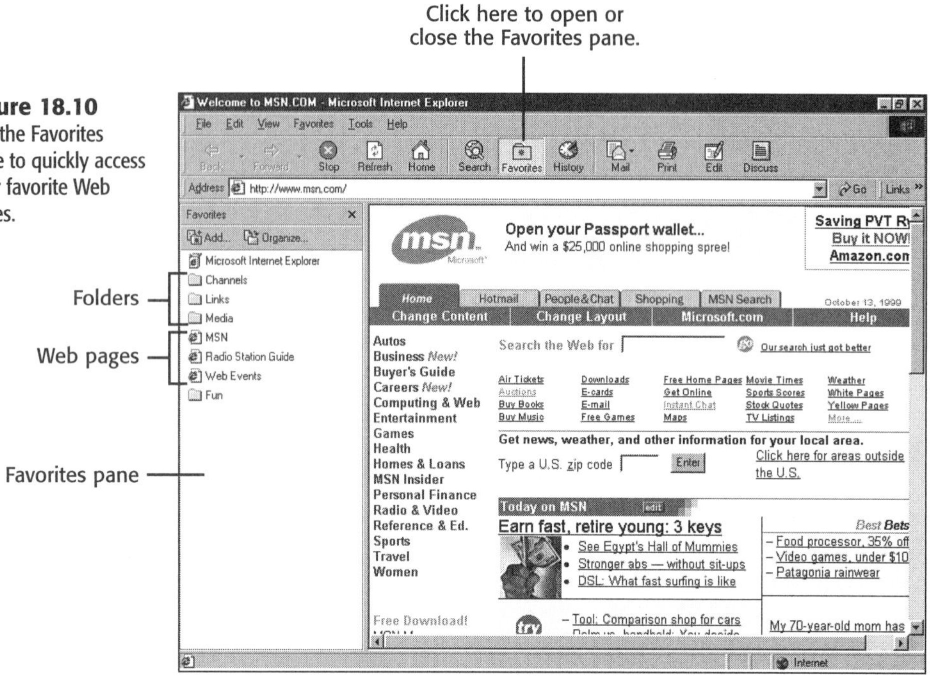

Figure 18.10
Use the Favorites pane to quickly access your favorite Web pages.

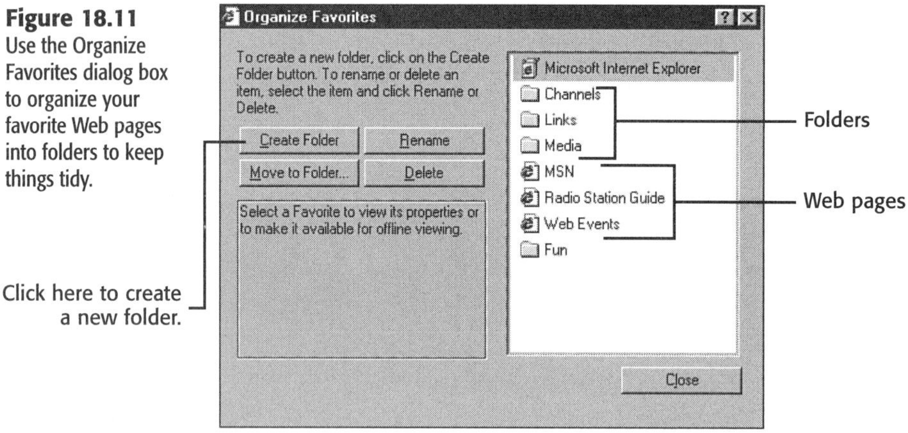

Figure 18.11
Use the Organize Favorites dialog box to organize your favorite Web pages into folders to keep things tidy.

2. Click on the item that you want to move, rename, or delete.
3. Do one of the following:
    - To delete the item, click the Delete button.
    - To rename the item, click the Rename button. Then, type the new name and press Enter.

- To move the favorite to a different folder, click the Move to Folder button. In the dialog box that appears, click the folder to move it to, and then click OK.
- To create a new folder, click the Create Folder button on the toolbar located at the top of the Organize Favorites dialog box. Type the name for the new folder, and press Enter.

Tip #112 from
Faithe Wempen

> The favorites in a folder always appear in alphabetical order. You can't change that. You can, however, rename them to achieve the order you want. For example, rename the item you want on top so that it begins with a number instead of letters; numbers come first on the list.
>
> In keeping with that thought, you can order all your favorites in a folder precisely by renaming each one to start with the number that you want it to be on the list.

4. Repeat step 3 for each of the items you want to change, and then click Close to exit the dialog box.

Saving Web Content for Offline Use

Web browsing can be addictive—there's so much great information out there! I rarely surf the Web without finding some unexpected treasure that I want to save for later rereading and enjoyment. Saving an item to the Favorites list is one way to mark it, but the item will be available only while you are online.

There are lots of ways to capture the information from a Web page and make it available offline. You can print a hard copy of it or save the page itself to your hard disk, for example. You can also subscribe to the page so that it is available through Internet Explorer even when you are not online. You will learn all those techniques in the following sections.

Printing Content from the Web

You can print any Web page easily. For a printout of the entire page (a single copy on the default printer), simply click the Print button. Or, to print with more options available, use the following procedure instead:

1. Display the page you want to print.

   If the page has multiple frames (that is, multiple panes separated by divider bars), click in the frame that you want.
2. Choose File, Print. The Print dialog box opens (see Figure 18.12).
3. Select the printer, page range, and number of copies.
4. If the page contains multiple frames, the Print Frames area of the dialog box is enabled, as it is in Figure 18.12. Select how you want the frames to be handled:
   - **As Laid Out on Screen**—Prints the page as it appears, with all frames together on the printout.

- **Only the Selected Frame**—Prints only the content of the frame you clicked in step 1.
- **All Frames Individually**—Prints each frame's content on a separate page.

6. Click OK. The page prints.

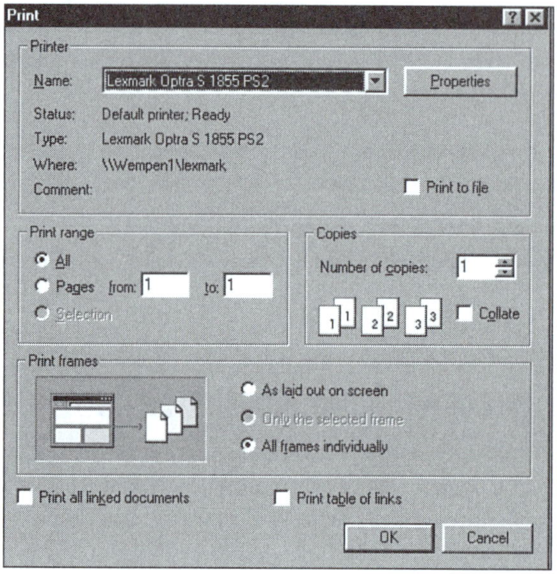

Figure 18.12
Set printing options, and then print the page.

You might have noticed in Figure 18.12 that there are a couple of special-purpose check boxes in the Print dialog box. They are

- **Print All Linked Documents**—Beware, this generates a lot of paper! It prints not only the current Web page but also all the pages that are hyperlinked to it.
- **Print Table of Links**—This prints a listing of all the hyperlinks on the page.

→ For general information about printing and Print dialog boxes, **see** "Printing Your Work," **p. 37**.

SAVING WEB PAGES ON YOUR HARD DISK

When you view a Web page, your browser does not save that whole page to your hard disk; it merely displays it onscreen. When you log off the Internet, that page will no longer be available for viewing until you log back on again.

You can save a Web page to your hard disk, however, so that it is available any time. You can also open and edit saved Web pages using Microsoft Word or some other program that supports that format.

Note

Some Web browsers include a caching feature that saves each page you view into a temporary file so that if you want to view the same page again later, it will load more quickly. However, this is not the same as really saving the page to disk yourself, because those saved temporary files are for the browser's use only; you can't work with them directly. You will learn to empty the cache in Chapter 19, "Customizing Internet Explorer."

You can save a Web page in four formats:

- **Web Page, Complete**—Saves the entire page, including any graphics, frames, and style sheets.
- **Web Archive for Email**—Saves all the information necessary to display the page in a single MIME-encoded file (for mailing in Outlook Express). If you don't have Outlook Express 5 installed, this choice will not be available.
- **Web Page, HTML Only**—Saves just the current Web page, not the graphics or other files.
- **Text File**—Saves just the text from the current Web page.

The default is Web Page, Complete. I use this to retrieve the contents of public-domain books online (such as at `www.greatliterature.com`), and I save the book files to disk. Then, I use Word to open the saved HTML files, and I can read them in Word whenever I want.

If a page contains many graphics, and you aren't interested in saving them, Web Page, HTML Only might be a better choice. This saves hard disk space by not saving anything except the text and the HTML formatting codes.

To save a Web page, follow these steps:

1. Display the page.
2. Choose File, Save As. The Save Web Page dialog box opens (shown in Figure 18.13).
3. Change the save location, if desired.

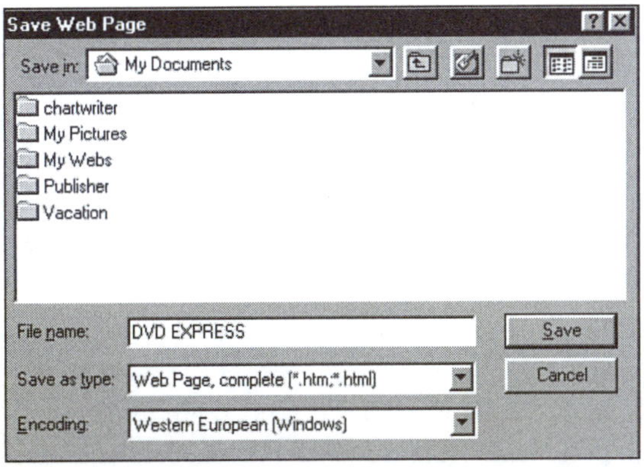

Figure 18.13
Save a Web page to your hard disk.

4. To change the filename (the default is the page title), type a different name in the File Name box.
5. Open the Save as Type drop-down list, and choose the format you want.
6. Click Save.

Note

You should not have to change the Encoding settings in the Save Web Page box; leave it set to Western European (ISO). This setting is primarily for saving Web pages written in languages that use different character sets than English.

Opening a Saved Web Page

To open a saved page later, choose File, Open, and then select the Web page to open, just as you would open a file in any program. You can be either online or offline; because the page is saved on your hard disk, your connection status doesn't matter.

The exception is if you have chosen the format Web Page, HTML Only, and the page has graphics or other elements that were not saved. In that case, when you load the page in Internet Explorer, you will have to be online, or those unsaved elements will not display.

Saving an Individual Graphic from a Web Page

To save a particular graphic that you find online, right-click it and choose Save Picture As. Then, use the Save Picture dialog box to save it in either JPEG or Bitmap format.

Caution

Most images used on Web pages are copyrighted, and you may not legally use them without permission. Nobody is going to come to your door and arrest you if you have an unauthorized picture of Bart Simpson on your desktop, but beware of reusing graphics that you have "borrowed" from other Web pages for any document or page you are going to distribute publicly.

Making Favorites Available for Offline Browsing

You learned earlier in the chapter how to add pages to your Favorites list so that you can revisit them later. However, the Favorites items are accessible only while you are online.

You can set certain favorites also to be available while you are offline, however. Further, you can set them so that all the pages linked to them are available, too. (You can go several levels deep with this!) That way, you can peruse an entire Web site at your leisure offline.

Here's how it works: When you turn on the Make Available Offline option for a page, Internet Explorer immediately transfers that entire page (and other related pages, if specified) to your hard disk, in a temporary folder. It waits there for you to choose it from the Favorites menu. Then, periodically (according to the schedule you specify) it updates the stored version of the page to synchronize it with the latest version on the Web.

To make a favorite available offline, follow these steps:

1. Choose Favorites, Organize Favorites.
2. Click the favorite you want to make available.
3. Click the Make Available Offline check box. A Properties button appears, as in Figure 18.14.

Figure 18.14
Select a page from the list, and then mark the Make Available Offline check box.

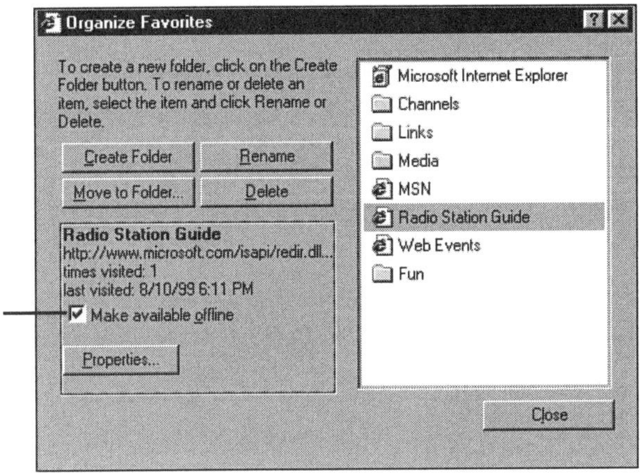

Part III Ch 18

4. Click the Properties button. The Properties box for that link appears.
5. Click the Schedule tab.
6. Choose a scheduling option for updating this page:
   - Only When I Choose Synchronize from the Tools Menu (the default)
   - Using the Following Schedule(s)

   If you choose the latter, you must create at least one schedule. Click the Add button, and specify a schedule in the New Schedule dialog box, shown in Figure 18.15. You can have different schedules for different links; some pages you might want to update daily, and others less often.

Figure 18.15
Create a schedule for automatic synchronization of offline content.

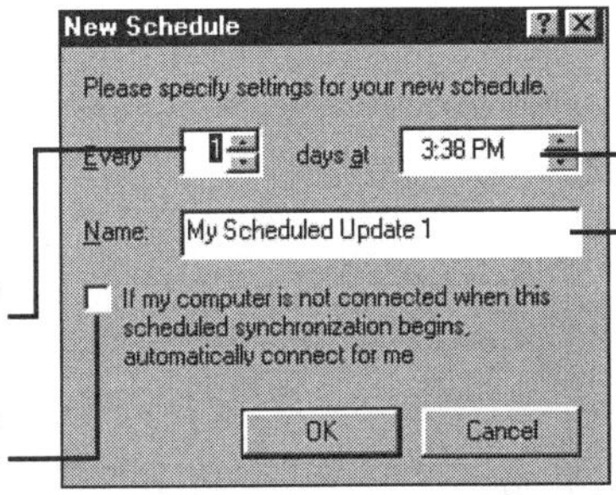

7. Click the Download tab (shown in Figure 18.16).

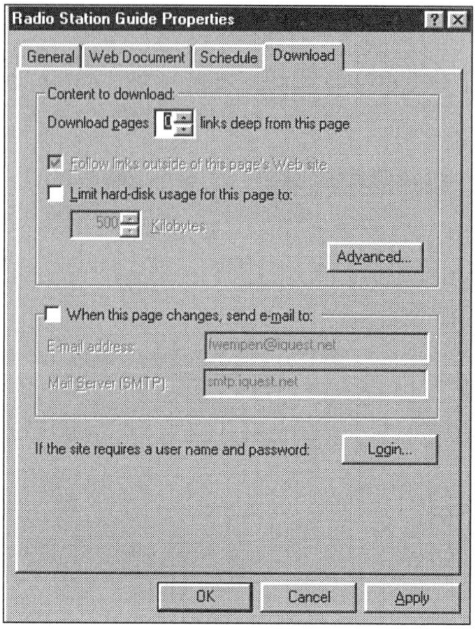

Figure 18.16
Specify how much information will be downloaded to your hard disk.

8. Set options for the associated pages:
   - Specify a number of levels of links you want to download in the Content to Download area. For example, to download all the pages linked from this page, choose 1. To download all that and all the pages linked to all those pages, too, choose 2.
   - To download only pages from this same Web site (that is, with the same domain address), deselect the Follow Links Outside of This Page's Web Site check box.
   - To limit the total amount of hard disk space that these downloads can consume, select Limit Hard-Disk Usage for This Page To, and then enter a number of kilobytes.
   - To omit images, sounds, and video, or ActiveX controls and Java applets, click the Advanced button, and deselect the undesired objects from the box that appears. (Then click OK to return.)
9. Set any other options for the page as needed:
   - If you want an email sent to you when the page changes, click the When This Page Changes, Send E-Mail To check box, and enter your email address and mail server.
   - If the page requires you to log in, click the Login button, and specify your user-name and password for that site.

10. Click OK, closing the Properties box for the page.
11. Click Close, closing the Organize Favorites box.

The chosen pages are immediately downloaded to your hard disk. You can now view them any time from the Favorites menu, even when offline.

TROUBLESHOOTING

STREAMLINING YOUR FAVORITES LIST

My Favorites list is too crowded and it's hard to find anything on it.

If your Favorites list becomes cluttered, even with subfolders in use, create new, general subfolders such as Work, Fun, Reference, and so on, and move other folders into one of those broad groupings. That way, your first-level Favorites menu will be small and manageable.

LOCATING CONTACT INFORMATION ONLINE

I'm trying to find someone's email address but can't locate it using the default search engine in Internet Explorer.

Try a different search engine. There are different search engines for people than for Web sites. Try `http://www.bigfoot.com`, `http://www.infospace.com`, or `http://www.worldpages.com`. Note that these sites are not always up-to-date—the best way to get people's email addresses is still to call them and ask them, if possible.

REFINING ADVANCED SEARCH QUERIES

The query structure I've used before successfully at one search site doesn't return the results I expect at other search sites.

If you aren't familiar with the syntax at a particular search site, it can be hard to develop a complex query that pinpoints what you want. I suggest sticking to one or two favorite search sites so you have a reasonable chance at memorizing the correct syntax for advanced searches.

CHAPTER 19

Customizing Internet Explorer

In this chapter

CHANGING THE WAY PAGES APPEAR ONSCREEN

You can customize the way Web pages appear in Internet Explorer. For example, you can change which page opens every time you start Internet Explorer, the way fonts are displayed, and even the colors used. A variety of customizing options help you get the most out of your Web-surfing sessions. The following sections detail some of the more popular customizing options.

CHANGING THE STARTING PAGE

By default, Internet Explorer always opens up the Microsoft Start page every time you use the program. Whenever you click the Home button on the Internet Explorer toolbar, you're returned to this page. Although this page makes a great starting page for every Internet session, you might prefer another page as your start page.

If you know the URL of another page you prefer to use as your home page, you can tell Internet Explorer to load this page as the default page.

To do so, choose Tools, Internet Options. The Internet Options dialog box appears, as shown in Figure 19.1. Enter a different URL into the Address box, or do any of the following:

- If you want to start with a blank page each time, click Use Blank.
- If you want to set the currently displayed page as the start page, click Use Current.
- If you want to reset to the default home page address, click Use Default.

Click OK to close the dialog box when you're finished. The next time you open Internet Explorer, the new home page loads immediately.

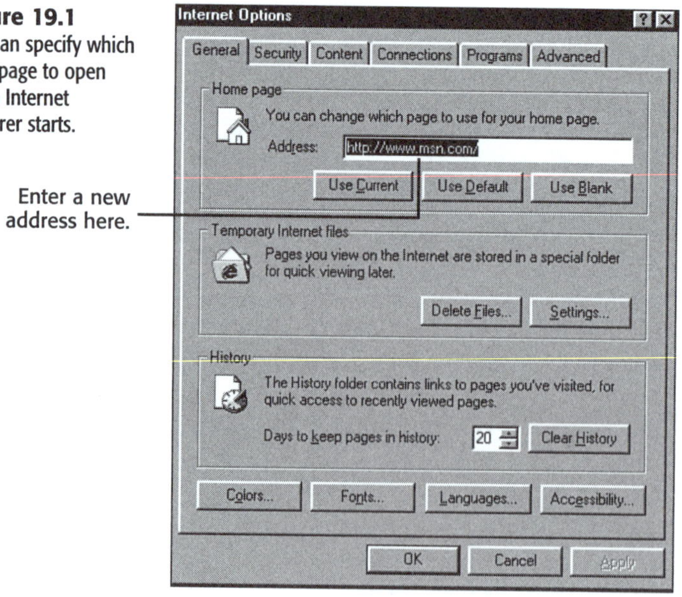

Figure 19.1
You can specify which Web page to open when Internet Explorer starts.

CHANGING THE DISPLAY FONT

Your Web browser settings determine the font and font size of text on displayed Web pages. If it is difficult to see the text in your browser window, you can make that text larger. Choose View, Fonts, and choose a larger size from the submenu that appears. The default is Medium, but you can choose Largest, Larger, Smaller, or Smallest. The latter two can help fit more words on the screen at once so that you don't have to scroll as much, if your vision can handle the smaller type.

CHANGING THE COLORS USED

If the font is chosen by the Web browser, not the Web page, what about the colors and background? These can go either way. Internet Explorer has settings for text color and background, but they are used only for pages that do not provide their own font color and background information. The default background in Internet Explorer is the same color scheme that you use in Windows. The Windows Standard scheme uses plain white with black text, for example.

You can also change the color of the underlined hyperlink text in the pages you view. The default is blue for unvisited hyperlinks and green for visited hyperlinks.

Tip #113 from *Faithe Wempen*

Internet Explorer uses a History list to keep track of which Web pages you have displayed. If a hyperlink refers to a page on that list, it's considered a visited hyperlink, and it displays in a different color. To clear this list, clear the History list. This process is explained in the section "Protecting Your Privacy," later in this chapter.

To change your colors in Internet Explorer:

1. Choose Tools, Internet Options. The Internet Options dialog box opens.
2. Click the Colors button. This opens the Colors dialog box shown in Figure 19.2.

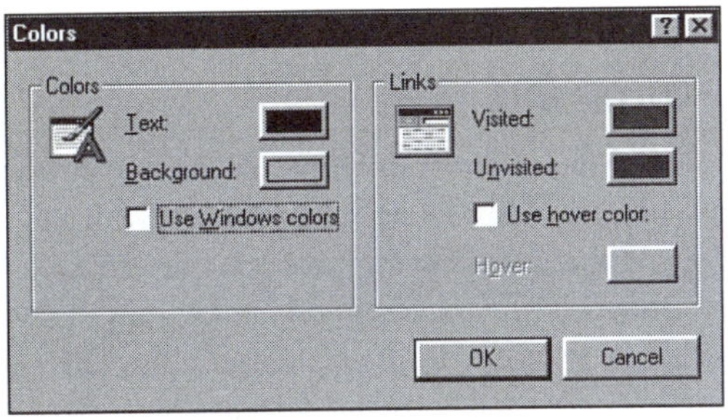

Figure 19.2
Use the Colors dialog box to change link colors and background colors.

3. If you want to override Windows colors, deselect the Use Windows Colors check box. (If not, skip to step 6.)

4. Click the Text button to pop up the Color palette (see Figure 19.3) for text, and click the color you want to use. (Choose a color that contrasts well with the color you want for the background.) Then click OK.
5. Click the Background button and do the same as in step 4 to choose a new background color (click OK when finished).
6. To change the color for visited hyperlinks, click the Visited button. In the Color palette that appears (see Figure 19.3), click a new color to use, and then click OK.

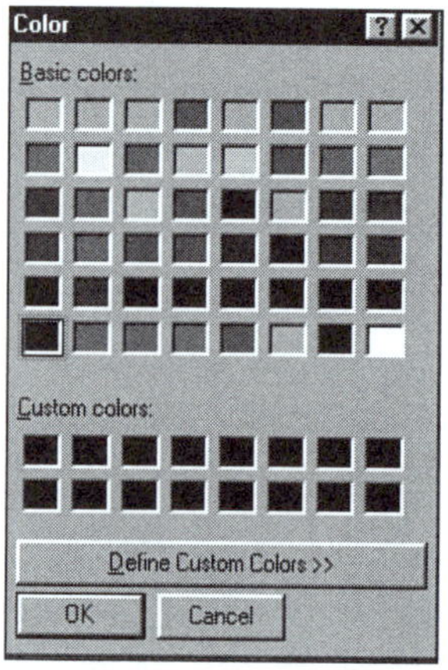

Figure 19.3
Use the same Color palette to choose text, background, and ink colors.

7. Click the Unvisited button and do the same as in step 6, choosing a new unvisited hyperlink color.
8. (Optional) If you want links to be a different color when you move the mouse over them, mark the Use Hover Color check box and select a Hover color.
9. Click OK to close the Colors dialog box.
10. Click OK to close the Internet Options dialog box and apply the new settings.

ENABLING AND DISABLING MULTIMEDIA

By default, Internet Explorer's multimedia options are all turned on because they enhance your Web-browsing experience. You can turn them off, however, if they aren't appropriate for you, or if you want to speed the page-loading process. For example, if you don't have a sound card, playing sounds does not do you any good, and loading the sounds into your computer's memory wastes time. To take a look at which multimedia options are turned on, choose Tools, Internet Options, and then click the Advanced tab. Scroll down the list to find the Multimedia heading, as shown in Figure 19.4.

Deselect the check box for any option you don't want. Most people want to leave Show Pictures marked because today's Web pages are so graphically based that you can miss out on a lot of content by not showing pictures. However, if you have a very slow modem (slower than 28.8KB), each page might take an unacceptably long time to load. Turning off the graphics can make each page load much faster.

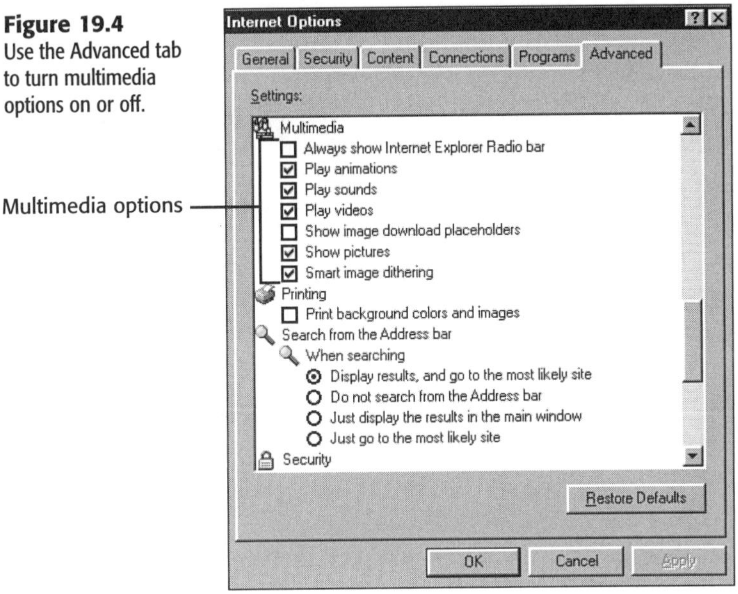

Figure 19.4
Use the Advanced tab to turn multimedia options on or off.

Figure 19.5 shows how a page loads when you turn off Show Pictures. Notice the placeholders for the images. If you want to display a certain graphic, you can click its placeholder to display it.

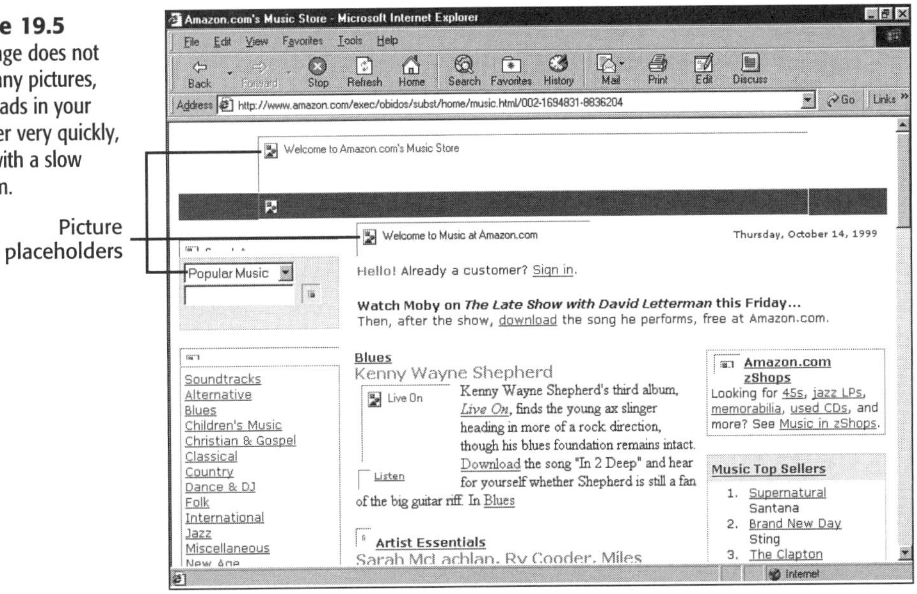

Figure 19.5
This page does not show any pictures, so it loads in your browser very quickly, even with a slow modem.

PROTECTING YOUR PRIVACY

You are in the best position to assess your need for computer privacy at the local level. Do many people use your home computer, or only you? Do you care whether other people who use your computer know what you've been looking at on the Internet?

There is also an Internet-wide privacy issue to consider. Whenever you send information to a site (such as entering keywords in a search engine), someone could intercept those keywords and find out what your interests are—in theory, anyway. The possibility is remote (in fact, you stand a greater chance of being struck by lightning in the next 24 hours). But this slim possibility keeps some people awake at night.

→ For information about search engines, **see** Chapter 18, "Looking Up Information Online."

Here are some settings you can use in the Internet Options dialog box to make your system more snoop-proof.

HIDING WHERE YOU'VE BEEN

If you don't want other people who use your computer to be able to find out what Internet sites you've visited, the following steps can help cover your tracks using the Internet Options dialog box:

- On the General tab, use the Colors button to set the color for the Visited and Unvisited links to the same color so that a link that you have visited before is not obvious to someone else using your computer.
- On the General tab, click the Clear History button to clear the list of sites that you've visited. (If you don't clear this, someone can click the History button on Internet Explorer to see where you've been.) Do this regularly. In this area, you can also choose the number of days to keep your history file. Choosing a larger number of days keeps larger lists of your surfing, whereas a shorter number of days cleans up your tracks on a more regular basis.
- On the General tab, you can control the storage of temporary Internet files on your hard disk. When you visit a page, its information is *cached* (temporarily saved) on your hard disk in a special temporary folder. That way, the next time you visit that page, it loads much more quickly because it pulls the saved copy unless the page has changed. The downside is that, like your History list, people can look at your saved temporary files and know where you've been. To clear the temporary files, click the Delete Files button. To prevent Internet Explorer from saving temporary files in the future, click the Settings button; then click the Never option button and click OK.

Now you can close the dialog box and resume surfing, secure in the knowledge that your secrets will remain just that.

Keeping Intruders Away

This section is mostly for the paranoid. Millions of people surf the Internet, and most of them visit really ordinary sites. Unless you feel that you have somehow been targeted for surveillance, you can forget about people outside your home snooping on you.

If you're still reading, though, you must be worried, so here you go.

Security Properties

First, there are global security settings. On the Advanced tab of the Internet Options dialog box, under the Security heading (see Figure 19.6), choose which warnings you want to receive. For example, you can set Internet Explorer to warn you each time you send information over the Internet that's redirected, so that you can assess your risk on a case-by-case basis.

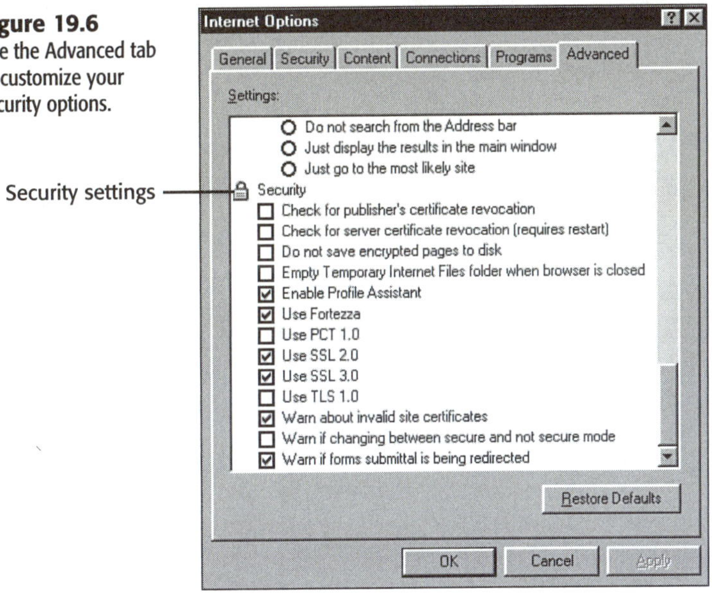

Figure 19.6
Use the Advanced tab to customize your security options.

Security Zones

Next, you can set up security zones from the Security tab of the Internet Options dialog box (see Figure 19.7). Internet Explorer divides the Internet into four zones that you can assign to a Web site, along with four security levels (High, Medium, Low, and Custom). The zones include

- **Local Intranet**—If your company uses a local network and has an intranet, you can mark the security level for pages found on the network. The default security level for this zone is Medium.

- **Trusted Sites**—Use this zone level to mark pages you believe are from trusted sites that you don't worry about downloading files from or exchanging information with; the default security level for this zone is Low.
- **Restricted Sites**—Use this zone level to mark sites you don't trust and aren't sure about downloading or running files from; the default security level for this zone is High.
- **Internet**—This is the default zone setting for all Web pages, and the default security level is Medium.

On the Security tab, shown in Figure 19.7, you can set a security level for various zones to which you assign Web pages. To change a setting for a site, select a zone from the Zone box; then choose a security level.

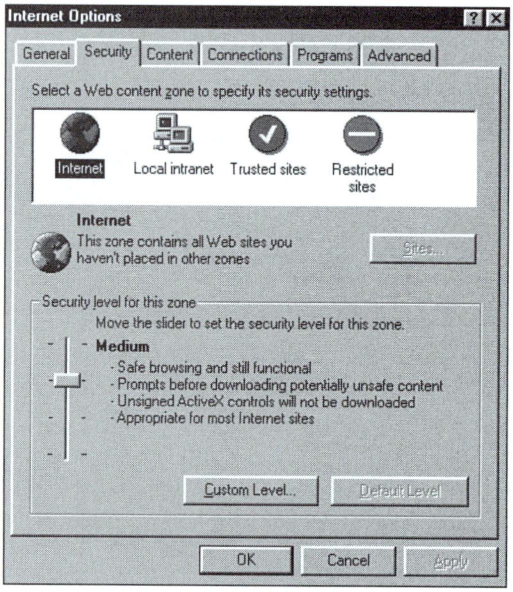

Figure 19.7
Set security zones and levels in the Security tab.

You can customize a security level by clicking the Custom Level button. This brings up a dialog box in which you can turn on/off permissions for certain kinds of Web-based programs to run on your PC, such as ActiveX and Java. You can also set up to accept or reject cookies from sites in that security zone.

Note

A *cookie* is a little text file placed on your hard disk to keep track of the fact that you've visited this page before. They're used to identify frequent visitors, so you don't have to reenter your information the next time you visit the site. Cookies make your Web browsing more convenient, but some people feel they are an invasion of privacy.

CERTIFICATES

The Content tab of the Internet Options dialog box has a section for *certificates* (see Figure 19.8). Certificates are like passcodes that prove that content is coming from a legitimate source. For example, when you download a file that appears to be coming from Microsoft, how do you know that some evil foreign government is not actually sending the file and pretending to be Microsoft? Microsoft sends a certificate with the download that says, "Yes, it's really us." Internet Explorer handles certificates more or less automatically, so you don't have to do anything with these controls—just feel good that they're there. (Advanced users can configure the use of certificates and even purchase their own digital certificates to positively identify themselves to others, but this is total overkill for the home user.)

Figure 19.8
Control the use of certificates here.

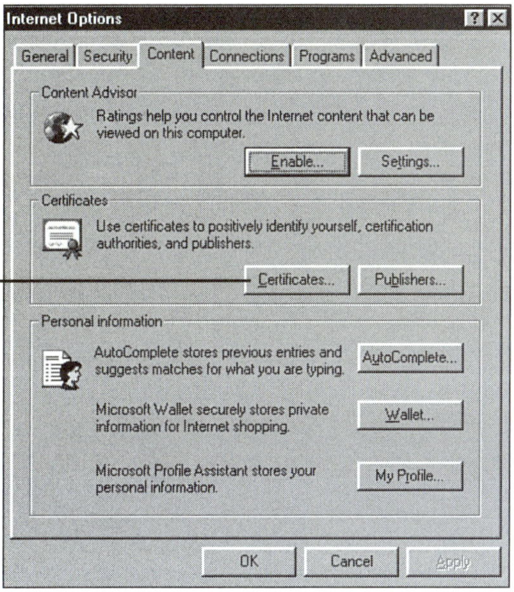

Click the Certificates button to change the settings.

LIMITING CONTENT ACCESS

If you are a parent of minor children who use your PC, you may be concerned about your kids being exposed to adult content online. This is a valid concern! Internet Explorer provides a content-rating feature that can help prevent some of the obvious smut from reaching your desktop. However, it is not perfect, and so it can't be relied on to filter out 100% of the material that you may find objectionable.

Caution

The Internet is not a day care center! Children should not be allowed to go online without an adult nearby, at least casually observing the action. Security measures and content filtering are helpful tools, but they are not a substitute for parental involvement in a child's online experience.

The Content Advisor works by comparing the settings you choose to the ratings for a particular site. Not all sites have ratings, so you can choose whether you want sites that have no rating to be viewable on your PC. (If you go to all the trouble of setting up content ratings, I strongly suggest that you block sites with no rating; many explicit sites are ratingless.) You can also specify a password that can be typed to override the block (so adults in the household may view sites that the children, who don't know the password, cannot).

To set up content restrictions:

1. Start in the Internet Options dialog box (Tools, Internet Options) on the Content tab.
2. Click the Enable button. The Content Advisor dialog box opens.

Note

If a Disable button is shown instead of Enable, content ratings are already on. Click Settings and enter the password when prompted to get to the Content Advisor dialog box needed for step 3.

If an Enable button is shown, but someone has already used content ratings on this computer in the past, you'll be prompted for the password when you click Enable. After you enable the rating system, the Content Advisor dialog box will not appear automatically; you must click Settings and enter the password again to get to it.

3. On the Ratings tab, set a rating for Language, Nudity, Sex, and Violence. Drag the slider bar to choose an acceptable level. For example, in Figure 19.9, the Violence rating is set to Level 2. A description of what that entails appears below the slider bar.

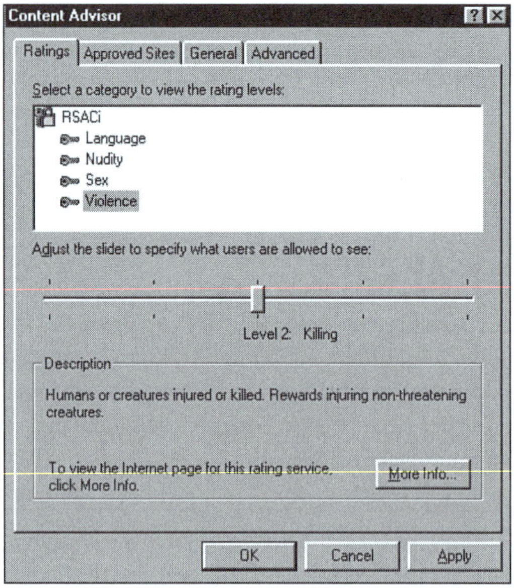

Figure 19.9
Set the allowable level for each of the four categories.

4. (Optional) To block or allow certain sites, type the address on the Approved Sites tab and then click Always or Never to set its status. For example, in Figure 19.10, the site `http://www.wempen.com` is set to always be viewable, regardless of its content, whereas the site `http://www.hardcore.com` is set to never be visible.

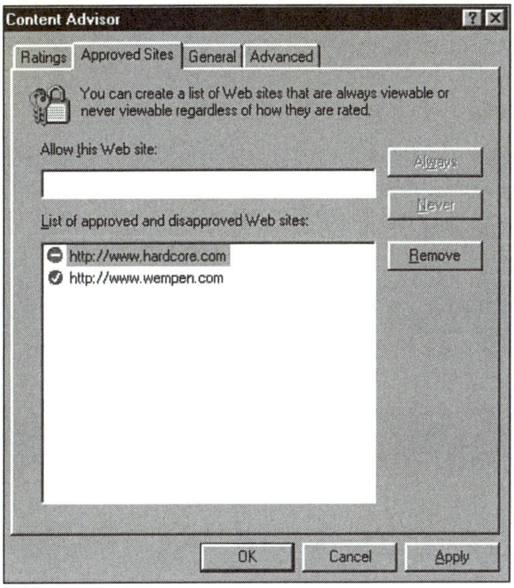

Figure 19.10
Specify certain sites to always or never be viewable.

5. On the General tab, do any of the following:
   - Select or deselect the Users Can See Sites That Have No Rating check box. If this is marked, all sites with no rating are assumed to be objectionable.
   - Select or deselect the Supervisor Can Type a Password to Allow Users to View Restricted Content check box.
   - Set a password by clicking Change Password.
   - Find and use other rating systems by clicking Find Rating Systems. (Some systems require you to pay to use them.)

Note

I intentionally skipped the Advanced tab in this dialog box because there's little here that most Web users would need. If you are using a special rating service that requires you to set up a ratings bureau or PICS rules, the service will provide instructions for setting the required options on the Advanced tab.

6. Click OK to accept the new settings.
7. If you chose to use a supervisor password, the Create Supervisor Password dialog box appears. Type a password (and then type it again to confirm) and click OK.

Note

If content ratings were enabled in the past on this PC, you may not be prompted for a password in step 7; it will use the existing password. You must click the Change Password button on the General tab to change it.

8. A message appears that the Content Advisor has been enabled. Click OK.
9. Click OK to close the Internet Options dialog box.

Try to visit some pages that are objectionable, to see whether the Content Advisor blocks them successfully. If you need to make changes to the settings, reopen the Internet Options dialog box (Tools, Internet Options) and click the Settings button on the Content tab.

To stop using content ratings, click the Disable button on the Content tab. When prompted for the password, type it and click OK.

Tip #114 from
Faithe Wempen

You can buy other, more comprehensive site-blocking software to use along with Internet Explorer (such as NetNanny) that enables you to block sites based on specific keywords you enter. (For example, you could block out all sites that use "hot sex" as keywords.)

Changing the Way You Connect to the Internet

When you set up your Internet connection, either when you first set up an Internet account or as directed in Chapter 17, "Internet Basics," you specified which modem you were going to use, entered a phone number for the connection, and so on. If you later get a different modem or the phone number changes, you might have to make a switch.

Changing the Dial-Up Connection Properties

If you get a new modem, you must change your Dial-Up Networking settings or create a new Dial-Up Networking connection.

You might not have realized it, but when you went through the setup procedure in Chapter 17, you created a Dial-Up Networking connection. To see it, open the My Computer window by double-clicking the My Computer icon on the desktop. Within that folder, double-click the Dial-Up Networking icon. A window appears, showing all the Dial-Up Networking connections on your system (see Figure 19.11).

To create a new dial-up connection (for example, if you have a second Internet service provider that you sometimes use), click the New Connection icon and follow the instructions onscreen.

To modify an existing connection, right-click its icon and choose Properties from the menu that appears. This displays the Properties dialog box for that icon (see Figure 19.12).

Figure 19.11
Locate the connection that you currently use to connect to the Internet.

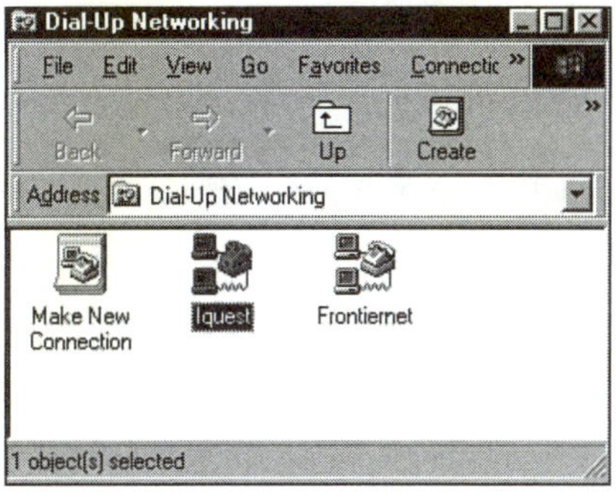

Figure 19.12
Changing the properties changes the way the connection is established and maintained.

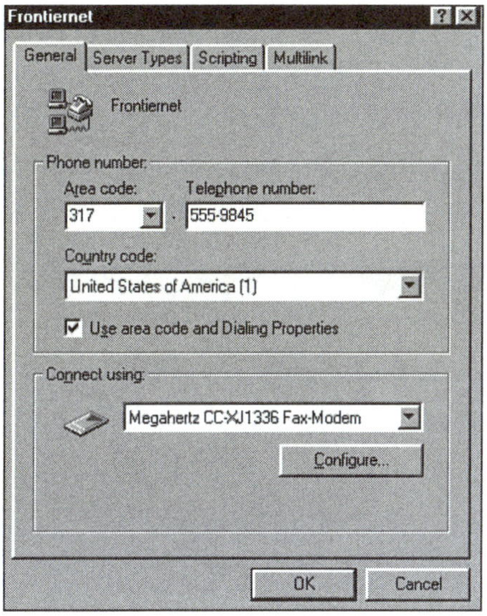

From this dialog box, you can perform the following functions:

- Change the phone number being dialed by entering a different number into the Telephone Number text box.
- Choose a different modem to use (if you have more than one) by selecting it from the Connect Using drop-down list.
- Change the IP address and the DNS address by clicking the Server Types tab and then the TCP/IP Settings button.

Click OK when finished with any of these functions to direct the system to accept your changes.

Changing the Dial-Up Connection in Internet Explorer

If you made changes to an Internet connection in the preceding section, you do not need to change anything in Internet Explorer as long as the name of the connection stayed the same. However, if you created a new ISP connection or changed the name of your existing one, you must inform Internet Explorer.

To choose a different dial-up connection in Internet Explorer:

1. Start Internet Explorer by double-clicking the Internet Explorer icon on your desktop.
2. If the Internet AutoDial dialog box appears, open the drop-down list and choose the connection you want to use. Then click OK.
3. The Connect To dialog box appears. Connect to the Internet as usual.
4. In Internet Explorer, choose Tools, Internet Options. The Internet Options dialog box appears.
5. Click the Connections tab.
6. Select your current Internet dial-up connection from the Dial-Up Settings list (see Figure 19.13).

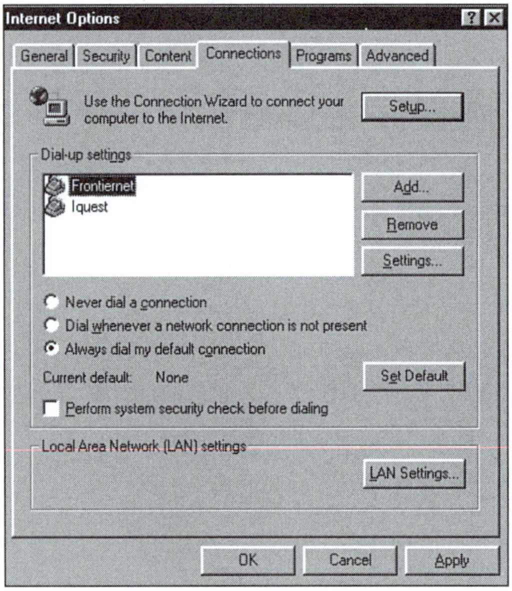

Figure 19.13
Select the dial-up connection to use.

7. Make sure that Never Dial a Connection is *not* selected below the list. You can choose either of the other two options.
8. Check the Current Default setting. If your chosen dial-up connection does not appear there, click the Set Default button. The word (Default) appears next to it on the list.
9. Click OK to apply the new setting.

➔ You might also need to change your Outlook Express setup if you have changed ISPs. **See** Chapter 20, "Working with Email and Newsgroups."

TROUBLESHOOTING

GAMES REQUIRE DIFFERENT SECURITY SETTINGS

I'd like to use a site that offers online chess and backgammon games, but it doesn't work in Internet Explorer.

If you are trying to play a game or do something interactive online but it doesn't work, you probably need to set your security settings differently. Contact the Webmaster at the Web site and ask if he or she is aware of any certain Internet Explorer settings you should change.

TROUBLESHOOTING YOUR MODEM

Windows indicates that my modem is installed correctly, but I can't make it connect to the Internet.

If you have a new modem that doesn't seem to be working, try running a diagnostic on it. To do so:

1. Double-click the Modems icon in the Control Panel.
2. Click the Diagnostics tab.
3. Click the modem you want to test.
4. Click the More Info button.

After about 30 seconds, various codes will appear if the modem is being recognized. (If not, an error message appears.) Some of the codes will say `ERROR` next to them; this is normal. If at least some of them report OK or some string of codes, the modem is working normally.

CHAPTER 20

Working with Email and Newsgroups

In this chapter

INTRODUCING OUTLOOK EXPRESS

Outlook Express is an email program that comes free with Microsoft Works Suite 2000 and with Windows 98. As its name implies, Outlook Express is a slimmed-down version of a larger program called Outlook that comes with Microsoft Office. This chapter focuses on Outlook Express. It handles your incoming and outgoing email, and it lets you read and post messages to newsgroups.

Note

If you have decided to go with an online service such as America Online, your email program is built into the service, and you won't be able to use a separate email program such as Outlook Express.

Dozens of other perfectly good email programs are out there, and most are available for free or trial download on the Web. Some of the most popular include Eudora, Pegasus, and Netscape Mail. Each has its own special set of features to recommend it; serious mailing list participants or managers like Pegasus, for example, because of its excellent sorting and filtering capabilities. However, this chapter covers only Outlook Express.

Outlook Express has a button on the Quick Launch toolbar; you can start it by clicking there. Or you can choose Start, Programs, Outlook Express.

Note

If the Internet Connection Wizard runs when you start Outlook Express, it means that your Internet connection has not yet been set up on this PC. Refer to Chapter 17, "Internet Basics," for help with it.

When you first start Outlook Express, it may open to an introductory screen like the one shown in Figure 20.1. From here you can click any of the various hyperlinks to do certain tasks, such as creating a message, setting up a newsgroup account, and so on.

When you click the Inbox icon in the folder tree or click the Read Mail hyperlink, you see your Inbox, shown in Figure 20.2. The Inbox is divided into three panes. The left pane lists the available folders, the same as in Windows Explorer. The top right pane lists the email messages in your Inbox, and the bottom right pane previews the selected email. As with most Windows programs, a toolbar located across the top provides shortcuts to the most common activities.

Besides the Inbox, Outlook Express uses several other special-purpose folders automatically for certain tasks:

- **Drafts**—Holds messages that you are currently composing. When you issue the command to send one, it moves to the Outbox.
- **Outbox**—Holds outgoing messages until they are sent to your ISP's outgoing mail server. After being sent, a message moves to the Sent Items folder.
- **Sent Items**—Holds a copy of each message you send, for you to refer to later.

- **Deleted Items**—Holds messages that you delete, in case you want to retrieve them. (They are destroyed eventually after a specified waiting period.)

Figure 20.1
Outlook Express's opening screen, unless you have set it to jump directly to the Inbox at startup.

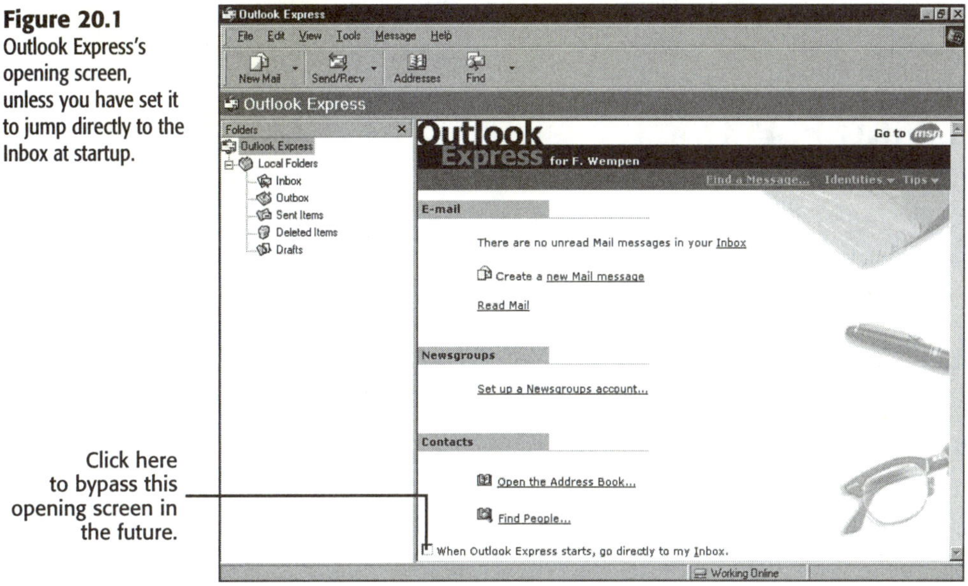

Figure 20.2
Familiarize yourself with the parts of the Outlook Express screen.

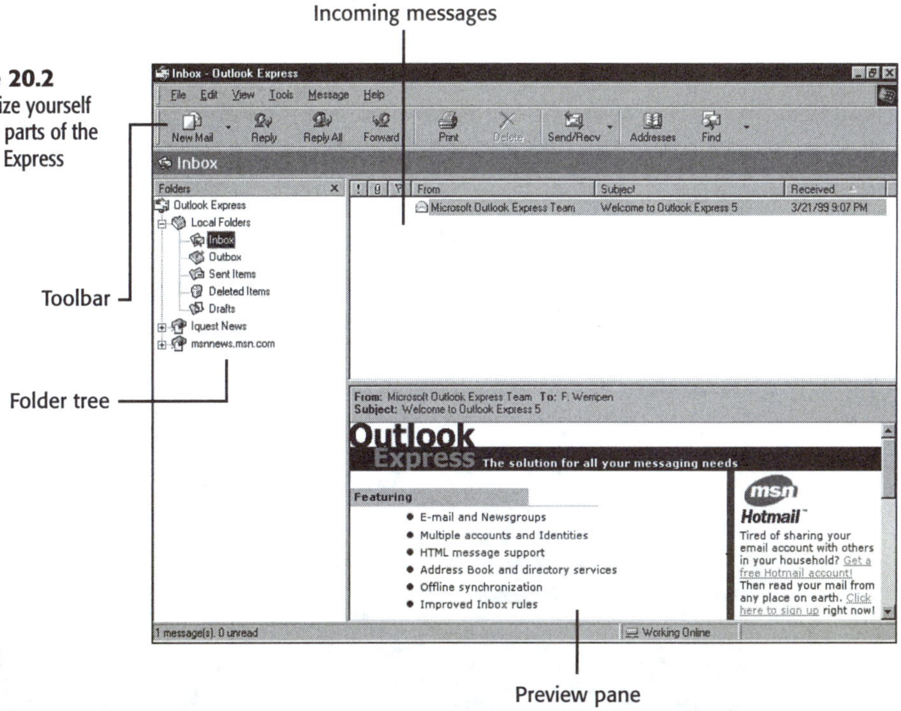

Outlook Express automatically uses each of these folders as needed; you do not need to do anything special to them. However, you can display a folder's content at any time by clicking its name in the folder tree.

→ To configure your Internet connection with the Internet Connection Wizard, **see** "Setting Up an Internet Connection," **p. 342**.

Receiving Email

Receiving email includes not only reading your new messages, but also deciding what to do with them afterward. You can delete them, print them, file them, and more.

Outlook Express may already be set up to receive new mail when you start the program (provided your Internet connection is established). To get your new mail at any time, choose Tools, Send and Receive, Send and Receive All. Or you can click the Send/Recv button on the toolbar.

Tip #115 from *Faithe Wempen*

If you have more than one mail account, you can send/receive from a specific one by choosing it from the bottom of the Send and Receive menu instead of choosing Send and Receive All.

New messages appear in your Inbox. Unread messages are bold, so you can distinguish them from messages you have already read (see Figure 20.3).

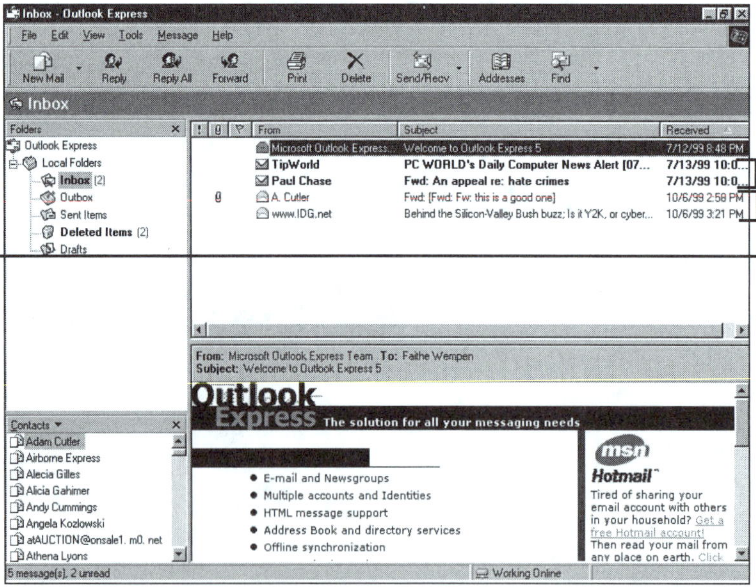

Figure 20.3
The Inbox contains several read and unread messages.

READING NEW EMAIL

Outlook Express gives you a Welcome email in your Inbox the first time you run it, so you will have some mail to work with. It's the first email on the list in Figure 20.3. Notice that the message is selected in the list of messages, and a preview of it appears in the Preview pane.

You can read all your mail from the Preview pane if you like, but you can also double-click the message in the list to open the message in its own window, as shown in Figure 20.4. This window features a message header area listing the sender, the date, the time, and the subject.

Figure 20.4
The Welcome message is displayed in its own window.

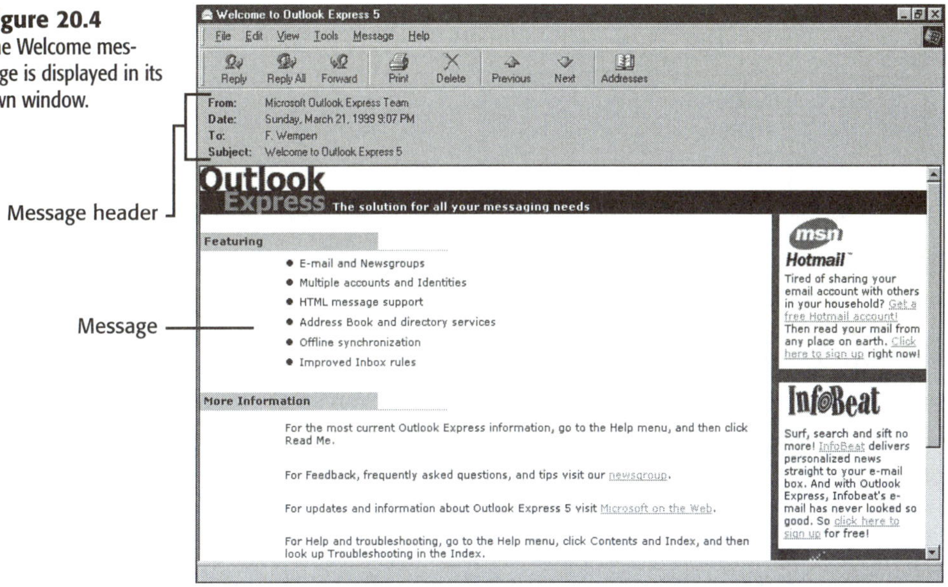

The Welcome message shown in Figure 20.4 is elaborately formatted, with graphics, different fonts, different colors, and so on. It looks a lot like a Web page in that regard! That's because it takes advantage of Outlook Express's capability to read HTML formatting in messages. But most of the messages you receive will probably be in plain-text format, like the junk advertisement shown in Figure 20.5 (which, by the way, is a total rip-off in my opinion, so don't even think about calling the number shown and ordering the product).

→ To add formatting to your own outgoing messages, **see** "Formatting a Message," **p. 400**

PART III
CH 20

PRINTING A MESSAGE

To print a message, either display it (by double-clicking it on the list) or simply select it on the list. Then to print it, click the Print button or choose File, Print. The latter method opens the Print dialog box, from which you can select the printer, the page range, the number of copies, and so on.

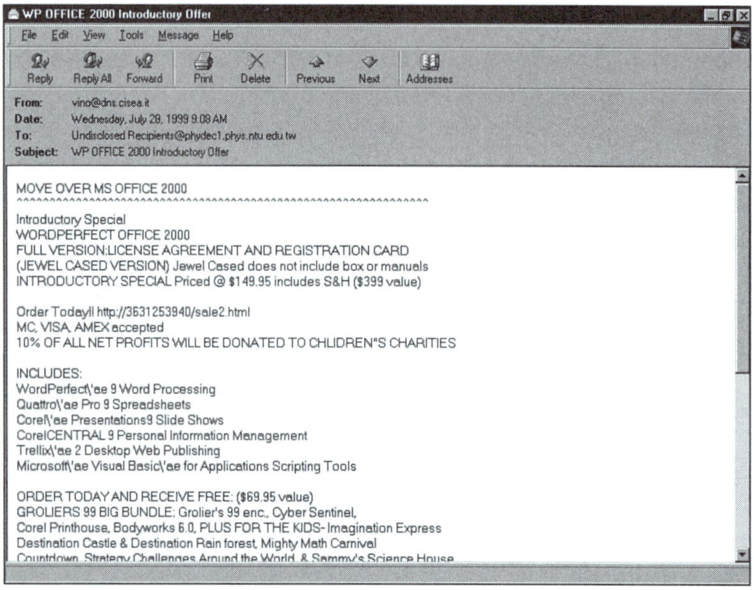

Figure 20.5
Most email messages from individuals come in plain-text format like this.

➔ For more information about printing, **see** "Printing Your Work," **p. 37**.

Reading and Saving an Attachment

Some messages come with attachments. An attachment can be any kind of file: a picture, a word processing document, a compressed archive (for example, a Zip file), or any other type. If a particular message has an attachment, a little paper clip appears next to it in the message list. When you open the message in its own pane, the attachment appears there, as shown in Figure 20.6.

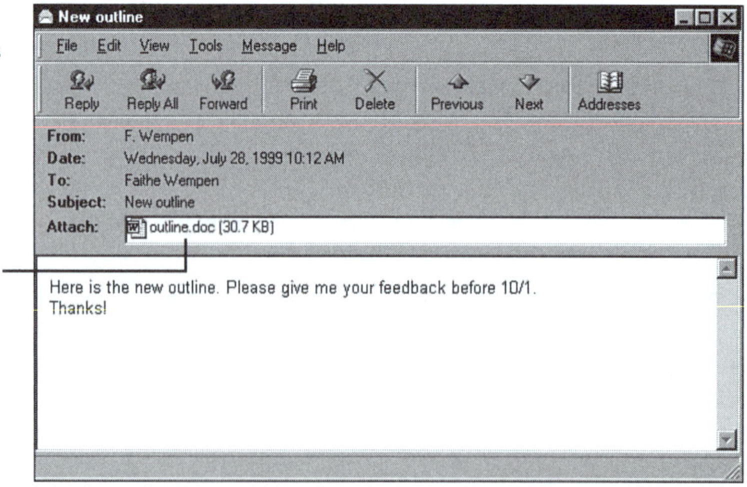

Figure 20.6
This message contains an attached word processing file.

1. Select the message on the message list, or double-click it to display it in its own window.
2. Choose File, Save Attachments. The Save Attachments dialog box opens (see Figure 20.7).

Figure 20.7
Save attachments to your hard disk using this dialog box.

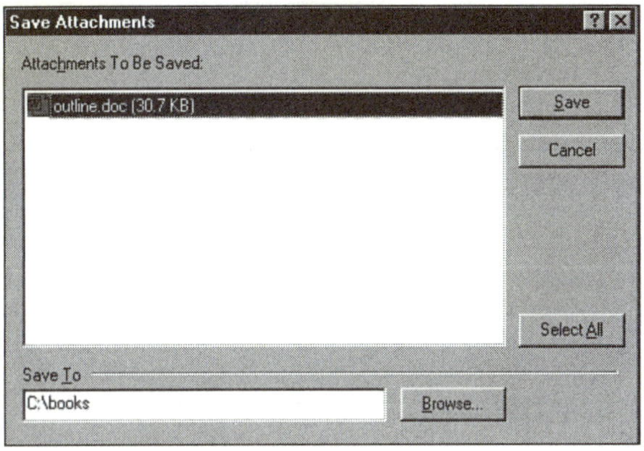

3. If needed, click Browse and choose a different folder in which to save the file.
4. Click Save. The attached file is saved to the specified location.

You do not have to save an attachment to view it. Simply do one of the following to open the attachment in whatever program it is associated with:

- Double-click the attachment name in the message (when the message is open in its own window).
- In the message Preview pane, click the large paper clip in the top-right corner. A menu opens showing the attachments. Click the attachment to open from that menu, as shown in Figure 20.8.

DELETING A MESSAGE

To delete a message, select it from the message list and press Delete, or click the Delete button. This moves the message to the Deleted Items folder.

Change your mind? You can undelete a message by locating the message in the Deleted Items folder and dragging it to the Inbox icon on the folder tree.

To delete a message completely so that there is no record of it, switch to the Deleted Items folder and delete it there. (Of course, you can't undelete the message after that.)

ORGANIZING INCOMING MAIL

It is perfectly okay to leave received messages in your Inbox as long as you like, but in time your Inbox will become crowded.

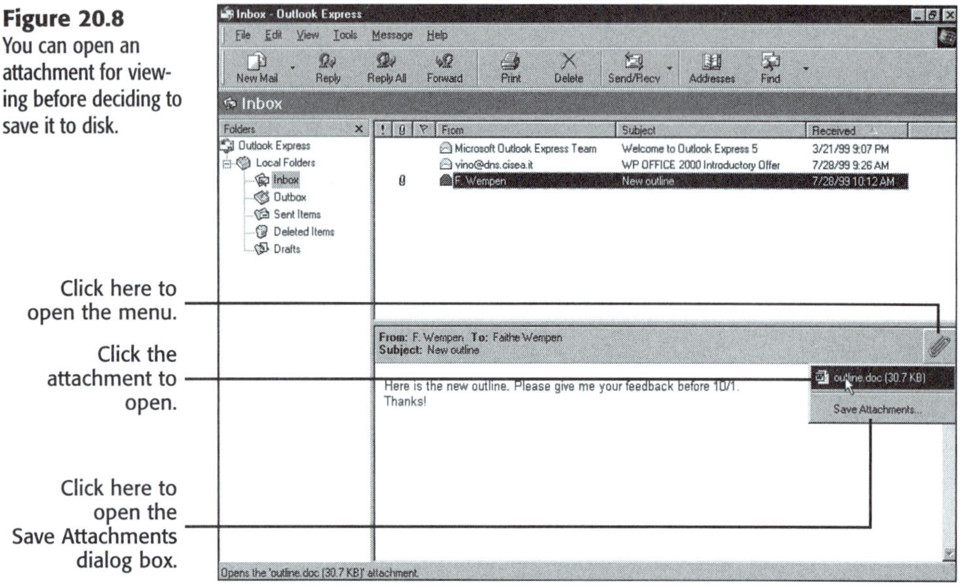

Figure 20.8
You can open an attachment for viewing before deciding to save it to disk.

If you get a lot of email (for example, if you participate in a mailing list), you may wish to create subfolders within your Inbox in which to organize the mail. For example, you could create a folder for each mailing list you participate in, and a folder for correspondence from your family, and a folder for advertisements that you may be interested in looking at when you have time.

To create a mail folder, follow these steps:

1. Choose File, Folder, New or press Ctrl+Shift+E. The Create Folder dialog box opens.
2. Click the Inbox to place the new folder as a subfolder of the Inbox.
3. Type a name in the Folder Name box.
4. Click OK. The new folder appears beneath the Inbox in the folder tree.

To move messages into the new folder, simply drag them from the Inbox's message list onto the new folder's name on the folder tree.

If it seems like a lot of work to drag each message where you want it—you're right. It is. Fortunately, you can create message-handling rules that do the work for you based on criteria you specify. The following section explains how to set it up.

CREATING MESSAGE-HANDLING RULES

Rules let you specify what should be done to a particular message based on one or more facts about it. Those facts could include who the sender is, what the subject line contains, what size the attachment(s) are, and so on. For example, suppose you belong to a mailing list called FunStuff. You could create a rule that automatically moved any messages addressed to the list into a special folder that you have created, called FunStuff.

To create an email-handling rule, follow these steps:

1. Choose Tools, Message Rules, Mail. The Message Rules dialog box opens.
2. Click the New button. The New Mail Rule dialog box opens. (If you have not created any rules yet, you won't need to click New; the New Mail Rule box appears automatically.)
3. Click a check box in the Select the Conditions for Your Rule list to indicate the type of conditions you want to set.

   For example, to base the rule on a particular email address (or group of addresses), in the Sender field, choose Where the From Line Contains People.
4. In the Rule Description area, click the hyperlink to open a box in which you can specify the condition.

   For example, in Figure 20.9, the hyperlink is `contains people`, and clicking it opens a Select People dialog box.

Figure 20.9
Select a type of condition, and then click the hyperlink to specify the exact settings.

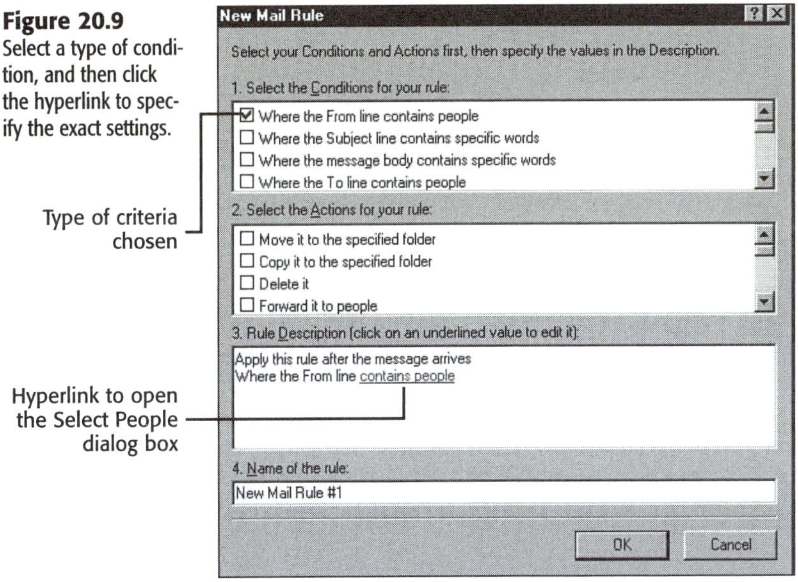

5. In the dialog box that appears (Select People, for example), set up the conditions for the rule. For example, in Figure 20.10 I have chosen two certain email addresses for the rule to apply to.
6. Click OK to return to the New Mail Rule dialog box. The conditions you specified now appear in the Rule Description area.
7. (Optional) Choose other criteria types from the Select the Conditions for Your Rule list, and set them up the same as you did the first one.
8. Choose an action from the Select the Actions for Your Rule list.

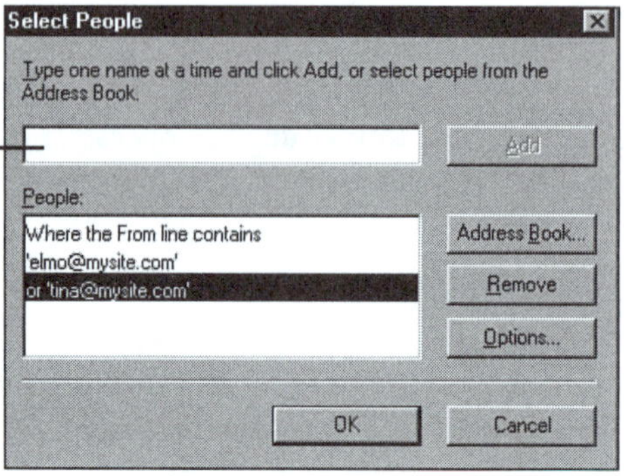

Figure 20.10
Specify the parameters for this part of the rule.

I typed each address here and clicked Add to place it on the list.

9. Click the hyperlink in the Rule Description area for the action you just added, and specify its parameters in the dialog box that appears. Click OK when finished.

   For example, if you chose Move It to the Specified Folder from the Actions list, you would click the word *specified* in the Rule Description to open a list of folders from which to choose.
10. Type a name for the rule in the Name of the Rule box. Make it descriptive—something you will understand later when you see it.
11. Click OK to create the new rule. The new rule appears in the Message Rules box.
12. Click OK to close the Message Rules box. Your new rule will be applied to any new incoming messages.

To modify or delete a rule later, return to the Message Rules box (Tools, Message Rules, Mail) and use the Remove or Modify buttons there.

Blocking Certain Senders

You can create rules (see the preceding section) that filter out some of the mail that you don't want. For example, you could create a rule that would delete all messages with the word *XXX* in the subject line without having them ever appear in your Inbox.

To block certain senders from sending you messages, you can create a rule, or you can use the Blocked Senders. The Blocked Senders list is a bit easier to set up than a full-blown rule, and you can quickly add senders to it on-the-fly. When you block a sender, any mail received from that sender is immediately moved to the Deleted Items folder.

To block a sender who has sent you a message, do the following:

1. Select a message from the sender.
2. Choose Message, Block Sender. A message appears that the sender has been blocked, asking whether you want to remove all messages from the sender now.

3. Click Yes or No.
4. If you chose Yes, a confirmation box appears; click OK.

You can also block mail from senders who have not sent you anything yet. When you do it this way, you can block email, newsgroup messages, or both for the sender.

To block any sender:

1. Choose Tools, Message Rules, Blocked Senders List. The Message Rules dialog box opens with the Blocked Senders tab on top.
2. Click Add. The Add Sender dialog box opens (see Figure 20.11).

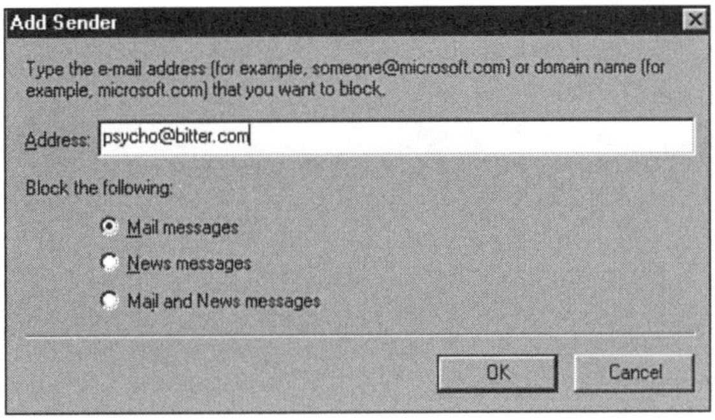

Figure 20.11
Enter the address of the sender to be blocked.

3. Type the address into the Address box.
4. Choose an option button describing what you want to block: Mail Messages, News Messages, or Mail and News Messages.
5. Click OK. The address appears on the list of blocked senders.
6. Click OK to close the Message Rules dialog box.

You can make changes to the list of blocked senders at any time. Just choose Tools, Message Rules, Blocked Senders List to redisplay the dialog box (see Figure 20.12). Then select or deselect the check boxes next to each address. To remove an address from the list completely, click it and then click Remove.

PART III CH 20

Figure 20.12
Manage your list of blocked senders here.

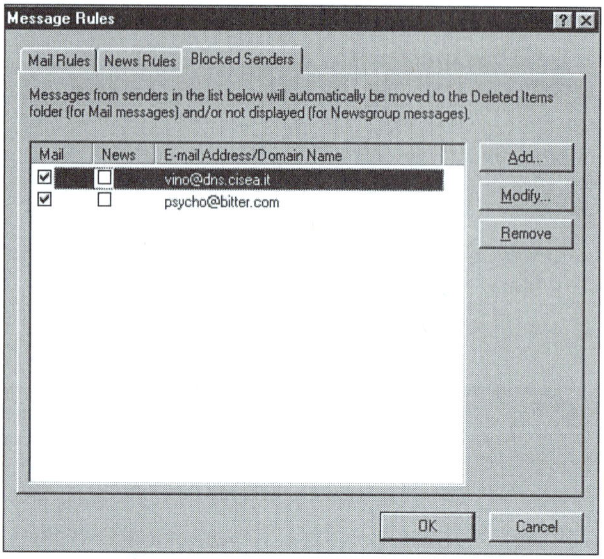

SENDING EMAIL

Now that you can handle your incoming mail with ease, it's time to tackle the other half of the equation: sending mail. You can reply to a message that you've received, or you can create a whole new message. You can rely on plain-text format (for maximum flexibility), or dress up a message with formatting (for greater impact). In the following sections, you'll learn how to create, format, and send messages to others.

REPLYING TO A MESSAGE

The easiest way to send a message is to reply to one that you've received. This is great because you don't have to look up the person's email address or the subject; when you reply, the correct address and the previous subject are inserted automatically.

When you reply to a message, the original message appears "quoted" below your reply. Each line of it is preceded by a symbol (such as >) that indicates the text is quoted and not original. You can type your reply above this quoted block, or you can insert the lines of your reply between the quoted lines to respond individually to certain points that the original writer made.

To reply to a message:

1. Select the message that you want to reply to, or open it in its own window.

2. Click the Reply button. A new message pane opens.
3. Type your reply (see Figure 20.13).

4. Click Send. The message moves to your Outbox.

   The message will be sent the next time Outlook Express is scheduled to send and receive messages.

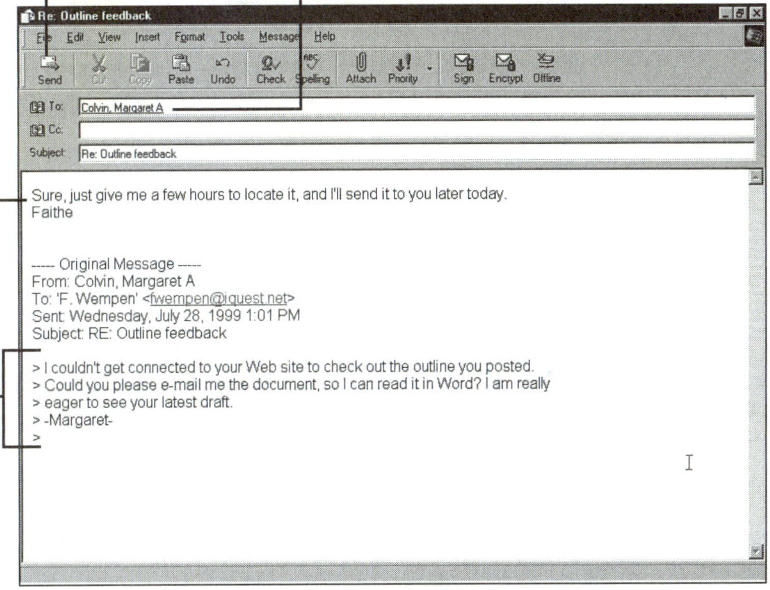

Figure 20.13
Type your reply to the original message and send it on its way.

5. To send the message immediately from the Outbox instead of waiting for the next scheduled delivery, click the Send/Recv button.

When you reply to a message, its icon changes in the Inbox to show a little arrow, like this: . You can use this to tell at a glance which messages you have sent replies to and which you haven't.

Note

In Figure 20.13, the recipient's full name appears instead of the email address. That's because I have set this recipient up in my Address Book under her full name. When I send the message, however, Outlook Express will look up her correct email address and use it.

➔ To work with the Address Book, **see** Chapter 7, "Using the Address Book."

COMPOSING NEW MESSAGES

Composing a new message is almost like replying, except that you need to specify the recipient's address. You can look it up in your Address Book, or you can type it.

To create a new message, follow these steps:

1. Click the New Mail button. A new message window opens.
2. Type the recipient's email address in the To box. Or select it from the Address Book, as described in the next section.

3. (Optional) To send copies to other recipients, type their addresses into the Cc box.

> **Note**
>
> Bcc stands for *blind carbon copy*. It is like a Cc except the other recipients don't see the name on their copy, so they don't know it was sent to the person.
>
> Outlook Express does not include the Bcc field on new messages, but you can choose names for Bcc copies when you select from the Address Book, as you will see in the next section.

4. Type a subject into the Subject box. This should be a descriptive title that will help the recipient know what the email is about.
5. Type your message in the Message area. Figure 20.14 shows a completed message, ready to send.

Figure 20.14
A ready-to-send message.

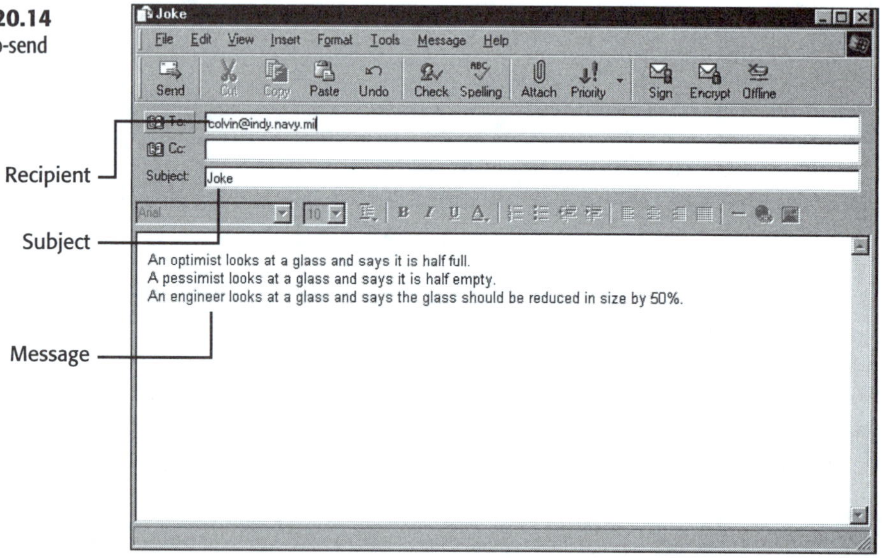

6. Click the Send button. The message moves to the Outbox.

7. To deliver the message immediately (before the next scheduled Send/Receive), click the Send/Recv button.

→ To control how often messages are sent and received automatically, **see** "Setting the Delivery Schedule," **p. 403**.

MANAGING ADDRESSES

Fortunately, you do not have to remember everyone's email addresses. You can store them in the Address Book and use them whenever needed. You worked with the Address Book in Chapter 7, "Using the Address Book"; now you will see how it interacts with Outlook Express.

Adding Addresses to the Address Book

There are several ways to add someone to your Address Book, as you saw in Chapter 7. One of the easiest is to copy the address from a message that you've received. The person need not have been the sender; he can be one of the other recipients.

To add an address book entry from a received message:

1. Display the message in its own window.
2. Choose Tools, Add to Address Book. A submenu appears.
3. Choose Sender to add the sender, or choose one of the other addresses on the submenu to choose one of the other recipients.

   A Properties box appears for the new address.
4. To file the person under his or her real name (not the email address), click the Name tab and type the correct First, Middle, and Last names into the boxes provided, as shown in Figure 20.15.

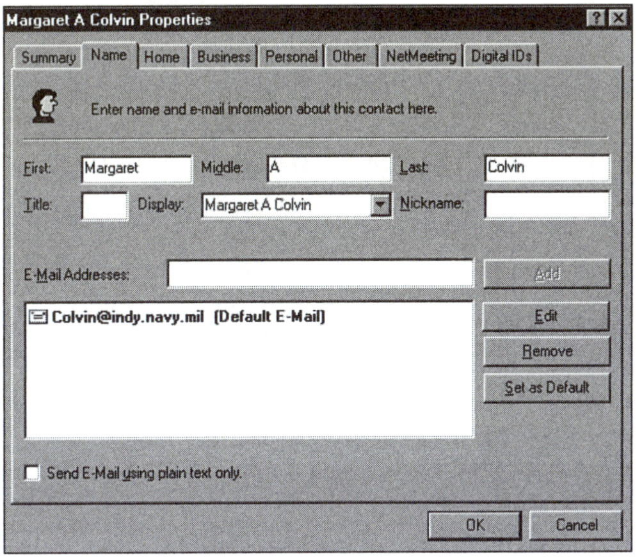

Figure 20.15
Type the person's full name on the Name tab if you want to use it for filing purposes.

5. (Optional) Fill in any other information about the person on the other tabs (such as Home, Business, and so on).

   This is not necessary to send email to the person, but you may want to keep the information for your own records.
6. Click OK, adding the person to your Address Book.

You can also add a new address to the Address Book "from scratch" (that is, without having received any mail from that person, as you learned in Chapter 7). Click the Addresses button on the Outlook Express toolbar as a shortcut to opening it.

Selecting Addresses for an Email

While composing an email, you can click the To: or Cc: button to open a Select Recipients box. It lists all the addresses in your Address Book and enables you to select any of them as primary recipients (To:), secondary or "copy" recipients (Cc:), and secret recipients (Bcc:).

To address an email message using the Address Book, follow these steps:

1. From the message composition screen, click the To: button or the Cc: button. The Select Recipients box appears.
2. Click a name on the list, and then click the To:, Cc:, or Bcc: button to move the name to the appropriate list. Figure 20.16 shows two primary recipients and one copy recipient.

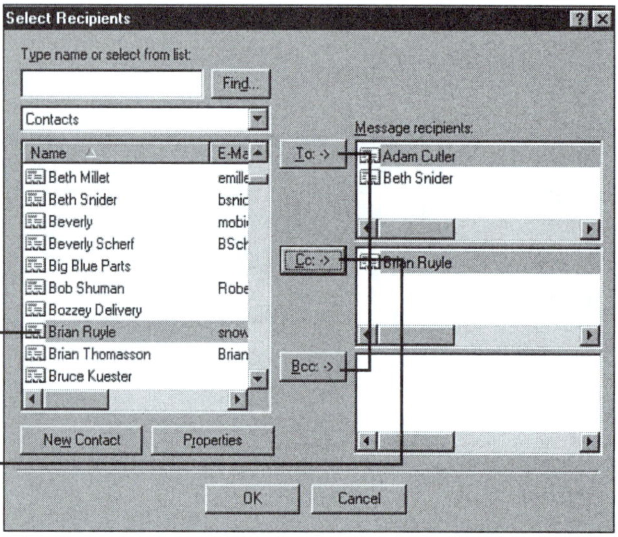

Figure 20.16
Choose who should receive the email in one of the three manners.

3. Repeat step 2 as needed to add more recipients.
4. Click OK. The names appear in the To: and/or Cc: fields in the message composition window.

You can also start a new email and address it to a single recipient directly from the Address Book. With the Address Book open, click a name, and then click the Action button on the toolbar and choose Send Mail from the menu that appears.

Formatting a Message

You can send messages in either Plain Text or Rich Text format. Rich Text allows you to apply formatting such as bold, italic, fonts, colors, bullets, and so on.

It might seem like a no-brainer: of course you want to use formatting if you can, right? Well, not necessarily. If you are sending email to someone whose email program cannot understand Rich Text formatting, your message will not look right on his screen. It would be better for you to send a plain-text message to such a person, because at least you can be confident in how it will appear on the other end. So how do you know? You don't. You can send a test message and find out whether it was received with formatting intact, or you can simply stick with text-only format and not have to worry.

But for now let's assume that you do want to include formatting in your message. When you click in the message area when composing an email, the Formatting toolbar may become available. If it does, you are already in Rich Text mode. If it doesn't, choose Format, Rich Text (HTML). (Conversely, you can switch to Plain Text mode by choosing Format, Plain Text.)

Tip #116 from *Faithe Wempen*

You can set a default format for new messages by choosing Tools, Options and choosing a Mail Sending Format from the Send tab.

Then just use the Formatting toolbar's buttons to format the message text as you type. It works the same way as the toolbar in Microsoft Word or most other word processing programs. Figure 20.17 shows the toolbar, along with a formatted message. Additional commands are also available on the Format menu that let you add backgrounds, use stationery, and work with Font and Paragraph dialog boxes. I won't go into the formatting in detail, because you worked with formatting in the Word section of this book.

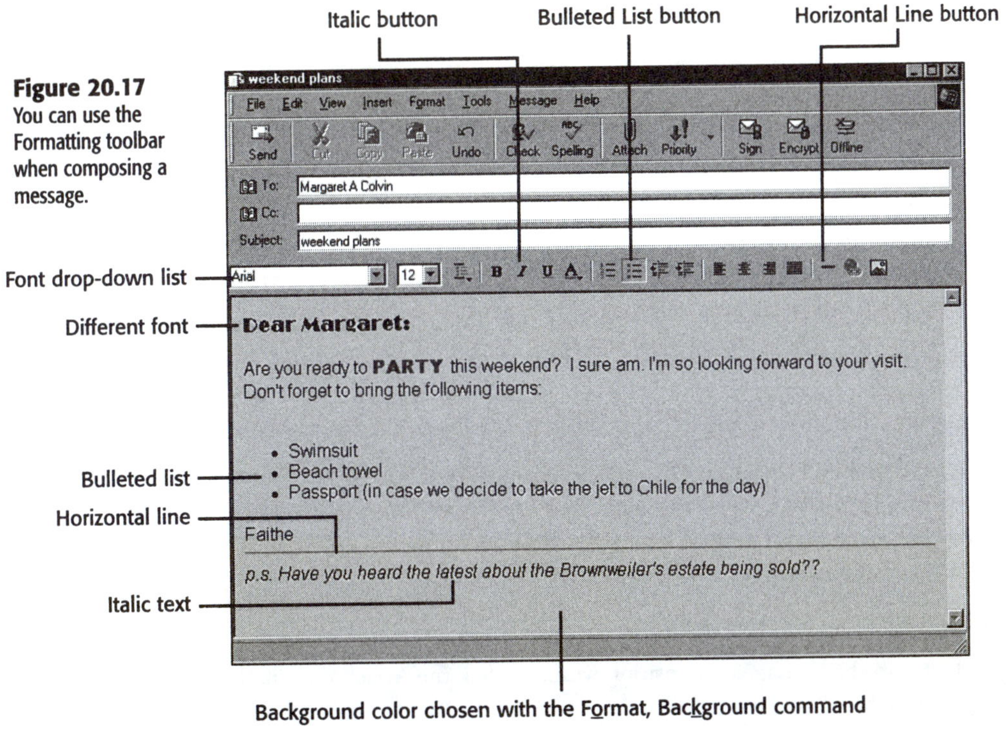

Figure 20.17
You can use the Formatting toolbar when composing a message.

If you are sending a message to someone whom you are certain has a compatible email program, you may want to take advantage of Outlook Express's Stationery feature. It uses a graphic as a background to the message, to make it look like you are typing on fancy paper. Figure 20.18 shows some stationery in use. To choose a stationery design, choose Format, Stationery. If the recipient can't use stationery in her email program, the stationery appears as an attached graphic file, which the recipient can simply ignore.

Figure 20.18
You can choose stationery to dress up the background of your message.

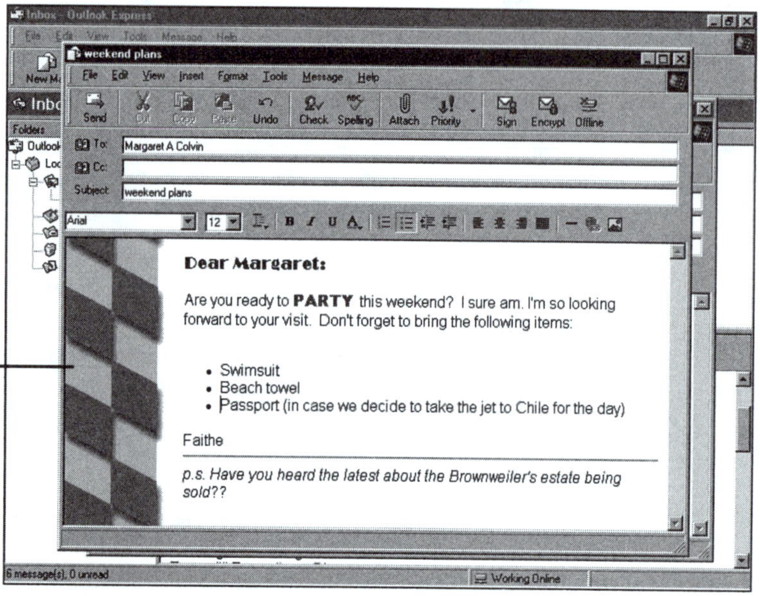

Graphic from stationery

SENDING ATTACHMENTS

You may sometimes want to attach files to your email messages. For example, I often send my editor updated versions of my outline as email attachments. I write the outline in Word, save it as a Word file, and attach it to my message; when my editor receives it, she saves it to her hard disk and opens it for viewing in her own copy of Word.

Before sending an attachment, you need to make sure that the person receiving your message has the appropriate program to open and read the attachment. For example, if you send an Excel file to someone who doesn't have Excel, the file will be all but useless to him.

As a workaround if you aren't sure, you can use the Clipboard (Copy and Paste) to copy text from a program such as Word, Excel, and so on directly into an email message. That way, the pasted information becomes part of the message and not an attachment that relies on a particular program to open it.

To attach a file to a message:

1. From the message composition window, click the Attach button. The Insert Attachment box opens.

2. Select the file to attach, changing drives and folders if needed.

   To select more than one file at once, hold down Ctrl as you click each file (in the same folder only).
3. Click Attach. The file(s) become attached to the email.
4. Finish and send the email normally.

Caution

Use a bit of discretion when emailing attachments to others. People with slow Internet connections will not appreciate the several minute wait required to receive a message containing a large attachment. In addition, some mail servers don't allow incoming attachments greater than a certain size and will lock up the person's mailbox if such an email is received.

Forwarding a Message

Forwarding a message is somewhat like replying to it, in that the original message's text is quoted. However, when forwarding, you specify the recipient. You might use Forward to send a joke that you have received to some other friends or to distribute a memo from your supervisor to the employees who report to you.

To forward a message:

1. Select the message from the list of messages.

2. Click the Forward button. A new message appears, containing the quoted text from the original message.
3. Enter or choose recipients as you normally would.
4. Type any comments you want to make in the Message area.
5. Send the message as you normally would.

As with replied-to messages, forwarded messages have a special icon in the Inbox, like this: , indicating that you have forwarded them.

Setting the Delivery Schedule

The *delivery schedule* is the interval at which Outlook Express connects automatically to your mail server to send and receive mail. The default setting is 30, which means Outlook Express will send and receive mail every 30 minutes, but you can change this to any interval. You can also specify that it should establish your Internet connection automatically as needed (or not).

To establish a delivery schedule, follow these steps:

1. From the Inbox, choose Tools, Options.
2. Click the General tab.

3. Set the following options in the Send/Receive Messages section:
    - **Play Sound When New Messages Arrive**—When enabled, this plays whatever sound is associated with new messages in the Sounds scheme. (Set this from the Sounds area of the Control Panel.)
    - **Send and Receive Messages at Startup**—When enabled, this sends and receives messages each time you start Outlook Express.
    - **Check for New Messages Every ___ Minutes**—When enabled, this sends and receives email at the specified interval.
    - **If My Computer Is Not Connected at This Time**—Choose what action to take from this drop-down list. Your choices are Do Not Connect, Connect Only When Not Working Offline, and Connect Even When Working Offline.

Tip #117 from *Faithe Wempen*

You can place Outlook Express in Offline mode so that it will not automatically connect to the mail server at the specified interval unless the If My Computer Is Not Connected at This Time option is set to Connect Even When Working Offline. To do so, choose File, Work Offline.

4. Click OK, closing the dialog box.

If you have multiple email accounts set up in Outlook Express, you can specify whether a particular account is to be included in a general Send/Receive Mail operation. To do so, follow these steps.

To include or exclude a mail account from automatic send/receive:

1. Choose Tools, Accounts.
2. Click the Mail tab if it is not already displayed.
3. Click the account you want, and then click Properties.
4. On the General tab, select or deselect the Include This Account When Receiving Mail or Synchronizing check box.
5. Click OK.
6. Click Close.

Working with Newsgroups

Newsgroups are like bulletin boards. One person leaves a message that everyone can read; someone else posts a reply (again, which everyone can read), and so on. The whole conversation is completely public, and hundreds or even thousands of people may be chiming in with their own posts on the subject. Chaotic? Yes. But *interesting*. You can post a request for help on a certain subject and receive dozens of informative replies from experts.

Outlook Express has a newsreader component that you can use to read and post to newsgroups. Many other newsreader programs are available, too, but because Outlook Express is free and already installed, this chapter uses it as the focus.

SETTING UP YOUR NEWS ACCOUNT

Your ISP probably provides a news server as well as a mail server, and its name is probably listed somewhere in the startup paperwork you received when you signed up. You will need that news server name to configure Outlook Express to read newsgroups.

> **Note**
>
> Your news server name is probably *news*-dot-whatever comes after the @ sign in your email address. For example, if your email address is `psycho@mysite.com`, your news server is probably `news.mysite.com`.

It's possible that the news server is already set up on your PC; perhaps someone else set it up, or perhaps the Internet Connection Wizard walked you through entering the needed information. If you see your news server listed on Outlook Express's folder tree (at the bottom), then it's already taken care of and you can skip the following steps.

To set up a news server:

1. Start Outlook Express if it is not already running.
2. Choose Tools, Accounts, and click the News tab.
3. Click Add, and then click News. The part of the Internet Connection Wizard that sets up newsgroup accounts runs.
4. Type the name by which you want to be known in newsgroup postings in the Display Name box, and then click Next.

   You may not want to use your real name here because newsgroup postings are very public.
5. Enter your email address in the Email Address box, and then click Next.
6. Type the news server name in the News (NNTP) Server box.

   This is probably something like *`news.yourprovider.com`*.
7. If the news server requires a logon, select the My News Server Requires Me to Log On check box.

   Some providers require you to log in to the news server with your username and password, to ensure that nobody except their members can access it. Other providers are more flexible and do not require this.
8. Click Next.
9. If you selected the check box in step 7, prompts appear for your username and password. Enter them and click Next. You won't see this if you didn't mark the check box in step 7.
10. Click Finish. The new news account appears on the account list.

11. Click Close to close the Internet Accounts dialog box. A message appears asking whether you want to retrieve a list of newsgroups from the server.
12. Click Yes.
13. Wait for the list of newsgroups to appear.
14. Subscribe to the newsgroups you want, as explained in the following section.

You should have to do the preceding procedure only once unless you want to use a different news server. For example, as a Microsoft beta tester, I have access to a special news server set up for testers to post messages. So I might add a new news account to Outlook Express by repeating the preceding steps for that new server.

Tip #118 from *Faithe Wempen*

Set up the news server `msnews.microsoft.com` to view a list of public newsgroups maintained by Microsoft. You can often get help with Microsoft products by reading here or by posting your own messages about problems you are having.

Subscribing to Newsgroups

Each provider decides which newsgroups it will carry on its server. More than 30,000 newsgroups are available, but some of them are pretty "adult" (and beyond!), so some providers choose to exclude some of the more disgusting ones. (Of course, "disgusting" is a matter of opinion, so if your provider doesn't carry a newsgroup you want, you can always ask for it to be made available, provided you have the guts to ask.)

The list of newsgroups may already be displayed if you just finished setting up your news account. If not, click the Newsgroups button on the toolbar to open the list (see Figure 20.19). Then select and subscribe to the groups you want, as explained in the following steps.

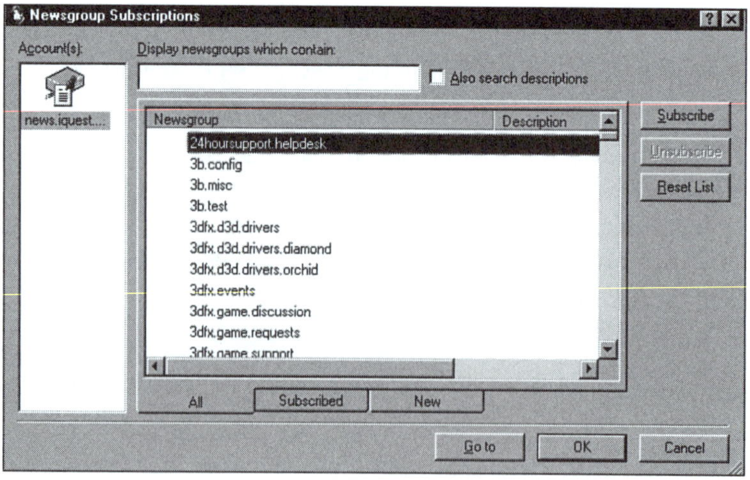

Figure 20.19
The list of newsgroups provided on my ISP's news server; yours may be different.

To subscribe to a newsgroup:

1. Start in the list of newsgroups (refer to Figure 20.19). If it doesn't currently appear, click the Newsgroups button.
2. Scroll through the list of groups to locate a group that interests you.

   OR

   Type a word or phrase describing a topic that interests you to narrow down the list only to groups that include that word in the name.

   For example, Figure 20.20 shows the list narrowed down to groups that contain "dogs" in the title.

Figure 20.20
You can narrow the list by typing words that you want to find.

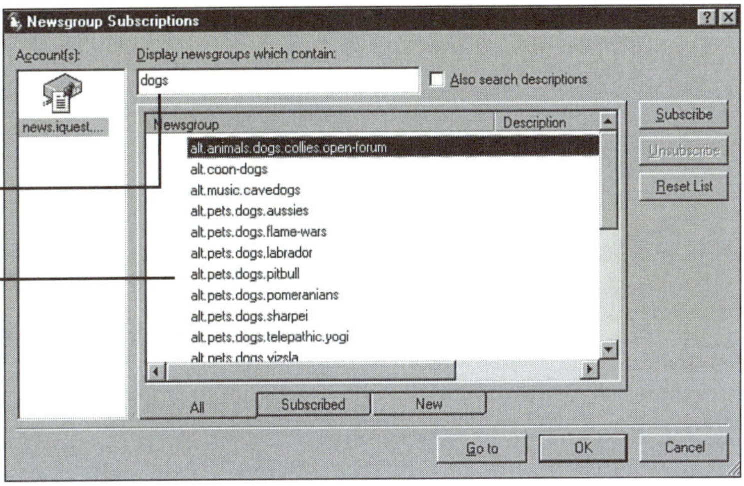

I typed here.

Each group on the list includes the word "dogs."

3. When you find a group that interests you, click it, and then click Subscribe.
4. Subscribe to other groups (steps 2–3). When you are finished, click OK.

You can subscribe to more newsgroups at any time simply by repeating the preceding steps.

To unsubscribe to a newsgroup, right-click it and choose Unsubscribe.

Retrieving Messages from Subscribed Groups

After subscribing to the groups you want, the newsgroups appear on a list in Outlook Express, as shown in Figure 20.21. (If you don't see this list, click the name of the news server in the folder tree.)

To retrieve the message headers in a newsgroup, click the newsgroup name. Its message subject lines appear in the upper-right pane, and a preview of the selected message appears in the lower-right pane, the same as in email. Figure 20.22 shows the new messages in one of my newsgroups, ready to read.

Figure 20.21
These are the newsgroups I have chosen to subscribe to.

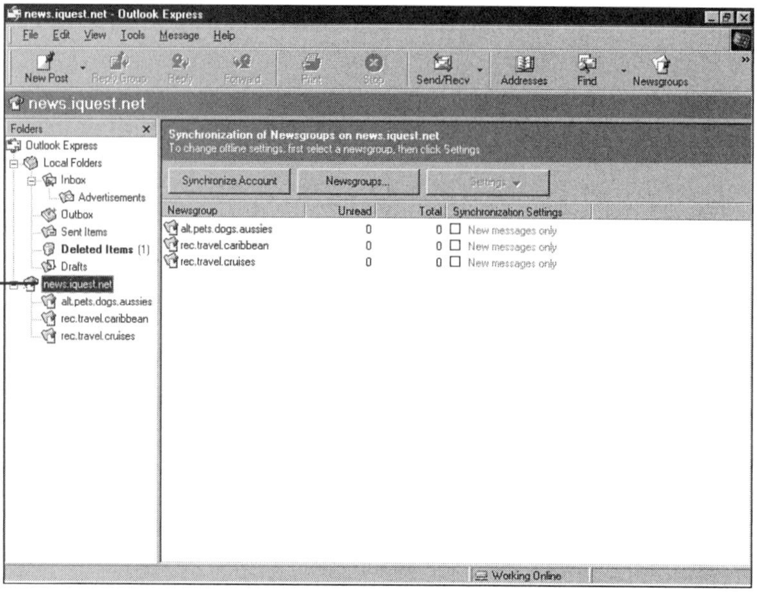

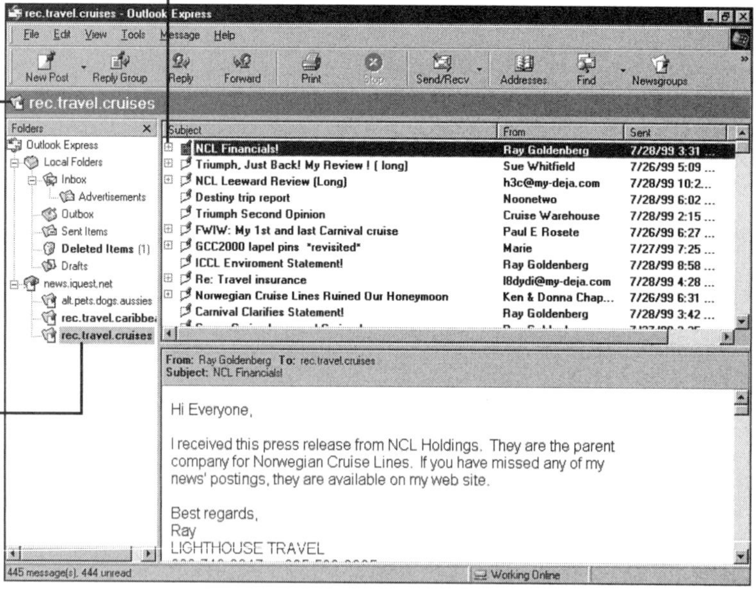

Figure 20.22
Here are the messages from the newsgroup `rec.travel.cruises`, one of my favorites for vacation daydreaming.

Outlook does not retrieve the entire message until you specifically choose that message to display. Instead, it retrieves the message headers. The headers contain information about the message, such as its subject line, its date, its sender, and its size. When you read a message, as you'll do in the following section, Outlook Express connects to the news server and downloads the message's actual content.

Tip #119 from
Faithe Wempen

Outlook Express retrieves only 300 message headers at a time. If the newsgroup contains more messages than that, you won't see them. However, you can ask it to retrieve 300 more by opening the Tools menu and clicking Get Next 300 Headers. You can repeat this until all message headers for the newsgroup appear, or until enough messages appear to make you sufficiently weary of reading them!

You can also set up Outlook Express to retrieve a different number of messages at a time. Open the Tools menu and click Options, and on the Read tab, change the Get ___ Headers at a Time setting to some other number.

READING A MESSAGE

Reading a newsgroup message is almost exactly like reading an email message. Click it to make it appear in the Preview pane, or double-click it to make it appear in its own window.

Replies to a message appear immediately beneath the original (refer to Figure 20.22 for examples). If you see a plus sign next to a message, click it to see the replies. Then read any of the replies the same as you would read a normal message.

An unread message appears in bold; already-read ones appear in regular text. This works the same as the messages in your Inbox, as you learned earlier in this chapter.

→ To read email messages, **see** "Reading New Email," **p. 389**.

SORTING MESSAGES

You can sort the messages according to any of the columns in the display by clicking the column name. For example, to sort by subject, click Subject. You can sort in ascending or descending order; click the same column heading again to toggle between the two. Figure 20.23 shows a newsgroup's content sorted by Subject.

You might want to sort by a particular column for several reasons. Here are some ideas to get you started:

- When scanning messages for information about a particular subject (for example, for information about Princess Cruises in the `rec.travel.cruises` group), sort by Subject.
- When scanning a newsgroup that contains graphics, messages that actually have graphical images tend to be larger than those that are replies and comments. Sort by the Size column to place all the larger messages together.
- When looking for posts from a particular sender, sort by the From column.

MARKING MESSAGES AS READ

When you read a message, it becomes marked as "read." It stops being bold on the message list.

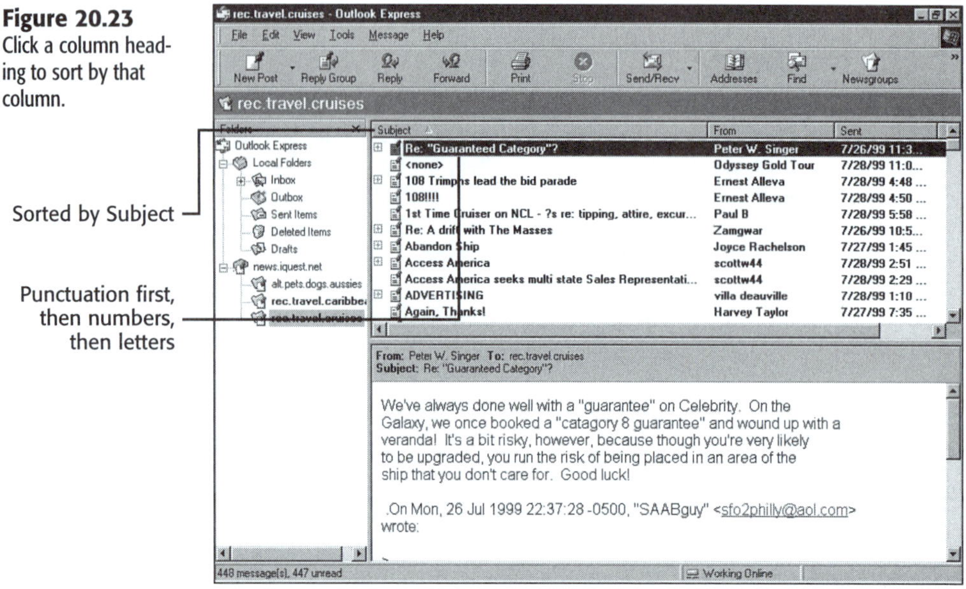

Figure 20.23
Click a column heading to sort by that column.

You may not be interested in reading every single message, especially those on a particular subject that you have no interest in. To mark a group of messages as read, select them, and then open the Edit menu and click Mark as Read. To mark the entire contents of the message list as read, choose Edit, Mark All Read.

Using Mark All Read affects only the displayed message headers in the current newsgroup; if more headers have not been downloaded yet (for example, if the 300-message limit has been reached and you have not yet selected Get Next 300 Headers from the Tools menu), those are not affected.

DISPLAYING OR HIDING ALREADY-READ MESSAGES

One important reason to mark messages as read is to prevent them from showing up the next time you view this newsgroup. That way, only the messages you have not yet seen will appear on the list.

Sometimes, however, you may want already-read messages to appear on the list. For example, you might want to refer back to a message that you read yesterday, having thought of an appropriately witty reply to it overnight.

You can choose whether to include read messages in the listing by opening the View menu, choosing Current View, and selecting Show All Messages or Hide Read Messages.

If you have set Outlook Express to hide read messages but they still appear, switch to another newsgroup and then back again. The list should change so that only the unread ones appear.

DOWNLOADING MESSAGES FOR OFFLINE READING

As I said earlier, by default only the message headers are downloaded. This saves a lot of time because you probably don't want to read every single message in the newsgroup anyway.

However, if you need to limit your time online, you may want to download the messages by doing the following steps so that you can read the messages offline:

1. Display the newsgroup you want to download from.
2. Choose Tools, Mark for Offline, Download All Messages Later. This marks all the messages in the newsgroup.
3. Choose Tools, Synchronize Newsgroup. The Synchronize Newsgroup dialog box opens.
4. Mark the Get the Following Items check box.
5. Choose All Messages.
6. Click OK. The messages are transferred to your PC.

Now you can hang up your Internet connection, and in Outlook Express choose File, Work Offline. The messages in that newsgroup will continue to be available for reading.

POSTING A REPLY

You can reply to a newsgroup posting either publicly or privately. Usually you will want to reply publicly, to share your information with others. (It's considered good manners to share in newsgroups.)

To reply to a message publicly, select the message and then click the Reply Group button. A message composition window appears, as shown in Figure 20.24.

Notice that the complete text of the message appears, along with the name of the person who wrote the message you are replying to. Compose your reply and click Send.

Caution

It is considered bad manners (that is, wasteful) to quote an entire posting in a public reply. Delete the parts of the original message that are not relevant to your reply, making your posting shorter overall.

To reply privately using email, select the message and then click the Reply button. Compose your email in the window that appears and click Send.

→ For more information about creating reply emails, **see** "Replying to a Message," **p. 396**.

POSTING A NEW MESSAGE

To post a new message in the active newsgroup, click the New Post button.

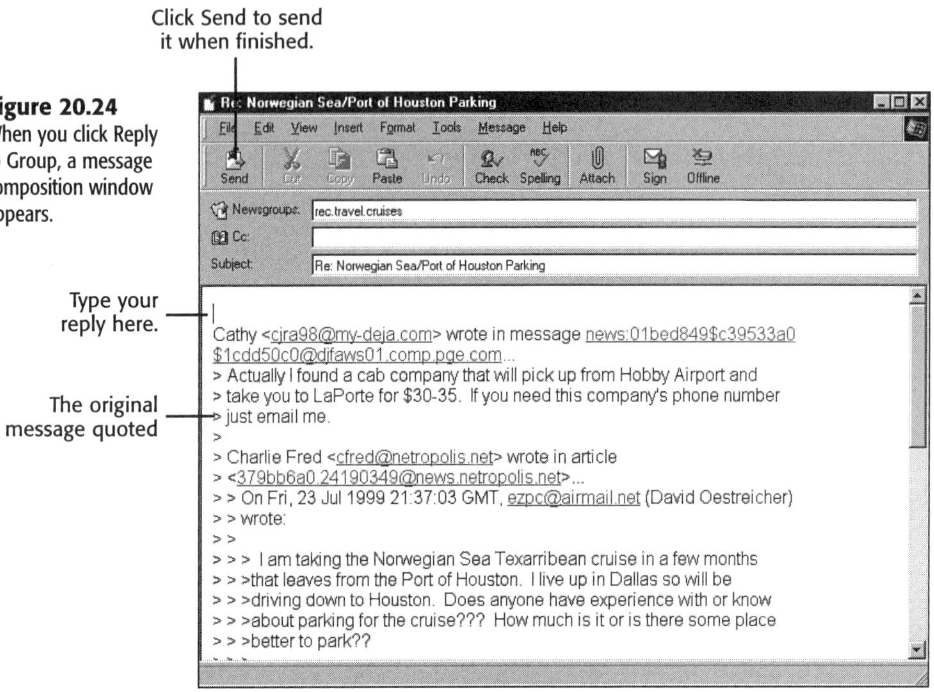

Figure 20.24 When you click Reply to Group, a message composition window appears.

Then fill in the subject and your message, as shown in Figure 20.25, and click Send. You do not specify a recipient; that information is already filled in based on the newsgroup that was active when you clicked the New Post button.

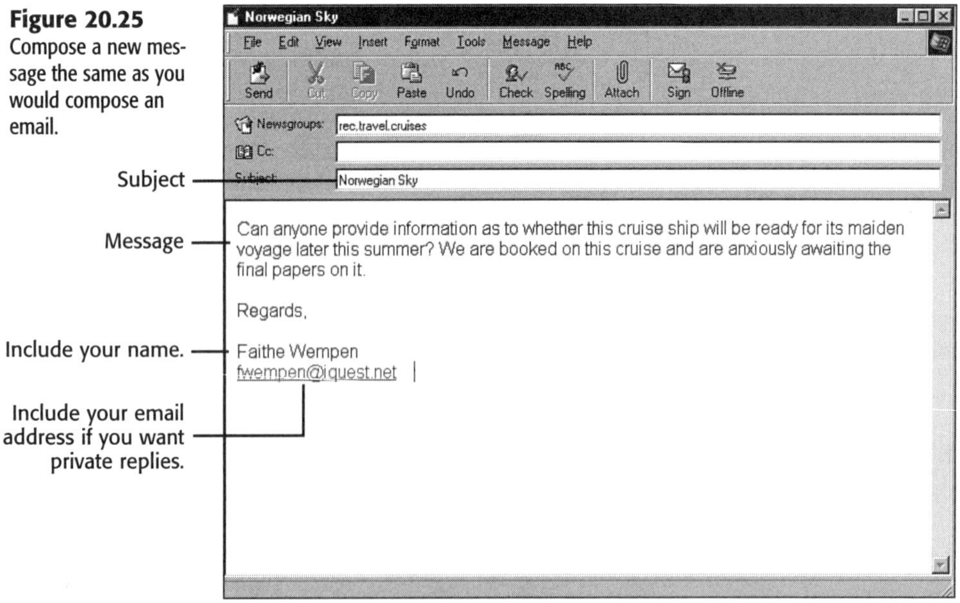

Figure 20.25 Compose a new message the same as you would compose an email.

TROUBLESHOOTING

MESSAGE CAN'T BE DELIVERED

I just sent an email message and got back a reply that said it couldn't be delivered due to a problem with the address. I know that the email address is right, though, because I send messages to that person a lot.

If you send an email message and it "bounces," meaning you get an error message saying the address you used doesn't exist, don't automatically assume that the address is wrong. The mail server for that address may be down temporarily. Wait a few hours and try again.

MAIL FILTERING PROGRAM WORKING TOO AGGRESSIVELY

I set up mail filters to screen out junk mail, but now some of my nonjunk mail isn't reaching me.

If you have mail filters set up to screen out junk mail, check your Deleted Items folder periodically to make sure that your filter did not delete an important message because it happened to have a word or phrase in it that you are filtering for. If you find a message deleted that shouldn't have been, adjust your filter criteria so that it won't happen again.

INBOX CLUTTER

I get a lot of email that I want to keep for later reference, but my inbox is getting so crowded that I'm having a hard time managing the volume.

If your Inbox is full of things that you just can't bear to delete, consider creating archive folders and organizing saved messages in them. For example, I create an archive folder for each month under the Inbox: Archive January, Archive February, and so on. Then at the end of each month I drag messages that I want to save for reference into the appropriate folder.

MULTIPLE IDENTITIES, ONE EMAIL PROGRAM

I use different mail accounts and identities for business and for pleasure. How can I use a single email program for all of them?

If you need to use different identities (such as a business email address and a work one) from within Outlook Express, you can set up identities. Choose File, Switch Identities, and then click the Manage Identities button to create new identities.

SUBJECTS HARD TO READ IN NEWSGROUP LISTING

Sometimes it's hard to tell what the subject of a newsgroup message is because of all the other columns crowding the Subject column.

If you are having trouble reading the subject lines in a newsgroup listing because the text gets cut off, resize the columns. You can reduce the size of the From and Sent columns, for example, and enlarge the Subject column. Simply drag between the column headings, the same as you do in a spreadsheet.

PART IV

USING MONEY

CHAPTER 21

Setting Up Your Accounts in Money

In this chapter

What Is Money?

Everyone knows what money is, of course, but how about Microsoft Money, the program? Microsoft Money 2000 is an all-in-one financial management tool designed for home users. It can help you keep your checking account balanced, remind you to pay your bills, check the current stock prices, plan future financial goals, and more. Money is also tightly integrated with the Internet, so you can have the most recent financial information available to you at all times, including stock updates. Whether you're using Money at home or with a small business, you can easily take advantage of the program's numerous features to help you gain control of your finances.

Note

The Standard version of Money comes with Microsoft Works Suite 2000, but a more powerful version called Microsoft Money 2000 Deluxe is also sold in stores. It contains some special features, such as enhanced planning and budgeting tools and more sophisticated investment tracking.

Starting Money 2000

If you haven't installed Money 2000 yet, do so now. After it's installed, you're ready to roll.

When you install Money, it places an icon for itself on your desktop. Double-click that icon, or choose Start, Programs, Microsoft Money.

➔ To install Money, **see** Appendix A, "Installing Microsoft Works Suite 2000."

Starting a New Money File and Profile

The first time you start Money, you're prompted to run the Setup Assistant. Click the Start Here button (an easy choice; it's the only button onscreen!) to do just that. The Setup Assistant then appears, as shown in Figure 21.1.

The first option, What Money 2000 Can Do for You, is a video tutorial that explains Money in very broad terms. It takes only 2 minutes; you may or may not want to watch it.

Most people want to jump in at the second option, Give Basic Financial Information, and work their way through the remaining options. The following sections explain each of the remaining options.

Providing Basic Financial Information

When you click Give Basic Financial Information, a wizard-like set of screens appears in sequence, prompting you for information about yourself and your financial picture. Figure 21.2 shows a sample screen from the process. Fill in the information requested, clicking Next to move to the next screen, until you're finished. When you reach the last screen, click Done.

Figure 21.1
The Setup Assistant presents a list of things to do, along with time estimates for each.

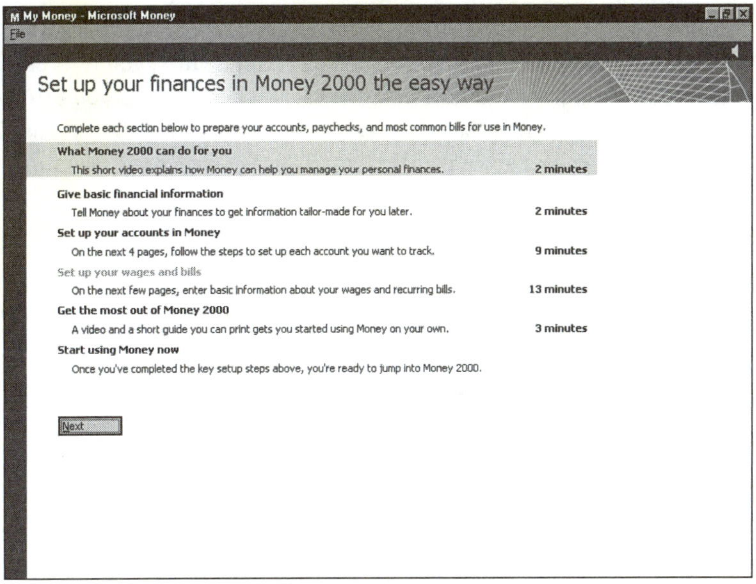

Figure 21.2
Enter the basics of your financial picture.

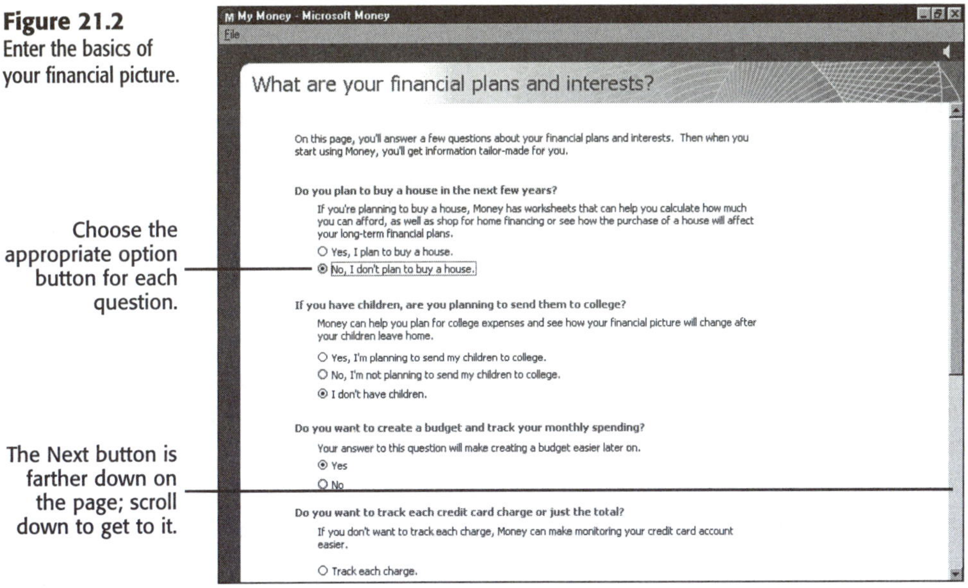

Note

As you complete each step in the Setup Assistant, its time estimate is replaced by Finished.

SETTING UP YOUR ACCOUNTS

When you click the Set Up Your Accounts in Money link, you're prompted to specify which account types you have and how many of each. Then it walks you through entering the account numbers, opening balances, and so on for each account. Figure 21.3 shows an example for a checking account. Work through the screens as prompted, until you return to the Setup Assistant.

Setting up your accounts is optional in the Setup Assistant. You can set up your accounts later if you prefer (for example, if you don't have your last bank statement handy for your starting balance). I'll cover setting up accounts in detail later in this chapter.

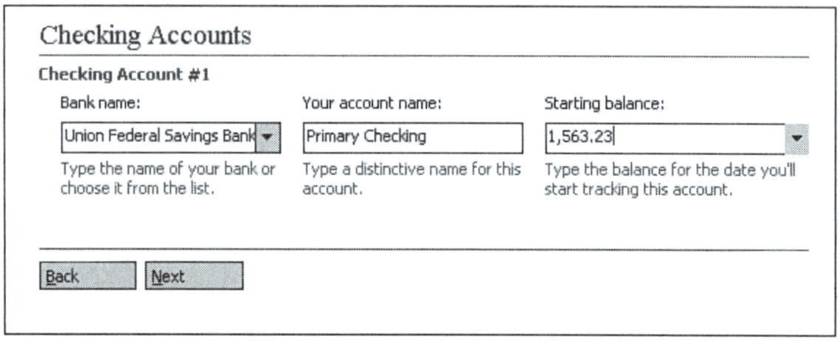

Figure 21.3
Set up each account by specifying the bank name, typing in a descriptive name for the account, and your starting balance.

Tip #120 from *Faithe Wempen*

When setting up an account, as shown in Figure 21.3, open the Bank Name drop-down list and see if your bank is listed there. If it is, choose it from the list rather than typing its name. This list of banks comes from Money's most recent data about banks that have online capabilities. Selecting your bank from this list will simplify your online setup later (in Chapter 25, "Online Banking and Bill Payments").

SETTING UP YOUR WAGES AND BILLS

Setting up wages and bills is optional. It takes a long time (13 minutes is the estimate), and unless you plan on using the budgeting feature in Money, the information isn't critical to enter.

This section of the Setup Assistant asks about your employer, the approximate amount of money you receive, and how often you get it. Figure 21.4 shows an example.

You are also asked about the bills you pay. You select the various bills from the list and indicate how many bills of each type you typically pay each month. Then you're prompted for the details of each bill. If you don't know the exact amounts and due dates, you can estimate. (These figures are for budgeting purposes only; entering info here does not make an entry in your bank account register.)

Many of the fields in Money have pop-up helpers. For example, to see a pop-up calculator, as shown in Figure 21.5, click the down arrow next to a numeric field, such as Est. Amount. To see a pop-up calendar from which to select a date, as shown in Figure 21.6, click the down arrow next to a date field.

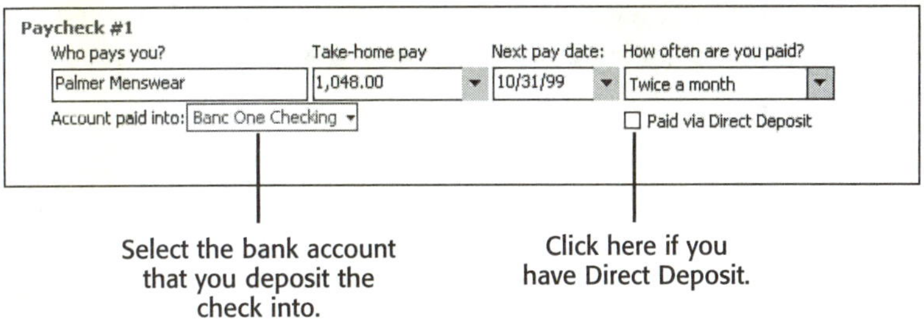

Figure 21.4
Enter the information about your paycheck.

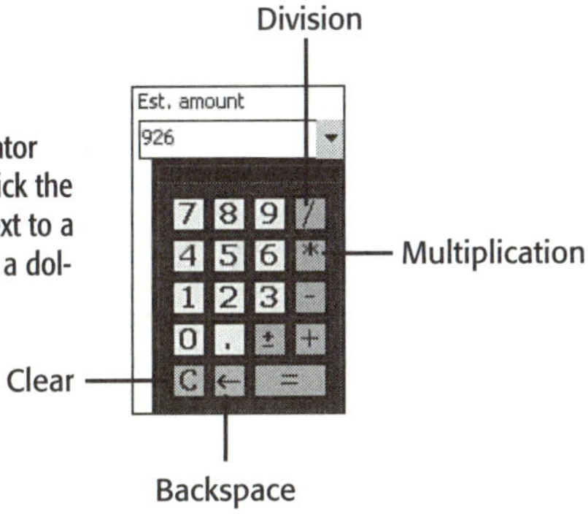

Figure 21.5
To see a calculator like this one, click the down arrow next to a field that holds a dollar amount.

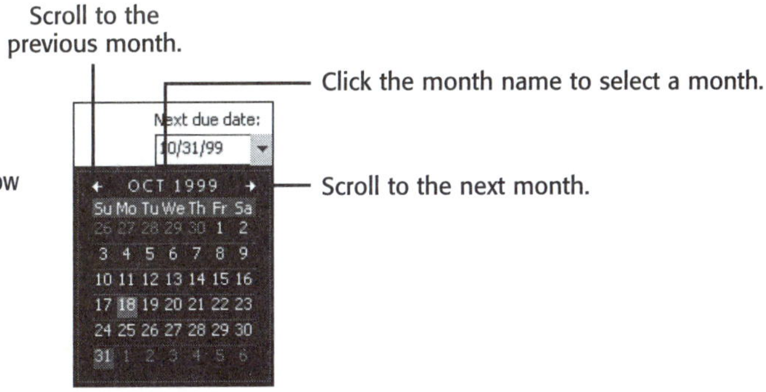

Figure 21.6
To see a calendar, click the down arrow next to a field that holds a date.

Note

You can also access a full-blown calculator by choosing Tools, Calculator or pressing Ctrl+K at any time in the program.

→ To learn about budgeting with Money, **see** "Setting Up a Budget," **p. 493**.

FINISHING UP THE SETUP ASSISTANT

If you want more tutorial assistance, go through the Get the Most Out of Money 2000 video. This explains how to use Money 2000 on your own after you exit the Setup Assistant.

Then, when you're ready to roll, click Start Using Money Now, and the Money home page opens. From this point on, every time you start Money, this home page is the first page you'll see. Figure 21.7 shows an example of it.

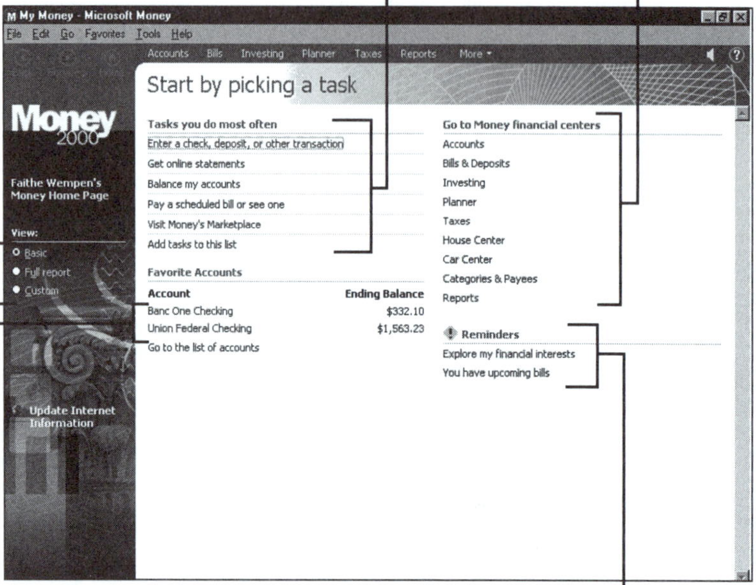

Figure 21.7
The Money home page greets you each time you start the program from now on.

STARTING A NEW FILE

The default Money file is called My Money; you can see its name in the title bar. You probably do not need other Money files, because you can store as many bank accounts and other financial records as you want in a single file.

> **Caution**
>
> Do not create a separate file to store each bank account that you have! This defeats Money's capability to show you an integrated picture of your finances as a whole.

However, if two people share the same computer but do not have intertwined finances, each person may want his or her own Money file. To create a new file, choose File, New, New File or press Ctrl+N. The New dialog box opens, as shown in Figure 21.8. Enter a file name into the File Name box, and click OK.

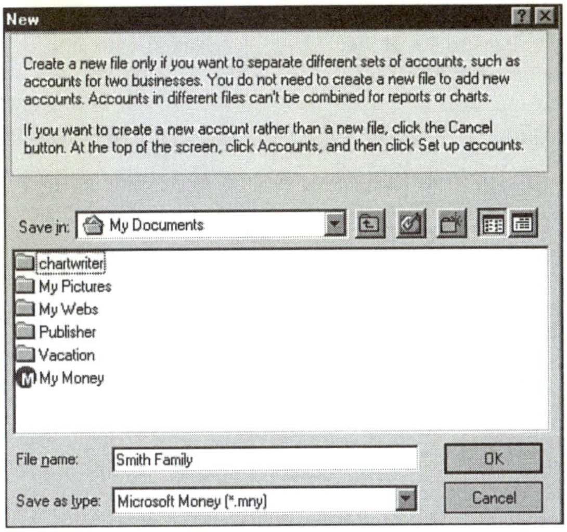

Figure 21.8
Create a new Money file if needed to store a separate set of finances.

NAVIGATING THE MONEY WINDOW

When you open Money 2000, you see the Money 2000 home page shown in Figure 21.7. The Money home page lets you see your current financial status at a glance.

Like most Windows-based programs, the Money window opens to reveal the familiar title bar and menu bar, but everything else might look a bit different to you. For one thing, at first glance there appears to be two menu bars. The top one (light gray) is a normal menu bar that opens drop-down menus. The second one (dark gray) looks like a menu bar, but it is actually a *navigation bar*; the words in it are hyperlinks that jump you to different parts of the program rather than opening menus.

Within some parts of the program, a secondary navigation bar may be onscreen, too, with more hyperlinks to jump to parts of the program. For example, in Figure 21.9, three separate bars are onscreen. Don't let these confuse you; just click the topic you want and you'll arrive where you want to go, whether it's through a menu or a hyperlink.

You can jump to the part of the program you want by selecting a command from the menu bar, by pressing shortcut key combinations, or by clicking one of the hyperlinks displayed.

Just like a Web browser program, the Money screen has Back and Forward buttons. The Back button takes you back to the previous screen you were working with; the Forward button moves forward again after the Back button has been used. This works the same way in Internet Explorer.

➔ To work with Back and Forward buttons in Internet Explorer, **see** "Using Internet Explorer," **p. 346**.

Home jumps back to the Money home page.

Menu bar

Navigation bar contains hyperlinks to the major parts of the program.

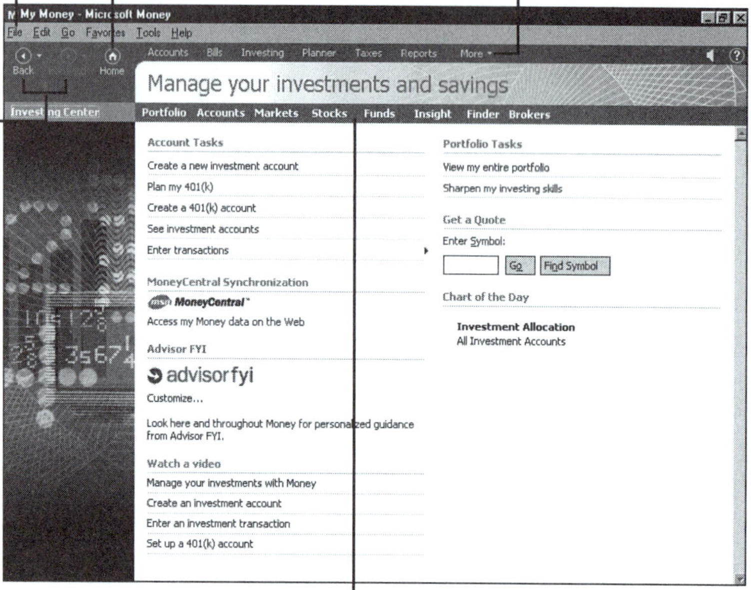

Figure 21.9
Don't let the several menu bars confuse you; only the topmost one actually opens drop-down menus. The others merely provide hyperlinks.

Back and Forward buttons work the same as those in Internet Explorer.

This secondary navigation bar contains hyperlinks to screens within the selected area of the program.

GETTING HELP WITH MONEY

Money's Help system is always ready to offer assistance. Simply choose Help, Help Topics on the menu bar, or click the question mark button in the top-right corner of the Money screen.

The Help system in Money works much like the Help system in the Works applications (Works spreadsheet, Works database, and so on). Figure 21.10 shows a sample Help screen with some key elements identified, and Table 21.1 explains the icons in the Help window.

Tip #121 from *Faithe Wempen*

Press the F1 key for immediate help related to the current task you're trying to perform. You can also right-click an item, select What's This? from the pop-up menu, and then click the item you want help with.

In addition to the Help tools at the top of the Help pane, you can use the Answer Wizard located at the bottom of the pane (see Figure 21.10). Click inside the Ask Money text box, type in your question, and then click the Search button.

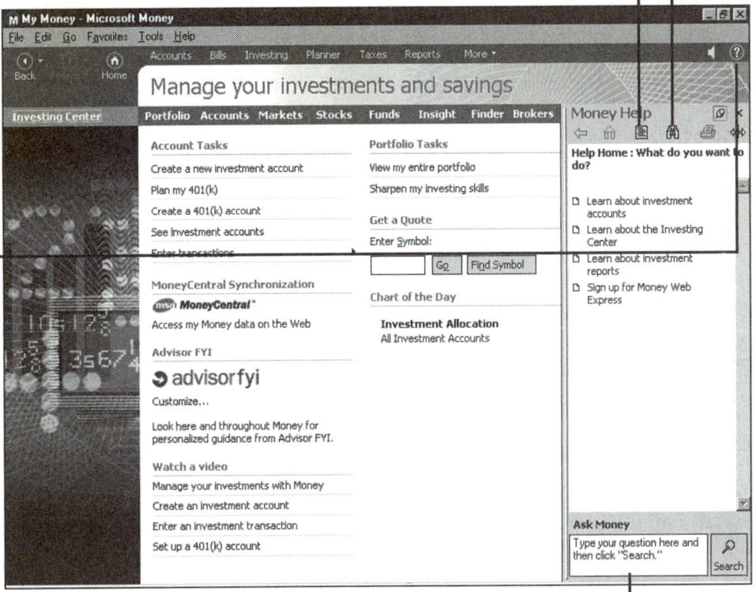

Figure 21.10
The Money Help window appears to the right of your main window.

Table 21.1 Help Icons

Icon	Description
	Moves back to the previous Help topic.
	Returns to the starting page of Help.
	Opens the Help contents, a listing of all the Money Help topics.
	Conducts a keyword search of Money's Help topics.
	Prints the current topic.
	Resizes the Help pane.
	Locks the Help pane in place.
	Closes the Help pane.

If Money's help topics aren't enough to assist you, you can also log on to the Internet and find more Money Help, provided you have Internet access. With your Internet connection running, choose Help, Microsoft on the Web; then select the page you want to visit. (For example, you might want to check out the Online Support page.)

→ To learn more about setting up an Internet account, **see** "Setting Up an Internet Connection," **p. 342**.

WORKING WITH ACCOUNTS

If you did not set up all your accounts during the Setup Assistant's session, you can set them up at your leisure. An *account* in Money is equivalent to an account at your bank or with your investment broker. Most users start out with at least a checking account. As you gain more experience using Money, you can also set up accounts for savings, credit cards, investments, loan accounts, and more. You can have numerous accounts in Money, and each can help you track your finances.

TYPES OF ACCOUNTS

Money offers many account types, and the choices can be overwhelming to a beginner. By far, the most common account types are Checking and Savings, but everyone's situation is different. You might find a use for at least one of the other account types listed in Table 21.2.

TABLE 21.2 ACCOUNT TYPES USED IN MONEY

Account Type	Used For
Assets	Valuable things you own, such as an art collection.
Bank	A generic type of bank account to cover any account that does not fall under Checking, Savings, or Line of Credit.
Cash	Day-to-day money that is not associated with any financial institution (for example, the money you carry around in your wallet).
Checking	A checking account through a bank or other financial institution.
Credit Card	Any credit card you use. (It need not be associated with one of your other bank accounts.)
Employee Stock Option	An account that tracks stock option grants you've received from your employer.
House	The equity you have in your home, and any changes in its market value.
Investment	Stocks, bonds, and mutual funds. Create one investment account for each brokerage statement you receive.
Liability	Money you owe that you don't pay interest on (for instance, money borrowed from a friend, short-term debt, taxes to be paid).
Line of Credit	Charge cards that directly debit (deduct from) an account.

Account Type	Used For
Loan	Amortized loans, such as a car loan. Do not include home loans; use the Mortgage type instead.
Mortgage	A home loan.
Other	Other expenses that do not fall into any other category.
Retirement	Any tax-deferred retirement plans such as IRA, SEP-IRA, 401(k), and so on.
Savings	Savings accounts (usually interest-earning). You can also keep track of checks and ATM transactions from such an account if you have those privileges.

Setting Up an Account

The procedure for setting up an account is basically the same for all account types. The details vary a little, and we'll look at those variations later in this chapter, but first let's take a look at account creation in general.

You'll practice in the following steps by setting up a checking or savings account because almost everyone has one of those. If you set up your accounts already using the Setup Assistant, you do not have to set them up again here; you can skip this section.

Before you set up an account, you should locate the pertinent financial records for it (your checkbook or passbook and/or a recent statement). These records provide the numbers that you need to enter into the program.

Here's how to set up a new checking or savings account:

1. Choose File, New, New Account. The New Account dialog box opens.

Tip #122 from *Faithe Wempen*

Another way to open the New Account dialog box is to click the Accounts hyperlink on the navigation bar, click Set Up Accounts, and then click Add a New Account.

2. Type the name of the financial institution in the Held At box, or choose from its drop-down list to use one for which you already have another account set up. Then click Next to continue.
3. If the name you chose does not match any of the names on the bank list that comes with Money, a dialog box appears, shown in Figure 21.11, from which you can choose it if you simply mistyped the name. Select the correct bank name, either from the list or from the Use button below the list (which shows what you typed in step 2). Then click Next.
4. Choose the type of account you want to set up. (The types were summarized in Table 21.2.) Then click Next.
5. Next, you're asked what you want to call this account. Type a "friendly" name that you will remember, but make sure that the name is unique enough that you won't confuse it with any of your other accounts. Then click Next.

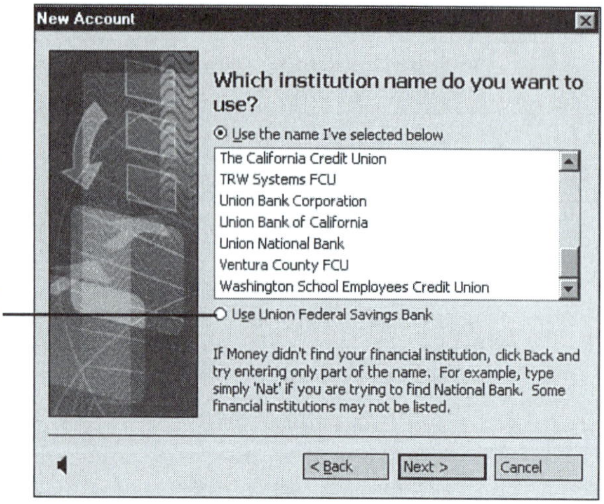

Figure 21.11
If your bank's name appears on the list, click it there; otherwise, choose the bottom option button to stick with what you typed originally.

6. When prompted for the account number, enter it. It should be at the bottom of your checks. If you don't have it, don't worry—just leave it blank for now. Click Next when finished.
7. In the What Is the Balance for This Account? text box shown in Figure 21.12, fill in your current account balance. Then click Next.

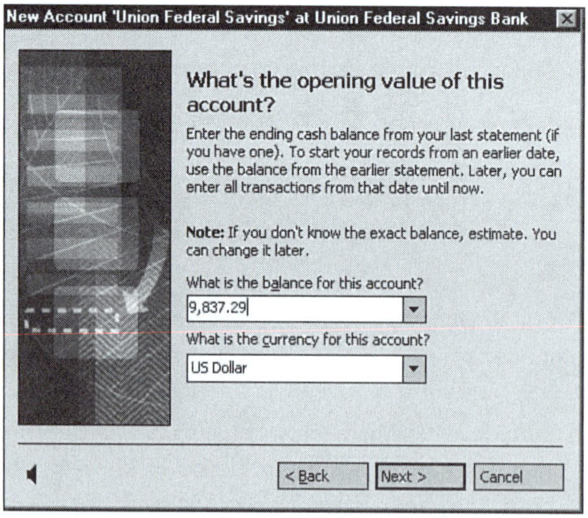

Figure 21.12
Enter the opening balance for the account based on your most recent bank statement.

Note

The figure for the *opening balance* can come either from your last bank statement or from your checkbook. If you enter it from your bank statement, it might be more accurate, but you will have to enter all the checks you have written since that statement. (Actually, that's not a bad thing to do because then they will be recorded in Money when it's time to balance with the next statement.)

8. Money asks whether you have other accounts with this same bank. Click the appropriate option button and then click Next.

Tip #123 from *Faithe Wempen*

Even if you do have other accounts at this same bank, you can answer No to the question in step 8 if you don't want to set up those other accounts right now.

9. Click Finish. You're finished! You're ready to use the account to enter transactions.

Note

If you want to set up the bank for online use right now, mark the Go to Online Setup check box before clicking Finish. However, this book doesn't cover that until Chapter 25, so leave it deselected if you want to follow along with the book.

→ To enter transactions into an account, **see** "Entering Transactions", **p. 444**.
→ To set up for online banking, **see** "Preparing for Online Banking," **p. 502**.

SETTING UP A CREDIT CARD ACCOUNT

Credit card accounts are a little more trouble to set up than regular bank accounts because they charge you interest and may have regular payments associated with them. To set one up, locate your account number and your last statement so that you'll know the amount of any outstanding balance.

When you choose Credit Card as the account type, you're asked some special questions in addition to those you saw with your checking or savings account. They include

- How much you owe on the credit card.
- Whether the card is a credit card or a charge card. Many people use these terms interchangeably, but a credit card is one where you don't have to pay the entire balance off each month (such as a VISA), and a charge card is one that is due in full each month (such as American Express).
- The interest rate you pay on your outstanding balance.
- If an introductory interest rate is in effect, what it is and how long it is in effect (see Figure 21.13).
- Your credit limit on the account.
- Whether Money should use the AutoBalance feature for the account. (This is recommended if you usually pay off the entire balance and don't want to track individual purchases in Money.)
- Whether you want the monthly payment to be included in your list of recurring payments in the Bill Calendar, so that Money reminds you when the bill is due.

Enter the interest rate and, if applicable, indicate any special limited-time rate in effect.

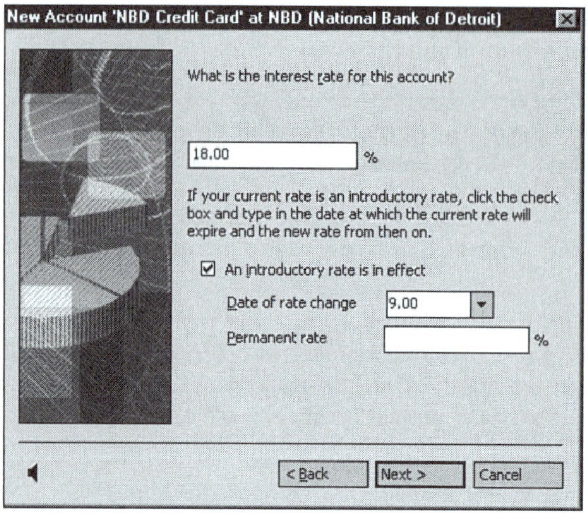

After filling in all the appropriate information, when asked whether you have other accounts at this bank, click No and then click Finish to end the procedure.

After you set up your credit card account, turn to Chapter 22, "Managing Bank Accounts and Loans," to learn how to enter transactions into the account. You will want to record each item you charge and each payment you make, and then balance the account against your monthly credit card statement, just like a regular bank account.

→ To enter transactions into an account, **see** "Entering Transactions," **p. 444**
→ To balance an account, **see** "Balancing an Account," **p. 461**
→ To work with the Bill Calendar, **see** "Tracking Bills to be Paid," **p. 468**

SETTING UP AN INVESTMENT ACCOUNT

If you have investments such as stocks, mutual funds, CDs, and so on, you can track them with one or more investment accounts. Here's an important point to remember: You should not set up a separate account for each individual stock you own. Instead, set up an investment account for each statement you receive.

For example, suppose that I have three stock portfolios: a portfolio of individual stocks that I trade through DLJ Direct (an online brokerage), a nonretirement portfolio of mutual funds through Scudder, and a mutual fund SEP-IRA through Scudder. I receive three statements each month: one from DLJ and two from Scudder. Therefore, I would set up three separate accounts in Money. I would then enter transactions into the appropriate accounts to describe the contents of each portfolio.

In this section, I'll show you how to set up each of your accounts, but they will be empty shells until you add your stock, bond, and mutual fund portfolio to them.

When setting up an investment account, you have a choice of account types:

- An *investment account* generically handles both regular and tax-deferred investment accounts. Use this for nonretirement accounts, regardless of the account's tax status. When setting up an account of the investment type, you are asked about the current estimated balances, and you can choose whether the account is tax deferred and whether you have an associated cash account.
- The *retirement account* type is especially for accounts that you will not be withdrawing from until you reach retirement age. This account type is automatically designated as tax deferred, and an associated cash account is automatically created.

Note

A *tax-deferred* account allows money to grow interest-free in the account until you withdraw it. For example, dividends on the stock might be used to purchase more stock, and you don't have to report the dividends as income on your taxes.

A *tax-deductible* account (usually a retirement account) allows you to deduct your contribution from your income on your taxes. For example, if you made $30,000 this year and contributed $2,000 to your IRA, your adjusted income would be $28,000. Tax-deductible accounts are almost always tax-deferred, too.

When entering an investment or retirement account, you need to decide how far back you want to go with it. Do you want to enter every buy and sell since you opened the account ten years ago? Or would you rather enter your current holdings as of today and go from there? It's your choice. Whatever starting date you choose, you will have to enter all the transactions between then and now.

To set up an investment account, follow these steps:

1. Choose File, New, New Account. The New Account dialog box opens.
2. Type the name of the brokerage or bank into the Held At text box and then click Next.
3. From the list of account types, click one of the investment types:

   Investment: for nonretirement accounts

   Retirement: for retirement accounts (excluding Education IRAs)

   Then click Next to continue.
4. Next, you're asked what you want to call this account. Type a "friendly" name that you will remember, such as **`Fidelity Mutual Funds`**.
5. If you chose Retirement in step 3, the account is automatically marked nontaxable. However, if you chose Investment in step 3, click the Taxable or Tax Deferred or Tax Free option button, whichever fits your situation (see Figure 21.14).
6. Next, you're asked whether you want to add your investments now. Choose Yes if you want to enter investments now or No if you want to do it later. Then click Next.

   Because we'll be devoting an entire chapter to investments later (see Chapter 23, "Managing Your Investments"), choose No to follow along with this book.

PART IV CH 21

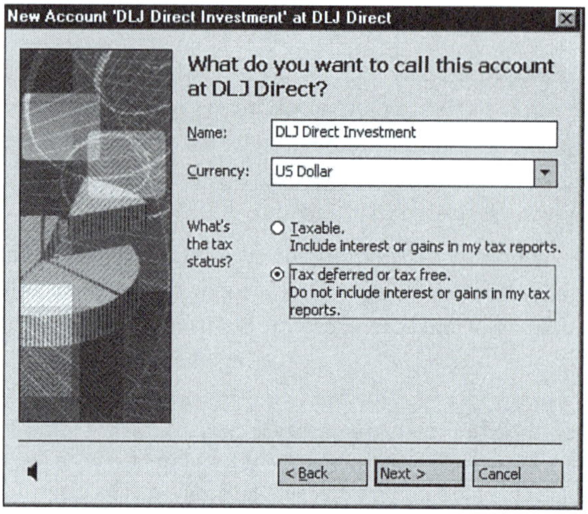

Figure 21.14
Enter a name for the account and specify its tax status (if non-retirement).

7. If you want, enter the estimated value of the securities in the account (do not include any uninvested cash), as shown in Figure 21.15. If you want, you can just leave this blank for a zero balance and enter each of your securities later.

Tip #124 from *Faithe Wempen*

You might want to briefly skip ahead to "Entering Your Current Holdings" in Chapter 23 and read about the benefits and drawbacks of estimating here in step 7 versus entering zero and filling in all your securities from scratch later, when you get to Chapter 23.

8. In the Cash field, enter any cash amount associated with this account. Most investment accounts have an associated cash account in which to store cash to be used for buying investments.
9. Click Finish. The account is now set up!

When you're finished setting up your investment accounts, you'll want to add your stocks and other holdings by entering Buy and Sell transactions. See Chapter 23 to learn how.

→ To add your holdings to the account, **see** "Entering Your Current Holdings," **p. 476**.
→ To enter stock sales, **see** "Recording Sales and Other Adjustments," **p. 482**.

SETTING UP A LOAN

If you have ever applied for a loan, you know that it feels like the application asks for your whole life story. There are so many questions! Money asks a ton of questions when you set up a loan, too, but there's a good reason. The more information you can provide about the loan, the better Money can help you manage it. Money can provide updated *amortization charts* that show you how many payments you have left at any given moment, tell you how much you've paid in interest on the loan this year (useful for tax time), and more.

You can set up to either borrow or lend money using the same account type: Loan. Because borrowing is more common than lending (unfortunately), let's look at how borrowing works. I'll use a car loan as an example here because many of us are making monthly payments toward our trusty vehicles.

Note Do not use the Loan type to set up a house loan; use the Mortgage type instead.

To set up a loan, do the following:

1. Choose File, New, New Account. The New Account dialog box opens.
2. Type the name of the financial institution or the individual who is loaning you money, and then click Next.
3. On the list of account types, click Loan. Then click Next. The New Loan Wizard appears.
4. Read the information that appears detailing this specific wizard and then click Next. Then read some more information detailing the collection of general data and click Next again.
5. Click Borrowing Money and then click Next. (If you are lending, the steps are only a little bit different from what's described here.)
6. In the Loan Name field, fill in a friendly name that you will easily associate with this loan, such as `Truck Loan`.
7. In the Make Payments To field, enter the name you will write on the check each month. This might not be the same as what you entered in step 2. Click Next when finished.

Note If you have already written a check to this payee (as explained in Chapter 22, you can open the drop-down list in step 8 and choose the payee from the list rather than typing the name from scratch. This is helpful if you know you have already made and recorded payments, but you don't remember the exact wording of the payee name.

8. Click the appropriate button to describe your interest rate: Adjustable Rate Loan (ARM) or Fixed Rate Loan. Then click Next.
9. The next several screens vary depending on your answer in step 9. Fill in the information as prompted regarding the loan terms and whether payments have been made. Click Next to move to the next screens until you get to the three-item list shown in Figure 21.15, with the second line (Calculate Loan) in bold lettering.
10. Click Next to continue.
11. Open the Paid How Often drop-down list and choose the payment frequency. (Monthly is most common.) Then click Next.

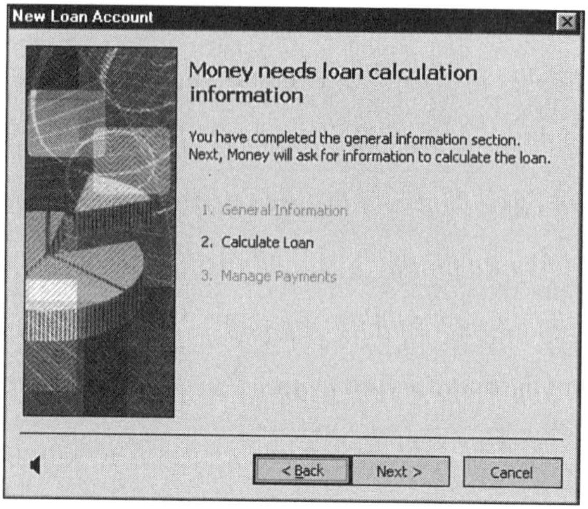

Figure 21.15
Pick up at step 10 when you see this screen.

12. Next, you're asked how interest is calculated on the loan. Click the option button corresponding to the method (Based on the Date Payment Is Due is the most common) and click Next.
13. The next few fields work as a group: Loan Amount, Interest Rate, Loan Length, Principal + Interest, and Balloon Amount. You can leave any one of these blank, and Money calculates it for you. On this first screen of the set, enter the loan amount into the Loan Amount text box, as shown in Figure 21.16, or leave it blank if that's the one you want to calculate. Click Next to continue.

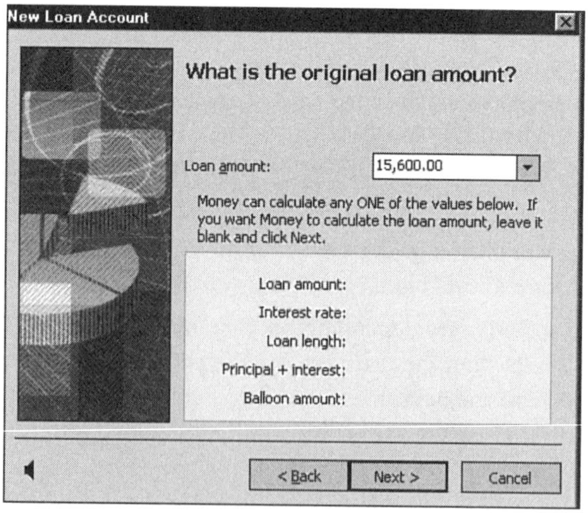

Figure 21.16
Enter the loan amount and then click Next to enter the value for the next line.

Note

When entering the Principal + Interest, do not include any taxes and insurance included with your payment. You will have the opportunity to enter these amounts later in the setup procedure.

14. On each of the next screens, enter the value as prompted, skipping the one (if any) that you want Money to calculate. When all information is entered, Money calculates the field you left blank and presents the calculation in a dialog box, as shown in Figure 21.17. Click OK to accept the calculated amount.

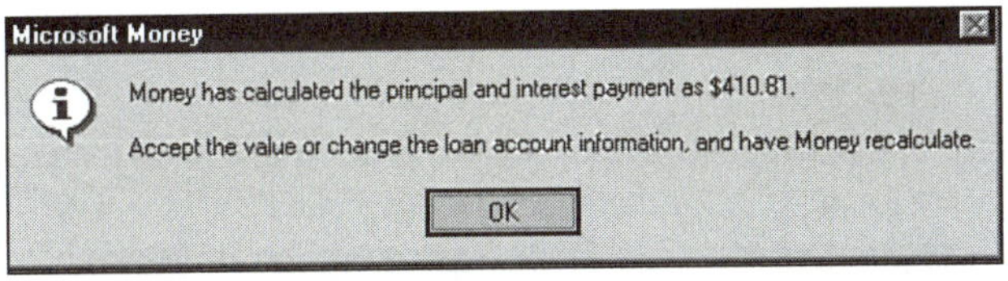

Figure 21.17 Money has calculated the loan amount based on all the other values entered.

15. Click Next to continue. The three-item list reappears, this time with Manage Payments highlighted. Click Next again to move on.
16. Choose the financial category and subcategory for the money spent on interest from the Interest Category Subcategory drop-down list. (We'll talk more about categories in Chapter 22.) For example, for a mortgage you might use Bills as the category and Other Loan Payment as the subcategory.
17. To the question Is This a House Mortgage? click Yes or No.
18. To the question Is the Interest on This Loan Tax Deductible? click Yes or No. Generally, interest on your primary home is deductible. Click Next to continue.
19. Next, you're asked about the extra amounts that go into your loan payment. Click the Other Fees button to display the Other Fees dialog box, shown in Figure 21.18.

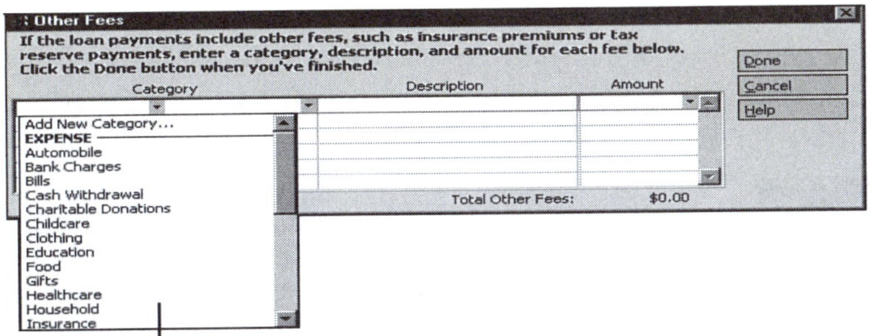

This drop-down list opens automatically.

Figure 21.18 Choose the appropriate categories and enter descriptions for the other fees that you pay into your mortgage or other loan account.

20. Choose the appropriate category and subcategory for your first line (for example, for homeowner's insurance, choose Insurance for the category and Homeowner's/Renter's for the subcategory).
21. Type a description into the Description field and an amount into the Amount field.
22. Repeat steps 20 and 21 for each additional amount that you pay in your loan payment (for example, other insurance payments or property taxes). Click Done when finished.
23. Click Next to go on to the scheduled payments screen.
24. If you want Money to remind you to make the payment each month, leave the Yes, Remind Me option selected. Then enter the next due date and choose which account to pay from. Or, if you prefer, click the No, Do Not Remind Me option to not be reminded. Click Next when finished.
25. Check out the summary of the loan that appears (see Figure 21.19) and then click Next.

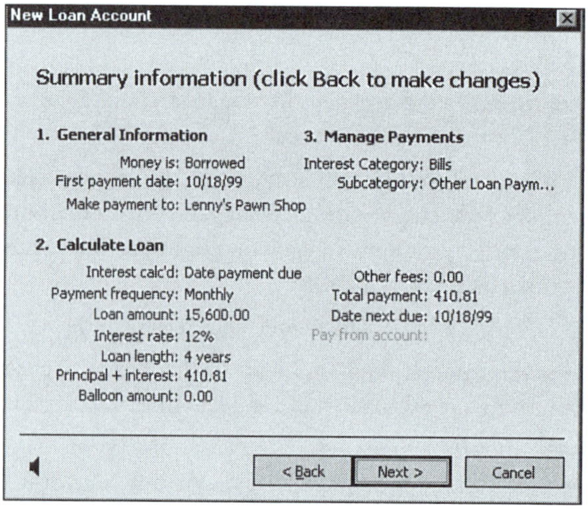

Figure 21.19
Money displays all the information you entered about the loan.

26. Next Money asks whether there is an asset to be associated with the loan. For example, if your loan is for an auto, you might associate your car or truck as an asset with the loan. If the loan is paying for a valuable asset, choose Yes. Then click Next.

Note

The value of an item is not necessarily just the amount you have paid on your loan. Home improvements you make can increase the value of a house, for example, and age and mileage can decrease the value of a vehicle.

27. If you answered Yes in step 26, you're asked which asset to associate the loan with. Choose it from the drop-down list, or if you don't already have an asset account set up for the item, type a new name into the box (for example, the house's street address or the name of your boat). Then click Finish.

If you chose to use an asset in step 26, and the asset didn't exist already, additional boxes appear asking for details about the new asset account. Fill in the blanks as prompted.

After setting up a new loan, you need to enter any payments you have made on the loan since its inception (or since the beginning of the year if you chose not to set up old payments from prior years).

→ To learn how to enter loan payment transactions, **see** "Entering Transactions," **p. 444**.

SETTING UP OTHER ACCOUNT TYPES

By now you can see that all account setups are basically the same, with a few variations specific to the account type. Just start a new account with File, New, New Account and follow the prompts presented to you.

MANAGING YOUR ACCOUNTS

You may sometimes need to modify your information for an account after creating it. For example, perhaps your bank has changed names, or you have closed an account (but still want it to be part of your historical records). You can make name changes, set account status, and lots more from the Set Up Your Accounts in Money screen.

1. Click Accounts on the navigation bar. The Accounts page appears.
2. Click Set Up Accounts under the Common Tasks heading at the left. A page appears, listing the activities you can perform on an account (see Figure 21.20).
3. Click the hyperlink that best describes what you want to do, and follow the prompts.

Tip #125 from *Faithe Wempen*

To quickly mark an account as open or closed, view the Accounts list (by clicking Accounts) and then right-click the account and choose either Account Is Open or Account Is Closed. The difference? Closed accounts do not appear on the account list by default. You can choose to show closed accounts by right-clicking a heading on the Accounts page (such as Bank Accounts) and deselecting Hide Closed Accounts.

You can also quickly rename or delete an account by right-clicking it and choosing Rename or Delete.

PART IV CH 21

Figure 21.20
Access account maintenance activities here.

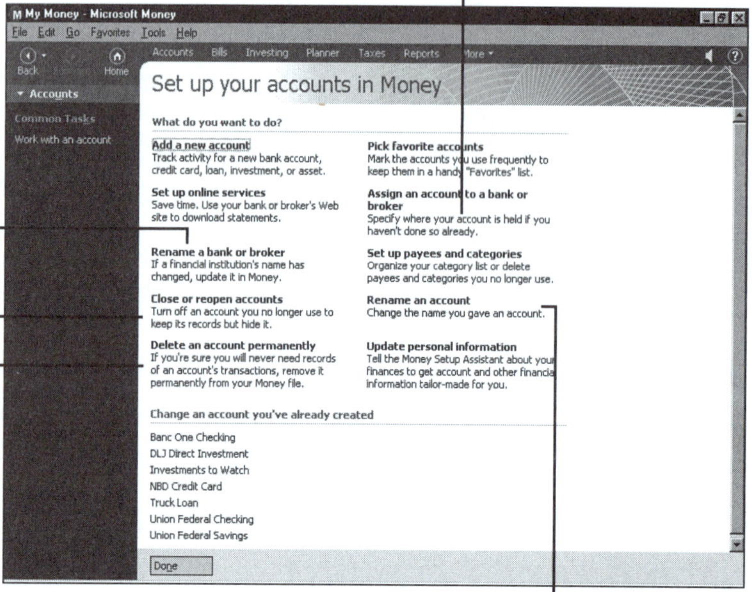

EXITING MONEY

Although you're not ready to close Money just yet, you might as well learn how so that you'll be ready when the time comes. If you need to leave Money for any reason, you can easily exit the program and reopen it again later. Any changes you make to your accounts are automatically saved, so you don't have to worry about saving your work.

When you exit Money, you are asked whether you want to *back up* your file. Backing up is different from saving. Backing up creates or updates a spare copy of your data file, in case something happens to the original. By default, Money attempts to back up to floppy disk, so make sure that you insert a disk into the floppy disk drive before selecting the Back Up Now button.

To exit Money:

1. Choose File, Exit. If you've left the default settings to Backup on Exit, a box appears, asking whether you want to back up your data file.

   The first time you back up, an Intro to Backup box appears. Click Back Up Now to get to the main Back Up to Floppy dialog box that you will see in the future each time (see Figure 21.21).

Tip #126 from *Faithe Wempen*

You can also click the Close (X) button on the Money program window, or press Alt+F4 to close the program.

Figure 21.21
Money asks whether you want to back up each time you exit the program.

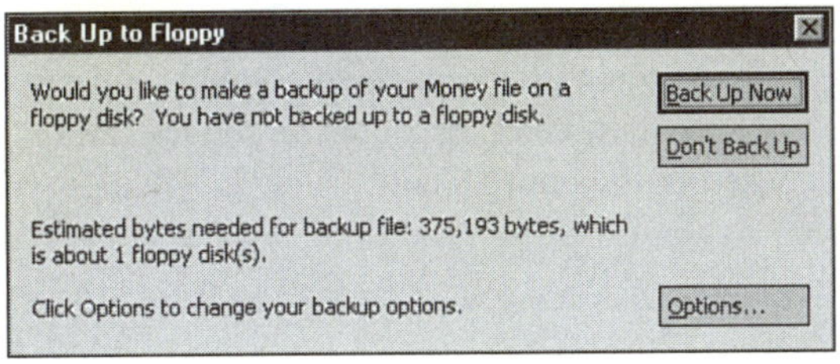

2. To exit without backing up, click the Don't Back Up button. Money exits, and you're done.

   OR, to back up, continue to step 3.
3. Do one of the following:
   - Insert a blank floppy disk into your drive and click Back Up Now.
   - Click the Options button to open the Backup Options dialog box. From there you can set the properties for your backup, including whether to back up automatically at a certain interval and where to back up to, if not to a floppy (see Figure 21.22).

Figure 21.22
You can set backup options from this dialog box.

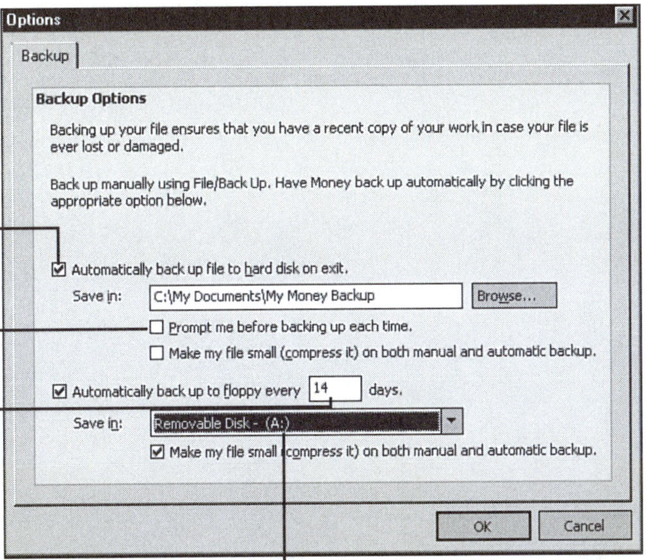

Clear this check box if you don't want backups.

Mark this check box to see a reminder each time you exit.

Set an interval for automatic backups.

Type a different path here if desired, such as a network drive.

TROUBLESHOOTING

WRONG ACCOUNT TYPE

After setting up an account, I found another account type that I would prefer to use for it. How do I change the account type?

If you realize you have assigned the wrong type to an account, you can change it without deleting and re-creating the account. Click Accounts on the navigation bar, and then right-click the account and choose See Account Details. Click the Change Type button to choose a different account type.

FAVORITE ACCOUNTS

I have lots of accounts, but only a couple that I work with frequently.

If you have too many accounts and tend to get lost in the list of them, set certain ones as Favorites. Only the accounts marked as Favorites appear on your home page. To set an account's Favorite status, right-click it and choose Favorite from the shortcut menu to place or remove the check mark next to it.

MISSING MONEY FILE

I created another Money file, and now I want to open the original one again. But I'm not sure where it's stored.

If you have forgotten where you stored a Money file or what you named it, check the bottom of the File menu. It lists the last four files opened. You can select the file you want to reopen from there without having to remember its location.

CHAPTER 22

MANAGING BANK ACCOUNTS AND LOANS

In this chapter

DISPLAYING THE ACCOUNT REGISTER

In Money, *transactions* are entered into account registers, and a *register* (a "page") exists for each account you created in Chapter 21, "Setting Up Your Accounts in Money." When entering a transaction, you have to make sure that you put it into the right register.

If the account appears under the Favorite Accounts heading on your home page, you can simply click its link to go directly to its register (see Figure 22.1).

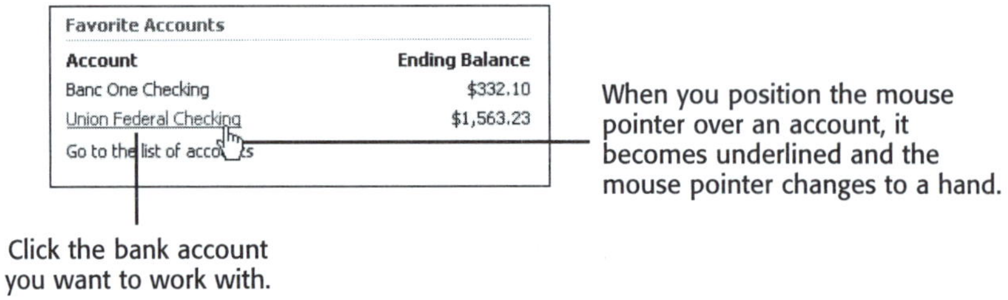

Figure 22.1
The Money home page displays links to your favorite accounts.

Tip #127 from *Faithe Wempen*

To add an account to be displayed on the Money home page, select the account from the Account Manager; then choose Favorites, Add to Favorites, or right-click the account and choose Add to Favorites from the shortcut menu. The account and ending balance now appear under the Favorite Accounts listing on the Money home page.

If a link to the account you want to work with does not appear on the home page, you can display the account register by first going to the Accounts page (see Figure 22.2) and then clicking the account's link from there.

You can go to the Accounts page in any of these ways:

- Choose Go, Accounts.
- Click the Accounts hyperlink on the navigation bar.
- Press Ctrl+Shift+A.

When you finally open an account register, your screen resembles Figure 22.3. Account registers vary slightly by account type, but they all have lines for transactions and a running total. Figure 22.3 shows an empty checking account register, ready for transactions to be entered.

Tip #128 from *Faithe Wempen*

If you are working in one account's register, you can switch to another account by clicking the green Accounts bar at the left side of the screen. This opens a drop-down menu of accounts that you can switch to.

Figure 22.2
Use Account Manager to view all your accounts.

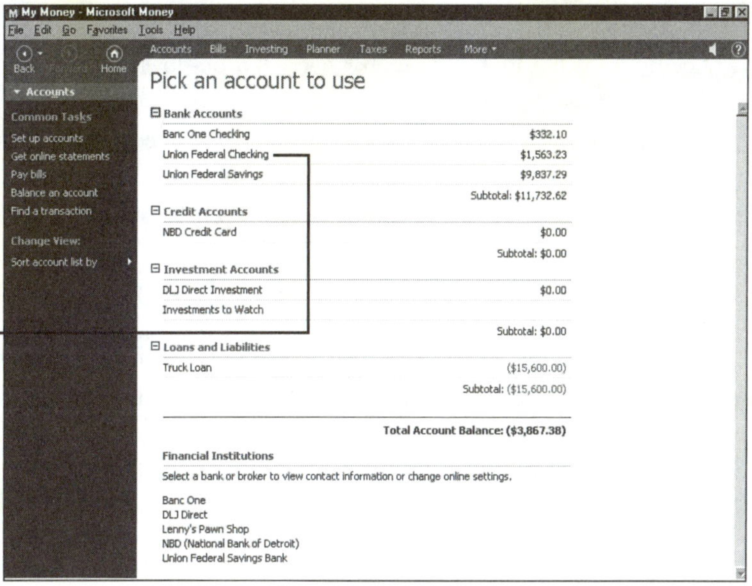

Figure 22.3
This checking account register is typical of most registers in Money 2000.

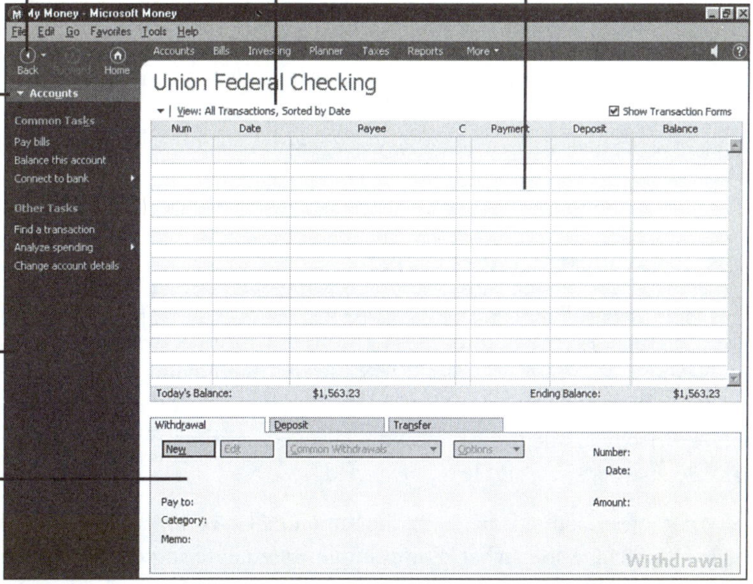

Let's review the controls in the register before going on:

- **Accounts**—Clicking this green bar opens a drop-down list so that you can switch to a different account's register quickly.
- **Activities Bar**—These hyperlinks help you perform common activities for this account. Items with a right-pointing arrow open a submenu.
- **Balance This Account**—This link opens a wizard that helps you reconcile your account with your bank statement.
- **View Menu**—Use this drop-down list to change the way you view transactions and in what order. The name of the current view appears to the right of the View drop-down arrow. For example, All Transactions, Sorted by Date is the view shown in Figure 22.3.
- **The Register Itself**—These are the columns into which you enter the transaction information. They include Num, Date, Payee, and so on.
- **Transaction Form**—The forms at the bottom of the register enable you to enter the transaction information in a more natural, friendly format, as you will see shortly. Tabs appear for each of the major transaction types: Check, Deposit, Transfer, and so on.

Tip #129 from *Faithe Wempen*

You can turn the display of transaction forms on or off with the Use Forms to Enter Transactions command on the View menu. You might, for example, turn off the forms so that you could see more lines of the register onscreen at once. To turn off the feature, select Enter Transactions Directly into the Register. To turn it on again, choose View, Use Forms to Enter Transactions.

→ For more information about accounts, **see** "Working with Accounts," **p. 426**.

→ To balance an account, **see** "Balancing an Account," **p. 461**.

→ For more about the choices in the View menu, **see** "Controlling How Transactions Are Displayed," **p. 460**.

Entering Transactions

In Chapter 21, you created the empty "shells" for each account and entered opening balances for each. Now you must enter all the transactions that have happened since that opening balance point. For example, if you entered the opening balance for your checking account as the balance from your last bank statement, you now need to enter all the checks you've written and deposits you've made since that time. So dig out your checkbook and any bank deposit receipts, and let's get started.

Entering a transaction is basically the same in all account types, although the individual fields may change somewhat. For example, when entering checks, you're asked for a check number, but when entering investments, you're asked for stock symbols and *commission fees*. If you just read carefully and enter what's requested, you should be fine. The easiest way to enter a transaction is to use the transaction form at the bottom of the register screen. Use the Tab key to move from field to field as you fill out the form.

To enter a check in a checkbook register, follow these steps:

1. Display the register for the checking account into which you want to record the check.
2. Click the New button on the Withdrawal tab in the transaction form area. Fields appear so that you can enter the check information, as shown in Figure 22.4. The cursor flashes in the Number field.

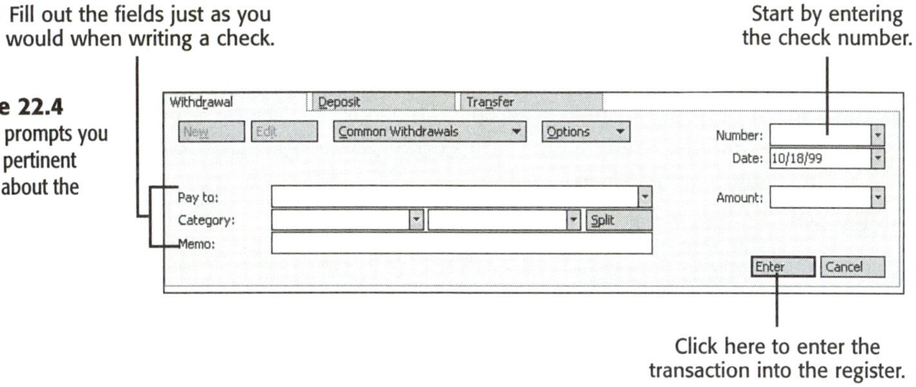

Figure 22.4 Money prompts you for the pertinent details about the check.

3. Do one of the following:
   - If you are writing (or have already written) the check by hand, enter the check number. After you enter a check number, Money increments that number for the next check you write. For example, if you enter 100 for this check, the next check you write will have 101 preentered in the Number field.
   - If you plan on printing a check from your computer (using special check paper you have bought), open the drop-down list in the Number field and choose Print This Transaction. When you do so, the Print Address dialog box appears, prompting for the contact information and account number for the payee. This is optional; you can click OK here without entering anything.
   - If you plan to send the check using online bill paying, choose Electronic Payment (E-Pay). This option will not be available if you have not yet set up online bill payment (see Chapter 25, "Online Banking and Bill Payments").
   - If the check is an electronic transfer from one bank account to another, choose Electronic Transfer (Xfer). The option won't be available if you don't have online banking set up for this account.
4. Today's date appears in the Date field. Change this value if needed (for example, if the check was written several days ago and you are catching up your Money register).

Tip #130 from
Faithe Wempen

As in any register, to move from field to field you can either press Tab or click in the field where you want the cursor to go.

By default, pressing Enter completes the transaction. However, some people like to use the Enter key to move between fields instead of Tab. Such folks must set up Money to work that way. Choose Tools, Options, click the Editing tab, and then place a check mark in the Use Enter Key to Move Between Fields check box. Click OK to exit the dialog box.

5. Click in the Pay To field and type the payee. If you've written a check to the payee before, Money autocompletes the name for you after you type the first few characters; if this happens, just press Enter to accept it. If Money makes the wrong assumption about the payee, continue typing to enter the correct name. You can also choose payees from the drop-down list in this field.
6. Enter the check amount in the Amount field.
7. (Optional) Choose a *category* (and a *subcategory* if appropriate) from the Category drop-down lists. (Categories are covered later in this chapter.)
8. (Optional) Enter any notes to yourself in the Memo field (use this field as you do the Memo line on handwritten checks).
9. When you're finished with the transaction, press Enter to complete it, or click the Enter button on the form.

→ For help setting up online banking and bill payment, **see** "Preparing for Online Banking," **p. 502**.

→ To work with categories, **see** "Categorizing Transactions," **p. 447**.

→ To split an entry among multiple categories, **see** "Splitting a Transaction Among Categories," **p. 451**.

Note

If you have enabled the Enter key to move between fields, as explained earlier, you can end the transaction by clicking the Enter button on the transaction form. If you don't do that, you must press Enter repeatedly until you have moved through the last field (Memo) to end the transaction.

After you enter the transaction, it appears in the register, as shown in Figure 22.5. To edit the transaction, double-click it to reopen the transaction form fields and make your changes.

Note

Depending on the category you select, you might see a Recurring Transaction Detected prompt after you press Enter to record the check. This is Money's way of helping you automate bills you need to pay often, such as utilities. Money can set up the transaction as a regularly scheduled payment to help you forecast your expenses. Click Yes to make the transaction a recurring expense, or No (you can always make it a recurring transaction later).

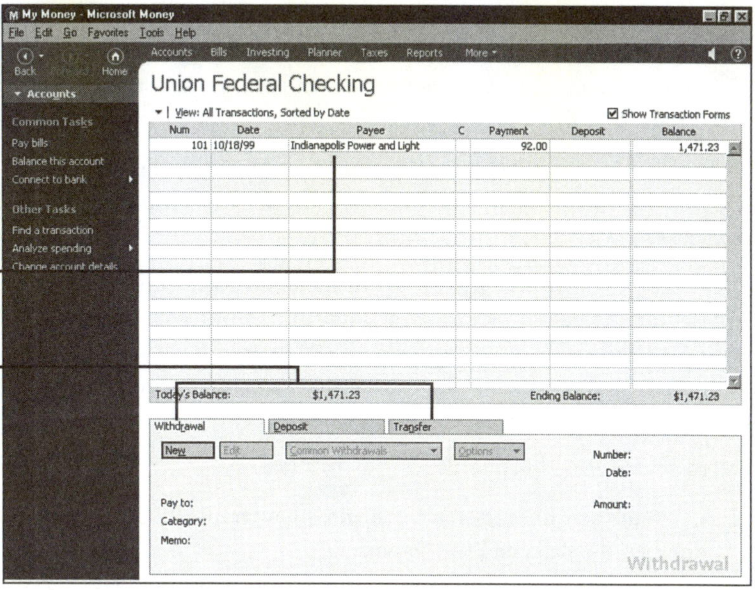

Figure 22.5 Use the transaction form to enter transactions of all types.

Entering other types of transactions is similar to entering a check. Just click the appropriate tab for the form you need and fill in the blanks:

- **Deposit**—Use this for all deposits into the account (except transfers from other accounts). The fields are basically the same as for a check.
- **Transfer**—This form has an additional field so that you can indicate which account the money is coming from and which it is going to. Such a transaction makes entries in both registers automatically. You can initiate a transfer from whichever register is more convenient—the one gaining the money or the one giving it.

You might occasionally have a situation in which the correct transaction type is not apparent. For example, if you're making a payment on a loan, would that be a check (because you're writing a check) or a transfer (because you're moving money from one account to another)? Technically, it's both. You would enter it as a check and then specify the loan account as the payee. The payment would then be added to the loan account's register, too.

Categorizing Transactions

Categories are used to classify your income and expenses so that you can create reports and charts later that show how you are spending and receiving money. For instance, if you categorize each check you write to the grocery store as Groceries, you can create a report that shows how much money you spend per month on groceries. *Subcategories* are further breakdowns of categories. For instance, if Food is the category, you might have Groceries and Dining Out as two subcategories. Categories are optional; you don't have to use them. However, many of Money's powerful features, such as reports, can't be used unless you use categories.

When you set up your Money account, it created a few categories automatically, which are ready for your use. As you're entering a transaction, you can skip over the Category line completely, or you can open the drop-down list and choose one. You can also type a new category on-the-fly.

You can set up categories in a couple of ways. One is to do it on-the-fly as you enter transactions. I like this method because it ensures that you create only the categories you'll really use.

Other people might prefer to set up all their categories and subcategories before they enter transactions (or before they enter any more). With this method, you can carefully plan your categories by looking at the complete list of existing ones and filling in the gaps for your own situation. This method also enables you to enter more detailed tax and description information about a category than the quicker on-the-fly method allows.

To create categories on-the-fly:

1. Open the account register and begin a new transaction. Enter the payee, the check number, the date, and the amount.
2. Move the cursor to the first Category field and type the name for the new category. Then press Tab to move to the next field. Before the cursor moves to the next field, a New Category dialog box appears, as shown in Figure 22.6.

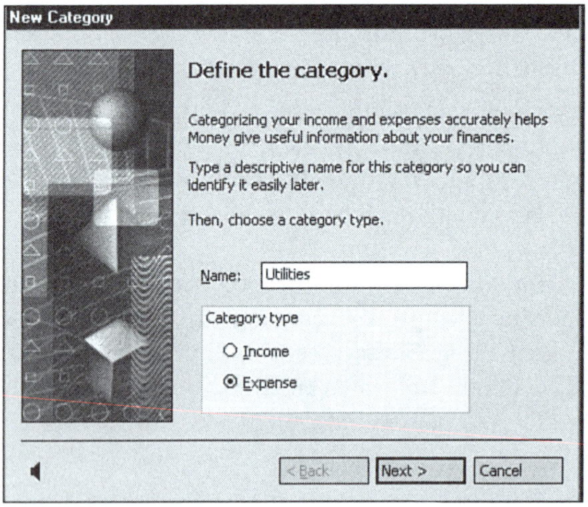

Figure 22.6
Use the New Category dialog box to set up a new category or subcategory.

Tip #131 from
Faithe Wempen

When inventing names for your categories, be as descriptive as possible. The more precisely you categorize your transactions, the more useful your reports and charts will be. For instance, Pay is not the greatest category name, especially if you have more than one job. Salary XYZ Corp. is better.

3. Click Income or Expense to specify the category type. Then click Next.
4. You're asked to place the new category in one of the preexisting tax and report category groups, as shown in Figure 22.7. Choose the item on the list that fits most nearly and then click Finish.

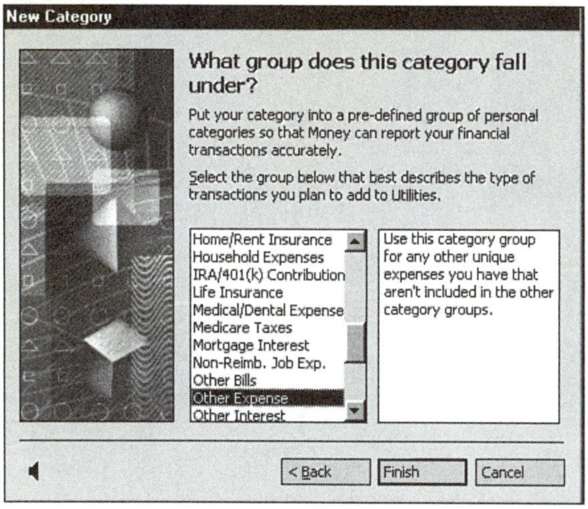

Figure 22.7 Choose the description that best fits your new category.

5. Complete the transaction as described earlier.

The other way to create a category is by working with the Payees and Categories screen. You can define categories here and immediately use them in a transaction.

To create a new category for later use:

1. Choose Go, Categories & Payees or press Ctrl+Shift+C. The Categories screen appears, with the categories you have set up so far (see Figure 22.8).
2. If you want to create a subcategory, first click the category to which it should be subordinate. If you're creating a top-level category, it doesn't matter which category is selected when you start.
3. Click the New button. The New Category dialog box appears with two choices: Create a New Category or Add a Subcategory To the category you selected in step 2. Click the option button you want and then click Next.
4. In the Name field, type the name for the new category. If you're creating a subcategory, use the Subcategory For drop-down list to assign it to a category. Click Next to continue.
5. Choose the group category to map the new category to, just as you did earlier in Figure 22.7. Then click Finish.

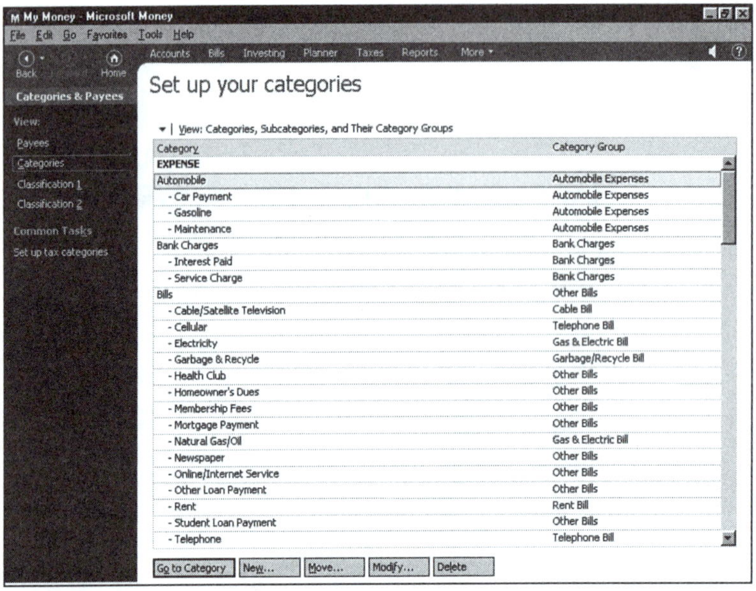

Figure 22.8 The Categories list neatly displays all your categories at once.

From the Categories screen (refer to Figure 22.8) you can also delete categories. Just select the category you want and click the Delete button. If the category has been used in one or more transactions, a dialog box appears, asking you to choose a different category to assign to those transactions. Do so and click OK, and you're finished.

To rename a category, right-click it and choose Rename, or select it and click the Modify button. A Modify Category (or Modify Subcategory) dialog box appears. Type the new name and click OK.

Tip #132 from *Faithe Wempen*

You can right-click any category or subcategory to get a shortcut menu. On this menu, you find commands equivalent to the four buttons at the bottom of the Categories screen. It's just another way to issue the commands—entirely optional.

To change the details relating to a category, follow these steps:

1. On the Categories page, select the category you want to work with and then click the Go to Category button at the bottom of the dialog box. (Or you can double-click the category name.)

   A screen of details for that category appears, showing the tax information, a history of transactions that used the category, and more (see Figure 22.9). Figure 22.9 shows a main category; fewer options are available when working with subcategories.

2. Do any of the following, as needed:
   - To rename the category, click the Modify button.
   - To create additional subcategories, click the New (Alt+W) button. This button is not available when you're working with a subcategory.

- To set up the category for *tax reporting*, click the Include on Tax Reports check box and then choose the appropriate tax forms and lines from the drop-down lists beneath it.
- Click the Go to Budget button to see how the category fits within your budget.
- To recategorize a transaction on the list, click it and then click the Change Category button.
- To change the group category, choose a different one from the Category Group drop-down list.

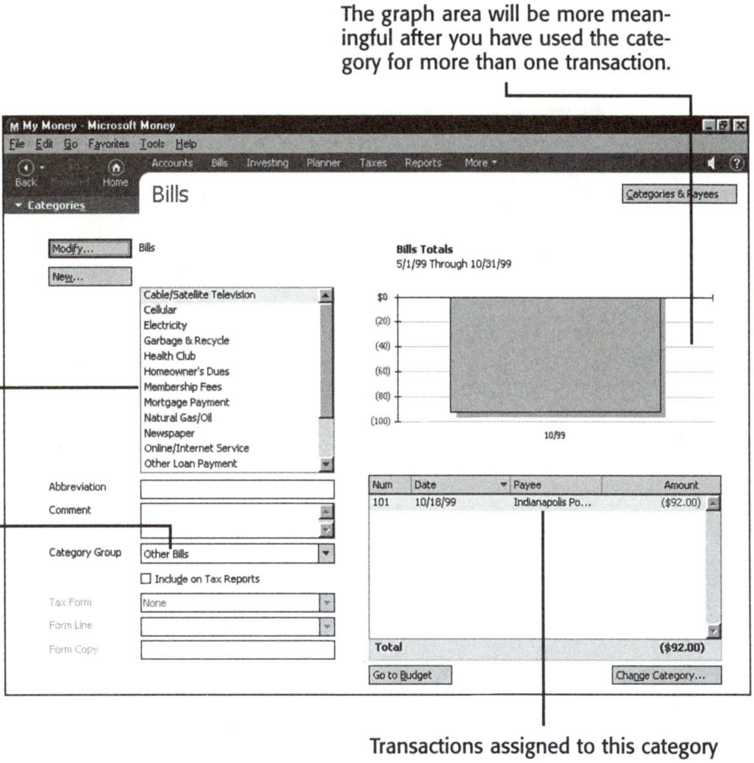

Figure 22.9
You can see all available information about the category at a glance on the Categories screen.

3. When you're finished working with the category, click the Back button on the Navigation bar to return to the list of categories.

→ To set up a budget, **see** "Setting Up a Budget," **p. 493**.

SPLITTING A TRANSACTION AMONG CATEGORIES

Have you ever written a single check for lots of different household items at one of those giant mega-superstores? It's oh-so-convenient to buy your groceries, hardware, lawn fertilizer, and home electronics at a single store. But then you get home and try to enter the check into Money. Uh oh. In the excitement of those discount prices, you loaded up your cart with lots of items, including a gallon-size jug of ketchup, a Thighmaster, and a new VCR. How in the world can you stuff all that into a single category?

You can't, of course. That's where the Split button comes in. Click it as you're entering a transaction, and you'll open a Split Transaction window. (You can also select Split from the Category drop-down list to do the same thing.)

In the Split Transaction window, you can enter lots of line items that all roll into a single check and categorize each line separately. For instance, you can put that keg-o-ketchup under Food:Groceries, the VCR under Furnishings:Electronics, and the Thighmaster under Leisure:Equipment. Just fill in the category, the subcategory, the description, and the amount of each item. Figure 22.10 shows how to apportion such purchases. Don't forget the sales tax! Click Done when you're finished.

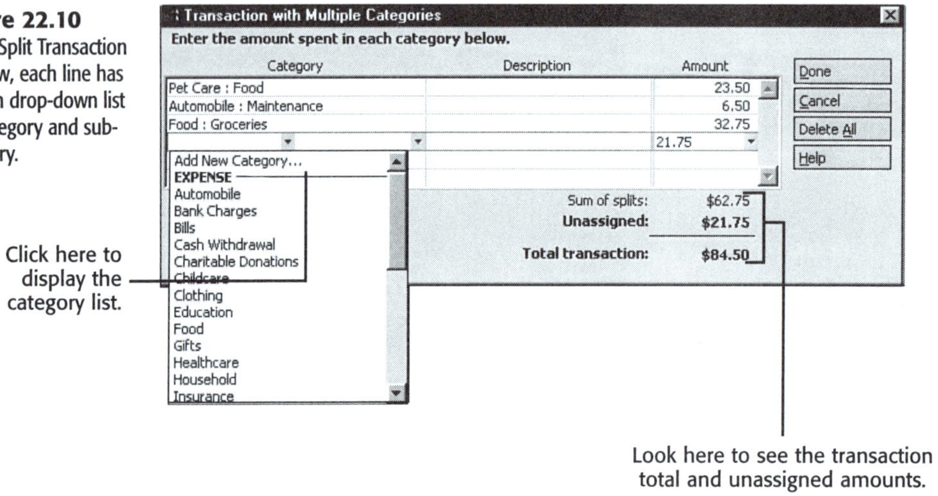

Figure 22.10
In the Split Transaction window, each line has its own drop-down list for category and sub-category.

PRINTING CHECKS

If you want, you can print checks directly from your printer instead of writing them with your actual checkbook. It requires special check paper, which can be rather expensive, but some people find it worth the expense.

Note

To get information about what kind of checks you can order and how much they will cost, choose Help, Ordering Checks.

If you want to print a check, you must indicate this by setting the Number field to Print This Transaction. You can do this for a whole batch of checks and then print them all at once. When you have checks to print, a Print Checks reminder appears to the side of the register.

TESTING YOUR PRINTER

Before you print checks for the first time, test your printer to determine how to feed in the paper. To do so, take a blank sheet of paper and draw an upward-pointing arrow on one side. Then feed the sheet of paper into your printer, arrow side up, point first, and print any document from any program (not necessarily Money). If the document comes out with the arrow on top and right-side-up, you know that you should feed your checks in exactly as you fed the test paper. If not, the test sheet demonstrates how you need to feed the paper (and thus your page of blank checks) into the printer.

Next, set up your printer for checks; choose File, Print Setup, Check Setup. This opens the Check Setup dialog box. Select the printer, the check type, and the source; then click OK.

PRINTING CHECKS

Money 2000 is very good at making the check printing process as friendly and as foolproof as possible. It provides a helpful wizard that steps you through the check-printing process. You just enter the requested information and go.

Note

Remember, before you can attempt to print any checks, you must first assign the Print This Transaction option to the checks you want to print. When recording the transaction, use the Number drop-down list and select Print This Transaction.

To print checks, follow these steps:

1. Set up your printer for checks, as described in the preceding section.
2. Click the Print Checks link on the Activities bar, or choose File, Print Checks. The Print Checks dialog box appears, shown in Figure 22.11.

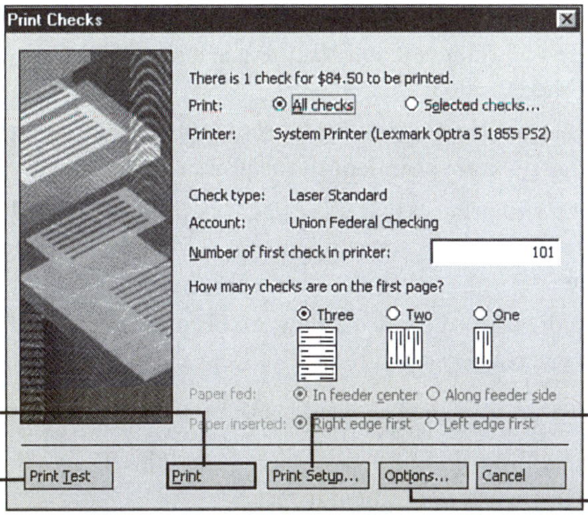

Figure 22.11
Use this dialog box to specify how you want the checks to print.

3. Choose the appropriate options in the dialog box. The options include
   - **Print**—Your choices are All Checks or Selected Checks. If you choose the latter, a box opens, prompting you to choose which checks you want among those with the check number set to Print that have not yet been printed.
   - **Number of First Check in Printer**—Enter the check number on the first check to be printed. Money automatically keeps track of the number of any others in the batch.
   - **How Many Checks Are on the First Page?**—A full sheet of checks contains three checks. If you have already used one or two of the checks, enter the number of checks remaining. Otherwise, leave it set at Three.
   - **Paper Fed**—Indicate how you will feed in the checks (applicable only if you're not using a full sheet).
   - **Paper Inserted**—Indicate which direction you are feeding in the checks. (If you are using less than a full sheet, you feed it in sideways, either left or right edge first.)
   - **Options**—To change any of the other information in the dialog box, such as the printer being used, click the Options button to open the Print Options dialog box.

Tip #133 from *Faithe Wempen*

Many print options are available–too many to list here. You might want to click the Options button to check them out, just so you'll know what's there. For example, you can set Money to prompt when a check is post-dated, and you can set an offset in inches that the printing should be moved over (in case your printer consistently misaligns the printing on checks).

   - **Print Setup**—Click here to reopen the Print Setup dialog box if you need to change the chosen printer.
   - **Print Test**—Click here if you want to run a check-printing test and don't mind wasting a check to do it.
4. Click the Print button to print the checks. A dialog box appears immediately, letting you know the check(s) have been sent to the printer.
5. Wait for the checks to print so that you can check them. Some additional controls appear (notably a Finish and a Reprint button), but don't click either one until the checks have printed.
6. After examining the printed checks, if they are okay, click Finish. If they aren't okay, make any adjustments needed and then click Reprint.

If you don't discover a printing problem until after you've clicked Finish, return to the register, open the Number drop-down list, and select Print This Transaction again. Then reprint the check as if you had not printed it yet.

FINDING A TRANSACTION

As you add more transactions to a register, it becomes increasingly difficult to find a particular one that you might need to check on. Did you pay $500 to the I.R.S. last month, or was it $650? How much was your electric bill at this time last year? You can find answers like these by finding the transaction and looking it up.

To find a transaction, you specify criteria based on all the information you know about that transaction. For example, if you know the payee and the date, you find the transaction based on that information. If you know only the amount, you can find all transactions with that amount. You can find transactions based on any field. Enter all the information you know—searches based on multiple fields provide narrower results.

To find a transaction:

1. Choose Tools, Find and Replace or press Ctrl+F. This opens the Find and Replace dialog box shown in Figure 22.12.

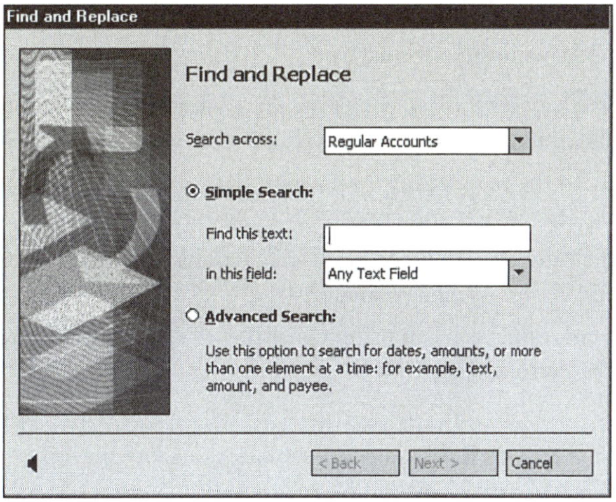

Figure 22.12
Use the Find and Replace dialog box to conduct a simple search of your transaction records.

2. Use the Search Across drop-down list to select the type of accounts you want to search.
3. Click the Simple Search option to perform a simple search for a transaction payee, category, amount, or so on. Click inside the Find This Text box and enter the data you want to locate. Use the In This Field drop-down list to select which field to search (select the Any Text Field option to search every field).
4. Click the Next button. The search results appear in another dialog box, shown in Figure 22.13.

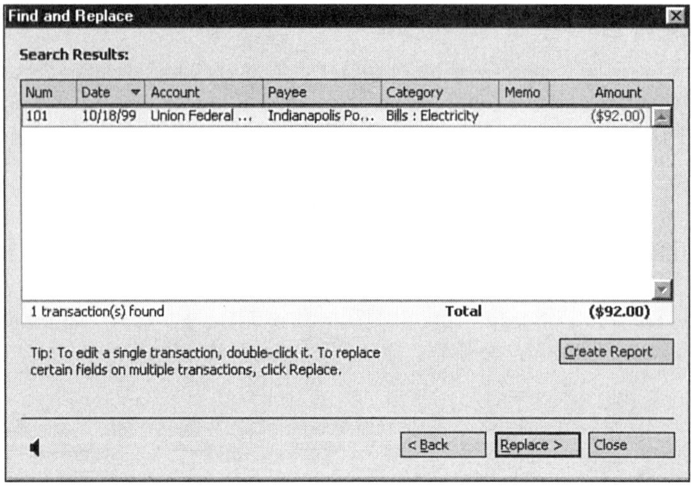

Figure 22.13
The results of the search show the date, the account, the category, and the amount of each transaction that meets the search criteria.

After finding a transaction or a group of transactions that meet your search criteria, you can do a variety of things with the information:

- To edit or take a closer look at one particular transaction, double-click it. This opens an Edit Transaction dialog box where you can make changes to each field as needed.
- To go quickly to the register for the account that a particular transaction is in, right-click the transaction and choose Go to Account.
- To change the category of one or more transactions on the list, select them and then right-click and choose Change Category.
- To create a report that you can print, consisting of the found transactions, click the Create Report button.
- To perform another search, click the Back button and enter new search criteria.
- If you are finished with the Find window, click the Close button.

To replace the transaction fields with different data, click the Replace button in the Find and Replace dialog box to reveal options for replacing data, as shown in Figure 22.14.

Select the transaction from the list box (click the check box to the left) you want to change. Click the Replace drop-down list and select the field containing the data you want to replace; then enter the new data into the With text box. Make sure that the Replace Only the Transactions I Checked Below option is selected; then click Next. Money asks you to confirm the replacement; click Finish.

In addition to performing a simple search, you can also perform an advanced search with Money's Find and Replace feature. Select the Advanced Search option in the Find and Replace dialog box (refer to Figure 22.12); then click Next to open the search criteria box, shown in Figure 22.15. Use the various tabs in this box to enter specific search criteria; then click Next, and Money finds any transactions matching your criteria.

Figure 22.14
Select the field to replace; then enter the new data for the field.

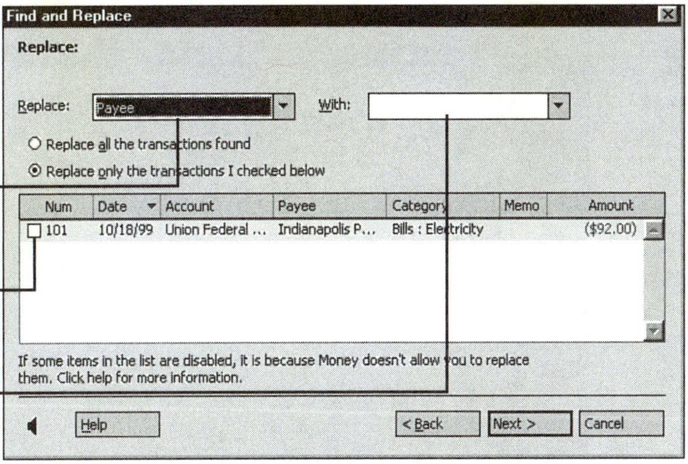

Select a field.

Select the transaction to replace.

Enter the replacement data.

Figure 22.15
You can also conduct a search by setting specific search criteria using the tabs in this dialog box.

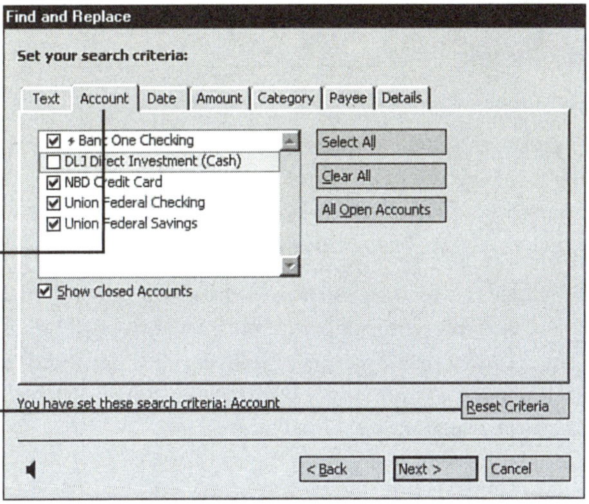

Click a tab to see the criteria on it.

Click here to clear all criteria.

➔ To learn more about reports, **see** "Viewing Reports and Charts," **p. 488**.

EDITING A TRANSACTION

To edit a transaction, go to the register where it is entered and double-click it. The transaction reappears in the Forms area below the register, as shown in Figure 22.16.

Tip #134 from
Faithe Wempen

You can also single-click the transaction and then click its Edit button to open it for editing, just as if you had double-clicked it.

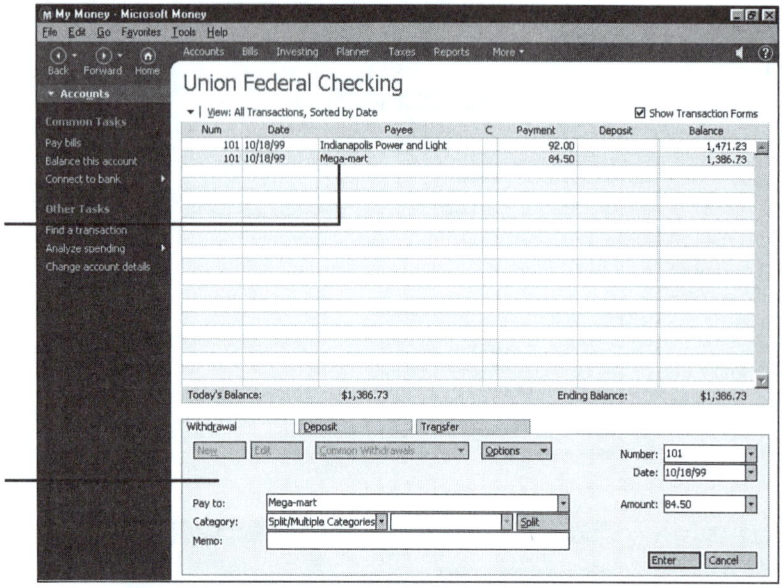

Figure 22.16
You can easily edit transactions you've previously recorded.

Click in the field you want to edit and make your changes directly in the text box or use the drop-down arrow to change the field. When you are finished making changes, click the Enter button or press Enter. (Exception: if you have set up the Enter key to move between fields, you must click the Enter button to complete the transaction.)

You can change all details about a transaction in the previously described way, except for its type. To edit the transaction's type, select the transaction from the transaction list; then choose Edit, Change Transaction Type To and select the appropriate type from the submenu: Deposit, Transfer, or Withdrawal. (Transfer may not always be available on this menu; it depends on the transaction.)

Voiding or Deleting a Transaction

You can get rid of a transaction in two ways, and each method is good for certain circumstances. Unfortunately, most people don't understand the difference between the two.

Note

I try to stay away from the word "cancel" to mean deleting or voiding a transaction, because cancel is often used in the financial world to refer to a check that has cleared the bank. A "canceled check" is not really canceled at all; it is cleared. *Deleting* and *voiding* refer to methods of negating the effect of the transaction.

Deleting is for transactions that were a mistake from the first—such as data entry errors. If you enter a transaction into the wrong account, for example, and you didn't want to move it to the correct account right away, you could delete that transaction and then reenter it later in the correct account. Or suppose that you entered a few bogus transactions just to practice, but they don't have any correlation to any real transactions you've ever made. Delete those, and you'll never see any trace of them again.

Voiding is kind of like taking a big rubber stamp and red inkpad and stamping VOID (or UNDO or WRONG) on a contract or bill. With voiding, the transaction stays in your register so that you can be reminded that it exists, but its income or expense isn't reflected in your account balance, and the transaction won't affect any of your reports or charts. You might void a paper check that you started to write and then made a mistake and tore up. That way, if you ever wonder what happened to that check number, you can look at your register and see that the check is void (rather than stolen).

Deleting a Transaction

To delete a transaction, just select it from the register list and press the Delete key on the keyboard. When asked if you want to delete the transaction, click Yes. It's gone immediately.

If you delete a transaction that has been reconciled (or voided), you'll get a warning message telling you this. Click OK to delete the transaction anyway. Be careful, however; deleting a reconciled transaction could mean an error in your account balance. (If your account balance matched your bank statement balance, and you delete a reconciled transaction, it will no longer match.)

Tip #135 from *Faithe Wempen*

You can also delete a transaction from the transaction form at the bottom of the transaction list. To do so, click the Options button and select Delete from its menu. You can also choose Edit, Delete from the menu bar.

Voiding a Transaction

To void a transaction, select it in the register and then choose Edit, Mark As, Void; or on the transaction form, click the Options button and choose Mark As, Void. VOID appears in the Balance column, as shown in Figure 22.17, letting you know that this transaction doesn't affect the balance.

The nice thing about voiding is that, unlike deleting, it's reversible. Just repeat the procedure to unvoid the transaction. Void is a toggle that turns on or off each time you select it.

Figure 22.17
A voided transaction is marked as such in the transaction record and on the transaction form.

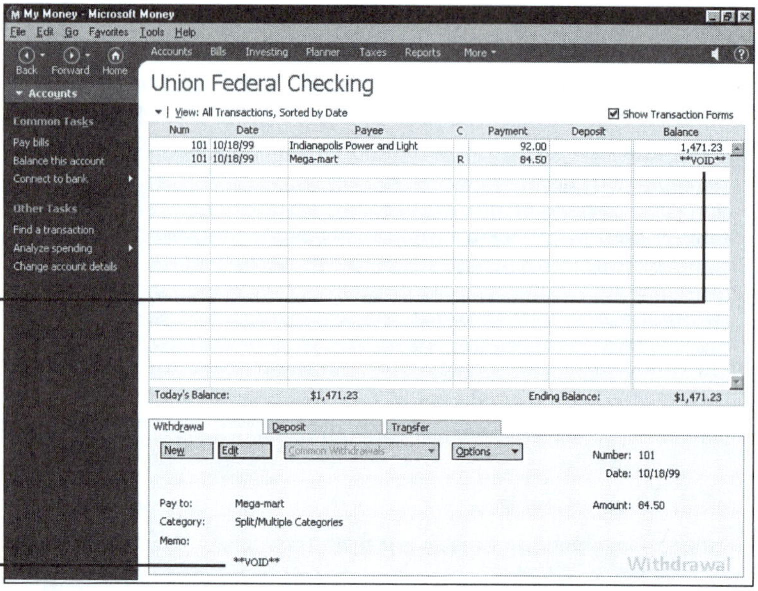

Voided transaction

The form is also marked void.

CONTROLLING HOW TRANSACTIONS ARE DISPLAYED

Each register has a View menu with commands that control how transaction records appear. To open the View menu, just click the View drop-down arrow at the top of the register window, as shown in Figure 22.18.

Figure 22.18
Use the View menu to control the register display.

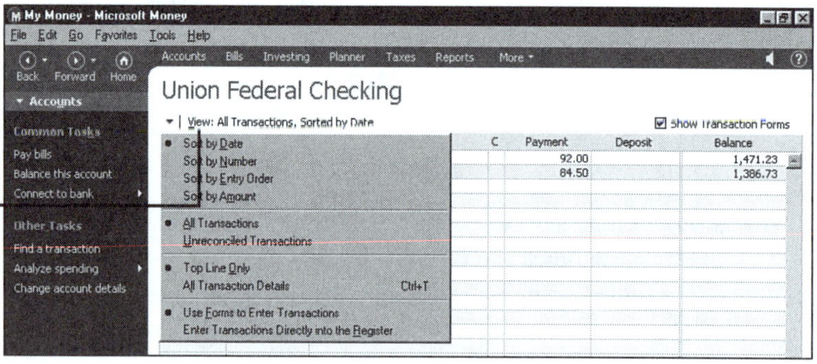

Click here to open the View menu.

The View menu is divided into several sections, each with its own set of mutually exclusive options. (It's just like option buttons in a dialog box.) Here's what you're looking at:

- **Sort By (Sort Order)**—The options in the first group control the order in which the transactions appear in the register. You choose between Sort by Date (the entry in the Date field), Sort by Number (the entry in the Number field), Sort by Entry Order (the actual order in which you inputted them), or Sort by Amount.

- **Which Transactions**—The second group of options controls whether some transactions will be hidden. You choose between All Transactions and Unreconciled Transactions (which are the ones that have not yet been balanced with your bank statement).
- **Transaction Detail**—The options in the third group control how much detail you see about each transaction in the register. By default, you see Top Line Only, which makes for a nice, compact register. (If you want to see the details of a transaction, just select it, bringing its details into the Forms area.) Your other choice is All Transaction Details, which expands the register to show all detail lines (see Figure 22.19). This is useful primarily if you turn off the transaction forms (see next bulleted item).
- **Transaction Forms**—If you want to see more lines of the register onscreen, select Enter Transactions Directly into the Register. You won't be able to use the forms to enter new transactions; however, you'll have to enter data directly into the register, which is somewhat more awkward. To turn the forms back on, select Use Forms to Enter Transactions.

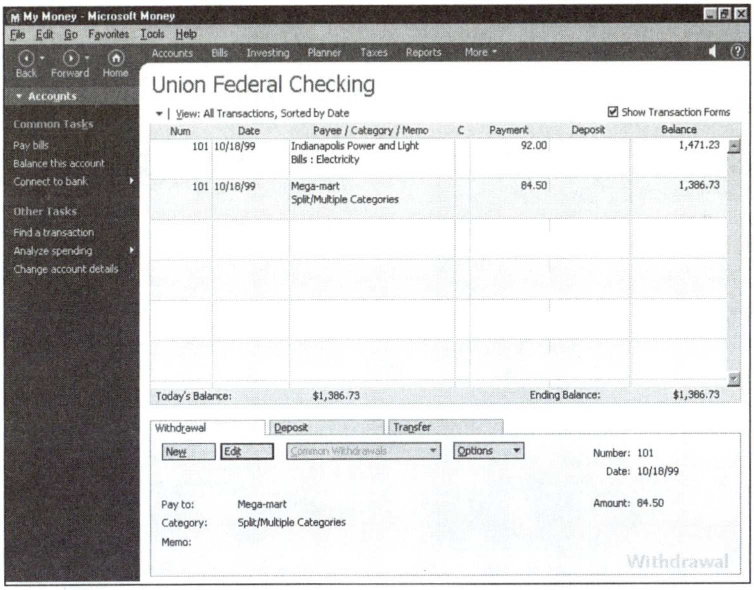

Figure 22.19
Transaction detail is set to All Transaction Details.

BALANCING AN ACCOUNT

I used to dread getting a bank statement in the mail because it meant an hour or more of frustration. I would find all the math errors I had made over the previous month. The bank statement would get littered with scribbles and check marks as I tried over and over to compare my poor, sloppy records with the bank's printout. With Money, however, balancing is considerably easier and takes only a few minutes.

Note

Money uses the term *balance*, but you may have heard the process called *reconciling*. It's the same thing. You compare your bank statement to your own records and identify and correct errors.

To balance an account:

1. Display the register for the account you want to balance.
2. Click the Balance This Account link on the Activities bar. A dialog box appears, explaining why you balance an account. Click Next to move on.
3. Next, you get to fill in some numbers, as shown in Figure 22.20. Enter the following data in the appropriate fields:
   - **Statement Date**—Enter the date from your bank statement.
   - **Starting Balance**—Don't change this; it's the ending balance from the last statement (or your opening balance you entered, if this is your first time). If your starting balance is wrong on your bank statement, call your bank.
   - **Ending Balance**—Fill this in with the ending balance from the bank statement.
   - **Service Charge**—Scan your statement quickly; if you were charged any service charges, enter them. You can categorize them if you want.

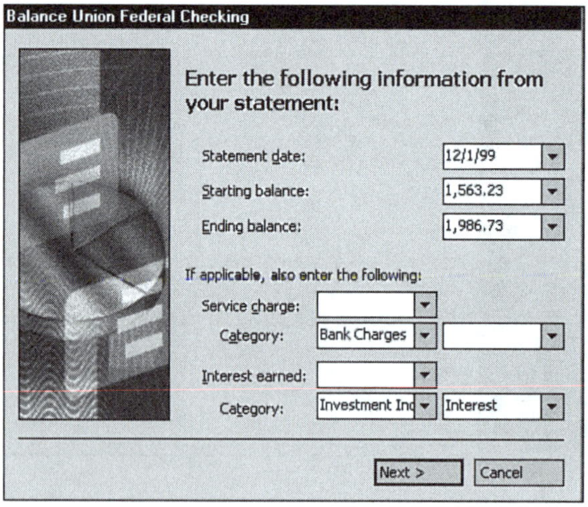

Figure 22.20
Enter all the pertinent details from the statement into this dialog box.

Caution

If you were charged fifty cents or a dollar each time you made an ATM withdrawal, these charges may not be neatly summarized in one spot on your statement. You may have to search for them, add them up in your head, and then enter that total in the Service Charge field.

- **Interest Earned**—If your statement shows that you accrued any interest, enter it. You can categorize it, too, if you want. Although you can enter the interest as a separate transaction and then mark it as cleared, it's much more efficient to just enter it here in the dialog box instead.

Note

If you need to stop reconciling your account—perhaps to tend to another task—click the Postpone button in the Activities bar. You can return to the reconciliation process again later and pick up where you left off. Any items you marked as cleared will stay that way.

4. When you've entered all the requested information, click Next to move on to the next step: clearing individual transactions.
5. Compare your bank statement with the list of unreconciled transactions onscreen (see Figure 22.21) and click in the C column to place a C next to each one that matches up.

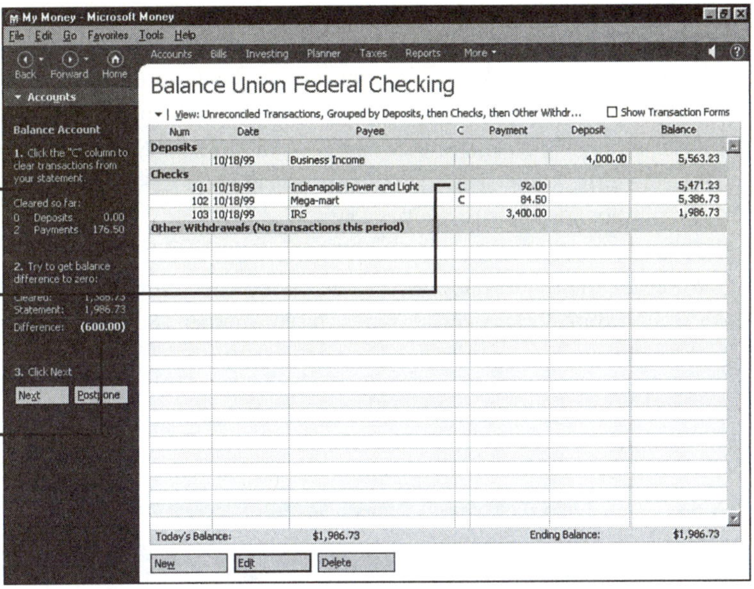

Figure 22.21
Click to place a C, meaning "cleared," in the C column.

Directions for balancing the account

Click here to mark the item as cleared.

Check the difference here.

6. When all the transactions on the bank statement have been accounted for, look in the Activities bar for the Difference line. It should read 0.00. If it does, congratulations! You balance! Click Next. (If you don't have 0.00, see the information that follows these steps.)

Tip #136 from *Faithe Wempen*

You can edit or add transactions as you balance. Just double-click a blank line on the register to open a new transaction form, or double-click an existing transaction to edit it.

7. A congratulatory box appears; click Finish. You're done. The transactions you marked with C have now changed to R, indicating they are fully reconciled.

If you can't seem to make it balance, look into these factors for causes:

- Does the ending balance you entered match the one on your bank statement? Check the number next to Statement on the balancing screen. If it's not the same as your statement's ending balance, click Postpone; then click the Balance button again to return to balancing, but enter the correct ending balance this time.
- Does the starting balance match that of your bank statement? In general, you shouldn't change the entry in the Starting Balance field. It comes from the ending balance of last month's bank statement or from your starting balance for the account if this is the first month. If a discrepancy exists, it may be a bank error, but if you're sure it's your own error, go ahead and change it.
- Did you enter all the transactions? Every transaction on your bank statement must match a transaction in Money. You might need to add transactions that don't appear in Money but should. Note that the reverse is not true, however; you might have transactions that appear in Money but not on your bank statement. That just means that those transactions have not yet been sent to your bank from the payee.
- Did you remember the service charges and interest? Not all banks statements label these clearly. Look closely at your bank statement to see whether these small additions or subtractions apply to your account.
- How about ATM withdrawals? ATM transactions are handy, but it's also easy to forget to record them in Money because there's no check stub to help remind you. Go through your pockets and/or purse to see whether you can find any unrecorded ATM receipts.

If you still can't find the problem, click the Next button anyway. Money presents several solution options, as shown in Figure 22.22.

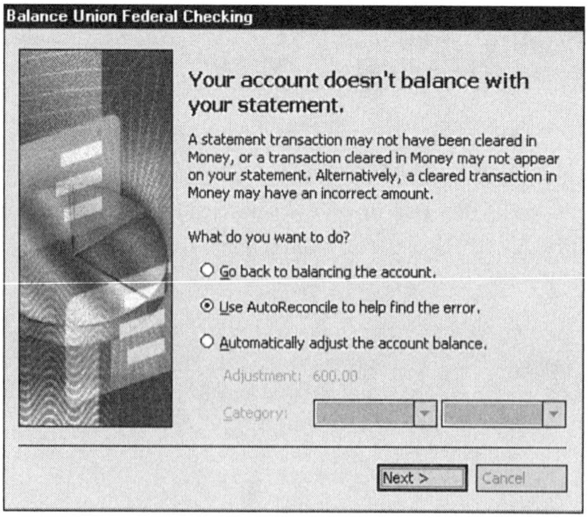

Figure 22.22
Money can sometimes help you identify the error causing the imbalance.

Your first line of defense should be to let Money's AutoReconcile feature try to find the problem. AutoReconcile looks for likely transactions that you might have marked incorrectly and reports them to you. Click the middle option button, as shown in Figure 22.22, to try it out.

What happens next depends on what AutoReconcile finds. If it can't find any obvious errors, it lets you know. However, if it finds a problem, it reports it in a dialog box. Figure 22.23, shows how I forgot to clear a transaction. Because it was for exactly the amount that my balance was off, AutoReconcile noticed it. To correct the problem, I can just click Yes. If AutoReconcile was mistaken, I could click No to tell it to keep looking or click Cancel to give up.

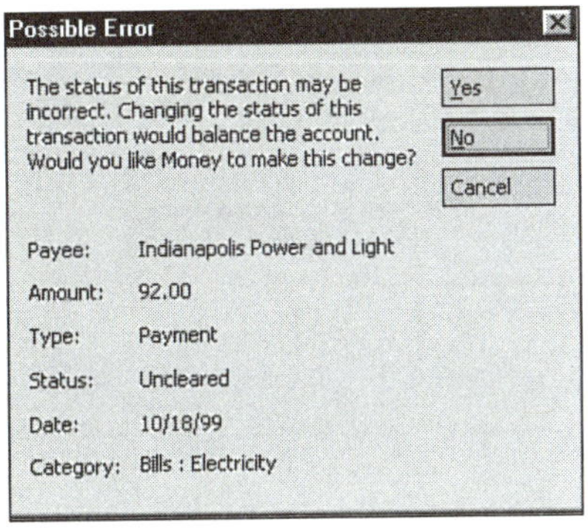

Figure 22.23 AutoReconcile alerts you to a possible problem.

If AutoReconcile is no help, you can adjust the balance using the controls shown previously in Figure 22.22. Click the Automatically Adjust the Account Balance option button. (You can categorize the adjustment if you want. If you don't, you'll be asked whether you want to.) Then click Finish. Congratulations, you're done.

CHANGING ACCOUNT DETAILS

Account details are little facts about the account that you don't need every day but that come in handy occasionally. They include the original starting balance for the account, the bank's name and address, and so on.

To view (and change) the account details, open the register you want to use. Then click the Change Account Details link in the Activities bar to see the details. Figure 22.24 shows the details for a checking account. You can change any of the information in any of the editable fields.

When you've finished, scroll down to the bottom of the page and click the Done button (which is not shown in Figure 22.24) to return to the register.

Figure 22.24
You can enter or change details about an account at any time.

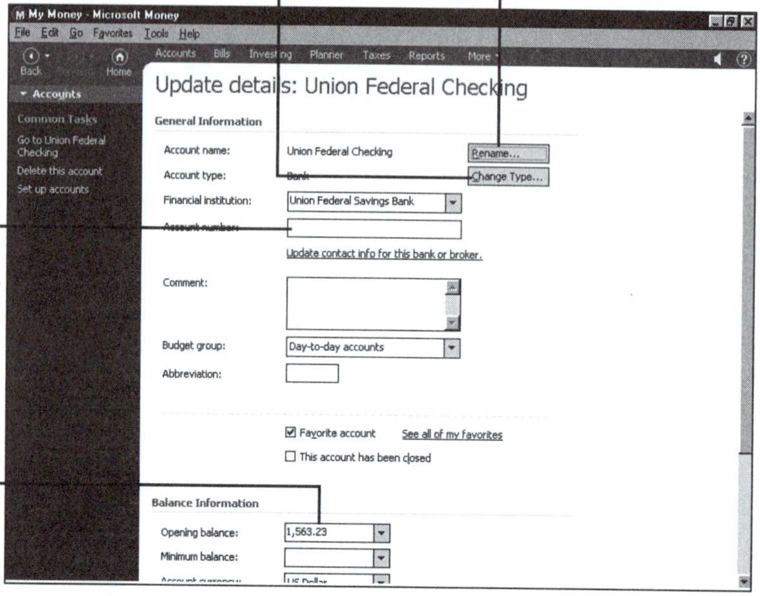

MANAGING PAYEES

Just as you can manage categories, you can also manage your list of payees. This isn't essential—you can get by just entering payees on an as-you-go basis. By working directly with the Payees list, however, you can enter extra information for each payee. Here are some perks:

- You can enter the payee's address so that it automatically prints on any checks that you print. This is great if you have to address an envelope for the payment, because the address is right there.
- You can record the payee's phone number so that it's handy in case you have a question. Also, in the case of credit card companies, if you ever lose the card, the phone number that you would call to cancel the card is right there.
- You can have Money remember your account number, if you have one, for that payee. This can be valuable for your own records and also for printing on the check. (Some companies ask you to write your account number on each check.)
- By entering payees up front, you ensure that you don't have several variations of the same payee on your list. Because you can create some reports by payee, it's important that all payments to the same payee be recorded as such. You won't have separate entries for Amoco, Amoco Oil, and Amoco Credit Card, for example, when they all refer to the same bill that you pay every month.

ENTERING A NEW PAYEE

Every time you write a check, you are entering a payee. That's one way to enter one. Another, more formal, way lets you enter payees that you have not written any checks to yet, for future use. That way, you can enter names and addresses for all the payees you pay frequently so that you don't have to go back later and enter their contact information individually.

To enter information about a payee separately from a transaction:

1. Choose Go, Categories & Payees, or press Ctrl+Shift+C.
2. Click the Payees link (in the Activities bar). A list of current payees appears.
3. Click the New button. A Create New Payee dialog box appears.
4. Type the name for the new payee and then click OK. The new payee is added to the list.

ENTERING OR CHANGING PAYEE DETAILS

The real value of the Payees list comes in entering details for each one. This is where you can record important addresses, phone numbers, and account numbers.

To enter payee details:

1. On the Payees list, double-click the payee you want to see details for, or click it once and then click the Go to Payee button. A details screen appears, as shown in Figure 22.25.

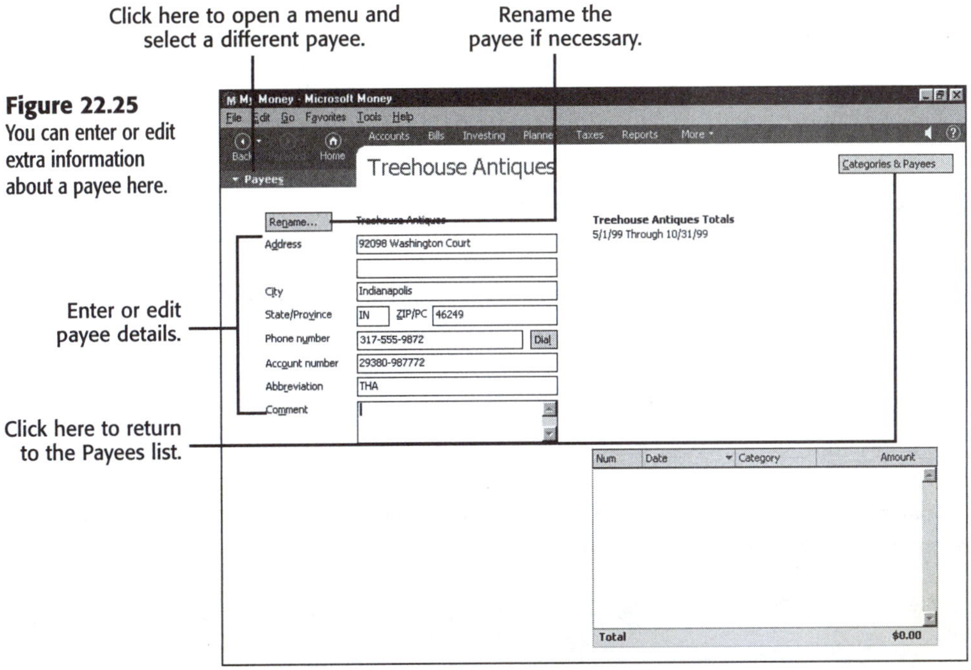

Figure 22.25
You can enter or edit extra information about a payee here.

2. Enter or change any information in any of the editable fields.

Note

In addition to payee details, the screen may show you a chart of your payments to the payee and a list of each payment made (in the bottom-right corner of the screen). You can also double-click any of the payments listed to have a closer look at a payment you have made to that payee. This is a great, informal way to get a report of all payments made to a particular payee without fussing with the Reports section of Money.

3. If you want to rename the payee, click the Rename button to open a box where you can enter a new name. The new name will be applied to all future transactions with this payee, but the payment history under the old name remains associated with it.
4. When you are finished working with this payee's details, do one of the following:
   - To work with a different payee, open the Payees drop-down list in the top-left corner of the screen and choose a different payee.
   - To return to the list of payees, click the Categories & Payees button in the top-right corner of the screen.

DELETING A PAYEE

If you find that your list of payees is cluttered with people or organizations that you did business with once but will never deal with again, go ahead and delete them. Deleting a payee does not affect any transactions you have already entered—that payee will still appear for that transaction. (This is *unlike* categories, where deleting a category wipes it out from all existing transactions, too.)

To delete a payee, select it from the Payees list and then click the Delete button (at the bottom of the screen). A message appears, asking whether you really want to delete it. Click Yes, and it's outta there.

TRACKING BILLS TO BE PAID

If you have many payments that you make on a regular basis, such as mortgage payments, car payments, or gym dues, you'll appreciate Money's Bill Calendar. If you have already set up a loan in Money (see Chapter 23, "Managing Your Investments"), you had the opportunity to create a scheduled payment at the end of that setup process. If you did so, you already have a scheduled payment.

Like a wake-up call in a hotel, a scheduled payment helps you meet your obligation. It reminds you 10 days in advance of the due date and even prints the check for you or makes the payment via modem. Believe me, it's much better than tacking up a Post-It note reminder on your refrigerator and hoping it doesn't fall off.

Tip #137 from *Faithe Wempen*

The 10-day warning is just a default. You're free to change it to be notified earlier or later, or not at all. Just choose Tools, Options, and click the Bills tab. In the Bill Reminder section, change 10 to some other number, and click OK.

To open Money's Bills & Deposits feature, click the Bills link on the Navigation bar, or choose Go, Bills & Deposits.

Scheduling Bills with Bill Calendar

All scheduled transactions are created and modified in the Bill Calendar. To see it, click the Go to Calendar link in the Activities bar. Figure 22.26 shows a sample Bill Calendar. Notice that it already has some payments set up. When you are done looking at it, click the Return to Paying Bills link.

Figure 22.26 Use Money's Bill Calendar to schedule regular payments.

Click here to schedule a new bill or deposit.

Click here to return to paying bills.

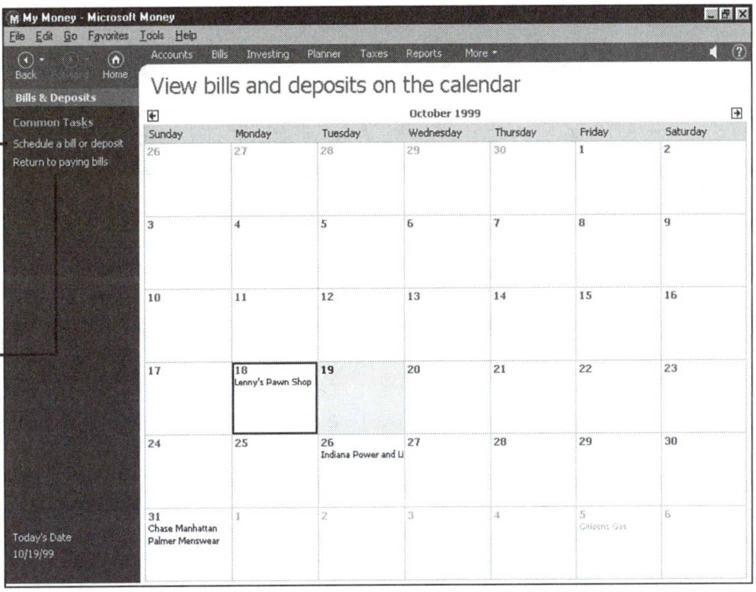

A scheduled transaction on the Bill Calendar need not be a check; it can be an automatic withdrawal from an account (for example, your gym membership) or a deposit (for example, the automatic Direct Deposit of your paycheck).

To create a new bill or deposit:

1. Click the Bills link on the Navigation bar, and then click the Set Up Bills and Deposits link on the Activities bar.
2. Click the New button. The Create New Scheduled Transaction dialog box opens (see Figure 22.27).

Tip #138 from *Faithe Wempen*

If you are in the Bill Calendar (refer to Figure 22.26), you can click the Schedule a Bill or Deposit link instead of performing steps 1 and 2.

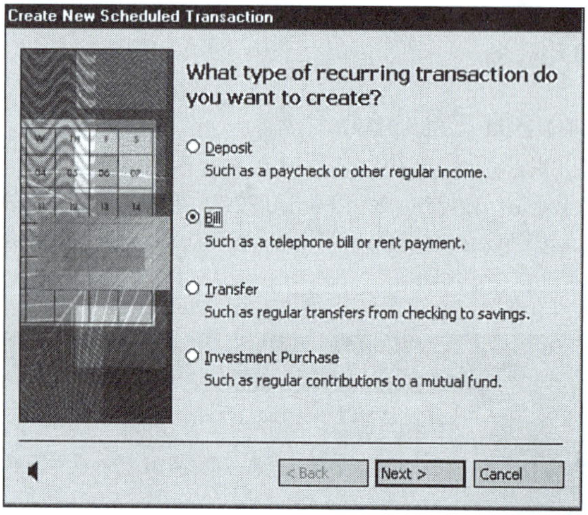

Figure 22.27
Begin by specifying the type of transaction.

3. Choose the option button for the type of transaction: Deposit, Bill, Transfer, or Investment Purchase. Then click Next.
4. In the next dialog box, shown in Figure 22.28, indicate the frequency of the transaction; then click Next to continue.

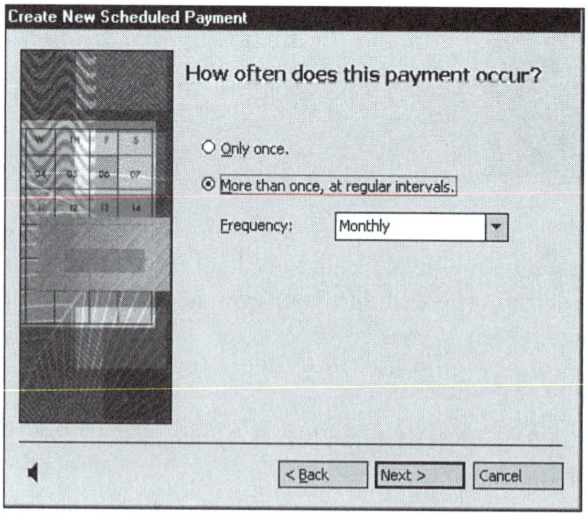

Figure 22.28
Using the options in this dialog box, tell Money how often the transaction occurs.

5. From the Payment Method drop-down list, choose how you will make the payment. Your choices are Write Check, Direct Debit, Other, or Print This Transaction. Then click Next.
6. Next, you are asked whether the bill is usually the same amount each time. Choose Yes or No. If you choose Yes, enter an estimated amount. Then click Next.
7. A dialog box appears in which you can enter or edit the transaction. Its fields and options depend on what transaction type you chose in step 3—for example, for a scheduled payment, it's called Create New Scheduled Payment dialog box (see Figure 22.29). Fill in the fields to describe the recurring transaction:
   - **Account**—Choose which account should pay or receive the payment.
   - **Pay To** (or from)—Choose the payee (or the person or company from whom a deposit is coming).
   - **Number, Date, Amount, Category**, and **Memo**—Use these fields as you would with any other transaction. For fields where the value will vary each time, such as Date, enter the appropriate value for the first time, and Money increments the others as appropriate.

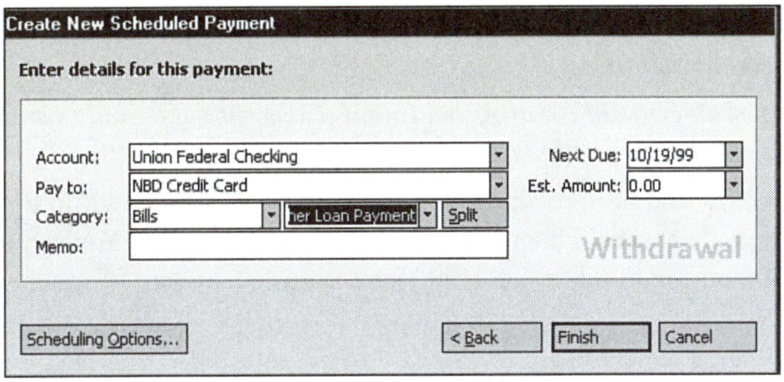

Figure 22.29
Enter information about the recurring payment or deposit.

8. Click Finish. Your payment is set up and ready to go.

To edit a recurring transaction, just double-click it on the list, or click it once and then click Edit Details.

To delete a recurring transaction, click it and click Delete. A dialog box appears, asking whether you want to delete one instance or all instances. Click the appropriate button.

TROUBLESHOOTING

DUPLICATE PAYEES

I have entered the same payee more than once with slightly different wording; how do I combine them into one entry?

If you don't enter a payee's name the same way each time (for example, IRS versus I.R.S.), you may end up with duplicate payees on the Payees list. You can delete the duplicates from the Set Up Your Payees screen without disturbing transactions that used it. You won't be able to view a list of transactions using that payee anymore, though.

CLASSIFICATION USAGE

I need to categorize transactions in more than one way. For example, sometimes I buy groceries for personal use and sometimes for charity; the purchases I make for charity need to be separated somehow for tax purposes, but I don't necessarily want to create two Groceries categories.

If using Categories isn't cutting it for you and you need more precise labeling, try using *Classifications*. Set them up on the Categories & Payees page. They let you categorize transactions at a higher, additional level, such as Family, Business, Job Expense, and so on.

PAUSING BILL PAYMENT

I am going on an extended vacation, and I want to skip some of the bill payments for services I won't use while I'm gone. How do I put them on "pause" without deleting them?

If you find that you need to skip one of the bill payments you set up for a few months, you don't have to delete the bill entirely from your Pay Bills page. You can use the Skip Transaction button to put it "on hold" for a specified amount of time.

CHAPTER 23

Managing Your Investments

In this chapter

A QUICK LOOK AT THE INVESTING GAME

Two kinds of investments exist—those that carry a risk and those that tie up your money for a certain period of time. Investments in the first category might or might not pay off; as with gambling, the higher the risk, the larger the potential prize. If you buy the stock of a company that's doing poorly, you can get a great deal, but there's a bigger chance that the stock's value will drop even further than that of a company that is doing well. *Certificates of Deposit*, or CDs, are examples of the latter category of investments. You buy a CD at a certain interest rate for a certain period of time. At the end of that time, you get your money back, plus the amount of interest that you agreed on. (*Money Market funds* and *bonds* are other variations on this theme.) These investments don't risk your principal (your original money you put in).

You'll do your investing through your bank or investment broker, so why would you want to enter the information into Money? There are a couple of reasons. Your investments are part of your larger financial picture, and you can't really understand how much you're worth unless you take them into consideration. Another reason is convenience. If you buy stock, for example, and write a check for it, you can enter a single transaction in Money to show that the cash was moved from one account (your checking) to another (your brokerage account).

Money recognizes two types of investment accounts: retirement and investment. In actuality, a retirement account is a type of investment account, but in this case, "investment account" means a nonretirement account. Retirement accounts usually have some tax benefit associated with them. You might have, for example, a *401(k)*, an *IRA*, a *Keogh*, or an *SEP-IRA*. These retirement accounts can consist of any of the investments that a regular investment account can contain.

Money considers any *nonretirement* account that either ties up your money for a certain time or has a certain amount of risk to be an investment. Such investments can include *bonds*, *CDs*, *Money Market funds*, *mutual funds*, *stocks*, *treasury bills*, *treasury notes*, and *treasury bonds*.

→ To learn how to put together net worth reports, **see** "Viewing Reports and Charts," **p. 488**.

PREPARING YOUR INVESTMENT ACCOUNTS

You'll store your investments in investment accounts; one for each bank or brokerage that you deal with. You might have already created these accounts when you set up Money in Chapter 21, "Setting Up Your Accounts in Money." If not, turn back to Chapter 21 now and create a new investment account.

It's important to remember the distinction between investment accounts and investments. An *investment account* summarizes all your holdings with a particular brokerage or bank. An *investment* is the individual stock or security that you buy or sell. For example, you might have 10 investments that you bought through Fidelity Investments (a brokerage). They would all be contained in a single account in Money.

If you followed along in Chapter 21, you now have at least one investment account. Check out what's there by clicking the Investing link on the Navigation bar. The Manage Your Investments and Savings screen appears. Then click the View My Entire Portfolio link to see the accounts you have set up (see Figure 23.1).

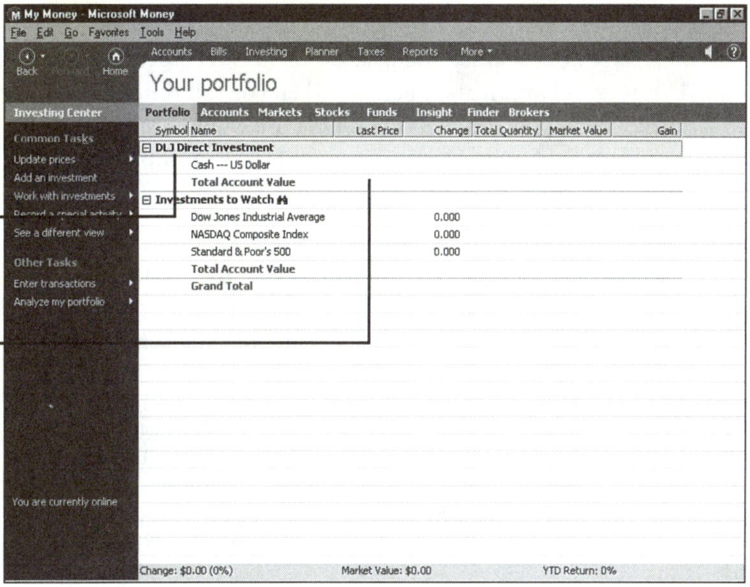

Figure 23.1 Money displays the investment account you set up earlier.

Note

If you need to set up another investment account, you can do so from here; return to the Manage Your Investments and Savings screen by clicking Back and then click the Create a New Investment Account link.

You can work with eight views in the Your Portfolio screen. To switch views, click See a Different View on the Activities bar to open a menu of them. You'll learn more about each view at the end of this chapter.

➔ To set up investment accounts, **see** "Setting Up an Investment Account," **p. 430**.

Stock options work a little differently than regular investments because you don't actually own the stock; you just have the option to buy it. If you need to enter a stock option, enter it as a new investment (as explained in the following section), and when asked what type it is, choose Employee Stock Option grant. This starts a wizard that walks you through the process of setting it up.

401(k) accounts are also a little different to set up. To set one up, click the Investing link on the Navigation bar and then click the Create a 401(k) Account link.

Entering Your Current Holdings

You can enter the holdings in your portfolio in one of two ways. You can start with a zero balance in your account and then enter Buy transactions to create the portfolio value, or you can enter your holdings with an Add Shares transaction. What's the difference?

When you enter a Buy, you are making a recording of the actual transaction that acquired the shares for you. The price you paid for them is recorded, along with any commission you paid. This is useful information because when you sell the investment, you will have to pay taxes on the *capital gain*, which is the selling price minus the buying price and commissions. If it's important for Money to calculate your taxable profits, you should build your portfolio this way.

In contrast, when you Add Shares, you are recording the fact that you own certain investments, but you are not recording how much you paid for them or on what date you acquired them. This is a much simpler way to enter your existing holdings into Money, but it does not provide the profit data and can't help you prepare tax reports.

Note

The step-by-step activities in this chapter focus mainly on stocks and mutual funds because these are the most common kinds of investments. But the procedures also work equally well for other investments, such as CDs and bonds. The only difference is that when you enter a fixed-value investment such as a CD, Money asks only for a total dollar amount invested, not a price per share nor the number of shares.

Entering Past Buys

When you created your investment account, you may have entered an estimated value for it that included all your current holdings. If you decide to build up your portfolio by entering all your past buys, you need to start with a zeroed-out account balance for the account.

To zero out an investment account balance so that you can enter past buys:

1. From the Your Portfolio screen (refer to Figure 23.1), click the name of the investment account. The register for that account opens.
2. Click Change Account Details in the Activities bar to see the details for the account.
3. Change the Estimated Value number to `0.00` (see Figure 23.2).
4. Click the Back link on the Navigation bar to return to Holdings view.

If the investment account has an associated cash account, you might want to increase its opening balance so that the money to "pay for" the investments that you'll soon be recording can come from somewhere. To do this, repeat the preceding steps, choosing the cash account in step 1 and changing the Opening Balance of that account.

To enter an investment, start from the register for the investment account. (You can get there by clicking the account name on the Your Portfolio screen or from the Accounts screen.) Then enter the transaction the same way that you would enter any other transaction in any account. There are minor differences in the fields, and you might be asked for more information about the particular stock or security you are buying, but it's really similar to what you've been doing with your regular accounts.

Figure 23.2
If you want to enter all your stocks from scratch, zero out the value of your investment account.

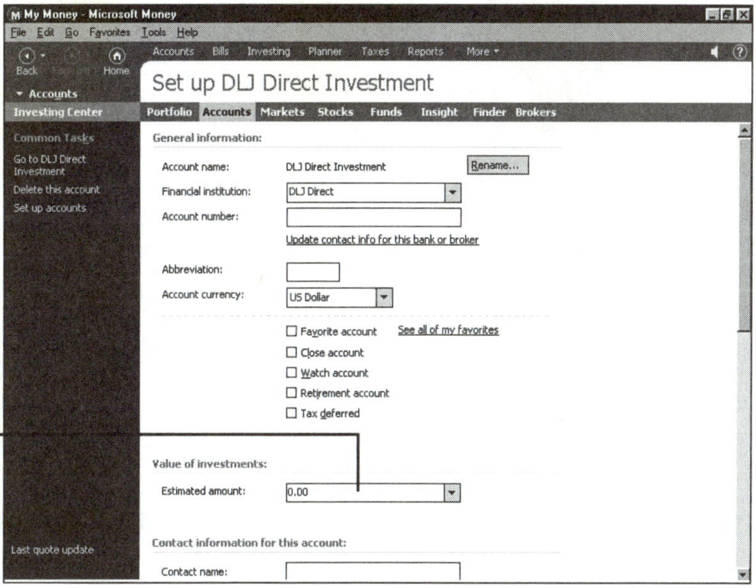

Enter a zero value here.

To enter a stock-buying transaction:

1. Display the account register for the investment account in which you want to enter the investment.
2. Click the New button. Fields appear so that you can enter the new investment, as shown in Figure 23.3.
3. In the Date field, enter the date when the transaction occurred. If you are entering stocks that you have already bought, make sure that you date the transaction accurately. (It will make a difference on your tax reports.)
4. In the Investment text box, carefully type the name of the stock or other investment.
5. Press Tab to move on. If this is the first time you have entered anything for this investment, a Create New Investment dialog box appears, as shown in Figure 23.4. (If not, skip to step 9 to fill in the Activity field.)
6. Click the appropriate button and then click the Next button.
7. Fill in additional details about the investment. The fields vary depending on the investment type; for stocks, for example, you are prompted for the stock symbol.
8. Click the Finish button. The dialog box closes, and the cursor moves to the Activity field.

Figure 23.3
Click the New button and begin filling in the fields.

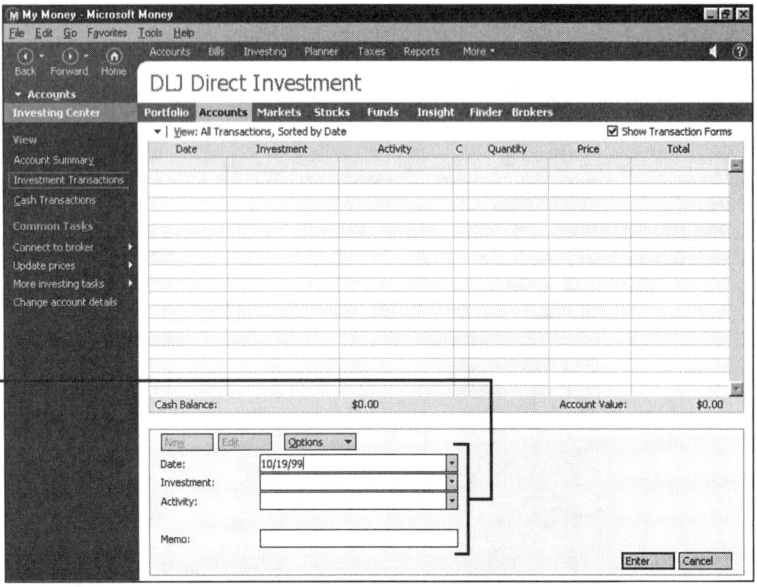

Fill in these fields.

Figure 23.4
Use these option buttons to specify what type of investment it is.

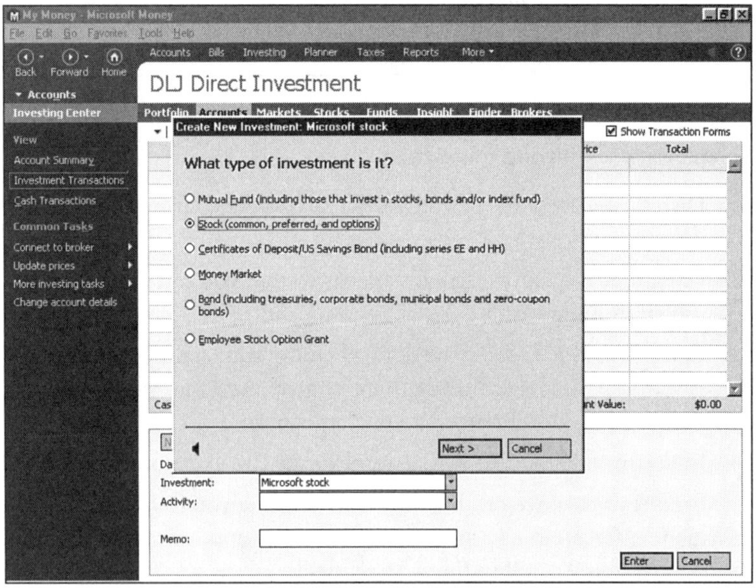

9. Choose Buy from the drop-down list. Additional fields appear on the form, as shown in Figure 23.5.

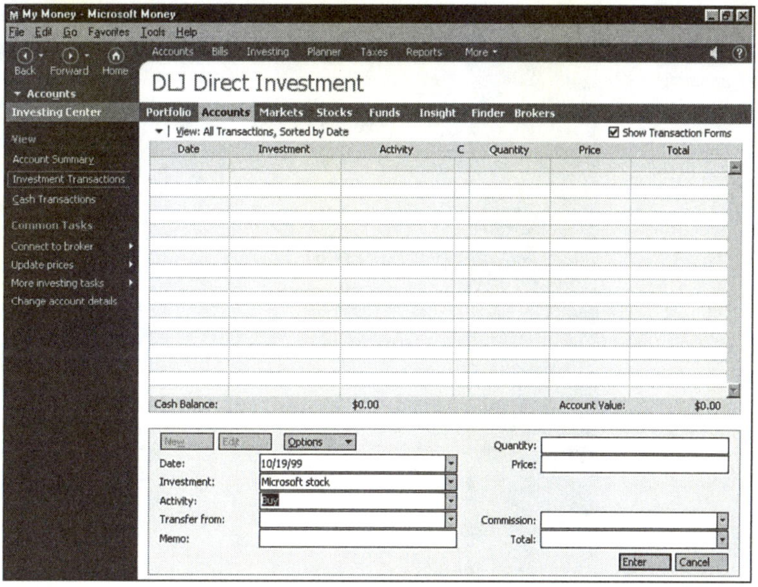

Figure 23.5
When buying a stock, you must enter the quantity bought and the price paid per share, as well as any commission paid.

10. Enter the Quantity, Price (per share), and Commission in the corresponding fields. Money calculates the amount in the Total field automatically.
11. If the money is coming from some other account (such as the associated cash account), select it from the Transfer From drop-down list. If you don't want to indicate where the money is coming from, leave this blank.

Note

If you leave the Transfer From field blank, a dialog box asks whether you want to track cash transactions for this account. If you choose No, Money won't use an associated cash account for this investment account.

12. Click the Enter button, recording the transaction.
13. Repeat these steps until you have entered all your past buys, so that all your current holdings are represented.

When you are finished entering, click the Investing link on the Navigation bar to return to the Your Portfolio screen and view your investment list (see Figure 23.6). This is an easy way to see whether you have missed anything. If you have, go back and add it.

If you have any sales to enter, or dividends or interest received, you can create new transactions for each action, changing the Activity type from Buy to the appropriate activity (Sell, Reinvest Dividends, and so on).

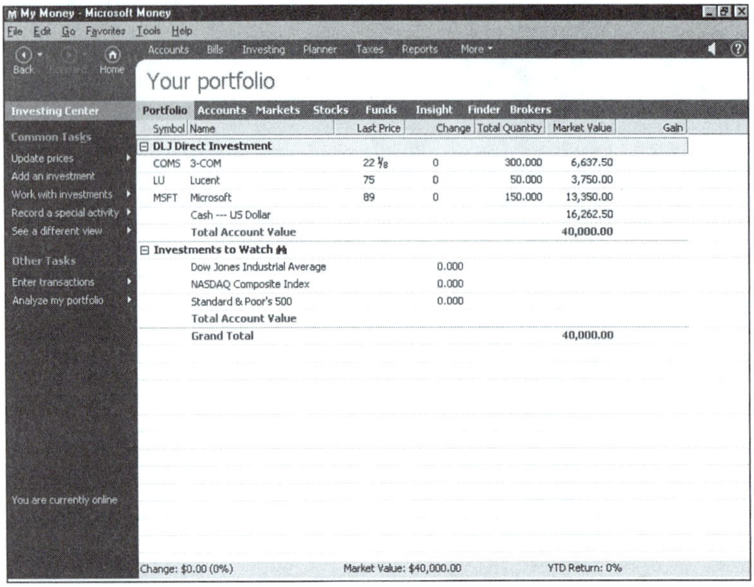

Figure 23.6
A sample investment portfolio containing three stocks.

Adding Shares

When you use the Add Shares activity, Money makes a note that you have a certain quantity of a certain investment. You can use this activity to build up a list of your portfolio holdings without having to know what date you purchased them or what price you paid. This is useful, for example, for a retirement mutual fund because it doesn't matter what you paid for the original shares.

To add shares:

1. Perform steps 1–8 of the previous procedure.
2. Choose Add Shares from the Activity drop-down list.
3. Fill in the remaining fields as needed.

> **Note**
> The Quantity field is required; the Price field is optional. The Total field computes automatically if you enter both quantity and price. You can also compute the Price field by entering the Quantity and the Total.

4. Click the Enter button or press Enter.

You also can use the Remove Shares activity to take shares out of an investment account without entering a Sell transaction. The difference? When you sell, Money takes the current value of the investment and transfers that money over to the associated cash account. When you remove shares, it removes them, and their value disappears from your Money account. You might remove shares from your account that have become worthless, for example, because the company went bankrupt.

UPDATING PRICES

You can update prices manually by entering the most recent prices from your local newspaper's financial section. But if you have an Internet connection, a much easier way to update the prices is to use Online Quotes. Let's look at both ways.

To manually update a price:

1. Start at the your portfolio screen.
2. Click the investment you want to update (on its line, but not directly on its name). The line becomes highlighted.
3. Click Update Prices on the Activities bar, and choose Update Price Manually from the menu that appears. The Update Price dialog box opens (see Figure 23.7).

Figure 23.7
You can manually enter the stock's new price here.

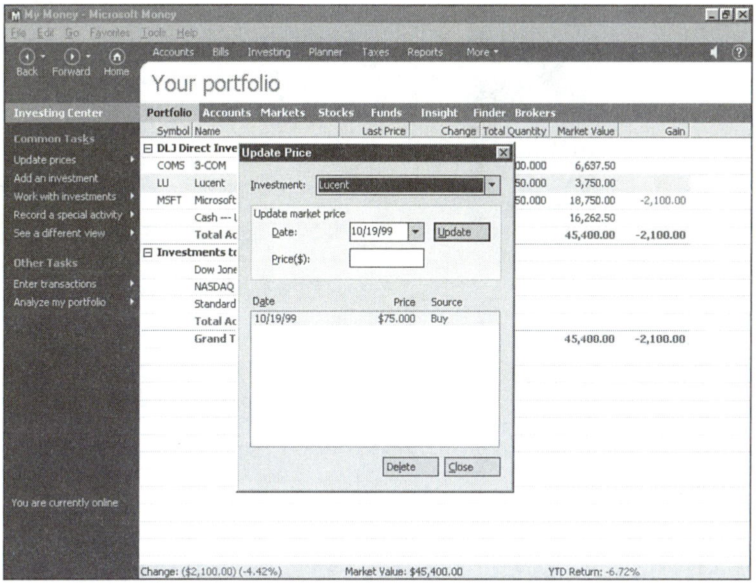

4. Enter the price in the Price($) text box.
5. Click the Update button.
6. If you want to update another stock's price, open the Investment drop-down list and select it. Then return to step 3. Otherwise, click Close.

It is easier to update the prices online, provided you have Internet access. To do so, follow these steps:

1. Establish your Internet connection.
2. Choose Tools, Update Internet Information. A Call Progress dialog box opens, and Money connects to the Internet.

3. Wait for the call to complete. When it is finished, a Call Summary dialog box appears (see Figure 23.8).

Figure 23.8
This call was successful.

This message denotes that your stock prices were updated.

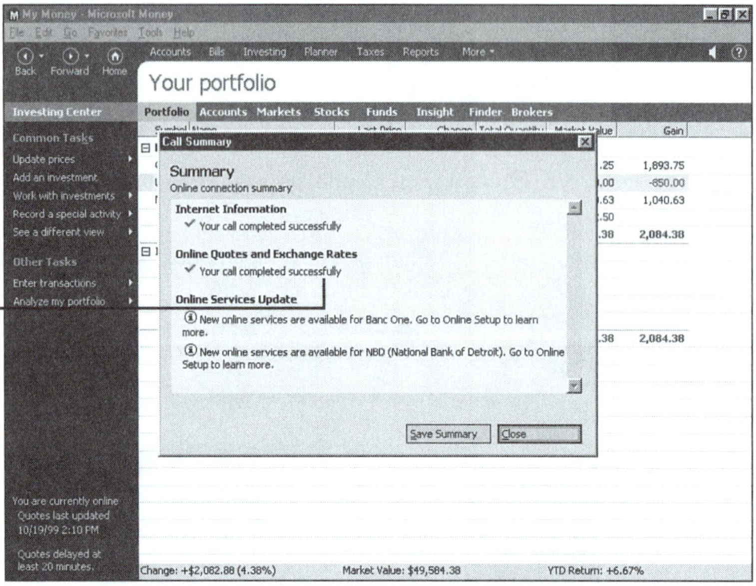

4. Click Close.

Tip #139 from *Faithe Wempen*

Another way to update prices is to click the Update Prices link on the Activities bar in the Your Portfolio window and choose Update Price Online from the menu that appears.

Recording Sales and Other Adjustments

You record investment sales and other transactions in the same way you record the buys. Just choose a different activity from the Activity drop-down list. The activities include Sell, Reinvest Dividend, Reinvest Interest, Short Sell, Cover Shares—almost any type of transaction that you can accomplish through your bank or investment broker. The fields might be slightly different for different transaction types, but they're mostly self-explanatory.

Recording Stock Splits

Sometimes when a stock's price gets fairly high, the company decides to *split* the shares. For example, if you had 100 shares of the stock at $100 per share, you now have 200 shares at $50 per share. You still have the same amount of money ($1,000), but you have twice as many shares.

Sometimes stocks split at odd rates (like 2 5/8 to 5) rather than the simple two-for-one. Money can handle any split ratio.

To record a stock split, do the following:

1. Select the stock you want to split from the Your Portfolio window.
2. Click the Record a Special Activity link in the Activities bar. A menu appears.
3. Click Record a Split from the menu. The Split Shares dialog box appears (see Figure 23.9).

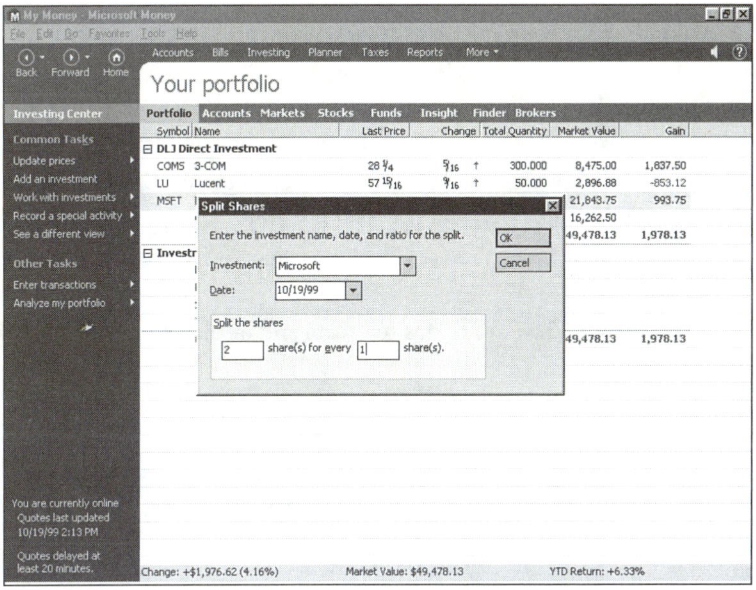

Figure 23.9
Money handles stock splits through this dialog box.

4. Confirm that the stock name is correct; if it's not, choose it from the Investment drop-down list.
5. Change the Date, if needed, to reflect the date of the split.
6. Enter the split ratio in the Split the Shares boxes. For example, if the stock is splitting two for one, enter **2** into the first box and **1** into the second.
7. Click OK. Money makes the change in your records.

UNDERSTANDING THE INVESTMENT VIEWS

Investment views are sort of like minireports. They show you your portfolio in different ways so that you can make different evaluations about it. The default investment view is Standard, which is what you see when you click the Investing link on the Navigation bar and then click View My Entire Portfolio. To choose another view, click See a Different

View in the Activities bar and then select a view from the menu that appears. Here's a brief description of each of the views:

- **Performance View**—Use this view to see the latest share prices, increases and decreases in the share price percentage, and the annual percentage of return. An example of Performance View is shown in Figure 23.10.
- **Return Calculations View**—Use this view to project how much money you will gain or lose on each investment over varying time periods, based on the current gains/losses. For example, suppose your favorite stock has gained 10% in 6 weeks. How much will it have gained in 12 months if it keeps up at its present course? This view can tell you.
- **Valuation View**—Check this view to compare your investments with the latest market price.
- **Quotes View**—View the most recent price of the security sold based on your last quote update, including changes in the price and the volume of shares traded.
- **Holdings View**—Click this view to see a list of your investment accounts and view the market value, quantity, and the total portfolio value.
- **Fundamental Data View**—Check this view to see historical trends in your share prices.
- **My Custom View**—Use this to create and display your own view that you set up yourself.

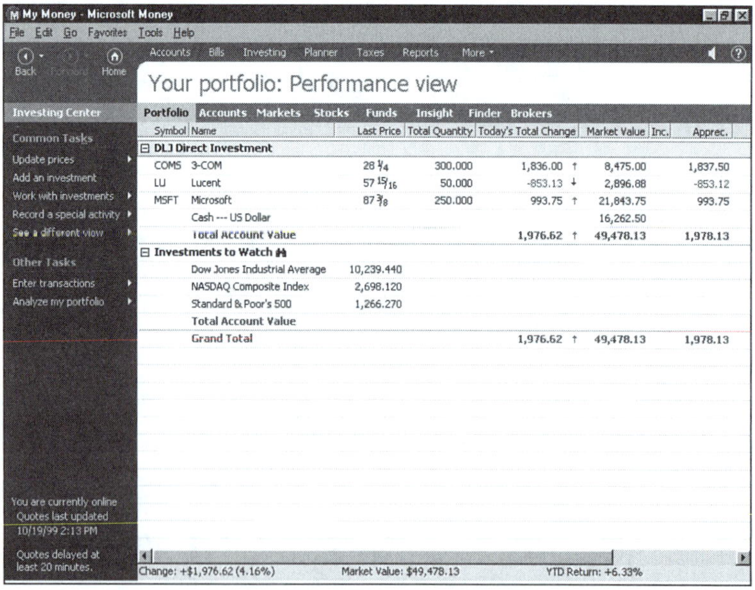

Figure 23.10
Performance View shows you how well your investments are performing on an annual percentage basis.

➔ To produce a variety of printed reports detailing your investment holdings, **see** "Printing Charts and Reports," **p. 492**.

TROUBLESHOOTING

PUZZLED BY INVESTMENT ACCOUNT CHOICES

I want to set up my retirement account in Money, but I don't know what kind of account it is. How can I get more information?

Click the Plan My 401(k) link on the Manage Your Investments and Savings screen. You can also get lots of good information about investment accounts from MSN Money Central.

INVESTING ADVICE NEEDED

I'm a novice at investing; how do people decide which stocks to buy or sell?

If you aren't sure what stocks to buy, check out the links on the secondary Navigation bar in the Your Portfolio window. In particular, check out the Finder link, which opens a page where you can search for investments based on criteria you specify.

BROKERAGE STATEMENT BALANCING

I have a statement from my brokerage; how do I use it to balance my account?

When you get a statement from your brokerage at the end of each month, use it to balance your account. However, you can't directly balance an investment account; there's no Balance command available. Instead, display the associated cash account and balance that one, entering any service charges, interest paid, or interest earned there. If you need to record stock transactions to balance with your statement, jump back to the regular investment account to do so.

MOVING INVESTMENT ACCOUNTS AMONG BROKERAGES

I've transferred one of my accounts to a different brokerage; how can I let Money know of the change?

If you transfer an account from one brokerage to another, you can move it in Money without reentering everything. Use the More Investing Tasks, Record a Special Activity, Transfer an Account command.

CHAPTER 24

Planning and Reporting

In this chapter

VIEWING REPORTS AND CHARTS

Reports are text-based summaries of your data; for example, a report could add up all the transactions categorized as Food:Groceries and tell you how much you spent last month for groceries. *Charts* are graphical summaries of the same data. I'll tend to talk about reports and charts as a single entity in this chapter. That's because (at least in Money) they're just two different, interchangeable views of the same data. Every Money report can be viewed as a chart and vice versa.

To use Money's reporting and charting tools, click the Reports link on the Navigation bar (see Figure 24.1). Then click a report type in the Activities bar to see a list of reports in that category.

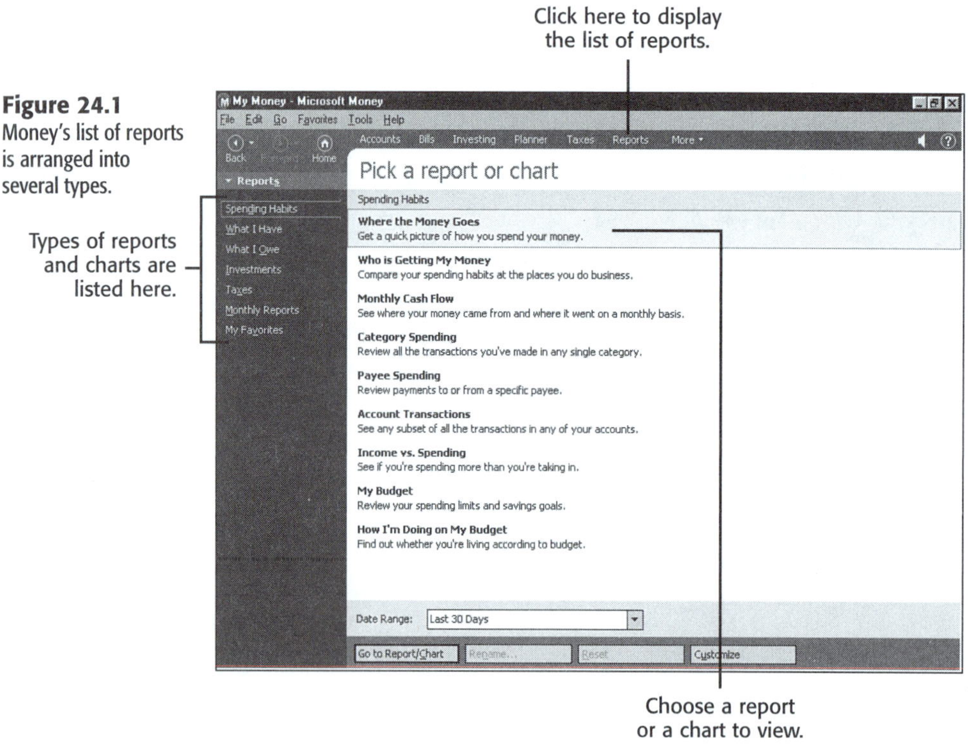

Figure 24.1
Money's list of reports is arranged into several types.

From the list of report and chart types displayed in the Activities bar, select the topic that best represents the report or chart you want to view. Each type you select displays a more detailed list of reports and charts. The procedure for viewing reports is the same for every report.

To view a report, do the following:

1. Click the Reports link on the Navigation bar, or choose Go, Reports, or press Ctrl+Shift+R. The list of reports appears (refer to Figure 24.1).

2. Choose a report type (Spending Habits, What I Have, and so on) from the list in the Activities bar.
3. Double-click a report name to view that report, or click it and then click Go to Report/Chart. Figure 24.2 shows a typical report.

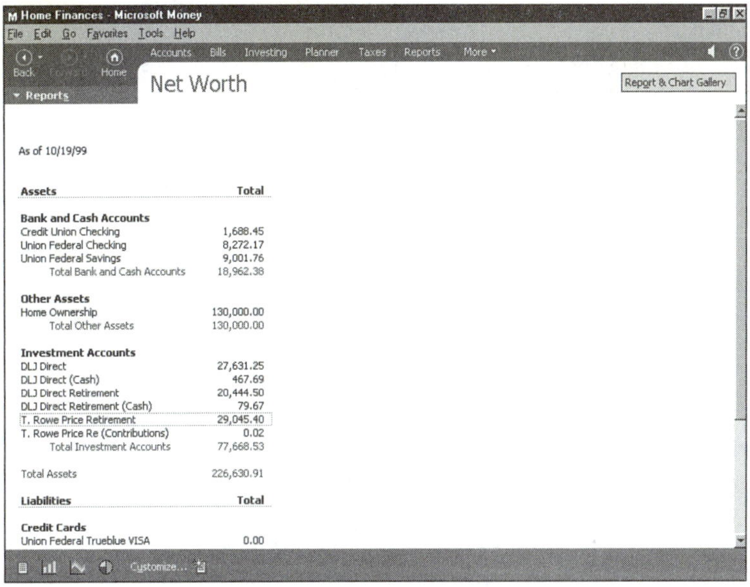

Figure 24.2
One of the many reports available in Money 2000.

4. To return to the list of reports, click the Back button on the Navigation bar or click the Report & Chart Gallery button.

To see details about a particular line item on the report, double-click it. The View Transactions dialog box opens, detailing the item. For example, Figure 24.3 shows what happens when I double-click one of the investment accounts listed in Figure 24.2. Click Close when you're finished with that dialog box.

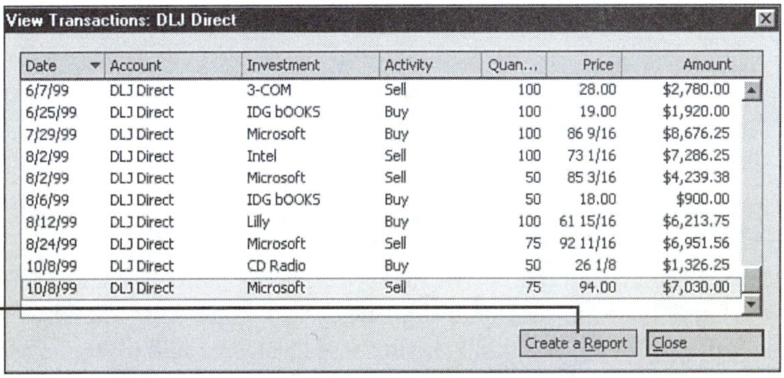

Figure 24.3
Double-click a report element to see a list of the transactions that it represents.

Click here to create a new report from the information in this dialog box.

CHANGING A CHART INTO A REPORT (OR VICE VERSA)

Although almost all the reports and charts listed in the Reports & Charts Gallery can be viewed either way, certain ones lend themselves naturally to one form or the other. The "natural" form of any item is what you see by default when you select and view the item. For instance, Net Worth is naturally suited to a report—it's highly detailed and text oriented. Net Worth Over Time, on the other hand, is more suited to a graphical format because the whole point is to see the general trend, not to read about individual transactions.

To change to the alternative form (report to chart or vice versa) or to change the chart type, click one of the format buttons at the bottom of the screen. For example, the Net Worth report from Figure 24.2 appears in Figure 24.4 as a pie chart.

Figure 24.4
Here's the same information shown in Figure 24.2, but in a pie chart.

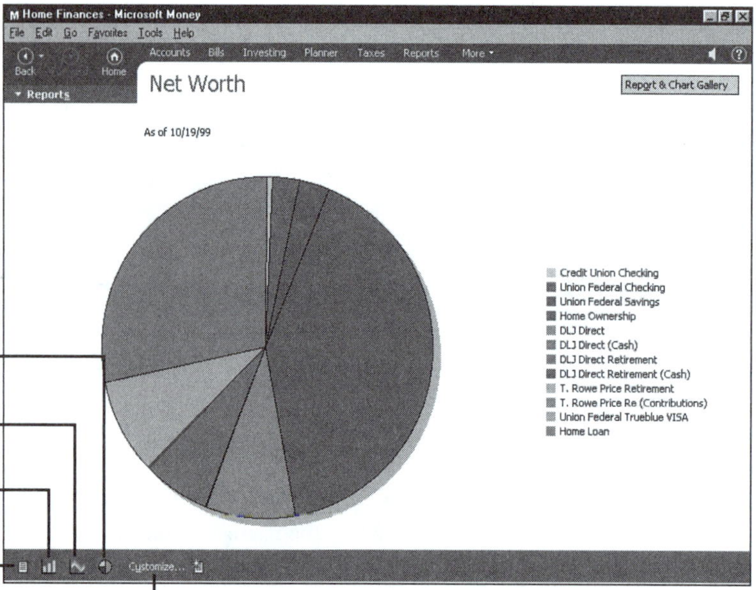

To put a report or chart back to its original format, select it from the Pick a Report or Chart screen and then click the Reset button. When asked to confirm, click OK.

CUSTOMIZING A REPORT OR CHART

Money's reports and charts are extremely versatile. You can change the report name, the time frame it encompasses, the chart type, the account(s) it accesses, and even the colors and patterns used if you think any of those changes would make the report more useful to you.

In most cases, Money uses (by default) the most useful chart or report format. When you need to customize, however, you can change all the same things on a chart that you can change on a report—and more. For example, you can choose a different chart type, change the way labels are displayed, and add 3D effects. These changes can give you a different perspective on your data, helping you think about your situation in different ways. For example, if a chart of your expenses isn't meaningful because there are too many categories, you might limit the report's scope to a single account and look closely at one account at a time.

To customize your report or chart, display the report or chart and then click the Customize button. The Customize Report dialog box appears, as shown in Figure 24.5. The dialog box has several tabs with options for customizing the report or chart. The exact tabs and controls within them depend on the specific report you are customizing; the reports that deal with individual transactions, for example, have more options.

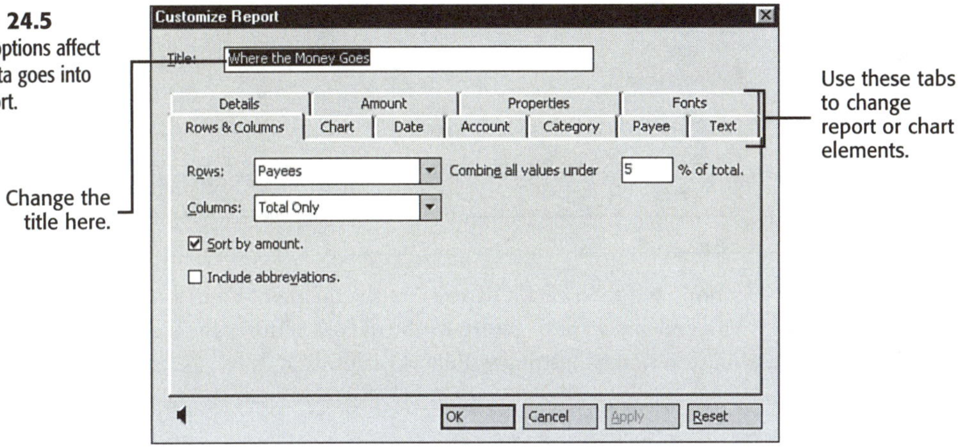

Figure 24.5
Report options affect what data goes into the report.

I won't go into every detail of this dialog box, but some of the highlights include the following:

- Enter a new title for the report in the Title text box.
- Use the Rows & Columns tab to specify what data appears in the rows or columns of the report.
- Click the Date tab to change the date range that's included in the report by selecting one of the preset ranges from the Range drop-down list. Or, if you prefer, type a range into the From and To text boxes.
- To use a different account, click the Account tab and select from the list.
- To specify which categories are shown, click the Category tab and choose which categories are listed.
- Use the Payee tab to change which payees are displayed in the report or chart.
- Use the Text tab to display only transactions with certain text criteria in the report.

- Click the Amount tab to specify which amounts appear in the report.
- Click the Details tab to specify transaction types and status.
- Use the Fonts tab to change the font used for the report or chart.
- Click the Chart tab, shown in Figure 24.6, to see options for changing the chart. You can display or hide legends and gridlines, change the chart type, and apply 3D effects.

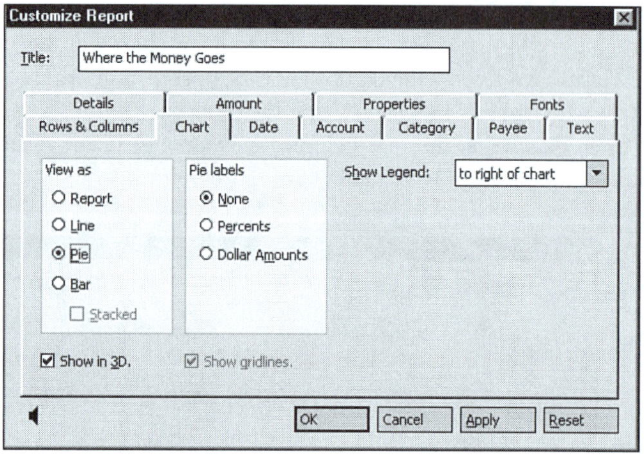

Figure 24.6
Use the Chart tab to make changes to the chart elements.

Make your selections and then click OK to close the dialog box and apply your changes. If you change your mind and want to return to the default settings for the report or chart, click the Reset button in the Customize Report dialog box.

PRINTING CHARTS AND REPORTS

When your chart or report is exactly the way you want it, you might want to share it with others (unless you were just creating it for your own satisfaction, which is fine, too). At that point, you're ready to print your chart or document and then make copies of the printout to share.

To print a chart or report, follow these steps:

1. Display the report or chart onscreen.
2. Choose File, Print, or press Ctrl+P, or right-click the report or chart and choose Print. The Print dialog box appears. Either Print Report or Print Chart appears at the top, depending on which you're printing (see Figures 24.7 and 24.8).
3. Set any options you want in the dialog box.

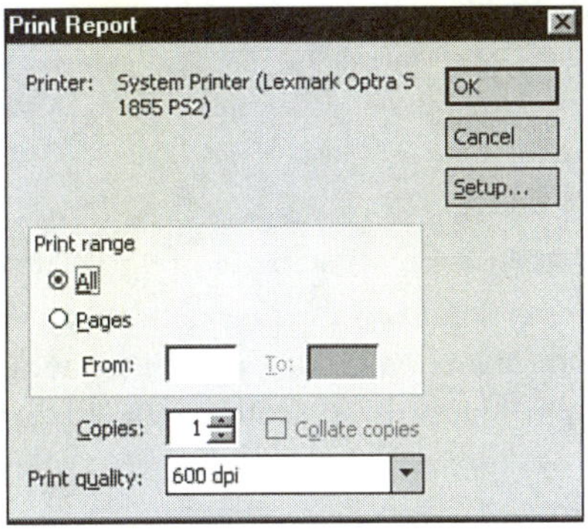

Figure 24.7
The Print Report dialog box appears when you print a report; it lets you choose which pages to print, the print quality, and how many copies to print.

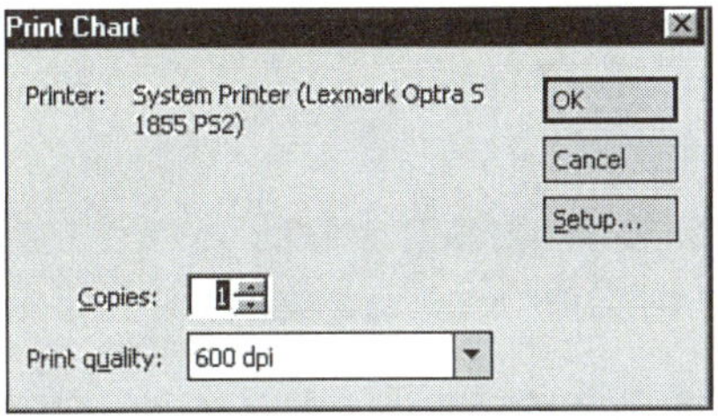

Figure 24.8
The Print Chart dialog box appears when you print a chart; it has options for designating how many copies to print and the print quality.

Note

The lower the print quality, the faster the document prints. Use the highest quality for a final draft. Some printers have only one print quality available; in that case, you're stuck with whatever is offered.

4. Click OK to print. The report or chart prints, and you have a handsome printout to share with the world.

You can use the Setup button in the Print dialog box to set some additional options for your printer. The available options vary depending on what kind of printer you have. You might be able to choose between Portrait and Landscape orientation, change the paper size, and choose which paper tray to use. You can also select a different printer, if you have more than one, from the Printer Name drop-down list in this dialog box. Check your Windows documentation for more information about setting up a printer.

SETTING UP A BUDGET

Use Money's Budget Planner feature to help you set up and maintain a budget. The Budget Planner can help you figure out where your money goes and what's left over after paying all the bills. You can quickly see your debt, plan savings goals, and fine-tune your spending.

Two major tasks involved with a budget are setting it up and sticking to it. Setting it up is the easy part, especially when you're working with an easy-to-use tool such as Money.

Tip #140 from *Faithe Wempen*

The deluxe version of Money that you can buy in stores contains many more planning and budgeting tools; the budget planner in the standard version of Money is only a small part of the total offerings. If you need more planning and budgeting features, you might consider investing in an upgrade.

To start Budget Planner, click the Planner link on the Navigation bar, or choose Go, Planner. Then click the Create a Budget link on the Financial Planner page to open the Budget Planner start page, as shown in Figure 24.9. From here you can start a new budget, track existing budgets, and forecast your spending and goals.

Note

If a budget has already been set up for this Money file, you'll see an Update My Budget link instead of Create a Budget. You'll learn how to update an existing budget later in this chapter.

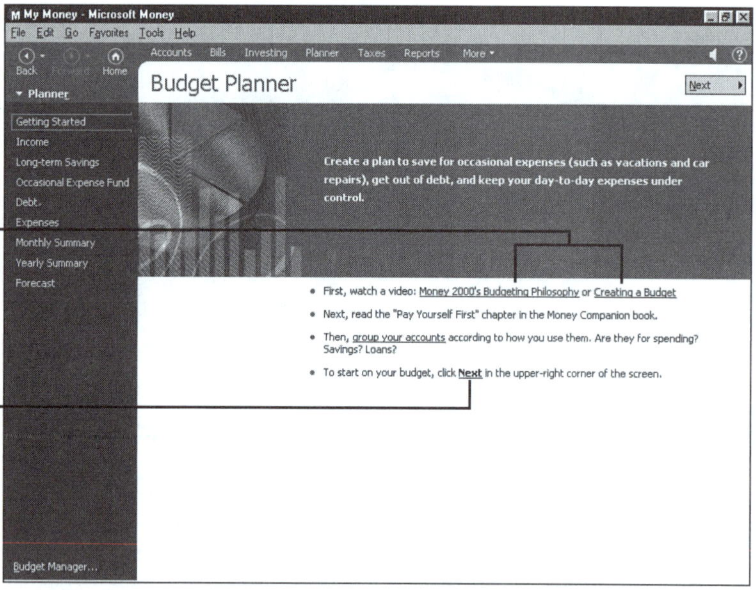

Figure 24.9
Use the Budget Planner to create and track a budget.

Tip #141 from *Faithe Wempen*

If you click the Planner drop-down arrow in the upper-left corner of the Planner screen, you can then select Budget Planner from the list to open the Budget Planner tool.

To set up a budget in Money:

1. From the Budget Planner page, click the Group Your Accounts link to open the Organize Accounts by Purpose dialog box shown in Figure 24.10.

Figure 24.10
Use this dialog box to specify money usage for each account.

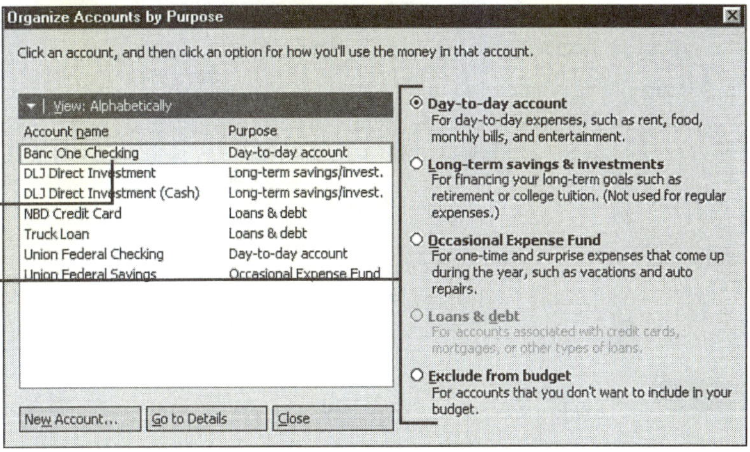

2. Select each account name and assign a use option. For example, select the checking account name and click the Day-to-Day Account option because you use your checking account to pay everyday expenses, such as rent, utilities, groceries, and other bills.
3. When you're finished assigning each account in the list, click the Close button.
4. Click the Next link on the Budget Planner page to open the Where Does Your Income Come From? page, shown in Figure 24.11.

Figure 24.11
Start your budget off by indicating your sources of income.

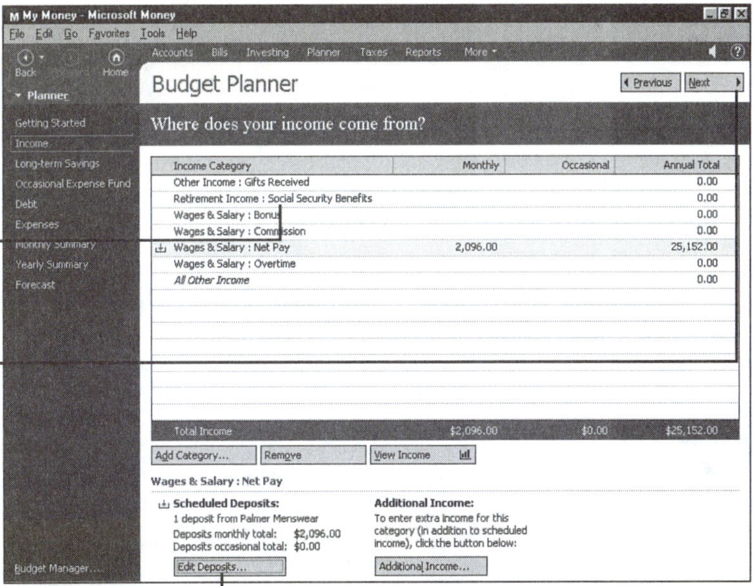

5. Select an income category at the top of the page. For example, to enter your net pay, select the Wages & Salary:Net Pay category.
6. Set up the scheduled income for the category. To do so, click Schedule Deposits (or Edit Deposits, if you already have a deposit set up), and then click New Deposit. The Create New Scheduled Deposit Wizard runs. Work through it to schedule your deposit.

Tip #142 from *Faithe Wempen*

This wizard not only helps you enter your expected income, but it can also help you split your pay stub data into multiple categories for tax or other reporting purposes.

Note

When you set up your account in Chapter 21, "Setting Up Your Accounts in Money," you may have set up a scheduled deposit, too. If so, you don't have to do it again now.

7. After setting up all scheduled deposits, click Close to return to the Budget Planner.
8. Set up any additional income for this category. To do so, click the Additional Income button. Enter or edit additional deposits here, the same as in step 6, and then click Close.
9. When you're finished entering amounts for each income category as needed, click the Next button (in the upper-right corner) to continue.

Tip #143 from *Faithe Wempen*

If you need additional categories to those shown in the Budget Planner, click the Add Category button and set up a new category. Money walks you through the steps necessary for adding a new category. To remove a category you're sure that you'll never need, select the category and click the Remove button.

10. The next step is to designate how much you want to put into savings (see Figure 24.12). The list box lists any scheduled deposits you might have set up. To add a new contribution to the list, click the New Contribution button to open a series of dialog boxes for specifying the amount. (You used this same series of dialog boxes to create a scheduled transaction in Chapter 22, "Managing Bank Accounts and Loans.") To edit a contribution, click the Edit button and make any necessary changes. Click the Next button to continue creating your budget.

Note

The amounts in the Occasional column (placed there by entering custom numbers) don't count toward the monthly budgeted amount. That's because such income is sporadic and shouldn't be used to calculate the regular monthly plan.

11. Next, Budget Planner asks what you want to set aside for occasional expenses, such as emergency funds or vacations. Use the New Contribution button to add a contribution to the list; then click Next to continue to the next phase.

Figure 24.12
The next step in creating a budget is to specify any long-term savings contributions.

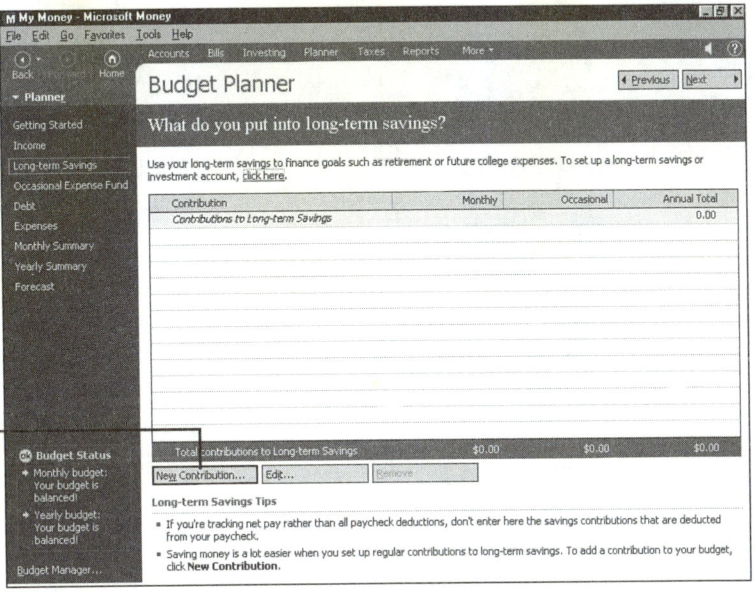

Click here to enter a new contribution.

PART IV CH 24

Tip #144 from *Faithe Wempen*

As you create your budget, use the Previous and Next buttons at the top of the window to move back and forth to view other pages.

12. Use the next page to review your debt and loans. The loans listed here are based on loan accounts you set up in Chapter 21. Click Next to continue.
13. The Expenses list box, shown in Figure 24.13, tells you how you spend your money based on transactions you've recorded in the account registers. To add new categories to the list, click the Add Category button. Be sure to include categories that cover all your expenditures, from monthly groceries to utilities and rent. Click Next when finished.

Tip #145 from *Faithe Wempen*

After you have been using Money for a month or so, AutoBudget lists budget categories based on the categories you used with transactions you recorded. To use AutoBudget, click the Create AutoBudget button to display the AutoBudget dialog box and verify the categories. Note: If you choose to use AutoBudget's categories, they will overwrite any existing category budget information you might have already entered.

14. The Monthly Summary page lets you see your monthly spending at a glance, showing the total income available and the total you need to spend on bills. Figure 24.14 shows an example. Click Next to continue.
15. The Yearly Summary page lets you see your income and expense totals for the year. Click Next to continue.
16. The last page in setting up your budget, the Forecast page, lets you see your budget forecast for the next 12 months. Click Finish to complete the budget planning process.

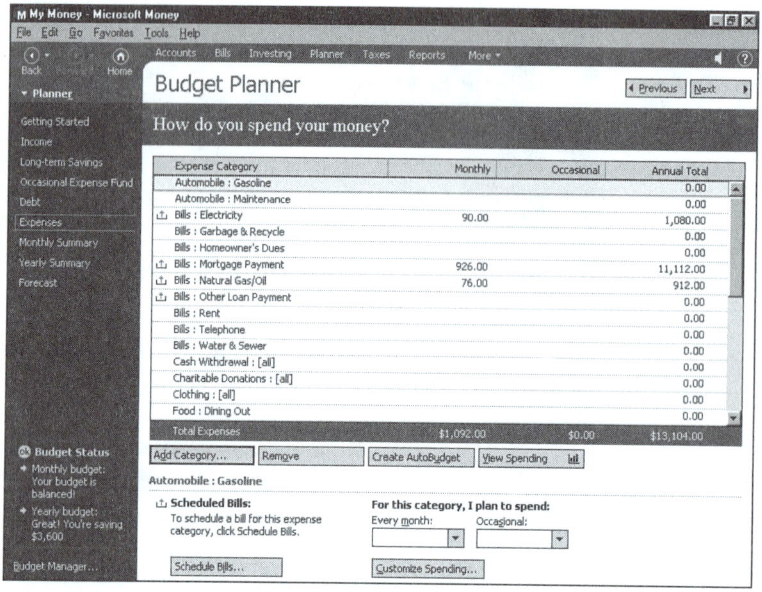

Figure 24.13
Use this page of the Budget Planner to specify categories detailing how you spend your money.

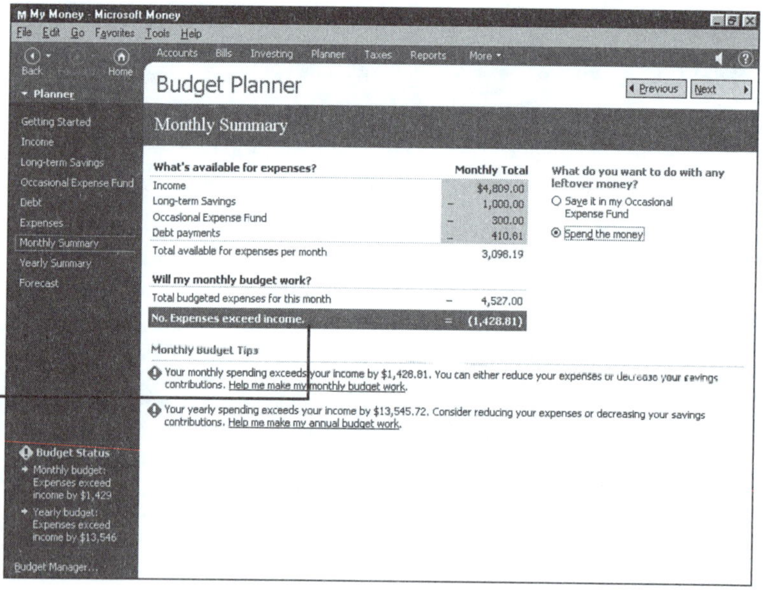

This indicator shows I'm over budget.

Figure 24.14
Oops! I'm over my monthly budget by $1,428.81. I'll need to click Previous and revise my budget amounts.

CHECKING UP ON YOUR BUDGET

The time-consuming part of budgeting in Money is over; now all you have to do is view the My Budget report to see how you're doing.

Tip #146 from *Faithe Wempen*

> If you are budgeting, it's essential that you categorize each income and expense transaction carefully to match the categories for which you have budgeted. If you are sloppy about entering transactions with the wrong categories (or none at all), your budget won't do you any good.

To view your budget reports, do the following:

1. Click the Reports link on the Navigation bar.
2. Click the Spending Habits button in the Activities bar.
3. Double-click the My Budget report on the list of reports. The budget report appears. This shows your original budget.
4. Now click the Back link on the Navigation bar to return to the Reports list.
5. Double-click the How I'm Doing on My Budget report to see how your actual spending compares to the budget.

If either report doesn't tell you what you want to know, you might try customizing it or changing the chart type. For example, personally, I don't get a lot out of the default How I'm Doing On My Budget chart. Instead, I click the Report button (at the far bottom-left corner of the screen) while viewing it to change the picture to a text-based report.

→ To customize a report or chart, **see** "Customizing a Report or Chart," **p. 490**.

TROUBLESHOOTING

CHART CUSTOMIZATION

I've customized a chart, but I don't like the customization. How do I change it back to the way it was?

Customization can sometimes make a chart or report less useful, rather than more useful. If you have customized a report to the point where it's not useful anymore, select it on the Pick a Report or Chart screen and then click Reset.

BUDGETING HELP

I would like to know more about the Budgeting feature in Money.

If you need more budgeting help than this chapter provided, check out some of the other links on the Plan Your Finances page. They include Create a Plan to Reduce My Debt, How Do I Balance My Budget?, and How Can I Track My Budget Progress?

I made some mistakes when entering my budget; how do I make changes to it?

You can return to the budget to make changes either by clicking the Previous button repeatedly until the screen that you want appears (if you have edited the budget since you started Money this time) or by clicking a link in the Activities bar while the Budget Planner is onscreen.

What does this Budget Forecast chart mean? I don't understand how to read it.

If you don't understand the chart presented by the Budget Planner for your budget forecast, click the Interpret the Forecast link to open the Help system to a page that explains it.

CHAPTER 25

Online Banking and Bill Payments

In this chapter

BANKING YOU CAN DO ONLINE

Money offers two kinds of online services: online banking and online bill payment.

Anyone can use online bill payment, regardless of his or her bank. It works through a service called CheckFree, which is completely separate from Microsoft. You sign up for an account with CheckFree, and for your monthly fee, CheckFree processes up to a certain number of payments for you.

You prepare your payments in Money by entering them in your register and setting the Number field to Electronic Payment (E-Pay). Then you click the Connect button in Money and connect to the CheckFree service either through the Internet (if you have Internet access) or direct-dialed with your modem. The payment information is sent to CheckFree, and it processes your request and sends a payment to the payee for you.

Note

CheckFree doesn't pay your payees with its own cash; it merely prints a computerized check with your own checking account number on it and mails the check for you. In some cases, where CheckFree and a certain payee have made an agreement, CheckFree authorizes that payee to make an electronic withdrawal from your checking account.

Online banking is totally different. Online banking works only with certain banks that have set up an online presence (usually through the Internet). You can pay bills through your bank's online banking and send letters to the bank, retrieve electronic copies of your statements, check on a particular transaction, and maybe more, depending on your bank. When you connect to your bank, you go to the bank's own Web pages; Money does not control the process and it's different for every bank.

Note

Some banks also offer their own version of online bill payment, which isn't related to CheckFree. The procedures for using it may be different than for using CheckFree, so you will need to check with your bank to find out how it interfaces with Money 2000 if you want to use their service instead.

To use Money's online features, you need Microsoft Money (obviously!) and a modem. Almost any modem will do, although faster is better. You also need access to a telephone line. Money 2000 works through the Internet by default, so you should establish your Internet connection before going online with Money.

PREPARING FOR ONLINE BANKING

The first step to establishing an online connection is to find out what online services your bank offers. Not all banks are up-to-date with Internet technologies, but if you're lucky, your banking service is, and you can readily tap into the power of the Internet to track and manage your finances. If your bank does not offer any services, you can always use CheckFree, an independent online bill payment service.

The setup procedure for online banking is different depending on the bank. Some banks set themselves up automatically for online usage; others require you to download a service update containing the latest features. Still others do not directly offer online banking at all.

To set up your bank for online services, do the following:

1. Click the Accounts link on the Navigation bar, displaying a list of accounts.
2. Click the Set Up Accounts link, displaying the Set Up Your Accounts in Money screen.
3. Click Set Up Online Services.
4. Click the account you want to set up. The Review Online Services for [bank name] screen appears. Depending on the bank, you will see one of the following:
   - **Online Setup Is Complete**—Some banks come with setup information built into Money 2000, so no setup on your part is required.
   - **Service Update Is Required**—Some banks want you to check for updated offerings online. To do so, click the Update button next to the message and follow the prompts.
   - **Set Up Online Services**—If Money does not recognize your bank as one that has online services pre-set, you will see this message. Click the Set Up button next to the message and follow the prompts to identify the bank.

Figure 25.1 shows the Set Up screen for the latter case. Note that the preceding messages refer only to the online services (top) portion of the screen, not the online bill paying.

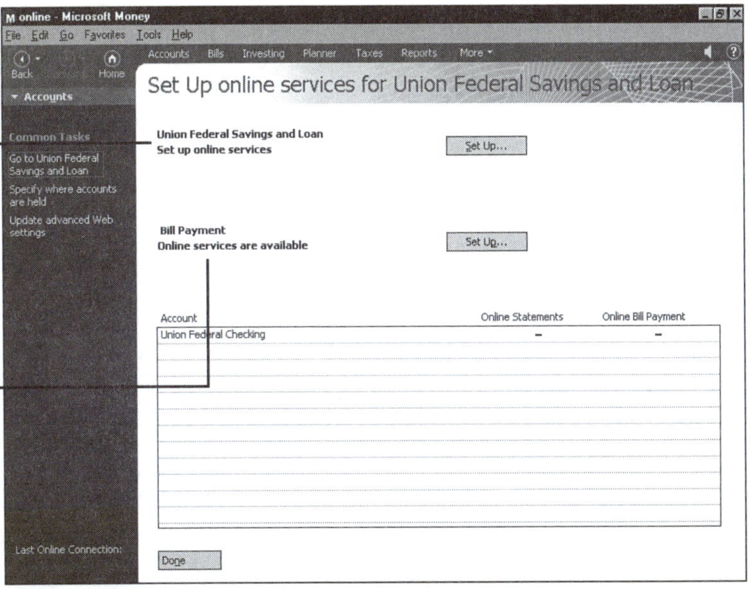

Figure 25.1
Check the Set Up Online Services screen to see whether your bank is currently set up.

Look here to see whether your bank is set up.

This part is for online bill payment, covered later.

To use Money for online banking, your bank must be on Money's list of approved banks for this purpose. If it's not, you'll be limited to online bill paying only. Therefore, the "Setup" for an unrecognized bank consists merely of trying to match up its name to one of the names of approved banks, as shown in Figure 25.2. If your bank isn't on the list, you can skip to "Paying Bills Online" later in this chapter to learn about online bill payment.

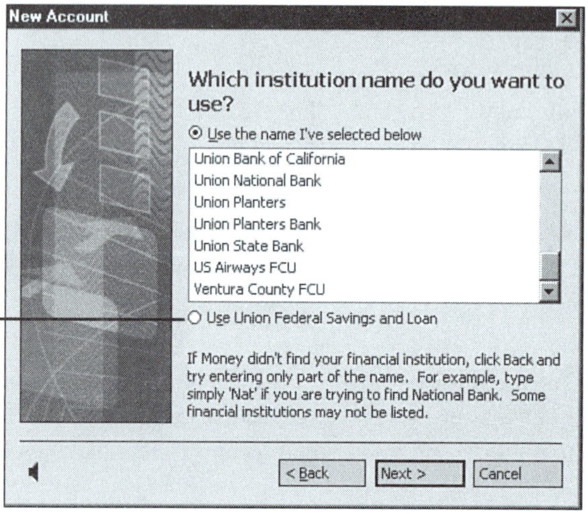

Figure 25.2
Try to find your bank on the list of institutions; if it's not there, it doesn't support online banking.

Note

Because more banks are offering new online services every day, there is a possibility that your bank does offer online service but Money 2000 doesn't recognize it. If that's the case, contact your bank and find out if there is a way to set up Money to work with it. You might also visit the Microsoft Money 2000 Web site (Help, Microsoft on the Web, Microsoft Money Home Page) and find out if an update is available that allows you to use your bank. If not, you can still bank online using your Web browser and then manually duplicate the transactions in Money 2000.

Banking Online

Online banking works intimately with your own bank. The Web page you visit and the information you retrieve from it come directly from your bank. Therefore, the procedures for each bank are different. However, most banks offer at least two basic features:

- **Online statements**—You can download a current bank statement. This is better than your monthly paper statement you receive in the mail because it is updated daily. If you have questions about whether a transaction has cleared, you can check the statement.
- **Online transfers**—You can transfer funds between accounts (as long as they're both at the same bank). Most banks usually require a trip to the local branch office to do this, but with online banking, you can do it from the privacy of your home.

To connect to your bank online, use Money to display its online services page. Money has its own built-in Web browser for this purpose. Do the following:

1. Make sure you are connected to the Internet.
2. In Money, display the register for the account.
3. Choose Connect to Bank, Go to [bank name] Web Site. Your bank's opening Web page appears.

   A prompt for a username (or Access ID, or some other wording) and password appear on the Web page, as shown in Figure 25.3.

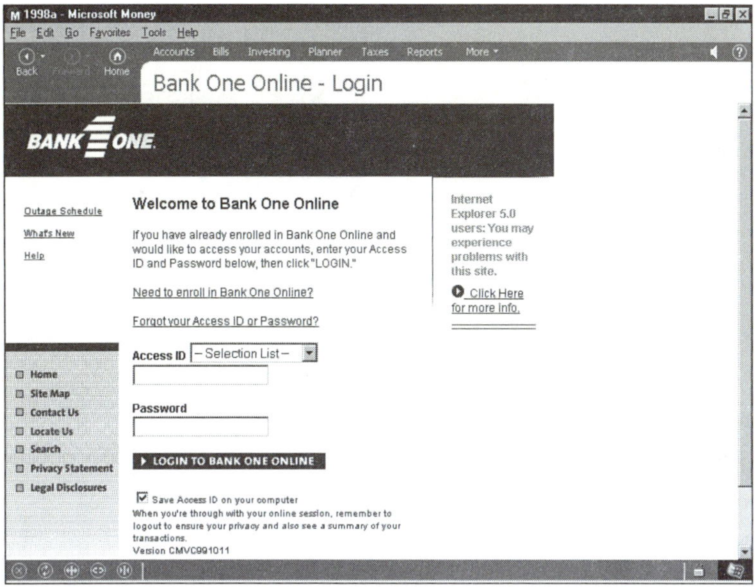

Figure 25.3
A typical bank log-in screen.

4. Enter your ID and password, and then click the Login button (which may have a different name, such as Enter, Continue, or Connect, depending on the bank).

Note

Some banks require you to go through an online enrollment process the first time you connect online. This doesn't mean you are signing up for an extra bank account. It just configures your existing bank account to work online.

Exploring Your Bank's Web Site

After you have logged in, you have access to the full Web site for your bank. You can follow any of the links there for various activities. Figure 25.4 shows an example.

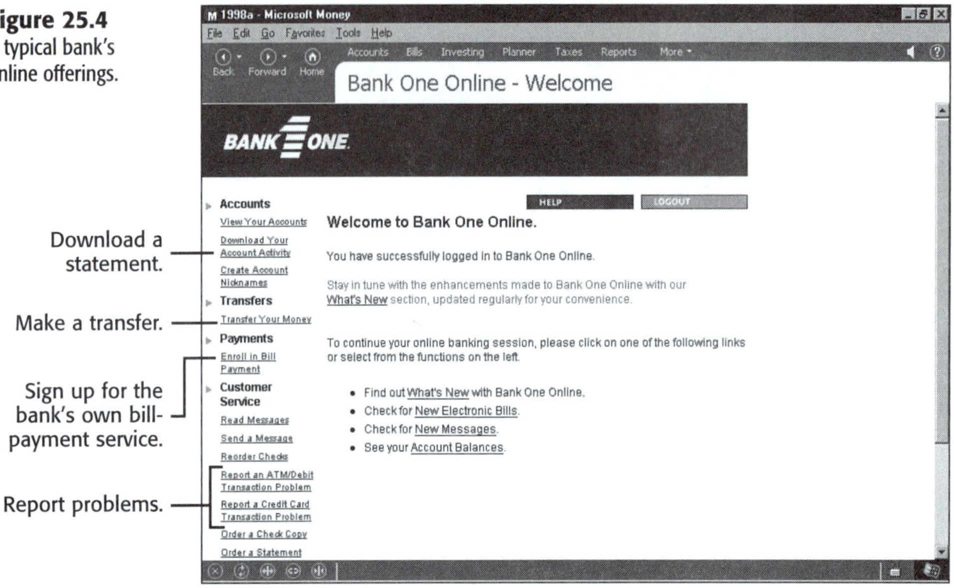

Figure 25.4
A typical bank's online offerings.

RETRIEVING A BANK STATEMENT

Almost all online banking services include online statements. You can view a list of all your account transactions online to compare against your records in Money.

Online statements work in one of two ways, depending on your bank. Some banks use an "active statements" technology that integrates seamlessly with Money so that you can reconcile (balance) your account directly in Money. Other banks enable you to download a QIF file (Quicken Information File—but don't worry, it works with Money, too), which you then import offline into a Money account. That's the method most banks use these days, so that's what I'll show you in the following steps.

To integrate a downloaded online bank statement with Money through a QIF file:

1. Use your online bank's Web site to download the statement in QIF format. The exact steps for this depend on your bank's Web page setup.

   When prompted, save the file in a location that you will remember.
2. Log out of your bank's Web site and display the register for the account that the statement is for.
3. Choose File, Import. The Import dialog box opens (see Figure 25.5).
4. Click Import. The Import QIF to Money dialog box appears.
5. Leave the first option selected (As a Statement from My Bank). Then click OK.

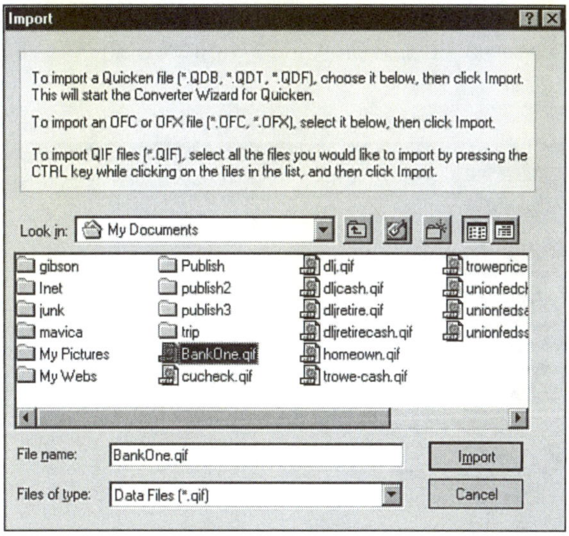

Figure 25.5
Select the QIF file that you just downloaded.

6. The first time you do this, you may be prompted to choose a money account, as shown in Figure 25.6. This appears if Money cannot determine which of your accounts the statement is for. Select the account from the Money Account Name drop-down list and then click Next.

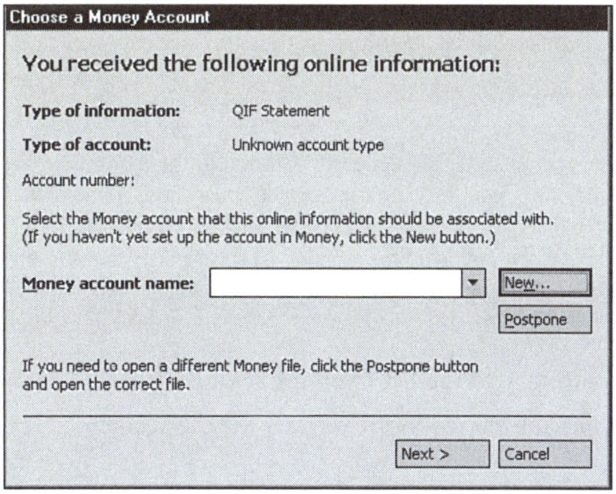

Figure 25.6
If prompted, select the Money account to use.

7. At the Summary screen, click Close. A screen appears in Money stating that you have statements to read.
8. Click the hyperlink for the statement to be read. Money integrates the transactions into your register.

If any transactions on the statement do not match up with transactions already in your register, they appear on a list, as shown in Figure 25.7. You can choose whether to add them to the register.

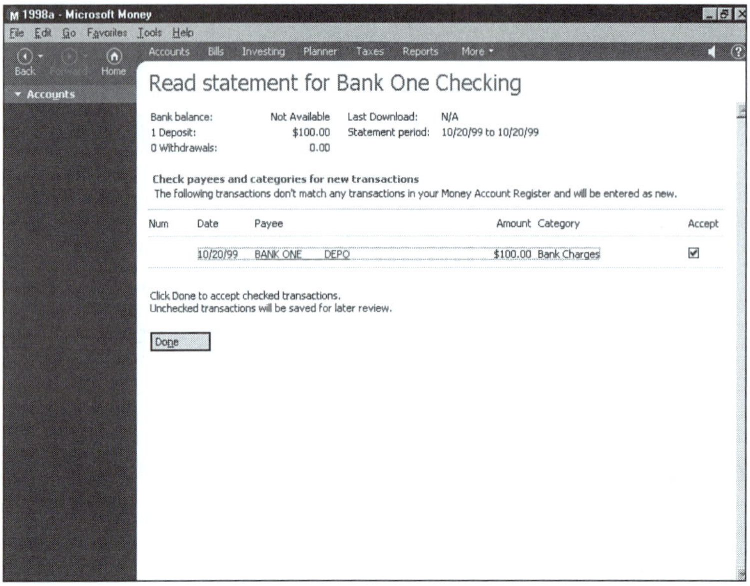

Figure 25.7
Money shows transactions that it cannot automatically enter.

9. Deselect the Accept check box for any of the transactions you don't want to enter in your register.

Caution

Do not automatically accept every transaction. There may be a valid reason why it does not belong in your register. For example, in Figure 25.7, the unmatched deposit shown is for the money I deposited to open my account. It's reflected in the opening balance I entered when setting up the account. If I accepted this transaction, my available balance for the account would show as double what I actually have.

10. Click Done. You return to the list of online statements.
11. Click Done again. You return to the register for the account.

Transferring Funds Online

Some banks support online transfers directly through Money. If yours does, you will be able to set the transaction type to Xfer in the Number box when entering a transfer in your register. After you do so, the next time you connect to your bank online, the transfer will take place.

If Xfer does not appear on the drop-down list for the Number box when you enter a transfer, your bank does not support this kind of transfer. In that case, you will need to make the transfer using your bank's Web site and then manually duplicate it in Money separately. To do so, follow these steps:

1. Connect to your bank's Web site and log in.
2. Use the Web site's controls to make the transfer between accounts.
3. Log off the Web site.
4. In Money, display the register for the account from which the money came.
5. Enter the Transfer transaction as you would normally.

Paying Bills Online

After you start paying your bills online with CheckFree, you'll never want to go back to writing checks by hand. It's very convenient—no stamps, no trips to the post office, and no writer's cramp in your hand.

Note

Your bank may also offer its own bill-payment service, independent of CheckFree. If so, it may work differently than what is described in this chapter.

Signing Up for Online Bill Payment

1. Click the Accounts link on the Navigation bar, displaying a list of accounts.
2. Click the Set Up Accounts link, displaying the Set Up Your Accounts in Money screen.
3. Click Set Up Online Services.
4. Click the account you want to set up. The Review Online Services for [bank name] screen appears.

Note

If you do not see a Set Up button next to Bill Payment, perhaps your bank integrates bill payment with online banking. Explore your bank's Web site for details.

5. Click the Set Up button next to Bill Payment. The Bill Payment Setup Wizard starts. Click Next to begin.
6. Choose a provider to use to pay bills (see Figure 25.8). Your bank may have instructed you to pick a certain provider; if not, choose either. You can review their plans and fees by clicking More Info next to one of them.

Note

The online bill-payment service (CheckFree or MI Bank) will deduct a service fee directly from your checking account each month to pay for the service. When you click the More Info button next to a provider's name during setup, you will see the most recent rate information.

7. Click Next.

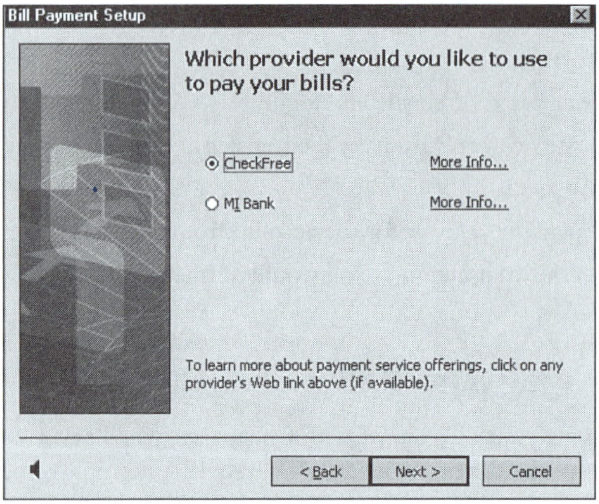

Figure 25.8
Select the provider for bill payment.

8. A message appears, telling which provider you selected; click Next to go on.
9. This next question is tricky. It asks whether you have an ID and password from your bank.

   Choosing No… takes you to one of two places. If your bank is on Money's online list, it allows you to connect to your bank's Web site to request that an ID and password be sent to you. If your bank is not on Money's list, it takes you to a message saying that you can't use Money for online banking for that account—but you knew that already.

   Choose Yes… if *either* of the following is true:

   - You actually do have an ID and password from your bank.
   - Your bank is not on Money's list of online banks. (Yes, I know you don't have an ID and password, but choose Yes anyway.)
10. Click Next. Prompts appear for your name, address, phone number, and Social Security number.
11. Enter the information into the boxes provided and click Next.
12. Choose the account to set up for online services from the list that appears, and then click Next.
13. Mark the Direct Bill Payment check box, and then click Next.
14. Enter your account number and routing number into the boxes provided. (You should be able to find both of these numbers on your checks.) Then click Next.

Note

The routing number is the 9-digit number in the bottom-left corner of your checks; the account number is the number to the right of it. There is no fixed length for account numbers; each bank does it differently.

15. When asked whether you want to set up another account (at the same bank, that is), choose Yes... to go back and do so, or click No, I'm finished. Then click Next.
16. Click the Finish button. This completes the bill payment setup.

After you sign up for online bill payment, the service you signed up with will send you a password that you can use to connect. You will need this password to complete the steps in the following section.

PAYING A BILL ONLINE

To pay a bill online after you have signed up for online bill payment, just set the check number for the transaction to Electronic Payment (E-Pay), as shown in Figure 25.9. Then connect using the Online window, and the rest is gravy.

Figure 25.9
Record an electronic payment in your register.

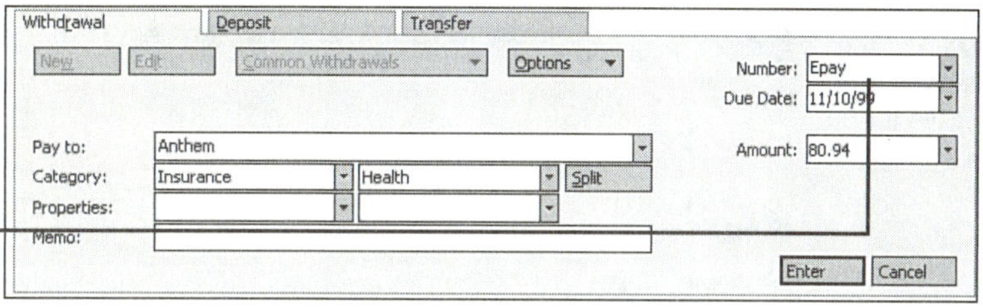

Set the payment type to Epay.

Here's how to pay a bill with online bill payment:

1. Display the register for the checking account from which you want to pay.
2. Start a new check transaction, but instead of entering a check number, open the drop-down list and choose Electronic Payment (E-Pay).
3. Complete the check normally. When you enter the payee, Money prompts you for the payee's address and telephone number and for your account number, as shown in Figure 25.10. Enter it and click OK to continue.

Note

Money records the payee information you enter when paying bills electronically in the Payee Details dialog box. Whenever you pay that payee in the future, the details are automatically sent with your online transaction.

CheckFree also automatically updates address and/or account numbers of payees with which it has established a special direct account. If you later view the payee's details and the address or account number seems to have been changed, don't change it back to the original settings because it will mess up the direct account function.

4. When you have completed the transaction, a Send Payments reminder appears to the left of the register telling you that you have transactions to send. Click it to open the Connect dialog box (see Figure 25.11).

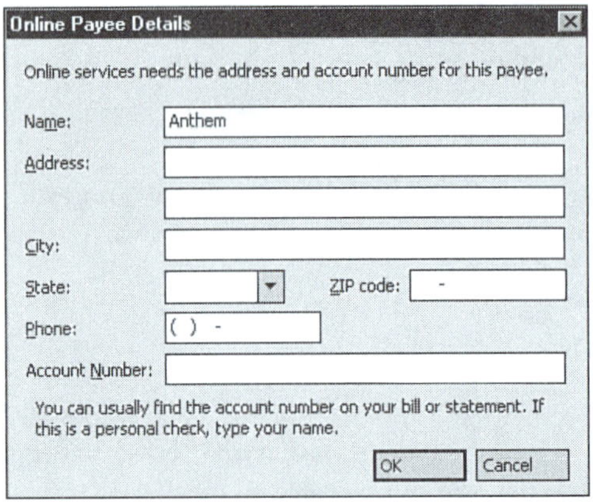

Figure 25.10
Enter payee contact information the first time you pay them.

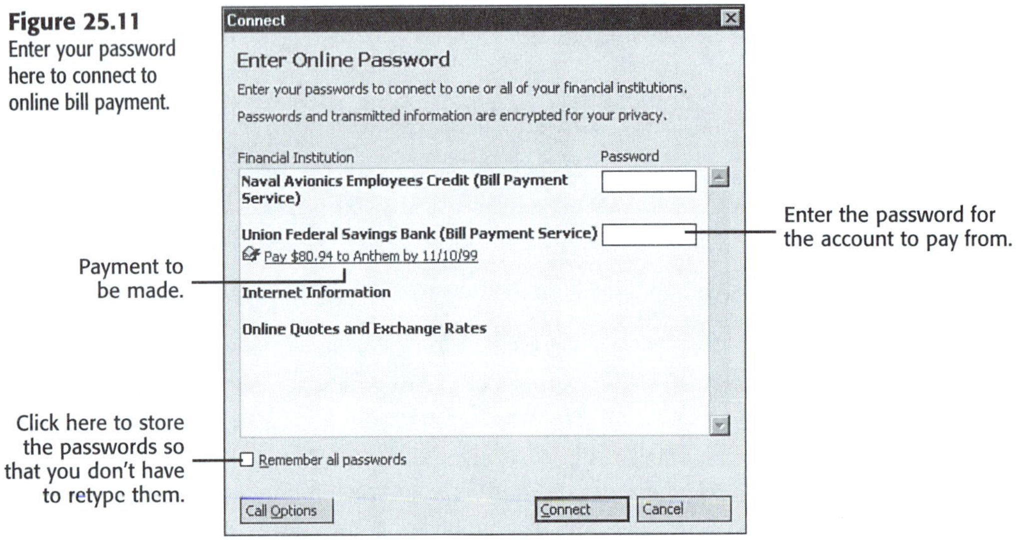

Figure 25.11
Enter your password here to connect to online bill payment.

5. Enter your password for the account from which to pay. (CheckFree will send you a password after you sign up.)

Tip #147 from *Faithe Wempen*

If you want Money to remember the passwords, mark the Remember All Passwords check box.

6. Click the Connect button in the dialog box. A Call Progress box appears.
7. Wait for the call to complete. When you see the Call Summary box telling you that your call was completed successfully, click the Close button to close the box.

TROUBLESHOOTING

ONLINE BANKING OFFERINGS

What will I see when I bank online with my bank?

At this time, online banking is rather a "free-for-all" with few established standards. Each bank has full control of its own Web site, so there's no way for me to describe what you might see there. Just follow the prompts, look for the obvious, and contact your bank directly if you get confused.

QIF STATEMENTS

Is there anything special I need to be wary of when downloading a bank statement in QIF format and integrating it in Money?

When downloading a QIF statement and integrating it into your Money account, make very sure that you have not duplicated a transaction. Check your register afterward and delete any duplicates that you find.

NO CHECK NUMBER WHEN PAYING BILLS WITH CHECKFREE

I am paying bills with CheckFree. I saw a message that my call was completed successfully, but there is no check number next to some of the transactions in my register. Did my payment go through, or not?

If you do not see a check number, the bill payment probably did not go through. Call CheckFree's toll-free customer service number and inquire.

CLEARING A BILL PAYMENT ERROR

I keep getting a message that my last call was interrupted and needs to be completed, but it never completes successfully. How do I get past this?

If you repeatedly get a message that the last call to online services was interrupted and needs to be completed, but the message never goes away, you can clear this by holding Ctrl and Shift while you click Cancel at the message box. However, this makes the status uncertain of any online payments that were included in that call to be completed. You may want to call CheckFree and verify their records against your register to determine which payments were made and which were not.

PART V

EXPLORING OTHER WORKS SUITE PROGRAMS

CHAPTER 26

Using Microsoft Home Publishing 2000

In this chapter

What Is Microsoft Home Publishing?

Microsoft Home Publishing is an easy-to-use program that helps you create beautiful greeting cards, invitations, labels, stationery—just about anything that's printed. If you don't have a color printer, you might end up buying one when you see all the fun, colorful items you can produce with Home Publishing 2000.

Home Publishing 2000 is part of Microsoft's home publishing line of products. The program taps into the wonderful designs and messages from Hallmark, the world-renowned source for quality cards and greetings. With Home Publishing you can whip up projects such as these:

- Create personalized greeting cards for a variety of occasions.
- Make your own invitations to parties and family or corporate gatherings.
- Utilize a variety of Hallmark papers (available at Hallmark stores everywhere) to print your messages.
- Create email greeting cards to send on the Internet.
- Personalize your cards using scanned photos.
- Add your own scanned photos to greeting cards.

In addition to these projects, you can also log on to the Microsoft Publishing home page on the Web and download add-on packs of more designs, some of which are free.

Tip #148 from *Faithe Wempen*

When you installed Home Publishing, Microsoft's Picture It! Express program was also installed, and you'll see a shortcut icon for it on the Windows desktop. You can use Picture It! Express to help you work with photos you scan in with a scanner. If you have a scanner hooked up to your computer, there's no end to the personalized cards you can create. For example, you can design your own family Christmas cards with a group photo to send to all your relatives. Be sure to check out the Picture It! Express program and see what it can do.

Starting and Exiting the Program

You can start Home Publishing through the Works task launcher or by choosing Start, Programs, Microsoft Home Publishing 2000. If you start it through the task launcher, you can start a new project at the same time by choosing one of the task launcher's publishing tasks. In this chapter, however, we'll deal with Home Publishing as a standalone application.

When you start Home Publishing, the first thing you see is the Creative Ideas tab, shown in Figure 26.1. It lists broad categories of projects. Click a category to see individual project templates within it.

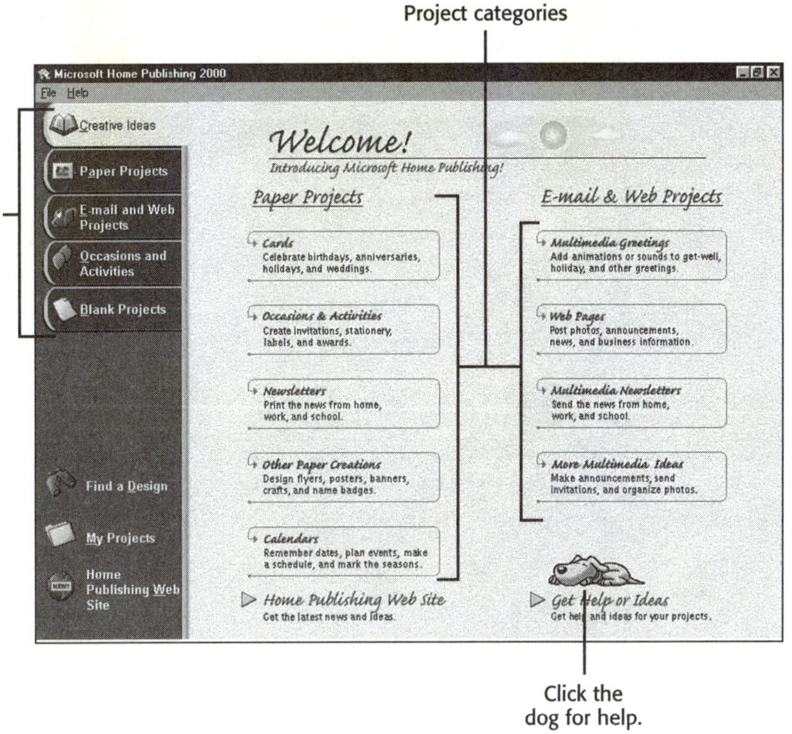

Figure 26.1
Welcome to Home Publishing 2000.

Note

You will need to insert one of the Home Publishing 2000 CDs (disks 4–6 in the Works Suite 2000 set) at some point during a project, so have your CDs ready.

To exit the program, click the Close button in the upper-right corner of the program window, or open the File menu and select Exit.

CREATING YOUR FIRST PROJECT

Ready to see how this works? Let's start with a greeting card because they're fairly straightforward. The skills you learn while creating this card can be applied to all the other projects. Although the remainder of this chapter focuses on the greeting card project type, be sure to check out the other project types available. The steps for completing the other project types are nearly the same.

Note

After you've worked with Home Publishing for a while, you may want to design your own cards and projects. You can do so at any time, starting with the Blank Projects tab in the main window, or you can create blank projects after choosing a project type. Either way, you're in the driver's seat.

To create a greeting card, follow these steps:

1. Click the Paper Projects tab. A list of paper projects appears (see Figure 26.2).

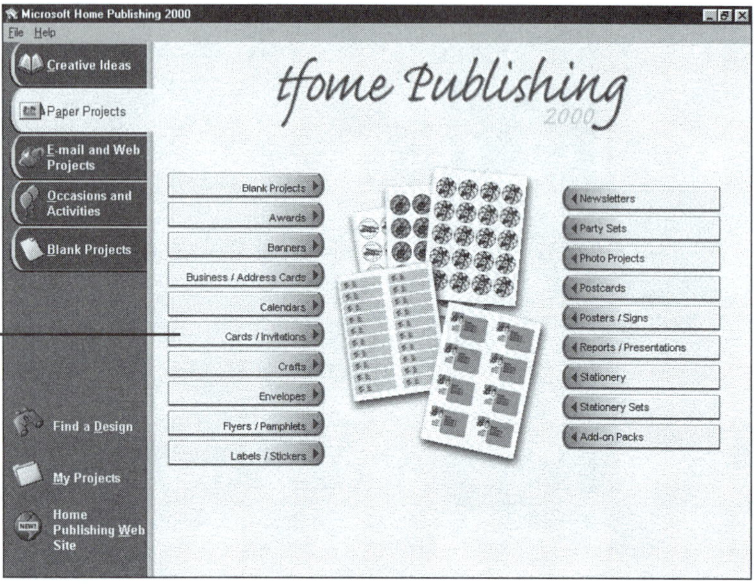

Figure 26.2
Select a paper project from any of these options.

2. Click Cards/Invitations. A list of occasions appears.
3. Click the occasion you want on the list (for example, Birthday). Some sample cards appear, as shown in Figure 26.3.

Note

At step 3 you may be prompted to insert a different CD into your drive.

4. Click a theme on the Themes list to specify the context for the card (for example, Love).
5. (Optional) Open the Style drop-down list and choose a card style (Cute, Funny, or Serious). Or leave this set to All to see all card choices.
6. Scroll through the list, looking at the cards. When you find one you want to work with, double-click it. The card appears in the editing window, as shown in Figure 26.4.

Tip #149 from
Faithe Wempen

When you click a card design, you see a preview of its message text on the right side of the dialog box. Keep in mind that you can customize this text later or even change it completely. Don't let the text be the defining factor on which card you choose.

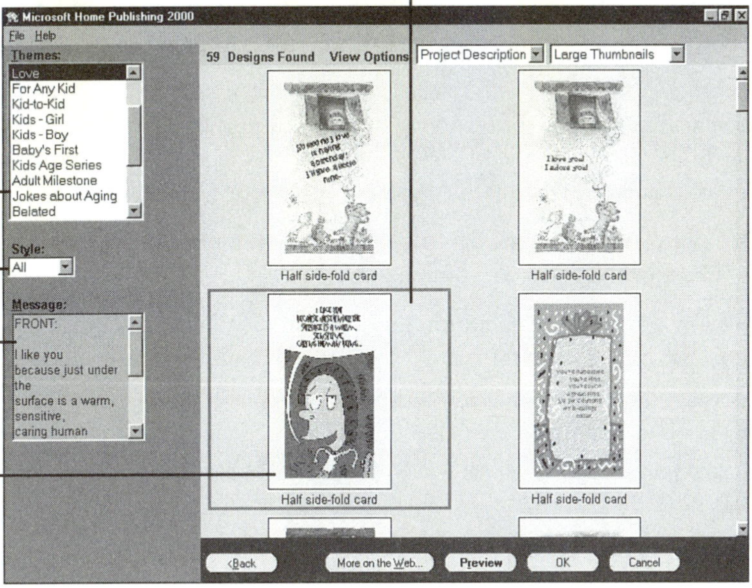

Figure 26.3
Choose the card you want to start with; you can modify it later.

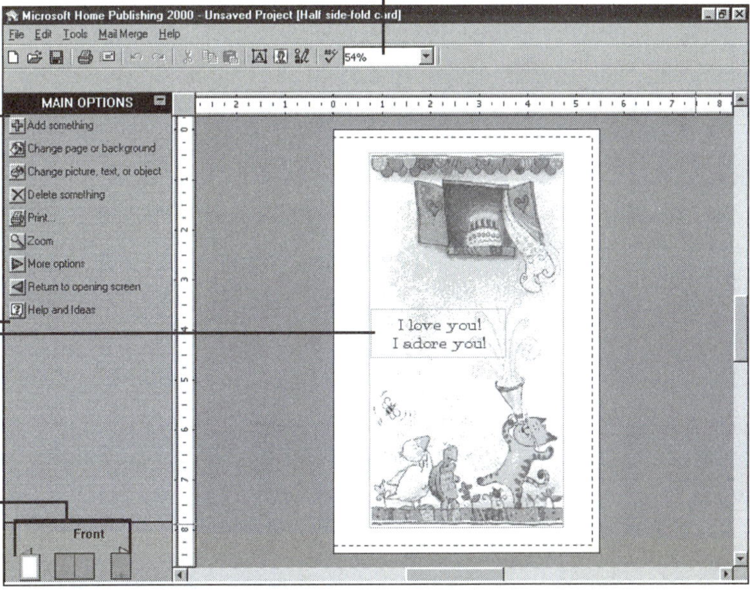

Figure 26.4
The card is ready for your customization.

Tip #150 from *Faithe Wempen*

> If you decide that you don't want that card after all, choose File, Close, and Return to Design Selection. This takes you back to Figure 26.3 to pick a different card.

Now you're ready to start working on the card to customize it to your specifications. Use one of the buttons in the Main Options pane to the left of the card, or follow along with the rest of this chapter for specific guidance.

In Figure 26.4, notice the buttons along the bottom left of the screen. Click one of these buttons to display that part of the card.

You can also use the Zoom drop-down list on the toolbar to change how you view your card. You can zoom in for a closer look or zoom out to see the entire page.

→ To change the font and font size, **see** "Changing or Adding Text," **p. 522**.

→ To resize, move, or copy text or graphics, **see** "Manipulating Objects," **p. 529**.

→ To print your card, **see** "Printing Your Work," **p. 532**.

Changing or Adding Text

To change text in an existing text box, click in it to place the insertion point inside its box, and then edit the text the same as you would in a word processor. Use the arrow keys to move the cursor, use the Backspace key to delete, and so on. You might want to change the message on the card. (I usually change the message to make it special for the person I'm sending it to, adding something about their hobbies or interests.)

You can also add an entirely new text box. For example, suppose that you want to add a new box under the inside message that says `Much love, Mom and Dad`.

You can add a new text box in either of two ways:

- Click Add Something from the Main Options, and then click Text on the menu that appears.

- Click the Add New Text button on the toolbar.

Either way, a text box appears in the middle of the current page; you will need to drag it where you want it. Then click inside it and type your text (see Figure 26.5).

Tip #151 from *Faithe Wempen*

> Don't worry about the outline around the text box. It won't print.

Note

> You cannot drag text boxes or other objects between pages on the card. If you realize that you need to put the text box on a different page of the card, select it and use cut and paste to move it to a different page.

Figure 26.5
Added text in its own text box on the card.

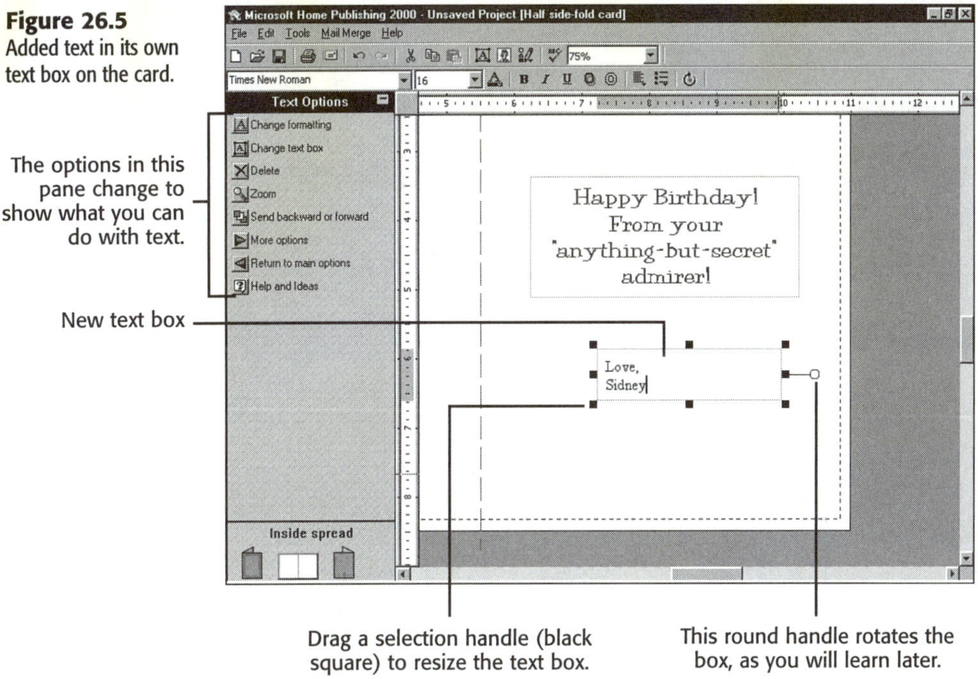

ADDING NONTEXT OBJECTS

Strictly speaking, everything is an *object* on your card (or other project). Each text box and each picture is a separate piece. You have already seen how to add text to a card, so now let's take a look at what else you can add.

PART V

CH 26

ADDING A PICTURE

Picture is this program's word for clip art. If you have worked with clip art in Word or Works, you know that clip art is predrawn art that you can use to enliven a plain space or illustrate a point. Follow these steps to see and use what Home Publishing has to offer.

1. Click the Add New Picture button on the toolbar. This opens the Select Picture File dialog box. (This is actually the Microsoft Clip Gallery, with a different name in the title bar.)

Note

Instead of step 1, you can also click Add Something from the Main Options and then click Picture from Clip Gallery.

2. Click a category to display the available clip art.

3. When you find a picture you want to use, click it and then click the Insert Clip button (see Figure 26.6).

The picture is immediately inserted in your card. You can move or resize it as needed.

Figure 26.6
Click the clip you want and then click the Insert Clip button.

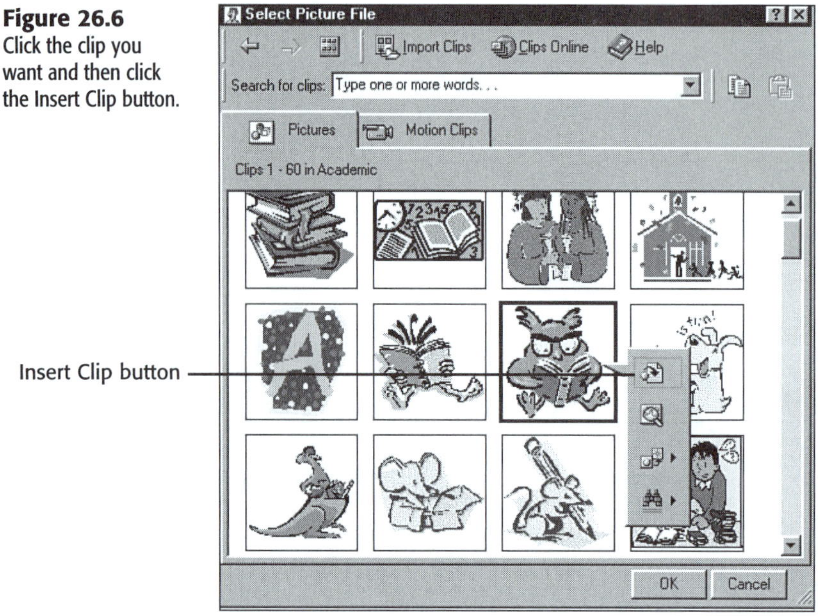

➔ To move or resize your picture, **see** "Manipulating Objects," **p. 529**.

Adding a Photo

The distinction between a photo and a picture (that is, a piece of clip art) is rather fuzzy. For practical purposes, let's just say that *clip art* is anything that shows up in the categories when you insert clip art in Home Publishing, and a photo is any other piece of art, such as a *scanned image* or something you've drawn in an art program such as Paint. That's not exactly accurate, but it's close enough without getting too technical.

Numerous photo projects are available in Home Publishing, and you'll find most of them under the Photo Projects category on the Paper Projects tab. Adding a photo is a lot like adding clip art. After choosing a design, double-click the photo placeholder on the project page to open the Clip Gallery and then locate the photo you want to use. Figure 26.7 shows a photo inserted on a photo project.

Home Publishing uses the Clip Gallery for selecting photos. If you've got photos stored in another folder on your computer (for example, ones you have scanned), you can import them into the gallery. Click the Import Clips button and locate the files.

Figure 26.7
You can insert photos into projects.

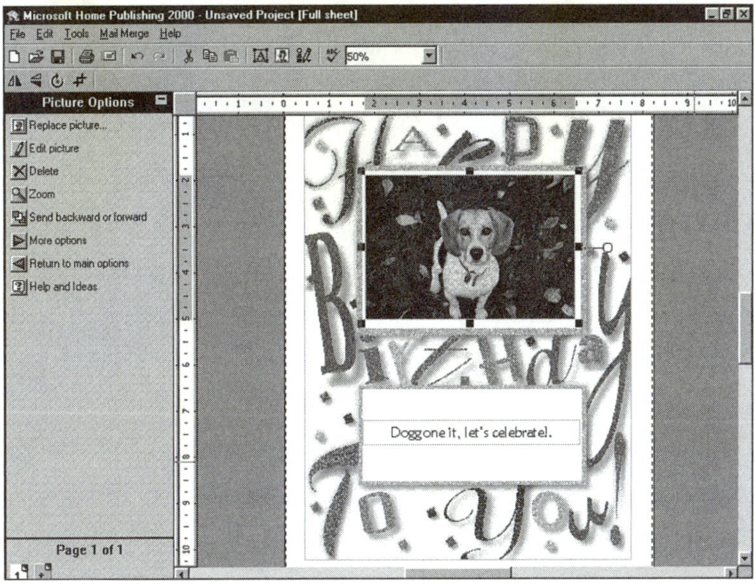

You can also place a picture from your own hard disk in a project (for example, a picture you have scanned). From the Main Options window, choose Add Something, Picture from Another Source. Then choose either My Computer to select an already-saved picture or Scanner or Digital Camera to operate your scanner now.

→ You can work the photo just like any other object; **see** "Manipulating Objects," **p. 529**.

ADDING SHAPED TEXT

Shaped text is another name for WordArt, which you might have encountered in Word or Works. It's a neat little utility that takes regular-looking text and twists, bends, and otherwise manipulates it to look cool. You can spend many hours playing with this feature.

Follow these steps to do some experimenting with shaped text:

1. Open the project page where you want to insert shaped text. For example, you may want to place the text on an empty page.
2. From the Main Options pane, choose Add Something, Other, Shaped Text. A palette of shapes appears, as shown in Figure 26.8.
3. Click the shape you want. The Edit Shaped Text dialog box opens.
4. Type the text you want to use. If you want to start a new line, press Ctrl+Enter.
5. Click OK. The text appears in the shape you chose (see Figure 26.9).

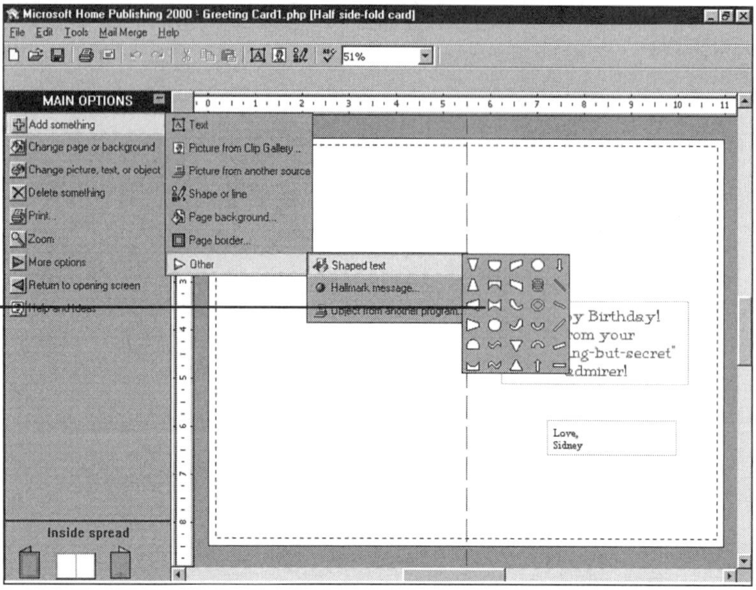

Figure 26.8
Select a shape to use for the text.

Click a shape for the text.

Drag a selection handle to resize it.

Drag this circular handle to rotate it.

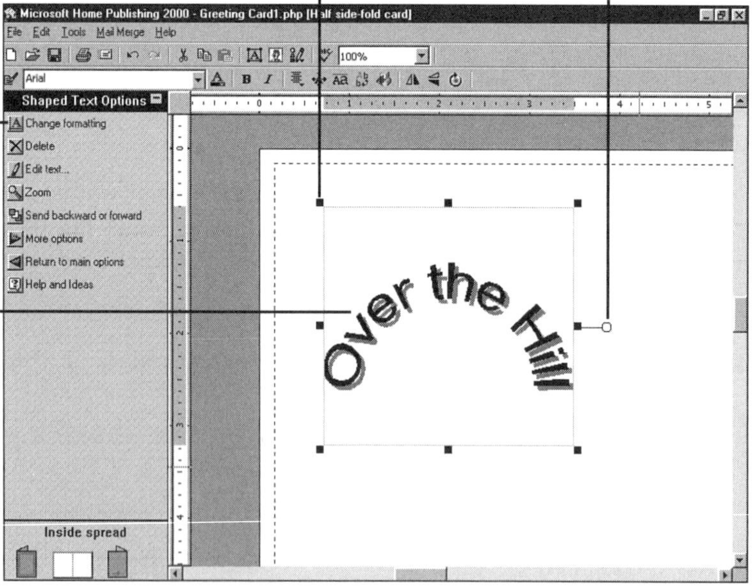

Figure 26.9
Your text will be squeezed into the shape you chose.

Click Change Formatting to open a menu of formatting options for it.

Shaped text

Now you are free to format the shaped text as you desire. Use the toolbar buttons shown in Table 26.1, or click Change Formatting and then select a formatting command from the menu that appears.

To change the font, select from the Font drop-down list on the toolbar, or choose Change Formatting, Font to use a dialog box. To change the outline or shadow around the text, choose Change Formatting, Shadow, or Change Formatting, Outline, respectively.

Table 26.1 Shaped Text Formatting Buttons

Button	Name	Action
	Text Color	Opens a palette of colors from which to choose.
	Bold	Makes text bold.
	Italic	Makes text italicized.
	Alignment	Opens a menu of alignments from which to choose.
	Stretch to Fit	Stretches the shaped text to fill its text box both vertically and horizontally. (Resize the text box to alter the look.)
	Same-Height Letters	Makes all letters the same height, including capitals.
	Vertical Text	Toggles between vertical and normal text.
	Replace Shape	Reopens the palette of shapes from which to choose.
	Flip Horizontal	Flips the text horizontally.
	Flip Vertical	Flips the text vertically.
	Rotate	Enables the text to be rotated.

Drawing Lines and Shapes

Home Publishing comes with some basic drawing tools, but don't get your hopes up too high—these are not sophisticated tools that you can use to get fancy results. Rather, they enable you to create basic lines and shapes to enhance the other parts of your project. For example, you could add a line to separate one section of text from another, or you could add a circle around a picture—that sort of thing.

To add a shape, click the Shape button on the toolbar. A menu presents four options:

- **Line**—Places a default-formatted, straight horizontal line on the page. You can then format it, move it, and/or rotate it as needed.
- **Shape**—Opens a palette of shapes. Choose a shape, and it appears on the page. You can then format it, move it, and so on.
- **Draw a Line**—Turns your mouse pointer into a crosshair. Drag with it to draw a line (not necessarily a straight one). Press Enter or click Done to finish.
- **Draw a Shape**—Turns your mouse pointer into a crosshair. Drag with it to draw a freehand shape. Or drag to draw the first side of a shape, then release the mouse button, and then move the mouse to extend the shape (see Figure 26.10). Click to place a corner, and then drag again to make another; when you are finished, press Enter or click Done.

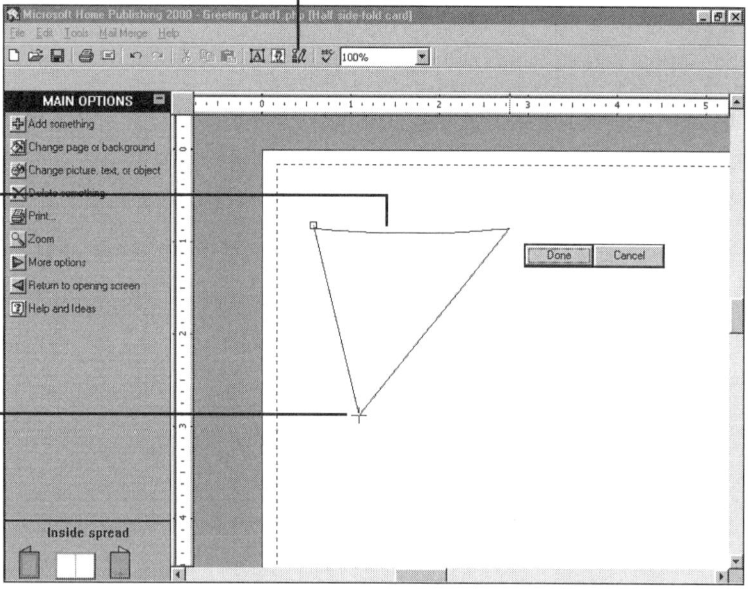

Figure 26.10
You can draw a freehand shape with the mouse pointer.

After placing a line or a shape, you will probably want to move or resize it. The next section explains moving and resizing.

To format a line or a shape, click Change Shape or Line and then choose from the menu that appears. For example, for a line, you can choose Line Color, Line Thickness, or Arrowhead.

Manipulating Objects

The default placement of objects is seldom the right placement. The generic elements you add, such as shapes, clip art, lines, text, and so on need to be modified to work well on your page. In this section, you learn how to do just that.

Note

As I mentioned earlier, everything on the page is an object, and all objects are manipulated in common ways. When you know how to work with a piece of clip art, for example, you also know how to do the same things to a picture, a text box, or some shaped text.

Resizing an Object

The best technique for resizing an object is dragging. When you select an object, it's surrounded by black boxes, called selection handles. You can drag a handle to resize the object.

1. Click the object so that selection handles (squares) appear around its border, as shown in Figure 26.11.

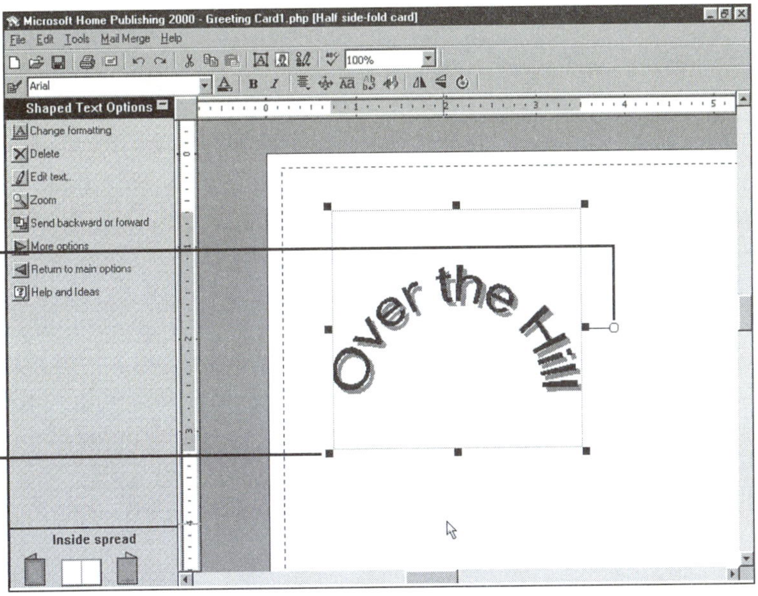

Figure 26.11
A selected object is surrounded by selection handles.

2. Point the mouse pointer at one of those handles so that the mouse pointer turns into a double-headed arrow.
3. Hold down the left mouse button and drag the handle to change the size of the object. A dotted outline shows where the new dimensions will be.
4. When you're finished, release the mouse button, and the object changes to its new size.

You can drag a side handle to resize in one dimension, or you can drag a corner handle to resize in two dimensions at once. To maintain the *aspect ratio* (the proportion of height to width), hold down the Shift key on the keyboard as you drag.

Repositioning or Moving an Object

First, let's get our terms straight. I'm using the term "reposition" to mean moving an object around on its same page. I'm using "moving" to mean transferring the object from one page to another.

To reposition an object, just point the mouse pointer at its middle so that the pointer turns into a four-headed arrow. Then drag the object to a different spot.

To move an object to another page, you have to use the cut-and-paste method. Select the object (by clicking it), and then click the Cut button on the toolbar.

Then use the tabs on the left side of the screen to display the page where you want it to go and click the Paste button.

The object probably will not be pasted at exactly the right spot on the new page, so it's likely that you will have to reposition it after it gets there.

Rotating and Flipping an Object

Depending on what object you have selected, you might see rotating and/or flipping buttons on the toolbar at the top of the screen. Click the object to select it and then click one or more of these buttons:

- **Flip Vertical**—Flips the object from top to bottom so that it's upside down.

- **Flip Horizontal**—Flips the object from side to side so that it's a mirror image of itself.

To rotate an object, hover your mouse pointer over the rotation symbol next to the object until your mouse pointer says ROTATE. Then drag up or down to start rotating the object. When you have the rotation just right, release the mouse button.

Tip #152 from *Faithe Wempen*

To undo a rotation (or any other action), choose Edit, Undo or press Ctrl+Z.

Cropping an Image

Some objects, such as photos, for example, allow cropping. This means you can eliminate some of the outside of the image and show just a certain part of it. For example, in Figure 26.12, the image on the left is the original, and the one on the right is a cropped and resized copy. The cropping makes the important part of the image more noticeable.

Figure 26.12
Cropping can improve a picture with too much extraneous detail.

To crop a picture:

1. Select the object and then click the Crop button on the toolbar.

> **Note**
>
> If you don't see the Crop button, make sure that an object is selected that allows cropping. You can crop only pictures and photos.

2. Position the mouse pointer over one of the selection handles, so that the word CROP appears.
3. Drag the selection handle to crop the object. Repeat for each side of the object until it is cropped the way you want it.
4. Click the Crop button again to turn off cropping.

Adding a Page Border

Page borders are a type of picture, but instead of hogging center stage, they play a supporting role around the edge of the page. Several kinds of page borders are available. Some are banners that run across the top and bottom of the page; others are graphical lines or little repeated pictures.

To add a page border:

1. In the Main Options pane, choose Add Something, Page Border. This opens a box of borders from which you can choose.

2. Choose a border category from the Select a Category drop-down list at the top of the box. (You can always choose a different one at any time in the process.)
3. Click a border name that you're curious about and see a preview of it in the Preview pane (see Figure 26.13).

Tip #153 from *Faithe Wempen*

To preview the border on your page without closing the Border dialog box, click the Preview button.

4. Specify the desired border size in the Border Size box. This refers to the height of the individual pictures that repeat to make up the border.
5. Click OK.

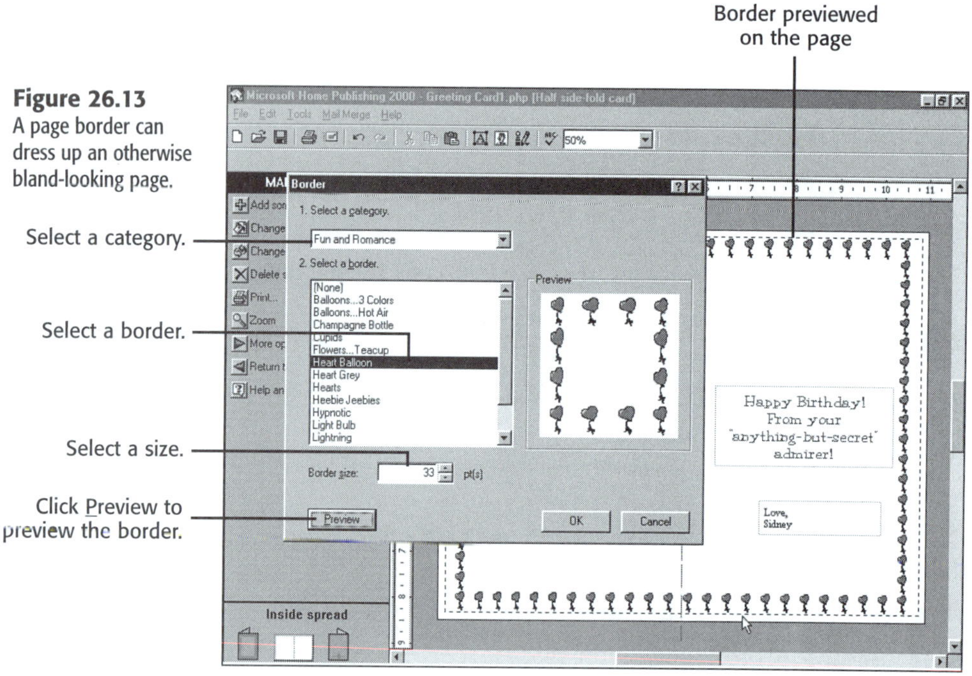

Figure 26.13
A page border can dress up an otherwise bland-looking page.

PRINTING YOUR WORK

You can print your work not only when you're finished, but at any time along the way to see what progress you're making. The onscreen display is pretty close to what the printout will look like, but sometimes it's nice just to hold the thing in your hands and admire it while you're thinking up ideas for the final touches.

Tip #154 from *Faithe Wempen*

If you have a color printer, by all means use it for your final printout. Home Publishing projects make extensive use of color, and you won't get the same cool results on a black-and-white printer. However, if you have both a black-and-white and color printer, you might want to use the black-and-white for your in-progress drafts because the cost per page is lower. (You don't want to use up all your expensive colored ink on a rough draft.)

When it's time to print the final copy, consider using some of that special glossy paper available for inkjet printers. It's expensive, but it makes the printouts look great.

To print your work:

1. Click the Print button on the toolbar, or click the Print option in the Main Options pane. The Print dialog box opens (see Figure 26.14).

Note

When you print, if you have not yet saved your project, you'll be prompted to do so. Click Yes (and follow the directions for saving in the "Saving a Project" section later in this chapter), or click No if you don't want to bother with that now. You can always save later.

2. The default printer is listed and one copy is selected for printing. Change the printer, the page range, and/or the number of copies, if desired, and then click OK to print.

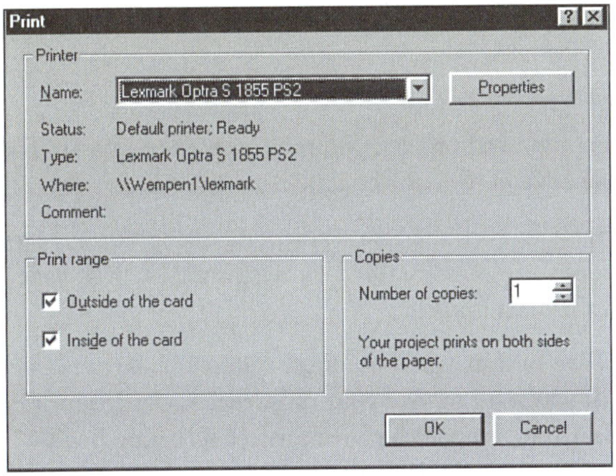

Figure 26.14
Print your work from Home Publishing.

Note

The first time you print in Home Publishing 2000 with a particular printer, you will be prompted to go through a printer test. Follow the onscreen instructions. You will need to do this only once.

3. Wait for the front of the pages to print. Then click OK.
4. Remove the printed pages from the printer and reinsert them as shown in the dialog box that appears. The animation will be different depending on your printer; Figure 26.15 shows one example.

Figure 26.15
Follow the example shown onscreen for reinserting the paper in your printer to print side two.

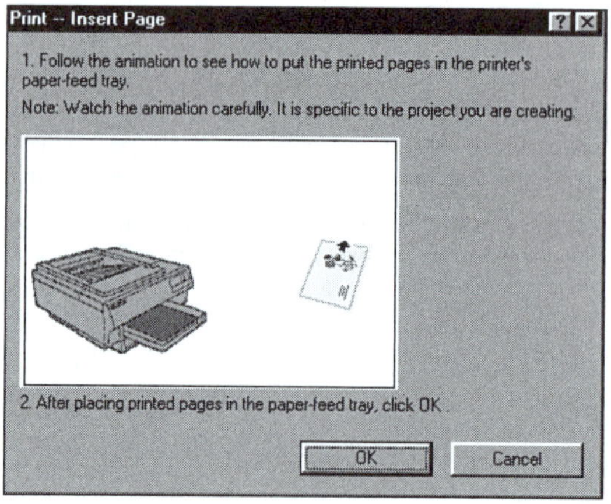

5. Click OK to print the second side.
6. Wait until the printer has finished; then click OK.

If the project did not print correctly (for example, if one side is upside down or both sides printed on the same side of the paper), try again, rotating the paper differently between sides one and two.

SAVING A PROJECT

Whenever you print an unsaved project, you're prompted to save it. That's one way to save. Another is to click the Save button on the toolbar at any time.

The first time you save a project, the Save Project As dialog box appears, as shown in Figure 26.16. Change the File Name to something more specific (such as **`Nancy Birthday Card`**). Then click Save. Your project is saved.

When you click the Save button again, the file is automatically saved to the name you previously assigned. If you want to save your most recent changes or type a different name to save it under a new name, reopen the Save Project As dialog box by choosing File, Save As. You might do this, for example, if you want to base a new project on an existing one.

OPENING A SAVED PROJECT

You can open a saved project in any of these ways:

- You can open one of the last four projects by selecting it from the bottom of the File menu.
- You can click the My Projects button from the main program window, select the project you want, and then click Open.
- You can choose File, Open at any time, select the project you want, and click Open.

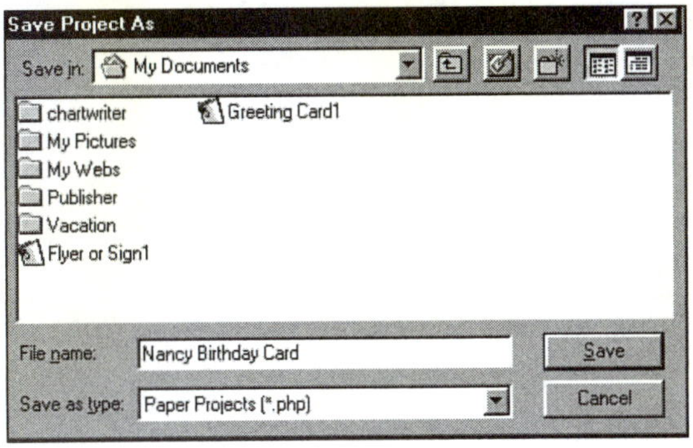

Figure 26.16
Change the default name for the project to something more meaningful and specific.

If you have a project stored in a different location (for example, on a floppy disk), you can access that location by clicking the Look In drop-down list.

CREATING EMAIL AND WEB PROJECTS

Although most of the projects you create with Home Publishing follow similar steps, email and Web projects work a bit differently, enough to warrant a brief discussion on the topic. You can send animated email greeting cards, create email stationery, create Web pages, and lots more.

To see a listing of the email and Web projects, click the Email and Web Projects tab from the opening screen. (Choose File, Close and Return to Opening Screen at any time to get there.)

As an example, let's look at making an email greeting card:

1. If you are not at the opening screen, choose File, Close and Return to Opening Screen.
2. Click the Email and Web Projects tab.
3. Click Greetings. A list of occasions appears.
4. Click the occasion you want. A list of designs appears from which to choose.
5. Click the theme you want from the Themes list.
6. Double-click the greeting you want. It appears for editing.
7. Make any changes to the project.
8. Choose File, Send by Email. The Send by Email dialog box appears.
9. Choose which email program you want to use. (If you are using Outlook Express, as you learned in Chapter 20, "Working with Email and Newsgroups," choose that.) Then click OK. A new message appears in your email program.
10. Address the message the same as you would any message. (Refer to Chapter 20 for help with Outlook Express.)

    Depending on the email program, the message appears either as an attachment or right there in the message pane.

11. Click the Send button, or do whatever you normally do to send a message in your email program. The message is sent.

When the recipient receives the message, it shows up as an attachment. When he or she opens the attachment, a mini-application within Internet Explorer (or the recipient's current Web browser) displays the card, as shown in Figure 26.17.

Figure 26.17
When viewing email greetings, the graphics are often animated onscreen.

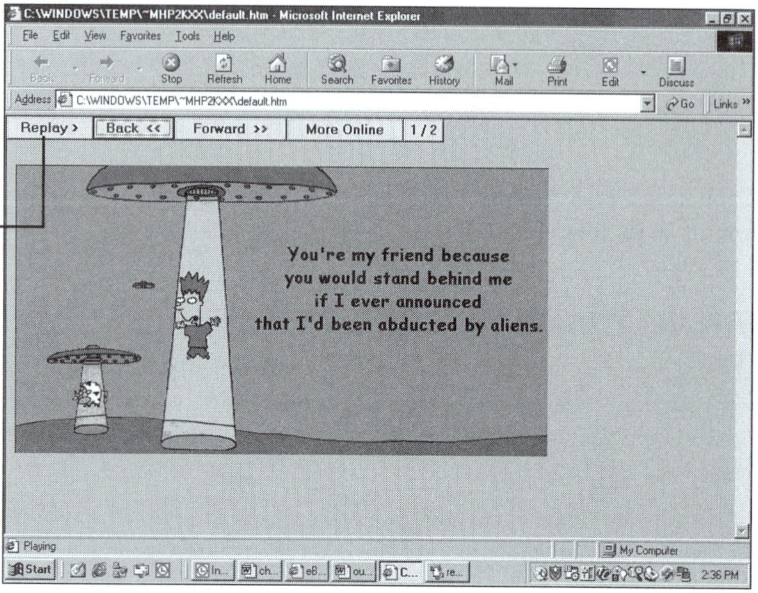

There's just not enough room in this book to show you all the great things you can do with Home Publishing, but you can explore all the options on your own. For example, you can change the sound effects used with email greetings, add reminders about upcoming events for which you need to make cards, or download more designs from the Web, as explained in the next section.

Exploring the Home Publishing Web Site

Home Publishing comes with some wonderful designs and art, but even more good stuff is out there and you can download it from the Web—some of it for free. The goodies are called *add-on packs*. All you need is a modem, an Internet account, and Internet Explorer.

You already know how to use Internet Explorer. Now all you need to know is, "How do I get this good stuff?" Easy.

1. Start your Internet connection.
2. On the main screen of Home Publishing, click the Home Publishing Web Site link.

3. Internet Explorer opens and a connection box appears (if you're not already connected to your Internet account). Click Connect and after a few seconds, the browser window displays the product home page.
4. Click the Add-On Packs hyperlink on the Web page that appears.
5. Now follow the links to find just the right add-on pack you want to download.

Be sure to check out all the other great stuff on the Web site. When you're finished, log off and return to Home Publishing and try out your new designs.

TROUBLESHOOTING

FREQUENT CD SWAPS

It seems like I'm always having to swap the CDs to give Home Publisher the files it needs.

If you find yourself having to swap CDs frequently when using Home Publisher, perhaps you would be better off installing a more complete version of the program. When you install Home Publisher, you have a choice of Compact, Standard, or Full installations; rerun the installation program and choose a different install set. (Remember, however, a more complete install takes up more hard disk space.)

CREATING A CONSISTENT LOOK

Is there an easy way to create coordinated items for an event, such as envelopes, invitations, and banners that all have a common theme?

If you want to create a set of items that all match one another, with common artwork or coloring for example, start on the Occasions and Activities tab and choose an occasion, such as Valentine's Day. Then choose a design and select from a full listing of projects that employ it (regardless of project type).

REMOVING BACKGROUND ARTWORK FOR BLACK-AND-WHITE PRINTING

I have a black-and-white printer, backgrounds don't look very good when printed. But when I try to remove the background from certain projects, nothing happens.

Some colored backgrounds are actually artwork; select a background image and press Delete to remove it. If you don't like how the project looks without it, you can always press Ctrl+Z immediately to replace it.

CHAPTER 27

Using Microsoft Encarta 2000

In this chapter

WHAT IS MICROSOFT ENCARTA?

Microsoft Encarta 2000 is an electronic version of a set of encyclopedias. Unlike book encyclopedias, however, Encarta offers much more than text and pictures. With Encarta, you can look up topics and view video clips, sound clips, and more.

Encarta is basically a giant *database* of information, including multimedia items. You can access the information in various ways:

- **Encyclopedia articles**—This is the equivalent of turning to an encyclopedia page in a book. Encarta's articles include text and pictures, as well as links to related articles.
- **Multimedia clips**—Many articles found in the encyclopedia's library include pictures, video clips, and sound clips. You can run a sound or video clip to see or hear more about a particular topic.
- **InterActivities**—As the name implies, this feature provides interactive learning tools for exploring more about a topic or a concept.
- **Categories**—Rather than looking up specific topics, you can also explore the encyclopedia by categories using Encarta's Explore feature.

That's just the tip of the iceberg when it comes to features offered in Encarta 2000. In this chapter, you learn how to use Encarta to look up topics, play multimedia files, try a knowledge-testing game, and tap into the Encarta Online Web site.

STARTING AND EXITING ENCARTA

To begin using Encarta, choose Start, Programs, Microsoft Encarta, Encarta Encyclopedia 2000. You can also start Encarta from the Task Launcher by choosing Encarta Encyclopedia from the Programs tab and then choosing an Encarta activity as a task. (Doing so will jump to a particular spot in the program, whereas starting the program from the Start menu will start you at the opening screen.)

Another way to start the program is to pop Disc 1 of the set into your CD-ROM drive. If Auto Insert Notification is turned on, Encarta starts automatically.

Note

If the Encarta CD was not in the drive, the first thing you'll see is a prompt telling you to insert it.

The Encarta home page, shown in Figure 27.1, is your home base for using the program. You can start Encarta's main features from this page. You'll also notice a title bar at the top of the program window and a menu bar for accessing commands. To return to this screen at any time, you can click the Home button on the menu bar.

Figure 27.1
Encarta's opening screen offers jumping-off places for all its features and activities.

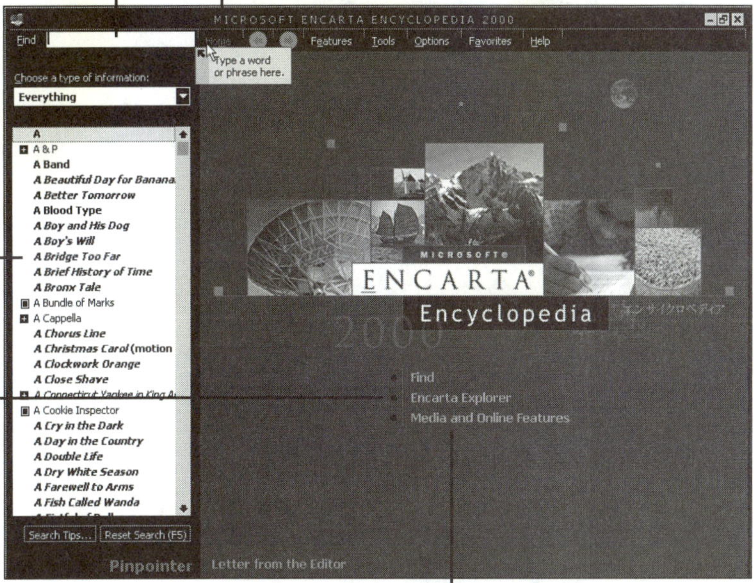

When you're ready to exit Encarta, click the Close (X) button in the top-right corner of the program window.

Looking Up a Topic

The library of encyclopedia articles is the largest part of Encarta. If you do not see the Pinpointer pane on the left (refer to Figure 27.1), click Find to display it. (Find appears twice on the home page: once in the top-left corner and once in the middle. Either will work.)

Encarta's Pinpointer search tool can help you look up articles, multimedia items, and more.

To open a topic in the Pinpointer pane's topic list, simply click the topic. Notice in Figure 27.2 that some topics have icons next to them. For example, a plus sign next to an entry means that there are more topic articles and media items to list. Click the plus sign icon to display the items. A minus sign means the subtopics have already been expanded; click it to collapse them again. Other symbols indicate pictures, video clips, sounds, or any of several other special types of entries.

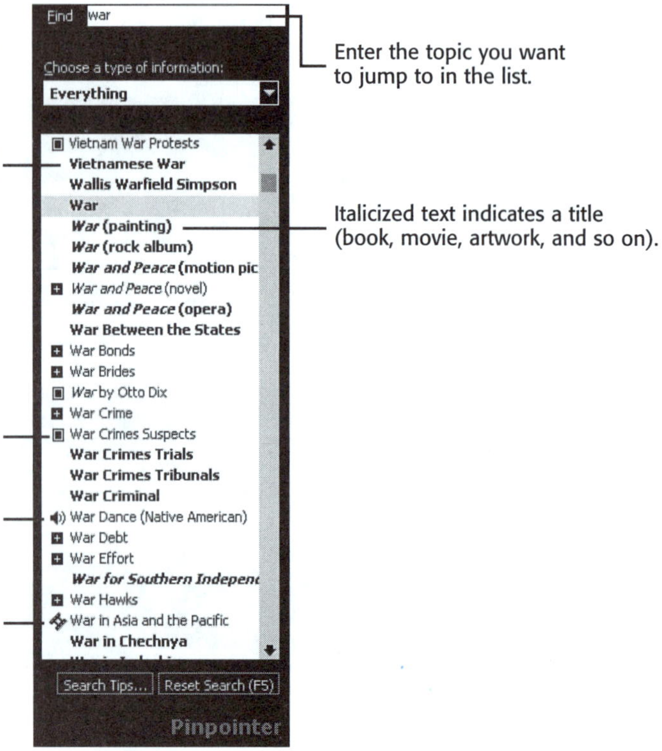

Figure 27.2
Look up encyclopedia articles from here.

The example used in the following steps walks you through the procedure for looking up the topic `dinosaur` using the Pinpointer pane, viewing a Contents page for dinosaur, and then viewing a related article. Follow along with the steps to view the article on your own computer.

1. From the Home screen, click Find, if you have not already done so. This opens the Pinpointer pane, as shown in Figure 27.1.
2. Click inside the Find text box at the top of the Pinpointer pane and type in the topic you want to search for. As you type, the list box scrolls alphabetically to the topics. For example, if you type **`dinosaur`**, the list displays the topics shown in Figure 27.3.

Tip #155 from *Faithe Wempen*

Almost all subjects are singular in Encarta. Avoid adding "s" to the end of the topic you are searching for, or Encarta might not be able to locate what you want.

3. To view an article or the Contents page, click the topic. For example, if you double-click the Dinosaur topic shown in Figure 27.3, the Dinosaur Contents page opens, as shown in Figure 27.4.

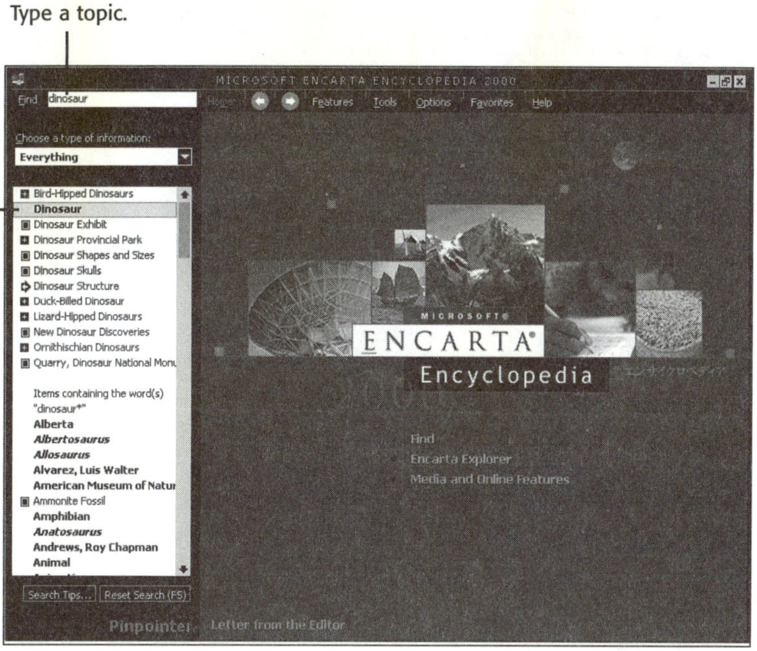

Figure 27.3
Typing words into the Pinpointer box narrows down the list of topics.

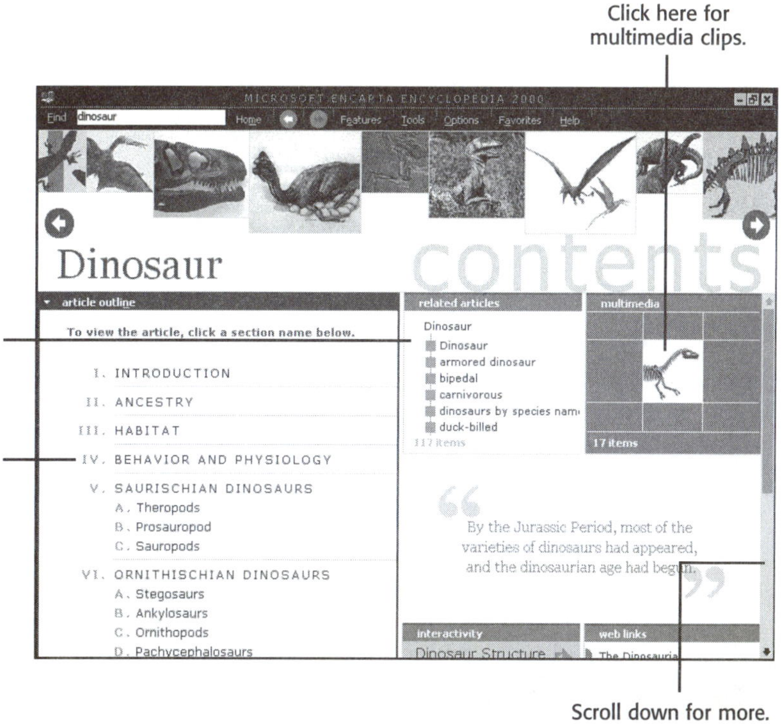

Figure 27.4
A Contents page has links to related articles and a media bar for viewing images and multimedia clips.

4. If you click the `Prosauropod` link in Figure 27.4, the article detailing the topic appears, as shown in Figure 27.5. Use the scrollbars to help you read the article.

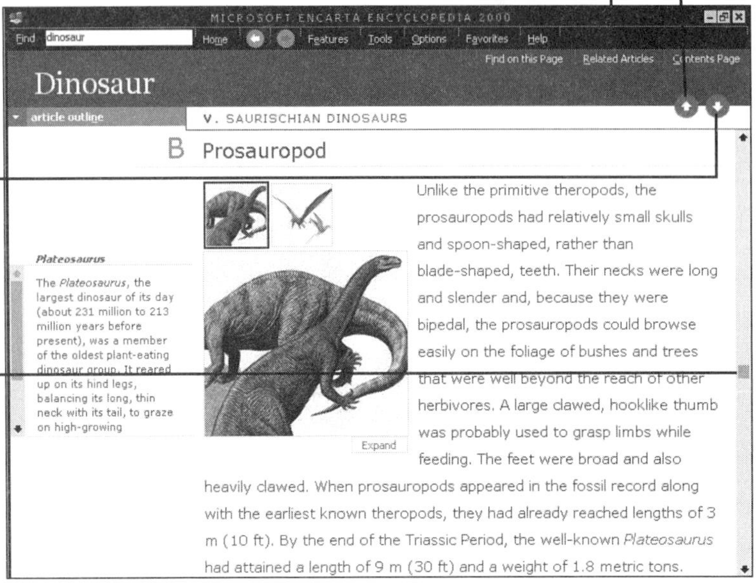

Figure 27.5
An article may include pictures and a scrollable sidebar.

5. To return to the previous page you were viewing, click the Back button (the left-pointing arrow) on the menu bar (refer to Figure 27.5).
6. To look up another topic, click inside the Find text box on the menu bar and enter a new topic.

You can also look up specific types of media. By default, the Pinpointer pane is set to look up all media forms. To look up only one kind, open the Choose a Type of Information drop-down list and select a particular media item. For example, Figure 27.6 shows the list of articles containing "dinosaur," with the list filtered to show only articles.

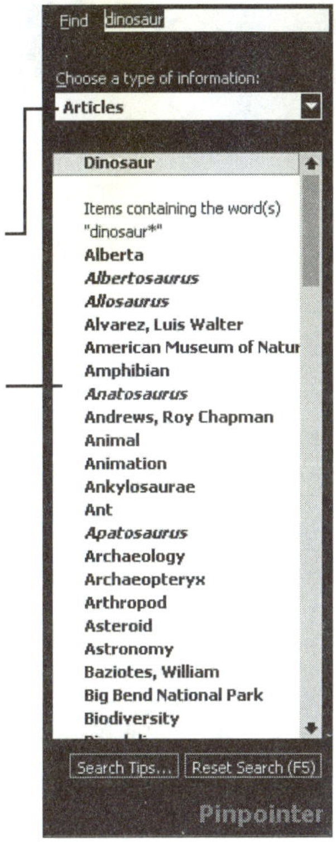

Figure 27.6
You can look up specific kinds of media items.

Working with an Article

When the article you want is displayed, you can scroll through and read the information. Use the vertical scrollbar on the right side of the article page to scroll up or down the article. A click on the Article Outline drop-down arrow, located on the far left side of the article page, displays an outline of the topic's related Contents page with links to other related articles (see Figure 27.7).

In addition to reading articles, you can do a couple of things with the article, as explained in the following sections.

Copying an Article

Suppose that you want to copy a part of the article into your word processor so that you can save it.

Note

Okay, technically that's plagiarism, but who among us hasn't "borrowed" the wording from an encyclopedia for a junior-high science report? But if you do copy from Encarta, you must cite your source in the report and not try to pass it off as your own writing.

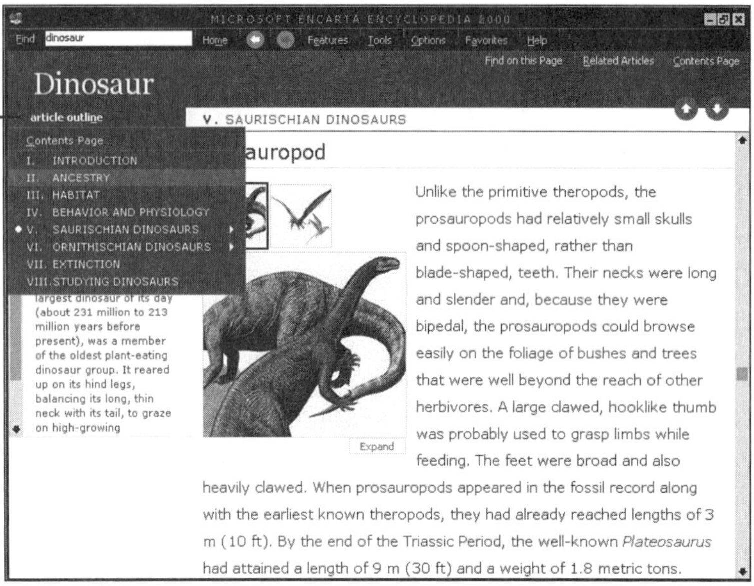

Figure 27.7
View the Contents in a menu format without leaving the current article.

Click here to open the menu.

1. If you want to copy only certain text, select it by dragging across it with the left mouse button held down. If you want the whole article, you don't need to do this.
2. Choose Options, Copy. The Copy dialog box appears, as shown in Figure 27.8.

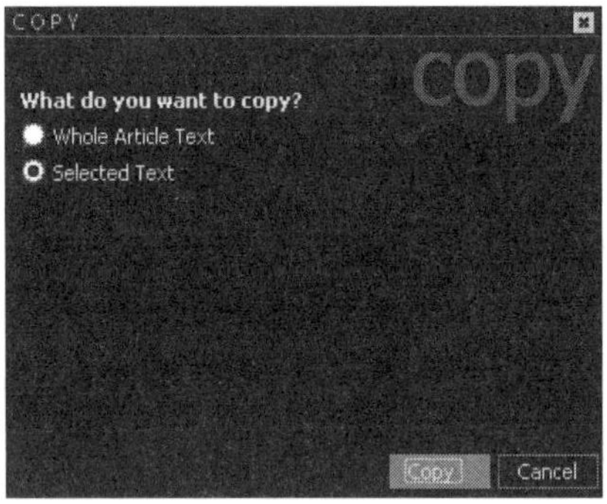

Figure 27.8
Use the Copy dialog box to copy the article to the Windows Clipboard.

3. If you selected text in step 1, click Selected Text. If you didn't, click Whole Article Text. The text is copied to the Windows Clipboard.
4. Open your word processing program (use the Start button). You don't need to close Encarta.
5. In the word processor, choose Edit, Paste. The material appears in the word processor.

PRINTING AN ARTICLE

You can print part or all of the article. If you want to print only part of it, select that part first. Otherwise, just go ahead and choose Options, Print. A Print dialog box appears, as shown in Figure 27.9. Select what you want to print (the exact choices vary depending on what you are viewing at the moment), and then click Print.

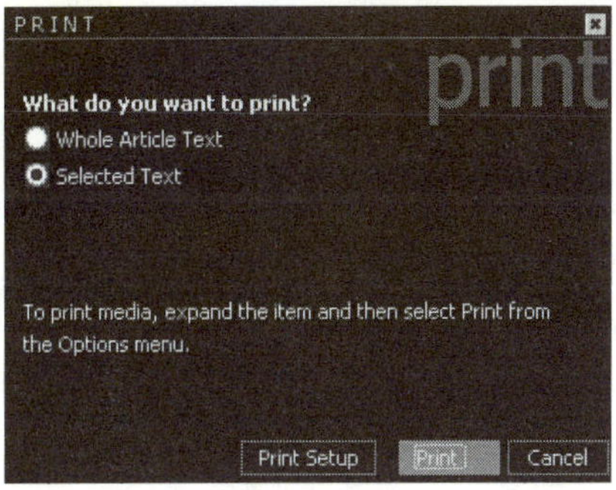

Figure 27.9
Use the Print dialog box to print portions of the article.

WORKING WITH THE MEDIA CLIPS IN AN ARTICLE

Many of the encyclopedia articles have at least one media item (a picture, video, sound, and so on); others have numerous media items to explore. Encarta media clips include sound, video and film clips, tables, maps, photos, and collages (these can include several of the other media clip types). Let's look at the United States (Overview) article to examine several of the media items you might encounter.

When you open a Contents page, a Multimedia box on that page provides a link to any available media clips. Click Multimedia to see a list of the available clips for the topic. Figure 27.10 shows the multimedia clip listing for "United States."

PLAYING SOUND CLIPS

Most computers today have speakers for hearing sound files. Encarta 2000 takes full advantage of this by offering all kinds of sound files with its articles.

To open a sound clip feature, click the media item containing a sound clip icon (which looks like a speaker). For example, when you click the United States Flag and Anthem in Figure 27.10, the clip plays. A progress bar appears under the placeholder graphic, as shown in Figure 27.11. If this were a video clip, a moving picture would appear in place of the placeholder graphic.

VIEWING MAP MEDIA

Some media items open maps. (The first entry in Figure 27.10, United States, does this.) When you choose it, a map appears.

Figure 27.10
This Contents page has a variety of media items.

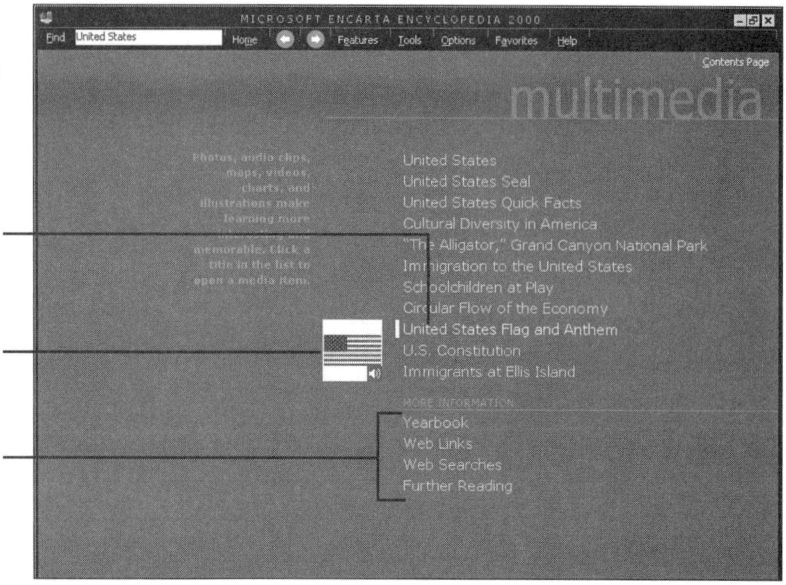

Figure 27.11
The clip appears onscreen and plays.

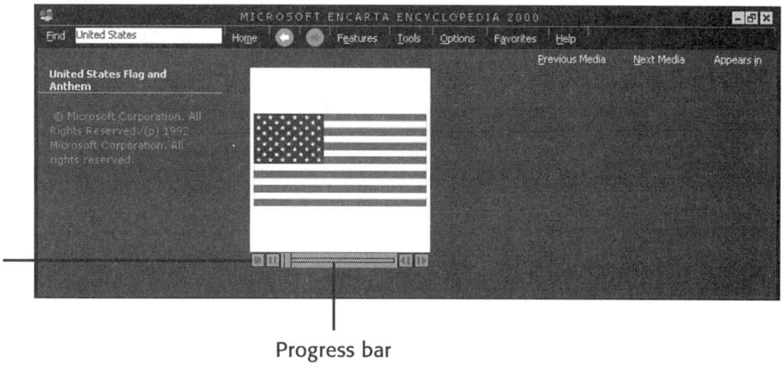

Sometimes the map may need to be expanded. For example, in Figure 27.12, you must click the Expand button to see the full map, shown in Figure 27.13.

Figure 27.12
Here's a map, but it's not expanded and so not very useful.

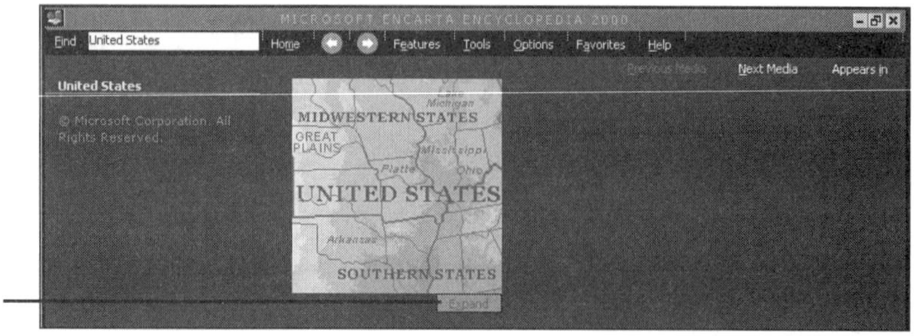

Figure 27.13
The same map after clicking the Expand button.

Zoom Out button

Find a Place listing

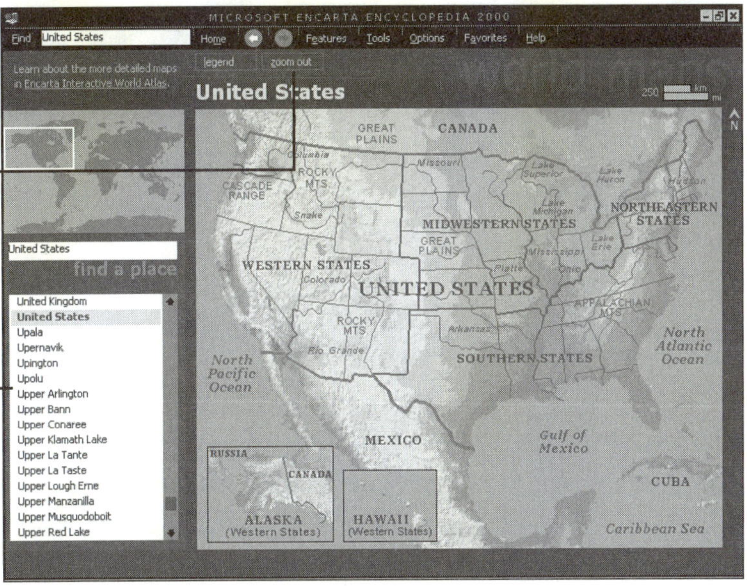

Click the map to zoom in on a particular spot; click the Zoom Out button above the map to zoom back out again. Use the Find a Place listing to the left of the map screen to search for a specific place on the map.

Tip #156 from *Faithe Wempen*

To find all the maps available in Encarta, choose Features, World Maps. This opens the World Maps feature with a global view of the world. You can then zoom in on any area you want to see.

Working with InterActivities

Encarta's InterActivities feature is an interactive article that's both a learning tool and an information resource. Depending on the topic, the activity itself might be a chart you can make changes to, a diagram you can build, or more. Like other media links, click an InterActivity to open the feature.

For example, perform the following steps to check out a dinosaur-related InterActivity:

1. Start by typing the word **`dinosaur`** into the Find text box and pressing Enter.
2. Open the Choose a Type of Information drop-down list and choose InterActivities. Encarta lists the Dinosaur Structure topic in the Topics list box.
3. Click the topic to open the InterActivity feature shown in Figure 27.14.
4. Follow the instructions for assembling the dinosaur skeleton. You can also read about the topic.
5. When finished, click the Back button on the menu bar to return to the previous screen.

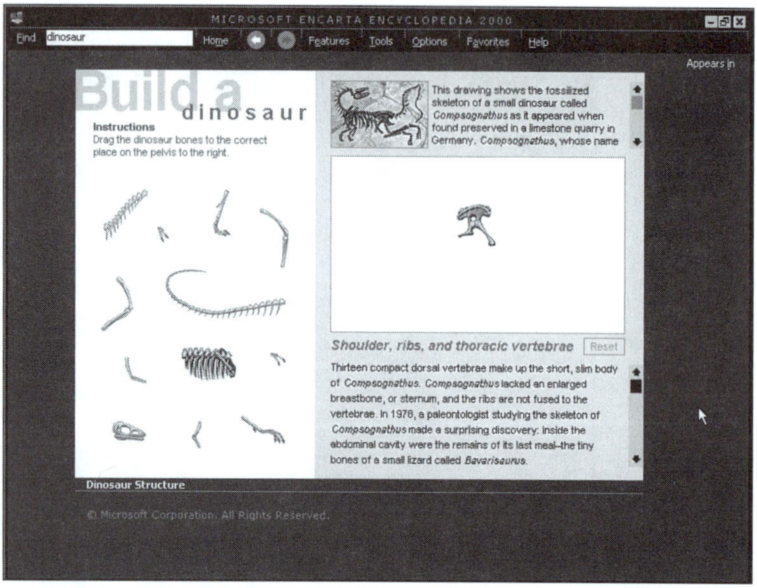

Figure 27.14
Use this InterActivity to build a dinosaur skeleton.

Encarta has all kinds of InterActivities you can explore. Some involve selecting various types of data from drop-down lists, manipulating graph data, science experiments, and more.

Tip #157 from *Faithe Wempen*

To explore only the InterActivity features found in Encarta, choose Features, InterActivities. This opens a central page listing links to all the topics containing InterActivities.

EXPLORING BY CATEGORY

Another way to use Encarta is to explore the encyclopedia by categories. Click the Home button on the menu bar to return to the Home page; then click the Encarta Explorer link. You can also choose Features, Encarta Explorer. Either method opens the Explore screen, shown in Figure 27.15.

Click the category you want to explore. This displays another screen like the one shown in Figure 27.15, this time detailing more categories (subcategories) from which you can choose. Continue selecting the category you want to explore, each time narrowing your topic. Finally, when the topic category is narrowed, a Contents page displays. From here, you can read topic articles and explore media items.

Figure 27.15
You can also explore your electronic encyclopedia via categories.

Click a category.

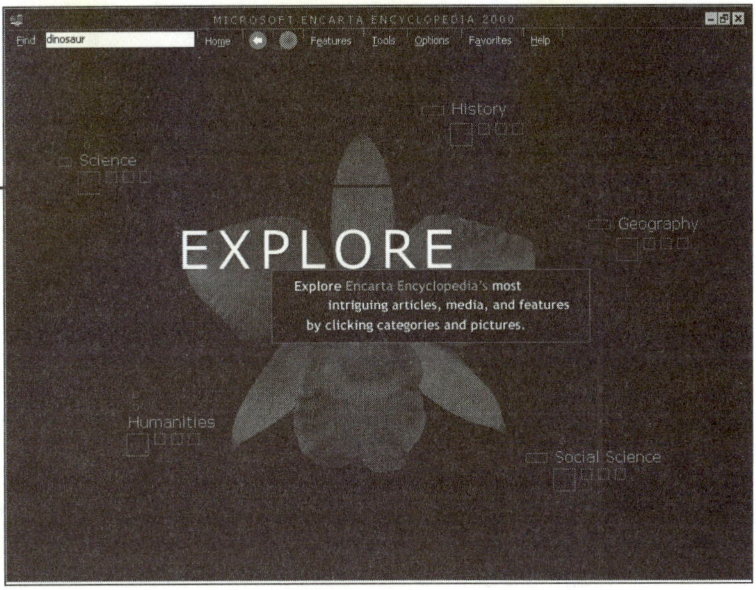

Playing MindMaze

If you like Trivial Pursuit, you'll love MindMaze. It's a great test-your-knowledge game designed for all ages. You can play it at any of three degrees of difficulty. Level 1 is appropriate for kids and for adults who either have not had a whole lot of education or who enjoy winning easily. The difficulty level progresses all the way up to Level 4, for people who find the questions on *Jeopardy!* insultingly easy.

The object of the game is to get to the top of the castle and answer the necessary questions to break the castle curse. To do this, you move through rooms in a castle to a stairway leading up. Each time you want to pass through a doorway, you have to answer a question correctly. (You get points along the way for correct answers, and speed of answering counts.) When you go up a stairway, you're on the next level, and you do the same thing again—navigate toward the stairway to an even higher level. Finally (presumably), you reach the top of the castle and break the curse, thus winning the game.

Along the way, you see various people and animals in the rooms. You can click them to "talk" to them (they talk to you, but you can't really interact), but talking to them is not an integral part of the game. It's just there to add interest.

1. Choose Features, MindMaze. The first thing you see is the entry door.
2. If you haven't played before, you need to enter your name. Click the New Player button, type your name, and then press Enter.
3. Click your name on the list and then click the front door to enter the castle.

4. Now you're in the main playing area. To reach the screen shown in Figure 27.16, click the doorway that you can see through the bars. The parts of the screen work as follows:
   - **Map**—You are the dot. Your goal (the next level's staircase) is the bracket. Each time you move through a room, the dot moves to a different square. This is how you can tell which room you should go to next. Like a maze, however, not all paths go through; some are dead ends. You may sometimes have to backtrack.
   - **Choose Area of Interest**—This lists the available question categories. Click the one you want, or click All Areas for a variety.
   - **Level**—Choose 1, 2, 3, or 4, depending on your knowledge level. You might want to start with 1 just to get the hang of the game.
   - **Picture**—This shows you what you're "seeing." You can click any person to show a blurb of what they're saying or click any door to go through it. (You will have to answer a question first, of course.)

Figure 27.16
This screen shows the major game-playing tools.

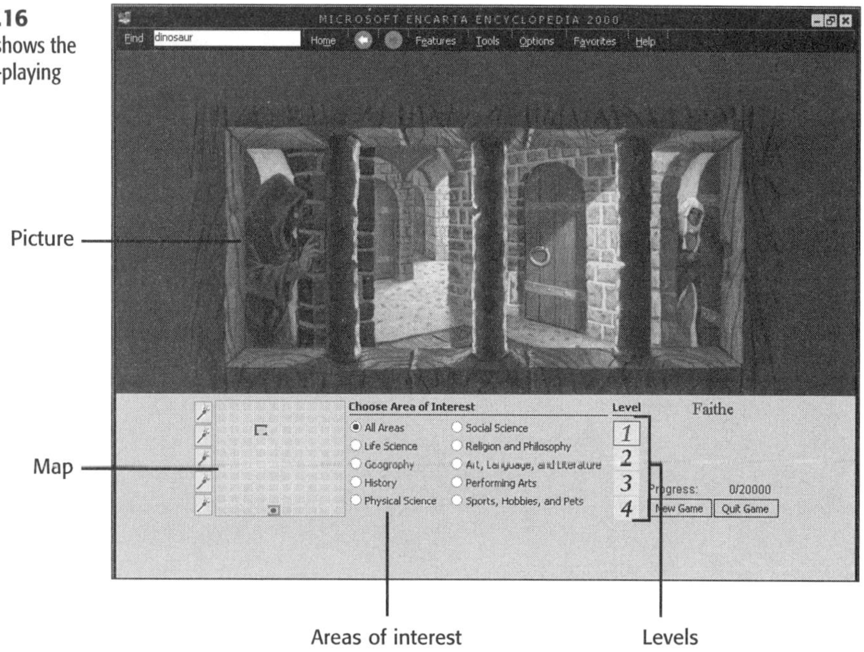

5. Click one of the doors. (Try the one on the left, for starters.) The view changes again. Now you're in a room.
6. (Optional) If a character is in the room, click him or her. Some text appears, showing a message. Click away from it to get rid of it. Some rooms contain objects that link you to articles; when your pointer turns to a hand over one of these objects, click to see the associated information.
7. To leave the room, click a door. If you have not been through this door before, a question appears (see Figure 27.17).

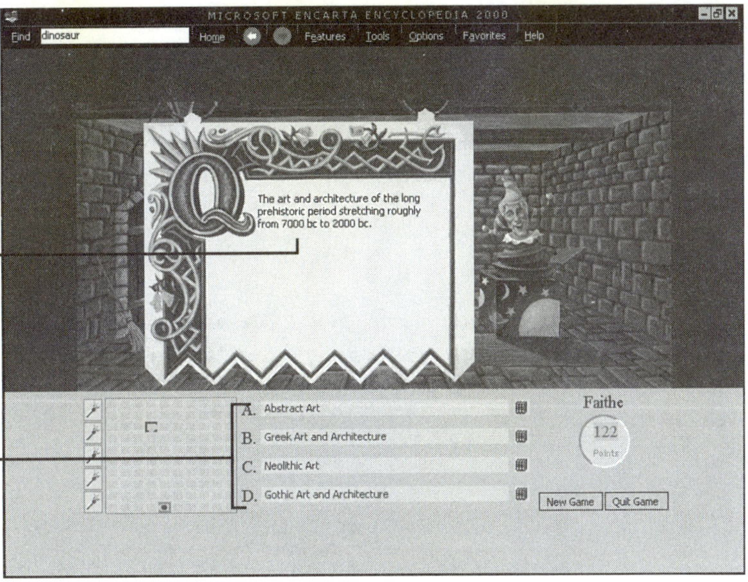

Figure 27.17
Answer the question by clicking answer A, B, C, or D.

8. Click the correct answer for the question, if you know it. If you don't, guess. (Incorrect answers just lower the points you get when you reach the right answer.) If you get it right, a box pops up to inform you of how many points you received for the correct answer. Click OK to move to the next room.

   If you're wrong, a box appears, telling you that you were incorrect and that you can try again. Click OK to get rid of the box and guess again.

Note

You can click the books icon next to any of the answers to see an encyclopedia article about that answer. This can help you determine which answer to pick.

9. In the next room, pick the door that looks most likely to take you in the direction you need to go. Consult the map as needed.

Tip #158 from *Faithe Wempen*

The five torches at the left are "cheats" that show you the floor's map along with the correct path to the stairway. Each time you click a torch, it is used up, so use your torches wisely.

10. Keep moving through the rooms until you come to the staircase. Then click it to go up to the next level.
11. Keep playing until you win or get tired!

If you need to quit for awhile, you can come back later and pick up where you left off. Just click the Close (X) button in the window's corner to end the game. The next time you return, choose your same name again at the entry door, and you'll be whisked back into the same spot.

GOING ONLINE WITH ENCARTA

Even with Encarta's wealth of data, you might find that you need more information on a topic. Perhaps you are looking up some obscure town that Encarta has only a paragraph or two about, or maybe you want up-to-the-minute information, and your copy of Encarta is several months old. Whatever the case, you will want to check out the online component to Encarta.

GETTING MORE TOPIC INFORMATION

To look for more information online, choose Media and Online Features from the opening screen, and then choose Web Links on the screen that appears. (You can also access this same listing by choosing Features, Web Links.) This opens an extensive alphabetical list of Web links, as shown in Figure 27.18. Click one of these links to visit a Web page on the subject.

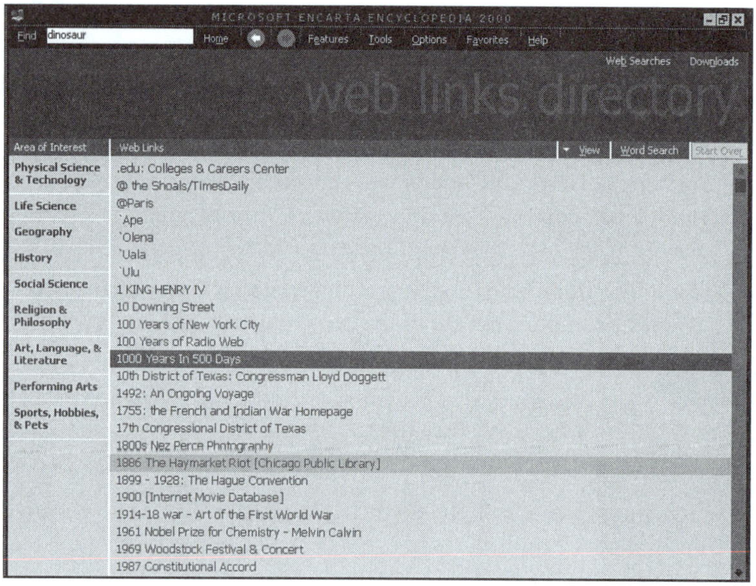

Figure 27.18
Browse topics online through this listing.

When you click a topic, a dialog box appears, describing the online resource and asking what you want to do. You can either copy the URL (for later visiting) or connect to this site now by clicking the button you want.

Tip #159 from
Faithe Wempen

As you are searching for more sources of information, don't forget the Internet itself. It's a vast, varied web of information, and the free sources online greatly outnumber the Encarta information and Microsoft's extra-charge update information combined. Turn back to Chapters 17 through 19 and try searching for the topic you want using an Internet search engine such as Yahoo! or Excite; you might turn up some of your best information that way, without even using Encarta.

Visiting the Encarta Online Web Site

You can also visit the Encarta Web site by choosing Tools, Encarta Online (or Help, Microsoft on the Web, Encarta Online, which is the same thing). This Web site offers an online version of Encarta (abridged), along with other helps and extra information.

Downloading Encarta Updates Online

You can download updates to Encarta to keep your copy fresh and current. To do so, choose Tools, Downloads and then click Update Encarta. The updates download automatically; a progress Window like the one in Figure 27.19 shows the progress. When it is finished, a message appears; click OK to return to Encarta or click Yearbook to go to the Yearbook (which is where you view the downloaded updates).

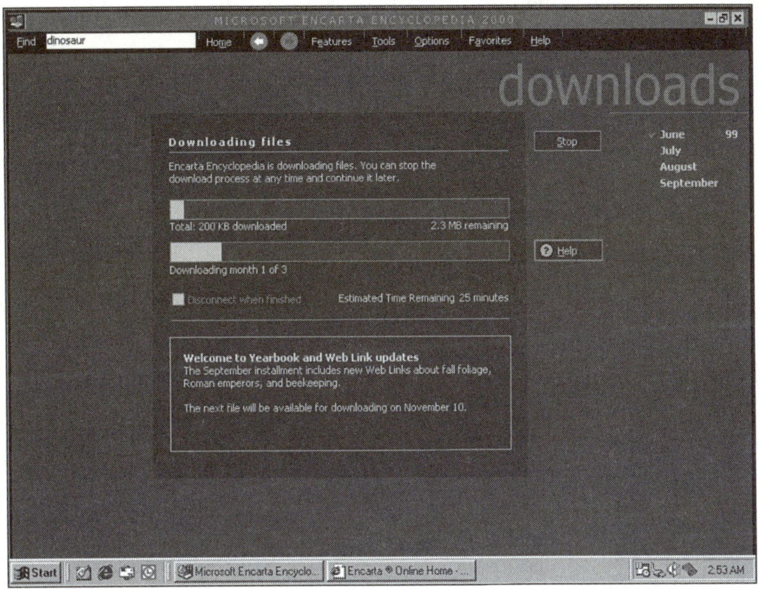

Figure 27.19
Updates download while you wait.

To view the latest updates, choose Features, Yearbook. A list of the new articles appears, and you can read one by double-clicking it. These articles are also integrated with the main database, so you can also find them by looking up their topics in the Pinpointer. The Yearbook merely provides a quick way of browsing what's new.

→ For information about getting an Internet connection, **see** "Setting Up an Internet Connection," **p. 342**.

→ Some of Encarta's online features require the use of Internet Explorer. If you aren't sure how to use that, **see** Chapters 17 through 19.

TROUBLESHOOTING

FEW ARTICLES FOUND

I'm looking up what I think is a common topic, but there aren't very many articles.

Make sure that the Choose a Type of Information drop-down list is set to Everything. By default it stays at whatever setting you chose last, and it limits the listing to only that type.

CLOSED CAPTIONING FOR AUDIO CLIPS

I don't have a sound card, but I would like to know what the sound clips are saying, especially the ones that are speeches from famous people.

Turn on closed-captioning by choosing Options, Closed Captions. Likewise, if you have a hard time reading small print on the screen, choose Options, Text Size, Large.

RETURNING TO FREQUENTLY USED ARTICLES

I sometimes have trouble finding an article again that I have looked at before.

If you keep losing track of articles that you frequently look at, create a Favorites list within Encarta. To add an article to your Favorites list, display it and then choose Favorites, Add to Favorites, the same as you do in Internet Explorer. To jump to a favorite article, select it from the bottom of the Favorites menu.

BETTER SEARCHES

I can't seem to get the hang of searching in Encarta; my searches seldom turn up the information I wanted.

If you aren't sure how to search, or if your searches don't seem to be very effective, click the Search Tips button at the bottom of the Pinpointer pane. This opens some search tip topics in the Help window.

CHAPTER 28

Using Streets & Trips 2000

In this chapter

WHAT IS STREETS & TRIPS 2000?

On-the-go users will really appreciate the inclusion of Microsoft's Expedia Streets & Trips 2000 in the Works Suite. If you're traveling by car, bus, plane, or train, getting there just got easier with this program. Streets & Trips 2000 is a detailed electronic road atlas that maps more than 5 million miles of U.S. roads. The program can help you plan routes, locate points of interest, look up specific addresses, book hotel rooms over the Internet, and more. Use Streets & Trips 2000 to do any of the following:

- Look up specific addresses anywhere in the U.S.
- Locate businesses, restaurants, and hotels, including addresses and phone numbers.
- Plan a route around town or across the country.
- Look up restaurants using the ZAGATSURVEY Restaurant Guide.
- Look up hotels using the Expedia Hotel Directory.
- Print out detailed driving instructions to guide you every step of the way to your final destination.
- Keep a record of sight-seeing stops you don't want to miss.

STARTING AND EXITING STREETS & TRIPS 2000

Before starting the program, make sure that the Streets & Trips 2000 CD (the red one in the Works Suite set) is inserted into your CD-ROM drive. The program may start immediately when you insert the CD. If it doesn't, choose Start, Programs, Microsoft Streets & Trips 2000.

When you first start Streets & Trips 2000, the Start Screen dialog box appears. From it you can click the button for the activity you want to perform (see Figure 28.1). You can plan a route, find a city or other location, look up an address, or open a saved trip or map.

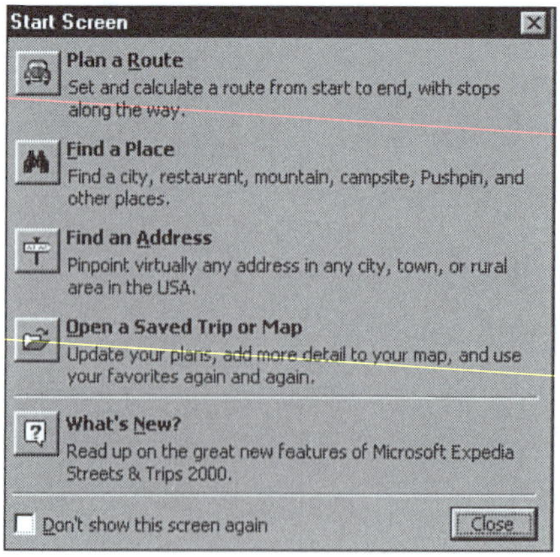

Figure 28.1
The Start Screen box provides shortcuts to common activities.

If you don't want to work with the Start Screen box, you can click Close to get it out of your way and perform an activity using one of the menus or toolbar buttons, as you will learn in this chapter. To reopen the Start Screen box at any time, choose Help, Start Screen.

Tip #160 from *Faithe Wempen*

To turn off the Start Screen box so that it doesn't appear automatically at startup, click the Don't Show This Screen Again check box in the Start Screen box. If you later decide to turn it back on again, display the Start Screen (Help, Start Screen) and deselect the check box.

Table 28.1 explains each of the Start Screen options. Each of these options on the Start Screen is also available through tools and menus in the program window.

TABLE 28.1 START SCREEN OPTIONS

Option	Description
Plan a Route	Use this to plan a trip from one location to another, including routes to take, stops to make, and so on.
Find a Place	Use this option to look up a city, a business, or a particular place on the map.
Find an Address	This option lets you find an address on the map based on portions of the address you enter, such as the street name or the city.
Open a Saved Trip or Map	Use this to retrieve a map or trip that you have worked with in a previous session and saved.

When you're ready to exit the program, use any of these methods:

- Click the program window's Close (X) button.
- Open the File menu and select Exit.
- Press Alt+F4 on the keyboard.

Tip #161 from *Faithe Wempen*

Use Streets & Trips 2000's Help features any time you need additional help with the program. Choose Help, Contents and Index to look up information about specific parts of the program.

NAVIGATING THE PROGRAM WINDOW

Before jumping in and using the program, take a moment to acclimate yourself to the program window (see Figure 28.2). It looks a bit different from the other Works Suite programs covered in previous chapters. Here are some of the elements you'll be working with:

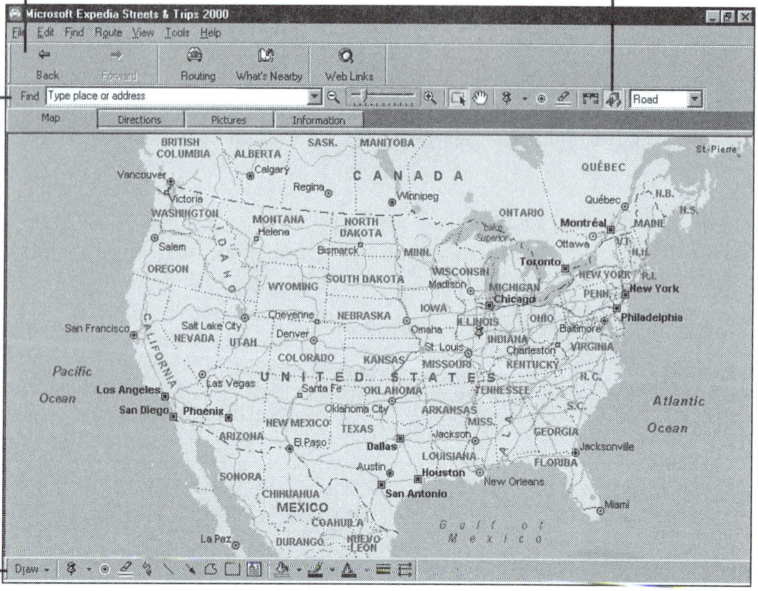

Figure 28.2
Familiarize yourself with the parts of the Streets & Trips 2000 screen.

- **Menu bar**—Contains drop-down menus from which you can select commands, the same as in any other program.
- **Standard toolbar**—Contains Back and Forward buttons (which work the same as in Internet Explorer) and Routing, What's Nearby, and Web Links buttons.
- **Mapping toolbar**—Contains controls for working with the map. You can zoom in and out, highlight certain areas, use the Find feature, and more.
- **Drawing toolbar**—Not shown by default, this toolbar contains additional buttons for annotating a map. You can draw lines and shapes on the map, highlight it, and so on. To display or hide the Drawing toolbar, click the Drawing button on the Mapping toolbar.
- **Map area**—The middle portion of the program window shows the map; you can zoom in and out for more or less detail.

Zooming In and Out

Streets & Trips 2000's zoom features are invaluable for viewing the map. You can choose from several zoom features, as shown in Figure 28.3.

- To zoom in your map view for a closer look of a particular area, click the Zoom In button on the toolbar.
- To zoom out, click the Zoom Out button.

Note

You can click the Zoom In or Zoom Out button as often as you like to zoom your view of the map.

- To select a zoom amount, drag the Zoom slider to the left or right.

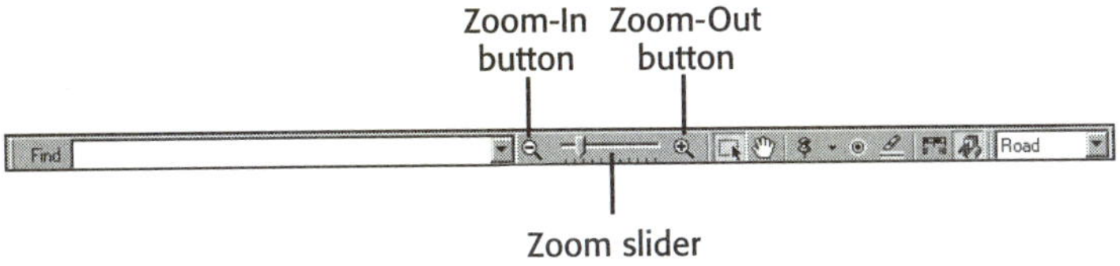

Figure 28.3
Zoom controls on the Mapping toolbar.

To zero in on a particular area of the map, use the Selection button. Click the button and then draw an outline on the area of the map you want to zoom in on, as shown in Figure 28.4. Then move the mouse pointer inside the selected area, and it changes to a magnifying glass with a plus sign. Click, and the display zooms in to that area.

Figure 28.4
Use the Selection button to draw an outline of the area you want to view.

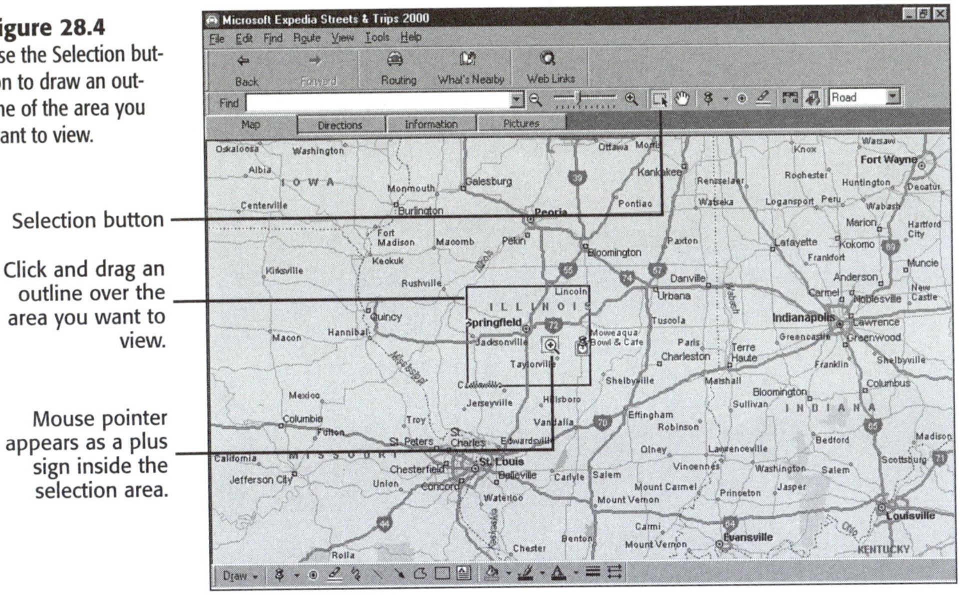

Tip #162 from *Faithe Wempen*

To zoom back out to the map of the United States, continental United States, right-click the map and choose Zoom, To North America.

MOVING AROUND THE STREETS & TRIPS 2000 MAP

You can move around the map display in several ways. If you move the mouse pointer to any edge or corner of the map area, the pointer takes the shape of a large arrow icon. When the pointer is a large arrow, click the mouse button to shift the map in that direction. For example, if you're pointing at the far-right edge of the map, the large arrow shape points east. If you click the mouse button, the map shifts to the left.

If you hold down the left mouse button, your view moves very quickly. This is the same principle involved in scrolling around a document page; use the arrows to scroll around the map.

Another way to move around the map is to use the Hand tool. Click the Hand button and then drag it on the map in the direction you want to move.

You can also use the Overview Map tool to move around the map. Choose Tools, Overview Map. When selected, this feature opens a small window on top of the map that gives you a zoomed-out view of the map area you're currently viewing—sort of a bird's-eye view. You can click and drag inside the Locator Map to change your view of the larger map beneath. Figure 28.5 shows an example of the Overview Map feature in use.

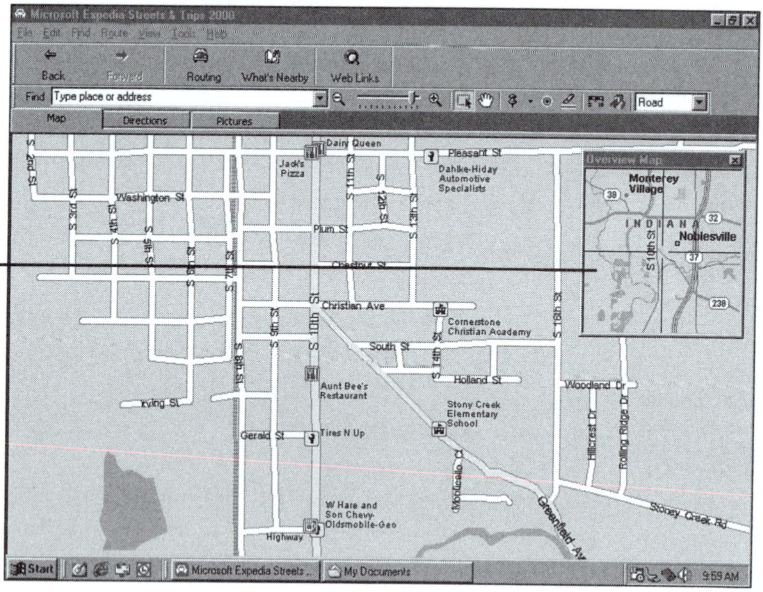

Figure 28.5
Use the Overview Map feature to put the current map view you're using in context with a larger area of the map.

To close the Overview Map, click its Close (X) button located in the right corner, or choose Tools, Overview Map again.

If you're looking for a specific geographic location, such as a particular latitude and longitude, you can find it with the Location Sensor tool. Choose Tools, Location Sensor. This opens the Location Sensor dialog box, as shown in Figure 28.6. The dialog box shows the state, the latitude, the longitude, and the time zone of the map area you're viewing.

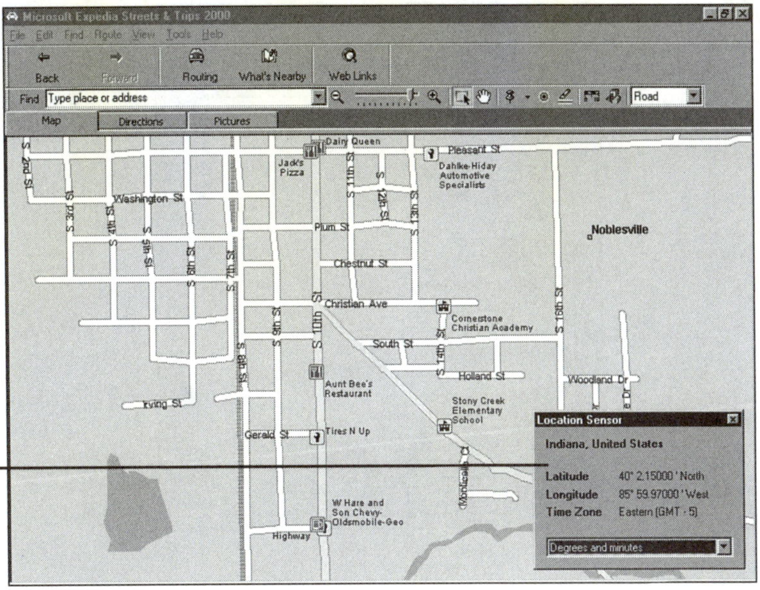

Location Sensor

Figure 28.6
Use the Location Sensor dialog box to gauge the latitude and longitude of the area you're viewing.

To close the Location Sensor tool, click its Close (X) button, or choose Tools, Location Sensor again.

Changing the Map Style

You have three style choices for your map: Road, Terrain, and Political. Each shows just what you would expect: Road (the default) shows the whole map in white, with the major highway lines in orange; Terrain shows mountains, bodies of water, and so on as different shades of green; and Political shows the states in different colors.

To choose a different map display, select from the Choose a Map Style drop-down list on the Mapping toolbar, or choose View, Map Style and select one of the styles from the submenu.

Seeing Points of Interest

What do you think of when you hear "points of interest?" Most people think immediately of the kinds of places that schoolchildren visit on field trips: museums, historical landmarks, and so on. But in Streets & Trips 2000, points of interest are definable. You can set it to show whatever places interest *you*, whether that's an art gallery or an ATM machine.

To define the points of interest to show, choose View, Show or Hide Points of Interest. The Show or Hide dialog box appears, as shown in Figure 28.7. Place or remove a check mark next to each category you want to show on your maps, and then click OK.

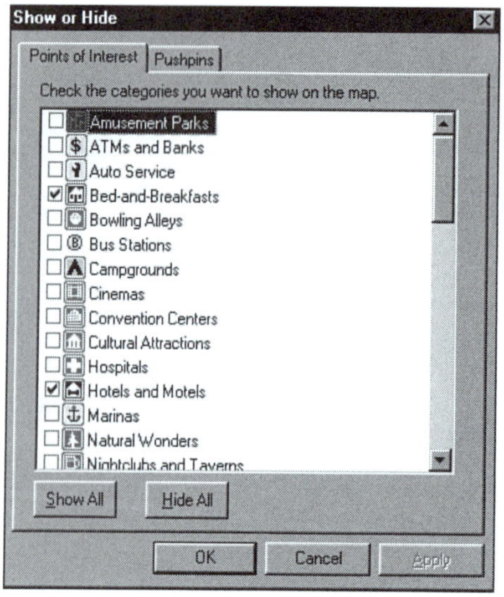

Figure 28.7
Use this dialog box to specify exactly what points-of-interest categories you want to appear on the map.

Note

Points of interest do not appear on the national map. You won't see them until you zoom in to a city. Then they will appear as colored icons (or colored dots, depending on the zoom level).

When you zoom in on a city so that you can see its individual streets, the points of interest appear along the streets, as shown in Figure 28.8.

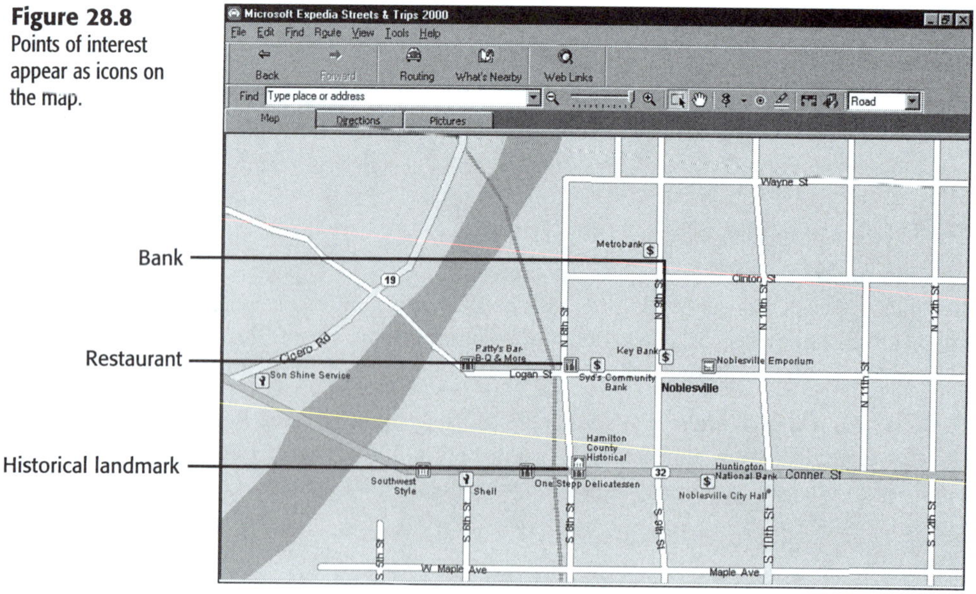

Figure 28.8
Points of interest appear as icons on the map.

Tip #163 from
Faithe Wempen

To see a legend of all the points-of-interest icons, choose Tools, Map Legend and then click Points of Interest. To close the legend, click its Close (X) button.

LOCATING ADDRESSES AND OTHER PLACES

The best part of any mapping program is being able to locate exactly where you want to go. With Expedia Streets & Trips 2000, you can look up all kinds of addresses, including residential and business addresses. As long as you know part of the address, Streets & Trips 2000 can help you locate the place. You can also look up restaurants and hotels—or just about anywhere you need to go.

Caution

Although Expedia Street's database of addresses is impressive, you won't find every address on the map. For example, you won't find streets for new housing additions. However, Streets & Trips 2000 comes pretty close and tries to match the address you enter as best it can. You also won't find every restaurant and hotel.

FINDING AN ADDRESS

Need a map to your newest client's office? Need to find the location of the nearest license branch? You can easily look up addresses for any city or town across the U.S. When it comes to locating addresses, you can be as specific or as vague as you want to be, and Streets & Trips 2000 will find the closest possible match. For example, if you know the street address but not the city, state, or zip code, Streets & Trips 2000 finds any matches and presents them to you as a list. You can then examine each one individually.

To look up an address:

1. Choose Find, Address. This opens the Find dialog box.
2. On the Address tab, enter as much of the address as you can. You can use abbreviations, such as St for street or Ave for avenue. You can leave boxes blank for which you don't have the information.
3. Click Find. Addresses that match that information appear at the bottom of the Find dialog box, as shown in Figure 28.9.
4. Click the address that most closely matches the location you want to look up, and the map automatically zeroes in on the address.
5. Click OK to close the Find box and examine the map. A pushpin appears, marking that address, as shown in Figure 28.10. You will learn more about pushpins later in this chapter.

Figure 28.9
The Find results show all matching addresses.

This street address was the sole criterion entered.

All these cities have an 801 Lowe Street.

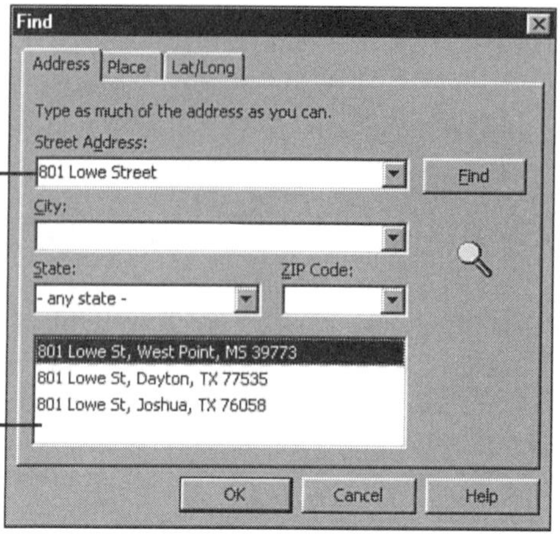

Figure 28.10
Streets & Trips 2000 identifies the found address on the map.

Pushpin

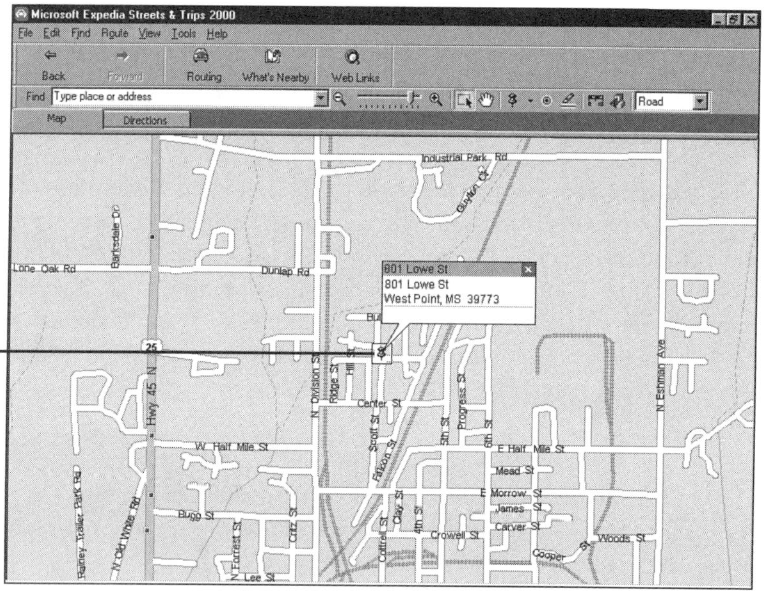

You can also find places in addition to addresses. A *place* is a named location. It can be a city name, a street name, a business, a landmark, and so on. To find a place, choose Find, Place. The Find dialog box appears again, but this time with the Place tab on top. Type a name into the Place Name box and click Find, and a list of places that contain what you typed appears. (Figure 28.11 shows an example. Notice that it also finds similar spellings, so you don't necessarily have to spell the name correctly.) Then click the one you want and click OK to jump to it.

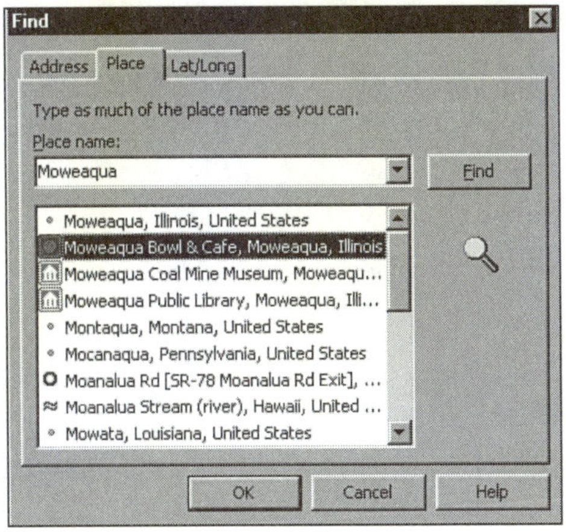

Figure 28.11
To find a place, enter a full or partial place name and click Find.

Tip #164 from *Faithe Wempen*

If you have an Internet account and Internet Explorer installed, you can tap into the Web Links feature for more information about the chosen place. Click the Web Links button on the Standard toolbar, and click OK at the confirmation box. This opens the Internet Explorer window, with information about the chosen location. For example, for some locations it may offer to show you a photo of the location from the Microsoft Terra Server.

Here's a great shortcut. Instead of working with Find, Address or Find, Place, you can simply type what you are looking for in the Find box on the Mapping toolbar. See Figure 28.12. For example, if you want to find a certain town, type its name there and press Enter. The Find dialog box appears, listing the found places or addresses, the same as if you had started from there.

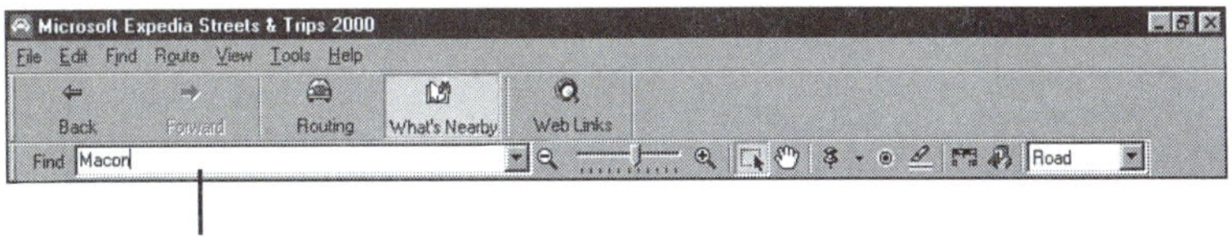

Type here and press Enter to search.

Figure 28.12
Type search words directly into the Mapping toolbar's Find box as a shortcut.

FINDING NEARBY FACILITIES

You can use the What's Nearby feature in Streets & Trips 2000 to locate hotels, restaurants, and other facilities near the chosen address. This can be very handy if you are planning a trip to the specified location and need to make a hotel reservation, for example. It can also help you make the most of a sightseeing trip by identifying cultural attractions you won't want to miss.

To find what's nearby a certain address, follow these steps:

1. Find the place or address, as you learned in the preceding section.
2. Click the What's Nearby button on the Standard toolbar. The What's Nearby pane opens to the left of the map.
3. Click the plus sign next to the category of interest to expand it.
4. Click the place you want to locate. It appears on the map with a box around it, as shown in Figure 28.13.

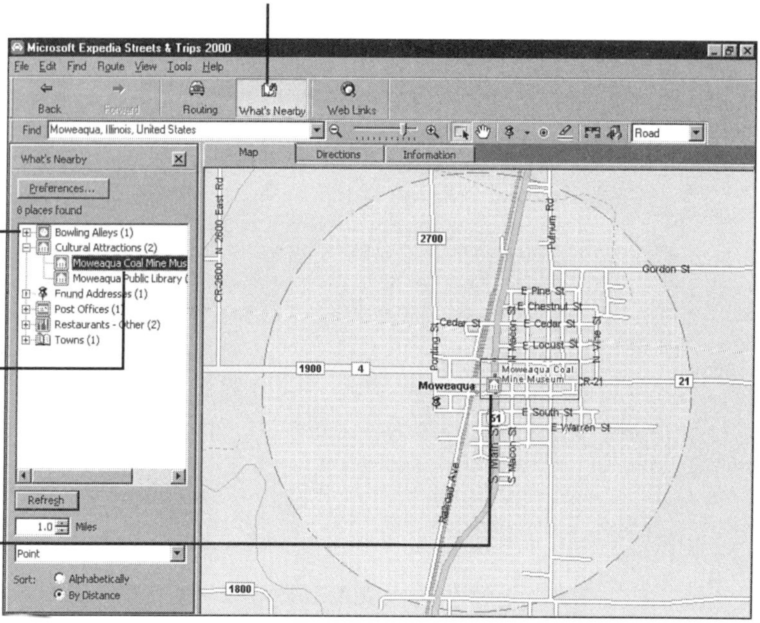

Figure 28.13
Find nearby places with the What's Nearby pane.

You can set some options for the What's Nearby feature, as follows:

- This feature displays a one-mile circle on the map, into which places must fall to be considered "nearby." You can change this to a larger circle by increasing the Miles value in the What's Nearby pane.
- This feature displays the types of places you have chosen for your Points of Interest. To change that, choose View, Show or Hide Points of Interest and select or deselect various types of places.
- This feature displays certain kinds of restaurants, lodging, and so on, based on your preferences. To set preferences, click the Preferences button in the What's Nearby pane to open a dialog box in which you can choose specific types of each amenity. (You can also choose your points of interest from there, too.)

GETTING INFORMATION ABOUT A PLACE

In the previous sections, you've learned how to find places, whether it be a restaurant, a hotel, an attraction, or some other type of facility. After you locate a place, you may want to get some more information about it.

Start with the place highlighted on the map (that is, with a box around its name and icon, as shown in Figure 28.13). Then click the Information tab, or right-click the place and choose Show Information. Information about the place appears, as shown in Figure 28.14.

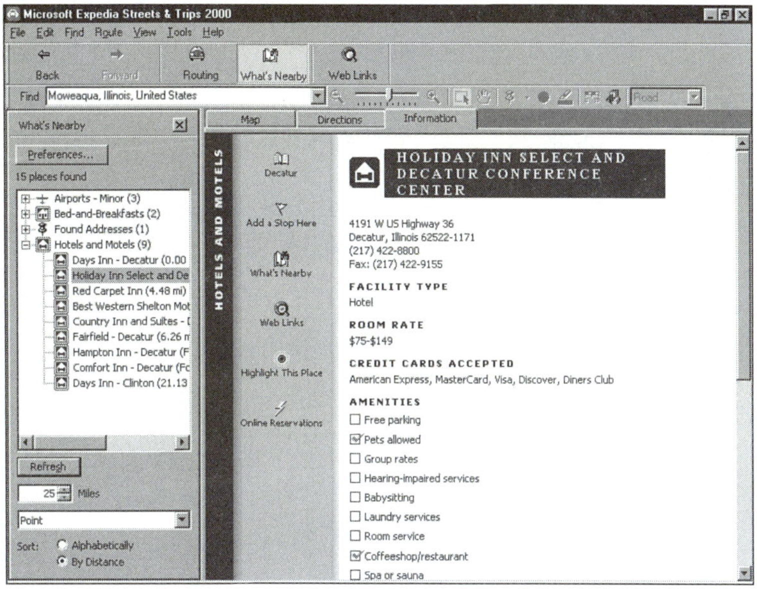

Figure 28.14
Information about the chosen place.

Tip #165 from
Faithe Wempen

Display the What's Nearby pane, and then click various attractions with the Information tab displayed to compare several places at a glance.

From the Information tab for a place, you can do any of the following:

- Click the icon for its city (Decatur, shown in Figure 28.14) to see information about the city.
- Choose Add a Stop Here to add the chosen place to an itinerary you are building. (More on this later in the chapter.)
- Choose What's Nearby to display nearby places in the What's Nearby pane.
- Choose Web Links to go to the Internet for more information.
- Choose Highlight This Place to put a marker on the map for this place for easy reference later.
- Choose Online Reservations (if available) to make a reservation using the Expedia travel service online.

WORKING WITH PUSHPINS

Streets & Trips 2000 lets you mark places you find on the map with pushpins—electronic versions of the real-life tacks used on bulletin boards. When you learned how to find an address earlier in this chapter, Streets & Trips 2000 marked the spot with a pushpin and a note about the address (which happened to be the location's street address).

You can mark a spot with a pushpin any time by clicking the Pushpin button on the Mapping toolbar and then clicking the map. To add a note, click inside the pushpin note text box and start typing. You can enter a title for the pushpin and note text about the pushpin. Figure 28.15 shows a pushpin marking a spot on the map.

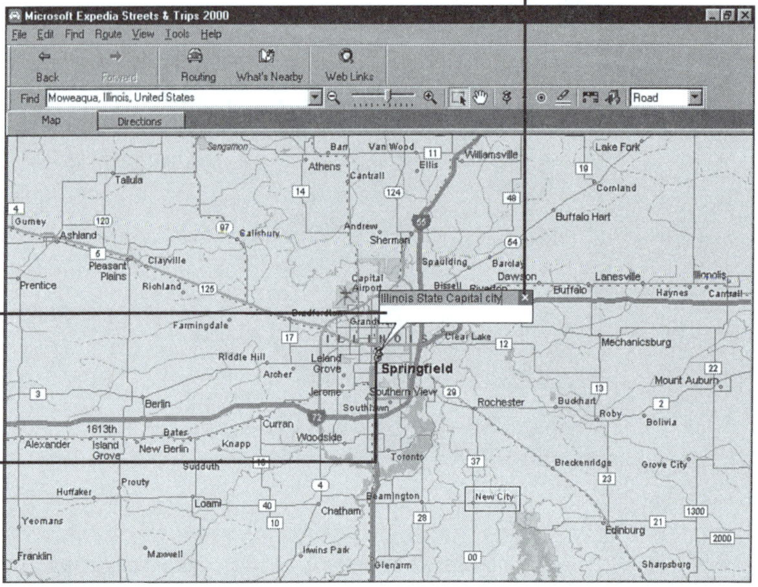

Figure 28.15
A pushpin marks a spot and highlights a specific area on the map.

Pushpins are useful because they make it easy to find a place again on the map.

To jump to a pushpin-marked location, do the following:

1. Choose Tools, Pushpin Explorer. The Pushpin Explorer dialog box opens (see Figure 28.16).
2. Click the set in which the pushpin you want is contained.

   By default, pushpins based on addresses you have looked up appear in the Found Addresses set, and pushpins you placed manually appear in the My Pushpins set.
3. Double-click the pushpin you want to revisit. The dialog box closes and the map displays that location.

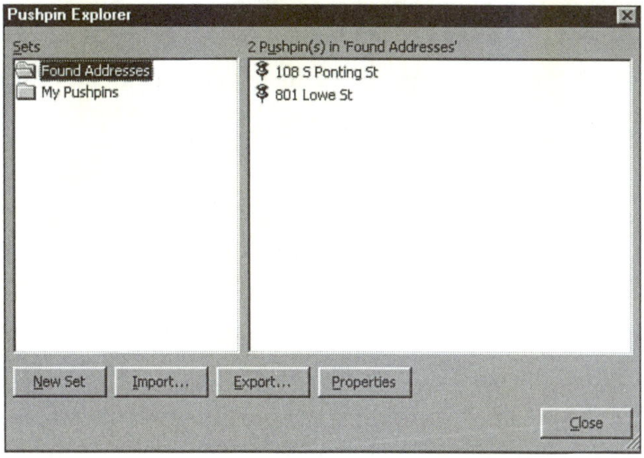

Figure 28.16
Use the Pushpin Explorer to select a pushpin location to redisplay.

You may have noticed that there are extra controls in the Pushpin Explorer dialog box. You can create your own pushpin sets, import and export sets, and set a pushpin's properties. Here are some tips to get you started:

- To move a pushpin from one folder to another, select the pushpin and then drag it to the left pane and drop it onto the folder you want to store it in.
- To create a new folder, click the New Set button and give the folder a name.
- To rename a pushpin, change its symbol, or set other options for it, select the pushpin and then click the Properties button.
- To delete a pushpin, select the pushpin and press Delete.

Tip #166 from *Faithe Wempen*

Right-click a pushpin on the map to display a pop-up menu of related pushpin commands. For example, to hide all the pushpins of a particular set, select the Hide Set command.

You can also choose different pushpin styles by opening the drop-down list on the Pushpin button (on the Mapping toolbar). Clicking its down arrow opens the palette shown in Figure 28.17. Click the pushpin style you want to use.

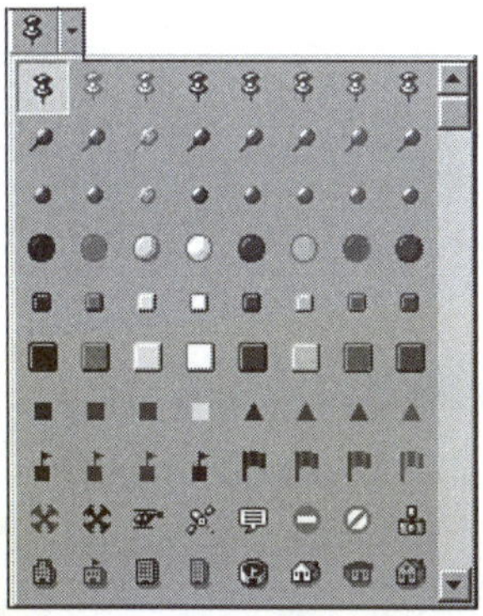

Figure 28.17
Select an alternate pushpin style if desired.

PLANNING A TRIP WITH STREETS & TRIPS 2000

Streets & Trips 2000 can help you plan a route to take, whether it's a trip across town or a trip across the country. You can plan a trip in either of two ways. You can let the Routing feature map out the route for you, or you can route it yourself directly on the map using the highlighter.

PLANNING A ROUTE WITH THE ROUTING FEATURE

The Routing feature helps identify the best roads to take to get from your starting point to your destination, taking into account the conditions and preferences you specify.

Note

"The best roads" is a rather subjective concept–some people think the best roads are the fast interstate highways; others think the best roads are the scenic ones. You can specify your own preferences.

1. Click the Routing button on the Standard toolbar. This opens the Routing pane to the left of the map (see Figure 28.18).

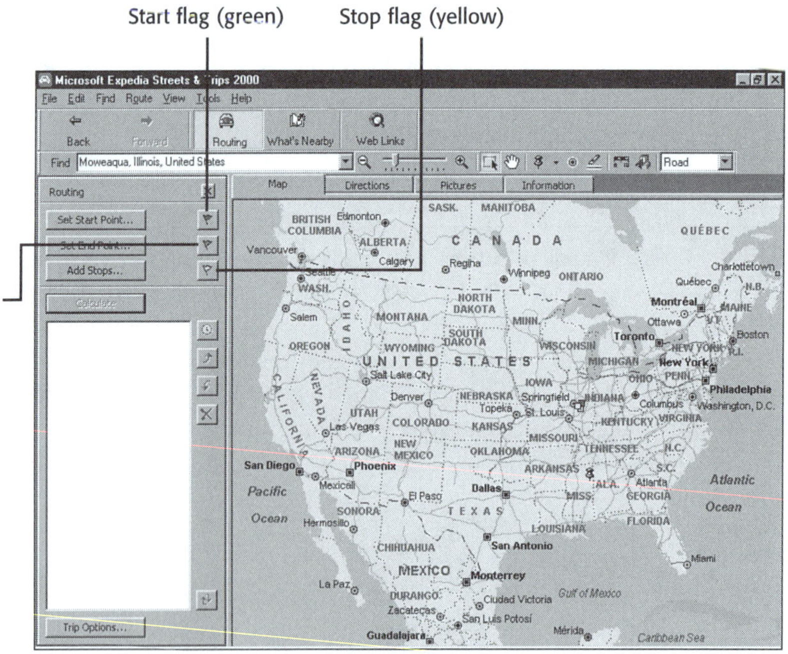

Figure 28.18
The Routing pane provides buttons to help you set the starting point, the ending point, and the stops for your trip.

2. Set the starting point. You can do this in either of the following ways:
   - Click the Set Start Point button, and then use the Find a Place to Start dialog box to locate an address or place, the same as you learned earlier in this chapter.

- Click the Green Flag button, and then click the map to mark the starting place. Zoom in or out on the map as needed.

3. Set the end point. You can do this in either of the following ways:
   - Click the Set End Point button, and then use the Find a Place to End dialog box to locate an address or place.

   - Click the Red Flag button, and then click the map to mark the ending place.
4. (Optional) If you want to include any certain landmarks or other points of interest on the trip, do either of the following:
   - Click the Add Stops button and then use the Find a Place For a Stop dialog box to choose places to stop.

   - Click the Yellow Flag button, and then click the map to mark a stopping place.
5. Click the Calculate button. The program calculates the quickest route and displays it on the Directions tab, as shown in Figure 28.19.

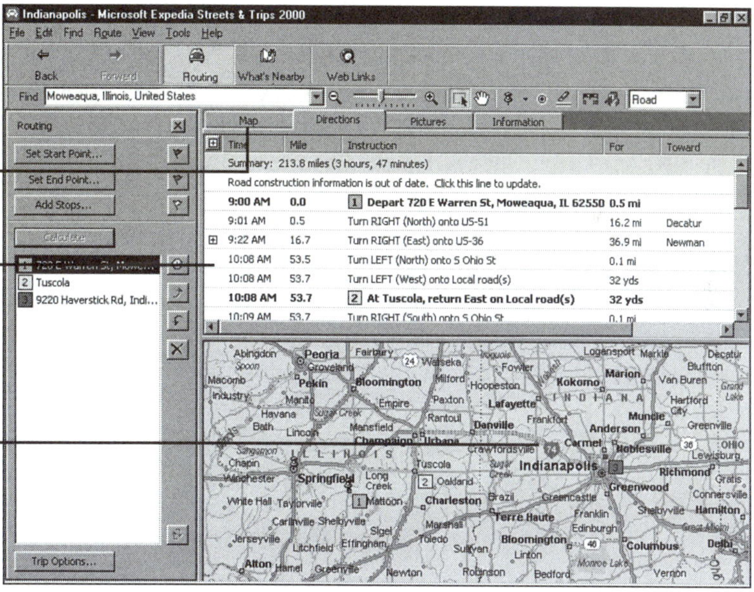

Figure 28.19
The trip route, automatically plotted for you.

Click here to see a larger map.

Driving directions

Map with route highlighted in green

Note

If you see a message that the road construction information is out of date, as shown in Figure 28.19, click that line and follow the prompts to download updated information from the Web.

6. (Optional) To save the route, click File, Save. Enter a name for the trip in the dialog box that appears, and click Save.

Note To open a saved trip later, choose File, Open.

7. (Optional) To print the route, choose File, Print, Map or Driving Directions. The Print dialog box opens.
8. Choose one of the options provided:
   - Print current map: to print only the map.
   - Driving directions: to print the directions. If you choose this, you can choose Directions Only, With Turn-by-turn Maps, With Strip Maps, or With Complete Trip Map. Choose whichever you think will be most helpful to you.
9. Set any other printing options desired (such as number of copies, page orientation, and so on). If desired, click the More Options button to open an extra dialog box with specific settings for the printout, such as placing each stop on a separate page.
10. Click Print to print the directions and/or map.

EDITING TRIP ROUTING

Now that you have a basic trip route planned, you may want to edit it. Perhaps you need to add a stop (or delete one), set some options, or rearrange the stop order. You can recalculate a trip after any change by clicking the Calculate button again. The following sections explain some edits you can make.

SETTING TRIP OPTIONS

Click the Trip Options button at the bottom of the Routing pane to open the Trip Options dialog box (see Figure 28.20). This dialog box contains four tabs. On each of these you can customize one aspect of the way the trip plans are calculated.

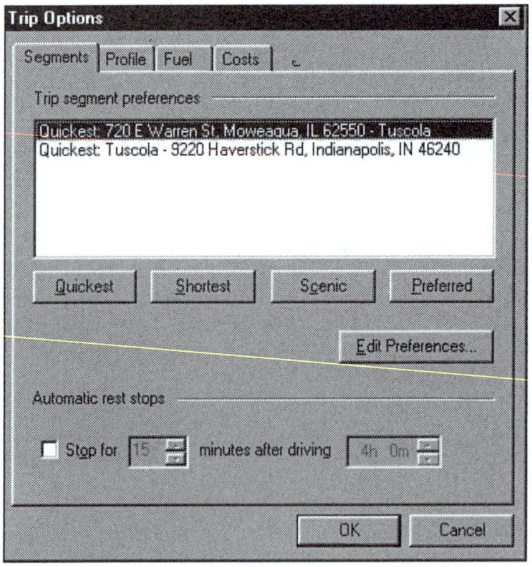

Figure 28.20 Fine-tune your trip parameters in this dialog box.

On the Segments tab:

- The default trip shows the quickest route, but you can click the Shortest, Scenic, or Preferred button for each segment, if you prefer. If you use Preferred, click the Edit Preferences button to adjust your custom settings.
- If you would like to program some rest stops into the total time calculation, mark the Stop For check box and enter the number of minutes to stop and the interval at which to stop.

On the Profile tab:

- Set your average driving speed in each of four categories: Interstate Highways, Limited-Access Highways, Other Highways, and Arterial/Major Roads.
- For multiday trips, enter information about your average driving day (start and end times).

On the Fuel tab:

- Enter the miles per gallon (both city and highway) that your vehicle gets. This information is important if you are calculating trip costs or if you want to use refuel warnings in your driving directions.
- To indicate fuel fill-up suggestions in your directions, mark the Include Refuel Warnings in Driving Directions check box. Then enter the tank capacity and set the warning levels.

On the Costs tab:

- Enter the fuel cost per gallon to calculate the trip cost based on fuel economy, or enter a fixed cost per mile.

ADJUSTING THE TRIP TIMING

The trip timing is the amount of time it will take to make the trip based on the driving times you specified in the Trip Options (see the preceding section).

To adjust the time for a segment, do the following:

1. Select the segment from the Routing pane.

2. Click the Time button in the Routing pane to open the Edit Time dialog box (see Figure 28.21).
3. To enter a stop at the end of the chosen segment, make sure the Stop For check box is marked, and enter a number of hours and minutes.
4. (Optional) If you want to arrive at the end of the chosen segment at a certain time, mark the Arrive At check box and enter the time.
5. (Optional) If you want to begin the chosen segment at a certain time, mark the Depart At check box and enter the time.

Figure 28.21
Enter any special times at which you want to arrive, depart, or stop.

6. Click OK to close the dialog box.
7. Click the Calculate button to recalculate the trip.

Rearranging or Deleting Trip Segments

If you want to rearrange your trip so that certain stops appear in a different order, use the Move Up and Move Down buttons in the Routing pane. Select the segment you want and then click one of these buttons to move it on the listing.

To delete a segment, select it and then click the Delete button.

Highlighting a Route

Another way to plan a trip is to highlight the route on a map by dragging a Highlighter tool. This does not calculate directions, but merely highlights a map that you can print and use in your travels. Follow these steps to try it:

1. Use the zoom tools to display both the starting point and destination point of the route you plan to take. (If it's a particularly detailed route, you can use the direction arrows to scroll the map as you go.)

2. Click the Highlight a Line button on the Mapping toolbar, or choose Tools, Road Highlighter. The mouse pointer becomes a crosshair.
3. Using the mouse, drag a line along the route you want to highlight. Don't worry that the line is very fat and covers up the road; it won't when you're done.

Tip #167 from *Faithe Wempen*

To clear the last segment you have drawn, click the Back button. If that doesn't work, delete the entire highlighted route: double-click the highlighted route so that the little black squares appear along it, and then choose Edit, Cut.

4. Click the Highlight a Line button again, turning off the highlighter. The route appears highlighted, with little black squares along the way, as shown in Figure 28.22.

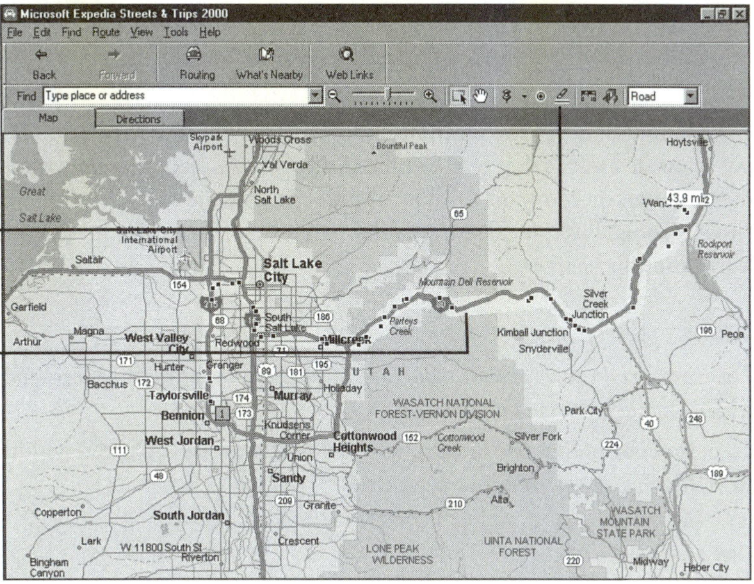

Figure 28.22
The route appears highlighted with color as you trace its path.

Highlight a Line button

Highlighted route (hard to see in this picture)

Those black squares along the highlighted route are not just for decoration; you can drag any of them to alter the highlight. For example, you might drag one to make the highlight conform more closely to a jog in the road.

To delete a highlighted route segment, select it (so that its black squares appear) and then choose Edit, Cut, or right-click it and choose Cut from the shortcut menu.

Tip #168 from
Faithe Wempen

A quick way to measure the distance between two points is to use the Measuring tool. Choose Tools, Measuring Tool. The mouse pointer becomes a crosshair. Drag it on the map to create a black line. At the end of the line is a measurement of the number of miles. Press Esc to end the measurement, and then press Delete to remove the black line from the map.

If you prefer to see the map distances measured in kilometers rather than in miles, choose Tools, Units, kms.

TROUBLESHOOTING

MORE HOTEL CHOICES

Streets & Trips doesn't have very many hotels listed for the city I'm traveling to. How can I get a more comprehensive listing?

If you can't find a hotel you want in the Streets & Trips 2000 program, try using Expedia.com online. Open your Web browser and go to `http://www.expedia.com`; then click Reserve a Room and search using the controls on the Web page that appears.

Too Many Pushpins

I've used Streets & Trips quite a bit, and my maps are starting to get very cluttered with pushpins.

You can hide some of the pushpins by choosing View, Show or Hide Pushpins. This opens the Show or Hide dialog box. On the Pushpins tab, place or remove the check mark next to the pushpin sets you want to show or hide. To control which pushpins appear in which set, choose Tools, Pushpin Explorer and drag pushpins from one folder to another, as you learned in this chapter.

Routing Preferences to Avoid an Area

There are certain parts of some cities that I would prefer not to drive through; how can I tell Streets & Trips not to route me through them?

To make your preference known, you can define an area to avoid with the Route, Avoid Area, Mark an Area to Avoid command.

Can't Print in Streets & Trips

Every time I try to print a map, I get an error message and the program shuts down.

As a workaround, you can select the information and/or map and then copy and paste it into another program, such as Microsoft Word, for printing.

PART VI

APPENDIXES

APPENDIX A

Installing Microsoft Works Suite 2000

In this chapter

Understanding the Installation Process

When you get a new Windows-based program, you usually have to run a *setup utility* before you can use it. The role of the setup utility varies from program to program, but some common things that setup utilities do include the following:

- Copy the files used to run the program to your hard disk. Some programs, such as Word, copy all the necessary files; others, such as Encarta, leave some of them on the CD and require you to pop the CD into your drive every time you want to use the program.
- Register the program with Windows, letting Windows know how to handle the data files for the program. For example, Word registers its document extension (.doc) with Windows so that when you double-click a file with a .doc extension, Word starts automatically.
- Install special *drivers* and *system files* that interact with Windows to help the program run. Some of these drivers must be loaded each time Windows starts; if you install a program that uses these, you are prompted to restart your computer after the setup utility has finished its work.
- Set up a command on the Start menu—and sometimes a desktop shortcut, too—that makes it easy for you to start the installed program.

Using the Works Suite Setup Program

Microsoft Works Suite 2000 is actually a bundled group of products, rather than one integrated program. When installing, you can choose to install every component or just certain ones. The Setup program then walks you through the steps necessary to install each program.

You may be prompted from time to time to insert different disks into your CD-ROM drive; just follow the prompts as needed. To get things started, insert Disc 1 of the Works Suite CD set into your CD-ROM drive. The Works Suite 2000 Setup screen (see Figure A.1) should appear automatically when you put in the disc.

If the Setup screen doesn't appear automatically, follow these steps:

1. Double-click the My Computer icon on the desktop.
2. Double-click the icon for the CD-ROM drive containing the CD.

If that doesn't work, right-click the icon for the CD-ROM drive and select AutoPlay.

If that still doesn't work, right-click the icon for the CD-ROM drive and select Open. Then, in the window that appears, double-click the Setup.exe icon.

Figure A.1
The opening screen of the Works Suite 2000 Setup program.

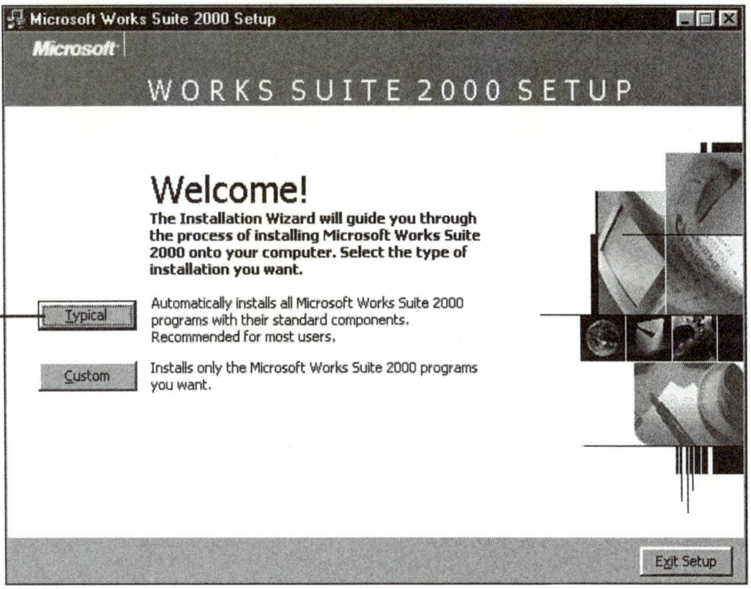

Typical is the right choice for most people.

Performing a Typical Install

A typical install is the best choice for most people. A typical install lets you choose which programs to install, but makes the other decisions for you automatically (such as the installation locations for files). It also runs the installation utilities for each program that you choose automatically in succession so that you do not have to start each installation separately.

1. Click the Typical button on the Welcome window.
2. Read the licensing agreement that appears, and click I Agree. A list of programs appears.
3. Deselect the check box for any of the programs you don't want (see Figure A.2).

   Works itself will be installed no matter what, but you have a say about the others.
4. Click the Install button.

Note

If you are using Windows 98 Second Edition or Windows 2000, you will see a warning about upgrading a version of Internet Explorer 5 in which the uninstall feature has been disabled. Click OK to move past this.

5. Follow the prompts to install each Works Suite component, inserting other discs as requested.

   A message box appears, letting you know how many more components remain to be installed, as shown in Figure A.3.

Figure A.2
You can choose which Works components you want.

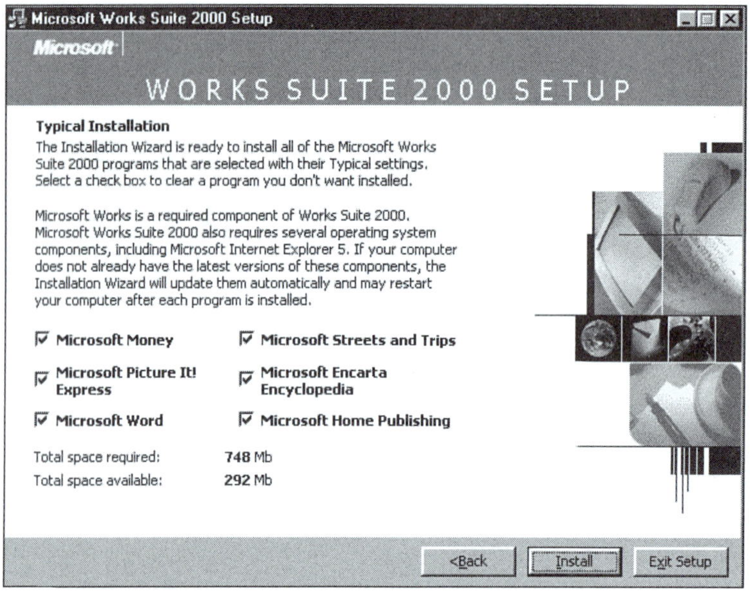

Figure A.3
Check your progress here during the installation.

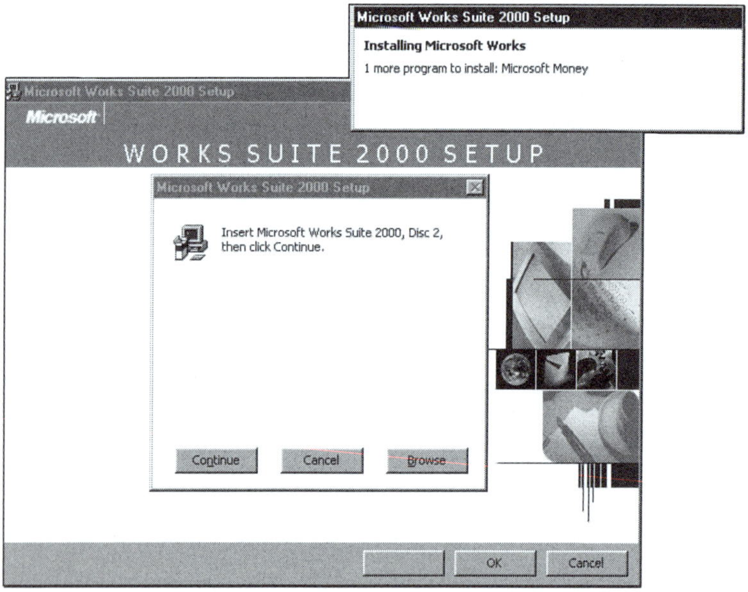

Note

Depending on your version of Windows and the components you chose to install, Windows may spontaneously restart itself during the installation process; this is normal.

6. If you chose to install Microsoft Word, a prompt appears asking for your CD key. Enter the 25-digit code from the yellow sticker on the back of your Works Suite disk package, and then click OK to continue.
7. Wait for the installation to complete.
8. When the last Works Suite component is installed, you may be prompted to restart your PC; click Yes. (Or, depending on which components you chose to install, your PC may restart itself automatically.)

Tip #169 from *Faithe Wempen*

If prompted to restart your PC, check the message box that tells you how many more programs to install. If the current one is not the last, save yourself time by choosing No.

9. After your PC restarts, the Setup window reappears. Click Finish to close it.

PERFORMING A CUSTOM INSTALL

A custom install lets you install each of the Works Suite programs separately, instead of as a group. Otherwise, the procedure is very similar to that of the Typical install you learned about in the preceding section.

1. Click the Custom button on the Welcome window. Buttons for each individual program appear, as shown in Figure A.4.

   Notice that Works itself is not represented here. That's because Works is installed no matter which options you choose.

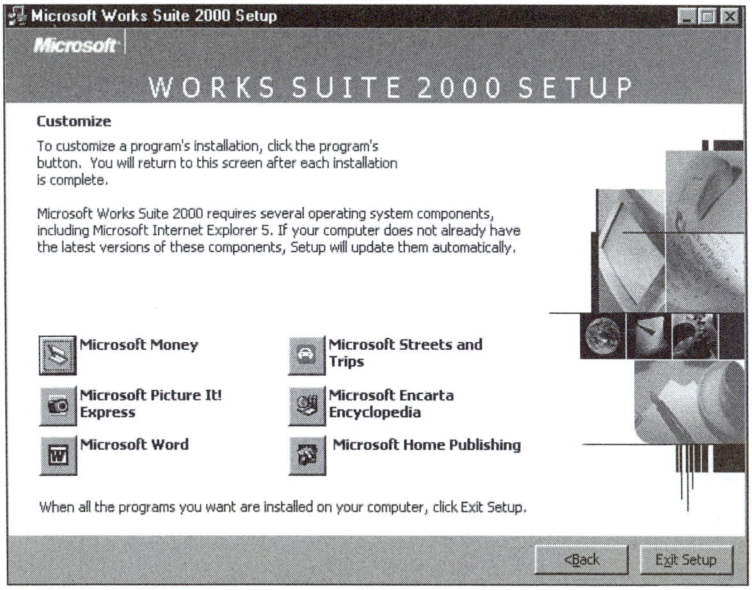

Figure A.4
The Customize screen lets you install one program at a time.

2. Click a button for the program you want to install.

Note

If you see a message that Works requires certain operating system components, click Continue to move past it. If you see a message about upgrading to Internet Explorer 5, click OK to go on.

3. When prompted, insert the requested disc from the Works CD set and click Continue.
4. Work through the prompts of the installation program that appears. If prompted to restart your computer, choose Yes to do so.
5. Repeat steps 2–4 to install another program, or click Exit Setup.

ADDING AND REMOVING

If you install a Works Suite component and decide not to use it, it's a good idea to uninstall it to free up space on your computer's hard disk drive. You can uninstall programs by returning to the Setup program. You can also install additional components at any time if you did not install them all on the first go-round.

When you insert the CD into your CD-ROM drive again, the Setup program may restart. If it does not, double-click the CD-ROM drive's icon in the My Computer window, or right-click it and choose Open. Then in the file listing, double-click the Setup icon.

The Setup program runs in Maintenance mode after your initial installation, as shown in Figure A.5. Use the Add button to add components or Remove to remove components.

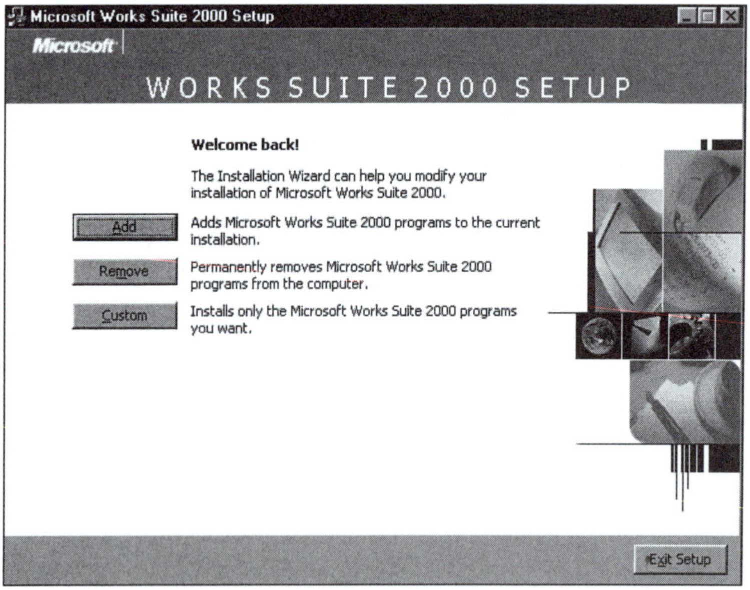

Figure A.5
You can easily add, remove, or reinstall Works Suite components from this window.

INSTALLING MICROSOFT WORKS ONLY

If you want to install only Microsoft Works and not the rest of the programs in the suite, you must use a different installation program than the one previously described. Follow these steps to get the ball rolling:

1. Insert Disc 2 of the Works Suite CD set.
2. Double-click the My Computer icon, and then double-click the icon for your CD-ROM drive.
3. Double-click the MSWorks folder.
4. Double-click the wks2000 icon. The Setup program runs.
5. Follow the onscreen prompts to install Works.

Caution

If you ever need to uninstall Works, double-click Add/Remove Programs in the Windows Control Panel, and then choose Microsoft Works 2000 from the list of installed programs to uninstall. Before you do so, however, make sure you have Disc 2 in your drive. Otherwise, the uninstall program won't be able to find the information it needs, and you'll see an error message.

APPENDIX B

GLOSSARY

401(k) A retirement plan through your employer. You make contributions and sometimes the employer does, too. Contributions are not taxed, but withdrawals are.

absolute reference A reference to a spreadsheet cell that, when copied to a different cell, retains its original reference. Absolute references are denoted with dollar signs in formulas, such as A5.

account In Money, any bank or brokerage account, or a nonbank holding such as petty cash.

account details In Money, the details about an account, such as the account number, the name and address of the bank, and the opening balance.

account number The unique identifier for a bank or a brokerage account.

active cell In a spreadsheet, the cell that is currently selected. All commands issued apply to the active cell, and the active cell's content appears in the formula bar.

address book A collection of addresses (physical or email, or both) from which to pick recipients.

alignment The way text in a paragraph or a cell positions itself in relation to the margins or edges. Alignment options include left aligned, right aligned, and centered.

amortization chart A chart that shows the split of each payment between the principal and the interest of the loan. As time goes by, more of each payment progressively goes toward principal and less goes toward interest.

arguments In a spreadsheet function, parameters that tell the function what cells to operate on and how. For example, the `=SUM` function's arguments are the names of the cells whose contents should be added.

arithmetic operators Math symbols in a formula that tell a spreadsheet how to calculate. Arithmetic operators include + (addition), – (subtraction), * (multiplication), and / (division).

attachment A binary file attached to a text-based email message. For example, you could send a text email to your boss, along with an attached Word file containing a report.

AutoComplete In Word, a feature that automatically completes a word or phrase based on the first few letters.

AutoCorrect In Word, a group of features that automatically corrects typing and form atting errors. The features included under AutoCorrect are AutoFormat, AutoComplete, and AutoText.

AutoFit A feature in the Works spreadsheet program that automatically changes the width of a column to exactly fit the longest line of text in it.

AutoFormat In Word, a feature that applies certain formatting, such as creating automatic bulleted or numbered lists or converting email addresses to active hyperlinks.

AutoFormat As You Type Special AutoFormat settings that apply the changes automatically as you type, rather than waiting for you to issue the AutoFormat command.

AutoPlay A Windows 95/98 feature that automatically runs a CD-ROM when you place it in your PC.

AutoShape A drawing tool in Word and other Microsoft products that enables you to place predrawn shapes, such as arrows, starbursts, and complex shapes.

AutoSum In the Works spreadsheet, a toolbar button that automatically applies the =SUM function and guesses which cells you want to find the sum of based on the active cell position.

AutoText In Word, a means of storing frequently typed phrases and paragraphs and inserting them into a document with a few keystrokes.

back up To copy important files from your PC's hard disk to an alternate location, such as a floppy disk or a tape drive, in case something happens to the originals.

balancing In Money, to reconcile a bank account with the statement you receive.

Bank Online The former name of the online banking portion of CheckFree, an online banking and bill payment service.

Bill Calendar In Money, a calendar that helps you track when your bills are due and reminds you to pay them.

boilerplate Material that is standard among many documents, such as a standard closing to a business letter.

bond An agreement by the issuer to borrow money and then pay it back with interest on a certain date. Bonds are often issued by governments and sometimes by companies.

bookmark *See* Favorites.

border A line or box drawn around certain paragraphs (in a word processor) or cells (in a spreadsheet).

cache A storage area for information from a program that keeps the information readily available in case it is used again. For example, Internet Explorer caches recently visited Web pages.

capital gain The profit you make when you sell a security (such as stock) or other investment (such as real estate) for more money than you initially paid.

category In Money, a means of classifying income and expenses for reporting purposes.

cell The intersection of a row and a column in a table or spreadsheet.

cell address area In the Works spreadsheet, the area to the left of the formula bar where the address of the active cell appears.

certificate On the Internet, a verification code sent to your Web browser designed to ensure that software being downloaded or run is actually from the source it claims to be.

Certificate of Deposit (CD) Like a bond, but purchased from a bank. You agree to let the bank use your money for a certain period of time, and the bank agrees to return it with interest on a certain date.

character formatting Any formatting that affects individual words and characters rather than entire paragraphs or pages.

character styles Styles (in Word) that apply character formatting, such as font changes and attributes.

chart A graphical representation of spreadsheet or other numeric data.

CheckFree An online banking and bill-paying service that you can sign up to use with Money.

clip art Predrawn artwork that you can use in your documents—for example, in Word and Works.

Clipboard A holding area in Windows where copied or cut material waits to be pasted.

column header The button with the shaded letter at the top of a spreadsheet column.

commission fees Brokerage fees that you pay when you buy or sell a stock or other security.

communications program A program that uses your modem to help your computer connect to and communicate with other computers over phone lines.

Concepts In Money, broad groups into which certain categories are divided.

context sensitivity The capability of a Help system to determine what you are working on and then provide help based on the context.

contiguous Touching one another. For example, a block of cells together in a spreadsheet consists of contiguous cells.

cookie A small file placed on your hard disk when you visit a Web site. The information in the file feeds back to the originating Web site when you visit it on subsequent occasions, letting the site owner know that you are the same person who has visited before.

criteria In a database filter, the specifications that data must meet to be included. For example, if you were filtering out all addresses in the 46240 zip code, having a 46240 zip code is the criterion.

cross-hair A "plus sign" cursor used to help align the mouse pointer precisely when drawing or placing graphics.

cursor The insertion point in a word processing document, or the thick border denoting the active cell in a spreadsheet. Sometimes erroneously used to mean the mouse pointer.

database A file created with a database program.

database program A program that helps you organize and manipulate data (such as addresses, phone numbers, descriptions, and so on).

decimal tab A tab stop that aligns the data with the decimal point. For example, you might use a decimal tab stop to align a column of numbers that have varying numbers of digits before and after the decimal point.

desktop publishing Page layout done in a computer application. For example, when you design a newsletter layout in Word, you are doing desktop publishing.

desktop shortcut An icon on your Windows desktop that provides a shortcut to running a program or opening a document or window.

dialog box A box that appears when you select certain commands prompting you for more information. For example, when you open the File menu and choose Print, a Print dialog box opens.

dividend Profit-sharing that you get from the company in which you hold stock. In addition to the profit you might make by buying stock at a low price and selling it at a high price, you also might receive quarterly dividend payments from the company for each share you hold, if the company is doing well.

DNS address Stands for domain name server address, one of several numeric settings that your Internet service provider might need you to specify in your Dial-Up Networking setup.

download To transfer files from a remote computer to your own (usually through a modem).

drivers Utility files that help Windows communicate with your system's hardware. For example, a driver tells Windows how to talk to your modem. Another driver tells Windows how to work with your video card.

drop-down list A list in a dialog box that drops down to display its choices when you click the down-pointing arrow to its right.

E-Pay *See* Electronic payment.

Easy Filter In Works database, one of two methods of filtering data. Easy Filter is the simple, easy-to-use method; Filter By Formula is the other, more complicated method.

Easy Text A text-insertion feature in Works that works like AutoText does in Word. *See* AutoText.

electronic mail *See* email.

electronic payment (E-Pay) A bill payment you make through a bill-paying service such as CheckFree instead of writing a check yourself.

electronic transfer A means of transferring funds online from one account to another rather than doing so at the bank.

email Electronic messages sent and received on the Internet.

Email client A program that helps you send and receive email on your PC (for example, Outlook Express).

Favorites A list of saved Internet addresses (URLs) in Internet Explorer that you can quickly access to visit those sites.

field code A code in a database or word processing document that substitutes a variable value when printed. For example, the code `&p` in a header or a footer inserts the correct page number on each page of the document.

fields Text boxes or lists in which you enter data or settings. For example, when you fill out a form, each individual text box (such as the one for Name or Address) is a field.

filter A set of criteria applied to data (for example, in a Works database) so that only the data you want is displayed. For example, a filter could weed out all addresses that do not have a certain zip code.

Filter by Formula In the Works database, one of two methods of filtering data. Filter by Formula enables you to create complex filters using multiple criteria. The other method is Easy Filter, a simpler filter type designed for beginners.

font A typeface, or style of lettering. Fonts included with Windows include Courier, Arial, and Times New Roman.

font style The attributes applied to characters, such as bold, italic, and underline. Do not confuse these with character style, which is a named style in Word that applies pre-specified fonts and font styles to text.

footer Repeated text at the bottom of each page of the document, such as the company name or the date the document was printed.

formatting Attributes you apply (usually to text) to change its appearance. Formatting can include font and size changes, bold, italic, and underline, and indenting.

formula In a spreadsheet, a notation in a cell that tells the program to process a function or perform a math operation with arithmetic operators. For example, `=A1+A2` adds the contents of cells A1 and A2.

Formula bar The area above the column headers in a spreadsheet that shows the current content of the active cell.

forum An area of the Internet that enables people to exchange ideas about a topic of interest. *See also* newsgroups.

function A named math operation that you can apply in a spreadsheet. For example, Works includes `=SUM`, which finds the sums of the contents of cells, and `=AVG`, which averages them.

GIF A graphics format popular on the Internet. GIF stands for Graphical Interchange Format and was originally developed for and popularized on the CompuServe online service.

graph *See* chart.

graphics filter A utility built into an application (such as Word or Works) that enables the application to open and use graphics files in various formats, such as PCX and BMP.

grayed out Currently unavailable commands or controls. The name comes from the fact that they often appear as gray letters rather than as black ones.

gridline In a spreadsheet, the gray lines onscreen that separate each row and column. These may or may not print, depending on the settings you have specified.

gutter The whitespace between two columns in a multicolumn layout, or the whitespace between the text and the binding in a book.

handles Black or white squares onscreen surrounding a selected graphics image. You can resize the object by dragging the handles. Handles do not print.

hanging indent An indent where the first line of the paragraph starts farther to the left than the subsequent lines.

hard page break A page break that you enter yourself with a command, in contrast to one that occurs naturally (soft page break).

header Repeated text at the top of each printed page, such as the company name or the name of the document.

home page A page that automatically opens as soon as you log on to the Internet. A home page is your starting point for exploring the rest of the Web. Also called a start page.

HTML Stands for Hypertext Markup Language, the formatting scheme used to create Web pages.

hyperlink A link to a Web page, usually on the Internet. Hyperlinks usually appear as underlined text in a different color from the surrounding text. Clicking a hyperlink opens the page that it represents.

increment buttons Small up and down arrow buttons next to a text box in a dialog box. Click these buttons to increment the numeric value in the text box up or down.

indent The amount that an individual paragraph is moved in or out from the rest of the document's margins. For example, some people like to indent the first line of each paragraph by five spaces.

Individual Retirement Account (IRA) A generic term that covers a wide variety of tax-deferred retirement plans. An individual can open an IRA through a bank or brokerage, or an employer can provide an IRA plan. Contributions may be tax-deductible, and earnings may be tax-deferred.

inline picture A graphic that is embedded in a document and treated like an individual character. For example, if the graphic were embedded between two words and those words moved on the page, the graphic would move, too. Contrast this to a floating picture, which moves independently of the text on the page.

input form In the Works database, the form you use in Form view to input new records into the database.

Insert mode A typing mode in a word processor in which existing text moves over to make room for additional text you type. Compare to Overtype mode.

insertion point The flashing vertical line onscreen that indicates where text you type will appear. Also called the cursor.

integrated program A program that combines several functions in one interface. Works is an example of an integrated program.

Internet A vast network of interconnected computers all over the world.

Internet service provider (ISP) A company that provides access to the Internet to consumers for a monthly fee.

investment In Money, an investment is a stock, a bond, a CD, or other security that you buy or sell.

investment account An account in Money that tracks all your investments with a single brokerage or bank.

IP address Stands for Internet Protocol address. One of several numeric settings that your Internet service provider may need you to specify in your Dial-Up Networking setup.

ISP *See* Internet service provider.

Java A programming language that creates programs that can be run from Web pages, regardless of the type of computer you are using (PC or Macintosh).

JPEG A graphics format popular on the Internet. JPEG stands for Joint Photographic Experts Group. JPEG files are smaller than other formats (such as GIF), so they are popular for displaying graphics on Web pages.

justified An alignment option that aligns a paragraph's text with both the right and left margins, inserting extra space between words and letters as needed so that each line begins and ends in the same spot.

Keogh A retirement plan for self-employed people. It works much like other IRAs—contributions are tax-deductible and earnings are tax-deferred, but withdrawals are taxable.

landscape A page orientation in which the page is wider than it is tall.

launch To start an application.

leader Repeated dots or other characters between text and the next tab stop, which help the readers' eyes follow the line. These are common in tables of contents.

link A connection between two files in Works, Word, or any other Windows-based program. Typically, one file is linked or embedded into another, such as a graphic in a word processing document. Whenever the source (the original graphic, for example) changes, the copy in the document changes too. *See also* object linking and embedding.

mail merge A technique that takes names and addresses from a database or other list and combines them with a standardized form letter to produce "personalized" copies for each recipient.

mail server A computer set up by an Internet service provider that handles incoming and outgoing email for its subscribers.

manual page break *See* hard page break.

mass mailing A group of letters or other documents created with a mail merge.

menu bar The bar across the top of most Windows programs listing the names of menus that can be opened.

merge To combine data from two or more files or programs. For example, you can merge addresses from a Works database with a form letter from the Works word processor.

merged cells Two or more cells in a table or spreadsheet that have been combined to form a single, larger cell.

modem A device in (or attached to) a computer that converts computer data to analog signals (sound) that can be sent over phone lines and that receives such data from other computers, translating it back into computer data.

money market fund A type of mutual fund that invests in short-term securities, such as T-bills. You can choose to have your invested cash in a brokerage account put into a money market fund so that it continues to earn while you are deciding what stocks to buy with it.

mutual fund A collection of stocks, bonds, and other securities managed by an investment professional. You buy shares in a mutual fund as if it were a single stock.

negative indent *See* outdent.

newsgroup A collection of related messages about a topic people have in common; for example, there is a computer consulting newsgroup, a dolphin newsgroup, an Irish music newsgroup, and so on.

newsgroups Public discussion forums on the Internet where users can post public messages and read messages posted by others.

Normal document template The default template used to start new documents in Word. Also called blank document.

object Any bit of text or graphics (or a whole file) that is copied, linked, or pasted into a document in a Windows-based application.

object linking and embedding (OLE) The process of creating dynamic links between data. For example, you might include a chart from Works in a Word document with a link so that when the chart changes in Works, the copy in the Word document changes, too.

OLE *See* object linking and embedding.

Online Layout view A special view in Word in which you can see all the document headings in a panel to the left of the main document window.

opening balance The amount of money that you start with in a Money account. You must enter all transactions that have occurred between the opening balance and the present balance.

operator *See* arithmetic operators.

orientation The direction that text runs on a page: across the short edge (portrait) or the long edge (landscape).

outdent A negative indent, where a particular paragraph begins to the left of the left margin or to the left of the rest of the paragraphs in the document.

Overtype mode A typing mode in which text you type replaces any text that is already there to the right of the cursor.

paragraph code An invisible code placed in a document by pressing the Enter key on the keyboard, indicating that a new paragraph should begin.

paragraph formatting Any formatting that affects entire paragraphs rather than individual letters or words.

paragraph styles Styles (in Word) that affect the entire paragraph rather than only individual letters or words. For example, a style might set the indents for a paragraph or the line spacing.

path The location of a particular file on your hard disk. Paths are written with the drive letter first, followed by each level of folder. For example, C:\Windows\System\thisfile.dll is in the System folder, which is in the Windows folder, which is on the C drive.

PIN number A secret code that you use like a password to identify yourself when doing online banking or bill payment in Money.

points A measurement of type size. A point is 1/72 of an inch. Can also be a measurement of blank space; for example, in Word, a paragraph can be set to have 12 points of space before or after it.

populate To enter or import data records into a database.

portrait A page orientation in which the page is taller than it is wide.

printer font A font that is built into your printer so that you can use it with any PC to which the printer is attached.

properties Additional ways to categorize Money transactions. They work like categories and are optional to use.

reconciling To compare the balance on your bank statement to the balance for an account in Money and then correct any discrepancies.

records Data in a database. For example, in an address database, each person's set of data (name, address, phone number) is a record.

register In Money, the area where you enter transactions for a particular account.

Registered Retirement Savings Plan (RRSP) A Canadian retirement savings plan. As in other plans, contributions are tax-deferred, but withdrawals are taxed.

relative reference In a spreadsheet formula, a cell reference that changes when copied to a different location. By default, all formulas use relative references. *See also* absolute reference for an alternative.

retirement account In Money, any account that tracks investments for retirement.

rollover A direct transfer of funds from one investment to another. For example, when changing retirement plans, you roll over the funds to the new plan rather than cashing out the old one so that you avoid paying taxes on the withdrawal.

routing number The number on a check that identifies the bank.

row header The gray button to the left of each row in a spreadsheet containing the row number.

sans serif A font without little "tails" on the letters. Block lettering is an example of sans serif. The opposite of serif, which is a font that does have tails on the letters.

scalable Capable of being resized. For example, TrueType fonts in Windows are scalable because you can use them at any size, from very tiny (8 points) to very large (72 points).

scanned image An image acquired by using a scanner. These are almost always bitmap images and may be saved in any of a variety of formats, such as TIF, JPG, GIF, PCX, or BMP.

scanner A device (much like a copier) that scans documents and images and then imports them into your computer in digital format so that you can modify and save them.

screen font A font designed specifically to be displayed on your screen. Some printer fonts and other fonts require complementary screen fonts so that your preview of your work onscreen does not appear jagged. TrueType fonts do not require screen fonts because they work equally well when printed and when displayed on the screen.

ScreenTip A note that pops up, explaining an object's purpose, when you position your mouse pointer over a toolbar button or other control.

scrollbars Bars along the right and bottom edges of a window that enable you to scroll the display to see parts of the document or window not currently visible onscreen.

search criteria In a database filter or a search utility in another application, the keyword(s) or criteria used to narrow a list or locate specific text.

search engine A Web site (usually a sophisticated, commercial one) providing a service that helps users find other Web sites on the Internet.

section A division in a Word document that has its own margin and column settings—and possibly its own headers and footers, too. Section breaks enable a single document file to have different margins, columns, and so on in different spots.

serialized A data type in a database that increments the value in the field for each record. For example, you might have a Record Number field that automatically numbers the records: 1, 2, 3, and so on.

serif A type of font that uses little "tails" on the letters to improve readability. The term "serif" can also apply to the little tails themselves.

server A computer that provides information or performs services for other computers.

Setup utility A program that helps you set up another program to run on your computer.

shortcut icon An icon (often on the Windows 95 desktop) that provides a pointer to an application or a document. You can double-click a shortcut icon to quickly open that program or document.

Simplified Employee Pension (SEP) A type of IRA retirement plan for small business owners and the self-employed. Contributions are tax-deductible, and earnings are tax-deferred.

smart quotes A feature of Word that converts straight quotation marks " to marks that point to the right or left, depending on their position in the sentence: "Smart Quotes."

soft page break A page break that occurs naturally in a multipage document. If you add or remove text, a soft page break adjusts itself. In contrast, a hard page break, which you insert yourself, does not automatically adjust.

sort To arrange data according to certain criteria. For example, you might sort an address database alphabetically, from A to Z, by the last name of the people.

special character A character not found on a standard keyboard, such as a copyright symbol ©.

split In Money, to divide a transaction's amount between two or more categories.

spreadsheet program A program that helps you track and calculate numbers in a grid of rows and columns.

start page *See* home page.

static The opposite of dynamic. A static copy of an object is not automatically updated when the original changes, whereas a dynamic copy is.

stock Shares of ownership in a company. Stocks fluctuate in value on a daily basis and sometimes pay quarterly dividends.

style Most commonly refers to a named set of formatting in a word processor. Can also refer to the attributes applied to a character, such as bold, italic, and underline.

Style Gallery An area in Word where you can view and transfer styles from various templates.

style sheets An obsolete term for a type of template that held only styles. In earlier versions of Word, you could attach a style sheet to a document to make a list of styles available. (Now you would attach a template to do this.)

styles Named formatting that you can apply to text in Word. For example, you might have a style called Heading 1 that formats text as 18-point bold Arial text with a 1/2-inch indent.

subcategory In Money, a category within a category. For example, in the Home category you might have subcategories for Utilities, Rent, and Maintenance.

subscribe Subscribing to a newsgroup (for example, Internet News) tells your news readers that you want to monitor the newsgroup and see the new message headings in it each time you log on to the Internet.

symbol A printed character that is not a regular letter or number. Some symbols appear on a normal keyboard, such as * and $; others are special characters.

syntax rules Rules for writing formulas and functions in a spreadsheet program so that they execute properly.

system files Files on your PC that start the PC and help keep it running.

tab stop A marker for a paragraph that determines where the insertion point will move when you press the Tab key.

table A grid of rows and columns, similar to a spreadsheet grid, in a word processing document.

task A template, a wizard, or a bookmark you select from the Works task launcher that points you toward an activity you want to accomplish.

TaskWizard An older name for a *task*. Earlier versions of Works used this term.

tax deductible You can deduct the amount you contribute from your income that you report to the IRS.

tax deferred You don't have to pay taxes on the income until you withdraw it from the plan.

Tax reporting Reports in Money that help you figure out your tax deductions and liabilities.

template A set of styles, margins, boilerplate text, and other formatting on which you can base new documents.

text wrapping *See* word wrap.

texture A graphics image of a certain surface type, such as wood or granite, that you can apply to text or to an object in place of a color.

title bar The colored bar across the top of a window that shows the program name.

toggle button A button or command that works like a light switch, changing its state each time you activate it.

toolbar A row of graphic buttons along the top or bottom of a window that provide shortcuts to common menu commands.

tools In Works, tools refers to the individual program components, such as Word Processor, Spreadsheet, and Database.

ToolTip *See* ScreenTip.

transactions In Money, any activity that results in a change of the balance in an account. Transactions include deposits, withdrawals, and transfers.

Treasury bill (T-Bill) Money that the United States government borrows from the purchaser for exactly one year.

Treasury bond (T-Bond) Like a treasury bill, except that the duration is 10 years or more.

Treasury note (T-Note) Like a treasury bill, except that the duration is 2 to 10 years.

TrueType A scalable type of font available in Windows programs. TrueType fonts have many advantages over other fonts, and most Windows users prefer to use them exclusively. Windows 98 comes with several TrueType fonts, and Microsoft Works Suite comes with many more, which are installed automatically when you install Word.

typefaces *See* font.

uniform resource locator *See* URL.

unprintable area The area at the edges of a piece of paper (usually about 1/4 inch on all sides) on which the printer cannot print. Only the most high-quality printers do not have this limitation. The capability of printing all the way to the edges of the page is called *bleeding*.

unvisited hyperlink A hyperlink that you have not yet explored on a Web page. Unvisited hyperlinks are usually a different color than visited ones so that you can tell them apart.

URL (pronounced "earl") An acronym for uniform resource locator, which is the electronic address of a Web page (for example, `http://www.mcp.com`) or another Internet resource. Entering an URL in your Web browser tells the browser to find and display the page at the address.

visited hyperlink A hyperlink that you have already explored on a Web page. *See also* unvisited hyperlink.

Web Short for World Wide Web.

Web browser A software program that enables you to navigate documents, or pages, on the Web. With most browsers, you can view both text and graphics in documents authored in the HTML format. The most popular browsers are Netscape Navigator and Microsoft Internet Explorer.

Web page An HTML document on the Internet that has its own unique address. (The term *page* does not refer to a printed page; a single Web page might take many sheets of paper to print.)

Web site A page or collection of pages on the World Wide Web that you can view with your Web browser.

weight The thickness of the letters in a typeface. For example, the Arial typeface comes in several weights, including Light, Regular, and Black (heavy).

wizard Any helper program that walks you through a complicated procedure with a series of question-and-answer dialog boxes.

word processor A program that helps you type and format text. Word is a word processor, and Works contains a Word Processor tool, also.

word wrap The feature in a word processor that automatically starts a new line of text when you reach the right margin of a line.

WordArt A feature in Word and Works that enables you to create stylized text in a variety of shapes and orientations, often with special shading, textures, or 3D effects.

worksheet *See* spreadsheet program.

World Wide Web (WWW) The graphical portion of the Internet, consisting of a vast network of interlinked Web sites.

INDEX

Symbols

A

C

D

E

F

I

J-K

P

Q

R

T

X-Z